Introduction to Programming Using

java™

An Object-Oriented Approach

----

second edition

DAVID M. ARNOW

SCOTT DEXTER

GERALD WEISS

Brooklyn College of City University of New York

PEARSON

Addison
Wesley

Boston San Francisco New York
London Toronto Sydney Tokyo Singapore Madrid
Mexico City Munich Paris Cape Town Hong Kong Montreal

Executive Editor	Susan Hartman Sullivan
Senior Acquisitions Editor	Maite Suarez-Rivas
Assistant Editor	Galia Shokry
Senior Marketing Coordinator	Lesly Hershman
Senior Production Supervisor	Jeffrey Holcomb
Project Management	Argosy Publishing
Copyeditor	Carol Noble
Proofreader	Kim Cofer
Composition and Art	Argosy Publishing
Text Designer	Leslie Haimes
Cover Designer	Joyce Cosentino Wells
Cover Image	© 2003 H. Kuwajima/Photonica
Prepress and Manufacturing	Caroline Fell

Access the latest information about Addison-Wesley titles from our World Wide Web site:
http://www.aw.com/computing

Many of the designations used by manufacturers and sellers to distinguish their products are claimed as trademarks. Where those designations appear in this book, and Addison-Wesley was aware of a trademark claim, the designations have been printed in initial caps or all caps.

The programs and applications presented in this book have been included for their instructional value. They have been tested with care, but are not guaranteed for any particular purpose. The publisher does not offer any warranties or representations, nor does it accept any liabilities with respect to the programs or applications.

Library of Congress Cataloging-in-Publication Data

Arnow, David M.
    Introduction to programming using Java : an object-oriented approach / David M. Arnow, Scott Dexter, Gerald Weiss.—2nd ed.
        p. cm.
    Includes index.
    ISBN 0-321-20006-3 (pbk.)
    1. Java (Computer program language) 2. Object-oriented programming (Computer science) I. Dexter, Scott. II. Weiss, Gerald. III. Title.

    QA76.73.J38A77 2003
    005.13'3—dc21

                                                            2003051401

ISBN 0-321-20006-3
1 2 3 4 5 6 7 8 9 10-PHT-06 05 04 03

About the Authors

David Arnow received his Ph.D. in Computer Science from New York University in 1981. Since then, he has been a professor in the Department of Computer and Information Science at Brooklyn College. Over this time his academic interests have included file system organization, distributed and parallel computing systems, and the use of logic in introductory CS courses. Since 1991, he has been a frequent contributor and reviewer of papers and tutorials for SIGCSE, FIE, and CCSC.

Scott Dexter is an assistant professor of Computer and Information Science at Brooklyn College of the City University of New York. He received his B.S. in Mathematics and Computer Science from Denison University and his M.S. and Ph.D. in Computer Science and Engineering from the University of Michigan. His research interests include network and multimedia security, formal methods, distributed computing, computer science pedagogy, and the politics of technology. He has been an invited speaker at meetings in Philadelphia, Toronto, Prague, and the People's Republic of China.

Gerald Weiss is a professor in the Department of Computer and Information Science at Brooklyn College where he has taught since 1980. He received a Ph.D. in Computer Science from New York University in 1986. Gerald has over twenty years of experience in compiler design and implementation, software systems, object-oriented development, and educational consulting, in both academic and corporate settings.

To my wife, Fern, my parents, Joseph and Lorraine,
and my children, Yocheved, Zvi, and Shlomo.

Gerald Weiss

To my partner, Jeanne, my parents, David and Sharon,
my sister, Katherine, and the Theoharis family.

Scott Dexter

To my wife, Barbara, my parents, Aron and Tessa,
and my children, Kera, Alena, and Joanna.

David M. Arnow

Preface

This book is intended as the primary text of an introductory course in programming. It assumes no programming background. The material covered is sufficient for a one- or two-semester sequence that would then be followed by a traditional CS2 (data structures) course.

To the Student

This book is an introduction to the art of computer programming in Java. It uses this popular language for a number of reasons:

- Java is an object-oriented language. Object orientation has become an essential approach of the software development community. Over the course of this text we will explain what makes a language object-oriented.
- Java is a relatively *simple* object-oriented language, at least compared to some others, such as C++. Although much of the complexity of C++ is in areas beyond the scope of our book, there are occasional pitfalls into which the beginning student can wander. Many of these *gotchas* cannot occur in Java.
- It borrows many features from other popular languages, most notably C and C++. This familiarity makes it attractive to users of those languages.
- It allows even the novice programmer to produce programs with fairly sophisticated user interfaces—that is, buttons, list boxes, scrollbars, and so on.
- It runs on many machines—PCs, Macintoshes, Sun workstations, and so on.
- It provides some fairly sophisticated facilities, including relatively easy access to networks and the Internet, making it attractive to many areas of programming.
- Programming in Java can be fun. As we pointed out above, even a relative newcomer can use the facilities provided by Java to write a program that looks nice and has sophisticated behavior.

Despite all the hoopla and fun, and despite the fact that you'll learn to use Java along the way, we have a very specific purpose: to get you to begin to think like a programmer. That means learning to analyze a problem, breaking it up into its component parts, and devising a solution. It also means practicing a lot. Programming is not learned simply from a book—you have to write lots of computer code. You won't be an expert by the end of this book, but if you pay careful attention and work at the programming exercises, you'll be on your way.

To the Instructor

In this text, we use the Java programming language to introduce students to programming. Our primary focus is on the process of developing software solutions to problems. This process cannot be achieved in the abstract but requires a description of much of the Java language and some of its class library, as well as a discussion of a number of programming techniques and algorithms. The preface elaborates on how we achieve these goals.

A FAQ (frequently asked questions) section can be found on this book's web site, www.aw.com/cssupport. It covers many of the topics in a question-answer form.

Changes to the Second Edition

In the second edition, we have retained and sharpened our commitment to an objects-early approach. In particular, the early chapters have been significantly reworked and expanded. Chapters 2 and 3, on working with objects, incorporate additional discussion and illustration of fundamental object-oriented programming concepts; we also emphasize and exploit the benefits of viewing programming as an act of modeling. We have expanded our treatment of the class definition process (Chapters 4 and 5) to provide a more carefully paced introduction with more examples. Class design now has its own chapter (Chapter 7), also with more and richer examples. These new examples are partially supported by the earlier introduction of some imperative programming concepts (such as primitive types, assignments, and conditionals); other imperative concepts (advanced conditionals, more primitive types, and simple counting loops) are covered in Chapter 6. The discussion of traversing collections has been rewritten to use counting loops and indexing; a brief explanation of using the Enumeration interface as an alternative appears in Appendix D. In this way, we bring discussion of this topic into closer alignment with our coverage of loop patterns, iteration, and the Vector collection. We have also reorganized the later chapters somewhat, most notably by removing the chapter of examples; some parts of this chapter are now distributed across the remaining chapters.

We have rewritten much of the GUI supplement material to provide tighter connections between the supplements and the concepts introduced in the main text of the chapter. See the GUI Supplements table of contents on xxxii for a brief overview.

Finally, we have moved all section exercises to the ends of chapters and added many new exercises.

Paradigm

Any introduction to programming must take a stand on the issue of paradigm choice. Our language platform is Java, so it is not surprising that our choice is object-oriented programming (OOP). However, although it is pretty clear what procedural and functional programming entail at the CS1 level, there are a variety of competing visions of what OOP at this level signifies. We concentrate on:

- Defining and using classes
- Issues of behavior and responsibility
- Using composition, rather than inheritance

A typical problem in this text is solved by identifying a primary object in the problem, describing its behavior, and then defining a class to provide that behavior. Usually a small number (often just one) of independent subsidiary classes are defined in the solution process. The solution is completed by writing a small imperative driver, in the form of a main method, for the primary object.

In the early 1990s there was some confusion regarding the relationships between OOP, procedural programming, and imperative programming. By now, it is generally well-understood that even though OOP and procedural programming are distinct paradigms, imperative programming is equally a part of both. Certainly, as soon as assignment enters the picture, one is doing imperative programming, and sending messages that change object state may be viewed as imperative programming as well. Thus, this text teaches both OOP and imperative programming from the start. However, just as the procedures-early approach, long popular in procedural CS1 classes, introduces the mechanics and use of procedure invocation prior to imperative devices such as conditionals and loops, so here we introduce the mechanics and use of message sending and object creation before conditionals, and class definition before iteration. The rationales in both cases are identical; it is preferable to introduce the paradigm first and develop the imperative devices in that context.

In procedural programming, the way to get a task done is to find a procedure that does it and then to invoke the procedure. If no such procedure exists, the programmer has to write one. In OOP, the way to get a task done is to find or create an object of a class whose behavior includes carrying out the task and sending the object a message. If no such class exists, the programmer has to write one.

Process

Our primary focus is the process of developing software solutions to problems. To this end, we introduce informal but methodical approaches to four areas:

- Developing a class specification from a problem statement
- Implementing a class given a class specification
- Constructing loops
- Constructing recursive methods

The first two of these approaches are introduced in a rudimentary way in Chapters 4 and 5, are fleshed out in Chapter 7, and used consistently thereafter throughout the book. The other two approaches are introduced with iteration and recursion, in Chapters 10 and 14, respectively. They, too, are used consistently thereafter, wherever iteration or recursion appear.

The consistent reuse of these methodical approaches is necessary so that students realize that methodology is not just something to which one pays lip service but that it can be genuinely useful in the development of solutions to problems.

The emphasis on process means that two common fixtures of introductory texts are rarely seen in this book: dissection of code and incremental modification of code (although the latter does appear in some extended examples and exercises). Dissection of code requires at the outset the presentation of a complete class implementation without development. It is followed by a careful analysis of the code. This approach is helpful in explaining how code works, but does not explain the process of developing code.

Many of the topics and their order in the text have been determined by our commitment to process. For example, before presenting the approach to class specification and definition, the student must be quite familiar with the idea of classes as repositories of behavior and the use of composition of classes. To that end, Chapter 3 discusses some of Java's predefined classes (including `BigInteger`, `Date`, and `GregorianCalendar`, and some of the i/o-related classes).

Language

As we elaborate on the process of program development, we introduce the features of the Java language. To prevent the discussion of the details of those features from digressing too far from the process of developing code, we often defer such discussions to special sections called Java Interludes. In these sections, we fill in the details of features introduced in the course of code development. We also use these sections to introduce language features that do not appear elsewhere but with which a CS1 student should have familiarity. Nevertheless, several features of the Java language are not covered, such as bit operations, concurrency, synchronization, and inner classes.

GUI Programming

Java's support for graphical user interface (GUI) programming is one of the reasons for its appeal in CS education—both to instructors and students. We have chosen to treat this topic in a series of GUI supplements, that is, special sections that appear at the end of each chapter. The main body of each chapter is entirely independent of these supplements. Each supplement introduces a new set of GUI tools and/or techniques in a context that reinforces the material introduced in the main body of its chapter.

The advantage of this organization is that it permits instructors to omit GUI programming altogether or introduce it at any time. It also serves to strengthen the focus of the main text on object-oriented programming rather than on language-specific features. Furthermore, it isolates the main body of the text from changes to the class library, primarily in the Abstract Window Toolkit (AWT) portion of the class hierarchy.

We have chosen to work exclusively with applets rather than applications in the GUI supplements for several reasons:

- It is easy to transform an applet into an application; the reverse is more difficult and in some cases impossible.

- The execution context of applets is more involved and therefore more worthy of a discussion in the text.
- Students love creating "cool" web pages and displaying their applets in them.

Broad coverage of the AWT is beyond the scope of this text. Our approach therefore is to address the following critical issues:

- Applet basics (Chapters 1 and 2)
- Layout—placement of components (Chapter 4)
- Event handling (Chapters 6 and 8)
- Precision in text and graphics (Chapters 5, 11, and 12)
- Threads (Chapters 11 and 14)

Along the way many useful AWT classes and methods are encountered.

Similarly, we have chosen to work almost exclusively with AWT rather than Swing (although we include a brief study of Swing as the final GUI supplement). Our reasons include the following:

- Unlike the change from JDK 1.0's event model to AWT's (JDK 1.1), the differences between AWT and Swing are primarily aesthetic, at least at the novice level.
- Swing introduces several complexities that are unnecessary for the beginner (for example the introduction of a content pane for component placement).
- The more interesting improvements only become understandable once inheritance, interfaces, and polymorphism are introduced (for example, the fact that all JComponents inherit from the AWT Container component allows placement of JComponents, e.g., icons, into other JComponents, e.g., buttons).

Flexibility

Every CS department has its own culture and its own goals for CS1. Even instructors who completely share our approach to OOP in CS1 may want to reorder or even omit some of the topics in this text. Accordingly, we have made every effort to make the introduction of many topics mutually independent. At the same time, we do want the topics in the book to build on each other. It's worth mentioning a few ways in which we resolved this tension.

Inheritance Inheritance is the subject of Chapter 12. However, an instructor who wishes to introduce this topic earlier in the course can go directly from Chapter 7 to Chapter 12 and work with the first two thirds of that chapter. The last third of the chapter addresses polymorphism and interfaces and uses material from Chapters 10 and 11.

Recursion Recursion is the subject of Chapter 14. However, an instructor who wishes to introduce recursion earlier in the course can go directly from Chapter 7 to Chapter 14 and work with the first third of the chapter, which does not involve arrays and vectors. On the other hand, an instructor who wishes to omit the topic of recursion can do so.

Exceptions   Exceptions are the subject of Chapter 13. However, the majority of the chapter is approachable directly after Chapter 7.

And, of course, the GUI supplements offer the instructors a great deal of flexibility with respect to the topic of graphic and event-driven programming. See the GUI supplement table of contents on page xxxii for a brief overview.

The dependency diagram summarizes these relationships.

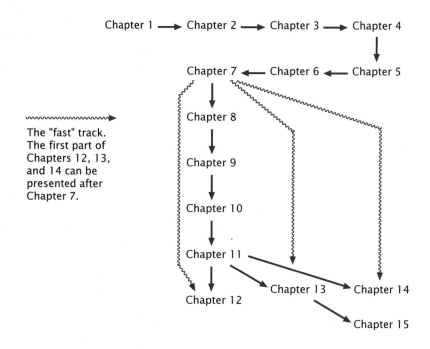

Input/Output

We believe that it is important to give students thorough experience with classes, objects, constructors, composition, cascading, and the concept of a class as a model before they go about the business of writing class definitions (beginning in Chapter 4). Chapter 3 presents a rich and involved discussion of these vital topics using a variety of example classes, including some of the classes in the java.io package.

Chapter 3 is integral to our sequence of exposition, but for the sake of those instructors who may have alternative approaches to preparing students for Chapter 4 and therefore wish to bypass Chapter 3, we have provided a very simple i/o package, AWIO in Appendix C, which may be used instead of Sections 3.9–3.12.

Typefaces in Code Examples

It would be useful now to identify the typefaces of the four elements that appear in code examples.

First there is the code itself:

```
class PrefaceExample {
    public static void main(String[] arg) {
            System.out.println("just an example");
    }
}
```

We often add comments to the code, notations that start with // or are surrounded by /* and */. These are intended to be notations that would actually be part of the code. The second line of the following code is an example of a comment:

```
class PrefaceExample {
    // Just print a short exemplary statement on the display.
    public static void main(String[] arg) {
        System.out.println("just an example");
    }
}
```

As we develop computer code, we will often make a notation that "holds the place" and represents code that is yet to be written. An example of such a place-holder (or pseudocode) appears in the fifth line of the following code:

```
class PrefaceExample {
    // Just print a short exemplary statement on the display.
    public static void main(String[] arg) {
        System.out.println("just an example");
        Additional output statements go here.
    }
}
```

Finally, explanatory remarks that would not normally be part of the code but serve to aid our presentation are placed in shaded screens around the code, often with arrows:

```
class PrefaceExample {
    // Just print a short exemplary statement on the display.          ←———— A comment
    public static void main(String[] arg) {                               A class with a
        System.out.println("just an example");                            main() method
        Additional output statements go here.
    }
}
```

An Annotated Overview of the Chapters—The Non-GUI Parts

Chapter 1: Jumping Into Java   Here we introduce the concept of programming as a means of creating models of situations. Our primary goal is to introduce the reader to ideas of classes, objects, and message passing as they are realized in Java. In addition, we present and explain an example of a program and discuss the mechanics of writing and running Java programs.

Chapter 2: Sending Messages and Performing Operations   In this chapter, the focus is on the mechanics of using objects by sending them messages and all that this entails. We elaborate on the three key ideas presented in Chapter 1—classes, objects, and message passing—and introduce additional OOP and imperative essentials: methods, arguments, return values, signature, prototype, overloading, reference variables, declarations, assignment, `int`s and arithmetic, and simple conditionals. The `String` and `PrintStream` classes are used to illustrate these ideas.

Chapter 3: Working with Objects and Primitive Types   The chapter begins by showing how to use a class's constructor to create objects. We continue to emphasize the theme of class as a repository for behavior. This idea is reinforced through an exploration of some of Java's predefined classes; we also explore how behaviors can be combined using cascading and composition. At the same time we introduce a few more imperative programming concepts (such as conditionals and `boolean` values) to increase the richness of our examples.

Chapter 4: Defining Classes   By this time, the student is quite clear about the first principle of OOP: If anything needs to be done, find an object that can do it and send it a message. Now we show the reader how to define new classes. This definition requires quite a bit in the way of mechanics, which we begin covering in this chapter: class definition structure, method definition structure, declaration, scope and use of parameters, local variables, instance variables, and the `return` statement. Amid all these necessary language details we try to maintain a focus on the concepts of *behavior*, *interface*, and *state*. Along the way we introduce a limited version of the methodical approach to class definition that is presented in the next chapter.

Despite the embryonic character of the approach, once we get through this chapter in our courses, we breathe our first sigh of relief. At this point we can give assignments that involve the definition of new classes. We are now doing OOP.

Chapter 5: Advanced Class Definition   In this chapter we cover some more mechanics of class definition: constructors, static methods, final values, and the keyword `this`.

Chapter 6: Inside the Method: Imperative Programming   Now that we have discussed the major issues of class definition, we turn to the topic of writing powerful methods. We continue with further examples of class definition, but here our focus is on imperative programming concepts (primitive data types and a wide selection of conditional statements, as well as an introduction to counting loops) that we can employ to provide the behavior our methods require.

Chapter 7: Class Design It is here that we introduce the methodical approach to class definition that we use consistently through the rest of the text. This approach starts by identifying the nouns in the problem statement. From there, a primary object is identified. This object's class is then implemented, with the implementation driving the determination of the additional classes needed in the problem. The implementation of a class entails defining its behavior and state. This straightforward "waterfall" approach is sufficient for most design problems that would be encountered by a CS1 student.

Chapter 8: Verifying Object Behavior This chapter is an overview of the need for and techniques for testing. It introduces the concept of test drivers and module testing. Additionally, it provides the reader with a starting point for the selection and construction of test cases.

Chapter 9: Working with Multiple Objects Here we introduce additional limited forms of iteration and the notions of a collection. The `while` loop is introduced and its mechanics are explained but, pending further discussion in the next chapter, its use is confined to the read/process loop pattern:

```
read
while (not eof) {
    process
    read
}
```

We also introduce a new `for` loop pattern:

```
for (i = 0; i < size of collection; i++)
    process element number i
```

The collection we use is the `Vector` class. This provides several advantages:

- The complexity of indexing is deferred until the student can get a handle on the processing of multiple objects.
- No new syntax is required. The vector is just another object and is managed by sending messages to it.

At the conclusion of the chapter we introduce arrays and illustrate some of the similarities and differences between arrays and `Vector`s.

Despite the limitations, once we get through this chapter in our courses, we breathe a second sigh of relief. At this point we can give assignments that are much more reminiscent of "real" applications, as distinct from utility classes.

Chapter 10: Designing Iteration   This is an in-depth chapter on an all-important CS1 imperative programming issue: the construction of loops. A survey of CS1 texts and courses reveals three approaches:

- The null approach—just imitate the code in the book
- Providing a set of loop patterns
- Some kind of methodical development technique, usually a watered-down formal method

In this chapter, we combine the last two of these. We present a methodical technique and then apply it to quite a few typical problems, identifying the results as loop patterns that we can refer to later.

Chapter 11: Maintaining Collections of Objects   This chapter focuses on algorithms for searching and sorting. We also go beyond the usual venue of collection objects and arrays to consider searching external files. In this connection, we take the opportunity to introduce Java threads.

Chapter 12: Extending Class Behavior   Our approach to inheritance is to emphasize the extending of the behavior of a superclass by a subclass. This is the way in which inheritance is most commonly used, especially by the beginning programmer—taking an existing class and adding state and behavior to produce a richer class. We do this in the context of those classes, both predefined and programmer-defined, introduced in Chapters 3–7 for the following reasons:

- The classes that we extend are already familiar to the student.
- The instructor may introduce inheritance earlier in the course, for example, immediately after Chapter 7, if it is so desired.

Extension of state, protected instance variables, overriding, and polymorphism are easily motivated in this context.

The instructor covering the GUI supplements may wish to cover at least the beginning of Chapter 12 somewhat early to give the student some appreciation of how inheritance allows even the beginner to implement complex windowed applications.

We also present an introduction to another use of inheritance: factoring out the common behavior/state of several logically related classes, producing a superclass and a class hierarchy. Again we emphasize the concept of behavior and modeling in which the various layers of the hierarchy model different abstractions of the objects.

Finally, interfaces are presented as a means of forcing a class to conform to a specified protocol.

Chapter 13: Exceptions   Another theme running through the text is that of responsibility-driven programming. Classes should be responsible for as much of their behavior as possible. The other side of the coin is the idea that classes should not be responsible for behavior that is not logically theirs. We present exception handling in this light—as a way for a method to signal an exceptional, not necessarily erroneous, situation to an invoker of that method. Though some knowledge of inheritance is necessary to fully appreciate the structure of an exception hierarchy, the first part of this chapter may be covered at a relatively early stage (after Chapter 7) in order to clarify the throws clause code present in many of the methods signatures.

Chapter 14: Recursion   In this treatment of recursion, we focus on its use as a programming tool. We start with extremely simple problems that some might consider inappropriately easy for recursion. These problems provide a context for developing an approach to constructing recursive solutions. We then take an obligatory detour and discuss how recursion is implemented, but we end that discussion with a stern admonition for the student to focus on how recursion is used and to ignore the implementation issue. We then move to two problems whose complexity cry out for recursion—generating permutations and the classical Towers of Hanoi problem—and end with a comparison of recursion and iteration.

When we get through this chapter in our courses we breathe a third sigh of relief. At this point, we have covered assignment, variables, expressions, numeric and logical and string types, interactive and file i/o, control structures, functions (methods), structures (classes), arrays, several algorithms, recursion, testing and debugging—all the traditional material of CS1. And of course we've done more: classes, objects, messages, plus any material from the GUI supplements that have been included. There are no more sighs of relief save the sigh when the final grades of the course are turned in to the registrar.

Chapter 15: Client/Server Computing   In this chapter we provide a brief introduction to network programming using Java. We lay out some fundamental ideas about the Internet (in particular, we describe the nature of a TCP connection) and use these ideas to support the development of simple HTTP and SMTP clients.

Appendices   The appendices include:

- A glossary of all the defined terms in the text (containing chapter terminology lists and terms from the GUI supplements)
- A description of how to write and run Java programs in a UNIX/Linux, Windows, or MacOS X environment
- An alternative set of classes supporting input and output that may be used in lieu of Java's predefined i/o classes.
- A brief discussion of using the `Enumeration` interface to traverse a collection.

Supplemental Materials

The following supplements are available to all readers of this book at www.aw.com/cssupport:

- Source code: All the completed classes and methods that appear in the text.
- JavaPlace access
- Errors: We have worked hard to avoid these and hope there are few. Here you can link to a list of errors that have been discovered.

The following instructor supplements are only available to qualified instructors. Please contact your local Addison-Wesley Sales Representative, or send e-mail to aw.csc@aw.com, for information about how to access them.

- Instructor's Manual with Solutions: This contains teaching suggestions, sample syllabi, and additional questions and problems that are suitable for homework. Also included are fully worked solutions to all exercises.
- Chapter by chapter test bank available as a Word file or in Test Gen format
- PowerPoint slides of all figures

Contact Us

We welcome questions, comments, suggestions, and corrections. Our email addresses are:

arnow@turingscraft.com
sdexter@brooklyn.cuny.edu
weiss@turingscraft.com

Acknowledgments

As everyone who reads the acknowledgments section of prefaces knows, textbooks are really the result of the collaboration and support of many people. The support we received from Addison-Wesley was first rate.

Thanks to Nathan Schultz, Lesly Hershman, and Katherine Kwack in Marketing; Patty Mahtani and Jeffrey Holcomb in Production; Joyce Cosentino Wells in Design; and Daniel Rausch and Edalin Michael at Argosy Publishing.

We are especially grateful to Galia Shokry and Maite Suarez-Rivas for their patience and encouragement.

Also essential to this effort were a host of reviewers: Michael Crowley, University of Southern California; Ralph Deters, University of Saskatchewan; Le Gruenwald, University of Oklahoma; David P. Jacobs, Clemson University; Chung Lee, California State University; Mike Litman, Western Illinois University; Yenumula B. Reddy, Grambling State University; Nan Schaller, University of Rochester; Esther Steiner,

New Mexico State University; and Shih-Ho Wang, University of California, Davis. From the first edition we thank the following reviewers: Jan Bergandy, University of Massachusetts Dartmouth; Robert H. Dependahl, Jr., Santa Barbara City College; Eileen Kraemer, Washington University in St. Louis; Ronald L. McCarty, Penn State Erie; David D. Riley, University of Wisconsin La Crosse; Jim Roberts, Carnegie Mellon University; Dale Skrien, Colby College; and Ken Slonneger, University of Iowa. These reviewers made many valuable suggestions and challenged us to refine and at times rethink our approach.

Our approach to CS1 using Java continues to mature along with that of the CS education community. Few of the ideas in this book are solely ours, but we hope we have managed to represent some of the best thinking of our fellow educators.

The customary place for acknowledgments to the family of the author is at the end. We are not ready to violate tradition, but the thanks we owe to our families for their support, encouragement, involvement, and love belongs not just at the end but at the beginning, the middle, and the end of the acknowledgments because that's where they were with us: all along, at every stage. During the course of the project, our families put up with absences, late nights, early mornings, obsessive muttering about "GUI supplements," unwashed dishes, late dinners, lots of take-out, and monopolization of the family computer, not to mention bouts of discouragement and worry. In spite of this, they gave us all the love and support one could dream of and we will never forget this. Thank you,

Barbara	Jeanne	Fern
Kera	David, Sharon, and Kathy	Yocheved
Alena	The Theoharis clan	Zvi
Joanna		Shlomo

| **David M. Arnow** | **Scott Dexter** | **Gerald Weiss** |

Table of Contents

LISTING OF JAVA INTERLUDES

LISTING OF GUI SUPPLEMENTS

Chapter 1

Jumping into Java

1.1 Computers and Programs

Because this is an introduction to computer programming and computer science, you might expect us to give you a straightforward definition of a computer. However, a good definition of a computer is not the starting point of the study of computer science—it is, perhaps, a midpoint. For now, we will live with our everyday notions of computers: They are the machines that compute taxes, help us write term papers, monitor airplanes, control car engines, help find the gene sequences in living things, and entertain us in various ways.

In this book, therefore, our focus will be on **programs**—texts that can make a computer do a task. Programs are written in a specialized language, called a **programming language**. The content of a program is called **code**. When a computer carries out or runs a program we say that it **executes** the code. Our goal is to teach you how to read and write programs using the Java programming language.

Java is a newcomer among the hundreds of programming languages. Because it was developed recently, its design reflects much of the wisdom acquired over the last few decades concerning program development and programming language design. This acquired wisdom is reflected in Java's design as an *object-oriented* language.

To get an idea of what Java code looks like, let's take a quick look at a small Java program:

```java
public class Program0 {
    public static void main(String[] arg) {
        System.out.println("Welcome To Java!");
    }
}
```

This program displays the greeting "Welcome To Java!" on the computer's screen. If you look closely, you will see this greeting embedded in the third line of the program. There is clearly a relationship between this code and a real event—the display of text on the screen.

In this chapter, we will explore this relationship and show you how to use objects in Java to write your first Java program.

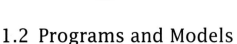

1.2 Programs and Models

Nearly all programs model something. What does it mean to model? A **model** is a simplified representation. It includes features that are considered important to its user while neglecting others. For example, when our first program displays "Welcome To Java!" our interest is only in the characters that are displayed, not their color, the brightness of the screen, or any other attribute of the display. A child's plastic car model may show the exterior details and the wheels, but leave out the engine and transmission entirely. A more sophisticated version might include a working engine and realistic interior details. Of course, the more realistic and detailed the model, the greater the effort and expense in its creation.

People constructed models long before there were computers. Consider the following example:

The service dispatcher for the Keyspan Gas company keeps track of 43 repair trucks in the Brooklyn area. She does this using a large map and numbered pushpins: Pushpin #1 represents repair truck #1, pushpin #2 represents repair truck #2, and so forth. The pins are pushed into the map and represent the most recent location of a particular vehicle. When a repair truck calls in a new position, the pin representing that truck is moved.

The dispatcher also must keep track of customer service requests. When a call for service comes in, the dispatcher places a thumbtack at the customer's location. When service is completed, the thumbtack is removed.

Even though the pushpins are clearly not repair trucks, the dispatcher refers to them as if they were, both in her mind and when talking about them with coworkers. Yet if she came to work one day and discovered that the pushpins were replaced by numbered carpet tacks, she would have no problem referring to the carpet tacks as "repair trucks."

The model is not a complete representation. For example, the thumbtacks on the map don't indicate the kind of problem the customers have. In spite of such apparent lapses, models are acceptable and useful if they *abstract* the important details (the ones that matter) and thereby get the job done.

Although there is a logical correspondence between elements of the model and what they represent, models are physically quite different from the things they represent. There is no way that anyone could look at the dispatcher's map out of context and know what the pins mean. One might guess they were locations of robberies in the last month, or particularly bad potholes, or especially nice restaurants. The meaning of the pins is not inherent in the map but is given by the dispatcher.

Models can also represent an imaginary or hypothetical world, such as "the city of the future." Furthermore, not all models are something physical that you can touch. A model may exist only on paper, or even just in someone's mind—a mental model.

For example, someone planning on financing her college education might hypothetically assume that she will find a certain amount of part-time work during the semester, full-time work in the summer, government loans, school financial aid, and so on. Writing these down and adding them up (in the hope that they will equal or exceed tuition) is an act of modeling. The numbers written down represent hypothetical amounts of money.

Every model, whether representing the real world or a hypothetical one, shares the following characteristics:

- Elements of the model represent other, more complex things; for example, pins can be used to represent repair trucks.
- These model elements exhibit consistent **behavior**; for example, pins indicate position and can be moved.
- The model elements can be grouped into different categories based on their common behaviors; for example, the thumbtacks appear and disappear. Once placed on the map, they are not moved until they are taken off the map. In contrast, the pushpins stay on the map all the time but can be moved about. (This reflects the reality that the repair trucks travel but customer locations either need service or they don't.)
- Actions external to a model element cause the behavior of the model element; for example, a hand moves the pin.

In the preceding example, the model elements are physical objects (pushpins, thumbtacks), the external actions came from a person, and even the behavior was in part carried out by a person. In programming, we dispense with these physical means and instead represent model elements and behavior within a program. At first, we will work with models much simpler than those described in this example. However, as we acquire more tools in the coming chapters, we will be able to build increasingly complex models in our programs.

1.3 Objects, Classes, and Messages

Model elements in Java programs are called **objects**. Objects that share a common behavior can be grouped into distinct categories called **classes**. Objects that work together to perform a task communicate with each other by sending **messages**. In this section, we begin our exploration of these fundamental ideas by using an analogy between a Java program and a corporation.

Objects

Specifically, let's consider the group of employees in a good-sized software development business. We will simplify our model of such a business by considering only a few kinds of employees and only a few of the tasks that these employees might perform. Such a business might have a president and a couple

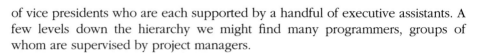

of vice presidents who are each supported by a handful of executive assistants. A few levels down the hierarchy we might find many programmers, groups of whom are supervised by project managers.

In Java terms, we would refer to each of the personnel in our model as an object. Indeed, if we were writing a Java program to simulate some activity of this company, we would model each of these individuals as a Java object: a `President` object, two `VicePresident` objects, some `ExecutiveAssistant` objects, many `Programmer` objects, and so forth.

Behavior

Although they may be working on different projects within the company, programmers behave similarly in our model: They generate code, they work a lot of overtime, and they sleep under their desks. In Java terms, we say that `Programmer` objects share a **common behavior**, meaning they do the same kinds of things. Vice presidents also do similar kinds of work, although their areas of responsibility may be different: They ask their staff for data, they generate reports, and they resign under pressure from shareholders. Thus, `VicePresident` objects also share a common behavior. Not surprisingly, `VicePresident` objects share a common behavior that differs from that shared by `Programmer` objects. The two kinds of objects model distinct categories of things (executives and programmers). In a Java program simulating this company, we would use objects with different kinds of behavior to model these different kinds of employees.

Messages

Just as no organization can function effectively without clear communication channels, so must Java objects be able to coordinate their efforts. Much of the daily communication within a modern business takes the form of email or voice mail: If one person needs to give information to another or request that someone perform some task, he might simply send an appropriate email message or leave a voice mail. This is how Java objects communicate with each other: by sending messages (note that these messages among objects are not actually email messages!).

Of course, the employees of a company have different training and responsibilities, so not everyone can respond appropriately to every message that might be sent. While it would make perfect sense to ask a programmer to prepare a demonstration of the current project for next Tuesday, making the same request of a vice president would give results that are unpredictable at best. Similarly, we wouldn't ask a programmer to gather financial data about the company, but vice presidents are presumably well-equipped to carry out this task. Clearly, the behavior of an object is closely related to the kinds of messages to which it is able to respond.

Let's think a little more about what constitutes a message: If the president needs a staff member to prepare a report, how does she craft the message? The message clearly has a sender (the president) and a receiver (the designated staffer). It also specifies the kind of task that needs to be performed: prepare a report. If this was the entirety of the message, though, the staff member would have difficulty figuring out what to do: He needs more detailed information specifying, say, that the report should summarize income and expenditures for the month of June.

In Java, messages are structured similarly: Each message sent must specify which object is to receive it (in Java, this object is designated with a **reference**), what task that object should perform in response, and any further details that must be supplied to describe the task adequately.

Java Programs

Moving away from the analogy we have been using, what have we learned about Java and Java programs? We know that a Java program, when it is running on a computer, is simply a collection of objects that correspond to the important elements of the problem being solved or the computation being performed. These objects are the main actors: Every object has a certain set of tasks (or behaviors) that it is able to carry out. For example, in the next section we will see that PrintStream objects are able to display text on the computer screen. Objects also send messages to other objects, asking them to perform one of their designated tasks. The behavior of an object is determined by what kind of thing it represents; no object can perform every task, but we expect objects representing similar things to behave similarly.

Classes

A category of model elements is called a *class* in Java. The fundamental job of a Java programmer is providing *class definitions*, or descriptions of how objects in each class must behave. These class definitions describe the kinds of messages objects in the class can receive and how they respond to these messages. Once a class has been defined in a program, objects of that class can be created when the program runs on a computer. Every object belongs to exactly one class and is said to be an **instance** of that class. Programming in Java amounts to nothing more or less than writing the definitions of classes and using those classes to create objects.

We will sometimes speak of a class's **responsibility**. By that we mean the set of behaviors that the class provides (or takes responsibility for). This is simply another way of specifying what the class is modeling. When we speak of *modeling*, we are concentrating on what sort of object the class is representing; when we speak of *responsibility*, we are focusing on how the object behaves.

If we were modeling our software company in Java, we would define a Programmer class. It would provide the behavior of Programmer objects and allow us to create Programmer objects, each an instance of the Programmer class. We would also define a President class, which would define the behavior of President objects and allow us to create new President objects.

Predefined Objects and Classes

Many programs have some behavior in common; for example, many programs display text on the screen. Must we begin work on every such program by defining classes that provide this common behavior? Fortunately, we don't have to reinvent the wheel constantly: Java comes with some classes and objects already defined. In addition, we can use classes and objects that we or other programmers have created and made available. In this way, program code can be reused to create increasingly powerful programs.

To begin exploring how to use objects in Java, we will work with one of these predefined objects.

1.4 Our First Object: A `PrintStream`

A program's purpose is to provide information. Most of the programs that we'll write will display information on a *monitor;* that is, they will show information on a computer screen. In this section we'll learn how to use one of Java's predefined objects to control a monitor.

Monitors play two roles. For people, monitors are devices to read information from. For programs, monitors are devices for displaying information. From the point of view of a program, the most important behavior of a monitor is that it can be told (by the program) to print out some **characters** (letters, digits, punctuation marks, spaces, etc.), and then some more characters, and then some more, and so on. Thus, to a program, a monitor is a device on which to print a continuing stream of characters.

Java provides a predefined class that models devices like monitors that can print a stream of characters. The class is called (appropriately) `PrintStream`. The `PrintStream` class is responsible for displaying a stream of characters. Objects that are instances of the `PrintStream` class can receive `println()` messages, which request that a given group of characters be printed out. All `PrintStream` objects share this `println()` behavior.

The `PrintStream` class does not model all the features that real monitors have. It does not, for example, provide any behavior that would change a monitor's background color. It just models the ability of monitors to display streams of characters.

Along with the predefined `PrintStream` class, Java provides a predefined *instance* of `PrintStream` that represents the computer's own monitor. In a Java program, the phrase `System.out` refers to this predefined `PrintStream` object. In the next section, we will see how a Java programmer can use `System.out` to send `println()` messages to this `PrintStream` object in order to elicit its `println()` behavior.

We mentioned above that `System.out` refers to a predefined `PrintStream` object. We say that `System.out` is a *reference* to that object. Figure 1.1 shows

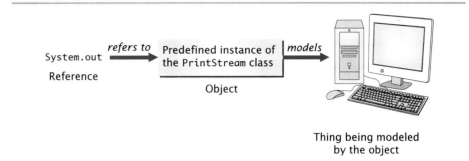

Figure 1.1
An example of a reference. Here the reference System.out refers to a predefined PrintStream object that models a monitor.

the System.out reference in use. A *reference* in Java is any phrase that is used to refer to an object.

1.5 Sending a Message to the System.out Object

A *message* in Java is a request for some desired behavior from an object. A message is composed of

- The name of the desired behavior (in the PrintStream class this behavior is named println()),
- Followed by any further details surrounded by parentheses.

The "further details" needed depend on the particular behavior. For example, the PrintStream object's println() behavior, which prints out a stream of characters, needs to know what characters to print. So, a println() message to a PrintStream object looks something like this:

println (*some-characters*)

In Java, we can specify a group of characters by writing them between double quotes. Such an expression is called a **string**. So to make the monitor display a greeting to a pair of users named Millicent and Micah, we must send the PrintStream object a message like the following

println("Welcome Millicent and Micah")

This Java message is shown in Figure 1.2.

To send a message, we must specify the **receiver**, that is, the object that is the recipient of the message. In Java we write a phrase consisting of

- A reference to the receiver object (for example, System.out)
- A period
- The message we want to send

Figure 1.2
Messages in Java.
A message contains
the behavior desired,
with further details in
parentheses.

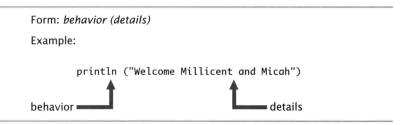

Form: *behavior (details)*

Example:

println ("Welcome Millicent and Micah")

behavior ──────→   ──── details

So to send our `println()` message to the `PrintStream` object we must write the following:

```
System.out.println("Welcome Millicent and Micah")
```

Figure 1.3 illustrates the parts of this Java message.

Figure 1.3
Messages in Java.
The *reference.mes-
sage* form is used to
send a message to a
receiver.

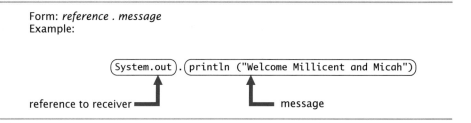

Form: *reference . message*
Example:

(System.out).(println ("Welcome Millicent and Micah"))

reference to receiver ────→   ──── message

When this is executed, the `System.out` object receives the `println("Welcome Milli-cent and Micah")` message and in response prints the greeting on the screen. In this example, pictured in Figure 1.4, `System.out` is a reference to the receiver of the `println()` message.

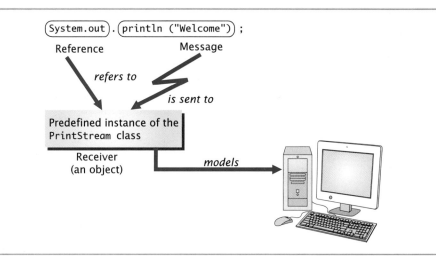

Figure 1.4
The role of the
receiver in sending
a message.

Java Statements

Sending a message to an object is an action that the programmer specifies and that the computer carries out when the program runs. In Java, all actions are specified in **statements**.

To turn a Java phrase that sends a message to an object into a complete Java statement, we add a semicolon at the end:

```
System.out.println("Welcome Millicent and Micah");
```

just as we add a period to complete a sentence in English. (See Figure 1.5.)

Figure 1.5
A statement that
sends a message.

```
Form: message-sending-phrase;
Example:
```

1.6 A Java Program

Much of the joy of programming comes from seeing our programs in action. Even a program that just prints an announcement is an important first step, and it *is* modeling something—a human being making an announcement. Suppose we want to write a program that displays the words "This is my first Java program" on the screen and right below that displays "but it won't be my last." The following ideas provide a guide for writing the program described.

- There is a predefined object (referred to by System.out) whose behavior includes displaying characters on the screen.
- The way to get the behavior is to send a message.
- The first part of the message must be the name of the method that provides the behavior (println()).
- The rest of the message must consist of arguments containing information the object needs to do the job (the line to be displayed).

Because there are two lines to be displayed, we must send two messages to the System.out object. This leads to the following kernel of a Java program, consisting of a pair of statements:

```
System.out.println("This is my first Java program");
System.out.println("but it won't be my last.");
```

To make this a valid Java program, we must choose a name for it and then surround it with some additional notation. Names in Java are called **identifiers**. An identifier is a sequence of letters, digits, or underscores. The first character must be a letter. A good name for this program is `Program1`. Using that name and adding the required notation, we can write our Java program as

```
public class Program1 {
    public static void main(String[] arg) {
        System.out.println("This is my first Java program");
        System.out.println("but it won't be my last.");
    }
}
```

For the rest of this chapter and Chapter 2, the first two lines

```
public class program-name {
    public static void main(String[] arg) {
```

and the last two lines

```
    }
}
```

will be the beginning and end of each program that we write.

Appendix B describes the steps you must take on a particular computer to type in and run this program. If you have a computer close at hand and wish to do so, you could skip ahead to that section now in order to find out how to run this program.

Java Interlude   *Identifiers, Statement Order, Format, and Comments*

The purpose of this book is to teach programming. Lest that all-important goal suffer from distractions involving the details of the Java language, we will frequently omit some details and variations from our discussion. To fill in the gaps and to review and summarize, we will periodically have Java Interlude sections, such as this one, that look solely at the language itself.

Java Rules

Just as English has a set of rules that tells us what an acceptable sentence is, Java has a set of rules that tells us what an acceptable program is. We call code *legal* if it does not violate these rules.

Identifiers

A class or a behavior must have a name—an identifier. Be careful: Java recognizes the distinction between uppercase and lowercase letters. That means that `system` and `System` are different identifiers! If you write `system` when you mean `System`, your program will not work. In Java, it is common for the name of each class and program to begin with a capital letter; other identifiers (such as method names) begin with lowercase letters.

Keywords

Keywords are special words with predefined meanings in the Java language. Words like `class`, `public`, `static`, and `void` are all keywords. `PrintStream` is not a keyword—it is the name of a predefined class.

The Order of Java Statements

The order of statements matters because they are executed by the computer in the order of appearance. So

```
System.out.println("One two three");
System.out.println("Four five six");
```

yields a different order of messages and therefore a different display on the screen than

```
System.out.println("Four five six");
System.out.println("One two three");
```

Program Format and Comments

The Java program that we wrote in the last section was written in a particular format. The statements of the programs were indented using the TAB key several times. Each statement appeared on one line, and one line never contained more than one statement.

The rules of Java are very flexible with respect to format. The chief format rule is that two adjacent identifiers or keywords must be separated by at least one space. Thus we could not legally write

```
classProgram1 ...
```

instead of `class Program1`. But we could legally have written the example program as

```
public class Program1 { public static void main(String[]
arg) { System.out.println(
"This is my first Java program"); System.out.println(
"but it won't be my last."); } }
```

Though legal, this code is very difficult to read. One of our goals when we write code is to make it readable. Readability is important because programs have to be periodically updated and also *debugged* (examined for errors and corrected) by people who often are not the ones who originally wrote them. At this point, it is too early to provide a detailed list of explicit formatting rules, but here is a start:

- Write one statement per line. If the statement is too long to fit on a line, break it up at some reasonable point and indent by one tab past the beginning of the statement.

- Use the TAB key, not the space bar, to indent. This will make it easier to have nicely aligned left margins.
- In general, imitate the style used in this textbook.

As we present additional features of the Java language, we will illustrate how to format them.

Comments

Java allows the programmer to write comments in the code. *Comments* are notes that are ignored by the computer, but that appear in the program in order to clarify it to the reader. There are two ways of writing comments in Java: surrounded comments and line comments.

Surrounded Comments

Any text that starts with /* and ends with */ is a comment. The /* and */ do not have to be on the same line. Thus,

```
/*
 * This program prints out several greetings.
 */
```

is a legal comment. (Note: There must be no space between the / and the *.)

Line Comments

Once // appears on a line, all text on the rest of the line is a comment. Thus,

```
// This program prints out several greetings.
```

is also a legal comment. (Note: There must be no space between the two / characters.)

Because comments are ignored by the computer, you can put them anywhere in your program.

As with program format, although the rules for comment placement are quite liberal, there are certain conventions. Here are a few guidelines:

- There should be a comment before the line that starts with the keyword `class`, indicating the purpose and behavior of the code.
- Comments should not explain how Java works. Assume that the reader of the program understands Java. Rather, comments should give insights not readily apparent from the code.
- Comments should not appear in the middle of a statement.

For example, we might comment the program from the last section in this way:

```
/*
 * Program1: Announces my first Java program experience and my intent to continue.
 */
```

```
public class Program1 {
    public static void main(String[] arg) {
        System.out.println("This is my first Java program");
        System.out.println("but it won't be my last.");
    }
}
```

1.7 Mechanics

Writing down a Java program on a piece of paper will not by itself make the computer do anything. First, the program has to be made accessible to the computer. Second, the program must be translated into a form that the computer can execute. Finally, the computer must be directed to execute, that is, carry out, the instructions of the translated program.

Fortunately, these three steps are quite easy to undertake, in part because there are programs that carry out each of these steps in a nearly automatic fashion. The precise details of these programs vary from one computer system to another. In this section we will describe the general steps. Details for some specific systems (including Windows, UNIX/Linux, and Macintosh) are provided in the appendices.

Accessibility

A program written on paper with pen is not accessible to a computer. To make a program accessible we need to create a file containing the program. A **file** is simply a collection of items of information that has a name and that can be stored on the disk of a computer system. Most computer application software (word processors, drawing programs, spreadsheets, etc.) involves the creation of files. For example, a user writes a letter in a word processor and wants to save it, so she directs the word processor software to save it in a file. To write a program and save it in a file we need an application program called an *editor*. An editor is similar to a word processor in that it allows the user to type in text that will be saved in a file. Where it differs is that it lacks text formatting, typeface control, and other word processing-oriented features (such as spell-check). Furthermore, a good editor program will have some features that help in writing programs (for example, displaying comments in a different color to readily differentiate them from program text).

So, step 1 involves starting an editor program, typing in the program, and saving the resulting changes in a file. Try this using the first Java program developed in this chapter:

```
/*
 * Program1: Announces my first Java program experience and my intent to continue.
 */
```

```java
public class Program1 {
  public static void main(String[] arg) {
      System.out.println("This is my first Java program");
      System.out.println("but it won't be my last.");
  }
}
```

Java has strict rules regarding the name of the file in which you save your Java program. The filename must be of the form X.java, where X is the name of the program. So this program would have to be stored in file named

`Program1.java`

Preparing for Execution: Translation

Even after the Java program has been stored in a file in the computer system, the computer cannot immediately carry out its instructions. That is because computers can only carry out instructions of languages that are much more primitive than Java. These languages are called *machine languages*. Each different kind of computer has its own unique machine language. Though simple, machine languages are so inconvenient for writing programs that they are almost never used. Instead, we use *high-level languages*, such as Java and C++, to write our programs. A bridge is needed between the high-level languages and the machine languages. Two such bridges are compilers and interpreters.

We can use a program called a **compiler** to translate the program from the high-level language to machine language. The compiler accepts a file that contains a high-level language program as input and produces a file containing a machine language program that is equivalent to the input.

Another approach is to use a program called an **interpreter**. An interpreter also uses the high-level language program as input, but instead of translating the whole program, it carries out the instructions of the program directly.

So, if a compiler encountered a program in a high-level language that contained instructions to print the numbers from 0 to 99, it would produce a machine-language program that contained instructions to print the numbers. On the other hand, if an interpreter encountered such a program, it would directly print the numbers from 0 to 99.

Execution

Once a program has been translated into machine code, we have to tell the computer to execute the program. On some computers, this simply involves pointing to an icon on the screen that represents the file containing the machine code and double-clicking the mouse; on other computers, we have to type the name of the file containing the machine code and hit the RETURN key. The details of how this is handled depends on a program called the *operating system*. Every computer system has such a program. Its chief task is to load translated programs into memory and set things up so that the computer will carry out the instructions in these programs.

Java involves a combination of the two approaches—compiling and interpreting. Java programs are translated using a Java compiler. However, the Java compiler translates the program not to true machine language but rather to an idealized form of machine language called Java bytecode. Suppose we have a file called X.java that contains Java code. When we invoke the Java compiler on this file, the result is called X.class and contains Java bytecode. Because this bytecode file does not contain real machine code, it cannot be directly executed by any computer. Rather, a Java interpreter is used. Note, however, that the Java interpreter does not interpret the Java program (that is, the statements in X.java)—rather it interprets the bytecode file (X.class) produced from the Java program. Figures 1.6 and 1.7 illustrate the processes of creating an executable program and then executing it.

There are two advantages to this scheme. First, because the Java program is translated to Java bytecode instead of real machine code, the resulting translation is not bound to any particular machine—it can be executed on any machine that has a Java interpreter. Second, because the Java interpreter has to interpret only the simpler bytecode rather than the more complicated Java program, it is relatively easy to write Java interpreters. These interpreters can then be embedded in other programs, notably web browsers such as Netscape Navigator and Internet Explorer (more about all these later). This makes it possible for people to write Java programs and put their translations (bytecode files) into their web pages, then for these programs to be carried out by computers of all varieties.

In order to start writing and running Java programs, ask your instructor, system administrator, help desk, or friend:

- What editor do I use? How do I invoke it?
- How do I invoke the Java compiler? How do I tell it what Java program file (.java file) to compile?
- How do I invoke the Java interpreter? How do I tell it what Java bytecode file (.class file) to interpret?

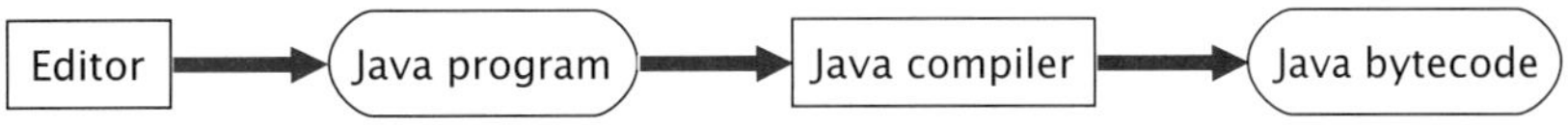

Figure 1.6
Creating an executable Java program.

Figure 1.7
Executing a Java program. The Java bytecode is interpreted by the Java virtual machine, which itself is a program running on the computer's hardware.

$$\boxed{\text{Editor}} \rightarrow (\text{Java program}) \rightarrow \boxed{\text{Java compiler}} \rightarrow (\text{Java bytecode})$$

$$(\text{Java bytecode}) \rightarrow \boxed{\text{Java interpreter}} \rightarrow \boxed{\text{Computer hardware}}$$

The appendices answer these questions for a few systems. However, if you are using a different system, or one that has been customized in some way, the answers may be different.

1.8 Time

In the previous section, we identified three activities that are done by programmers: writing the program, compiling the program, and running the program. Different issues arise in each of these phases, and it helps to refer to the time period in which each activity takes place: program-writing time, *compile-time*, and *execution-time* (also called *run-time*).

Some aspects of programming occur at one time but not another. Consider comments in a program. They are added to the program at program-writing time. They are ignored by the compiler at compile-time, and do not even exist at execution-time.

Or consider the errors that may occur during programming. They may be made by the programmer at program-writing time. They may be detected at compile-time or execution-time. For example, suppose we mistakenly wrote our first program as

```java
public class Program1 {
    public static void main(String[] arg) {
        Sistem.out.println("This is my first Java program");
        Sistem.out.println("but it won't be my last.");
    }
}
```

We would be informed of the mistake (`Sistem` instead of `System`) at compile-time. That is, when we invoke the compiler to translate this Java program into bytecode, the compiler will detect the error, print an error message such as

```
Program1.java:3: package Sistem does not exist
        Sistem.out.println("This is my first Java program")
            ^
1 error
```

and refuse to complete the translation (no `.class` file will be produced).

On the other hand, if our intention is to write additional Java programs, but we mistakenly wrote

```java
public class Program1 {
    public static void main(String[] arg) {
        System.out.println("This is my first Java program");
        System.out.println("but it will be my last.");
    }
}
```

the Java compiler would not detect the error of printing `will be my last` instead of `won't be my last`. How could it know our intentions? The compiler will produce a `.class` file, and it won't be until execution-time, when we run the program, that we will have a chance to notice the error. Unlike a compile-time error, however, there will be no obvious indication in the output that an error has occurred. Rather, we must be familiar with the program's purpose, be aware of the expected output, and see that the expected result was not produced.

Summary

Programs are texts that make a computer carry out a task. Java is a programming language that can be used to construct such texts. From another perspective, programs can be viewed as models. In Java, the basic model elements are called objects. Objects are grouped together in categories on the basis of common behavior. These categories are called classes. In this chapter, you have seen a Java program that displays a greeting on a computer screen by sending a message to an object that models a computer screen. This object is an instance of a class called `PrintStream`, a class that models output pathways. `PrintStream` is one of many predefined classes that Java provides. Later in this text, you will learn to define your own classes.

To send a message in a Java program, we specify the receiver object and the message itself. The receiver is specified using a reference—a phrase that refers to an object. For example, `System.out` is a reference to the object that models a monitor. The message is specified by the name of the desired behavior (`println`, for example) and additional information in parentheses.

At the heart of the Java programs that we considered here is a sequence of Java statements—phrases that send messages, written with semicolons after them.

Once a Java program has been written it needs to be translated by the Java compiler into Java bytecode before it can execute on the computer. The instructions in the translated program can then be interpreted—carried out—by the Java interpreter.

Key Terms

behavior Any action that may be taken by an object.

character A distinct elementary symbol, often corresponding to a single keyboard keystroke; letters, digits, punctuation marks, spaces, and tabs are all examples of characters.

class A category of objects that share the same behavior.

code A section of text written in some programming language such as Java.

common behavior The behavior shared by objects in the same class. It is this behavior that defines the class.

compiler A program that translates code written in a high-level programming language into machine language.

execute To carry out instructions of program code.

file A collection of information that has a name and that can be stored on a disk of a computer system.

identifier A sequence of characters which may be used as a name in a Java program. An identifier typically consists of an alphabetic characters (A–Z, a–z) followed by zero or more alphanumeric characters (A–Z, a–z, 0–9).

instance A particular object of a class.

interpreter A program that directly carries out the statements of a high-level programming language.

Java The name of one of the most recent and popular programming languages; also the one used in this text.

keyword A word with a special, predefined meaning in Java language.

message The mechanism by which an object's behavior is invoked. A message consists of the name of the behavior along with further details.

model A representation of something. Models are usually simpler than the object they are representing; they contain only those aspects relevant to the user of the model.

object An entity in Java that models something; a member of a class.

program A Java text that can be compiled and executed.

programming language A specialized language for writing programs.

receiver An object to which a message is sent.

reference A value or expression that refers to an object, thereby allowing us to send messages to the object.

responsibility The set of behaviors that a class provides.

statement A sentence of the Java programming language. A statement represents an action to be carried out.

string A group of characters written between double quotes.

Questions for Review

1. Can an *object* belong to more than one class?
2. What is a *message* composed of?
3. What is the importance of proper *indentation*? What about program *comments*?
4. Describe the development process of a program from its creation through its execution.
5. What are the advantages of Java bytecode?

Exercises

1. Colleges use different models of their students in the process of planning and allocating resources. What attributes of a student are important in the registrar's model? The financial aid office's model? The admissions office's model? Which features are unimportant to each of these models?

2. Consider the following situation. A proofreader for a publisher checks a manuscript for spelling errors. The manuscript is in English but also contains some words in French, German, and Latin. The proofreader uses four dictionaries, one for each of these languages, and looks up each word in the manuscript. Identify the relevant classes and objects here.

3. Consider a software system that supports traffic control at a large airport. Air traffic controllers need a view of all air traffic, ground controllers need a view of ground traffic, and every aircraft needs to be assigned to a controller at every moment. Identify the relevant classes and objects. What kinds of messages might need to be sent among objects?

4. Consider a chess player, playing the great game. To model this activity, what would the relevant classes and objects be? (If you don't know chess, pick another game, for example, checkers or Othello.)

5. `System.out` refers to a predefined Java `PrintStream` object that allows sending output to the monitor. Java also provides another predefined `PrintStream` object, referred to by `System.err`, which allows a separate stream of characters to be sent to the monitor. What specific behavior do these two `PrintStream`s have in common? What kind of message could you send to `System.err`?

6. Write a string consisting of the characters in the first word of this sentence.

7. Write a Java statement that makes the monitor display your full name.

8. Consider the statement that you wrote in Exercise 7. Identify the following elements: the reference, the message, the name of the behavior.

9. Write a statement that displays a greeting to Millicent and Micah by sending a message to `System.err` instead of `System.out`. (See Exercise 5.)

10. Write a program that prints out your name and your complete address.

11. Write a program that prints out a message that is obviously false.

12. Write a program that does absolutely nothing.

13. For each program you wrote above, add an appropriate comment in the program.

14. Look at the following program. Determine whether it is a legal Java program. Will it run correctly? Is there anything wrong with it?

```
/*
 * MyName: Displays my name to the user
 */
public class MyName {
    public static void main(String[] arg) {
    System.out.println("718-951-4193");
    }
}
```

15. Look at the following program. Determine whether it is a legal Java program. Will it run correctly? Is there anything wrong with it?

```
public class MyName public
static void
main(String[] arg) {System.out.println(
"718-951-4193");}}}
```

16. Write a program that prints out the first two lines of itself.

17. In the previous exercise, you wrote a program that reproduces itself partially. Have you ever heard of programs that do that entirely? What are they called? Moving beyond the world of programming, what sorts of things in the real world reproduce themselves? What do you make of this common attribute?

Introduction: Web Pages, HTML, and Applets

The interest in Java displayed by the computer world has centered upon the ability of Java programs to be run across the Internet. An essential element of this capability is the fact that Java makes it relatively easy to write programs that employ fancy *graphical user interfaces* (GUI), that is, interfaces that use graphic elements such as buttons, menus, scrollable windows, and images to communicate with end users.

We will introduce you to this aspect of Java in supplementary sections at the end of each chapter. The examples will often draw upon material covered in the chapter proper, but will incorporate it into a program with a GUI suitable for deployment on the World Wide Web. In order for you to gain the most from these supplements, you will need a basic level of familiarity with the web and HTML.

Browsing the World Wide Web

If you have never "surfed the web," that is, used a web browser application such as Netscape to access World Wide Web sites, you should *stop reading at this point and make arrangements to do so*. It is not difficult, and having the concrete experience of at least one session with Netscape or the equivalent is necessary for the rest of this section to have much meaning for you. So, *if you haven't done so before, go surf the web.*

Web Pages

When we surf the web, our screen jumps from one page to another as we click on various pieces of text and graphics. These *web pages* are the basic unit of information on the World Wide Web. Their significance to our endeavor is this: To place a Java program on the Internet, it must be embedded in a web page. Shortly, we will see how to do just that, but first we must learn a bit more about web page construction.

HTML: HyperText Markup Language

A web page is defined by a file containing a mixture of two constructions:

- Ordinary text (just words, like this very line)
- Special notations called *tags,* which control the appearance of the text (**bold-face** versus regular font, for example), bring in pictures, set up *links* to other web pages, and so forth.

The set of rules that govern the construction and use of tags is called HyperText Markup Language, or HTML. We can say, therefore, that a web page is defined by an HTML file. Our purpose here is not to show you how to create a state-of-the-art web page; you won't need very much HTML knowledge to deploy the Java programs you create in these supplements. But you will need to generate a little bit of HTML in order to embed Java in a web page.

HTML File Structure

HTML files should be structured in the following way:

```
<HTML>
<HEAD>
    <TITLE>
        Place the title of your web page here.
    </TITLE>
</HEAD>
<BODY>
        Write the content of your web page here: text, tags, and so on.
</BODY>
</HTML>
```

The elements <HTML>, <HEAD>, <TITLE>, and so on are tags; in HTML, tags consist of

- An open angle bracket, <
- A tag word (not case-sensitive—upper- or lowercase characters are allowed)
- Possibly some additional information, depending on the tag
- A close angle bracket >

Many HTML tags have matching *closing tags*; for example, <BODY> is matched with the closing tag </BODY>. The tags above are used to describe the HTML file's structure: The text that appears within <TITLE>...</TITLE> becomes the window title of the web browser document window. The HTML that appears within <BODY>...</BODY> is the content of the web page.

Active Content

HTML is a fantastic tool that makes it possible to organize information in new and useful ways and to present this information to a truly worldwide audience. However, it has a number of limitations. One of these is its passive character. Once downloaded onto the web browser's display area, it can only present the information that it carries. It can't interact with the user and produce new information based on that interaction. In other words, HTML does not compute (hence it is *not* a programming language). Using HTML, you cannot put up a web page that invites a customer to input specifications of an order and respond with a suggested model number, price, and anticipated delivery date. All you can do with HTML is present a list of models, prices, and similar information. The customer can only pore over them to make a decision.

This limitation is overcome by all sorts of supplements and extensions to HTML. One of these extensions is the *Java applet*. A Java applet is a Java program that is referred to in a web page and is downloaded by the browser along with the web page. Once downloaded into the browser, it starts executing. It can invite the user to type in input, or click and drag on graphical icons. It can respond to these actions and display images or text.

Writing Applets

Applets use the GUI facilities that are provided with Java. These are not part of the language proper; they belong to a package of predefined classes known as the *abstract window toolkit* (AWT). Most of the code in the following sections will employ language constructs that are covered in the first several chapters of this book. Early on, we may not understand exactly how a piece of code fits into the big picture, but we will at least understand what it does at the statement level.

However, there will be some "magic" (i.e., portions of code whose purpose or even basic meaning cannot be discussed until later—this will obviously occur more frequently in the beginning and less as we progress). Our attitude toward this is *do as we do* (i.e., play with the code presented in the following sections and build upon it). For example, in the following sample piece of code, you will see the method invocation:

```
g.drawString("Welcome to Java.",20,20);
```

Modifying (playing with) the arguments will give you a sense of how the coordinates (20,20) work and how this method behaves. We will provide examples and some explanation, but you will have to experiment and learn to read existing documentation.

The *Java Application Programming Interface* (API) is a description of the classes and methods distributed with Java. This documentation can be accessed via the World Wide Web (ask your instructor or administrator for details, or jump ahead to the end of Chapter 3). All the classes and methods used in these sections are documented in the Java API. In addition, other related methods of interest (e.g., changing colors or fonts) will often be documented nearby. You should feel free to experiment with such methods. You may crash your program, but that too is part of the learning process.

Reading documentation is an essential skill any computer scientist must acquire. It is also often a multipass effort, sometimes because the documentation is not particularly well written, other times because we do not yet have the full prerequisite background. Do not be discouraged if you cannot make much sense out of the API at first. Frequent contact with it will make you familiar with its "geography," and you will eventually feel comfortable with it.

In summary, the following sections are a break in approach from the main parts of the chapter. They are intended to be fun, as well as instructive. Remember, though, that these sections are more like the bumper car ride in an amusement park than driving in the city, and things may get quite bumpy at times.

Our First Applet

Let's start with the following simple applet

```java
import java.awt.*;                          // Our first applet
import java.applet.*;
public class FirstApplet extends Applet {
    public void paint(Graphics g) {
        g.drawString("Welcome to Java.", 20,20);
    }
}
```

This is just the applet version of the program we encountered at the beginning of the chapter, which began as follows:

```java
public class Program0 {
   public static void main(String[] arg) {
```

There is almost a line-by-line correspondence between the two:

- The `import` lines indicate that the applet requires predefined classes from both the AWT and the applet packages; we'll see more of this in Chapter 3.
- The two lines after `import` and the two lines that end the applet correspond to their counterparts in `Program0`.
- In an applet, we have no `PrintStream` object available; one way to display text is to send a `drawString()` message to a `Graphics` object instead of using `println()`.

A `Graphics` object models the drawing behavior of a portion of a computer screen; that is, it will respond to messages requesting that rectangles be drawn, background colors be set, current font information be returned, and so on. One of these methods, `drawString()`, allows a string to be displayed at a particular position on the screen. This method requires three additional pieces of information: first, the string to be displayed, then two numbers specifying the horizontal and vertical coordinates (x and y, respectively) of the starting position of the text on the screen (i.e., the location at which the first character is displayed).

Embedding an applet in a web page means arranging for it to be downloaded as part of a web page and executed by the web browser. To embed the `First-Applet` applet, do the following:

- Compile `FirstApplet.java`, yielding `FirstApplet.class`.
- Include the following HTML code in a web page:

```html
<APPLET CODE="FirstApplet.class" WIDTH=300 HEIGHT=60>
</APPLET>
```

(The class file must be in the same directory or folder as the HTML file and, depending on the system, the access permissions may have to be changed—you may have to consult your instructor, system administrator, or help desk for details.)

A complete HTML file for this applet might be as follows:

```
<HTML>
<HEAD>
    <TITLE>Hw1</TITLE>
</HEAD>
<BODY>
    <HR>
        <APPLET CODE="FirstApplet.class" WIDTH=300 HEIGHT=60>
        </APPLET>
    <HR>
    <A HREF="FirstApplet.java">The source.</A>
</BODY>
</HTML>
```

In addition to the structuring tags discussed above, this HTML file uses the `<HR>` and `<A>...</A>` tags. The `<HR>` tag causes a horizontal line (or "horizontal rule") to appear when the page is displayed. The `<A>` tag allows us to provide a *link* to another document on the web. Here, the HREF indicates that we are providing a link to another location. The text in double quotes (which are optional) gives the location: in this case, the file `FirstApplet.java`, which we assume is in the same directory as the HTML file and `FirstApplet.class`. When the web page is displayed, the text between the closing > of the `<A>` tag and the `</A>` closing tag (in this case, `The source.`) will have an appearance that distinguishes it from regular text (typically, underlined and in a different color).

When this web page is accessed, the web browser will detect the APPLET tag and download the `FirstApplet.class` file. The web browser creates a `Graphics` object and associates it with part of the screen. The size of the screen portion associated with the `Graphics` object is determined in part by the WIDTH and HEIGHT specifications in the APPLET tag. At some point, the browser starts executing the applet, and, like `main()` in the programs in the chapter, `paint()` executes. In the above example, it simply invokes the `drawString()` method of this `Graphic` object, and the text `"Welcome to Java."` appears on the screen (see Figure 1.8).

Shapes and Colors

Besides drawing `Strings`, `Graphics` provides the following simple geometric object drawing methods:

- `fillOval()`
- `fillRect()`
- `drawOval()`

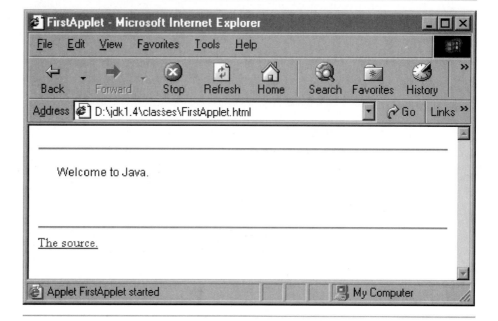

Figure 1.8
Executing the
FirstApplet applet.

- drawRect(): These four methods each require four numbers specifying the *x,y* coordinates and width and height of the shape to be displayed
- drawLine(): Requires four numbers specifying the *x,y* coordinates of the start and end of a line

For example:

```
import java.awt.*;                    // Our first applet: a variation
import java.applet.*;
public class FirstApplet extends Applet {
    public void paint(Graphics g) {
        g.fillOval(20,20,120,160);
    }
}
```

In addition, the AWT provides a Color class and Graphics.setColor() method that allow us to change the display color. Colors are described using three integers that specify the amount of red, green, and blue, each on a scale of 0 to 255. To change the color to purple, we create a Color object that represents purple and then send a setColor() message to the Graphics object before displaying our graphics. For example, we can continue to modify our first applet as follows:

```
public void paint(Graphics g) {
    Color c = new Color(180,10,120);
    g.setColor(c);
    g.drawString("This is everyone's first applet.",20,20);
}
```

Lots of red and blue, but not too much or it will be too light; there is almost no green.

The AWT also provides several predefined colors, named Color.red, Color.yellow, Color.green, and so on, that we can use instead of creating new Color objects.

Suggested Experiments

1. Write a small HTML file that sets up a web page containing your name, centered and in boldface. The title of the page should also be your name.

2. Write a Java program whose output is the complete HTML code that you created in the previous exercise.

3. Take all three versions of FirstApplet and experiment with the arguments to all the methods. Try making beautiful and hideous colors, big bold print, and fine print suitable for disclaimers. Replace fillOval() with the other geometric object-drawing methods.

4. Write an applet that displays a circle of one color inside a square of another color. What, if any, is the relationship between the size and dimension of the circle and the size and dimension of the square?

5. Write an applet that displays a square of one color inside a circle of another color. What, if any, is the relationship between the size and dimension of the circle and the size and dimension of the square?

6. Write an applet that displays the sentence "This is a test." on one "line" with each word displayed in a different color. What's especially tedious about this task?

Chapter 2

Sending Messages and Performing Operations

2.1 Introduction

Chapter 1 presented some fundamental Java concepts that enabled us to create our first program. In that program, we sent a message to a predefined object of the `PrintStream` class in order to print an announcement on the screen.

In this chapter we will continue our exploration of the use of Java's predefined objects. As we proceed, we'll acquire some additional tools and techniques that will be useful in working with all objects.

2.2 Using `PrintStream` Objects

In the last chapter we sent messages of the form

println("*something to display*")

to the `PrintStream` object to which `System.out` refers. When the `PrintStream` object receives such a message, the string of characters in double quotes is displayed on the monitor and the *cursor* (which indicates where the next character will appear) moves to the beginning of the next line.

A similar message we can send to a `PrintStream` object is of the form

print("*something to display*")

As with `println()`, the characters in the double quotes are displayed. There is one difference, however, in the `PrintStream` object's behavior. When the `PrintStream` object receives a `print()` message, the cursor does not advance to the next line. Thus, the next character displayed will be on the same line. For example

```
System.out.print("JA");
System.out.print("VA");
```

displays

```
JAVA
```

on the monitor, while

```
System.out.println("JA");
System.out.println("VA");
```

displays

```
JA
VA
```

on the monitor. Repeatedly invoking `print()` builds a single line of output. Invoking `println()` guarantees that the next character displayed will appear on a new line.

`PrintStream` accepts a second form of the `println()` message, one that requires no additional information. Sending such a `println()` message, as in

```
System.out.println();
```

causes the `PrintStream` object referred to by `System.out` to display subsequent output on the next line without displaying any characters first. Note that even though there is no string of characters in double quotes, the parentheses are still required in the message:

```
println()
```

Here is another example:

```
System.out.print("The Java");
System.out.println();
System.out.print("Programming Language");
```

displays

```
The Java
Programming Language
```

Java Interlude   *References, Methods, and Messages*

A *reference* in Java is any phrase that refers to an object. We use references in Java to identify the object we wish to send a message to. Strictly speaking, `System.out` is not an object, but a reference to one. However, rather than writing the cumbersome phrase, "the object to which `System.out` refers," we shall often simply write "the `System.out` object." This usage is acceptable provided we remember that `System.out` is a reference to the object, not the object itself.

As we saw earlier, it is **behavior** that distinguishes objects in one class from those in another class. In Java, object behavior is specified by *methods*. A **method** is a section of Java code within a class that provides a particular behavior. Associated with every method is an identifier that names the method: the **method-name**.

A class's methods determine the kind of messages that can be sent to objects of that class. You already know three of the PrintStream class's methods:

- println, with additional information (a string of characters)
- println, with no additional information
- print, with additional information (a string of characters)

Because the PrintStream class has these methods, every PrintStream object has them too. The additional information items that are sometimes provided in a message are called the **arguments**. The print() and one of the println() methods of PrintStream each require one argument.

W. ᵗʰ these terms in mind, we can give a more precise form for a message:

method-name(arguments)

Some methods, as we shall see, require more than one argument.

Overloading Methods

The PrintStream class has more than one method by the name of println(). The methods are distinguished from each other by the arguments they require; in Java terms, we say that they have different **signatures** (that is, their names and arguments are different). One println() requires a string of characters as an argument; the other requires no argument at all. The methods are distinct; they model different, though related, behaviors. Methods of the same name but different signatures in the same class are said to be overloaded. The practice of designing classes with such methods is called **overloading**.

When a Message Is Sent

Java statements are ordinarily executed by the computer in the order in which they appear. However, when a **message** is sent to an object (the receiver), the execution of the sending code is suspended until the receiver acts on the message by executing the method indicated by the method-name in the message. Eventually, the receiver finishes executing its method. At that point, the execution of the sending code is resumed. We say in that case that the method (of the receiver) *returns* to the sending code.

Sending a message to an object is often called *invoking the method*. For example, in

```
rocket.launch()
```

we are sending a launch() message to the object referred to by rocket. We may also say we're invoking the launch() method of that object.

Identifiers, Again

Java has certain conventions for selecting names. The first letter of a class name should be uppercase (as in PrintStream). The first letter of a method name should be lowercase (as in `print()` and `println()`). All other letters should be lowercase except where needed to make it easy to see multiple words within an identifier—that's why we write `PrintStream` instead of `Printstream`.

2.3 The `String` Class

Another class that Java predefines is named `String`. It models a sequence of characters (letters, digits, punctuation marks, spaces, or special symbols). Such sequences are commonplace (license plate numbers, names, a line in a love letter, an entire essay).

In Java, any group of characters in double quotes, like

`"Welcome to Java Programming"`

is a reference to a `String` object that models that precise character sequence. Thus, `"Welcome to Java Programming"` is a reference to a `String` object modeling the characters W, e, l, and so on. We have already seen this kind of a reference; it is the argument we send in `println()` and `print()` messages to `System.out`, as shown in Figure 2.1. `String` references of this kind are called **String constants**. (See Figure 2.2.)

What can we do with a reference to a `String` object? We have already seen one use—as an argument to a message:

`System.out.println("Welcome to Java Programming!");`

We have seen references to `PrintStream` objects used to identify receivers of messages. In the statement above, `System.out`, a reference to a `PrintStream` object, identifies the receiver of a `println()` message. Sending messages to objects is

Figure 2.1
A `String` object is referenced within quotes.

Figure 2.2
`String` constants: References to `String` objects. `"Hello"`, a `String` constant, is a reference. It refers to a `String` object that models the character sequence H e l l o.

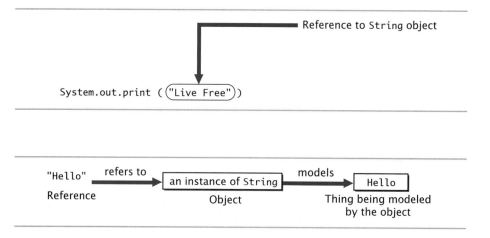

how we elicit their behavior. Similarly, we can use references to String objects to identify receivers of messages for String objects.

PrintStream objects can receive print() and println() messages. What kind of messages can we send to String objects? That question is the same as each of the following two questions:

- What behavior does the String class provide?
- What methods does the String class provide?

One of the methods String provides is called toUpperCase(). The toUpper-Case() method requires no arguments. To send a toUpperCase() message to the String object that "ibm" refers to, we follow the form:

reference. method-name(arguments)

and write

"ibm".toUpperCase()

The receiver of the toUpperCase() message is the String object to which the String constant "ibm" refers. Figure 2.3 illustrates the process of sending a toUpper-Case() message.

You might think that this method changes the *receiver*, making it all uppercase. However, the designers of the String class decided that a String method should never change the String itself, but rather produce a new String object with the desired change. So, the toUpperCase() method creates a new object, one that is also an instance of the String class. This object has the same characters as the original except that all the letters are uppercase.

A new object is useless unless there is a way to reference it. So besides creating a new, all-uppercase String object, toUpperCase() provides a reference to this object. In Java lingo we say that toUpperCase() **returns** a reference to the new object. Alternatively, we say the **return value** of toUpperCase() is a reference to a String object. This return value is represented by the phrase that sent the message in the first place. That means that

"ibm".toUpperCase()

Figure 2.3
Sending a toUpper-Case() message. The toUpperCase() message is sent to the String referred to by "ibm".

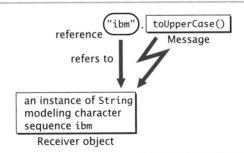

not only sends a `toUpperCase()` message to the `"ibm"` object, but also represents the return value from `toUpperCase()`, which is a reference to the newly created `"IBM"` object. See Figure 2.4 for an illustration of a returned reference.

What can we do, then, with an expression like `"ibm".toUpperCase()` if it represents a reference to a `String` object? Remember, we can take two actions with references. We can

- Send messages to the object the reference refers to
- Send the reference itself as an argument in a message to another object

For example, because one of the `println()` methods of `PrintStream` allows a `String` reference as an argument, we could write

```
System.out.println("ibm".toUpperCase());
```

We can thus use the reference returned by `toUpperCase()` as the argument in the `println()` message. In effect, we are using a reference to the `String` `"IBM"` as an argument.

Figure 2.4
A returned reference to a new object. The entire expression `"ibm".toUpper-Case()` is the reference returned by `toUpperCase`.

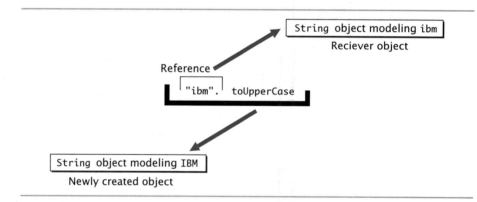

2.4 Methods, Arguments, and Return Values

We have so far encountered four methods: (1) `print()`, (2) `println()` with an argument, and (3) `println()` without an argument, provided by the `PrintStream` class, as well as (4) `toUpperCase()`, provided by the `String` class. The `print()` and `println()` methods do not return a reference to an object, but the `toUpper-Case()` method does. The latter does not receive any arguments, whereas the `print()` and `println()` methods both receive a reference to a `String` object, a reference such as `"hello, world"`.

As we proceed, we will learn many more methods of these and other classes in Java. Becoming familiar with a method means knowing what it returns and what argument(s) it receives. Here are the characteristics of the four methods encountered so far:

CLASS	METHOD	RETURN VALUE	ARGUMENTS RECEIVED
PrintStream	println	None	None
PrintStream	println	None	Reference to a String object
PrintStream	print	None	Reference to a String object
String	toUpperCase	Reference to a String object	None

The signature of a method consists of its name and a description of its arguments. The **prototype** of a method consists of a description of its return value along with its signature. The preceding table gives us information about the prototypes (and therefore the signatures) of four methods.

2.5 Reference Variables

A **variable** is an identifier that can be given a value, as in the letter x in "let x be 5." It is called a variable because it can contain different values at different times; that is, its value can vary. A **reference variable** is a variable whose value is a reference.

Reference variables allow us to save a reference for a later or repeated use. For example, suppose we had an identifier line that had somehow been given the following reference value:

"xxxxxxxxxxxxxxxxxxxxxxxxxxxxxxxxxxx"

Such a variable is called a *String reference variable*, because the reference it is given is a reference to a String object.

If we wanted to print three lines of xs, we could write

```
System.out.println(line);
System.out.println(line);
System.out.println(line);
```

When the argument is evaluated, the value of the variable replaces the variable. It is as if we had written

```
System.out.println("xxxxxxxxxxxxxxxxxxxxxxxxxxxxxxxxxxx");
System.out.println("xxxxxxxxxxxxxxxxxxxxxxxxxxxxxxxxxxx");
System.out.println("xxxxxxxxxxxxxxxxxxxxxxxxxxxxxxxxxxx");
```

If at various places in our program we needed to print a line of xs of this sort, it is easier to use line than to type the same number of xs out each time.

If we wanted a line of uppercase Xs, we could write

```
System.out.println(line.toUpperCase());
```

Again, the value of the variable, a reference to a String of xs, replaces line. The toUpperCase() message is sent to the String of xs, creating a String of Xs. It is as if we had written

```
System.out.println("xxxxxxxxxxxxxxxxxxxxxxxxxxxxxxxxxxxxx".toUpperCase());
```

Declaring Reference Variables and Saving References

To introduce a reference variable in a Java program, we write the class of the object to be referenced followed by the name (an identifier of our choice) of the reference variable:

```
String       greeting; // Will refer to a String modeling a greeting.
PrintStream  output;   // Will refer to the same PrintStream object that
                            System.out does.
```

These statements (note the required semicolon!) are called declarations. A **declaration** is a statement that introduces a variable in a program. It supplies an identifier that will be the name of the variable and a type, such as String or PrintStream, that establishes what kind of value the variable can possess. The first declaration establishes that greeting is a variable that can contain a reference to a String object, and the second establishes that output is a variable that can contain a reference to a PrintStream object. We say that we have *declared* greeting as a String reference variable and output as a PrintStream reference variable. Until a variable is declared in a program, we can't use it. Any attempt to do so will result in a compile-time error.

A newly declared variable has no value. To give a variable a value, we use an **assignment statement**:

```
greeting = "Hello";
```

This statement *assigns* to greeting the reference "Hello" so that they both refer to the same object. We could then write

```
System.out.println(greeting);
```

instead of

```
System.out.println("Hello");
```

Figure 2.5 illustrates the result of executing greeting = "Hello";.

The general form of the assignment statement is

variable = value;

Figure 2.5

String **reference variables and** String **objects. The** String **constant** "Hello" **and the variable** greeting **refer to the same object. Therefore,** "Hello" **and** greeting **can be used interchangeably to send messages to this object or to refer to it in an argument.**

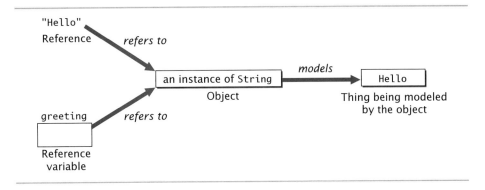

The *value* is *assigned* to (saved in) the *variable*. The value must have the same type as the variable.

To make output refer to the same PrintStream object as System.out, we may write

```
output = System.out;
```

We could then write

```
output.println("Hello");
```

instead of

```
System.out.println("Hello");
```

It is convenient to use a reference variable to hold a returned reference from a message. For example, we might have

```
String  bigGreeting;
bigGreeting = greeting.toUpperCase();
```

This code makes bigGreeting refer to the new String object returned by the receiver of the greeting.toUpperCase() message. If we need to use the reference to the new String repeatedly, we can write

```
System.out.println(bigGreeting);
System.out.println(bigGreeting);
System.out.println(bigGreeting);
```

instead of repeatedly sending toUpperCase() messages to greeting:

```
System.out.println(greeting.toUpperCase());
System.out.println(greeting.toUpperCase());
System.out.println(greeting.toUpperCase());
```

Variables and Assignment

Variables

A variable is an identifier that can have a value. One kind of value—the only kind we've seen so far—is a reference to an object. To create a variable, we must *declare* it by indicating the type of value it may contain, followed by the identifier that names the variable. The form of a **declaration** statement is

type   identifier;

Alternatively, if there is more than one identifier of the same type to declare, we can use this form:

type   identifier1, identifier2, . . .;

The convention for naming variables is the same as for methods: Start with a lowercase letter. If the variable is intended to be a reference variable, then we must write, in place of *type*, the name of the class of the object. For example,

```
String s;
```

makes the identifier s the name of a reference variable, one that can contain a reference to a String object. Strictly speaking s is not a variable—it is the *name* of a variable. The variable itself is actually a small portion of the computer's internal memory. However, most of the time we will not make that distinction and we will speak of "s, the variable," meaning the variable that is named s.

Assignment

Variables are given values by assignment. Until a variable is assigned a value, it cannot be used for any purpose. An assignment statement has the form

variable = value;

We often speak of the *variable* as the *left-hand side* of the assignment, and the *value* as the *right-hand side*. The variable must have already been declared, and the value must be consistent with the variable's declared type. For example, given the declarations

```
String      s;
PrintStream p;
```

these assignment statements are legal:

```
s = "Hello";
p = System.out;
```

but these are not:

```
s = System.out;    // Wrong! Can't assign a PrintStream reference to a String variable
p = "Hello";       // Wrong! Can't assign a String reference to a PrintStream variable
```

Consider the assignment

```
String t =  "Red tape holds up bridge";
```

The variable t now contains a reference to the same String object that "Red tape holds up bridge" refers to. This assignment doesn't keep us from subsequently making t refer to some other object of the String class, for that is what it means to be a variable: Its value varies.

Assignment Is Not Equality

Consider the assignment

```
t =  "Springtime";
```

This statement is an *imperative*, a direct order to the computer to make the value of the variable t be a reference to the String object referred to by the String constant at that point in the program. It does *not* assert that t already refers to the String object "Springtime" or that t will always be associated with this object. One thing, and only one thing, is certain in connection with this statement. Immediately after it is executed by the computer, the variable t refers to the same String object referred to by "Springtime". However, it is entirely possible that the very next statement in the program could change the value of t again. Consider the sequence

```
t = "Springtime";
t = "Wintertime";
```

Although it is unlikely that this sequence of statements would be useful, it is perfectly legal. It illustrates the way in which a variable contains a value. These two statements will be executed by the computer in the order in which they appear. After the first statement above is executed, the value of t is a reference to the String object "Springtime". Any previous value contained in t is lost. Immediately after the first assignment, the second statement is executed, after which t refers to the String object "Wintertime". Now, the reference to the String object "Springtime" is gone. (See Figure 2.6.) Variables *remember* (contain) only one thing at a time, the last value they were assigned. In particular, reference variables refer to only one object at a time.

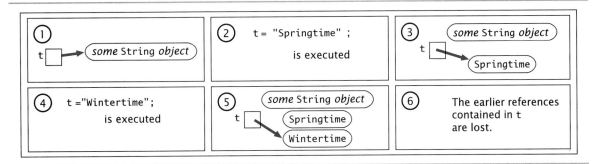

Figure 2.6   The references in t change.

Initializers

Variable declarations may include an **initializer** that specifies the initial value we want the variable to have. Thus, if we know this initial value when we declare the variable, we can write, for example,

```
String s = "Hello";
```

rather than

```
String s;
s = "Hello";
```

Reference Variables and Objects

A reference variable refers to just one object at a time, but several reference variables may simultaneously refer to the same object:

```
String     s, t;
s = "Springtime";
t = s;
```

Here the first assignment makes s refer to the same object that the String constant "Springtime" refers to. The second assignment makes t refer to the same object that s refers to. In the end, two variables, s and t, are referring to the same object. This process is illustrated in Figure 2.7.

A Subtle but Important Point: Two Roles for Variables

We said above that a variable is an identifier that can have a value. Variables serve as a program's memory as it executes. Memory can be used for two different, though related, purposes:

- Storage of information for possible future use, like memorizing a fact for a test
- Retrieval of information for immediate use, like remembering the fact during the test

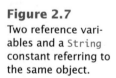

Figure 2.7
Two reference variables and a String constant referring to the same object.

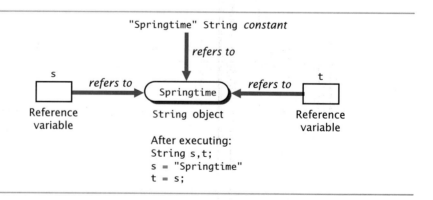

The role that a variable plays—storage or retrieval—depends on whether it is on the left or right side of the = in an assignment statement.

Consider the following code:

```
String  s;        Here s has the role of storing and "Bob" the role of retrieving a value.
String  t;        Here t has the role of storing and s the role of retrieving a value.
s = "Bob";
t = s;
```

In the first assignment statement, the value "Bob" is *saved* in s, which appears on the left side of the =. In the second assignment statement, s is on the right side of the = and its value is *retrieved* and assigned to t. When it appears on the left side, s is a variable whose old value is discarded and is assigned a new value; when it appears on the right side, s retrieves a value.

Variables are Independent

Consider again the above code. The last assignment,

```
t = s;
```

guarantees only that after it is executed, t will have the same value as s. If we then change s by assigning a new value to it

```
s = "Payroll";
```

the value of t does not change. The assignment of s to t did not set up a permanent equality relationship between s and t, it just copied the value of s to t at the time of executing the assignment. Variables are independent of each other—their values can vary independently.

Constants are Not Variables

Constants such as "Bob" are not variables and cannot be assigned to. The word **constant** itself means something unchanging, something that does not vary. "Bob" cannot have its value changed. Thus the following line

```
"Bob" = s;
```

is illegal. Only something that can store a value can be on the left side of the assignment operator.

Statements

So far we have encountered three kinds of Java statements (also summarized in Table 2.1):

- Declarations
- Assignment statements
- Message-sending statements

Declarations may include initializers or not, as

```
String name;
String name = "William";
```

The right-hand side of an assignment statement can be a value that comes from invoking a method on an object that results in a value, as in the following statement:

```
bigGreeting = greeting.toUpperCase();
```

An example of the last kind of statement can be seen in the following `println()` message to the `System.out` object:

```
System.out.println("Bonjour, tout le monde");
```

TABLE 2.1 THREE KINDS OF STATEMENTS

STATEMENT	PURPOSE	EXAMPLE
Declaration	Create a variable	`String   s;`
Assignment	Associate value with variable	`s = "Hey!";`
Message-sending	Send a message to an object	`System.out.println(s);`

Variations

The computer executes the statements in Java in the order that they appear. Order can be very important. If you want to fry an egg, it is not a good idea to put the egg in the pan first, heat it for three minutes, and then crack it. However, some variations in the order of statements are possible. Consider the following program:

```
public class Program1 {
   public static void main(String[] arg) {
      String  greeting;
      String  bigGreeting;
      greeting = "Yo, World";
      bigGreeting = greeting.toUpperCase();
      System.out.println(greeting);
      System.out.println(bigGreeting);
   }
}
```

The program prints out "Yo, World" (the `String` object that `greeting` refers to) and then prints out the uppercase version "YO, WORLD" (referred to by `bigGreeting`).

Alternatively, we could have written:

```
public class Program1 {
    public static void main(String[] arg)  {
        String  greeting;
        greeting = "Yo, World";
        String  bigGreeting;
        bigGreeting = greeting.toUpperCase();
        System.out.println(greeting);
        System.out.println(bigGreeting);
    }
}
```

Declarations can come anywhere provided they precede any appearance of the variable.

or

```
public class Program2 {
    public static void main(String[] arg) {
        String  greeting = "Yo, World";
        String  bigGreeting = greeting.toUpperCase();
        System.out.println(greeting);
        System.out.println(bigGreeting);
    }
}
```

Declarations can include assignments to the variable. (These are called initializations.)

2.6 Imperative Programming: Doing the Work

We've spent a lot of time exploring one of the fundamental ideas behind Java programming: accomplishing a task by sending a message to an appropriate object. We're already able to write programs that, though small, still display moderately interesting behavior simply by sending messages to objects in Java's predefined classes.

As we saw in Chapter 1, the idea of programming by sending messages closely mirrors how many complex tasks are achieved in "the real world." For example, once an architect has designed a house, she then builds it by sending a message (i.e., a blueprint) to a contractor. The contractor may lay the plumbing and wiring by sending messages to a plumber and to an electrician. Coordinating the plumbing and the wiring (as well as the many other tasks involved in constructing the house) will require many messages among the builders.

But while much effort goes into sending all these messages, sooner or later the workers will have to apply their own particular skills, making decisions and carrying out the (often repetitive) tasks they have been trained to do. The carpenters will have to determine in what order to construct the many parts of the house, pound nails over and over again, and decide what kind of saw to use to cut the lumber; the electricians will have to screw on a multitude of wirecaps, determine how to wire the circuit breaker, and decide what gauge wire to use for different sections of the wiring; the plumbers will have to go through the correct sequence of tasks to install the kitchen sink. And everyone will have to make sure that their work conforms to the local building code. Doing this kind of work doesn't rely primarily on sending messages (although the electricians may have to coordinate with the carpenters to ensure that the circuit breaker is adequately supported). Instead, it depends on the knowledge and skill that these individuals have acquired.

In the same way, while most programming work involves determining what messages to send to which objects, programmers also need to write code to "do the work"—to perform some calculation, to make a decision, to perform some repetitive task. This type of programming is known as **imperative programming**: Instead of sending a message to some object, we are directly commanding the machine to perform some fundamental computational task for us.

In this chapter, we will take a brief look at two important aspects of imperative programming: working with numbers and making simple decisions. In the next several chapters, we will occasionally present sections that focus on other aspects of imperative programming.

Integer Types and Arithmetic

From the 1940s, when the first computers were used in code breaking, nuclear reaction simulation and ballistic calculations, to the present graphical environments where drawing shapes and determining the width of a line of characters in a proportional font are common tasks, numerical processing has been a prime constituent of the "work that is to be done." Performing arithmetic computations is a fundamental function of a computer. Java, therefore, makes it easy for us to manipulate numeric values. How are these values represented? A little thought suggests that numbers have characteristics that distinguish them from objects: Where objects are *active*, exhibiting behavior that may model some real world action, numbers are *passive*, being manipulated by operations like addition and subtraction. Following this intuition, Java does not offer predefined classes to provide numeric processing. Instead, it gives us a built-in data type, `int`, that represents integers. Along with this data type, Java provides the basic arithmetic operations such as +, -, *, and /, which may be used to construct standard arithmetic expressions such as

```
x + (y / z)
```

and

```
rate * hours
```

Printing of integers is provided by the (overloaded) `print()` and `println()` methods of `PrintStream`, which accept an `int` as an argument:

```
System.out.println(rate*hours);
```

On the whole, the use of `int` corresponds closely to our intuitive notion of arithmetic expressions using integers.

Built-in, or **primitive data types** are so called because they are closely related to the computer's hardware—for example, computers are designed to manipulate numbers easily—and therefore bypass much of Java's object-based structure. So, unlike objects, primitive data types have no methods or instance variables—an integer value is the only thing associated with a value of type `int`.

Just as we can use reference variables to store references to use later, we can use "primitive" variables to store primitive data values. Variables of this kind can be treated in much the same way as variables that refer to objects. They can (and must) be declared. The statement

```
int  i;
```

declares a new variable i; rather than containing a reference to an object, though, i will contain an `int` value. We may use primitive data types in assignment statements. For example,

```
i = 7;
```

has the effect of storing the `int` value 7 in the variable i. These two statements can be combined as

```
int i = 7;
```

if we want to provide an initial value for i.

Earlier we saw that when we assign a value to a reference variable, the text on the right side of the assignment statement can be quite simple or much more complex, as long as it provides a reference to an object of the appropriate class. We've seen both of these assignment statements:

```
s = t;
bigGreeting = greeting.toUpperCase();
```

Similarly, when assigning to an `int` variable, we can assign simple values (like 7), or we can use more complex expressions that represent integer values. These few statements

```
int i = 10, j = 15, k = 7;
int answer;
answer = (k + 17) * (j - (i / 2));
```

will store the value 240 in answer.

The Basic Arithmetic Operators

These complex expressions are constructed using the familiar arithmetic operators, some of which are listed in Table 2.2. These operators can be applied to int variables and values to represent a new int value; for example

```
base * height / 2
25*quarters + 10*dimes + 5*nickels * pennies
```

are valid expressions (assuming that all the variables involved are of type int) that could be used in assignment statements such as

```
area = base * height / 2;
```

Because we are dealing with integers (whole numbers) only, / means integer division. The quotient is an integer and the remainder is ignored. This means that 17/3 is 5, and the remainder, 2, is discarded. To calculate the remainder, or *modulus*, we write 17%3. For example,

```
i = 97;
quotient = i / 10;
remainder = i % 10;
```

stores 9 in quotient and 7 in remainder.

TABLE 2.2   BASIC ARITHMETIC OPERATORS

OPERATOR	OPERATION
+	Addition
–	Subtraction
*	Multiplication
/	Division
%	Remainder

Precedence

There is a potential for ambiguity in expressions with more than one operator. An expression is *ambiguous* if there is more than one way of interpreting it. Consider the expression 5+3*2. This might be interpreted to mean either 16 (if we do the addition 5+3 first and then multiply by 2) or 11 (if we do the multiplication 3*2 first and then add the result to 5).

Java, along with most programming languages and mathematics itself, uses **precedence rules** to resolve such ambiguities. For example, multiplication and division have higher precedence than addition and subtraction and are therefore done first. In the case of 5+3*2, this forces the second interpretation (* before +) and the result is 11. As usual, parentheses can be used to override precedence. If, in 5+3*2, we want the addition to be performed first, we must write (5+3)*2. If you were thinking that the multiplication is obviously performed first, that's precisely because these precedence rules have become second nature for you.

Parentheses can also be used for clarity or when a programmer is uncertain of the precedence rules. As you learn more of the Java language, you will encounter many more operators. As the number of operators grows, so does the number of precedence rules. It is perfectly acceptable to use parentheses to guarantee the desired interpretation. Thus, you may write 5+(3*2) instead of 5+3*2. The precedence rules are just shortcuts that allow us to use fewer parentheses. Table 2.3 lists some of Java's operators and their precedence.

TABLE 2.3   COMMON JAVA OPERATORS IN ORDER OF DECREASING PRECEDENCE

OPERATOR	OPERATION
++, --	Increment, decrement
*, /, %	Multiply, divide, modulus
+, -	Add/concatenate, subtract
<, >, <=, >=	Less/greater than, less/greater than or equal
==, !=	Equal, not equal
=, +=, -=, /=, *=, %=	Assignment, assignment and operation

Compound Assignment Operators

Assignments involving arithmetic expressions often take the following form:

x = x *op some-value*

where *op* is an arithmetic operator. For example,

```
yearToDate = yearToDate + currentWages;
```

or

Op

```
salary = salary * 1.20;    // 20% raise
```

This pattern occurs so often that Java provides special operators to handle such assignments. The above statements can be rewritten as

```
yearToDate += currentWages;
```

and

```
salary *= 1.20;              // 20% raise
```

These operators are known as *compound assignment operators*. The effect is to view the variable on the left-hand side of the assignment as both an operand to the arithmetic operator and as the target of the assignment. Each of the above arithmetic operators has a corresponding compound assignment operator, as shown in Table 2.4.

TABLE 2.4 RELATED BINARY AND COMPOUND ASSIGNMENT OPERATORS

OPERATOR	COMPOUND ASSIGNMENT	EFFECT
+	+=	Add and assign
–	–=	Subtract and assign
*	*=	Multiply and assign
/	/=	Divide and assign
%	%=	Take remainder and assign

We strongly advocate the use of these operators, and we will always write x += 3 instead of x = x + 3. This is not because we are lazy typists. It is a matter of minimizing the likelihood of error. If our purpose is to add 3 to x, x = x + 3 is more error prone than x += 3 because we could mistype the second x (hit c instead, for example). This is especially true for long identifiers. If the mistyped identifier is not a variable name, the compiler will catch the error. However, if it is a name of a variable (for example, customerName1 instead of customerName2), we could introduce an error that is murderously difficult to track down.

One characteristic of operators is that they produce values. This is true of compound assignment operators as well. Therefore they can be embedded in larger expressions:

```
x = y + (z += w);
```

The result of an assignment operator is the value assigned to the left-hand side. In the above example, the value of the expression z += w would be z + w because that is the value assigned to z by the compound assignment +=.

In this book we will not embed assignment operators in larger expressions, nor do we recommend doing so. The proper use of such expressions is often misunderstood, and their misapplication can result in code that is hard to understand, frequently incorrect, and difficult to debug.

Interestingly, our familiar assignment symbol, =, is also an *assignment operator* and therefore also produces a value (the value assigned to the left-hand side) just as the compound assignment operators do. We will use this fact in one way only: in a multiple assignment, as in

```
x = y = z = 0;
```

Here, z is assigned the value 0. The value of *that* operation is 0, which is assigned to y. The value of *that* operation is then also 0, which in turn is assigned to x.

Increment/Decrement

The most common arithmetic operations in a program are adding and subtracting 1:

```
x = x + 1;        // Also written as x += 1;
```

and

```
x = x - 1;        // x -= 1;
```

As before, Java provides us with special operators for these assignments. The above two statements may be rewritten as

```
x++;
```

and

```
x--;
```

The first is called an *increment operator* because its effect is to increment (increase) its operand by 1. The second is called a *decrement operator* because it decrements (decreases) its operand by 1. (There are two other increment/decrement operators: ++x and --x. For our purposes they have the same effect as the pair presented above.)

Because the operand is itself modified (as opposed to producing a result by being added to 1), the following are illegal:

```
6++;     ◄——————————————— No good—can't modify a literal!
```

and

```
(x + y)++;   ◄——————————— No good—can't modify an expression!
```

Like the assignment operators, the increment and decrement operators result in a value and can appear as operands of larger expressions, and as in the case of assignment operators, we strongly caution against doing so.

EXAMPLE Average of three ints.   We can illustrate the use of these operations with a simple program that calculates the average of three integer values. Recall that to calculate an average of a list of numbers, we first find their sum, then divide the sum by the size of the list (in this case, we are working with just three numbers, so we'll divide by 3). Let's write our code to mirror this process very closely. First, we must declare and initialize three int variables:

```
int num1 = 11;
int num2 = 4;
int num3 = 21;
```

We must also declare a variable that will hold the sum of the three integer values, and we need a variable to store the result of the average calculation:

```
int sum;
int average;
```

We can then compute the average with the following two statements:

```
sum = num1 + num2 + num3;
average = sum / 3;
```

We finish by adding two lines that produce the output of the program; we also include the lines necessary to make this a complete Java program. The final product is

```java
public class Program2 {
  public static void main(String[] arg) {
      int num1 = 11;
      int num2 = 4;
      int num3 = 21;
      int sum;
      int average;
      sum = num1 + num2 + num3;
      average = sum / 3;
      System.out.print("The average is ");
      System.out.println(average);
  }
}
```

Notice that this program uses both object-oriented and imperative techniques to do its work. Output is accomplished by invoking appropriate methods, but these two statements

```
sum = num1 + num2 + num3;
average = sum / 3;
```

use no references and send no messages yet are the statements that accomplish much of the work of the program.

Order of Operations

We could have chosen to calculate the average using just one variable and one statement—that is, by doing the whole calculation at once. Doing it that way would look like this:

```
int average;
average = (num1 + num2 + num3) / 3;
```

It's important to note that because Java's precedence rules require that expressions be evaluated by performing division and multiplication before addition and subtraction (just as we are taught to do in algebra), we had to use parentheses in the expression to calculate average—without them, the expression

```
num1 + num2 + num3 / 3
```

would be evaluated by dividing only num3 by 3 and adding this value to num1 + num2—which would give us a very different result.

2.7 Using String Methods

We have already encountered the toUpperCase() method of the String class. Table 2.5 gives information about its prototype and the prototypes of some other methods of the String class.

TABLE 2.5 **PROTOTYPE INFORMATION FOR SOME String METHODS**

METHOD	RETURNS	ARGUMENTS
toUpperCase	Reference to a String object	None
toLowerCase	Reference to a String object	None
length	int value	None
trim	Reference to a String object	None
concat	Reference to a String object	Reference to a String object
substring	Reference to a String object	int value
substring	Reference to a String object	int value

The length() method returns the number of characters in the receiver String object.

All of the other methods return a reference to a newly created String object, one that is based on the receiving String object and the arguments. For example, the toUpperCase() and toLowerCase() methods return references to new String objects that are uppercase-only or lowercase-only versions of the receiving String.

The trim() method creates a copy of the receiving String, but removes spaces and tabs from the beginning and end.

The concat() method creates a new String consisting of the characters of the receiving String object followed by those of the String object referred to by the argument, as in the following statements:

```
String  s, t, u;
s = "ham";
t = "burger";
u = s.concat(t);
```

As a result of the last assignment, u refers to a newly created String, "hamburger". We say that "ham" and "burger" have been *concatenated* (joined). Figure 2.8 presents a diagram of the process of receiving a concat() message.

String concatenation is so common an operation that the Java designers felt compelled to represent it with a simple operator symbol in order to provide the same convenience that is associated with arithmetic operations. Thus, the expression

Figure 2.8
Receiving a `concat()` message. When given a `concat()` message, the receiver object produces a new `String`, consisting of its characters concatenated with the characters of the argument `String`.

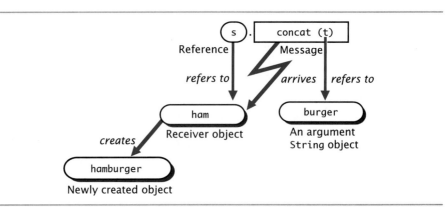

string1 + string2

is a Java shorthand for

string1.concat(*string2*)

Furthermore, the operator +, when used with a `String` operand, is defined to allow primitive data types, such as `int`, to appear as the other operand. When they do, they are automatically converted to their `String` representation.

This notation is particularly useful with `System.out.print()` and `println()`. For example, we may write something like

```
System.out.println("The value of x is " + x);
```

The `substring()` method creates a new `String` consisting of a subset of the characters in the receiving `String` object. It does so by assuming the positions are numbered 0, 1, 2, starting from the left (counting from 0 is very common in programming languages such as Java, even though it's hard for humans to get used to). Java considers a substring at position 3, say, to include the character at position 3 (which is the fourth character because we're numbering from 0) all the way to the end of the `String`. These positions are illustrated in Figure 2.9.

In the one-argument version of `substring()`, the argument specifies the position of the first character that will be part of the new `String`—and all succeeding characters are included. Here is an example; the process of receiving a `substring()` message with one argument is illustrated in Figure 2.10.

```
String  s, t;
s = "hamburger";
t = s.substring(3);
```

Now `t` refers to "burger", because 3 is the position of "b" in the receiving `String` object shown in Figure 2.9, and all the succeeding characters are part of the new `String`.

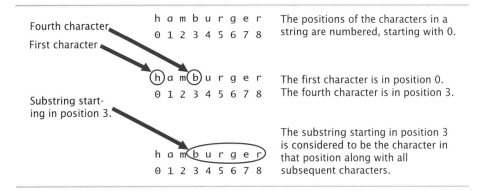

Figure 2.9
String positions and substrings.

The positions of the characters in a string are numbered, starting with 0.

The first character is in position 0.
The fourth character is in position 3.

The substring starting in position 3 is considered to be the character in that position along with all subsequent characters.

Figure 2.10
Receiving a sub-
string() message.
Given a substring()
message with one
argument, the receiv-
ing object produces a
new String, starting
with the character in
the position indicated
by the argument and
going to the end.

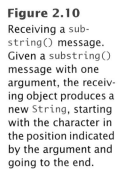
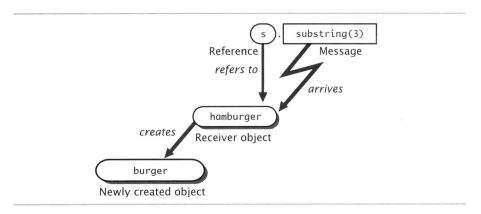

In the two-argument version of substring(), the first integer argument specifies, as before, the position of the first character that is to be part of the new String. All succeeding characters up to *but not including* the character whose position is given by the second argument are incorporated into the new String object. The role of the two integers is shown in Figure 2.11.

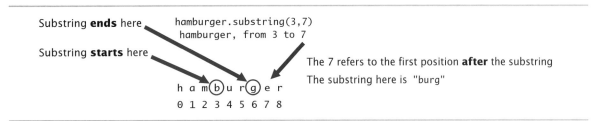

Figure 2.11   Substrings specified by two integers. The first integer specifies the position of the first character in the substring(). The second integer specifies the position after the last character of the substring().

For example, consider the role of 3 and 7 in the following statements:

```
String  s, t;
s = "hamburger";
t = s.substring(3,7);
```

As a result of the last assignment, t refers to "burg", because 3 is the position of "b" in the receiving String and all the succeeding characters, up to but not including position 7 ("e"), are part of the new String.

Empty Strings

A String object that has an empty sequence of characters is called an *empty* String. "" is a reference to such a String. The empty String returns 0 as its length. Thus, "".length() equals 0.

EXAMPLE Initials of a name. Let's write a program that will, given a first, middle, and last name, print the initials. In particular, our program will print out the initials of "John Fitzgerald Kennedy", where the three names are modeled as distinct String objects. We can sketch our program using the usual boilerplate, along with declarations of and assignments to three String variables used to represent the first, middle, and last names of the former president:

```
public class Program3 {
    public static void main(String[] arg) {
        String  first = "John";
        String  middle = "Fitzgerald";
        String  last = "Kennedy";
        ... rest of program goes here ...
    }
}
```

The initials can be modeled using a String,

```
String  initials;
```

and can be constructed from three other String objects: the first initial of the first, middle, and last names. For convenience, let's use String reference variables for these as well:

```
String  firstInit, middleInit, lastInit;
```

An initial of a name is the first character (position 0, according to Java's scheme for numbering characters in Strings). If we send a substring() message to the name, indicating to start with position 0 and not include position 1, the resulting String will consist of just the first character. We can pick up each initial this way:

```
firstInit = first.substring(0,1);
middleInit = middle.substring(0,1);
lastInit = last.substring(0,1);
```

All that remains is to concatenate the three initials into a String object, a reference to which is assigned to initials. We do this by making initials refer to
the String object that results from concatenating firstInit with middleInit and
then concatenating that object with lastInit. The reference that results, stored in
initials, can be used as an argument in a println() message.

```
initials = firstInit.concat(middleInit);
initials = initials.concat(lastInit);
System.out.println(initials);
```

We could alternatively use the + notation for concatenation and write

```
initials = firstInit + middleInit + lastInit;
```

The entire program to print out the initials we are seeking is as follows:

```
public class Program3 {
    public static void main(String[] arg) {
        String  first = "John";
        String  middle = "Fitzgerald";
        String  last = "Kennedy";
        String  initials;
        String  firstInit, middleInit, lastInit;
        firstInit = first.substring(0,1);
        middleInit = middle.substring(0,1);
        lastInit = last.substring(0,1);
        initials = firstInit.concat(middleInit);
        initials = initials.concat(lastInit);
        System.out.println(initials);
    }
}
```

EXAMPLE Average length of three Strings.   Because the length() method
of the String class returns an int value, we can use that method in combination
with some arithmetic operators to find the average length of a few strings. We begin
with the usual boilerplate, and we initialize three String variables:

```
public class Program4 {
    public static void main(String[] arg) {
        String s1 = "deoxyribonucleic";
        String s2 = "hippopotamus";
        String s3 = "a short ride in a fast car";
            find lengths, then compute average
    }
}
```

We can use the length() method to get the lengths of these Strings; we'll need to
store these values in variables so we can then use them to compute the average.

```
int length1 = s1.length();
int length2 = s2.length();
int length3 = s3.length();
```

We can then compute and output the average:

```
int average = (length1+length2+length3) / 3;
System.out.print("The average length is ");
System.out.println(average);
```

So the complete program is

```
public class Program4 {
    public static void main(String[] arg) {
        String s1 = "deoxyribonucleic";
        String s2 = "hippopotamus";
        String s3 = "a short ride in a fast car";
        int length1 = s1.length();
        int length2 = s2.length();
        int length3 = s3.length();
        int average = (length1+length2+length3) / 3;
        System.out.print("The average length is ");
        System.out.println(average);
    }
}
```

EXAMPLE Finding the middle character of a String. Let's write a program that displays the middle character of "antidisestablishmentarianism", which at one time was the longest word in the English language. A word can be modeled as a String. We can sketch our program using the usual boilerplate, along with a declaration of and assignment to a String variable to represent our long word this way:

```
public class Program5 {
    public static void main(String[] arg) {
        String  word = "antidisestablishmentarianism";
        ... rest of program goes here ...
    }
}
```

The middle character of a String is itself a sequence of characters (a single character in this case) and can thus be modeled as a String (one with a length of 1!). We can use a String reference variable, middle, to refer to it:

```
String  middle;
```

Sending a substring() message to word could create a String composed of just that middle character. All we need to do is specify the starting position of the substring. This position must be the middle of the String, and the first position after the substring, which will be one position beyond that:

middle = word.substring(*the middle position of* word, *the position after that*);

To find the middle of word we must determine its length. The length() method of String provides us with this information. Given the length of a String, its middle can be found by dividing by 2:

word.length()/2

The position after the middle can be found by dividing the length by 2 and adding 1:

1+word.length()/2

We can use these two expressions as arguments to the substring() method:

middle = word.substring(word.length()/2, 1+word.length()/2);

The completed program is as follows:

```
public class Program5 {
    public static void main(String[] arg) {
        String  word = "antidisestablishmentarianism";
        String  middle;
        middle = word.substring(word.length()/2, 1+word.length()/2);
        System.out.println(middle);
    }
}
```

Running this program yields the output:

s

Smart and Helpful Objects

Wait a minute! What kind of a string does the String class model, anyway? Whoever heard of getting a substring from a String by "sending the string a message" to do so? That's like sending the number 27 a message to "add 68 to yourself and tell me the result." It's faintly ridiculous to think of numbers as having the ability to add themselves, so what are we doing with Strings that know how to find substrings of themselves?

The answer to this objection is this. In Java, we have the freedom to design our classes any way we choose. The wisest choice is one that makes the object a helpful one, one that can, on request, carry out any useful operation related to that object. By providing methods such as toUpperCase() and substring(), the Java class designers are following that principle.

2.8 Imperative Programming: Simple Conditionals

Until now, our programs have been simple, in the sense that they have consisted solely of assignment statements and the invocation of methods. This lack of complexity is also a lack of flexibility. For example, we have no way of writing a method that takes one action or another depending on circumstances. This section introduces **conditional execution**—the ability to execute some code contingent upon some condition. This will enable us to write more flexible code and create programs that are more sophisticated models.

In order for our programs to be flexible they must be able to respond differently to different situations. This requires the ability to test a value and carry out some action depending on the result of the test.

The `if` Statement

The `if` statement allows us to do just that. Here's an example:

```
if (age < 17)
  System.out.println("Must be accompanied by parent.");
```

The *condition* tested by this `if` statement is whether the value of the variable age is less than 17. If this condition is true, then the `println()` *action* is carried out. We can test values returned from method invocations as well:

```
if (ZIPCode.length() != 5)
  System.out.println("Invalid ZIP code.");
```

The operator `!=` is read as "not equal."

The `if` statement may take another form that provides two alternative execution paths—one for a true outcome, the other for a false one:

```
if (age < 17)
  System.out.println("Must be accompanied by parent.");
else
  System.out.println("Enjoy the show!");
```

Just as in the first form of the `if` statement, the first action is carried out if the condition is true; the `else` is now followed by an action to be carried out if the condition is false.

`if` statements, then, take this general form:

```
if (condition)
      statement1
else
      statement2
```

where the `else` portion may be omitted if no action is necessary when the condition is false.

Note that

- The condition of the if statement must be surrounded by parentheses.
- If *condition* is true, *statement1* (the true portion) is executed; otherwise *statement2* (the false portion) is executed.
- The *statement* portions (both true and false) are restricted to a single statement. If we wish to execute more than one statement as a result of *condition* being true or false, we surround the statements with braces {} to create a **compound statement**, which is considered a single statement:

```
if (x > y) {
    System.out.print(x);
    System.out.print(" is greater than ");
    System.out.println(y);
}
else    {
    System.out.print(x);
    System.out.print(" is not greater than ");
    System.out.println(y);
}
```

compound
statements

Conditions

The condition must be an expression that evaluates to true or false. For the moment we'll restrict ourselves to conditions that are comparisons of two numerical values. These comparisons use the familiar relational operators shown in Table 2.6.

TABLE 2.6   JAVA'S RELATIONAL OPERATORS

OPERATOR	MEANING
<	Less than
>	Greater than
==	Equal to (note the pair of equal signs)
<=	Less than or equal
>=	Greater than or equal to
!=	Not equal to

EXAMPLE Middle of a String, again. Suppose that in the middle-of-the-String example earlier we wanted to be a little more precise. When applied to a String of even length, like "home", our code determined the middle character to be the one just after the true midpoint of the String ("m" in the case of "home")

We can rewrite our program using a conditional statement so that in the case of odd-length Strings, we display, as we did before, the single character that lies at the middle, while in the case of even-length Strings we display the two characters that bracket the middle ("om" in the case of "home"). To construct our program, we'll being by designing the code we want to execute in each condition. When the String has odd length, we can use the same computation we used in the first version of this program:

```
middle = word.substring(word.length()/2, 1+word.length()/2);
```

If the String has even length, we need to extract the substring that contains the previous character as well; we do this by subtracting 1 from the starting position:

```
middle = word.substring(word.length()/2-1, 1+word.length()/2);
```

What is the condition we need to test? We need to know whether the String has even or odd length, so we need to examine the value of word.length(). We can use the % (remainder) operator to find out the remainder after this value is divided by 2—if the remainder is 1 the length is odd; otherwise, the length is even (and in this case the remainder will be 0). Our if statement will therefore take this form:

```
if (word.length() % 2 == 1)
    this is the odd case
else
    this is the even case
```

Combining all these pieces, our finished program looks like this:

```
public class Program5 {
    public static void main(String[] arg) {
        String  word = "home";
        String  middle;
        if (word.length() % 2 == 1)           Is the length odd?
            middle = word.substring(word.length()/2,
                              1+word.length()/2);   Same calculation as
                                                    before
        else
            middle = word.substring(word.length()/2 - 1,  Get previous char-
                              1+word.length()/2);   acter as well
        System.out.println(middle);
    }
}
```

EXAMPLE Testing a trimmed String. Let's write a program that uses the String.trim() method to trim a String, then uses a conditional statement to test whether the String was actually shortened as a result. We'll begin with the usual program boilerplate and declare a String that we wish to trim as well as a String variable that will refer to the trimmed String:

```
public class Program6 {
   public static void main(String[] arg) {
      String  beforeTrim = "   spacy   ";
      String  afterTrim;
```

Then we trim the String and compare the lengths of the two Strings:

```
      afterTrim = beforeTrim.trim();
      if (beforeTrim.length() == afterTrim.length())
         System.out.println("String is no shorter.");
      else
         System.out.println("Shortened the string.");
}
```

In this case, the length of beforeTrim is 10, and the length of afterTrim (which has the value "spacy") is 5; because these are not equal, the output of the program is

```
Shortened the string.
```


EXAMPLE Printing multiples.   Sometimes the utility of imperative programming arises simply in the performance of tedious tasks (like the carpenters pounding hundreds of nails). Here's a fragment of a program that just prints out the first few multiples of 7:

```
int base = 7;
int multiplier = 1;
int result;

result = base * multiplier;
System.out.println(result);
multiplier += 1;

result = base * multiplier;
System.out.println(result);
multiplier += 1;

result = base * multiplier;
System.out.println(result);
multiplier += 1;
```

```
result = base * multiplier;
System.out.println(result);
multiplier += 1;
```

We'll see in Chapter 6 that we can make tasks like this much easier for the programmer to describe.

Summary

In this chapter we used some of Java's predefined objects to write a few simple programs. Behavior of objects is implemented by the methods their class provides. Messages consist of method names and a parenthesized list of additional information called arguments. Each method is characterized by its signature: its name and the number and type of arguments that it expects to receive. A class may provide more than one method of the same name, so long as their signatures are distinct. This is called overloading.

When a message is sent to an object, the sender is suspended while the object executes the method that was invoked. Some methods return a reference value to the sender of the message. This is called a return value. The type of a method's return value together with its signature is called the method's prototype. When a method does not return a value we say its return-type is void.

Values may be assigned to variables. These are identifiers that may be associated with a value. A variable may have only one value at a time. Assignment to a variable is destructive in the sense that any previous value will no longer be associated with the variable.

Variables are established in a program by declarations—statements that indicate the type of the variable and its name (identifier). Only values that are compatible with the declared type of the variable may be assigned to it.

In this chapter we also made the further acquaintance of two of Java's predefined classes, PrintStream and String. We encountered three of PrintStream's methods: print(), println() with a String argument, and println() without an argument. We also encountered a half-dozen String methods: toUpperCase(), toLowerCase(), concat(), substring(), trim(), and length().

Imperative programming involves sending instructions directly to the computer, rather than to some Java object. Numerical calculations and making decisions are two forms of imperative programming. Integers can be represented as values of type int; these values can be manipulated and combined using the usual arithmetic operations. Decision making is carried out by *conditional* or if statements that test a condition in order to determine which action to take.

Key Terms

argument Information provided in a message in addition to the method-name.

assignment The association of a value with a variable; the new value replaces any previous value associated with the variable.

assignment statement A statement that results in an assignment; the statement consists of the name of the variable being assigned, the assignment operator =, and an expression that gives the value that is assigned to the variable.

behavior Any action that the object may take; any change it may undergo or characteristic it may reveal.

compound statement One or more statements surrounded by braces that are thereby treated as a single statement.

conditional execution The ability to selectively execute code depending on some true or false condition.

constant An entity whose value may not be changed after initialization.

declaration A Java statement that introduces a variable into a Java program. A declaration of a reference variable specifies the name (identifier) of the variable and the class of object to which it may refer.

imperative programming Programming by commanding the computer to perform a fundamental computational task.

initializer An optional portion of a variable declaration specifying the variable's initial value.

message The mechanism by which a method is invoked. A message consists of a method name followed by a (possibly empty) argument list.

method A self-contained section of code belonging to a class that defines a specific behavior for that class. It is referred to in a message by its method-name.

method-name The identifier associated with a method.

overloading The practice of having a class provide different—though highly related—methods of the same name; the methods are distinguished by the types of arguments they receive, that is, their signatures.

precedence rules Rules describing the order in which to perform a sequence of operations.

primitive data type A data type provided as part of the language definition rather than through a class definition. No class or methods are associated with the data type.

prototype A method's name along with a description of its return-type and arguments.

reference variable An identifier that may be assigned a reference to an object of a particular class.

return The action of the receiver of a message providing a value that is given to the sender; the value replaces the phrase that sent the message.

return value The value given back to the sender by the receiver of a message.

signature A method's name along with a description of its arguments.

String constant A sequence of characters embedded in double quotes, e.g., "Hello". The constant is a reference to the String object consisting of the characters between the quotes, in our case, the characters Hello.

variable An identifier that can be given a value.

Questions for Review

1. What is the purpose of a *declaration*?
2. What is a *message* composed of?
3. Can a *reference variable* refer to more than one object at the same time? At different times?
4. Can more than one *reference variable* refer to the same object?
5. What does the *assignment statement* do?
6. Give two examples of *overloading*.
7. Why does Java have primitive data types?
8. How does a primitive data type differ from an int?
9. What are the basic operations for int?
10. What are the two forms of the if statement?
11. What are relational operators?

Exercises

1. Write two different sequences (each containing three statements) that display a single line, "Malice toward none, charity for all," on the monitor.
2. Write the words "System Unavailable" on separate lines, double spaced.
3. For each Java statement on the following page, identify the reference, the method-name, and the arguments (or indicate if there are none).

```
System.out.print("Ad Astra Per Aspera");
car54.ask("Where are you?");
smart.get();
x.y("a","b");
smart.get(x);
```

Which, if any, of these represent overloaded methods?

4. What is meant by the term *invoking a method?*

5. Which of the following are valid references to `String` objects? Of those, which are `String` constants?

```
'This is a test.'
"unesco".toUpperCase()
"An injury to one is an injury to all."
"imf".touppercase()
```

6. Which of the following are references? For those that are, identify the class of the object that is referred to and briefly describe the object.

```
System.out
System.out.println("hello, world");
"hello, world"
"hello, world".toUpperCase()
toUpperCase()
```

7. Deduce the signature of the "mystery" methods in each of these statements:

```
x.mystery1("gallop",System.out);
y.mystery2("fee", "fie", "foe", "fum");
System.out.println(z.mystery3());
```

8. Write declarations of three `String` reference variables that are intended for use as references to your first name, your last name, and your full name. Choose appropriate identifiers for these variables.

9. Write code that makes the three variables of the previous exercise refer to `String` objects representing your first, your last, and your full name.

10. Declare another `String` reference variable and save in it a reference to an all-uppercase version of your last name. Use the `toUpperCase()` method and one of the variables that you have used in the previous two exercises.

11. Write expressions for each of the following:

   - The average of the `int` variables a and b.
   - The circumference of a circle with radius r.
   - Increase the value of the `int` variable i by 10.

12. Give three different ways of adding 1 to an `int` variable in Java.

13. Use parentheses to indicate three different orders of operation for each of these expressions. What is the value of each parenthesized expression?

```
3 + 4 * 10 - 2
100 / 4 + 6 * 2
```

14. Write a complete program that declares and initializes four int variables, multiplies them, and prints the result.

15. Write a complete program that prints two int values, their quotient, and their remainder.

16. Experiment with integer arithmetic. Write a program that contains various interesting expressions and see what the behavior is. For example, try dividing 0 by a number, and dividing a number by 0. What happens when you multiply two large numbers? Does Java limit the size of integer constants it allows you to write?

17. Which, if any, of the String methods discussed in this chapter are overloaded?

18. Suppose you had a reference variable, stuff, containing a reference to a String object. Write Java code that does the opposite of what the trim() method does. Specifically, your code should cause the reference variable spaceStuff to refer to a String containing the same String as stuff, preceded by three spaces and followed by two spaces.

19. Write Java code that assigns two Strings to the String variables longStr and shortStr (make sure that longStr is longer than shortStr). Cut off the end of longStr so that it's the same length as shortStr; assign this string to cutStr.

20. Suppose you had a reference variable, x, containing a reference to a String object that you knew contained exactly three distinct characters (like "abc" or "9=3"). Write Java code that displays every permutation of this String. For instance, if the String were "abc", the output would be

```
abc
acb
bac
bca
cab
cba
```

Your code will use the reference variable x, some of the String methods you have learned, and both the print() and println() methods of System.out.

21. Write a Java program that starts by creating a three-character String object such as "abc" and then, using the code you wrote in the previous exercise, displays every permutation of these characters.

22. Write a complete Java program that finds the longest substring of a String whose length is exactly a multiple of 10. To do this, it should remove up to nine characters from the end of the string. (Hint: Use the % (modulus) operator.)

23. Write a complete Java program that uses the String.trim() method to trim a String, then prints out the number of characters that were removed.

24. Write a complete Java program that prints the first five characters of a String, the middle five characters of the String, and the last five characters of the String.

25. Write a conditional statement that will invoke the boiler.shutdown() method if the value returned from gauge.getTemperature() exceeds 100.

26. Write a conditional statement that assigns the smaller value of a and b to smaller. (a, b, and smaller are all int variables.)

27. Write a conditional statement that outputs "The string is empty" if the length of String s is 0, and otherwise prints out the first character of s.

28. Answer questions 26 and 27 again using *different* conditional statements.

29. Suppose you are given the following code:

```
String   first = "someone's first name";
String   last  = "someone's last name";
```

where each String starts with some unknown number of spaces followed by a first or last name. Write a fragment of code that creates a String containing the initials of the first and last name and print it out.

30. Write a complete Java program that concatenates two Strings, placing the shorter one before the longer.

31. Given the following code:

```
String   x = "Studebakers of yesteryear";
String   y = "banana freak";
System.out.println(x.substring(0,4)
        .concat(x.substring(15,16)).concat(y.substring(0,1))
        .concat(y.substring(8)));
```

a. What is printed out?

b. Draw a diagram, showing every object that is created at some point in the execution of this code. Label each object with the phrase of the above code that refers to it. Show, using arrows, the order in which the objects are created.

Painting and Positioning Graphics

Now that we have the tools to do arithmetic in Java, we can turn to creating applets that create and display more interesting graphics. Our focus in this supplement will be solely on "passive" graphics (like lines, shapes, and text). In the Chapter 4 supplement we'll begin studying interactive elements (like buttons and check boxes); we'll see that those elements are generated and displayed a bit differently.

Centering a Circle

After experimenting with the applet and drawing methods (drawString(), draw-Oval(), etc.) from Chapter 1, you should have a sense of how the *x,y* coordinate system in Java works; you should also have a grasp of how the arguments to these methods work. Specifically, the point (0,0) is located in the top left corner of the drawing area, with *x* increasing to the right and *y* increasing downward. The coordinates passed to drawString() specify the left end of the imaginary line on which the text rests; the coordinates passed to drawRect() give the top left corner of the rectangle and the dimensions of the rectangle; the coordinates passed to drawOval() give the top left corner and dimensions of the "bounding rectangle" of the oval.

Keeping all this in mind, let's turn to writing an applet that draws a single circle centered in the applet's display area. First, what method should we use to draw the circle? Our developing Java intuition suggests that we use drawCircle(), but in fact there is no such method. Instead, we can observe that a circle is just an oval with the same width as height, so we can use drawOval() with equal width and height arguments. So a first attempt at writing this applet would look like this:

```
import java.awt.*;        // First attempt
import java.applet.*;
public class CenterCircleApplet extends Applet {
   public void paint(Graphics g) {
      g.drawOval(20,20,50,50);
   }
}
```

The oval drawn by this applet has width 50 and height 50; that is, it's a circle with diameter 50. So now we have a circle, but it's probably not centered. Remember that the size of the applet's display area is given by the HTML code that embeds the applet, such as

```
<APPLET CODE="FirstApplet.class" WIDTH=300 HEIGHT=60>
</APPLET>
```

69

Our first attempt will display a *centered* circle only if the WIDTH and HEIGHT values are carefully set for us (they must both be 90—why?). It'd be much better if we could design our applet to respond to the dimensions imposed on the applet and position the circle accordingly. The good news is that it's straightforward to discover these dimensions within the applet code itself: We simply write

```
getSize().height
```

to get the height of the applet, and

```
getSize().width
```

to get its width. (Yes, there is a little magic happening here, but it should be clear *what* these phrases do, even if it's not clear *how* they do it.). How can we use this information to center the circle? Consider the picture in Figure 2.12. From this picture we can tell that the *x*-coordinate of the top left corner of the circle is the same as the width of the *x* margin. We can also see that the width of the applet is equal to the diameter of the circle plus two times the *x* margin. In other words, the *x* margin is

```
xMargin = (appletWidth - diameter) / 2;
```

We can calculate the *y* margin using the height of the applet in similar fashion:

```
yMargin = (appletHeight - diameter) / 2;
```

At this point, we have calculated all four values to be passed to drawOval(): the coordinates of the top left corner (xMargin and yMargin) and the width and height (both diameter, assigned some fixed value). Because the value of diameter is fixed, we could just pass, say, 50 for the last two values, but if we later decide to modify the applet it may be easier to have this value stored in a variable that we can manipulate.

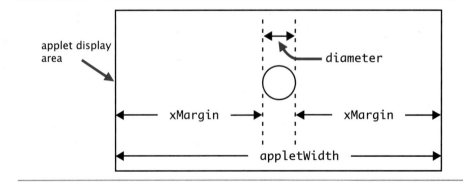

Figure 2.12
Centering a circle.

Now we can offer a second (successful) attempt at our `CenterCircleApplet`:

```java
import java.awt.*;          // Second attempt
import java.applet.*;
public class CenterCircleApplet extends Applet {
    public void paint(Graphics g) {
        int diameter = 50;
        int appletWidth = getSize().width;
        int appletHeight = getSize().height;
        int xMargin = (appletWidth - diameter) / 2;
        int yMargin = (appletHeight - diameter) / 2;
        g.drawOval(xMargin,yMargin,diameter,diameter);
    }
}
```

Centering Text

We can center a piece of text using very similar computations. Suppose we want to write an applet that displays `"X marks the spot"`. Just as with the circle, the we'll compute the x coordinate of the left end of the string with a calculation something like

```java
int xMargin = (appletWidth - textWidth) / 2;
```

What's less obvious in this case is the value of `textWidth`. It's certainly not a value that we (as programmers) assign as we did for the circle's diameter. Even more challenging, a little reflection suggests that this value isn't *any* fixed value: For example, the widths of these three strings are dramatically different:

X marks the spot

X marks the spot

X marks the spot

Although the text of these strings is the same, the width of the strings changes as we alter aspects of the *font* in which it is displayed.

The `Graphics` objects we've been using have a default font they use to display text. The AWT provides a `Font` class that enables the programmer to define new fonts for the applet's display. Fonts are specified by naming a font family (`"TimesRoman"` or `"Helvetica"`, for example), a font style (`Font.PLAIN`,

Font.BOLD, or Font.ITALIC), and a number specifying point size (12 is typical). Once we create a Font object representing our desired font, we pass this to the Graphics object using the method

```
void setFont(Font f)
```

For example, we might modify the paint() method of our first applet as follows:

```
public void paint(Graphics g) {
    Font f = new Font("Helvetica", Font.ITALIC, 18);
    g.setFont(f);
    g.drawString("This is everyone's first applet.",20,20);
}
```

So, there's no way for us to assess the width of the string "X marks the spot" without some knowledge of the font in which it will be displayed. To provide this knowledge, the Graphics class (which keeps track of the current display font) has a getFontMetrics() method that returns a reference to an instance of the FontMetrics class. Thus, we can write

```
FontMetrics fm = g.getFontMetrics();
```

to obtain a reference to g's FontMetrics instance.

FontMetrics offers a number of methods relating to font measurements; in our situation the most useful are these:

```
int stringWidth(String s)    // Returns width of s
int getHeight()              // Returns height of typeface
```

Using these methods in composition with getFontMetrics(), we can discover the dimension of our String as it will be displayed by the applet:

```
String s = "X marks the spot";
FontMetrics fm = g.getFontMetrics();
int textWidth = fm.stringWidth(s);
int textHeight = fm.getHeight();
```

Now we can complete our text-centering applet:

```
import java.awt.*;
import java.applet.*;
public class CenterTextApplet extends Applet {
    public void paint(Graphics g) {
        int appletWidth = getSize().width;
        int appletHeight = getSize().height;
        String s = "X marks the spot";
        FontMetrics fm = g.getFontMetrics();
        int textWidth = fm.stringWidth(s);
        int textHeight = fm.getHeight();
```

```
        int xMargin = (appletWidth - textWidth) / 2;
        int yMargin = (appletHeight - textHeight) / 2;
        g.drawString(xMargin,yMargin+textHeight,s);
    }
}
```

Note that because the coordinates passed to drawString() specify the position of the bottom left corner rather than the top left corner, we have to add textHeight to yMargin in order to achieve the correct vertical positioning. (In truth, this String will not be perfectly vertically centered because the getHeight() method measures the space from the top of one line to the top of one below it, including an appropriate amount of space between the lines.)

Self-Sizing Traffic Light

We'll finish this supplement with an example that performs an additional kind of calculation. We'll write an applet that produces a crude drawing of a traffic light. (See Figure 2.13.)

Drawing the light will involve positioning the three lights (drawn in red, yellow, and green) and the rectangular box that contains them. As in our previous examples, we'll display the traffic light centered in the applet, but in addition we'll determine the dimensions of the traffic light based on the dimensions of the applet. More specifically, we want the proportions of the light to remain fixed regardless of its actual size—for simplicity, we'll say that the height of the light will be three times its width—but the size will be determined by the size of the applet's display area.

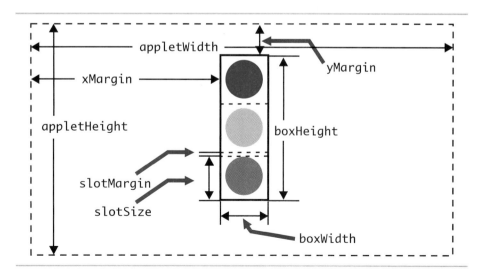

Figure 2.13
Traffic light with measurements.

We'll proceed by first deciding on the size and position of the box, then we'll figure out where to place the lights. We've already decided that the box will be centered, that its height will be three times its width, and that its width will be
somehow determined from the applet's dimensions. Thus our applet will begin as

```java
import java.awt.*;
import java.applet.*;
public class TrafficLightApplet extends Applet {
    public void paint(Graphics g) {
        int appletWidth = getSize().width;
        int appletHeight = getSize().height;
        Calculate boxWidth somehow
        int boxHeight = boxWidth * 3;
        int xMargin = (myWidth - boxWidth) / 2;
        int yMargin = (myHeight - boxHeight) / 2;
        g.drawRect(xMargin,yMargin,boxWidth,boxHeight);
```

What should the width of the box be? If our goal is to make the size proportional
to the applet display area, then the width of the light should be related to the
width of the applet; let's say (more or less arbitrarily) that the width of the box
should be one fifth the width of the applet. But there's another constraint to consider: If the height of the box is going to be three times its width, then the width
can be no more than appletHeight/3—otherwise the light will be taller than the
applet itself. So we have two possible ways to calculate the width:

```java
int boxWidth = appletWidth/5;
```

and

```java
int boxWidth = appletHeight/3;
```

To resolve this contradiction, we simply have to observe that the width of the
box should be the *smaller* of these two values. That will guarantee that the height
of the box never exceeds the height of the applet; if the display area is sufficiently tall, then the light will be one fifth the applet's width.

We can use an if statement to determine the correct value of boxWidth: we'll just
compare the two possible values and set boxWidth to be the smaller.

```java
int boxWidth;
if (appletWidth/5 < appletHeight/3)
    boxWidth = appletWidth/5;
else
    boxWidth = appletHeight/3;
```

Positioning the Lights

To position the lights within the box, we first note that because the height of the
box is exactly three times its width, we can divide the box into three square

"slots" inside which we will position the lights. Each slot has width and height `boxWidth`. The lights themselves shouldn't extend to the edges of each slot, so we'll set the diameter of each light to be

```
int diameter = 3 * boxWidth/4;
```

To make sure that the lights are centered within each slot, we calculate a margin (because the slots are square, this margin will serve as both "x margin" and "y margin"):

```
int slotSize = boxWidth;
int slotMargin = (slotSize - diameter) / 2;
```

Now we simply use these quantities to determine the position of each light. First, each light will have the same x coordinate, `slotMargin` units inside the left edge of the box, or

```
int lightXCoord = xMargin + slotMargin;
```

The y coordinates of each light are easy to calculate now: The topmost light is placed `slotMargin` units below the top of the box, or

```
yMargin + slotMargin
```

The middle light will be placed one `slotSize` below the top light, or

```
yMargin + slotMargin + slotSize
```

and the bottom light will be two `slotSizes` below the top light:

```
yMargin + slotMargin + 2*slotSize
```

Completing the Applet

Finally, before we actually display the lights, we must specify their colors. We can take advantage of some of the predefined colors provided by the `Color` class: `Color.red`, `Color.yellow`, and `Color.green`.

Now we can complete our traffic light applet:

```
import java.awt.*;
import java.applet.*;
public class TrafficLightApplet extends Applet {
    public void paint(Graphics g) {
        int appletWidth = getSize().width;
        int appletHeight = getSize().height;
        int boxWidth;
        if (appletWidth/5 < appletHeight/3)   Calculate size and position of box
            boxWidth = appletWidth/5;
        else
            boxWidth = appletHeight/3;
```

```
int boxHeight = boxWidth * 3;
int xMargin = (myWidth - boxWidth) / 2;
int yMargin = (myHeight - boxHeight) / 2 ;
g.drawRect(xMargin,yMargin,boxWidth,boxHeight);

int diameter = 3 * boxWidth/4;        Calculations for sizing and
int slotSize = boxWidth;              positioning lights
int slotMargin = (slotSize - diameter) / 2;
int lightXCoord = xMargin+slotMargin;

g.setColor(Color.red);                // set color of top light
g.fillOval(lightXCoord,               // x coordinate of all lights
        yMargin+slotMargin,           // y coordinate of top light
        diameter,diameter);           // dimensions of all lights

g.setColor(Color.yellow);             // set color of middle light
g.fillOval(lightXCoord,
        yMargin+slotMargin+slotSize,  // y coordinate
        diameter,diameter);

g.setColor(Color.green);              // set color of bottom light
g.fillOval(lightXCoord,
        yMargin+slotMargin+2*slotSize, // y coordinate
        diameter,diameter);
    }
}
```

Suggested Experiments

1. Write an applet that displays your first name in red, 10-point Times Roman font and below that displays your last name in orange, 14-point Helvetica. (Hint: You will have to use drawString() twice with different coordinates.)

2. Write an applet that displays three concentric, filled circles of different colors, centered in the applet's display area. The sizes of the circles should be proportional to the size of the display area.

3. Write an applet that displays the first few lines of a song or poem, centered in the applet display area and bordered by a rectangle.

Chapter 3

Working with Objects and Primitive Types

3.1 Introduction

I n Chapter 2, we learned how to use objects. Specifically, we learned how to use references to objects in order to send messages to them. Most of the objects we used were Java's *predefined objects*. The set of predefined objects we have seen is quite small—String constants, System.out, and a couple of others. To accomplish anything useful, we will need to create objects ourselves. In this chapter we will learn how to use Java's predefined classes to do just that.

A class always models something. The predefined classes that we have chosen as examples in this chapter model calendars, time zones, very large integer values, disk files, Internet sites, and various modes of input and output. We will start the discussion with a familiar class: String. This will lead us, by the end of the chapter, to writing programs whose reach extends out to the Internet. At the same time, we will study some additional imperative programming techniques: using primitive data types other than int and writing more complex conditional statements.

3.2 Creating Objects

Creating Objects with Constructors

In order to use predefined classes to their fullest, we need to be able to create new objects that belong to these classes. Every class has one or more methods that are used to create an object of that class. These methods are called **constructors** (because they construct the object). The name of a constructor method is *always* the same as its class. So the String class has a constructor method called String().

Like all methods, constructors may or may not require arguments. The String class has several constructors; one of the most commonly used takes a reference to an existing String object as an argument:

```
String("hello world")
```

This message requests that the newly constructed String represent the characters h e l l o   w o r l d. That is, the new object will be a copy of the one referred to by the argument.

Messages must be sent to an object. But in the case of constructors, we don't yet have an object—we are trying to create one. In Java, we use the keyword new to arrange for the creation of an object that can receive this message and to invoke the constructor method as follows:

```
new String("hello world")
```

This creates a String object and sends it the message String("hello world"). Because a constructor's only purpose is to aid in the construction of an object, it can be invoked only with the new keyword during object creation. The constructor returns a reference to the newly created object. Therefore, the expression

```
new String("hello world")
```

both creates a String object and is a reference to the created object.

The new keyword denotes an **operation** to be performed. An operation is an action that results in a value. The value of the new operation is a reference to the newly created object. An **operator**, such as new, is a symbol or keyword that represents an operation.

Reference Variables to the Rescue

The new operator gives us a reference to a newly created object, but unless we save that reference for future use, we will not be able to continue sending messages to the object. At this point reference variables, introduced in the previous chapter as a convenience, become essential. By declaring a reference variable and assigning it the result of the new operation, we can continue to use the reference to the newly created object, as follows:

```
String s, upper, lower;
s = new String("Hello");
upper = s.toUpperCase();
lower = s.toLowerCase();
System.out.println(s);
```

In this code, the reference returned by the new operation is used three times: twice to specify a receiver of a message and once as an argument in a message.

Java Interlude   *Origins of Objects*

Overloading and Default Constructors

The String constructor is intentionally overloaded so that when given no arguments, it produces an empty String, as follows:

```
String  empty = new String();      The same as new String("")
```

A constructor that takes no arguments is called a **default constructor** because it is the constructor that is invoked unless the programmer explicitly indicates otherwise.

Where Do Objects Come From?

Sometimes we get new String objects by using the new operator. Other times we get them by invoking methods that return references to String objects that these methods themselves created using new. We have already seen the following six methods, as shown in Table 3.1 that return references to newly created String objects:

TABLE 3.1　String **METHODS THAT RETURN REFERENCES TO NEWLY CREATED** String **OBJECTS**

METHOD	ARGUMENTS
toUpperCase	None
toLowerCase	None
trim	None
concat	Reference to a String object
substring	An int
substring	Two ints

Remember that although the last two methods have the same name, substring, they are different methods because they have different signatures; that is, they receive different sets of arguments.

We will encounter many other methods in other classes that also return references to newly created Strings.

Immutable Objects

Once created, String objects are never changed. Concatenation, trimming, and taking a substring never affect the receiver object. Rather, they create a new String object. The String class did not have to be designed this way—the designers of Java chose to make Strings unchangeable, that is, *immutable.*

Cascading

Consider this fragment of code from the last chapter:

```
initials = firstInit.concat(middleInit);     Now initials is "JF"
initials = initials.concat(lastInit);        Now initials is "JFK"
```

The value we assign to initials in the first line, "JF", is a reference to an object that is just an intermediate step in building the String "JFK". It is used just once—in the second line, where we send a concat() message to it—and is replaced by "JFK", as shown in Figure 3.1.

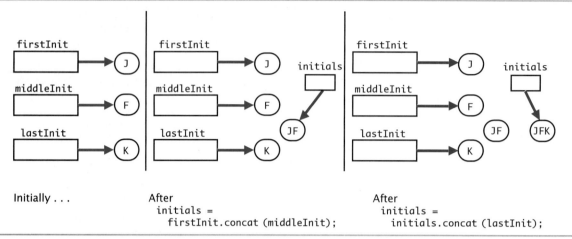

Figure 3.1 Repeated assignment.

In some sense, the first assignment is a waste: The value given to `initials` is changed immediately in the next line. We can avoid this by directly using the reference returned by `firstInit.concat(middleInit)` to send a `concat()` message to the `"JF"` String object:

```
initials = firstInit.concat(middleInit).concat(lastInit);
```

When the right-hand side is executed,

- A `concat()` message (with `middleInit` as argument) is sent to `firstInit`.
- The `firstInit` object returns a reference to a new `String` object (`"JF"`).
- Another `concat()` message (with `lastInit` as argument) is sent to the new `String` object whose reference was just returned.
- A reference to yet another new `String` object is returned.

This sequence is called **cascading**. It is the process of sending a message to an object to create a new object, which in turn is sent a message to create another new object, which in turn is sent a message to create yet another new object, and so on. (See Figure 3.2.)

Composition

Alternatively, for the same task of printing out the first, middle, and last initials, we could have written

```
initials = firstInit.concat(middleInit.concat(lastInit));
```

When the right-hand side of this statement is executed,

- A `concat()` message (with `lastInit` as argument) is sent to `middleInit`.
- The `middleInit` object returns a reference to a new `String` object (consisting of the middle and last initials).

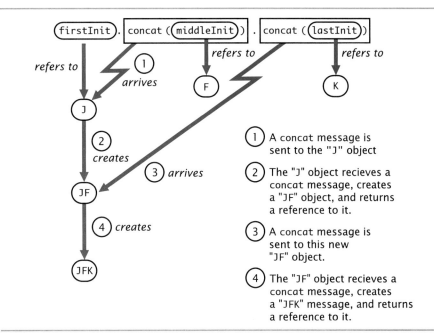

Figure 3.2
Cascading. In cascading, a message is sent to the object returned by a message and, in turn, a message is sent to the object returned by that message.

- The reference to this new object is sent as an argument in another concat() message.
- A reference to yet another new String object is returned.

This sequence is called **composition**. It is the process of sending a message to an object to create a new object whose reference is used *as an argument* in a message. In turn, this may yield a reference to another new object, which then could be used as an argument in yet another message, and so on. Figure 3.3 shows composition.

In cascading, the results of messages are used as receivers of additional messages; in composition, the results of messages are used as arguments in additional messages. Taken to an extreme, cascading and composition can rapidly lead to unreadable and error-prone code. Used judiciously, they lead to terse, elegant code.

3.3 Imperative Programming: The boolean Type

In Chapter 2 we introduced conditional statements, in which different actions are taken depending on the value of a condition. We looked at several examples of conditions based on relational operators, such as age < 17 and word.length() % 2 == 1. These conditions are expressions, just as 5 + 13 is an expression, but while arithmetic expressions have integer values, conditions take values *true* or

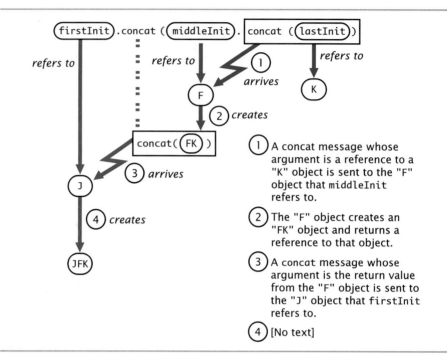

Figure 3.3
Composition. In
composition, the
return value of one
message becomes
the argument of
another message.

① A concat message whose
argument is a reference to a
"K" object is sent to the "F"
object that `middleInit`
refers to.

② The "F" object creates an
"FK" object and returns a
reference to that object.

③ A concat message whose
argument is the return value
from the "F" object is sent to
the "J" object that `firstInit`
refers to.

④ [No text]

false. These are called **Boolean** values. Like `int`, `boolean` is a primitive data type.
The `boolean` type models the behavior of a truth value which is why it has
exactly two possible values: `true` or `false`. We can declare variables of type
`boolean`, assign `boolean` values to `boolean` variables, construct `boolean` expressions, pass `boolean` values as arguments, and receive `boolean` values from methods. But most significantly, we can use any `boolean` expression as a condition.

boolean **Values and Variables**

The values `true` and `false` have their expected behavior:

`if (true)` *statement1* is executed.
        statement1
`else`
        statement2

and

`if (false)` *statement2* is executed.
        statement1
`else`
        statement2

We can also declare boolean variables:

```
boolean isFreezing;
```

set them:

```
if (temp < 32)
   isFreezing = true;
else
   isFreezing = false;
```

and, finally, use them:

```
if (isFreezing)
   System.out.println("Brrrrrr!");
```

As you can see, names for boolean variables are chosen to reflect their use as a condition: isFreezing, hasVacation, containsCoupon, and so on.

Just as it's possible for a method (such as String.length()) to return an int value, it's often desirable to have methods that return boolean values. Such methods are often called **predicate methods**. Because they return boolean values, we can use them as conditions in if statements.

For example, the String class contains a predicate method, equals(), that tests to see whether the receiver and its argument are identical. We can write

```
if  (s1.equals(s2))  s1 and s2 are both of type String.
   System.out.println("s1 has the same characters as s2");
```

boolean **Expressions**

The condition temp < 32 is an expression that contains the relational operator, <, and its two operands, temp and 32. The result of the operation is a boolean value (i.e., true or false), and therefore we say that this is a **boolean expression**. Such expressions are also called *logical expressions*.

Because temp < 32 results in a boolean that can be assigned to isFreezing, we can dispense with the if statement entirely and simply write

```
isFreezing = temp < 32;
```

Assigning the result of a boolean-valued expression to a boolean variable is a standard *idiom* in Java. Loosely speaking, an idiom of a programming language is a technique or approach that displays familiarity with the language, just as an idiom of a spoken language such as English shows familiarity with *that* language. A job interviewer, for example, might gauge job candidates' fluency in a language by seeing which idioms they know.

We can now provide a precise definition for what constitutes a valid condition: Any expression of type boolean is valid as the condition of an if statement.

3.4 Working with Objects

In each of the following sections, we present one or more predefined classes that provide useful behavior. In each case, we first present an overview of the items the classes model, followed by a brief demonstration of how to use the class. The purpose of these sections is not to provide an in-depth study in the use of these classes, but rather to illustrate and reinforce the use of objects as they have been presented in this and earlier chapters.

Most everyday tasks require more than one action. For example, to go grocery shopping, you may have to dig out your car keys, get together a shopping list, and grab your cash, credit card, and coupons. You use your car to drive to the store, where you grab a circular to see what's on sale. When you've filled your cart, you bring it to a register, check out, and place your purchases into a bag.

Programming tasks also can rarely be accomplished with a single object or class. Our simplest programs have worked with System.out and String objects, already two objects of two different classes. As applications get more complex and sophisticated, the number of objects increases substantially. The examples that follow illustrate the use of several classes in a single application.

3.5 Dates and Calendars

The manipulation of date and time is integral to many programming applications. Payroll systems require computation of hours worked, weeks of vacation allowed, years of seniority. Listing a directory of files on your computer displays a creation date for each file, in addition to the filename and size. Java offers several classes that support the modeling of dates. These classes together provide for date display, date arithmetic—that is, the ability to determine, given a starting date and interval, what the ending date will be—time zone support, and a host of other date-related facilities.

The class GregorianCalendar models the concept of the modern, Western calendar (known as the Gregorian calendar, hence the class's name). The class is responsible for maintaining and representing information about the months of the year, days of the week, leap years—all the conventions of a particular calendrical system. Other calendar-related classes could be introduced, representing various other conventions such as the Hebrew, Chinese, or Islamic calendars.

While the GregorianCalendar class is responsible for calendar-related issues, the actual modeling of a particular instant in time is the responsibility of the Date class. We will use Date, along with the TimeZone class (which models time zones) in conjunction with the GregorianCalendar methods.

Using the GregorianCalendar, Date, and TimeZone Classes

Let us first create a GregorianCalendar object using the class's default constructor:

```
GregorianCalendar now = new GregorianCalendar();
```

This creates an object representing the current time according to the Gregorian calendar, in the current time zone. The reference variable now holds a reference to this object.

The first thing we can do with this calendar object is query it for the current time by sending it a getTime() message:

```
Date d = now.getTime();
```

This method returns an object of class Date corresponding to the current time. The reference variable d holds a reference to this object. We can then print out the value of the Date object:

```
System.out.println(d);
```

Using composition, we can combine these two messages into a single statement and eliminate the intermediate Date reference variable:

```
System.out.println(now.getTime());
```

Executing this piece of code produces

```
Thu Dec 13 10:30:04 EST 2002
```

We can also query now for the local time zone by sending it a getTimeZone() message. (When you adjust the date and time on your computer, one of the options is to specify the time zone in which you are located—it is this information that is used by the GregorianCalendar class.)

```
TimeZone timeZone = now.getTimeZone();
```

Properly printing out a TimeZone requires invocation of its getDisplayName() method, returning a String:

```
String s = timeZone.getDisplayName();
```

This String can then be printed:

```
System.out.println(s);
```

Again, these statements can be combined, this time using a combination of cascading and composition:

```
System.out.println(now.getTimeZone().getDisplayName());
```

The TimeZone object returned by the now.getTimezone() invocation becomes the receiver of a getDisplayName() message—an example of cascading. The result of the getDisplayName() method invocation (a String) is then used as an argument to the println() method—an example of composition. Executing this piece of code produces:

```
Eastern Standard Time
```

Using a different (overloaded) constructor of GregorianCalendar, we can create an object corresponding to a particular date. This constructor accepts integers representing the year, month, and day of month as arguments. The only catch is that January's number is 0, so each month is one less than what we are used to. To create an object corresponding to February 29, 2004, we write

```
GregorianCalendar leapDay =
    new GregorianCalendar(2004, 1, 29);   // 1 -> February
```

We can then print out the date to see the corresponding day of the week:

```
Sun Feb 29 00:00:00 EST 2004
```

Finally, we can use the isLeapYear() predicate method to determine whether a particular year is a leap year:

```
if (gregorianCalendar.isLeapYear(2096))
    System.out.println("2096 is a leap year.")
else
    System.out.println("2096 is not a leap year.");


if (gregorianCalendar.isLeapYear(2100))
    System.out.println("2100 is a leap year.");
else
    System.out.println("2100 is not a leap year.");
```

3.6 Imperative Programming: Other Integer Types

The int type models the set of integers ranging from approximately −2 billion to 2 billion. Today, in commerce, administration, engineering, and science, 2 billion is often a small number. Numbers greater than 2 billion are needed to describe the federal deficit, the annual sales revenue of a major corporation, and hours of TV that U.S. residents watch.

Java provides a numeric primitive data type, long, that models the set of integers ranging from approximately −9 quintillion to 9 quintillion. A quintillion is a million times greater than a trillion. In commerce and administration, there are no quantities that get anywhere near this large.

The long type is identical to the int type (in terms of operators and behavior) except that long literals can be used to represent values whose magnitude exceeds 2 billion:

```
long    x = 2000L,  y = 1000L,  z = 1000000000L;
y  =  y * x;      ◀──────────  y is now 2 million—could have used an int for y.
y  =  y*1000L;   ◀──────────  y is now 2 billion—still could have used an int for y.
y  += z;  ◀──────────  y is now 3 billion—good thing we used a long for y.
y  *= x;  ◀──────────  y is now 6 trillion—a small long.
```

One minor difference between int and long is that long literals have an L appended to them.

Why Have an int at All?

Why shouldn't everyone just use long? The reason is twofold. First, longs require twice as much space in memory as ints (64 bits instead of 32 bits). So, when a program uses a large number of numeric variables, using longs increases its memory requirements. Sometimes we know with certainty that int will be adequate. In those cases we should use int and save the space.

There is an even more important reason, although it is one that is likely to decrease in relevance in the future. Many computers today are only 32-bit machines; therefore, they cannot carry out 64-bit arithmetic—the kind that involves longs—with anywhere near the efficiency with which they process ints (using 32-bit arithmetic). This factor is becoming less important as companies continue to introduce new 64-bit computers, such as DEC's Alpha, Sun's Ultrasparc, and Intel's Itanium.

Mixed Type Arithmetic

Java allows int values to be assigned to long variables because there is no chance of information being lost: If *n* is an integer whose magnitude is less than 2 billion, it certainly is an integer whose magnitude is less than 9 quintillion. Thus, we can write

```
long    x, y z;
int     j=55, k;
x =   98; ◄──────────── Assign an int literal to a long variable: OK
y =   j; ◄───────────── Assign an int variable's value to a long variable: OK
z =   2*j; ◄─────────── Assign an int expression's value to a long variable: OK
```

However, we cannot write

```
j  =  y; ◄──── Illegal: Can't assign a long to an int, even if the long value is within the int's range
k  =  32L; ◄── Illegal: Can't assign a long to an int, even if the long value is within the int's range
```

If we *must* assign a long value to an int and are certain that it will fit the int's range, we may write

```
j  =  (int) y; ◄──────── Acceptable
k  =  (int) 32L; ◄────── Acceptable
```

Preceding the expression with the conversion type (int) in parentheses promises the Java compiler that the long value will be small enough to fit in an int at execution time, when the program runs. This notation is called **casting**, and we often say we are *casting a long to an int*.

Other Integer Types: short **and** byte

Java provides two other integer types as well, short and byte. These represent even smaller ranges of integers and, accordingly, require less memory. A short models the set of integers from –32768 to 32767 and requires 16 bits of memory, half that needed by an `int`. A `byte` models the set of integers from –128 to 127 and requires 8 bits of memory, half that needed by a `short`.

The mixed arithmetic rules involving `short` and `byte` are based on the same principle as `long` and `int`: If information might be lost as a result of an assignment, an explicit *cast* is required.

3.7 BigInteger

The `long` integer type supports numbers in the range –9,223,372,036,854,775,808 to 9,223,372,036,854,775,807. This range is more than sufficient for just about any numeric application we might encounter. However, there are a few specialized situations that call for exceptionally large numbers. One of these is cryptography—the creation and use of codes for the purpose of privacy and security. Any traditional code can be easily broken by an inexpensive computer. Modern secure codes require computers in their creation as well as in their decipherment and in attempts to "break" them. Because such codes employ numbers of immense size, easily exceeding the range of `long`, the `BigInteger` class provides useful behavior to the modern cryptographer.

Using `BigInteger`

We create a `BigInteger` object by passing its constructor a `String` representing the number, such as

```
BigInteger codeKey1 = new
  BigInteger("5647335678535677546787654356778555433");
BigInteger codeKey2 = new
  BigInteger("1234561234535677546787654356778555433");
```

Basic arithmetic operations are available through the methods `add()`, `subtract()`, `multiply()`, and `divide()`. (Comparison and several other operations are also provided.) Each of these methods takes a second `BigInteger` object as its argument and returns a `BigInteger` object representing the result of the operation. Thus,

```
BigInteger sum;
sum = codeKey1.add(codeKey2);
```

calculates the sum of `codeKey1` and `codeKey2` and assigns the result to `sum`.

Let's write a program that prints out the product of `codeKey1` and `codeKey2` divided by 3. Once those two values have been declared, we can compute their product as

```
BigInteger dividend = codeKey1.multiply(codeKey2);
```

Although 3 can be easily represented as an `int`, because it is to be used in an operation involving a `BigInteger`, we must work with it as a `BigInteger` as well:

```
BigInteger bigThree = new BigInteger("3");
```

We can then perform the division

```
BigInteger result = dividend.divide(bigThree);
```

and print the result:

```
System.out.println(result);
```

The program in its entirety, then, is

```
import java.math.*;
public class BigIntProgram {
    public static void main(String[] arg) {
        BigInteger codeKey1 = new
          BigInteger("564733567853567754678765435677855433");
        BigInteger codeKey2 = new
          BigInteger("123456123453567754678765435677855433");
        BigInteger dividend = codeKey1.multiply(codeKey2);
        BigInteger bigThree = new BigInteger("3");
        BigInteger result = dividend.divide(bigThree);
        System.out.println(result);
    }
}
```

Alternatively, we can use cascading and composition to combine several statements and write

```
System.out.println(codeKey1.multiply(codeKey2).
                    divide(new BigInteger("3")));
```

Java Interlude

Packages and the import Statement

Note the first line of `BigIntProgram`:

```
import java.math.*;
```

This statement, known as an **import directive**, is required because of the way Java's predefined classes are organized. Java provides hundreds of predefined classes grouped into **packages** according to their purpose. For example, the `java.math` package contains classes that support mathematical calculations. As we will see in the rest of this chapter, the `java.io` package contains classes that allow us to do input and output. The `java.lang` package includes classes, such as `String`, that are central to the language itself.

Every class in Java belongs to a package (even the ones created by people other than the Java language designers). The full name of a class is given by the name of the package it belongs to, followed by the name of the class. For example, the full name of the String class is java.lang.String, while the full name of the BigInteger class is java.math.BigInteger. With the exception of the classes in java.lang, Java expects us to refer to classes by their full names. Using this naming system, the first few lines of BigIntProgram would look like this:

```
public static void main(String[] arg) {
    java.math.BigInteger codeKey1 = new
        java.math.BigInteger("5647335678535677546787654356778555433");
    java.math.BigInteger codeKey2 = new
        java.math.BigInteger("1234561234535677546787654356778555433");
```

Java provides the import directive because typing full class names becomes tedious very quickly; if a class is inside a package named in an import directive, it can be named with its simple name—that is, without the name of its enclosing package.

3.8 Introduction to Input

Every useful program must interact with its environment. A program that doesn't somehow announce its result—maybe by printing a message, creating some complex visual display, or perhaps providing data for another program—may as well not be run. Similarly, most programs are influenced by external factors—such as data entered by the user, the contents of a web page, the current time, or the geographical location of the computer running the program. We've already seen that Java contains several predefined classes that model some of these factors; we've also seen that the System.out object models the standard output behavior of printing messages to the screen. In the next few sections we'll focus on the predefined classes that model the processes both of outputting data (not just to the screen!) and of getting **input** data—sometimes, but not always, provided by the user typing at the keyboard. We'll begin by studying how a program can take input data from a text file; this will allow us to discuss all the essential elements of the input process. Then we'll look at situations where input data comes instead from a keyboard (typed in by the user) or from any web page on the Internet.

A computer's input and output mechanisms rely on many specialized pieces of hardware and software that must be carefully coordinated. As in any other large, complex project, a reliable input/output system must be structured so that responsibilities are clearly assigned and coordination channels universally agreed on. While every kind of input and output is fundamentally about transmitting data (e.g., from the keyboard to the processor, or from the processor to disk storage), each different "flavor" (e.g., input from the keyboard versus input from the web) has particular characteristics that require the data to be processed differently. We will see that Java's input and output classes have been carefully designed to reflect these relationships.

Overview of File Input: From Disk to Program

So far, our programs' interactions with their environment have involved simply displaying information on the monitor (specifically, printing streams of characters via System.out). But computer systems also store and retrieve data using files on disks—all the Java programs you've written have been saved as a disk **file**, and when the Java compiler processes them, it must in turn read the contents of that file. One advantage of storing data in files on a disk is *persistence*: Screen information lasts only as long as it is on the screen and may be easily lost—data stored in a file lasts much longer. If we need to perform several computations with a set of data (such as the results from a scientific experiment), it is much more efficient to store the data in a file to be read when needed rather than to retype the data (with a lot of typos, probably) each time. Another advantage of disk files is their *capacity*: much more data can be stored in a disk file than can be displayed on the screen or even printed conveniently on a printer.

In order to understand how data flows from a file into a Java program, we'll first look at an overview of the tasks that need to be performed. Then we'll consider the Java classes that are responsible for performing those tasks and show how they work together.

What must we do to enable a program to process data from a file? Reading data from a file into program variables requires two basic steps:

- Accessing information about the disk file—this includes the location of the file (so we can get to the data), and the length of the file (so we know when we're finished reading the file). This information is usually stored in the disk's directory. The information associated with a file is modeled by the Java class File; we'll see later that this class does *not* model the contents of the actual file, only information about it.
- Transferring the data from the file on disk to our program.

We'll see that this transfer requires the efforts of a handful of Java classes that take responsibility for different phases of the transfer processs. Figure 3.4 diagrams the process of reading text data; the three unlabeled rectangles represent classes whose names and responsibilities we will discuss in the next few sections. The first step is to read data from the disk directly; this data is passed on a stream of bytes (that is, as a sequence of numerical values—not text). Next, these numerical values are transformed into a sequence of character values; these characters are then combined to produce a String.

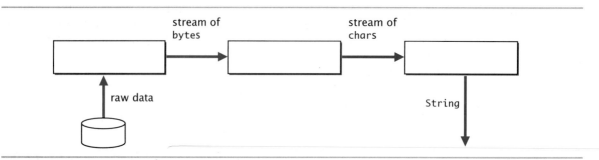

stream of
bytes

stream of
chars

raw data

String

Figure 3.4   Overview of the file input process.

From byte to char: The Case for Unicode

Originally, most computer systems recognized text based only on Latin characters—the English alphabet, punctuation, and a handful of European symbols. This character set, limited to about 120 characters, became known as the American Standard Code for Information Interchange (ASCII) character set; this was the standard for many years. The amount of memory required to hold a single ASCII character became known as a *byte*. One of the uses of Java's byte primitive type is to hold ASCII character values. Recall that byte values can store integer values from −128 to 127; ASCII values are represented by assigning character values to the numbers 0 to 127.

As the Internet proliferated, it became desirable to allow representations of other languages (such as Arabic, Hebrew, Chinese, and so forth) and their associated alphabets. An expanded character set, known as Unicode, was introduced to accommodate a wide variety of alphabets (including all characters in the ASCII set as well). Because there are many more possible Unicode characters than ASCII characters, a Unicode character requires a larger amount of memory. The Java primitive type char is used to contain Unicode character values, and the Java String class uses Unicode-based chars to store the characters that compose a String.

Despite the attractiveness of Unicode, most disk files are still composed of bytes representing ASCII characters. These files may have been created by editors, word processors, or other programs, designed before Unicode was introduced, that can manipulate only ASCII files. Alternatively, because ASCII takes up less room than Unicode, a file may be saved in ASCII for the sake of space efficiency. In either case, ASCII-based files contain their data as bytes.

This produces a conflict: much of the data we will want to input is byte (ASCII) based, while Java Strings require char (Unicode) based data. As we shall see, Java provides classes to resolve this conflict.

From chars to String: Obtaining Lines of Text

Reading the contents of a file character-by-character is primitive way of performing input—sometimes we might be interested in the individual characters that make up a file, but often it will be more natural to think of the contents of the file in larger units, such as lines. For this reason, Java provides a mechanism for converting a stream of characters into a sequence of `Strings`, each of which represents one line of the file. (See Figure 3.5.)

3.9 The `File` Input Process

Class `File`: Accessing Disk File Information

The `File` class is responsible for providing access to information about a disk file. For example, this class has methods that will tell us whether a named disk file exists, in which directory the file resides, the length of the file, and the date it was created and last modified. The `File` class is *not* responsible for providing access to the *contents* of disk files, but `File` objects are used by classes that do access the contents of these files.

The constructor for `File` accepts a file's name (a `String` reference) as its argument, as follows:

```
new File(filename)
```

An example of this follows:

```
File    f1, f2;
f1 = new File("letterToJoanna");
f2 = new File("letterToMatthew");
```

These statements create two `File` objects that refer to files named `letterToJoanna` and `letterToMatthew`.

When a `File` object (as above) is created, it does not create a corresponding file (that is, a file with the same name). That is, if no file named `letterToJoanna` exists on the disk, the construction

```
f1 = new File("letterToJoanna");
```

will not create it. Keep in mind that a `File` object in a Java program merely represents a possible file and does not guarantee that it exists. We can use the predicate method `exists()` to find out whether a file actually exists on disk. If the corresponding file does exist already, the `File` object provides methods that model some common file operations.

Figure 3.5
Transforming character stream in to `String`.

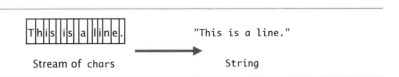

For example, we can delete a file, using the delete() method. To remove a file named junk, we can write the following:

```
File    f;
f = new File("junk");
if (f.exists())
    f.delete();
```

We can also rename a file. Suppose we have a file named junk and we want to change its name to garbage. We create two File objects, one representing junk the other representing garbage, as follows:

```
File    f1, f2;
f1 = new File("junk");
f2 = new File("garbage");
```

and then we use the renameTo method, as follows:

```
f1.renameTo(f2);
```

Although useful, these methods have not given us the means to create a file that does not exist nor have they given us the means to read from or write to a file. Table 3.2 summarizes the File methods we have learned.

TABLE 3.2   SOME File METHODS

METHOD	RETURNS	ARGUMENTS	ACTION
exists	boolean	None	Determines whether the disk file exists
delete	boolean	None	Deletes the file
renameTo	boolean	Reference to a File object	Renames the file

Notice that delete() and renameTo() each return a boolean value; this is used to indicate whether or not the operation was successful (for example, our program might try to delete a system file that may not be deleted). If we are not concerned about this possibility we may simply ignore the return value, as we did above; otherwise we can use a conditional statement to respond appropriately:

```
if (f.delete())
    System.err.println("Error deleting file.");
```

Class FileInputStream: Reading bytes from a Disk File

While the File class provides access to information about the file residing on disk, it provides no support for transferring data from the file into memory. Classes that support the behavior of transferring data from some source into memory are categorized as *input streams*. Java provides several such classes; for reading data from disk files, Java provides the `FileInputStream` class. A `FileInputStream` object is created by providing it with information about the file to be read in. This is done by passing a `File` object as argument to the constructor:

```
File f = new File("file1.dat");
FileInputStream fis = new FileInputStream(f);
```

The class also provides another constructor that accepts a filename (as a `String`) that provides a convenient shortcut for the above two statements:

```
FileInputStream fis = new FileInputStream("file1.dat");
```

We will encounter several such *convenience* methods—methods that are not actually necessary but are supplied to make life easier for the user of the class. In our case, the `FileInputStream` convenience constructor eliminates the need for an explicit `File` object.

Class `InputStreamReader`: **Transforming** bytes to chars

As we discussed in the overview, Java's `char` type supports the Unicode character set rather than the limited ASCII character set. Because many files stored on disk are still represented in ASCII (that is, as `bytes`), Java provides the `InputStreamReader` class, whose responsibility it is to transform a stream of `bytes` into a stream of Unicode `chars` suitable for processing in a Java application.

We create an `InputStreamReader` object by passing as an argument to its constructor an input stream object whose `bytes` we wish to turn into `chars`. With our `FileInputStream` `fis` object of the previous section, we can write:

```
InputStreamReader isr = new InputStreamReader(fis);
```

Class `BufferedReader`: **From a Stream of** chars to `String`

While an `InputStreamReader` object does produce data in a form usable by a Java program (a sequence of characters), this is not necessarily the form that is easiest for us to use as programmers. Usually we view text files not as sequences of characters but as sequences of *lines*. The `BufferedReader` class is responsible for transforming a stream of `chars` (as provided by an `InputStreamReader`) into a sequence of `Strings`.

Creating a new `BufferedReader` object is very similar to creating the other objects in the chain we've been building: We pass an `InputStreamReader` object to its constructor, like this:

```
BufferedReader br = new BufferedReader(isr);
```

The `BufferedReader` class provides a method, `readLine()`, that returns a `String` corresponding to one whole line of text in the associated file. We can then manipulate this `String` using any of the `String` methods we've studied already.

The Result: Opening a File for Input

Here is the final sequence of object creations:

```
File f = new File("file1.dat");
FileInputStream fis = new FileInputStream(f);
InputStreamReader isr = new InputStreamReader(fis);
BufferedReader br = new BufferedReader(isr);
```

Or, employing composition, we can directly obtain our desired BufferedReader object without explicitly declaring the intermediate objects:

```
BufferedReader br =
   new BufferedReader(
     new InputStreamReader(
       new FileInputStream("file1.dat")));
```

The following table summarizes the roles of the classes involved in file input.

SOURCE	EXAMPLE OF SOURCE	CLASS	RESULT
disk file	File("file1.dat")	FileInputStream	stream of bytes
stream of bytes	FileInputStream	InputStreamReader	stream of chars
stream of chars	InputStreamReader	BufferedReader	lines (Strings)

EXAMPLE Displaying the contents of a file.   Let's begin with a simple example: a program that displays on the screen the first few lines of the file example.txt. Our program will first have to set up a BufferedReader that will read lines from example.txt, then alternately read a line from the file and display the line on the screen using System.out.

Creating the BufferedReader is done just as it is above:

```
BufferedReader br =
   new BufferedReader(
     new InputStreamReader(
       new FileInputStream("example.txt")));
```

Then we can use the readLine() method of BufferedReader to read the first line of the file. We need to save a reference to the line in order to print it out, so we declare a String reference variable first:

```
String line;
line = br.readLine();
```

Then we display the line on the screen:

```
System.out.println(line);
```

The entire program is as follows:

```java
import java.io.*;
public class DisplayFile {
    public static void main(String[] arg) throws Exception {
        BufferedReader br =
          new BufferedReader(
            new InputStreamReader(
              new FileInputStream("example.txt")));
        String line;
        line = br.readLine();
        System.out.println(line);
        line = br.readLine();
        System.out.println(line);
        line = br.readLine();
        System.out.println(line);
    }
}
```

What Can Go Wrong?

As our programs further interact with their computing environment—reading from data files, for example—there are more opportunities for them to fail through no fault of their own. For example, the program above is perfectly correct, but if someone runs it in a directory where there is no file called example.txt, it will fail. Java requires that the programmer acknowledge potential failures of this kind by adding the phrase throws Exception to the boilerplate, as we have done above. If the phrase is omitted the compiler will issue an error. The phrase means that it is conceivable that an unrecoverable error might occur because of a problem in the computing environment, and as a result the program might terminate abruptly. We will learn more about this issue and exceptions in general in Chapter 14.

3.10 Keyboard Input

We said earlier that file input was the most complicated form of input; let's look now at obtaining input from the keyboard. This kind of input is a bit simpler only because we don't have to expend effort identifying which of many input sources we wish to use—while there are many possible data files, there is only one keyboard. Moreover, just as Java makes output to the monitor easy for us by predefining System.out, keyboard input is represented by the predefined object System.in.

Java treats the keyboard as a stream of bytes, which means that System.in is an InputStream object (though not a FileInputStream object, because the keyboard is not a file). We can apply familiar techniques to this object in order to create a BufferedReader object corresponding to the keyboard (see Figure 3.6):

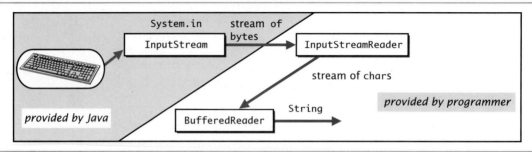

Figure 3.6   Overview of keyboard input.

```
BufferedReader keyboard =
    new BufferedReader(
        new InputStreamReader(System.in));
```

Let's use these new tools to write a program that reads a single noun from the keyboard and displays its plural on the screen. We don't yet have the tools to come close to doing this correctly, so we will assume that merely adding an *s* to a word correctly results in the plural form (thereby ignoring words like *fox* and *baby*).

We write a comment defining the meaning of the program followed by the usual first two lines of boilerplate notation and then the above code fragment, as follows:

```
import java.io.*;
/*
 * Plural: Displays the plural form of the word typed on the keyboard.
 *          Uses the naive and wrong (!) approach of just adding s.
 */
public class Plural {
    public static void main(String[] arg) throws Exception {
        BufferedReader keyboard =          // Models a keyboard that reads
            new BufferedReader(            //    lines as Strings
                new InputStreamReader(System.in));
                                            // Models a keyboard that reads
                                            //    a stream of characters
        String inputLine;                  // Models a line of input.
        inputLine = keyboard.readLine();

            Rest of the program goes here . . .

    }
}
```

All that remains is to arrange to display the String as intended. We will send a print() (not a println()) message to System.out with the word read from input as an argument. We send print() instead of println() because we want the s to appear on the same line as the word, not on the succeeding line. Then we will send a println() message with "s" as an argument in order to display the s and complete the line, as follows:

```
System.out.print(inputLine);
System.out.println("s");
```

Here is the complete program:

```
import java.io.*;
/*
 * Plural: Displays the plural form of the word typed on the keyboard.
 *              Uses the naive and wrong (!) approach of just adding s.
 */
class Plural {
    public static void main(String[] arg) throws Exception {
        BufferedReader keyboard =          // Models a keyboard that reads
            new BufferedReader(            //    lines as Strings
                new InputStreamReader(System.in));
                                           // Models a keyboard that reads
                                           //    a stream of characters
        String inputLine;                  // Models a line of input.
        inputLine = keyboard.readLine();
        System.out.print(inputLine);
        System.out.println("s");
    }
}
```

Interactive Input/Output

One characteristic distinguishing keyboard input is that it directly involves a human being, often termed an **end-user** (of the program). In practice, end-users are almost never the authors of the programs that they use. Millions of people use Microsoft Word—only a handful of them had a role in writing that program.

Because end-users (or *users* for short) are not the authors of the programs they use, they cannot be expected to know automatically what to type on the keyboard and when to type it. A program that expects input from a keyboard must, in order to be useful, provide that information to the users as it runs. It must display messages such as "Please enter your PIN now" and "Sorry, that choice is not correct--please make your selection again." These **prompts** tell the user what to type on the keyboard. The flow of data between users and programs is referred to as **interactive** input and output.

Consider `Plural` from the previous section. The program includes the following line:

```
inputLine = keyboard.readLine();
```

It expects the user to type in a word that is to be made plural. But how will the user know that this is expected? The `readLine()` method waits silently for the user to type in a line—it cannot offer any guidance. The solution is to display a prompt, such as, `"Type in a word to be pluralized, please"` just before the `readLine()` message is sent to `keyboard`. We know how to display such a string to the user: We must send a `print()` message to `System.out` prior to reading in the line, as follows:

```
System.out.println("Type in a word to be pluralized, please ");
         inputLine = keyboard.readLine();
```

A general form for interactive input and output is as follows:

```
System.out.println(prompt goes here);
string reference variable = keyboard.readLine();
possibly compute something (using, for example, concatenation)
System.out.println(output string goes here);
```

3.11 File Output

We began the book by talking about how to send output to the screen using the predefined object `System.out`. After thinking about performing input from disk files for a while, it shouldn't be hard to imagine situations in which we might want to send our program's output to a file rather than to the screen—it might generate more output than can easily fit on the screen, or it might be generating data that we want to save for longer than a few seconds.

Sending our output to a file involves a series of steps very similar to getting input from a file. We begin with a `File` object corresponding to the output file (which may or may not actually exist). For example, we might want to send our output to a file called `"prog1out.dat"`:

```
File outFile = new File("prog1out.dat");
```

In order to send output to this file, we must associate it with a stream of data—not an input stream, this time, but an *output stream*, specifically a `FileOutputStream`. A `FileOutputStream` object represents a stream of bytes going *to* a disk file, just as a `FileInputStream` object represents a stream of bytes coming *from* a disk file. We can create a `FileOutputStream` object either by passing a `File` object to its constructor or by using one of its convenience constructors and passing only the filename:

```
FileOutputStream outStream = new FileOutputStream(f1);
```

or

```
FileOutputStream outStream = new FileOutputStream("prog1out.dat");
```

Although a `File` object does not directly correspond to a disk file, a `FileOutput-Stream` object corresponds to a real stream of data that must go somewhere, so part of the constructor's responsibility is to ensure the existence of a disk file to receive the data. Thus, it checks to see whether a disk file with the specified name exists, and if one does not, it creates one.

As in the case of input, a stream of `bytes` is not often the most natural way to think about the output our programs generate, so Java provides a predefined class that allows us to work with output more naturally. A `PrintStream` object is created by passing a `FileOutputStream` object to the `PrintStream` constructor.

Now we can put all the pieces together:

```
PrintStream outPrintStream = new PrintStream(
    new FileOutputStream("prog1out.dat"));
```

Note that we went from a stream of `bytes` (a `FileOutputStream`) directly to an object we can program (with a `PrintStream`) without creating an intermediate object that generates a stream of characters. This is because the `PrintStream` class provides overloaded `print()` and `println()` methods that automatically produce text representations of Java data types.

EXAMPLE Maintaining a backup of screen output.   Suppose we want our program to maintain a disk file copy (named `backup`, say) of the screen output that it generates. Let's assume this is an improvement of `Program1`. We write the program as before but add the code needed to create a new file, `backup`, with an associated `PrintStream`. Then, whatever we write to `System.out`, we also write to this `PrintStream` object, as follows:

```
import java.io.*;
class Program1Backup {
   public static void main(String[] arg) throws Exception {
      PrintStream        backup;
      FileOutputStream   backupFileStream;
      File               backupFile;
      backupFile = new File("backup");
      backupFileStream = new FileOutputStream(backupFile);
```

```
        backup = new PrintStream(backupFileStream);
        System.out.println("This is my first Java program");
        backup.println("This is my first Java program");
        System.out.println("... but it won't be my last.");
        backup.println("... but it won't be my last.");
    }

}
```

3.12 Network Computing: An Introduction

In this section you will learn how to write programs that read publicly available information from the Internet—from the White House web site in Washington D.C., for example, or from New York radio station sites.

Network Concepts

Before jumping into Java code, we need a quick overview of some basic network concepts.

A **computer network** is a group of *computers* that can directly exchange information with each other. This is usually accomplished by connecting the computers with a wire of some kind.

The **Internet** is a group of *computer networks* that allows a computer on one network to exchange information with a computer on any of the other networks. The networks are connected to each other by means of special telephone lines or satellite relays. You can get on the Internet by getting a connection to one of those networks that are part of the Internet and installing the necessary software on your computer. You can then communicate with every machine on the Internet because of the following:

- Each computer on the Net (as we call the Internet for short) has a unique **Internet address**.
- The software on the computers on the Net can forward information to the correct computer, provided that information comes with a proper Internet address.

The Internet addresses of machines on the Net are Strings like "www.whitehouse.gov" or "home.netscape.com" or "machine1.somestateu.edu".

Information on the Internet is organized into units called **network resources**. These resources may be pictures, audio segments, videos, plain text, and so on. Usually, a resource is simply a file stored on some machine that is on the Net. Each resource is available from a particular machine on the Internet. Each resource is uniquely identified by a Uniform Resource Locator, abbreviated **URL** and pronounced "earl."

What's especially nice about URLs is that they are not just arbitrary unique identifiers (like Social Security numbers), but they have several parts, each of which has a meaning, as follows:

PART	EXAMPLE	PURPOSE
Protocol	`http`	Identifies the kind of software that is needed to access the data
Internet address	`www.yahoo.com`	Identifies the computer with the resource
Filename	`index.html`	Identifies the file on the computer holding the resource

These pieces are put together to form an URL as follows:

protocol: *// internet address/filename*

A `://` separates the protocol from the machine address, and a / separates the Internet address from the filename. For example, the URL

`http://www.yahoo.com/index.html`

means "use World Wide Web" software (*protocol*: http) "to contact the www. yahoo.com" (the Internet address of the computer that has this resource) "to access index.html" (the filename for the resource). (See Figure 3.7.)

Network Input

Reading input from World Wide Web resources in a Java program is as simple as reading input from a disk file. Again, the key is to obtain an `InputStream` that provides the fundamental behavior of modeling a stream of input (in this case from a web site).

The Java class library provides a class, `URL`, to model URLs. The `URL` class provides a constructor that takes a `String` argument (the URL as we would write it) as follows:

`URL u = new URL("http://www.yahoo.com/");`

Figure 3.7
The components of
an URL.

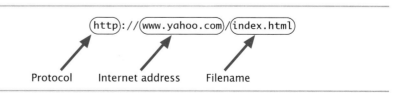

It also provides a method, openStream(), which takes no arguments but returns an InputStream, as follows:

```
InputStream ins = u.openStream();
```

This method does quite a bit of work behind the scenes: It sets up communication software on your side, initiates contact with the remote machine, waits for a response, sets up the connection, and then constructs an InputStream object to model the connection, returning a reference to this object.

Once we have an InputStream like this, we are in business: We can easily construct a BufferedReader object (as we did for file and keyboard) and then read from the remote resource, as follows (see Figure 3.8):

```
InputStreamReader isr = new InputStreamReader(ins);
BufferedReader remote = new BufferedReader(isr);
... remote.readLine() ...
```

EXAMPLE Reading From a Web Page. Here is a program that reads and prints out the first five lines of the White House's web page:

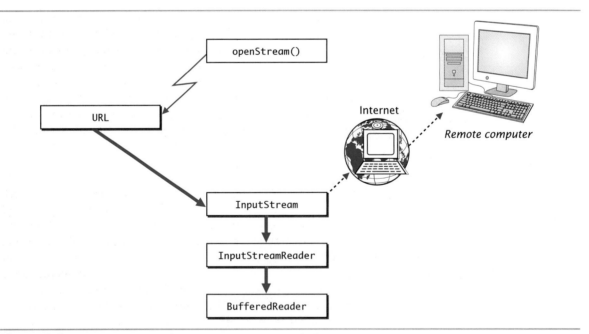

Figure 3.8 A BufferedReader for reading a web site on the Internet.

```
import java.net.*;
import java.io.*;
class WHWWW {
    public static void main(String[] arg) {
        URL    u = new URL("http://www.whitehouse.gov/");
        InputStream  ins = u.openStream();
        InputStreamReader  isr = new InputStreamReader(ins);
        BufferedReader  whiteHouse = new BufferedReader(isr);
        System.out.println(whiteHouse.readLine());
        System.out.println(whiteHouse.readLine());
        System.out.println(whiteHouse.readLine());
        System.out.println(whiteHouse.readLine());
        System.out.println(whiteHouse.readLine());
    }
}
```

Java Interlude

Java Documentation

The Java Application Programming Interface

Java's Application Programming Interface (API) is the set of classes and methods that are made available to the programmer; all the classes we have looked at so far are part of the Java API. The Java API includes hundreds of classes, many of which contain 20 or more methods. Becoming an excellent Java programmer certainly does *not* require memorizing even a significant fraction of this API, but it does mean being able to navigate the API *documentation* efficiently. Sun provides this documentation on the web; as of this writing, the documentation for the latest version of Java's API is at `http://java.sun.com/j2se/1.4.1/docs/api/`; documentation for past (and future) versions can be found at `http://java.sun.com/apis.html`.

Contents of the API Documentation

The API documentation contains descriptions of every package, class, method, and variable in the API, as well as signatures for each method. Reading the API documentation can be frustrating at first, mainly because understanding how one class or method works often requires understanding something about several other classes (for example, it's hard to use a `BufferedReader` properly without knowing something about `InputStreamReaders` and `InputStreams`). As the range of Java programs you write expands, your familiarity with the API will increase. In the next few paragraphs, we'll look at how Sun's documentation is organized; by studying the documentation for some familiar classes (like `String` and `BigInteger`), you should start to get a sense of how to use the API.

Layout of the Documentation Pages

Figure 3.9 shows the main sections of the API documentation. In the top left corner is a list of all the standard Java packages (such as java.io and java.math). In the lower left is a list of classes; initially, this frame lists *all* of the standard Java classes, but clicking on a package listed in the top left reduces the class listing to the classes in the selected package. The rest of the window is occupied by an "information" frame: Clicking on an item in the lower left frame (a package name, a class name, etc.) causes information on that item to appear in the main frame.

Looking Up the String Class

Let's use the API documentation to try to learn more about the String class: Are there other useful String methods? Are there other interesting things about the String class that we haven't discussed?

Because we know the name of the class we're interested in, we can just look up String in the (alphabetical) list of "All Classes" provided in the lower left frame. Clicking on "String" brings up new content in the information frame (see Figure 3.10). At the beginning of the class description, we see that String belongs to the

Figure 3.9
The Java API documentation pages.

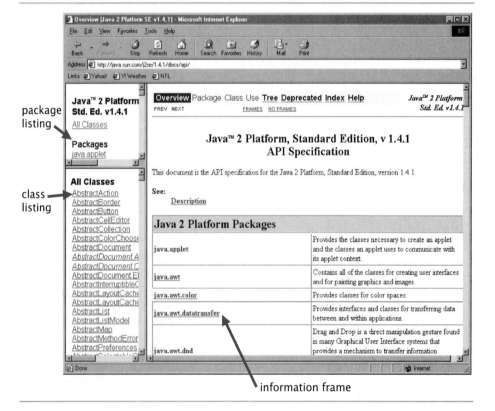

information frame

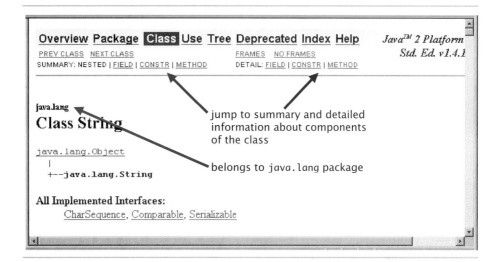

Figure 3.10
Some documentation on the String class.

java.lang package; scrolling down a bit gives us a page or so of descriptive text about the class. Either by scrolling down further or by using the links at the very top of the page, we can get more specific information about components of the class (such as methods). Figures 3.11 and 3.12 show method summaries and method details from the String class documentation. Notice that although these portions of documentation mention unfamiliar things (a class called Object, something called NullPointerException, and the value null), there's still enough accessible information to let us figure out how to use these methods.

Figure 3.11
Some method summaries for the String class.

Method Summary

char	**charAt**(int index) Returns the character at the specified index.
int	**compareTo**(Object o) Compares this String to another Object.
int	**compareTo**(String anotherString) Compares two strings lexicographically.
int	**compareToIgnoreCase**(String str) Compares two strings lexicographically, ignoring case differences.
String	**concat**(String str) Concatenates the specified string to the end of this string.

startsWith

```
public boolean startsWith(String prefix)
```

Tests if this string starts with the specified prefix.

Figure 3.12
Detailed documenta-
tion for the starts-
With() method of the
String class.

Parameters:
    prefix - the prefix.
Returns:
    true if the character sequence represented by the argument is a prefix of the character
    sequence represented by this string; false otherwise. Note also that true will be returned
    if the argument is an empty string or is equal to this String object as determined by the
    equals(Object) method.
Throws:
    NullPointerException - if prefix is null.
Since:
    1.0

Summary

In this chapter we have learned to create new objects, instances of Java's pre-defined classes. This requires the new operator, followed by a message to the newly created object that invokes its constructor. The constructor is a special method, used in the creation of an object. The name of the constructor is always the same as the name of its class. Like other methods, constructors may require arguments.

Conditions are expressions of the boolean primitive type, which models true/false values. In addition, boolean expressions are created from boolean variables and the literal values true and false. boolean expressions may also be created using operators such as <.

Integer values are modeled by several primitive data types—int, long, short, and byte—which require different amounts of storage space and represent values of different magnitudes. Casting can sometimes be used to facilitate assignment between values of different types.

The BigInteger class is used to model integer values too large to be represented as long values. The Date, GregorianCalendar, and TimeZone classes model different aspects of dates and times. Cascading and composition are often used to coordinate the efforts of several objects.

We were introduced to some of the classes that Java provides to support input and output. We learned how each of these classes provides just the behavior needed to model a particular input or output service. To create the object with the behavior that we wanted we had to create a sequence of objects, each used in the creation of the next. This can be done with multiple assignments or by composition of constructors with the new operator.

For example, to create a BufferedReader object that would allow lines to be read from a disk file, we had to create a File object, use the File object to create a FileInputStream object, and use that object to create an InputStreamReader object that finally could be passed to the BufferedReader constructor.

We were introduced to classes that model URLs and network connections to URLs. These allowed us to create objects that model URLs and the behavior of Internet connections.

Key Terms

boolean A primitive data type modeling true and false values.

boolean expression An expression evaluating to a boolean value.

cascading A technique in which the result of one method invocation is used as the receiver of a second method invocation.

casting A notation indicating to the compiler the true nature of a value.

composition A technique in which the result of one method invocation is used as an argument in a second method invocation.

computer network A collection of computers, connected by wires, that can exchange data with each other.

constructor A method that is invoked when an object is created. The name of the constructor method is the same as the corresponding class name.

default constructor A constructor that is invoked if no other constructor is explicitly selected.

end-user A person who is using a program, usually not the author of the code.

file A named collection of data on the disk.

import directive A statement that permits classes in a package to be named using its simple name rather than its full name.

input Information from outside the program that is provided to the program.

interactive An arrangement of bidirectional and alternating data flow between user and program.

Internet A rapidly growing, very widely used global network of networks.

Internet address A String, such as www.aw.com, that identifies a machine on the Internet.

network resource A resource, usually a file, that is available to users on machines other than the one on which the file is stored.

operation An action in Java that results in a value.

operator A symbol or keyword representing an operation (e.g., the identifier `new` represents the operation that creates an object).

package A named group of related classes.

predicate method A method whose return value is `boolean`.

prompt A `String` that is written to the screen to tell an end-user what kind of input should be entered next.

URL A unique identification of a network resource, including the Internet address of the machine on which the resource is stored, the filename of the resource, and the protocol (such as HyperText Transfer Protocol, or HTTP) that should be used to access the resource.

Questions for Review

1. What does the `new` operator do?
2. When is a *constructor* invoked? How is it invoked? What is its purpose?
3. What is the purpose of the `import` directive?
4. What are the differences among `byte`, `short`, `int`, and `long`? How can you convert a value from one type to another?
5. How can a Java program create or remove a file?
6. Why does the phrase `throws Exception` appear now in our code?
7. How do you read a line of text from a keyboard? From a file? From an Internet file?

Exercises

1. Write a fragment of code that uses the `new` operator to construct a `String` object that models the title of the textbook, *Introduction to Programming Using Java*. Print the title both in all CAPITALS and in all lowercase letters by sending `toUpperCase()` and `toLowerCase()` messages to the newly created object.

2. Is the following a legal Java statement? Explain why or why not. If it is legal, what does it do?

```
System.out.println(new String("second exercise"));
```

3. Is the following a legal Java statement? Explain why or why not. If it is legal, what does it do?

   ```
   String s = new String("third exercise").toUpperCase();
   ```

4. Given the declarations

   ```
   String s1 = "elephant";
   String s2 = "grasshopper";
   ```

   what are the values returned by the following message invocations?

   ```
   s1.substring(4).concat(s2.substring(5))
   s1.toUpper().concat(s2)
   s2.substring(s1.length()).substring(1,2)
   ```

5. Write a boolean expression to test whether the reference held by the String variable magicWord is equal to "pomegranate".

6. Write a statement that assigns to the boolean variable isEven the value of an expression that is true if the value of the int variable numberOfSocks is even. (Hint: Use the % operator.)

7. Use cascading and composition to write a single statement that outputs the date of your birthday.

8. Write a fragment of code that uses getDisplayName() and String methods to print only the current month.

9. Write a fragment of code that will print the name of your local time zone in all uppercase letters.

10. How much memory space is required to store the following variables?

    ```
    int mySalary = 30000, max = 123456789;
    short yourSalary = 20000;
    long counter = 1;
    ```

11. Experiment with casting by writing three small Java programs that incorporate the following declarations and assignments.

    - ```
      int x;
      long z = 75L;
      x = z;
      ```

    - ```
      int x;
      long z = 75L;
      x = (int) z;
      ```

    - ```
      int x;
      long z = 5000000000L;
      x = (int) z;
      ```

    Have each program print out the final value of x. Before you compile and run each program, try to determine what will happen.
      ```

12. Write a Java program that prints the result of 904300557126582647297712363 divided by 238886393911202347.

13. Write a Java program that uses the `BigInteger.mod()` method to determine whether 772459822236028242391256237 is divisible by 3, 7, 11, and/or 13.

14. Write a program that reads three lines from the file `threelines.txt` and prints them out in reverse order and uppercase.

15. Write a program that reads six lines from the file `sixlines.txt` and outputs on a single line the last five characters of each line. (Hint: You only need to declare one `String` variable.)

16. Write a program that prompts the user for a `String` to be printed three times, reads the `String`, and prints it out three times.

17. Write a program that prompts the user for his or her first, middle, and last names, then prints his or her initials.

18. Most computer systems provide a utility or other means for removing a file. Write a program that does this. It should prompt the user for the name of a file to delete. After the user types in the filename, the program deletes it.

19. Write a program that changes the name of a file. It prompts the user for the original name of the file and then for the new name of the file. After the user types in both names, the program makes sure that the original file exists and that no file with the new name exists. It then either renames the file accordingly or prints out an error message and stops.

20. Write a program that reads five lines from `fivelines.txt` and copies those lines to `fivemorelines.txt`.

21. Write a program that prompts the user for a filename, then writes the alphabet into that file.

22. Write a program that asks the user to enter three different strings, then prints the longest one to the file `longstring.txt`. (Hint: Start by initializing the variable `String longestStr = ""`.)

23. Write a program that prompts for and reads a `String`. The program should then construct an URL for `http://www.X.com/`, where X is the `String` read in, and arrange to print the first five lines of the resource at that site. If the user types in "ibm," the first five lines from `http://www.ibm.com/` will be printed.

24. At the time of this writing, the U.S. Census Bureau's estimate of the world population can be found in the tenth line of the following URL: `http://www.census.gov/cgi-bin/ipc/popclockw`. Write a program that prints that line and only that line.

25. Rewrite the program in exercise 20 of Chapter 2 so that it prompts for and reads a three-character string, and prints all permutations of the string's characters.

26. Write a program that takes a file named `ford`, renames it `lincoln`, and then creates a file called `ford` that contains the single line `"get a horse"`.

27. Write a program that models a psychiatrist by asking the user (patient) what the problem is. Upon getting the user's response, the program asks "Why do you say '...whatever the response was...'?" When the user answers this question, the program responds, "That's very interesting. We can talk more about that next session." Sample session (user input in bold):

```
What are you thinking of today?
I'm depressed.
Why do you say 'I'm depressed'?
I didn't say you're depressed, I said I'm depressed.
That's very interesting, we can talk more about that next session.
```

28. Write a program that prompts the user for the name of an URL or file. If the user's response begins with "http" treat the user's response as an URL; otherwise treat it as a filename. Your program's output should look approximately like this:

```
At time ...  the first 5 lines of the URL ... are
 .

 .

 .

```

Use the GregorianCalendar and Date classes to print the date; replace the word "URL" with the word "file" if the user provided the filename.

Toward Animation

In the previous two GUI supplements, we focused solely on static, passive applets that just displayed something on the screen. Now that we've explored some of the tools for creating applets, we can create an applet that takes advantage of some of the applet infrastructure's support for animation. In the process, we'll examine a few more details of the life cycle of an applet.

The idea behind animation is to display in rapid sequence a series of images that differ from each other only minutely. One issue we will have to address is how to refresh the screen between frames: If we don't remove the image displayed in one frame before we display the next, we'll have a growing trail of overlapping images rather than a single image that appears to be moving. We can take advantage of the applet infrastructure to do this work, freeing us to focus on how to generate the appropriate sequence of frames. The applet we develop now will have almost all the necessary ingredients of a proper animation, but due to our focus on the applet life cycle, the sequence of frames will be displayed far too slowly to create a perception of movement. In Chapter 4 we will use these techniques to write an applet that does perform a simple animation.

The Almost-Animation

Our animation will be moving slowly, so in order to make the shift from one frame to the next easily perceptible, we'll make the difference unmistakable: Our animation will display a rectangle that flips back and forth between red and blue. At normal animation speeds, this would just appear as a dizzying purplish flicker, but in this context it will allow us to see clearly what happens between one frame and the next.

To begin, let's first write an applet that will just draw a single rectangle with no animation:

```java
import java.awt.*;
import java.applet.*;

public class FlipperApplet extends Applet {   // incomplete
    public void paint(Graphics g) {
        g.setColor(Color.red);   // or g.setColor(Color.blue);
        g.fillRect(0,0,100,100);
    }
}
```

This animation-free code is not very complicated. Let's look at how to alter this code to introduce some animation-like behavior.

The Applet Life Cycle

As you have probably concluded by now, the code between the line

```
public void paint (Graphics g) {
```

and its matching } is responsible for determining how the applet is displayed—that is, how it "paints itself" on the screen. We've already seen that the applet paints itself when it starts executing, but there are other situations in which this may occur.

For example, suppose we have a browser window open on our computer with an applet (such as the TrafficLightApplet from the last chapter) running on it. We temporarily move another window over the browser window, obscuring the applet, and then remove the obscuring window to reveal the applet again. What do we see? In the case of TrafficLightApplet, we see the traffic light image once again. How does that work? One possibility is that some part of the computer's operating system remembers what was under the obscuring window; when it detects the window has been moved out of the way, it redisplays what was there before. This is not terribly practical, though, for a number of reasons. Storing the "underneath" images requires significant storage space. Further, it's not clear how many layers of images would have to be remembered (what if we had four or five windows stacked on top of each other?). Even worse, it's not clear whether we want the system to remember the *entire* window or only the portion that is obscured (and how should it identify that portion?). Ultimately, this is far too much work for the system to do—it could prevent more urgent tasks from being completed on time.

Instead, the system relies on each window to decide whether and how to redisplay itself: The system just keeps track of which windows are obscuring other windows. When a window is uncovered, the system sends a message to the underlying window, asking it to redraw itself on the screen. Different applications may respond to these messages differently, but in the case of a browser window in which an applet is executing, a "redraw" message from the system causes the paint() code to be executed.

In the rest of this supplement, we'll modify the paint() code of FlipperApplet to take advantage of this "manual" animation. That is, we'll change FlipperApplet so that each time we cover and redisplay the window in which the applet is running, the color of the rectangle will change.

Implementing the Animation

Now that we know that the key to our animation is in the paint() code, we have to determine how to take advantage of this aspect of the applet's behavior. Let's start with the first time the paint() code is executed—when the applet is first loaded. What needs to happen? Two things: First, we need to display a rectangle of some color (let's say that we'll start by displaying the rectangle in red). Second, we need to make sure that the *next* time the paint() code is executed, the rectangle is displayed in blue. To do that, we can use a variable that will keep track of what color to use for the next rectangle. Because we only have two colors to consider, we can just use a boolean variable whose value we'll test to determine what color to use. Here's another version of FlipperApplet that implements this idea:

```
import java.awt.*;
import java.applet.*;

public class FlipperApplet extends Applet {
    public void paint(Graphics g) {
        if (red)         // should I draw in red?
            g.setColor(Color.red);
        else
            g.setColor(Color.blue);
        g.fillRect(0,0,100,100);
    }
    private boolean red=true;   // start with red
}
```

If we run this applet, though, nothing appears to happen: The color of the rectangle never changes. The value of red is initialized to true, but nowhere does its value get changed. This corresponds to the second responsibility of the paint() code we mentioned above: It has to make sure that the next time it executes, it switches colors. Thus, sometime after the display color is set, we need to flip the value of red from true to false (and vice versa):

```
import java.awt.*;
import java.applet.*;

public class FlipperApplet extends Applet {
    public void paint(Graphics g) {
        if (red)         // should I draw in red?
            g.setColor(Color.red);
        else
            g.setColor(Color.blue);
        g.fillRect(0,0,100,100);
        if (red)              // flip value of red
            red = false;
        else
            red = true;
    }
    private boolean red=true;   // start with red
}
```

We can make our code a little shorter by taking advantage of one of the operators that applies to `boolean` values: instead of writing the `if (red)` ... code, we can write

```
red = !red;
```

The ! (read as "not") operator by definition produces the opposite of the value to which it is applied, so `!true` is `false` and `!false` is `true`.

Observing the Life Cycle

Now we can run this applet and explore the circumstances under which the `paint()` code is executed. As we have seen, when an applet is loaded into the browser window, it automatically displays itself on the screen. Thus, the first execution of the `paint()` code occurs when the applet is initially loaded.

If no external events "disturb" the applet, the `paint()` code will never again be executed; that is, the applet will not try to redisplay itself unless the window containing it is told by the system to redraw itself. When might that happen? Certainly, if the window containing the applet is minimized or "iconified" and then restored, the contents of the window will have to be redrawn—thereby causing the `paint()` code to execute. If we put the window containing the running `Flipper-Aplet` through this sequence, we'll see the rectangle initially displayed as red; after minimizing and restoring the applet, the rectangle will appear in blue.

If we cover the applet's window with another window, then uncover it, the rectangle should reappear in red—when the window is redisplayed, the `paint()` code is executed again, switching the color back to red.

Suggested Experiments

1. Write an applet that displays the string `"This is paint job #x"` where the value of x increases each time the `paint` code is executed. Use a variable to keep track of the value of x; this variable should be declared after the `paint` code (just as `red` is in the `FlipperApplet` example). Use `drawString()` to display the string; you can use the + operator to build the string itself (i.e., `"This is paint job #"+x`).

2. Write an "almost-animation" applet in which a rectangle switches between one side of the display and the other. Try to write the code to change the rectangle's position without using a conditional statement.

Defining Classes

4.1 Introduction

I n the previous chapter's discussion, we focused mainly on the mechanics of using classes in Java: creating new objects, employing cascading and composition, and expanding the utility of reference variables. We also touched on some aspects of the issue that will be occupying us for the next several chapters: class design. The predefined classes we used in the last chapter are part of Java's core classes because they meet some common programming need. The `BigInteger` class is designed primarily for cryptography in electronic commerce. The `Date` and `Calendar` classes were designed to deal with time. Moreover, each class is responsible for different aspects of time, but the classes are designed to work with each other. The classes that make up Java's input/output (i/o) framework are designed to be flexible enough to model an extraordinarily wide variety of input and output sources.

That flexibility is a mixed blessing, though. Once we've mastered the essential layered design of the i/o framework, it's not difficult to learn how to use a different input source. Unfortunately, that same flexible design becomes an inconvenience (at best) when we actually write a program. In order to write to a file, we have to go from `File` to `FileOutputStream` to `PrintWriter`. Arranging to read a web site (`URL` to `InputStream` to `InputStreamReader` to `BufferedReader`) makes the file output setup seem simple in comparison.

Are we as programmers therefore condemned to cumbersome compositions each time we want to read a web site or write to a file? Do we have to accept the inadequate (for our purposes) behavior of existing classes because some other programmers chose to design them that way? Fortunately, no. We can define our own classes to provide the behavior that we require.

In this chapter, we focus on the mechanics of creating simple classes. In later chapters, we look at some more advanced aspects of class definition, and we study how to design a class (or classes) to solve a particular problem.

4.2 Class Definition: Methods

We start with a class that has a very narrow responsibility: to write the current date and time to a log file. Specifically, objects of this class (which we'll call `Logger`) will respond to just two messages—`log()` and `logWithTZ()`—which will cause the object to print the date and time to a file called log. The log() message will cause just the date and time to be printed; logWithTZ() will cause the name of the local time zone to be printed as well. Figure 4.1 shows this class.

Class	Logger
Methods	log(), logWithTZ()
Behavior	Writes current date/time to file
New Concept	Class and method definition

Once we have defined this class, we will be able to use it just as we've used Java's predefined classes. For example, we will be able to declare new Logger reference variables:

```
Logger x;
```

create new Logger objects:

```
x = new Logger();
```

and send these objects messages:

```
x.log();
x.logWithTZ();
```

We already know how to write the code that will print the date and time using GregorianCalendar and PrintStream objects:

```
PrintStream logps;
GregorianCalendar now;
logps = new PrintStream(new FileOutputStream("log"));
now = new GregorianCalendar();
logps.println(now.getTime());
```

Figure 4.1
The Logger class.

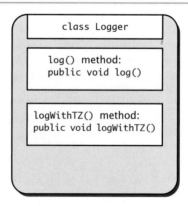

To print out the time zone in addition, we write

```
PrintStream logps;
GregorianCalendar now;
logps = new PrintStream(new FileOutputStream("log"));
now = new GregorianCalendar();
logps.print(now.getTimeZone().getDisplayName() + " ");
logps.println(now.getTime());
```

In order to specify that these code fragments should be executed when a Logger object receives a log() message or logWithTZ() message, we must incorporate these two code fragments into a class definition:

```
class Logger {
   public void log() throws Exception {
      PrintStream logps;
      GregorianCalendar now;
      logps = new PrintStream(new FileOutputStream("log"));
      now = new GregorianCalendar();
      logps.println(now.getTime());
   }
   public void logWithTZ() throws Exception {
      PrintStream logps;
      GregorianCalendar now;
      logps = new PrintStream(new FileOutputStream("log"));
      now = new GregorianCalendar();
      logps.print(now.getTimeZone().getDisplayName() + " ");
      logps.println(now.getTime());
   }
}
```

The phrase

```
class Logger {
```

indicates that this is the beginning of the definition of a class named Logger. The } on the last line signifies the end of the definition. These brackets, { and }, are called **delimiters** because they set the limits (beginning and end) of the class definition within the program text.

Between these two delimiters are the definitions of two **methods**, log() and logWithTZ(). The method definitions consist of a **prototype** such as

```
public void log() throws Exception
```

and a method body such as

```
{
    PrintStream logps;
    GregorianCalendar now;
    logps = new PrintStream(new FileOutputStream("log"));
    now = new GregorianCalendar();
    logps.println(now.getTime());
}
```

The prototype starts with the keyword **public** (this is optional, as we will see later). Following this is the **return-type**—the type of value that the method returns. The keyword **void** is used for methods, such as log(), that return no values. Following the return-type is the method's name and a pair of parentheses. Because this method uses file output, we must add the phrase throws Exception to the prototype just as we did in Chapter 3.

The method body contains the sequence of statements that is executed when the method is invoked (that is, when an instance of the class receives a message with the same signature as the method). When the closing brace } is reached, the method terminates. The sender of the message can then resume execution. (See Figure 4.2.)

Notice that the bodies of both log() and logWithTZ() contain declarations of the variables logps and now. In Java, variables declared in the body of one method cannot be used or accessed by any other methods. Variables of this kind are called **local variables**. So, even though these variables have the same names, there is no possibility of confusion: In the body of logWithTZ(), now.getTime() refers to the variable now that was declared in logWithTZ(). On the other hand, if we had written logWithTZ() as

```
public void logWithTZ() throws Exception {
    Missing local variable declarations!
    logps.print(now.getTimeZone().getDisplayName() + " ");
    logps.println(now.getTime());
}
```

the compiler would have complained that the variables logps and now are not declared. Even though logps and now were declared in log(), those declarations are completely independent from the body of logWithTZ().

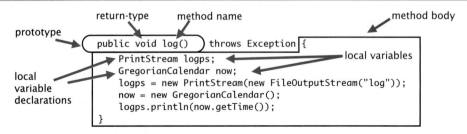

Figure 4.2   Structure of a simple method definition.

Using the Logger **Class**

All the classes we have used so far have been predefined ones provided by the Java distribution itself. Now we have our own, Logger. How do we use it?

First, we create a file, Logger.java, containing our class definition. At the beginning of the file we insert the following, because the Logger class uses Print-Stream objects:

```
import java.io.*;
```

Second, we compile the Logger.java file. If there are no errors, this produces the file Logger.class. Once we have compiled the class, we can write a simple program that creates Logger objects (Figure 4.3) and sends them log() and log-WithTZ() messages, as follows:

```
class UseLogger {
    public static void main(String arg[]) {
        Logger logger1, logger2;
        logger1 = new Logger();
        logger1.log();
        logger2 = new Logger();
        logger2.logWithTZ();
        logger2.log();
    }
}
```

Figure 4.3
Creating new Logger objects. We can create new instances of the Logger class just as we would with any other Java class.

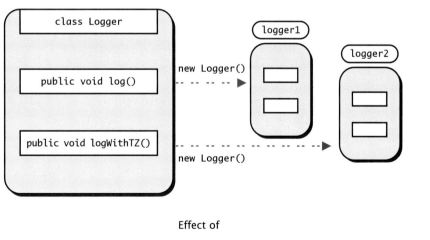

Effect of

```
logger1 = new Logger();

logger2 = new Logger();
```

Using a class we've defined ourselves is just like using any other class: We declare a reference variable that will hold a reference to an object of that class; we use `new` to create the new object; and then we may send messages to that object.

Basic Class Definition

Defining a class is a two-step process:

1. Identify the messages to which an object of the class should respond.
2. Write a method definition for each message, describing how the object should behave when it receives the message.

As we're defining the methods, we don't have to worry about declaring variables with the same name in different methods, because the compiler treats local variables completely independently of each other.

4.3 Class Definition: Instance Variables

Let's consider a class that, instead of simply recording the current time, functions as a stopwatch. This class, which we will call `Stopwatch`, will model the sort of stopwatch that provides just two behaviors: starting the watch and reporting how much time has elapsed since it was started. Each time we start the `Stopwatch`, then, we effectively reset the time elapsed to 0. To reflect these two behaviors, our class will have two methods: `start()` and `showElapsedTime()`. Thus, a Stopwatch object will be able to receive `start()` and `showElapsedTime()` messages.

Class	Stopwatch
Methods	`start()`, `showElapsedTime()`
Models	Simple stopwatch
Behavior	`showElapsedTime()` prints number of seconds since last `start()` message.
New Concept	Instance variables

We will be able to use objects of this class to time actions. For example:

```
Stopwatch sw;
sw = new Stopwatch();
sw.start();
System.out.println("How long does this println take?");
sw.showElapsedTime();
```

See Figure 4.4 for a sketch of the class.

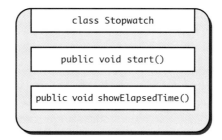

Figure 4.4
The Stopwatch class.

Before we **implement** the class by writing its method bodies, we should consider how we can take advantage of existing classes and methods. The GregorianCalendar and Date classes are obvious candidates: What methods do they provide that might help us compute elapsed time? Both of these classes deal with "absolute," or calendar-based, time, so there is no direct way to represent the "start" moment as 0. But the Date class does provide a method called getTime() that returns a long value indicating how many milliseconds have elapsed between the current moment and midnight on January 1, 1970. If a Stopwatch object saves this value when it receives a start() message, and does the same when it receives a showElapsedTime() message, the difference will be the number of milliseconds elapsed since the watch was started. We can then simply divide this value by 1,000 to determine the number of seconds elapsed.

In the previous section, we discussed the independence of local variables—variables declared in one method can't be used or accessed by other methods. At that point, independence was an asset; we could use the same names for these variables knowing that the compiler would not be confused. But now we will see that this can be an obstacle. Why? Let's see what happens when we use local variables in our method implementations.

The start() method of the Stopwatch class simply records the current time (in milliseconds) in the long variable startTime:

```
public void start() {          What's wrong with this code?
    Date now = new Date();
    long startTime = now.getTime();
}
```

The showElapsedTime() method uses another Date() object to record the time when showElapsedTime() is invoked. It then subtracts this time from the value of startTime, divides by 1,000, and outputs the result:

```
public void showElapsedTime() {    What's wrong with this code?
    Date now = new Date();
    long currTime = now.getTimeinMillis();
    long startTime;
```

```
        long difference = (currTime - startTime)/1000;
        System.out.print(difference);
        System.out.println(" seconds have elapsed.");
    }
```

What's wrong with this code? When the start() method is invoked, it assigns a value to startTime; when showElapsedTime() is called it computes the difference between currTime and startTime. However, these two startTime variables are completely independent. One is local to start(), and the other is local to show-ElapsedTime(). When showElapsedTime() finds the difference between currTime and startTime, startTime hasn't even been assigned a value. (This by itself will generate a compiler error, because Java does not allow local variables to be used before they are assigned a value.)

The difficulty here is that information from one method invocation (i.e., when the start() method was called) needs to be remembered until another method (showTimeElapsed()) is called. Information of this kind—that needs to persist across several of an object's method invocations—is known as the **state** of the object (see Figure 4.5). At this point, the only way we can store information "inside" an object is to use local variables, but a method's local variables have no meaning outside of that method. Thus, we need another way to store the information corresponding to an object's state in a way that will be remembered by the object across multiple method invocations. That is, we need a kind of variable whose value can be both set and accessed by any method of an object. Such a variable must be declared outside any method.

In the case of the Stopwatch class, the start() method is responsible for setting the value of startTime, and showElapsedTime() needs access to that value in order to compute the elapsed time. We need to store that value in a variable that can be accessed by *all* the methods in the class. Such a variable is called an **instance variable** because it belongs to the entire object (instance) and not to

Figure 4.5
The Stopwatch class needs to maintain information corresponding to its state.

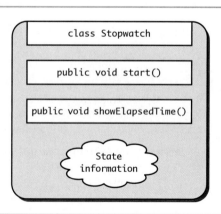

any one particular method. Declarations of instance variables, therefore, must occur inside the class definition but *outside* any of the methods. These declarations have the same form as the declarations we have encountered so far, except that we will start the declaration with the keyword **private**. Although these declarations may appear anywhere in the class definition (at the beginning, at the end, or even in between method definitions), one standard practice is to declare them at the end. (See Figure 4.6.)

Now we can write the start() and showElapsedTime() methods properly. Both of these methods will use a variable called startTime, but neither method will declare this variable. Instead, it will be declared at the end of the class as an instance variable:

```
class Stopwatch {
    public void start() {
        GregorianCalendar now = new GregorianCalendar();    Not declared
        startTime = now.getTimeInMillis();                   in this
    }                                                        method...
    public void showElapsedTime() {
        GregorianCalendar now = new GregorianCalendar();
        long currTime = now.getTimeInMillis();
        long difference = (currTime - startTime)/1000;      ...nor in this
        System.out.print(difference);                        method...
        System.out.println(" seconds have elapsed.");
    }
    private long startTime;          ...but here, outside
}                                    all methods.
```

Of course, both start() and showElapsedTime() still use local variables to hold values and references that are used only inside their respective method bodies. Most methods we write will use both instance and local variables to perform their tasks. Although we could have declared every variable in the class (now, currTime, difference) as instance variables instead of local variables, we will declare as instance variables only those that must be—that is, those whose values are used by more than one method within the class.

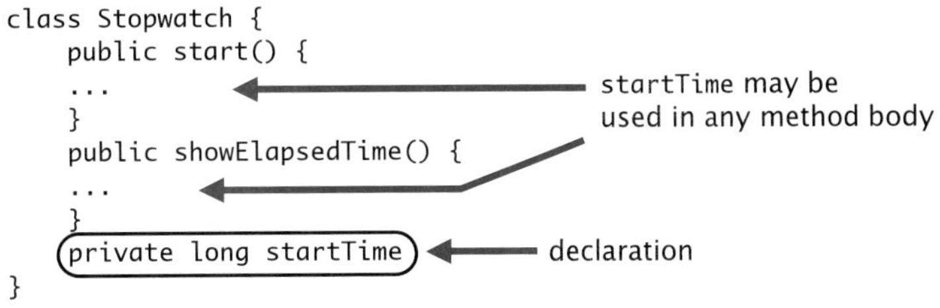

Figure 4.6

Accessing an instance variable.

```
class Stopwatch {
    public start() {
        ...                          ◄──────────    startTime may be
    }                                                used in any method body
    public showElapsedTime() {
        ...              ◄──────────
    }
    (private long startTime)  ◄────── declaration
}
```

Using the StopWatch Class

Once we have defined the StopWatch class, we can use it to time events in programs that we write. For example, suppose a long-distance runner wanted a program to help her train. The program would ask her to hit ENTER when she starts her run, then hit ENTER when she returns, and it would output the number of seconds she took.

This program will interact with a StopWatch object three times: first to create the object, again when the run begins (which we'll mark by sending a start() message to the StopWatch), and finally when the run ends (which we'll indicate by sending a showElapsedTime() message to the StopWatch). Our code, then, will begin like this:

```
class LonelyLongDistanceRunner {
    public static void main(String args[]) throws Exception {
        BufferedReader keyboard = new BufferedReader(
            new InputStreamReader(System.in));
        Stopwatch timer = new Stopwatch();
        System.out.println("Hit Enter on your way out!");
        keyboard.readLine();
```

At this point timer refers to a newly created StopWatch object, but its startTime instance variable has no meaningful value. This variable won't be given a value until timer receives a start() message later.

Once the readLine() message is sent to keyboard, keyboard waits patiently for a line of text, which by definition will arrive when the user hits ENTER. Because we don't care about what the user types before she hits ENTER (probably she won't type anything at all) we won't store a reference to the String returned by read-Line(). Once readLine() returns, we need to start the StopWatch and then wait for another ENTER:

```
        timer.start();
        System.out.println("Don't forget to hit Enter
                            when you get back!");
        keyboard.readLine();
```

Now timer's startTime variable holds the time when the run began, and keyboard is waiting for our runner to return. As soon as she hits ENTER, we'll send a showElapsedTime() message to the object referred to by sw, causing it to calculate the elapsed time and print it to the screen:

```
        timer.showElapsedTime();
        System.out.println("Go take a shower.");
    }
}
```

Using Instance Variables

As we design a class and its methods, we may determine that objects of the class will need to maintain state. That is, information used or created during the execution of one method may need to be available to methods that execute later. State information must be saved using instance variables, thereby making it available to all methods of the class (see Figure 4.7).

4.4 More on Methods: Return Values

Next, let's define a class that will help us count events instead of measure time. Such a class models a device sometimes found in the hands of theater ushers—a button on top, when clicked, causes the count to be increased by one, and the face of the device displays the current value of the counter. Another button causes the value of the counter to be reset to zero. This class, called Counter, will have three methods: one, which we will call increment(), to advance the value of the counter; one, which we will call getValue(), to report the current value of the counter; and one, called reset(), to set the value back to zero.

Class	Counter
Methods	increment(), getValue(), reset()
Models	Simple counter
Behavior	getValue() returns number of increment() messages since the last reset().
New Concept	Return values

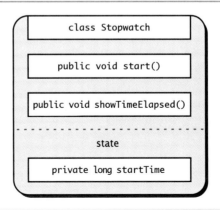

Figure 4.7
Using instance variables to store state information. The state of the Stopwatch class is maintained in the startTime instance variable.

The getValue() method will be used just as we have used other methods that return int values. For example, we might use the length() method of the String class in this way:

```
String s = "junk";
int l = s.length();
```

We will use getValue() similarly:

```
Counter c = new Counter();
int v = c.getValue();
```

Each of the class's methods, increment(), getValue(), and reset(), works with the value of the Counter itself. That is, each Counter object must maintain a value as part of its state: The value that increment() increments is the same value that getValue() reports. So, like the Stopwatch class, Counter will use an instance variable. Because this variable will store the current value of the counter, we'll call it count. Because a new Counter object hasn't had the opportunity to count anything yet, when the object is created its count value should be initialized to 0. Like other variables, instance variables can be initialized when they are declared, so we will declare count as

```
private int count = 0;
```

See Figure 4.8 for a sketch of the Counter class.

Unlike the Stopwatch class, the Counter class should not report its value by printing it to output. Instead, its value should be available to the program so that it can be used, for example, to see if some maximum capacity has been exceeded

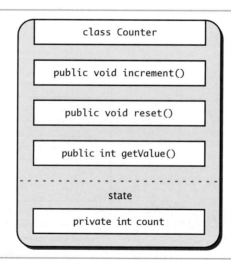

Figure 4.8
The Counter class.

or to estimate expected revenues. In earlier chapters, we have used many methods that made their results available to the program by *returning* values (either references or primitive type values). For example, the String.length() method returns an int value that reports the number of characters in a String. This value can then be used in further calculations and String operations. We need to use this mechanism in our getValue() method:

```
public int getValue() {
    return count;
}
```

Here, we specify the return-type as int (instead of void). In addition, we use the keyword **return** to specify the value that the method should return to its caller. In this case, the method performs no calculation but simply returns the value of the instance variable count.

The remaining methods are equally brief: reset() sets the value of count to 0 and increment() adds one to the current value of count:

```
public void reset() {
    count = 0;
}
public void increment() {
    count ++;
}
```

Here is the entire class definition:

```
class Counter {
    public void reset() {
        count = 0;
    }
    public void increment() {
        count ++;
    }
    public int getValue() {
        return count;
    }
    private int count = 0;
}
```

Using the Counter **Class**

We can use more than one instance of the Counter class to keep track of several different kinds of occurrences as our program runs. As a simple example, we'll write a program that asks three people whether they prefer purple or yellow, then outputs the color that earned the majority of preferences. The users will

enter their preferences as Strings (for simplicity we'll assume that anything that isn't "purple" means "yellow"), and we'll track the total responses using Counter references named purpleCounter and yellowCounter:

```
class PurpleVsYellow {
    public static void main(String args[]) throws Exception{
        BufferedReader keyboard = new BufferedReader(
            new InputStreamReader(System.in));
        Counter purpleCounter = new Counter();
        Counter yellowCounter = new Counter();
```

When the objects referred to by purpleCounter and yellowCounter are created, both of their count members are assigned the value 0.

```
        System.out.print("Person #1, do you prefer purple or yellow? ");
        String response = keyboard.readLine();
        if (response.equals("purple"))
            purpleCounter.increment();
        else
            yellowCounter.increment();
```

At this point, one person's preference has been processed, so one of the Counter objects' count value has increased to 1.

```
        System.out.print("Person #2, do you prefer purple or yellow? ");
        String response = keyboard.readLine();
        if (response.equals("purple"))
            purpleCounter.increment();
        else
            yellowCounter.increment();
        System.out.print("Person #3, do you prefer purple or yellow? ");
        String response = keyboard.readLine();
        if (response.equals("purple"))
            purpleCounter.increment();
        else
            yellowCounter.increment();
```

Now all preferences have been processed. We don't know precisely what state each of the Counters is in (that depends on the nature of the responses), but to output the "winner," we will send getValue() messages to each Counter so that we can compare their count values:

```
        if (purpleCounter.getValue() > yellowCounter.getValue())
            System.out.println("Purple wins.");
        else
            System.out.println("Yellow wins.");
    }
}
```

Return Values versus Output: Stopwatch **Revisited**

The Stopwatch class provides information about elapsed time by printing it directly to System.out. That is, the showElapsedTime() method interacts directly with the user and does not communicate with the part of the program that invoked showElapsedTime(). Return values and output (whether via System.out or some other output-generating object) are both techniques by which a method can provide information to its environment. Return values allow a method to report only one piece of information; furthermore, this value is reported only when the method terminates. But values reported this way can influence the further execution of the program. For example, they can be used in the condition of an if statement such as

```
if (myString.length() > 0)
    . . .
```

Reporting results to output allows us much more flexibility—we can output as many values as we like, and we can do so in the middle of a method (for example, if we need to prompt the user for further information). However, values sent to output can't be used by the program to decide what to do next. In our long distance runner example above, we might have wanted to print a message appropriate to her time—"That's a personal best!" or "You've done better than that," or "Someone forgot to eat her fortified wheat flake cereal this morning." Because those results were printed directly to the screen, however, there was nothing for us to do after calling showElapsedTime().

We can easily modify our Stopwatch class, though, to use return values instead of output. All we need to do is add another method similar to showElapsedTime() that returns the elapsed time instead of printing it out. Because this value will be used by some other part of our program, we don't have to worry about making it readable; instead, we should try to make it as usable as possible. So this value we will return as a number of milliseconds:

```
public long getElapsedTime() {
    GregorianCalendar now = new GregorianCalendar();
    long currTime = now.getTimeInMillis();
    return (currTime - startTime);
}
```

This requires two modifications to showElapsedTime(): replacing the output statements with a return statement, and changing the return-type from void to long.

Using Return Values

If we want to make the result of a method available for use by the code that invoked the method, we should report that result by returning it. We must both specify the return-type in the method's prototype and use the keyword return to indicate what value to return to the method invoker.

4.5 Imperative Programming: Finding the Minimum

Let's consider another use our long distance runner might make of the Stopwatch class. This time, she's going to run three laps and use the Stopwatch to find her best (lowest) time. As she completes each lap, she'll hit ENTER, which will record her lap time and restart the Stopwatch for the next lap.

Finding the smallest value in a sequence is a common programming task. As with any programming task, there are several ways this can be done, but we will focus here on one of the simplest. We will use a single variable (call it bestSoFar) to keep track of the runner's best time so far. For every new value we consider, we just check to see whether it's better than the best so far. If it isn't better, we can ignore it. If it is better, we assign its value to bestSoFar. This way, as we go through the sequence of values, bestSoFar will never get worse, and each time we see a better value, bestSoFar will improve. At the end of the sequence, best-SoFar will hold the best value in the entire sequence.

The Java code for considering one value of the sequence is just an if statement. In our example, we are considering a sequence of long values (corresponding to lap times), and the "best" value is the smallest one. If the variable lapTime contains the next value for us to consider in the sequence, then the code for considering it would be

```
if (lapTime < bestSoFar)  // if lapTime is the lowest time so far
    bestSoFar = lapTime;   // then it becomes the value of bestSoFar
                           // (otherwise, don't change anything)
```

What should happen when we consider the first value in the sequence? At that point it is the only value we have considered so far, so it is certainly the best so far. So we need to make sure that bestSoFar gets assigned the first value, no matter what that first value is. This means we must be careful about the initial value of bestSoFar. If it is initialized to 0, for instance, the new lapTime value will never be less (i.e., better) than bestSoFar, and we will never change the value of bestSoFar. In the end, we will be claiming that the runner's best time was 0—another sports scandal in the making!

To avoid this, we should initialize bestSoFar to the *worst* possible value. That way the first value, no matter how bad it might be, will still be better than best-SoFar. Because we're trying to find small values, the worst value possible is the largest possible long, which is 9223372036854775807L.

We have captured the essence of our approach: In order to find a minimum value, we'll use a variable to store the smallest value we've seen so far. We'll initialize it to the *maximum* possible value, and for every value we consider, if it's smaller than the smallest so far, we update the value of the smallest so far.

Now we can begin writing our lap-timing program.

```
class LonelyLapRunner {
   public static void main(String args[]) throws Exception{
      BufferedReader keyboard = new BufferedReader(
         new InputStreamReader(System.in));
      Stopwatch sw = new Stopwatch();
      long bestSoFar = 9223372036854775807L;
      System.out.print("Hit Enter to start!");
      keyboard.readLine();
```

The first time our runner hits ENTER, she's just starting her first lap, so all we have to do is start the Stopwatch and wait for another ENTER.

```
      sw.start();
      System.out.print("First lap in progress...");
      keyboard.readLine();
```

At the end of the first lap, we need to find out the lap time, restart the Stopwatch for the next lap, and check to see whether we need to update the minimum lap time:

```
      long lapTime = sw.getElapsedTime();
      sw.start();
      if (lapTime < bestSoFar)
         bestSoFar = lapTime;
      System.out.print("Second lap in progress...");
      keyboard.readLine();
```

At the end of the second lap, we simply repeat the process:

```
      long lapTime = sw.getElapsedTime();
      sw.start();
      if (lapTime < bestSoFar)
         bestSoFar = lapTime;
      System.out.print("Third lap in progress...");
      keyboard.readLine();
```

At the end of third and final lap, we again find the lap time and update bestSo-Far, if necessary. Then we can output the best time, which is simply the value stored in bestSoFar:

```
      long lapTime = sw.getElapsedTime();
      if (lapTime < bestSoFar)
         bestSoFar = lapTime;
      System.out.print("Your best time is ");
      System.out.println(bestSoFar/1000);
   }
}
```

Variables, Declarations, and the return *Statement*

Declaration Order

As we have seen, a class in Java is defined by declaring a set of variables and methods. Objects, that is, particular instances of a class, are characterized by this set.

The particular order of the variable and method declarations within the braces ({...}) of the class is irrelevant. Any order is legal. However, we will adopt the convention of always placing method declarations at the beginning of the class, followed by variable declarations.

The return Statement

The sender of the message cannot proceed until the method invoked by the message *returns*. This is accomplished either by executing the Java return statement, or, if the method's return-type is void, by reaching the closing brace of the method.

A void method may alternatively have an explicit return statement—with no return-value—as follows:

```
public void writeTwice(String s) {
    System.out.print(s);
    System.out.println(s);
    return;
}
```

In the case of void methods, the return serves merely to stop the execution of the method and allows its invoker to proceed. For methods that return values (such as value() in the Counter class), the return statement does more—it specifies the value that is returned. Because of this additional role, in a method that returns a value, the return statement is mandatory; it does not suffice to reach the closing brace.

Methods can return only one value for a given invocation. For example, it's impossible to write a method that returns two Strings, say "Flower" and "Power". One could concatenate the Strings in some way (making "Flower-Power" or "PowerFlower") and return the result, but then we are back to returning a single value.

Variables and Their Lifetimes

In the previous class definitions, we encountered variables declared in the following different contexts:

- As *local variables* (declared somewhere within the braces of a method body)
- As *instance variables* (declared within the braces of a class definition but not within any method)

Local variables are variables that are automatically created when the method is invoked, and they disappear when the method terminates. Their *lifetime* is the same as that of the method invocation. Furthermore, local variables are not *visible* outside the method in which they are defined. Given a method with a local variable s, no other method can refer to that particular s. If three methods each have a local variable s, in essence, there are three different variables s. Consider the following:

```
public String getGenre() {
    String  s = "classic rock";
    return s;
}
String getFormat() {
    String  s;
    s = "no commercials";
    return s;
}
```

The assignments to s in getFormat() will not affect the local reference variable s in getGenre(). Even if we remove the declaration of String s in getFormat(), the reference variable s in getGenre() cannot be modified by getFormat()—it will continue to refer to the same object—and the compiler will complain that s is undeclared in getFormat().

Instance variables have the same lifetime as the object to which they belong. An instance variable is created when its object is created, and it vanishes when that object vanishes. Instance variables can be accessed by any method in the class. If an instance variable is declared with an initialization, each new instance of the class will be created with the instance variable appropriately initialized. Unlike local variables, instance variables do not have to be initialized before they are used (Java gives these variables values automatically if the programmer doesn't). If we do choose to initialize them, though, we can initialize them when they are declared, just like any other variable. For example, if we had written

```
private long startTime = 37L;
```

in the Stopwatch class, then every new Stopwatch object would be created with startTime initialized to 37.

4.6 Still More on Methods: Parameters

Now, let's use Java's object-oriented capability to design a class that encapsulates the minimum-finding algorithm we developed in Section 4.5. We will then be able to use instances of this class anytime we need to find the minimum of a sequence. Our Minimizer class won't model anything from the physical world;

instead it will model the abstract idea of "a minimizer." Indeed, in order to decide what methods this class needs, we need to focus only on how it should behave, without worrying about the algorithm it will use. This behavior is very simple: First, we should be able to ask `Minimizer` objects to `check()` the next value in the sequence, and second, we should be able to `get()` the value of the minimum so far. Additionally, a `reset()` method similar to that of the `Counter` class will make the `Minimizer` more usable.

Class	`Minimizer`
Methods	`check()`, `get()`, `reset()`
Models	General-purpose minimum finder
Behavior	`get()` returns the smallest value passed to `check()` since the last `reset()`.
New Concept	Parameter

Before we turn to implementing this class, let's briefly consider how it will be used. For example, let's begin to rewrite the `LonelyLapRunner` program using a `Minimizer` object. The original `LonelyLapRunner` program used the variable `bestSoFar` to keep track of the runner's best time. In the new version we'll use a `Minimizer` object. So we'll replace

```
long bestSoFar;
```

with

```
Minimizer minTime = new Minimizer();
```

In the original version, when the `StopWatch` gave us a new `lapTime` value

```
long lapTime = sw.getElapsedTime();
```

we compared it with `bestSoFar` to determine the minimum time:

```
if (lapTime < bestSoFar)
   bestSoFar = lapTime;
```

This `if` statement does the work that will now be taken over by the `Minimizer` object—specifically, by its `check()` method. When we send a `check()` message, we need to provide the value to be checked (in this case, `lapTime`). Thus, `check()` messages must include one argument. The `if` statement above, then, will be replaced by the message

```
    minTime.check(lapTime);
```

We are including the value of `lapTime` in the `check()` message sent to the Minimizer. This value must be accessible in the body of the method; in Java we accomplish this by writing a variable declaration in the prototype of `check()`:

```
public void check(long nextValue) {
```
nextValue holds the value of the argument;
we can use it anywhere in this method body.
```
}
```

Variables like nextValue that are declared in the method's prototype are called **parameters**. When the method is invoked, the parameters are initialized with the values of the **arguments** provided in the invoking message (see Figure 4.9). Thus, when this check() message is sent from the body of LonelyLapRunner, nextValue is initialized to the value of lapTime. See Figure 4.10 for a sketch of the Minimizer class.

Figure 4.9
Invoking a method with parameters.

Figure 4.10
The Minimizer class.

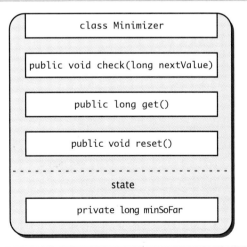

The remaining methods, get() and reset(), require no parameters: get() returns the current value of the best time so far (a long value), and reset() returns the Minimizer to its original state. Because all three methods need access to the value of the best time so far, this must be maintained as the object's state; thus we must also declare an instance variable minSoFar. As we discussed in the context of LonelyLapRunner, minSoFar should be initialized to the largest possible value. So far, then, we have a skeleton of the Minimizer class (without method bodies) like this:

```
class Minimizer {
    public void check(long nextValue) {
    }
    public long get() {
    }
    public void reset() {
    }
    private long minSoFar = 9223372036854775807L;
}
```

The method bodies are short. The reset() method just sets the value of minSo-Far back to 9223372036854775807L, and the get() method returns the current value of minSoFar. Finally, the check() method compares the value it receives as the nextValue parameter with the current value of minSoFar and updates minSo-Far if necessary. Thus, the complete class definition is

```
class Minimizer {
    public void check(long nextValue) {
        if (nextValue < minSoFar)
            minSoFar = nextValue;
    }
    public long get() {
        return minSoFar;
    }
    public void reset() {
        minSoFar = 9223372036854775807L;
    }
    private long minSoFar = 9223372036854775807L;
}
```

Using the Minimizer Class

Let's finish our rewrite of LonelyLapRunner using a Minimizer object. As we discussed, instead of using a bestSoFar variable directly in our program, we'll let the Minimizer keep track of the best for us. Below is the rewritten program with all the Minimizer-related changes in **bold**:

```
class LonelyLapRunnerWithMinimizer {
    public static void main(String args[]) throws Exception{
        BufferedReader keyboard = new BufferedReader(
            new InputStreamReader(System.in));
        Stopwatch sw = new Stopwatch();
        Minimizer minTime = new Minimizer();
        System.out.print("Hit Enter to start!");
        keyboard.readLine();
        sw.start();
        System.out.print("First lap in progress...");
        keyboard.readLine();
        long lapTime = sw.getElapsedTime();
        sw.start();
        minTime.check(lapTime);
        System.out.print("Second lap in progress...");
        keyboard.readLine();
        long lapTime = sw.getElapsedTime();
        sw.start();
        minTime.check(lapTime);
        System.out.print("Third lap in progress...");
        keyboard.readLine();
        long lapTime = sw.getElapsedTime();
        minTime.check(lapTime);
        long bestTime = minTime.get();
        System.out.print("Your best time is ");
        System.out.println(bestTime/1000);
    }
}
```

Each of the `if` statements in the original version has been replaced by `check()` messages, and at the end of the program we must `get()` the final minimum value from the `Minimizer`.

Using Parameters

We declare parameters in method definitions precisely when the messages that invoke that method will include at least one argument. Each parameter declaration corresponds to an expected argument and vice versa, and the parameter values are initialized to the argument values when the method is invoked. Apart from the manner of their declaration and initialization, parameters work and can be used exactly like any other local variable.

4.7 State and Behavior

We saw in the case of `Counter` that it is possible for a program using this class to have multiple instances of `Counter`, used to count different things. Each such instance shares the same methods but possesses its own instance variable; that is, each instance maintains its own state.

Objects belonging to the same class therefore share the same **behavior**; that is, the same methods can be invoked on these objects. Yet at the end of our Purple-VsYellow program, when the two Counter objects each received a value() message, they returned different values. This is because each object of class Counter contains its own copy of the count instance variable, and these may contain different values—maybe purpleCounter's count variable would be 3 and yellow-Counter's count would be 0. That is, although purpleCounter and yellowCounter *behave* identically when they receive a count() message, the results are different because their *states* are different.

So, two objects of the same class have the same behavior but usually have different state.

4.8 Class Definition: Putting It All Together

Let's bring these ideas together in the context of slightly more complicated class, TypingTutor. The heart of the class will be a test() method that prints a practice string (such as, "The quick brown fox jumps over the lazy dog") and asks the user to "echo" it back. It will time the user while he types in the string, and when he's done it will either tell him that he didn't type the string perfectly or it will report how many seconds he took. In order to make the class useful, we'll assume that the test() method can be called several times in a row. We'll want to be able to report meaningful information, such as the lowest time on any of the tests and the total number of perfect responses. For additional flexibility, we'll allow the practice string to be changed, at which point the accumulated statistics will be reset.

Before we proceed, let's decide that all the "reporting" to be done by this class will be done by returning values from various methods—no reports will be printed on the screen by the class. We will leave it up to the programmer using the TypingTutor class to decide whether and when this information should be output.

Identifying Methods

What methods should our class have? We established right from the start that it will have a test() method; what should its prototype be? Its role is to report either a time or imperfect typing. From our implementation of the Stopwatch class we know that it's easy to report a time as a long value representing milliseconds, which suggests that test() should return a long. But how will we report the presence of a typing mistake? We can return a value that can't possibly be interpreted as a valid time—that is, a negative value. test() also needs to know what practice string to test with. At this point this could be provided either as a parameter to the method or as an instance variable for the class; we'll postpone our decision on that until we have more of the class sketched out. So far, we've decided that `test()` will have one of these prototypes:

```
public long test()
```

or

```
public long test(String)
```

The class should also report on the lowest time turned in for any attempt using the current practice string. Therefore, we need a method `getLowestTime()` that will return a `long` (number of milliseconds) value. Similarly, we will need a `get-NumPerfect()` method that will return the number of perfect tests using the current string. This can be returned as an `int`. Neither of these methods will get arguments—they will have to get their information from the state (instance variables) of the object. So their prototypes will be

```
public long getLowestTime()
public int getNumPerfect()
```

Finally, we need a method that will change the practice string. This method doesn't need to return any values, but it does need a reference to the new practice string, so its prototype will be

```
public void setPracticeString(String newString)
```

Let's sketch our class definition so far (see Figure 4.11):

Figure 4.11
The `TypingTutor` class.

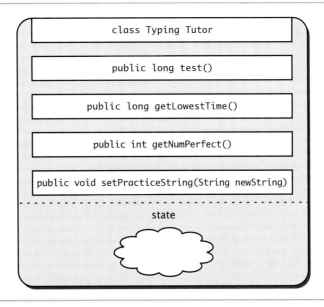

```
class TypingTutor {
   public long test()   OR   public long test(String) {
   }
   public long getLowestTime() {
   }
   public int getNumPerfect() {
   }
   public void setPracticeString(String newString) {
   }
   instance variables to be determined
}
```

Determining the State

If we consider the data used by these methods, we can see that TypingTutor objects must maintain a state that is more complicated than our earlier examples. Both test() and setPracticeString() need access to the practice string, so we will need an instance variable for it. Moreover, this variable should be initialized to some meaningful string, so it will be declared as

```
private String practiceString =
                  "The quick brown fox jumps over the lazy dog";
```

The getLowestTime() and getNumPerfect() methods need access to the lowest time and number of correct tests, respectively, each of which must be determined by the test() method. Therefore these values will also have to be maintained in the object's state. Furthermore, we can note that these two behaviors (tracking the lowest time and counting perfect responses) are precisely what the Minimizer and Counter classes were designed to do. So these instance variables will be instances of these classes:

```
private Minimizer lowestTime = new Minimizer();
private Counter perfectCount = new Counter();
```

Now we can make a more detailed sketch of our class:

```
class TypingTutor {
   public long test() {   Using instance variable instead of parameter
   }
   public long getLowestTime() {
   }
   public int getNumPerfect() {
   }
   public void setPracticeString(String newString) {
   }
   private String practiceString =
                  "The quick brown fox jumps over the lazy dog";
   private Minimizer lowestTime = new Minimizer();
```

```
        private Counter perfectCount = new Counter();
}
```

Implementing `test()`

Because the `test()` method is the key to this class, we'll begin with its implementation. Recall that this method will first print the practice string, then ask the user to type in the string. The method will then determine whether the string was typed correctly and, if so, determine how long the user took to type it. As we established above, `test()` will return a `long`; because it will be taking input from the keyboard, we will need to add `throws Exception` to its prototype. Therefore we know that the prototype of `test()` is

```
public long test() throws Exception
```

In order to be fair to users, we'll let them decide when to start the clock, so after we output the practice string, we'll ask them to hit ENTER to begin. We'll also create the `Stopwatch` object that we'll use to time the user's typing:

```
BufferedReader keyboard = new BufferedReader(
  new InputStreamReader(System.in));
System.out.println("String to type: " + practiceString);
System.out.println("Hit Enter to begin... ");
StopWatch sw = new Stopwatch();
String inputString = keyboard.readLine();        Detect ENTER.
System.out.println("\nType!\n");           One last prompt
```

Before the user starts typing, we need to start the `Stopwatch`. Then we'll read the user's input and get the elapsed time.

```
sw.start()
inputString = keyboard.readLine();
long typeTime = sw.getElapsedTime();
```

Once we have the string entered by the user, we need to determine whether it was typed correctly. That is, we need to compare it to the value of `practiceString` using the `String.equals()` method:

```
if (practiceString.equals(inputString))
```

If the string was entered correctly, then we have to do a few things. First, we have to submit the typing time to the `Minimizer` so it can keep track of the user's best performance so far and increment the `Counter` to keep track of the number of perfectly typed responses. Then we return the typing time.

```
{
    lowestTime.check(typeTime);
    perfectCount.increment();
    return typeTime;
}
```

If the string was not typed correctly, we simply need to return a value indicating that a mistake was made. Because no typing time can be less than 0, we'll use a return value of –1 to indicate the mistake:

```
else
    return -1;
```

The complete `test()` method, then, is

```
public long test() throws Exception {
    BufferedReader keyboard = new BufferedReader(
        new InputStreamReader(System.in));
    System.out.println("String to type: " + practiceString);
    System.out.println("Hit Enter to begin... ");
    StopWatch sw = new Stopwatch();
    String inputString = keyboard.readLine();
    System.out.println("\nType!\n");
    sw.start()
    inputString = keyboard.readLine();
    long typeTime = sw.getElapsedTime();
    if (practiceString.equals(inputString)) {
        lowestTime.check(typeTime);
        perfectCount.increment();
        return typeTime;
    } else
        return -1;
}
```

Implementing the Other Methods

The implementations for `getLowestTime()` and `getNumPerfect()` are short: They return a single value. In order to return the lowest typing time, we send a `getValue()` message to the object referred to by `lowestTime`; the value returned by `getValue()` is the value that `getLowestTime()` itself returns. Similarly, `perfectCount.getValue()` gives us the number of perfect responses, which `getNumPerfect()` then returns:

```
public long getLowestTime() {
    return lowestTime.getValue();
}
public int getNumPerfect() {
    return perfectCount.getValue();
}
```

`setPracticeString()` is a little more complex because in addition to changing the value of `practiceString`, it must also reset the values of `lowestTime` and `perfectCount`.

```
public void setPracticeString(String newString) {
   practiceString = newString;
   perfectCount.reset();
   lowestTime.reset();
}
```

The complete class definition, then, looks like this:

```
public class TypingTutor {
   public long test() throws Exception {
      BufferedReader keyboard = new BufferedReader(
         new InputStreamReader(System.in));
      System.out.println("String to type: " + practiceString);
      System.out.println("Hit Enter to begin... ");
      StopWatch sw = new Stopwatch();
      String inputString = keyboard.readLine();
      System.out.println("\nType!\n");
      sw.start();
      inputString = keyboard.readLine();
      long typeTime = sw.getElapsedTime();
      if (practiceString.equals(inputString)) {
         lowestTime.check(typeTime);
         perfectCount.increment();
         return typeTime;
      } else
         return -1;
   }
   public long getLowestTime() {
      return lowestTime.getValue();
   }
   public int getNumPerfect() {
      return perfectCount.getValue();
   }
   public void setPracticeString(String newString) {
      practiceString = newString;
      lowestTime.reset();
      perfectCount.reset();
   }
   private String practiceString =
                       "The quick brown fox jumps over the lazy dog";
   private Minimizer lowestTime = new Minimizer();
   private Counter perfectCount = new Counter();
}
```

Using the TypingTutor **Class**

We can use the TypingTutor class to provide most of the functionality of a simple typing program. Our program will ask the user to type each of two strings three times apiece and report the best time typed for each one. The first string will be the default string associated with the TypingTutor class, so our program will begin as follows:

```java
import java.io.*;

class Test {
   public static void main(String[] arg) throws Exception {
      TypingTutor tutor = new TypingTutor();
```

Because our program invokes a method (TypingTutor.test()) that throws Exception, we must also declare that our program throws Exception. Then we begin by declaring a TypingTutor reference variable tutor and creating a new TypingTutor object to which tutor will refer. Because the instance variables of TypingTutor were declared with initializers, tutor's instance variables are in the correct initial state and we can begin using the object.

We'll test the user three times, and after each test we'll report back to the user what the time on the test was or, that he or she made an error:

```java
      long result = tutor.test();  // First test
      if (result > 0) {
         System.out.print("Your time was ");
         System.out.println(result/1000 + " seconds.");
      } else
         System.out.println("You did not type correctly.");
      System.out.println();

      result = tutor.test();        // Second test
      if (result > 0) {
         System.out.print("Your time was ");
         System.out.println(result/1000 + " seconds.");
      } else
         System.out.println("You did not type correctly.");
      System.out.println();

      result = tutor.test();        // Third test
      if (result > 0) {
         System.out.print("Your time was ");
         System.out.println(result/1000 + " seconds.");
      } else
         System.out.println("You did not type correctly.");
```

Each test() message causes the Minimizer's instance variables lowestTime and perfectCount to be updated (if appropriate), so at the end of this battery of tests, the objects referenced by these variables hold the number of perfect tests and the user's best time out of all three. Now we can report the user's best time—unless he or she never typed correctly, in which case we'll report that instead. The first thing to check, then, is the number of perfectly typed tests. If it's not 0 we'll report the best time; otherwise we'll report on the failed tests:

```java
int perfCount = tutor.getNumPerfect();
if (perfCount > 0) {
    long lowestTime = tutor.getLowestTime();
    System.out.print("Your best time was ");
    System.out.println(lowestTime/1000 + " seconds.");
} else
    System.out.println("You failed all 3 tests!");
```

To change the practice string for the next battery of tests, we send a setPractice-String() message to tutor:

```java
tutor.setPracticeString("Exotic zebras jaywalk with impunity.");
```

Now the value of the practice string has been changed. In addition, the instance variables lowestTime and perfectCount have been reset, and we are ready to test the user on the new string, using exactly the same code:

```java
long result = tutor.test();   First test
if (result > 0) {
    System.out.print("Your time was ");
    System.out.println(result/1000 + " seconds.");
}
else
    System.out.println("You did not type correctly.");
System.out.println();

result = tutor.test();      Second test
if (result > 0) {
    System.out.print("Your time was ");
    System.out.println(result/1000 + " seconds.");
}
else
    System.out.println("You did not type correctly.");
System.out.println();

result = tutor.test();      Third test
if (result > 0) {
    System.out.print("Your time was ");
```

```
            System.out.println(result/1000 + " seconds.");
        }
        else
            System.out.println("You did not type correctly.");
    }
}
```

Method Patterns: get and set

In the TypingTutor class, three methods are closely tied to the class's instance variables: setPracticeString(), getNumPerfect(), and getLowestTime() are primarily responsible for changing the value of practiceString and returning the values of perfectCount and lowestTime, respectively. Methods such as these are called **accessor methods** because their main function is to access instance variables. Such methods are common in a wide variety of classes, so a naming idiom has developed: The names of methods that change the value of an instance variable typically begin with set, and names of methods that return the value of an instance variable typically begin with get. As in the TypingTutor class, not every instance variable will give rise to a pair of get/set methods—that will depend on the required behavior of the class. Similarly, the behavior of these methods may exceed what is suggested by their names, just as setPracticeString() actually changes the value of *all* the instance variables.

Java Interlude

Declarations, Access, and Objects

Parameters

Like all local variables, parameters are automatically created when the method is invoked, and they disappear when the method terminates. Their *lifetime* is the same as that of the method invocation. Unlike other local variables, which must be initialized in the method body, parameters get their initial values from the arguments that were part of the message that invoked the method. The arguments must correspond in number and, on a one-to-one basis, match the parameter types.

Given a method with prototype

```
void f(String s, PrintStream p)
```

here are some valid and invalid messages:

```
f("hello", System.out)  ◄──────── Valid: Arguments match parameters in number and type.
f("hello")  ◄──────── Invalid: Too few arguments.
f("hello", "goodbye")  ◄──────── Invalid: First argument/parameter type mismatch.
f("hello", System.out, "bye")  ◄──────── Invalid: Too many arguments.
```

Like all local variables, parameters are not visible outside the method in which they are defined. Because of this common characteristic, we often consider parameters to be a special kind of local variable. The primary distinction is that parameters are initialized automatically via the arguments of the invoking message, while local variables must be initialized in the body of the method.

Access Control: `public` versus `private`

A class definition contains method definitions and instance variable declarations. **Access** to a method or variable is the ability to use it. Code inside the class can access all methods and instance variables declared in the class. By using the keywords **public** or **private**, we allow or prevent code outside the class from accessing these methods and variables. When we use the keyword `public`, we make the method or variable accessible to all code outside the class. When we use the keyword `private`, we prevent the method or variable from being accessed outside of the class. This is called **access control**.

How do we decide whether to use `public` or `private`? In this text we will use the following simple but very effective rule:

> If we must make it accessible outside the class, we make it `public`; otherwise, we make it `private`.

The methods that we want to be used in messages from (that is, accessible by) code outside the class should be `public`. Later, we will see that some methods do not need to be accessible from outside the class—they will just help us implement some of the `public` methods. We will be able to declare these "helper" methods as `private`. Likewise, instance variables are present only for the sake of implementing the methods, so these we make `private` as well.

Because local variables and parameters are not visible outside the methods in which they're declared, they are not accessible outside these methods either. That is why the keywords `public` and `private` don't apply to them.

Objects Access Their Own Methods

All methods and variables declared in a class, whether they are declared `public` or `private`, are accessible by the methods of the class. So, a `private` method can be invoked *only* by another method of the class, and a `public` method can be invoked either from outside the class or by other methods of the class.

For example, we might have chosen to implement a `reset()` method of the `TypingTutor` class that cleared the values of the `Counter` and `Minimizer` but didn't change the practice string:

```
public void reset() {
    lowestTime.reset();
    perfectCount.reset();
}
```

We could then have used this method in our implementation of the `setPracticeString()` method:

```
public void setPracticeString(String newString) {
    practiceString = newString;
    reset();     Send self a reset() message.
}
```

Note that this `reset()` message has no apparent receiver; in this case the Java compiler understands that the message's receiver is the same object that is sending the message. Figure 4.12 shows what happens when a `TypingTutor` object implemented this way receives a `setPracticeString()` message.

Objects and Their Lifetimes

An object lasts as long as some reference variable, somewhere, refers to it. When no such variable exists anymore, the object is automatically destroyed by Java. Thus, while object creation in Java is a matter of the programmer explicitly requesting it with the `new` operator, object destruction is a quiet affair. No announcements, just a hidden occurrence when the last reference to an object is itself destroyed. The upshot is that when it comes to objects, we don't have to worry. Once we create them, as long as we have some reference to them, they won't go away.

Figure 4.12
An object sends a message to itself. When a `TypingTutor` object receives a `setPracticeString()` message, it first assigns to `practiceString`, then sends itself a `reset()` message.

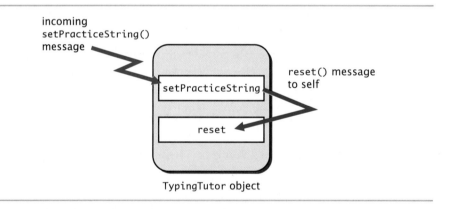

Summary

A class definition consists of a group of method definitions and declarations of instance variables enclosed in the class definition delimiters. A method definition consists of the prototype of the method followed by the method body—a sequence of Java statements enclosed in braces. The prototype consists of the return-type of the method (possibly `void`), the name of the method, and a parenthesized list of parameter declarations.

We have encountered three kinds of variables. Local variables are variables declared within a method. They must be initialized explicitly by the programmer. Parameters are variables declared within a method prototype. They are initialized with the values given by the arguments of the invoking message. Both local variables and parameters are created each time the method is invoked and destroyed each time the method returns. Both local variables and parameters are visible only to the method in which they are declared; as a result, different methods may declare local variables and parameters of the same name. Instance variables are declared outside of method bodies. They are created when the object is created and last throughout its lifetime. Instance variables are used to store information that must be preserved between message invocations. The values of the instance variables determine the state of the object.

Key Terms

access The ability to use a method or variable.

access control The ability to allow or prevent access to a method or variable.

accessor method A method whose behavior is either to assign a value to or return the value of one of the class's instance variables.

argument Information provided in a message in addition to the method-name and ultimately made available to the method via a parameter; one of the two ways that methods get needed information.

behavior Any action that the object may take, any change it may undergo, or any characteristic it may reveal as a result of a method being invoked.

delimiter A marker indicating a beginning or ending; in Java, braces mark the beginning and ending of method bodies and class definitions.

implement Provide the code that realizes a design.

instance variable A variable that is declared within a class but outside of any method; its purpose is to store information needed by methods to be preserved in between invocations. Each object has its own set of instance variables that have their own unique values—it is these values that distinguish one object from another. The entire set of the instance variables of an object define its state.

local variable A variable that is declared within a method; it exists only during the invocation of the method and is used as a temporary convenient holder of information.

method A self-contained section of code belonging to a class that achieves a specific behavior for that class. A method consists of a return-type, method-name, and parameter list, all of which form the method's signature, and the section of code that is called the body of the method.

parameter A variable that is declared in the parentheses of a method signature and whose purpose is to store the value of the corresponding argument; naturally, the type of the argument and the parameter must match in some sense.

private A keyword modifier in a method definition or instance variable declaration that *prevents* access to a method or variable from any code outside the class.

prototype Part of a method definition that consists of return-type, method-name, and argument list in parentheses.

public A keyword modifier in a method definition or instance variable declaration that *allows* access to a method or variable from any code outside the class.

return A verb keyword that allows a method to terminate its own execution and allows the sender of the message to resume execution; additionally, the `return` statement allows the method to send some information back to the receiver.

return-type The first part of the prototype; it specifies what kind of information will be returned by the method.

state The collection of values of the instance variables of an object at any given time.

void Return-type of methods that do not return a value.

Questions for Review

1. Describe the steps that must be taken from designing a class to using it in a program.
2. What are instance variables? Why are they necessary? Why can't they be declared within methods?
3. What sources of information are available to a method?
4. How can a method convey information to the sender?
5. When designing a class, should we consider its *behavior* or its *state* first?

Exercises

1. Write a class `FirstClass` with a single method, `first()`, that prints "This appears to be my first class" to `System.out`.
2. Write a class `NamePrinter` with methods that print each of your names (first, middle, last) to `System.out`. (For example, you might call these methods

first(), middle(), and last(), or family() and given().) Write a program that uses NamePrinter to print your name in various formats (such as "John Quincy Adams" or "Adams, John Quincy").

3. Write a class StringThing with two methods, upperize() and lowerize(). Each of these methods reads a string from System.in; upperize() outputs the string in all uppercase letters; lowerize() outputs the string in all lowercase letters. Write a program that uses the StringThing class.

4. Write a class called LastCall with methods yoo(), hoo(), foo(), and getLast(), and a String instance variable lastCalled. Methods yoo(), hoo(), and foo() set the value of lastCalled to "yoo", "hoo", or "foo", respectively, and getLast() prints the value of lastCalled to System.out.

5. Write an irritating version of Stopwatch that uses an instance variable callCount which is initialized to 10. Each time showElapsedTime() is called, callCount decreases by 1. When callCount becomes 0, every subsequent call to showElapsedTime() causes only the message "Due to planned obsolescence, this Stopwatch is no longer operational" to be output.

6. Write programs that use each of the classes in the previous two exercises and makes sure that the methods are implemented correctly.

7. Add a returnLast() method to the LastCall class (see Exercise 4) that returns a String reference rather than printing to output. Write a simple program that uses the modified LastCall class.

8. Write a class called KeyboardInput with a single method, get(). When a KeyboardInput object receives a get() message, it should return a String containing a line of input from the keyboard.

9. Write a Maximizer class that, instead of finding the *minimum* long considered so far, finds the *maximum* long so far. Use it in a program that reads in five test scores and outputs the highest.

10. Write an Adder class with reset(), add(), and sum() methods. The add() method takes a single long parameter, the sum() method returns the sum of all values received by add() so far, and reset() resets the object.

11. Write a ThreewayLamp class that models the behavior of a lamp that uses a three-way bulb. These bulbs have (curiously) four possible states: off, low light, medium light, and high light. Each time the switch is activated, the bulb goes to the next state (from high light the next state is off). The ThreewayLamp class has a single method, switch(), which takes a single int parameter indicating how many times the switch is activated; assume this will be not be negative. The switch() method should simply print to System.out a message indicating the state of the bulb after it has changed.

12. Rewrite the Logger class so that each of its methods takes a String parameter containing a message that is written to the log along with the date/time.

13. Implement a class called FileCopier. One method, called setSource(), takes a single argument, a String argument specifying the name of a file that contains

at least three lines. The other method, called copyTo(), also takes a String argument, one that specifies the name of a file to be written to. The copyTo() method writes the first three lines of the file it was instantiated with to the file given by the argument.

14. Write a class called InitialFinder that has a single method, getInitials(). This method takes three String parameters corresponding to a first, middle, and last name, and it returns a reference to a String containing the initials of this name. For example, if an InitialFinder object receives a getInitials("John","Fitzgerald","Kennedy") message, it should return a reference to "JFK".

15. Write a class called DimmerSwitch that models a kind of dimmer switch. This type of switch has two behaviors: Pushing it turns it on or off; rotating the switch, if it is on, increases or decreases the brightness of the light. Your class should include a getBrightness() method that returns an int between 0 (off) and 100 (full brightness).

A Simple Animation

Now that we have studied some of the techniques of class definition, let's revisit the FlipperApplet from the last chapter:

```
public class FlipperApplet extends Applet {
    public void paint(Graphics g) {
        if (red)
            g.setColor(Color.red);
        else
            g.setColor(Color.blue);
        g.fillRect(0,0,100,100);
        red = !red;
    }
    private boolean red=true;
}
```

We can now see that red is an instance variable; it is used by the applet to "remember" what the next invocation of paint() should display. We now understand that if red has been declared inside paint(), this memory would be lost because local variables (declared within methods) are recreated each time the method is invoked. Furthermore, we can observe the following:

- We have defined a class called FlipperApplet.
- FlipperApplet apparently contains a single method, paint().
- The paint() method has a single parameter g, a reference to an object of the Graphics class.

Understanding the behavior of this class hinges on understanding the following:

- That the class FlipperApplet is an applet. This is a result of the phrase extends Applet.
- The behavior of a Graphics object, in particular the setColor() and fill-Rect() methods.

At some point, the browser will use the class definition of FlipperApplet to create a FlipperApplet object. Eventually, the browser will invoke the paint() method, just as the Java interpreter invokes the main() method of a program. Before doing so, the browser creates a Graphics object. A reference to this object is passed to paint().

The extends Keyword

Let us return to a pair of words that appeared in the definition of our first applet class:

```
public class FirstApplet extends Applet {
```

It is far too early in our exploration of Java to explain these words in full, but we can make a few remarks about their impact on the class `FlipperApplet`, which we are defining. In particular, there is a predefined class called `Applet`. As a result of this clause, `extends Applet`, our `FlipperApplet` class possesses all of `Applet`'s methods without our having to write so much as an open brace. These methods provide basic behavior for applets. Any time we want to customize that behavior, we can do so by defining our own method to replace one of those that are predefined in `Applet`. `FlipperApplet` does this. It provides its own method, `paint()`, to draw the desired rectangle on the web page.

A Bouncing Ball Animation

In this supplement, we improve on the animation techniques from the previous supplement. Specifically, we will no longer rely on external events, like the minimization of a window, to cause `paint()` to be invoked. Instead, our applet will make use of the `repaint()` method, which tells the applet to redisplay itself even if no external phenomenon makes it necessary to do so.

The animation itself will consist only of a bouncing ball. That is, we'll display a small ball (i.e., a circle) moving back and forth. Its vertical position will not change; it will remain approximately halfway between the top and bottom of the applet's display area. See Figure 4.13.

As we mentioned in the previous supplement, animation works by displaying a series of images that differ from each other slightly; these differences create the perception of motion. Because we will use the applet's `repaint()` method to display the sequence of frames, we can focus on the calculations necessary to *generate* the sequence of frames.

Identifying Variables

A good approach is to use a variable for each distinct piece of information that enters the problem or its solution. Already, we can identify a few variables:

```
int xPos,         // Current x-coordinate of ball
    xVelocity,    // Distance traveled per frame
    diameter,     // Ball's diameter
    myWidth,      // Width of applet display
    myHeight,     // Height of applet display
    yPos;         // Halfway between top and bottom
```

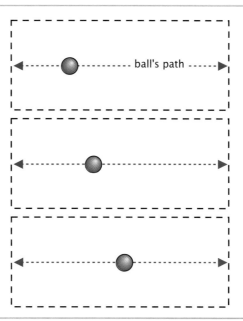

Figure 4.13
Three successive frames in the animation performed by BouncingBallApplet.

We still need to determine which of these should be an instance variable and which should be a local variable of paint(). At first glance, it might seem that all variables could be declared as local to paint(): Because we have written no other methods that would use these values, there couldn't be any need to share values among several methods. But a closer analysis shows that this is not the case. Like FlipperApplet, this applet needs to remember some information (specifically, the value of xPos and xVelocity) from one invocation of paint() to the next. Storing this information in variables local to paint() will not work, because those variables exist only while paint() is executing; each new invocation of paint() will create its own (freshly initialized) local variables. Thus, xPos and xVelocity, like red, must be declared as instance variables—in effect, these instance variables are used to facilitate communication between one invocation of paint() and the next.

The remaining variables can be declared locally in paint(). Because their values never change, each invocation of paint() can safely create its own copy of these variables.

At this point, we have the following skeleton of our BouncingBallApplet:

```
public class BouncingBallApplet extends Applet {
   public void paint (Graphics g) {
      int myWidth;
```

```
        int myHeight;
        int yPos;
        int diameter;
            .
            .
            .
    }
    private int xPos;
    private int xVelocity;
}
```

Assigning Initial Values

As we begin to think about our animation algorithm, we will first make a few arbitrary decisions to clarify the scenario. The animation will begin with the ball on the left side of the applet (i.e., at *x*-coordinate 0), the ball's diameter will be 10 units, and from one frame to the next the ball will move 5 units. Thus, we can provide initializers for a few of our variables:

```
private int xPos = 0;
private int xVelocity = 5;
int diameter = 10;
```

The values of myWidth and myHeight are determined, as before, by the assignment

```
int myWidth = getSize().width      // Width of applet display
int myHeight = getSize().height;   // Height of display
```

and the value of yPos, the ball's *y*-coordinate, will be determined by the value of myHeight:

```
int yPos = myHeight/2;     // Halfway between top and bottom
```

At this point, then, we have

```
public class BouncingBallApplet extends Applet {
    public void paint (Graphics g) {
        int myWidth = getSize().width;
        int myHeight = getSize().height;
        int yPos = myHeight/2;
        int diameter = 10;
            .
            .
            .
    }
    private int xPos = 0;
    private int xVelocity = 5;
}
```

Moving the Ball

Of these values, only xPos, yPos, and diameter directly determine how we will draw a single frame. To display the ball in its correct position for the frame we will send a fillOval() message to the Graphics object in paint():

```
g.fillOval(xPos,yPos,diameter,diameter);
```

Indeed, of these values only xPos will change from one frame to the next. The remaining variables—xVelocity and myWidth—will be used to compute the new value of xPos.

Once we display the current frame, using fillOval() as above, we need to determine the ball's next position. As a first attempt, we can observe that the value of xVelocity is intended to represent the distance the ball will move between frames. So, perhaps we can update xPos by saying

```
xPos += xVelocity;
```

Thus, the first frame is drawn with the ball's top left corner at x-coordinate 0; after this statement xPos will advance to 5, causing the ball in the next frame to be drawn at x-coordinate 5.

This will work perfectly until the ball reaches the right edge of the applet. At that time, if we continue to increase the value of xPos, the ball's position will move off the applet's display area. Instead, we want the ball's direction of motion to reverse so that it begins moving back to the left edge. That is, if the width of the applet is 300, then we should display a ball at x-coordinate 295, increment xPos by 5, display a ball at x-coordinate 300, and then *decrement* xPos by 5, effectively bouncing the ball off the right edge of the applet.

While we're considering this problem, we should also note that we'll face the opposite situation when the ball returns to the left edge. At that point, rather than continuing to decrement xPos, we should bounce the ball off the left side and begin incrementing xPos again.

To solve this problem, let's try to state it more succinctly. The essential behavior we'd like to capture when the ball reaches the right edge is "if the ball's position is on the right edge of the applet, then reverse direction." We can use a conditional statement that tests the values of two of our variables to implement this behavior as follows. First, the "if" part:

```
if (xPos > myWidth)
```

That is, the ball has reached the right edge of the applet precisely when the ball's x-coordinate has exceeded the width of the applet. If this is the case, we want to reverse direction; that is, instead of adding 5 we should start subtracting 5. This is most easily done by negating the value of xVelocity:

```
xVelocity = -xVelocity;
```

After this happens, the statement that we used on the preceding page,

```
xPos += xVelocity;
```

will have exactly the effect we desire: Now the value of xVelocity is −5, so this statement will cause 5 to be subtracted from xPos, moving the ball back toward the left edge.

If we turn to the situation when the ball reaches the left edge, we see that we need almost exactly the same code. To test whether the ball has reached the left edge, we write

```
if (xPos < 0)
```

If it has, then we again want to reverse the ball's direction. Where before it was moving in the "negative" direction, we want it to begin moving in the "positive" direction. We accomplish this with exactly the same negation of xVelocity:

```
xVelocity = −xVelocity;
```

The Nearly Complete Applet

Here's the applet code we've generated so far:

```
public class BouncingBallApplet extends Applet {
    public void paint (Graphics g) {
        int myWidth = getSize().width;
        int myHeight = getSize().height;
        int yPos = myHeight/2;
        int diameter = 10;
        g.fillOval(xPos,yPos,diameter,diameter);
        if (xPos > myWidth)
            xVelocity = −xVelocity;
        if (xPos < 0)
            xVelocity = −xVelocity;
        xPos += xVelocity;
    }
    private int xPos = 0;
    private int xVelocity = 5;
}
```

The logic here is impeccable, except for one glaring omission: This code will only display one frame of the animation. At this point, our applet is not so different from FlipperApplet—each invocation of paint() displays one frame, but the only way for paint() to be invoked more than once is to force its window to redisplay.

To rectify the situation, we'll modify our paint() method to ensure that it *will* be invoked again. We accomplish this by writing

```
repaint();
```

after our recalculation of xPos. By invoking the applet's repaint() method, we ask the applet to redisplay itself as soon as is convenient. It's important to keep in mind that the redisplay is *not* immediate. Some number of milliseconds will elapse first. Also, when the redisplay does take place, the paint() method is executed again in its entirety—including the recalculation of the ball's position *and another invocation* of repaint(). So the process of fillOval() ... recalculate ... schedule another paint() continues indefinitely.

Stopping the Animation, Crudely

At this point, our paint() method looks like this:

```java
public void paint(Graphics g) {
    int myWidth = getSize().width;
    int myHeight = getSize().height;
    int yPos = myHeight/2;
    int diameter = 10;
    g.fillOval(xPos,yPos,diameter,diameter);
    if (xPos > myWidth)
        xVelocity = -xVelocity;
    if (xPos < 0)
        xVelocity = -xVelocity;
    xPos += xVelocity;
    repaint();
}
```

The cycle of animation generated by this code repeats as long as the applet remains active (until, for example, a different page is loaded into the browser). If we want the animation to stop before that point, we need to terminate the paint()/repaint() sequence somehow. One way of doing this is just to count how many times the paint() code is executed, and to stop the applet after some threshold is reached. To do so, we need one more instance variable:

```java
private int counter = 0;
```

After each recalculation of xPos, we'll increment the value of counter:

```java
counter++;
```

And before asking the applet to repaint() itself, we'll check the value of counter to see whether it's time to stop:

```java
if (counter < 2000)
    repaint();
else
    stop();
```

Just as repaint() asks the applet to redisplay itself, stop() tells the applet to stop its execution, thereby bringing the animation to an end. The complete applet, then, is

```java
import java.awt.*;
import java.applet.*;
public class BouncingBallApplet extends Applet {
    public void paint (Graphics g) {
        int myWidth = getSize().width;
        int myHeight = getSize().height;
        int yPos = myHeight/2;
        int diameter = 10;

        g.fillOval(xPos,yPos,diameter,diameter);
        if (xPos > myWidth)
            xVelocity = -xVelocity;
        if (xPos < 0)
            xVelocity = -xVelocity;
        xPos += xVelocity;

        counter++;
        if (counter < 2000)
            repaint();
        else
            stop();
    }
    private int xPos = 0;
    private int xVelocity = 5;
    private int counter = 0;
}
```

Suggested Experiments

1. Animate a rectangle that bounces up and down rather than across the screen.

2. Animate a circle that, rather than moving across the screen, grows and shrinks. Keep the circle centered, so that both its diameter and the coordinates of its top left corner will change together.

3. Modify BouncingBallApplet so that the size of the circle diminishes as the ball approaches the center, then expands as the ball moves toward the edges.

4. Animate a circle that travels around the edges of the applet's display area.

Advanced Class Definition

I n Chapter 4, we introduced the mechanics of class definition with a focus on the most important aspect of a class: the behavior of its instances. Our main concern was with method definitions (their prototypes, including parameters and return-types, and their bodies), although we saw that instance variables, defined outside any method, were crucial for providing certain kinds of behavior. In this chapter, we will consider other kinds of desirable behavior and study the class definition techniques that support them.

5.1 Customizing New Objects: Constructors

An object's *state* is the set of values stored in the object's instance variables. We have seen that in some cases, the *initial state* of an object is very important: a new Minimizer object, for example, needs to start with the maximum possible value stored in the instance variable minSoFar. To arrange this, we declared minSoFar with an initializer that ensured that every new Minimizer object was created with the correct value stored in minSoFar.

When we design another class, we may determine that the initial state of its instances is not so important. In the Stopwatch class, for example, we did not specify an initial value for startTime because this value becomes significant not when a Stopwatch object is created but only after it receives a start() message.

There is a third possibility: that the initial state of an object is essential but can not be known to the designer of the class; it is, instead, determined by the user of the class. We've experienced this as class users already. Recall from Chapter 3 how we prepared to read input from the file file1.dat. The first thing we needed to do was create a new File object:

```
new File("file1.dat")
```

Here, we specified that the initial state of this new object should somehow be associated with the file file1.dat. As we saw in Chapter 3, every class has one or more methods, called *constructors*, that are automatically invoked when a new instance is created. Our class definitions up to this point have not included constructors; with such classes the Java compiler automatically generates a simple default constructor. Next, we'll consider adding constructors to some of the classes we defined in Chapter 4.

The TypingTutor **Class**

The TypingTutor class definition specifies a very particular initial state for each new TypingTutor object: Each contains new Counter and Minimizer objects and has practiceString initialized to "The quick brown fox jumps over the lazy dog." Some parts of this initialization are known to the designer because they are required by the class's own logic. In particular, the Counter and Minimizer objects *must* be in their own proper initial states. The practiceString, though, does not need to be initialized to this particular string. Indeed, the class would be more flexible if users could specify their own initial string. Let's add a constructor to this class that will allow users to do just that. For example, a new TypingTutor object might be created with a declaration such as

```
TypingTutor tt = new TypingTutor("I'm liking I's.");
```

To make it possible to create a TypingTutor object in this way, with a customized string, we will have to write a constructor definition that accommodates a String argument. Constructor definitions closely resemble method definitions, with two important distinctions. First, the name of the constructor is *always* the same as the name of the class. Second, constructor prototypes specify no return-type—not even void. Constructors are automatically invoked in conjunction with new; the constructor itself returns no value, although the whole "new phrase" is itself a reference to the newly created object. Like any other method definition, constructors may have parameters. The constructor that is invoked above, then, will have the prototype

```
public TypingTutor(String practice)
```

The parameter holds a reference to the user's desired practice String. Our job in the constructor is to get that reference into the appropriate instance variable. To accomplish this, in the body of the constructor we will assign practice (the parameter) to practiceString (the instance variable). We can also, if we choose, initialize the other instance variables at the same time:

```
public TypingTutor(String practice) {
   practiceString = practice;
   lowestTime = new Minimizer();
   perfectCount = new Counter();
}
```

With this constructor, the initializers for the instance variables are redundant, so we rewrite the instance variable declarations as

```
private String practiceString;
private Minimizer lowestTime;
private Counter perfectCount;
```

Now whenever a user creates a TypingTutor object, she must also provide the initial practice string. The modified class now looks like this:

```
public class TypingTutor {
    public TypingTutor(String practice) {
        practiceString = practice;
        lowestTime = new Minimizer();
        perfectCount = new Counter();
    }
    public void setPracticeString(String newString) {
        practiceString = newString;
        lowestTime.reset();
        perfectCount.reset();
    }
    public long test() throws Exception {
        .

        .

        .

    }
    public long getLowestTime() {
        return lowestTime.getValue();
    }
    public int getNumPerfect() {
        return perfectCount.getValue();
    }
    private String practiceString;
    private Minimizer lowestTime;
    private Counter perfectCount;
}
```

Defining Overloaded Constructors

In Chapter 3, we saw that some predefined classes have more than one constructor. For example, the GregorianCalendar class has both a default constructor, which creates a GregorianCalendar object corresponding to the current moment, and a constructor that accepts three ints (year, month, and day of month) and creates an object corresponding to midnight on that day. For example, we could declare a new GregorianCalendar object using either of these two constructor invocations:

```
GregorianCalendar now = new GregorianCalendar();
GregorianCalendar millennium =
    new GregorianCalendar(2001,0,1);   // Remember month usage
```

We can design our own classes in the same way. The Logger class we designed allowed us to log the current time to a file, but it did not allow a user of the class to specify the name of the log file—the class was designed to write to a file named log. This meant that every Logger object was forced to write to the same file. Let's modify the class design to allow the name of the log file to be specified whenever a new `Logger` instance is created. We want our new version of the class to allow the user to create instances in one of two ways:

```
Logger l = new Logger();
```
Write to default file `log`.

or

```
Logger err = new Logger("error.log");
```
Write to file `error.log`.

Thus, we will need to add constructor definitions with prototypes

```
public Logger()
public Logger(String logfile)
```

Even though these two methods have the same name, the compiler can distinguish them by analyzing the number and type of their parameters. Thus, if a `Logger` constructor is invoked as

```
Logger x = new Logger("crash.log");
```

then the constructor with the second prototype above will be invoked. But if a `Logger` constructor is invoked as

```
Logger x = new Logger();
```

then the constructor which takes no parameters will be invoked (and the object referred to by x will log to the file `log`). This technique is called *overloading*, because a single method name may bear the burden of several different behaviors.

Before we look at the implementation of these constructors, we should determine whether any other aspects of the class will change as a result of this design modification. Here is the original class definition:

```
class Logger {
   public void log() throws Exception {
      PrintStream logps;
      GregorianCalendar now;
      logps = new PrintStream(new FileOutputStream("log"));
      now = new GregorianCalendar();
      logps.println(now.getTime());
   }
   public void logWithTZ() throws Exception {
      PrintStream logps;
      GregorianCalendar now;
      logps = new PrintStream(new FileOutputStream("log"));
      now = new GregorianCalendar();
      logps.print(now.getTimeZone().getDisplayName() + " ");
      logps.println(now.getTime());
   }
}
```

Note that the filename log is "hard-coded" into the two method bodies. If we re-design the class to allow the user to designate the log file, both of the noncon-structor methods will need access to that information. In the case of the construc-tor that takes a String reference as a parameter, we need an instance variable to store that reference:

```
private String fileName;
```

The constructor's job is to assign the parameter logFile to the instance variable fileName. The other methods will then use the fileName reference rather than "log" to create their PrintStream objects. Thus, this constructor will be imple-mented as

```
public Logger(String logFile) {
    fileName = logFile;
}
```

The other constructor, which takes no parameters, will just assign "log" to fileName:

```
public Logger() {
    fileName = "log";
}
```

Now the log() and logWithTZ() methods will use the String referred to by fileName as the name of the file to which to write. Here is the modified Logger class with new constructors, new instance variable, and modified method implementations:

```
class Logger {
    public Logger() {
        fileName = "log";
    }
    public Logger(String logFile) {
        fileName = logFile;
    }
    public void log() throws Exception {
        PrintStream logps;
        GregorianCalendar now;
        logps = new PrintStream(new FileOutputStream(fileName));
        now = new GregorianCalendar();
        logps.println(now.getTime());
    }
    public void logWithTZ() throws Exception {
        PrintStream logps;
        GregorianCalendar now;
        logps = new PrintStream(new FileOutputStream(fileName));
```

Use value of fileName.

```
        now = new GregorianCalendar();
        logps.print(now.getTimeZone().getDisplayName() + " ");
        logps.println(now.getTime());
    }
    private String fileName;
}
```

Let's consider this modified class. If we examine how `fileName` is used by the `log()` and `logWithTZ()` methods, we notice that both methods use it in exactly the same way: to create and initialize a `PrintStream` object. Each method in the class, then, uses `fileName` only to initialize its own local `PrintStream` reference. What happens if we try to move this `PrintStream` initialization code into the constructors?

```
public Logger() {
    logps = new PrintStream(new FileOutputStream("log"));
}
public Logger(String logFile) {
    logps = new PrintStream(new FileOutputStream(logFile));
}
```

Using this approach, `logps` becomes an instance variable, because its value is used by the constructors as well as the other methods in the class. Therefore, we must replace the declaration

```
private String FileName;
```

with

```
private PrintStream logps;
```

Now the `log()` and `logWithTZ()` methods need not declare `logps`; they can just use it:

```
public void log() throws Exception {
    GregorianCalendar now = new GregorianCalendar();
    logps.println(now.getTime());
}
public void logWithTZ() throws Exception {
    GregorianCalendar now = new GregorianCalendar();
    logps.print(now.getTimeZone().getDisplayName() + " ");
    logps.println(now.getTime());
}
```

The difference between these two options (using a `String` instance variable versus using a `PrintStream` instance variable) is significant: using `PrintStream`, a `FileOutputStream` object is created—in this case by a constructor—only when a new `Logger` object is created. Using `String`, we create a `FileOutputStream` object much more frequently—each time a method is invoked. This is important because whenever a FileOutputStream object is created, if the file associated with it already exists, the contents of the file are destroyed. Thus, the original Logger class has a characteristic that is probably undesirable: After a sequence of log() and/or logWithTZ() messages, the log file will only contain the time of the *last* message!

Here is the complete final version of the Logger class:

```java
class Logger {
   public Logger() {
      logps = new PrintStream(new FileOutputStream("log"));
   }
   public Logger(String logFile) {
      logps = new PrintStream(new FileOutputStream(logFile));
   }
   public void log() throws Exception {
      GregorianCalendar now = new GregorianCalendar();
      logps.println(now.getTime());
   }
   public void logWithTZ() throws Exception {
      GregorianCalendar now = new GregorianCalendar();
      logps.print(now.getTimeZone().getDisplayName() + " ");
      logps.println(now.getTime());
   }
   private PrintStream logps;
}
```

By using a PrintStream instance variable, and thereby creating a FileOutput-Stream object only once for each Logger object, we ensure that the log file contains the output from *all* messages sent to the Logger object since its creation. Because the constructor is *always* the first method that is invoked, we can be confident that logps will have a meaningful value whenever any of the other methods are invoked.

Java Interlude

Constructors, Initializers, and Overloading

Default Constructors

When a constructor takes no arguments, it is called the **default constructor** for a class. If a class definition includes no constructor definitions, the compiler automatically provides a default constructor that performs no initializations. If a class includes *any* constructors, though, the compiler will provide no others. Thus, the modified TypingTutor class, which includes one constructor that receives a single

`String` parameter, has no default constructor. An attempt to create a `TypingTutor` by declaring

```
TypingTutor tt = new TypingTutor();
```

will cause a compilation error because there is no default constructor for `TypingTutor`.

Constructors and Initializers

Both constructors and instance variable initializers allow us to provide initial values for the instance variables of a class. The following two class definitions are exactly equivalent:

```
class Example {
    public print() {
        System.out.println(x);
    }
    private int x = 10;        Using initializer
}
```

```
class Example {
    public Example() {        Using constructor
        x = 10;
    }
    public print() {
        System.out.println(x);
    }
    private int x;
}
```

Overloading

Java allows multiple methods—including constructors—within a class to share the same name. These methods must have different *signatures*, however. When an object receives a message, the method that responds to the message is determined by matching the name *and parameter type(s)* of the message. Thus, this is a legal class definition:

```
class OverloadedExample {
    public foo(int x) {
        System.out.println(x);
    }
    public foo(String x) {
        System.out.println(x);
    }
    public foo(Minimizer x) {
        x.check(12L);
    }
    public foo(String x, int y) {
```

```
        if (y < 0)
            System.out.println(x);
    }
}
```

Several of the foo() methods take exactly one parameter, but the compiler distinguishes them by analyzing the parameter's *type*. Similarly, two of these methods take a String as a first parameter, but these two methods are distinguished by the total number of parameters they receive.

5.2 Example: A Name Class

Now that we can define classes using constructors, let's define a new class that incorporates constructors from the outset. Consider an item as simple as a person's name. We might be tempted to model it as a String, but we would find that String's behavior does not directly provide the behavior we want from a Name. For example, the String class provides no way of identifying the "first name" part of a String. Instead, we will have to build our own Name class.

Determining the Behavior

Given a Name object, we would like to do the following:

- Get the initials as a String object.
- Get the name as a String object in last name, first name order.
- Get the name as a String object in first name, last name order.
- Add or replace a title (such as Sir or Ms. or Mr.).

This is just one possibility. Another designer might have chosen a different set of behaviors.

Interface

Once we've identified the behavior, we can start to consider how our Name class will provide this behavior—that is, what kinds of messages objects of the class will receive. At this point we are only concerned with the relationship between the class and a programmer using the class. We don't yet have to figure out the details of how the class's behavior is implemented.

A programmer's interaction with a class is determined by the prototypes of the methods of the class: In order to use the class, a programmer needs to know only the names, parameter-types (if any), and return-types (if any) of each method of the class. This collection of information is called the **interface** of the class.

As a first step, let's imagine how a Name object would be used if it provided a method for each of the behaviors listed above. Before we can discuss using a Name object, though, it would be useful to decide how a Name object should be created, that is, what kind of constructor(s) the class should provide. At the very least, we should be able to instantiate a new Name object, based on first and last names, as follows:

```
pres = new Name("Calvin","Coolidge");
```

Now we can consider what methods the class should use to provide its behavior:

METHOD DESCRIPTION	INTENDED USAGE
Method to get the initials as a String object	String s0; s0 = pres.getInitials();
Method to get the full name as a String object in last, first form	String s1; s1 = pres.getLastFirst();
Method to get the full name as a String object in first, last form, preceded by an optional title	String s2; s2 = pres.getFirstLast();
Method to add a title or replace an existing title	pres.setTitle("President");

Notice that the arguments to the constructor do not include a title. This is our choice (as designers of this class). Our rationale is that not everyone has a title. Furthermore, a title, unlike a first or last name, is not a permanent aspect of a name. We thus provide a setTitle() method to permit the addition or modification of a title.

The constructor example above (new Name("Calvin","Coolidge")) informs us that the constructor prototype will be as follows:

```
Name(String first, String last)
```

We know that the constructor has two String parameters because our example passes two String arguments in "new Name ("Calvin","Coolidge")."

The setTitle() method requires one String parameter and returns nothing. Its prototype is as follows:

```
void setTitle(String newTitle)
```

The methods whose names start with get all return references to Strings, but none of them are given arguments, so they don't need parameters. Their prototypes are as follows:

```
String getInitials()
String getLastFirst()
String getFirstLast()
```

At this point, we can write a skeleton of the Name class definition:

```
class Name {
    public Name(String first, String last) {
    }
    public String getInitials() {
    }
    public String getLastFirst() {
    }
    public String getFirstLast() {
    }
    public void setTitle(String newTitle) {
    }
}
```

This skeleton shows that we have completely determined the *interface* of the class: We have provided all the information (method names, their parameter types, and their return-types) that someone using this class will need. Now we can begin developing the *implementation* of the class.

Implementing the Name Class

The first step we will take in writing the methods (including the constructor) is identifying instance variables. This requires that we identify the information that each method needs. Information needed by more than one method must be stored in an instance variable. Both the getFirstLast() and getLastFirst() methods, as well as the constructor, need access to first name and last name values, so we need instance variables

```
String    firstName;    // Will refer to the first name of this Name
String    lastName;     // Will refer to the last name of this Name
```

Similarly the title, needed by both setTitle() and getFirstLast(), must be an instance variable. We then have the following:

```
class Name {
    public Name(String first, String last) {
    }
    public String getInitials() {
    }
    public String getLastFirst() {
    }
    public String getFirstLast() {
    }
    public void setTitle(String newTitle) {
    }
```

```
    private String firstName;    // Will refer to the first name of this Name
    private String lastName;     // Will refer to the last name of this Name
    private String title;        // Will refer to the title part of this Name
}
```

Declaring an instance variable does not by itself give the variable a useful value. How are the three instance variables to get values? To answer that question, we must ask another: How is information provided to the Name object?

The specifications for the Name constructor indicate that the first and last names are Strings sent as arguments when a Name object is created, as follows:

```
public Name(String first, String last) {
}
```

When the constructor is invoked, its parameters, first and last, refer to the two String arguments.

It is the job of the constructor method to make the instance variable firstName refer to the same String object that parameter first refers to, and likewise for lastName with respect to last, as follows:

```
firstName = first;
lastName = last;
```

What about title? The specifications imply that until setTitle() is invoked, there is no title in the Name. This is certainly in accordance with our intuitive understanding of names and titles. What value can be given to the instance variable title to reflect this? There are several possibilities, but the one that is most convenient is to make title refer to an empty String, as follows:

```
title = "";
```

Putting these statements together, we complete our constructor:

```
public Name(String first, String last) {
    firstName = first;
    lastName = last;
    title = "";
}
```

A properly written constructor means that as we write the bodies for get-Initials(), getLastFirst(), and so on, we can be sure that firstName is a reference to a String object representing the first name, lastName is a reference to a String object representing the last name, and title is a reference to a String object representing the title. Alternatively, we might say that a properly written constructor guarantees that the object is in a well-defined, acceptable *state* when it receives its first and subsequent messages.

The setTitle() method assigns its parameter to the corresponding instance variable as follows:

```
public void setTitle(String newTitle) {
    title = newTitle;
}
```

By making this assignment, the setTitle() method ensures that the Name object's *state* will change appropriately (i.e., incorporate the new title) when it receives a setTitle() message.

The other methods return references to String objects, so each of them will use a return statement. In each case, the return value is obtained by concatenating the instance variables in a particular order and returning the resulting reference.

Let's see how this might work in the getLastFirst() method. Our task is to create a String object consisting of the last name, followed by a comma, followed by a space, followed by the first name. A cascade of concat() method invocations does the trick nicely:

```
lastName.concat(", ").concat(firstName)
```

Or we can use the + operator:

```
lastName + ", " + firstName
```

This results in the value that we are supposed to return (i.e., if our Name was created with arguments "Mary" "Smith", the resulting String would be "Smith, Mary"). Thus, getLastFirst() can be written as follows:

```
public String getLastFirst() {
    return lastName + ", " + firstName;
}
```

Observe that the getLastFirst() method does not change the Name object's state; that is, it does not modify any instance variables. It does, however, return information that is derived from the state of the object.

By analogy, we can write the getFirstLast() method, keeping in mind that the title is meant to be part of the newly constructed String, and that although there is no requirement for a comma, there must be a space between the title and first and last names, as follows:

```
public String getFirstLast() {
    return title + " " + firstName + " " + lastName;
}
```

The getInitials() method is similar, except that we need to use the substring() method in the way that we did in Chapter 2:

`x.substring(0,1)`   Return substring starting at position 0 with length 1

Here x is a reference to a `String`. This `substring()` message returns the first character of the `String`. Using that method to get the initials of `firstName` and `lastName`, we may write `getInitials()` as follows:

```
public String getInitials() {
    String  s;
    s = firstName.substring(0,1);
    s = s.concat(".");
    s = s.concat(lastName.substring(0,1));
    s = s.concat(".");
    return s;
}
```

Here we chose not to use cascading because of the number of methods that needed to be invoked. To do so would result in the following unreadable mess:

```
return firstName.substring(0,1).concat(".").
        concat(lastName.substring(0,1)).concat(".");
```

The Completed Name Class

Putting this all together, we have the following complete definition of the `Name` class:

```
class Name {
    public Name(String first, String last) {
        firstName = first;
        lastName = last;          Establishes the initial state.
        title = "";
    }
    public String getInitials() {
        String  s;
        s = firstName.substring(0,1);
        s = s.concat(".");
        s = s.concat(lastName.substring(0,1));
        s = s.concat(".");
        return s;
    }
    public String getLastFirst() {
        return lastName + ", " + firstName;
    }
    public String getFirstLast() {
        return title + " " + firstName + " " + lastName;
    }
    public void setTitle(String newTitle) {
        title = newTitle;          Modifies the state.
```

```
    }
    private String firstName;
    private String lastName;    }    Defines the state.
    private String title;
}
```

Using the Name **Class**

To illustrate how the Name class can be used, we'll write a simple program that reads in a few strings (for first name, last name, and title), creates a Name object, and then uses Name methods to print out the name in different formats. First, we'll declare the variables we'll need:

```
import java.io.*;
class UseName {
    public static void main(String arg[]) throws Exception {
        Name    n;                        // The name we are modeling
        String  first, last, title;
        BufferedReader keyboard = new BufferedReader(
            new InputStreamReader(System.in));
```

We then prompt the user to provide a first name, last name, and title, and we store references to those Strings as follows:

```
        System.out.print("First name, please: ");
        first = keyboard.readLine();
        System.out.print("Last name, please: ");
        last = keyboard.readLine();
        System.out.print("Title, please: ");
        title = keyboard.readLine();
```

Then we get to the point of this exercise: We use the String objects to create a new Name object and then send it a setTitle() message. Next we print the results of sending getInitials(), getLastFirst(), and getFirstLast() messages. The program is completed as follows:

```
        n = new Name(first,last);
        n.setTitle(title);
        System.out.println(n.getInitials());
        System.out.println(n.getFirstLast());
        System.out.println(n.getLastFirst());
    }
}
```

Outputting Objects: Modifying the Name **Class**

In our original design, the Name class itself does not read Name objects nor does it print them out. The responsibility for input and output rests entirely with the *user* of the class. UseName, for example, reads String objects that it uses to send to the

Name constructor to create a new Name object, and then it receives String objects of various sorts (for example, the initials or the name in last, first format) from the Name object and prints them out. UseName handles all the input and output.

Sometimes it is desirable to enable a class to take responsibility for its own input and output. When this is needed is a class design issue that we won't address now. Instead, we'll focus on the mechanics of how we can provide this capability to a class, using the Name class as our context.

We start with output. In the case of output, we can assume that a Name object already has been created—otherwise, there would be nothing to output. We need the ability to send a message to this object instructing it to write itself out, as follows:

```
Name      someName;
someName = new Name(...);
...
```

Send message to someName indicating that it should be output.

To do this, we will design a print() method for Name that performs output. What should the behavior of this print() method be? In particular,

- In what form should the Name be output? (First last? Last, first? How should the title be displayed?)
- Where should the output go?

The first question is harder to answer. Many choices are possible and there is no such thing as a right answer. Of course, one could write a different method for each potentially desirable choice, but "method clutter" has its own disadvantages. We will arbitrarily decide to write the Name out in "Title First Last" format.

We might take the same approach to the second question and arbitrarily decree that the output should go to standard output or to some particular file. However, if we are going to the trouble of adding a method to the Name class, we ought to make it as broadly useful as possible and not limit it to a single output target. This means that the method should not take the responsibility of choosing the output target—the responsibility for that choice should be left up to the sender of the print() message. Therefore, the sender will have to provide information to let the method know where to target the output. How can this be done?

All along, we have done output by sending println() or print() messages to a PrintStream object. As designers of the Name class, we can insist that the output target be a PrintStream object. With this choice, we demand that the sender of the print() message for Name pass a reference to a PrintStream object—the target of the output—as an argument. The prototype of the print() method then is as follows:

```
public void print(PrintStream target)
```

This means that System.out could be passed as an argument because System.out is a reference to a PrintStream object. For example,

```
someName.print(System.out);
```

The sender could pass a reference to a different `PrintStream` object if desired. The possibilities become intriguing. For example, we can use this method to write out a `Name` both to the screen and to a data file:

```
Name karpis = new Name("Alvin","Karpis");
karpis.setTitle("Public Enemy Number One");
PrintStream mostWanted;
mostWanted = new PrintStream(
            new FileOutputStream("Americas.Most.Wanted"));
karpis.print(System.out);     Print to System.out.
karpis.print(mostWanted);     Print to the PrintStream referred to by mostWanted.
```

With this code fragment, we have printed "Public Enemy Number One Alvin Karpis" to both standard output and the disk data file ("Americas.Most.Wanted") to which the `PrintStream` reference mostWanted refers.

Implementing the `print()` method is straightforward. If we were writing the `Name` object to `System.out`, we would write the following:

```
    System.out.print(title);
    System.out.print(" ");
    System.out.print(firstName);
    System.out.print(" ");
    System.out.print(lastName);
```

However, now we wish to use the `PrintStream` that the user sent as an argument. This is the parameter `target`, and so we write (showing the complete method here) the following:

```
void print(PrintStream target) {
    target.print(title);
    target.print(" ");
    target.print(firstName);
    target.print(" ");
    target.print(lastName);
}
```

5.3 Providing Class Behaviors

We now turn to input. We want the ability to send a message asking that a `Name` object *be created* from input. Immediately we have a problem. Messages are sent to objects, but we don't have an object to send a message to. We are sending a message in order to create an object. We can't send a message to a `Name` object; instead, we'd like to stretch the idea of sending messages and send a message to the `Name` class (if that were possible) and ask it to create a `Name` object from input for us.

In Java, this *is* possible. It is accomplished with a special kind of method: a **class method**, also known as a **static method**. Class methods are associated only with a class and never with a particular object of their class. As a result,

- Class methods must be invoked independently of any instance of the class. They are invoked by using the class name as the receiver of the message. That is, invoking a class method looks like this:

  ClassName. *staticMethodName*() ;

- Class methods may not access any instance variables (because the receiver is not an object, there are no instance variables).

These methods are defined in the same way as other methods (which we call **instance methods** when we need to distinguish them from static methods), except that the keyword `static` appears before their return-type.

We will therefore write a static method for the `Name` class to do input. Again, we use a static method because it is invoked without association with a `Name` object. We will call our input method `read()`. This `read()` method will

- Be a static or class method
- Create a `Name` object using data it has read from input
- Return a reference to the newly created `Name` object

We expect that it would be used as follows:

```
Name n = Name.read(...)     Notice the use of the class name.
```

As in the case of our `print()` method, in designing our static `read()` method we must address the following two questions:

- In what format will the data for the `Name` be?
- Where will the input come from?

We will require that the first name appear on a line by itself in the input and the last name appear on a line immediately following. As was the case for output format, this is an arbitrary choice.

We will design our method so that the responsibility for designating the input source rests with the invoker of the method. Accordingly, we require that a reference to a `BufferedReader` object be passed as an argument to `read()`.

First, we write the prototype for `read()`. It must be `static` and return a `Name` reference, and it receives a `BufferedReader` parameter, as follows:

```
public static Name read(BufferedReader br)
```

This allows a user of the `Name` class to read a `Name` from either a file (called `name.list` in the following example) or the keyboard. Here is a program fragment that uses the newly added input/output facilities of the `Name` class:

```
Name              n1,n2;
FileInputStream   f;
BufferedReader    inFile, keyboard;
keyboard = new BufferedReader(new InputStreamReader(System.in));
f = new FileInputStream(new File("name.list"));
brFile = new BufferedReader(new InputStreamReader(f));
n1 = Name.read(keyboard);    Input Name from keyboard.
n1.print(System.out);
n2 = Name.read(inFile);      Input Name from file.
n2.print(System.out);
```

Now that we have the prototype for the read() method and an understanding of how it will be used, we can write its body. The method

- Reads in the first and last names using the BufferedReader parameter, br:

```
String first = br.readLine();
String last = br.readLine();
```

- Uses the strings as arguments to the Name constructor to create the desired Name object:

```
Name n = new Name(first,last);
```

- Returns the reference to the brand new Name object:

```
return n;
```

Putting it all together, we have

```
public static Name read(BufferedReader br) {
    String first = br.readLine();
    String last = br.readLine();
    Name n = new Name(first,last);
    return n;
}
```

Note that this static method does not replace the constructor for the class. Instead, it does a little bit of work (reading in some strings), and then invokes the class's constructor.

The Revised Name Class and Its Use

With the additional methods introduced in the previous two sections, the revised Name class now is as follows:

```
class Name {
    public Name(String first, String last) {
        firstName = first;
        lastName = last;
```

```
            title = new String("");
        }
        public String getInitials() {
            String  s;
            s = firstName.substring(0,1);
            s = s.concat(".");
            s = s.concat(lastName.substring(0,1));
            s = s.concat(".");
            return s;
        }
        public String getLastFirst() {
            return lastName + ", " + firstName;
        }
        public String getFirstLast() {
            return title + " " + firstName + " " + lastName;
        }
        public void setTitle(String newTitle) {
            title = newTitle;
        }
        public void print(PrintStream target) {
            target.print(title);
            target.print(" ");
            target.print(firstName);
            target.print(" ");
            target.print(lastName);
        }
        public static Name read(BufferedReader br) throws Exception {
            String first = br.readLine();
            String last = br.readLine();
            Name n = new Name(first,last);
            return n;
        }
        private String firstName;    // Will refer to the first name of this Name.
        private String lastName;     // Will refer to the last name of this Name.
        private String title;        // Will refer to the title part of this Name.
}
```

Here is an example program that uses the new version of the Name class to read a
name from standard input and print it out, after adding the title "His Honor, the
Mayor":

```
class MakeMayor {
    public static void main(String[] arg) throws Exception {
        Name mayor;
```

```
        mayor = Name.read(new BufferedReader(
                          new InputStreamReader(System.in)));
        mayor.setTitle("His Honor, the Mayor");
        mayor.print(System.out);
    }
}
```

Java Interlude

Static Methods

Our First Program, Revisited

Look back at any of the programs from the preceding chapters, such as our very first one, which follows:

```
import java.io.*;
class Program0 {
    public static void main(String[] arg)  {
        System.out.println("Welcome To Java!");
    }
}
```

We can now see that programs, such as Program0, are themselves classes. Every class that can exist as a program must, as we mentioned in Chapter 1, have a main() method. We are now in a position to explain some more of the boilerplate. We see that the main() method is static; that is, it is not associated with an instance of the Program0 class. This is for a good reason. Execution of the program has to begin somewhere. In a sense, it is the Java interpreter that invokes the main() method. But it does so at the outset of program execution, before any objects from our code could have been created. In general, it is the task of the main() method to start the process of creating objects and invoking their methods (which in turn may create additional objects and lead to additional method invocations).

We can also understand the use of the keyword public. It is there to make it possible for main() to be invoked by something outside the class—namely, the Java interpreter.

Predefined Static Methods

So far, we have identified two applications for static methods:

- When reading in data from a BufferedReader and then using that data to create an object. There was no object to invoke a method upon—it was precisely the creation of the object that we were trying to achieve. We thus declared read() to be a static method.
- The main() method was declared static because at the outset of program execution, there were no objects to invoke methods upon.

We now present a third situation that calls for a static method. Consider primitive type values (e.g., `int`, `long`, `short`, etc.). The set of `int` operators, for example, that the Java language provides is small. If we need to compute the absolute value of an `int` or raise one `int` to the power of another, we must use a method. But `int`s are not objects and thus can't receive messages. What can we do about this? We can use static methods: If a value to be manipulated is a primitive type rather than an object, we use a static method for precisely the reason that there is no receiver.

Java supplies several classes consisting of static methods that manipulate primitive types. For example, the `Math` class contains various mathematically oriented methods, including the `abs()` method:

```
class Math {
   ...
   public static int abs(int a) {...} // Returns the absolute integer value of a.
   ...
}
```

Remembering that static methods are invoked by including the class name in the position of the message where the receiver normally goes, `abs()` can then be passed the integer whose absolute value is to be obtained:

```
int i = -2;
int j = Math.abs(i);◀──────── After this statement, j contains 2.
```

Although static methods could be placed in any class (as they are not associated with any receiving object), we apply some common sense guidelines regarding where to put them. Classes such as `Math` usually contain logically related methods, in this case methods that are mathematical in nature: logarithmic and trigonometric functions, and so on. Input methods, which create an object from input data, are best placed in the class of the object that they create.

Reading Primitive Values

On the topic of input, recall what we have learned about input so far: We know how to use the `readLine()` method of `BufferedReader` to read a string from an input source. We also know how to use this method in the body of a static method (such as `Name.read()`) in order to create a new object from input data. What we lack is the ability to read primitive values—we don't know how to ask the user for an `int` value, then read this value and store it in an `int` variable. To do this, we use the composition of two methods: The first reads in a `String` object from the stream, and the second transforms the characters of that `String` into a number, as follows:

- Read a line from the data file into a `String` object, using `readLine()`. For example, reading in a line containing 465 results in the `String` object "465" (note this is still a `String`; it is not yet an `int`).
- Convert (transform) the `String` value ("465") into the `int` value 465 using the static `parseInt()` method of the predefined class `Integer`.

The word *parse* means to break up a portion of text into its component parts. In our case, we are breaking up the String object, which consists of a sequence of digits, and reconstructing it into an int. The preceding two steps translate into

```
String s = br.readLine();        ←——————  Need s only briefly.
int i = Integer.parseInt(s);     ←——————  Convert s to int.
```

or more succinctly,

```
int  i  =  Integer.parseInt(br.readLine());
```

Note that the line read in *must* be capable of being turned into an integer value; otherwise the Java interpreter produces an error. Thus, input such as

```
2
75
-1
```

are fine, but an error will occur for

```
Hello
57 40
12o      ←——————  Lowercase o, not a zero.
```

For each primitive data type, Java provides a corresponding *wrapper* class: Integer, Long, Short, Byte, and so on. These classes allow us to "wrap" primitive type values in an object; they also contain a variety of useful methods for manipulating primitive data type values, including static methods such as parseInt(), parseLong(), parseShort(), and so on.

5.4 Tracking Class-Wide Information: Static Variables

The Counter class from Chapter 4 allows us to create objects that help us count occurrences of particular events. What if we needed to find out how many things had ever been counted by all the Counter objects—a sort of "global" count—in our program? For example, we might have Counters corresponding to several entrances to a theater, or Counters created and used at different points in time.

As a first attempt at solving this problem, we might try simply sending each Counter object a getValue() message and summing the results. This is inadequate for several reasons. First, the Counters themselves might be used in several different parts of our program—for example, several different methods might use locally declared Counter reference variables. It would be impossible to send all these objects a getValue() message from some "central" location in our program, because these variables are accessible only from inside the methods that declared them. Second, the getValue() method only returns the number of items counted since the last reset() message was received. If we wanted to keep track of everything ever counted by a Counter, we'd have to remember to record the

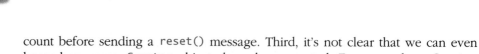

count before sending a reset() message. Third, it's not clear that we can even know how many Counter objects have been created. For example, a Counter might be created and used in the body of an if statement—that is, it might only be created under some specific circumstances.

We'll have better luck if we observe that this piece of information—the total life-time count accumulated by all Counter objects—is best recorded by the Counter class itself. Just as the behavior of Name.read() is associated with the Name class because no Name object could sensibly receive such a message, the value of this "total count" should be associated with the Counter class because there is no sen-sible way to extract this information from the population of Counter objects.

The variable we'll use to maintain this information is called a **class variable** or **static variable**. Static variables are declared just like instance variables but with the addition of the keyword static before the type:

```
private static int globalCount = 0;
```

Static variables can be initialized just like any other variable; the initialization takes place before the class is ever used.

Using Static Variables

Once we have the static variable globalCount, how should we use it? We will need to modify existing methods of the class—specifically the increment() method—so that the value of globalCount is incremented each time any Counter object receives an increment() message:

```
public void increment()
    count++;
    globalCount++;
}
```

As we've decided that the globalCount value is useful, we should also provide some way of accessing it from outside the class: We'll define another method, getGlobalValue(). It's also possible that someone would want to reset this value at some point, so we'll also define a method globalReset(). We have a choice to make: Should these methods be static or instance methods? Both are legitimate possibilities: Every instance method can access any static variable and invoke any static method; static methods can access only static variables and invoke only static methods (instance variables and methods are off limits because static meth-ods aren't associated with an instance). If we write them as instance methods, then to invoke them we would write code like this:

```
Counter c = new Counter();
. . .
int x = c.getGlobalValue();
```

That is, we would invoke these methods by sending a message to any Counter object. If we write them as static methods, then invoking them would look like this:

```
int x = Counter.getGlobalValue();
```

That is, we invoke them by "sending a message" to the Counter class itself.

In this case, because these methods only access a static variable, it's best to define these methods as static methods: The value we're accessing is maintained by the class, so it should be the responsibility of the class (rather than objects of that class) to provide access to it. Thus, our modified Counter class definition is

```
class Counter {
    public void reset() {
        count = 0;
    }
    public void increment() {
        count++;
        globalCount++;
    }
    public int getValue() {
        return count;
    }
    public static int getGlobalValue() {
        return globalCount;
    }
    public static void globalReset() {
        globalCount = 0;
    }
    private static int globalCount = 0;
    private int count = 0;
}
```

5.5 Defining Constant Values: final

Consider computing a value based on some formula. For example, suppose we are writing software to provide partial automation of a highway tollbooth. In our design, we might have a Tollbooth class with a calculateToll() method. If the toll system calls for a charge of $5 per axle and $10 per half-ton, we might write code to calculate this charge as follows:

```
int  tollDue  =  5*axles + 10*(totalWeight/1000);
```

Although this is perfectly correct, there are two legitimate objections to it:

- Code is meant to be read by others. The reader does not necessarily know the meaning of literals like 5 and 10 here; the reader may think that the 1000 suggests some kind of metric conversion.
- If politicians raise the tolls and 5 must be replaced by 6, for example, we do not want to search our method implementations for the formula. Also, if the

toll calculation appears in several places, it is possible to overlook one occurrence, thereby introducing an error in our class.

The values 5 and 10 in the preceding formula are sometimes referred to as *magic numbers* because they seem to come from nowhere. A better approach is to assign them to variables with descriptive names. If we use ordinary instance variables, we might inadvertently change their values. To avoid this, Java allows us to declare variables that are constant in nature. That is, once initialized with a value, they cannot be assigned another value:

```
static  final  int
    DuePerAxle  =  5,
    DuePerHalfTon  =  10,
    TonInPounds  =  2000,
    HalfTonInPounds  =  TonInPounds/2;
```

The keyword `final` states that the variable's value is *final*—once it has been initialized, it can never change again. We have already seen the `static` keyword; it states that this variable belongs to the class (`Tollbooth`), not each individual instance. Remember, however, each instance shares access to these static variables.

The toll-due formula may now be rewritten as follows:

```
int  tollDue  =  DuePerAxle*axles + DuePerHalfTon*
                        (totalWeight/HalfTonInPounds);
```

Predefined `final` **Values**

Many of Java's predefined classes provide definitions of useful constant values. For example, inside the definition of the `Long` class is the following declaration:

```
public static final long MAX_VALUE=9223372036854775807L;
```

Knowing this, we can rewrite the `Minimizer` class as follows:

```
class Minimizer {
   public void check(long nextValue) {
      if (nextValue < minSoFar)
         minSoFar = nextValue;
   }
   public long get() {
      return minSoFar;
   }
   public void reset() {
      minSoFar = Long.MAX_VALUE;
   }
   private long minSoFar = Long.MAX_VALUE;
}
```

The behavior is unchanged, but now it's easier to see how `minSoFar` is supposed to work.

Similarly, inside the `BigInteger` class are the following declarations:

```
public static final BigInteger ZERO;
public static final BigInteger ONE;
```

Keeping this in mind, we can use the phrase `BigInteger.ONE` instead of typing `new BigInteger("1")`.

The `Calendar` class defines

```
public static final int JANUARY=0;
public static final int FEBRUARY=1;
public static final int MARCH=2;
```

and so on. Recall that Java's month numbers are offset by one from our usual numbering; these constants allow us to forget about that peculiarity and instead create new `GregorianCalendar` instances like this:

```
GregorianCalendar leapDay =
    new GregorianCalendar(2004,Calendar.FEBRUARY,29);
```

Java Interlude

Working with Objects

"Dot" Notation

From early in this book, we have been using "dot" notation to send messages to objects. This notation allows us to send a message to a particular object by first giving a reference to the desired object, then specifying the message (and its parameters) to send to the object; the dot separates the reference name from the message name.

We've also seen that we can generalize this idea to accommodate class methods; in addition to expressions like

```
pres.getFirstLast();
```

that send messages to objects, we can also use expressions like

```
Counter.getGlobalValue();
```

that invoke class methods by using a class name rather than an object reference before the dot.

We can also use dot notation to access *variables*. For example, in the previous section, we used a constant static variable by writing

```
Long.MAX_VALUE
```

We still have a class name before the dot, but after the dot we now have the name of a static variable declared in that class.

Dot notation is not always necessary; for example, in our modification of the Counter class earlier, we wrote

```
globalCount++;
```

Here, because this code is part of the definition of the Counter class, we did not need to use the name of Counter explicitly. It would have been perfectly legitimate, however, to write this statement as

```
Counter.globalCount++;
```

Access Control Revisited

Until now, our rule regarding public and private designations has been to make all methods public and all variables private. This is a sensible rule because it reflects the separation of state and behavior: Methods provide behavior and so must be accessible from outside the class; variables maintain an object's state and so must *not* be manipulated from outside the class.

Similar reasoning applies to static methods and variables: Static variables maintain the "state" of the class and, therefore, are manipulated only by instance or class methods. Thus static variables are private and static methods are public.

Variables that are declared as static final represent an exception to our rule: They are almost always declared as public instead of private. Remember, though, that other variables are declared as private to prevent their manipulation from outside the class; because these variables are declared as final, their values are not permitted to change at all. Furthermore, these variables are used to declare constant values that may be useful or necessary to users of the class; declaring them as private would defeat this purpose.

The this Keyword

Occasionally, as we write method implementations, it is useful to be able to refer to the object through which the method is invoked. For example, it is common practice, in some situations, to use the same name for a method parameter as for an instance variable—this technique "self-documents" that the parameter value will be used to alter the value of the instance variable. As an example, consider the Name class, with its instance variable title. Suppose we started writing the setTitle() method as

```
public void setTitle(String title) {
```

to suggest that the instance variable title would be updated using the value of the parameter. Then the body of the method would consist of the statement

```
title = title;
```

which seems odd, at best. In fact, this will compile properly, but it will not have the desired behavior—both occurrences of title refer to the parameter; the instance variable's value is not changed.

We can specify that the title on the left side of the assignment refers to the object's instance variable title by writing

```
this.title = title;
```

instead. Here, this is a reference to the object whose setTitle() method is invoked; thus, this.title designates the title instance variable belonging to that object.

We can also use this to make it easier to overload constructors. Recall the two constructors for the Logger class:

```
public Logger(String logFile) {
    logps = new PrintStream(new FileOutputStream(logFile));
}
public Logger() {
    logps = new PrintStream(new FileOutputStream("log"));
}
```

Notice that these two constructors do nearly the same thing—they both use a String to create a PrintStream. In fact, the action of the second constructor is identical to the action of the first constructor if it had been passed "log" as its argument. We can act on this observation as follows: If, at the beginning of a constructor body, the word this is followed by parentheses (which may contain arguments), then the appropriate constructor for the class is invoked. Thus, we can rewrite the second constructor as

```
public Logger() {
    this("log");
}
```

Here, this followed by ("log") tells the compiler to look for *another* constructor of the class, one that is declared to take a single String parameter, and invoke that. This constructor invocation may be followed by other code and initializations as necessary.

Representing an Object as a String

In deciding how to output Name objects, we chose to write a print() method that received a PrintStream reference as an argument because we wanted it to be easy for the user to indicate the output target. By taking advantage of a convenience built in to Java, we can create an equally attractive alternative. Specifically, suppose we declare

```
Name pres = new Name("Calvin","Coolidge");
```

and later write

```
System.out.println(pres);
```

This seems as if it will generate a compiler error, because the compiler expects a `String` argument for `println()`, not a `Name` argument. At the same time, this does make a certain kind of *intuitive* sense; a human reader of this code could reasonably guess that we wanted to print out a `String` that somehow represented the value of `pres`. Furthermore, if we could do that, we could also write something like

```
anotherPrintStream.println(pres);
```

to print `pres` to a destination other than the screen.

Java provides a built-in mechanism that allows us to do exactly this. When the compiler sees a non-`String` reference where it expects a `String`, it checks to see whether the class of that reference defines a method with prototype

```
public String toString()
```

If so, the compiler causes a `toString()` message to be sent to the object referred to; the `String` returned is the `String` that will be output. So, in the case of our `Name` class, if we define a method

```
public String toString() {
    String output = title + " " + firstName + " " + lastName;
    return output;
}
```

then

```
System.out.println(pres);
```

will cause

```
Calvin Coolidge
```

to be printed to the screen.

If the prgrammer did not explicitly define a `toString()` method, a "default" definition of the method will be used, printing some generally unhelpful information about the object.

Comparing Two Objects

Suppose that we read in two `Name` objects and then wish to determine whether they represent the same name. How can we do this? Here is one possibility:

```
BufferedReader keyboard = new BufferedReader(
            new InputStreamReader(System.in));
Name n1 = Name.read(keyboard);
Name n2 = Name.read(keyboard);
```

```
if (n1 == n2)
   System.out.println("Same name?");
else
   System.out.println("Different names?");
```

If we put this code fragment in a program, however, the output will *always* be Different names? To see why, we have to consider carefully what kinds of things n1 and n2 are: They are references to Name objects. The line

```
if (n1 == n2)
```

is essentially asking if the values of n1 and n2 are the same—that is, if they *refer to the same object*. It's clear from their declarations that they do not. So this way of testing equality doesn't ask the right question—we want to know if the *states* of the objects referred to by n1 and n2 represent the same name. The ability to answer this question cannot be built into the Java compiler the way the ability to compare int values is. To understand why, we only have to examine the question itself: What does it mean for two Name objects to represent the same name? Our first response might be: "if their respective instance variables are equal." That's a perfectly legitimate response. But what about the Names President Calvin Coolidge and Mr. Calvin Coolidge and Mister Calvin Coolidge? Are they the same? That is, should a different title mean that the two Names are not equal? Perhaps.

Now, neither of these two options is clearly better than the other—we'd really have to know more about how the Name class was going to be used in order to choose one sensibly. But it's important to recognize that the decision is one we expect the *programmer* to make, not the compiler. In Java, a programmer describes how to decide whether two objects are equal by providing the class with an equals() method. This method takes a reference to an object as a parameter, and returns a boolean value. Thus, the prototype of this method in our case will be

```
public boolean equals(Name n)
```

To implement our first choice (insisting that all instance variables are equal), we can first observe that if two Name objects are equal, then their String representations as returned by toString() will be equal. We can test the equality of these values by first sending a toString() message to this, which will return a String reference. Then we can send an equals() message to that String. As a parameter to the equals() message, we will send the reference returned by n.toString(). The complete method, then, is

```
public boolean equals(Name n)
   this.toString().equals(n.toString());
}
```

With this method defined, we can then test the equality of n1 and n2 in our example above by writing

```
if (n1.equals(n2))        Or n2.equals(n1), equivalently
   System.out.println("Same name.");
else
   System.out.println("Different names.");
```

The complete Name class, including toString() and equals(), is as follows:

```
class Name {
   public Name(String first, String last) {
      firstName = first;
      lastName = last;
      title = new String("");
   }
   public String getInitials() {
      String  s;
      s = firstName.substring(0,1);
      s = s.concat(".");
      s = s.concat(lastName.substring(0,1));
      s = s.concat(".");
      return s;
   }
   public String getLastFirst() {
      return lastName + ", " + firstName;
   }
   public String getFirstLast() {
      return title + " " + firstName + " " + lastName;
   }
   public void setTitle(String newTitle) {
      title = newTitle;
   }
   public void print(PrintStream target) {
      target.print(title);
      target.print(" ");
      target.print(firstName);
      target.print(" ");
      target.print(lastName);
   }
   public static Name read(BufferedReader br) throws Exception {
      String first = br.readLine();
      String last = br.readLine();
      Name n = new Name(first,last);
      return n;
   }
   public String toString() {
      String output = title + " " + firstName + " " + lastName;
```

```
        return output;
    }
    public boolean equals(Name n)
        this.toString().equals(n.toString());
    }
    private String firstName;
    private String lastName;
    private String title;
}
```

5.6 Input Methods Revisited: Testing for End of Input

Many of the methods we have encountered return references as their return value: toUpperCase(), substring(), and the read() method of the Name class, for example. Usually these methods return a reference to an actual object, but occasionally we would like to return some indication that no object can be returned. This could happen in the read() method if no data remains in the file—if no data is present, then no object can be constructed.

The null Value

The keyword null is used in precisely such a situation. Unlike all other references, which refer to objects, null refers to *no object*. In addition, null may be assigned to reference variables of *any* class, and a reference variable can be tested to see if it contains null:

```
String s;
s = null;
if (s == null);    True
    ...
```

Using null in read() Methods

The readLine() method reads in a line of data from an InputStreamReader and returns an reference to a String object that is created from that line. In the event that there are no more data in the file (a condition known as *end-of-file*), read-Line() returns a null rather than a String object.

We wish to design our read() methods to mimic this behavior, returning null when there are no data to be read in. Let us modify the read() method of the Name class to include this feature. Specifically, we make the following modifications to this method: If the result of either of the readLine() invocations returns a null, indicating end-of-file, we will return null as the return value of our method:

```
public static Name read(BufferedReader br) throws Exception {
   String first = br.readLine();
   if (first == null)
      return null;
   String last = br.readLine();
   if (last == null)
      return null;
   Name n = new Name(first,last);
   return n;
}
```

Summary

A constructor is a method that is automatically invoked when an instance of a class is created. Constructors may receive parameters but have no return-type. A class definition may include several constructors that take different numbers and types of parameters.

One of the first steps in defining a class is developing the interface: the set of method names along with their parameter-types and return-types. Then the definition is filled in by identifying instance variables and implementing methods.

Class definitions may also include class methods that are not associated with any object of the class. Instead, these methods are invoked by using the name of the class in place of the receiver of the message. Class methods, also known as static methods, are commonly used to produce a new instance of the class based on external information such as input data. Wrapper classes such as `Integer` and "utility" classes such as `Math` also provide many useful static methods.

Variables can also be associated with classes rather than with objects. Class, or static, variables allow us to keep track of information that can't be associated with a particular instance of the class (such as the number of instances of the class that have been created). Variables that are declared as `final` do not change their value after initialization; that is, they are constant. Classes may define constant values by declaring `static final` variables.

Java provides several conveniences for manipulating objects. The keyword `this` always serves as a reference to the object whose method is currently executing. The `toString()` method provides a way for the compiler to convert an object into a `String` implicitly. The `equals()` method is universally used to test two objects for equality.

Key Terms

class method A method that is not associated with any particular object of a class but rather with the class itself. As a result, it can be invoked without reference to an object. Such a method is also called a static method.

class variable A variable that is not associated with any particular object of a class but rather with the class itself. As a result, it can be manipulated without reference to an object. Such a variable is also called a static variable.

default constructor The constructor automatically provided for a class if the programmer does not specify one; it takes no arguments.

instance method A method that is associated with a particular object of a class and therefore must be invoked via a reference to an object.

interface The collection of names, parameter-types, and return-types of all methods of a class.

static method A class method.

static variable A class variable.

Questions for Review

1. Why are constructors necessary? Why might a class need to provide more than one constructor?

2. Why are static methods necessary? Why can't a static method access instance variables?

3. Explain when a `public` variable might not be accessible to a method declared in the same class.

4. What techniques for creating instances of a class are available to users of that class?

Exercises

1. Modify the `Logger` class so that `Logger` objects that send their messages to `System.out` or `System.err` can be created. (Hint: Add another constructor.)

2. Modify the `Counter` class so that `Counter` objects initialized to a counter value other than 0 can be created.

3. Modify the `ThreewayLamp` class (see Exercises 11 of Chapter 4) so that `Three-wayLamp` objects can be created in a particular state: `"off"`, `"low"`, `"medium"`, or `"high"`. Add a constructor that takes a single `String` parameter.

4. Define an `Address` class. Proceed as in the development of the `Name` class in Section 5.2: determine its interface, identify instance variables, and implement its methods.

5. Define a `BankAccount` class. It should provide at least the following: a constructor that takes a name and an account number, `deposit()` and `withdraw()` methods, a `getAccountBalance()` that returns the number of dollars available, and an `isOverdrawn()` method that returns a `boolean`.

6. Write a static read() method for the Counter class that creates a Counter object initialized to a value read in from input (you will need to use Integer.parseInt()).

7. Modify any of our existing classes by adding a static method numCreated() that returns the number of instances of the class that have been created. Use a static variable to keep track of the count.

8. Modify the TypingTutor class by adding a static method getLongest() that returns a reference to the longest String used as a practice string.

9. Define a Robot class that has a constructor that takes two String parameters: a name and a model number (e.g., Robot r = new Robot("Robbie","R–128")). Each Robot created is assigned a unique serial number, starting at 1. The identify() method returns a String consisting of its name, model, and serial number. For example, r.identify() might return "Robbie R–128 37". Write a program that creates three Robots and prints their identifications.

10. Implement toString() and equals() methods for the Counter and Minimizer classes.

11. By modifying the Name class, design and implement a FullName class that represents names that may have a middle name and suffix (such as "Jr." or "Esq.") in addition to a title and first and last names.

Creating Controls and Interaction

Our first applet merely displayed a string on a web page—that's no big deal; we can do that with HyperText Markup Language (HTML) and not bother with Java. In our last supplement, we developed a simple animation—a little more exciting, but still just something that the user passively watches. Recall that the primary purpose of Java on the web is to provide active content—that is, web pages that can dynamically interact with users (web surfers) and compute things in response to that interaction. To do this, there has to be a means for communication between the program and the web user.

The Java class libraries provide an assortment of such communication means, all of them part of a graphical user interface. In other words, Java provides menus, text choices, buttons, check boxes, and an assortment of various graphical devices, all aimed at providing different means of communication between an applet and the user. In this section we will begin our exploration of these. In the process, we'll develop a modified version of our `FlipperApplet`, one in which the color of the rectangle "flips" only in response to a button click. Our executing `ButtonFlipperApplet` will look something like Figure 5.1. To create this applet, we have to address two topics:

- How to make the applet create "controls" such as buttons and place them on the screen
- How to make the applet respond to user interaction with these controls

More on the Life Cycle of Applets

Before we start throwing controls around, however, we need to learn a bit more about the life cycle of applets. When an applet is first loaded into the browser, the browser invokes its `init()` method. This always happens! You may be startled,

Figure 5.1
The executing
`ButtonFlipperApplet`.

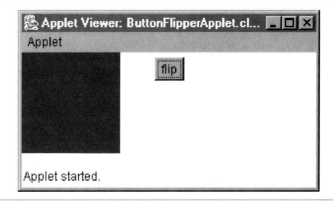

because our earlier applets did not have such a method. Remember, though—the FirstApplet class, the BouncingBallApplet class, and so on, possess all the methods of the Applet class, which they may replace with their own methods, such as paint(). The paint() method is invoked whenever the system detects the need for the applet to be displayed anew on the screen (for example, when it is first loaded, or later if something covered it up on the screen and then was moved). The init() method, on the other hand, is called just once, when the applet is first loaded into the browser. Its intended role is suggested by its name, *init*, that is, doing the initial setup for the applet. It is in the init() method that we must set up the controls that we want our applet to have, as follows:

```
public void init() {
        Carry out necessary setup here
}
```

Creating and Displaying Controls

Buttons that appear in the interface are modeled by Button objects. The Button constructor takes a String as an argument that will serve as a label in the button itself. So, our init() method will contain this Button constructor invocation:

```
Button flipButton = new Button("flip");
```

Creating controls is only part of what we must do. We must also accomplish the following:

- The controls should appear in the applet.
- The applet should be able to respond to the user's interactions with the controls.

The add() method, one of the methods that our applet possesses, handles the first of these. After we create a control, we pass a reference to it as a parameter to add() in order to display it. At this point, then, our ButtonFlipperApplet looks like this:

```
import java.awt.*;
import java.applet.*;
public class ButtonFlipperApplet extends Applet {
    public void init() {
        Button flipButton = new Button("flip");
        add(flipButton);
    }
}
```

Drawing the Rectangle

If we compile and execute this applet, the only thing that appears on the screen is a button labeled "flip"—clearly, this version of the applet does not include code to draw the rectangle. In the original FlipperApplet, this was done in the paint() method, which, in addition to drawing the rectangle, was also responsible for flipping the color of the rectangle. In ButtonFlipperApplet, we intend the color to flip only in response to a button click, so, at least initially, we'll give paint() only the responsibility of drawing the rectangle:

```
public void paint(Graphics g) {
   if (red)
      g.setColor(Color.red);
   else
      g.setColor(Color.blue);
   g.fillRect(0,0,100,100);
}
```

As before, we will also need to declare red as an instance variable:

```
private boolean red = true;
```

Handling Events

When we execute this version of the applet, we see a display that appears to be what we want. It's missing an important part of its behavior, though: Clicking the button elicits no response from the applet.

In order to respond to the button, the applet must somehow be *notified* when it is clicked on and then take some action. In our example, when the "flip" button is clicked on, we want the color of the rectangle to switch from red to blue or vice versa.

Clicking on a button on the interface is an example of an *event*. Think of an event as something the user does in the graphic interface to get the program's attention: clicking on a button, moving or clicking the mouse, closing a window. When an event occurs, there are three objects of interest:

- The object causing the event, for example, the button (when it is clicked). This object is called the *event source*.
- An object representing the event. For example, the event associated with clicking a button is represented by an ActionEvent object—so called because clicking a button usually indicates the user's desire for some action.
- The object that should respond to (or *handle*) the event, for example, our ButtonFlipperApplet object. This object is called the *listener*.

In our example, the only event that matters is clicking the "flip" button. When that button is clicked, the three objects of interest (see Figure 5.2) are

- The object referenced by flipButton—the event source
- An ActionEvent object to represent the click of the button

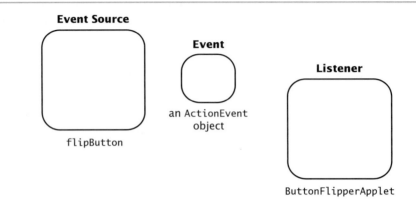

Figure 5.2
The three objects involved in handling an event.

- Our `ButtonFlipperApplet` object, which should handle the click by changing the color of the rectangle. It, therefore, is the listener.

When an event occurs, the source creates the corresponding event object. We would like the source object then to notify the listener that the event has occurred by sending it an event notification message. This message should pass the newly created event object as an argument. This can work only if

- The source knows which particular object is the listener.
- The listener object implements a method corresponding to the event-notification message it will receive; this method will handle the event.

These two requirements won't be met unless we program them into our applet. We have to tell the source (in our case, `flipButton`) which object is the listener (in our case, `ButtonFlipperApplet`), and we have to write the `ButtonFlipper-Applet` method that will handle the click event.

In our example, when the user clicks the button, the `flipButton` object (our event source) creates an `ActionEvent` object. It then sends an `action-Performed()` message to the `ButtonFlipperApplet` listener, with the `Action-Event` object as an argument. This can work only if

- The `flipButton` is aware that the `ButtonFlipperApplet` is a listener.
- The `ButtonFlipperApplet` object provides a method called `actionPerformed` that accepts an `ActionEvent` argument. (See Figure 5.3.)

To tell `flipButton` that the `ButtonFlipperApplet` is the listener, we send `flip-Button` an `addActionListener()` message, passing a reference to the `Button-FlipperApplet` object as an argument. We do this in the `ButtonFlipperApplet`'s `init()` method after creating the `flipButton` object:

```
flipButton.addActionListener(this);
```
Remember: this refers to the object executing this code (the `ButtonFlipperApplet` object).

This sends the `flipButton` object a message (`addActionListener()`) telling it that the applet object (`this`) should be sent an event notification message (`actionPerfomed()`) when the button is clicked. (See Figure 5.3.)

Now that we've made sure that `flipButton` will send a message to the applet, we must also make sure that applet has an `actionPerformed()` method. This is the method where we can specify what actually happens when the button is clicked:

```
public  void  actionPerformed(ActionEvent  ae)  {
    code to handle the event
}
```

When this method is invoked, we know that the button has been clicked, so we then need to do the following:

- Switch the color of the rectangle's display.
- Ask for the applet to be redisplayed (with the new color for the rectangle).

Therefore, the `actionPerformed()` method will be implemented as

```
public void actionPerformed(ActionEvent e) {
    red = !red;
    repaint();
}
```

To complete the applet, there are two small changes we must make in order to enable event handling. First, we need to add

```
import java.awt.event.*;
```

Figure 5.3
Sending an event-notification message. The `ActionEvent` object is created by `flipButton` as passed as an argument in the `action-Performed` message.

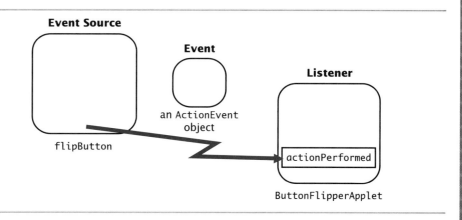

at the top of the applet. Second, we need to modify the prototype of the applet by adding the phrase implements ActionListener. Because not every applet is equipped (by virtue of methods like actionPerformed()) to handle events, we must indicate to the Java compiler that this applet *is* so equipped. The final form of the applet is

```java
import java.awt.*;
import java.applet.*;
import java.awt.event.*;

public class ButtonFlipperApplet extends Applet
implements ActionListener {
    public void init() {
        flipButton = new Button("flip");
        flipButton.addActionListener(this);
        this.add(flipButton);
    }

    public void paint(Graphics g) {
        if (red)
            g.setColor(Color.red);
        else
            g.setColor(Color.blue);
        g.fillRect(0,0,100,100);
    }

    public void actionPerformed(ActionEvent e) {
        red = !red;
        this.repaint();
    }

    private Button flipButton;
    private boolean red=true;
}
```

Note that, unlike the original FlipperApplet, occluding or minimizing the applet does *not* cause the rectangle's color to change. The paint() method is still invoked in this situation—as it is with every applet—but the behavior of paint() has changed. Because paint() is no longer responsible for changing the rectangle's color, and is instead responsible only for displaying the rectangle using the current color, simply redisplaying the applet will not affect the rectangle's color. Only a click of the button will have that effect.

Suggested Experiments

1. Write a modified version of the `BouncingBallApplet` in which the next frame will be displayed only in response to a button click. (You may want to increase the "velocity" of the ball or decrease the width of the applet so that the ball will bounce after just a few clicks.)

2. Write an applet that displays the string `"The button has been clicked x times,"` where the value of *x* increases by one each time the applet's button is clicked.

3. Write an applet that initially displays the string `"Hello"`. The applet will have one button; each time this button is clicked, an additional `'o'` is concatenated to the displayed string (so it appears as `"Hello"`, `"Helloo"`, `"Hellooo"`, and so on).

Chapter 6

Inside the Method: Imperative Programming

6.1 Introduction

Until now, most of our discussion has centered on the object-oriented aspects of programming in Java—sending messages, defining classes, creating objects, and so on. This discussion has been augmented with short presentations of some of Java's imperative programming constructs, such as primitive data types and conditional statements, along with some simple algorithms. Now that we have introduced some of the fundamentals of object-oriented programming, in this chapter we will fill in much of Java's imperative programming framework: We'll consider the rest of Java's primitive types, we'll introduce a limited form of *iteration*, or repetition, and we'll look at more complex forms of Boolean expressions and conditional statements. We will begin this exploration by considering some examples from engineering and scientific computation.

6.2 A Metric Conversion Class

In some parts of the world, the metric system of measurement has yet to be fully accepted. Instead, it co-exists with the "English" system, which uses units such as inches, feet, and miles. Therefore, we frequently need to be able to convert measurements from one system to the other. In this section, we'll develop a `Metric` class that will perform some of the necessary calculations. A complete class of this kind would provide methods for many different conversions, but for simplicity's sake we will focus on converting from feet to meters (other conversions would be treated similarly). We will provide two methods related to this conversion. One, `convertFeetToMeters()`, will take as a parameter a measurement in feet—say, 3.5—and return the equivalent number of meters. The other, `printFeetToMetersTable()`, will take as a parameter some number of feet—say, 10—and print out a table containing the conversions for 1 foot, 2 feet, and so on, up to the parameter value.

Modeling the Numbers of Measurement

Before we begin implementing these methods, we need to address one issue: How can we represent a number like 3.5? We have already seen that Java provides some facilities for representing numeric values: In Chapters 2 and 3 we discussed the primitive type int and the related types long, short, and byte, all of which are used to represent different ranges of integer values.

Integers are the numbers of *counting*. If we want to know, for example, how many students are taking calculus this semester, we could either multiply the number of sections being offered (suppose there are five) by the number of students in each section (say, 30) to arrive at the solution—or we could directly count each student. Assuming all the sections are full, we would arrive at the same value. Furthermore, as long as we count carefully, the precision of our result cannot be questioned—the only reason for saying that the number of students in a university is "around 16,000" is that we have chosen not to count carefully.

In measurement, we often obtain numbers that are *not* integers but that have fractional parts (6.5 or 3.14159, for example). In this situation, precision is *always* an issue. We can measure the length of a desk and come up with 1.45 meters. But is it really 1.45 meters? If a more careful measurement yields 1.47 meters, then our first measurement was just plain wrong. But if a more careful measurement yields 1.452, then we can't say the first was wrong—it just wasn't as precise as the second. The first measurement has a precision of three digits, while the second has a precision of four.

Precision issues affect calculations based on measurement. Suppose a photograph measures 6.4 inches long and 3.3 inches wide. We might claim that its area is 6.4 * 3.3 = 21.12 square inches. Is this reasonable? We measured each linear dimension with a precision of two digits, so how can the calculated area have a precision of four digits? In fact, it can't: If a more precise measurement shows that the dimensions are, for example, 6.41 by 3.32, then the resulting calculated area is 21.28, which shows that our first calculation was incorrect.

Scientists and engineers avoid this problem by recognizing that when we multiply two measured values, the precision of the result can't be better than the least precise of the measured values. So in our first area calculation, the scientifically correct value is 21 square inches, with a precision of two digits.

So, most of the numbers used in scientific and engineering applications have a different behavior from integers or even from the set of real numbers from mathematics. In the integer world, 64 * 33 is 2112, but using the number of measurement it is 2100: The answer 2112 implies four digits of precision, but each of our measurements has only two digits of precision.

The float and double Primitive Data Types

In computer science, numbers that have this behavior are called **floating-point numbers**. The term derives from the way computer hardware handles operations involving these values and the way these values are represented in memory.

Java provides two primitive data types for modeling floating-point behavior: **float** and **double**. The float data type models floating-point numbers with approximately 7 digits of precision, `double` with 15 digits of precision. The range for both of these greatly exceeds that of `int`, which only represents integers between −2 billion and 2 billion (approximately). The largest value a `float` can have is

   340282350000000000000000000000000000000

or

   3.4028235×10^{38}

or, as we would write it in Java:

   `3.4028235E38f`

The smallest positive value a `float` can have is

   0.000000000000000000000000000000000000000000000014012985

or, in scientific notation,

   $1.4012985 \times 10^{-45}$

or, as we would write it in Java,

   `1.4012985E-45f`

Exactly the same range applies to negative numbers represented as `float` values. The range for `doubles` is even huger, ranging from $2.2250738585072014 \times 10^{-308}$ to $1.79769313486231570 \times 10^{+308}$ (and similarly for negative values).

A `float` and an `int` take up the same amount of memory. So how can the `float` represent numbers from

   −340282350000000000000000000000000000000

to

   340282350000000000000000000000000000000

when an `int` can only represent numbers from −2147483648 to 2147483647? It's simple: The `float` can't represent *all* the numbers in that huge range, only those with seven or eight digits of precision. For example, a `float` can't represent 1,234,567,089, which is a perfectly good `int` value! The closest it can come to this value is 1,234,567,000.

Implementing `convertFeetToMeters()`

Both the parameter and return value of the `convertFeetToMeters()` method are numbers of measurement, so their types should be either `float` or `double`. Unless we know ahead of time that seven-digit precision will be adequate, we should use `double` for both in order to make our method as generally useful as possible. Thus, the prototype for the method is

```
public double convertFeetToMeters(double feet)
```

The method body is straightforward: We just need to multiply `feet` by the number of meters per foot, which is exactly 0.3048, and return the result:

```
public double convertFeetToMeters(double feet) {
    return feet * 0.3048;
}
```

As we discussed in Chapter 5, it is better to avoid using "magic numbers" like 0.3048 in our code—someone reading this method might be able to guess what this number represents, but we don't want people reading our code to have to guess. Instead, we'll add a constant definition to the `Metric` class:

```
public static final double METERSPERFOOT = 0.3048;
```

This approach has two advantages. First, we can rewrite `convertFeetToMeters()` to make it more readable:

```
public double convertFeetToMeters(double feet) {
    return feet * METERSPERFOOT;
}
```

Second, anyone using this class can, if desired, access this constant value directly by writing

```
Metric.METERSPERFOOT
```

The `printFeetToMetersTable()` Method: Iteration

The heart of our `printFeetToMetersTable()` method will be a fragment of code that repeatedly computes and prints foot/meter conversions for a sequence of values. This is a new programming technique: Up until now we have written programs that dealt with one object or one value at a time—`check()`-ing a single value in a `Minimizer`, printing a single `Name`, converting a single measurement from feet to meters, and so on. What we can do for one, though, we often would like to do for many: `check()`-ing a sequence of input values in a `Minimizer`, printing a list of `Name`s, printing a table of measurement conversions. Once we have determined how to perform a single calculation, we should be able to repeat that calculation as many times as desired.

Iteration (the ability to perform an action repeatedly) is the second of the techniques that alter the flow of program execution—the other being the conditional, which we introduced in Chapter 2. Much of the power of programming comes from this ability. Our conversion calculation is a simple matter of multiplying two values; however, performing that calculation for fifty or one hundred values becomes a tedious, repetitive, and thus error-prone (for humans) task. Computers, on the other hand, do not get bored and are not subject to the errors that arise from repetition and quantity.

Our `printFeetToMetersTable()` method will take a single `int` parameter called `maxFeet`, representing a number of feet, and will print a line containing conversion information for 1 foot, 2 feet, and so on, up to maxFeet. Because the method only generates output, it will return nothing, so its prototype is

```
public void printFeetToMetersTable(int maxFeet)
```

For example, if the value of maxFeet is 7, then the output should look like this:

```
Feet       Meters
1          0.3048
2          0.6096
3          0.9144
4          1.2192
5          1.524
6          1.8288
7          2.1336
```

Our strategy is to take one piece of code that converts one measurement in feet into meters and repeat this maxFeet times. This code can invoke the convert-FeetToMeters() method to perform the conversion, then print out a line of the table. We haven't yet determined where to get the value to be converted, but the code will look something like this:

repeat maxFeet *times:*
```
    double feet = to be determined
    double meters = convertFeetToMeters(feet);
    System.out.println(feet + "          " + meters);
```

We want to repeat this maxFeet many times, but arrange for feet to take a different value (1, 2, 3, and so on) each time. Furthermore, we need to keep count of how many times this code has been executed so that the iteration process stops at the right time. The way to remember something in a program is to store it in a variable, so we'll need a variable to keep track of the count. Such **counter** variables are traditionally (yet another programming idiom) named i, j, or k. After each conversion calculation, we'll increase the value of i by one and compare it to maxFeet to see whether it's time to stop.

Implementing a Counting Loop with for

This form of iteration, known as a **counting loop** because it performs a task a specified number of times, is most easily implemented using a for statement. The for statement has two parts: a *header*, which controls how the iteration proceeds, and a *body*, which describes the calculation to be performed within each iteration. We determined the loop body above:

```
    double feet = to be determined
    double meters = convertFeetToMeters(feet);
    System.out.println(feet + "          " + meters);
```

We know enough about our iteration to write the header: The iteration is to start at 1, stop when the calculation for maxFeet is completed, and increment the value being calculated by 1 from one iteration to the next. To express these conditions, we write

```
for (int i=1; i <= maxFeet; i++)
```

Every `for` loop header has three sections separated by semicolons (see Figure 6.1). The first is the *initialization assignment*, which takes place once before any iterations occur; here we declare a counter variable `i` and initialize it to 1. The second is the *loop condition*, a `boolean` expression that describes whether the loop should continue: As long as its value is `true` the loop will continue. The third is the *increment*; this describes how the counter value changes from one iteration to the next.

Now that we've described how our iteration should operate and developed most of the loop body, we need to determine the value assigned to `feet` each time the loop body is executed. Notice that the value being converted is very closely related to the value of `i` (i.e., the count of *how many* conversions have been performed): After we convert 1 foot to meters, one conversion has been made; after we convert 2 feet to meters, two conversions have been made. This continues until the count reaches `maxFeet`; after `maxFeet` has been converted, the iteration should stop. Thus, we can simply use the value of `i` as the value to be converted:

```
double feet = (double) i;
```

We used this technique, called *casting*, in Chapter 3 to convert a `long` value to an `int`; similarly, we use it here to convert an `int` value to a `double` value. We may write the complete loop as follows:

```
for (i=1; i <= maxFeet; i++) {
    double feet = (double) i;
    double meters = convertFeetToMeters(feet);
    System.out.println(feet + "         " + meters);
}
```

To make the output a little more readable, we'll print out some column headings before executing the `for` statement. Here is the entire `Metric` class:

```
class Metric {
    public double convertFeetToMeters(double feet) {
        return feet * METERSPERFOOT;
    }
```

Figure 6.1

Parts of a `for` loop header.

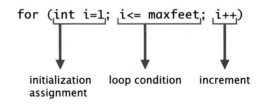

```
public void printFeetToMetersTable(int maxFeet) {
    System.out.println("Feet     Meters");
    for (i=1; i <= maxFeet; i++) {
        double feet = (double) i;
        double meters = convertFeetToMeters(feet);
        System.out.println(feet + "        " + meters);
    }
}
public static final double METERSPERFOOT = 0.3048;
}
```

Java Interlude   *float, double, **and the** for **Statement***

Printing float and double

As was the case with int, the println() and print() methods of PrintStream are overloaded to accept and then display floats and doubles.

Rather than print gigantic Strings such as

     340282350000000000000000000000000000000

the format for printing floats and doubles borrows from scientific notation:

     3.4028235×10^{38}

Because superscripts are traditionally not easy to print, the power of 10 is represented by the letter E followed by the value of the exponent:

     3.4028235E38

Float and Double Wrapper Classes

Just as Java provides an Integer wrapper class corresponding to the primitive type int, it also provides classes Double and Float corresponding to the primitive types double and float. These classes provide, among others, the static methods parseDouble() and parseFloat(), which work exactly as the Integer.parseInt() method does: They each take a String parameter representing a numeric value and convert that String into a value of the appropriate type.

float and double Literals

Literals of type float and double can be written using the scientific notation style. The decimal point, the fraction, and the exponent may all be omitted. Thus, the following literals are equal: 98.6, 986e–1, 0.986e2, and 9.86e1. To distinguish float from double, float literals must have a trailing f, as, for example, 3.14159f. To distinguish them from int literals, double literals with no decimal point or exponent (i.e., those that look like int literals) must have a trailing d, as, for example, 98d.

Using `float` and `double`

Despite their profound differences with integer types, the syntax for using `float` and `double` is comfortingly similar to that for `int`. Consider the following code that computes the area of a circle whose radius is 12:

```
double area, radius;
radius = 12.0;
area = 3.14159*radius*radius;
```

The familiar `int` operators +, –, *, and / (not % though!) are used. The general meanings are the same, but the behavior is different.

For example,

```
int        j = 1222333444;
float      x = 1222333444.0f;

System.out.println("j =" + j);
System.out.println("x =" + x);
j = j + 1;
x = x + 1.0;
System.out.println("j =" + j);
System.out.println("x =" + x);
```

displays

```
j = 1222333444
x = 1.22233344E9
j = 1222333445
x = 1.22233344E9
```

The increment to `j` changed its value as expected; the increment to `x` did not because only the most significant seven digits or so are maintained in a `float`.

When to Use `float` and `double`

By now it should be clear that `float` and `double` were designed for a very specific purpose: to model numbers related to measurement. When you encounter scientific or engineering problems that demand this data type, the need will be obvious.

Often, `double` is used in contexts that have nothing to do with measurement. It is used for the following reasons:

- `double` supports fractions (digits past the decimal point).
- `double` has a great enough precision (around 15 digits) so that as long as the values stay within the 100 trillion range, no additions will be lost (as we saw happened with `float` earlier).

Thus, you may find that some programmers will represent dollar quantities—things that are ultimately counted, not measured—with `doubles`, making the calculation of cents or other fractional parts easier.

On the other hand, you will find that `doubles` (and `floats`) are legitimately used in graphical calculations. That's because graphics involves geometry (a word meaning "*measurement* of the Earth").

A useful rule is this: Floating-point arithmetic is acceptable when you are satisfied to compute a result just within a certain precision.

Mixed Type Arithmetic

The rules governing assignment between `doubles` and `floats` follow the same principle as `long` and `int`: If it is certain that no information will be lost, the assignment is legal. Thus, `float` may be assigned to `double`, but the reverse requires a cast.

When mixing integer types and floating-point types, the general rule is that integer types may be assigned to floating-point types, but the reverse requires a cast. Be warned, however, that assigning a `long` to a `float` or `double` can result in information being lost. The idea is that `float` or `double` can represent numbers at least as large as the largest `long` but without the same degree of precision.

The Execution of a `for` Statement

As we saw earlier, every `for` statement has four components: an initialization assignment, a loop condition, an increment, and a body. Figure 6.2 shows how these components are related. The initialization assignment is executed first, then the loop condition is tested. Note that it is possible for the loop condition to be `false` the first time it is tested—in our case, this could happen if the value of `maxFeet` is 0, for example. If the condition is `false`, the loop stops and the statement following the `for` statement is executed. If the condition is `true`, then the body of the loop is executed, followed by the increment. Then the loop condition is tested again; this process continues until the condition becomes `false`.

Figure 6.2
Execution of the `for` statement.

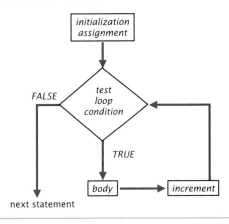

6.3 Approximating the Value of π

In this section we will use floating-point numbers and `for` loops to perform a more complex mathematical computation: approximating the value of π. To accomplish this, we will use a technique known as *Monte Carlo calculation*—so called because it relies on probability rather than direct computation, just as the gamblers at the casinos of Monte Carlo rely (fallaciously) on probability to bring them profit.

Suppose we have a square dartboard such as the one shown in Figure 6.3, with the top third shaded. Imagine that we have a completely unskilled dart tosser— he's a total klutz who has no control over the placement of the darts, so they strike the board in completely random locations. We'll consider only the darts that actually hit the square, and we'll ignore the ones that hit the wall and the people next to him. If our dart-tosser lands 300 darts on the board, about how many of them should land in the shaded area? Because the dart placement is completely random, we expect the 300 darts to be spread fairly evenly across the board—no part of the board is more likely to receive a dart than any other. The shaded area represents one third of the board, so approximately one third of the 300 darts—98 or 104 or some similar number—should land in the shaded area. Thus, the fraction of darts landing in the shaded area should be very close to the ratio of the shaded area to the area of the entire board. Of course, it is unlikely that *exactly* 100 darts will land in the shaded area, so our result is only approximate—but if we wanted a more accurate answer we could (in principle) toss 30,000 or 30 million darts.

In this example, the utility of tossing darts isn't completely clear: If we know the shaded area takes up one third of the board, why do we need to bother tossing a bunch of darts? But consider the dartboard in Figure 6.4: What is the area of the shaded portion? This is very difficult to determine directly, but our random dart-tossing technique will work just fine. If we toss a thousand darts at the board and 248 of them land in the shaded area, we can conclude that the shaded part occupies about a quarter of the board.

Figure 6.3
A square dartboard.

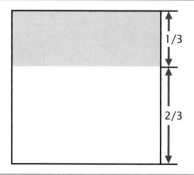

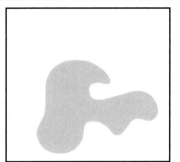

Figure 6.4
What is the area of
the shaded portion?

How can we use this technique to calculate an approximate value for π? If we use it to determine the area of a circle inscribed in a square dartboard, we can use the result to calculate the value of π. Consider Figure 6.5: We have

radius = r

Because the radius is half the width of square, we know that

side of square = $2r$

When we toss darts at the board, the fraction of darts in the circle will tell us approximately the ratio of the area of the circle to the area of the square. What should this ratio be? The area of a square is the square of the length of its side, so

area of square = $(2r)^2 = (2r) \times (2r) = 4r^2$

and the area of a circle is defined to be

area of circle = πr^2

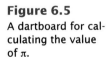

Figure 6.5
A dartboard for cal-
culating the value
of π.

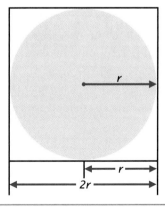

so the ratio of the area of the circle to the area of the square is

$$\text{ratio of areas} = \frac{\text{area of circle}}{\text{area of square}} = \frac{\pi r^2}{4r^2} = \frac{\pi}{4}$$

Thus,

$$\pi = 4 \times \text{ratio of areas}$$

so, we can estimate π by computing

$$\pi = 4 \times \text{fraction of darts in the circle}$$

Modeling the Dartboard

To perform this calculation, we will model the random dart thrower along with the circle-in-a-square dartboard by implementing three classes:

CLASS	MODELS	RESPONSIBILITY
Toss	One dart's location on the dartboard	Produces random tosses; Toss object "knows" where it lands.
Dartboard	A dartboard with a circle marked on it	Keeps track of how many Toss objects strike within circle.
MonteCarloPi	A klutzy guy who takes advantage of his inability to throw darts in order to compute π	Arranges for Toss objects to strike the Dartboard; Asks Dartboard for fraction striking circle; Computes π.

Writing the main() Method

To determine exactly what kind of behavior we'll need to provide in the Dartboard and Toss classes, let's begin by writing the MonteCarloPi class, that is, the main() method of our program.

We will allow the user to specify the number of darts to be tossed at the board, so we'll first prompt the user for this value and read in the response:

```
public class MonteCarloPi {
   public static void main(String[] a) throws Exception {
      BufferedReader br = new BufferedReader(
                          new InputStreamReader(System.in));
      System.out.print("How many darts should I toss at the board? ");
      String s = br.readLine();
      int numberOfDarts = Integer.parseInt(s.trim());
```

Then we need to create a Dartboard to receive the darts. Although the size of the dartboard doesn't matter to our calculation, both our Dartboard object and our

Toss objects (which represent locations on the board) need to be in agreement about the size of the board. MonteCarloPi will be responsible for ensuring this by providing size information to these objects; in the case of Dartboard, the easiest way to do this will be by passing the radius of the circle as a parameter to the Dartboard constructor:

```
double radius = 1.0;
Dartboard d = new Dartboard(radius);
```

Next, we need to model tossing numberOfDarts darts at the board. Note that this requires repeatedly tossing a single dart. This requires a counting loop that will iterate numberOfDarts times with each iteration modeling one dart toss. Thus, the header of this loop will be

```
for (int i=1; i <= numberOfDarts; i++)
```

To simulate each dart toss, we need to create an instance of Toss corresponding to a randomly placed dart, then "toss" it at the dartboard. To create the Toss object, our first instinct might be to invoke a Toss constructor. But the constructors of a properly designed Toss class won't provide the behavior we desire: Because the Toss class models any kind of dart toss (random or not), it wouldn't be sensible for the Toss default constructor to create a random toss. Alternatively, we could pass random numbers as parameters to a constructor describing the location of the toss, but the randomization of the tosses should be the responsibility of the Toss class. Instead, we'll use a static method of Toss to get an instance representing a random toss, just as we used static methods in Chapter 5 to create an instance based on values read from input. As we mentioned above, we need to communicate the size of the board to the Toss object to make sure it has a sensible location, so to create this Toss instance we'll write

```
Toss t = Toss.getRandom(radius);
```

where the static method getRandom() returns a reference to a Toss object representing a random dart toss. Once we have the instance, we'll send a strike() message to the Dartboard d, with t as a parameter, to model the dart striking the dartboard:

```
d.strike(t);
```

Thus, the entire loop is

```
for (int i=1; i <= numberOfDarts; i++) {
    Toss t = Toss.getRandom(radius);
    d.strike(t);
}
```

After we toss the darts at the board, all we have to do is learn what fraction of them struck inside the circle and use that value to calculate π. Because the Dartboard object is responsible for keeping track of where each dart lands, it must also be responsible for calculating the fraction of darts that landed inside the circle. Thus, we just need to send d a message asking for the value of that fraction, then multiply that value by 4.0 (note that these values are doubles, not ints), and output the result:

```
double fractionIn = d.getFractionIn();
double pi = 4.0 * fractionIn;
System.out.println("Pi is approximately " + pi);
```

The completed class is

```
public class MonteCarloPi {
    public static void main(String[] a) throws Exception {
        BufferedReader br = new BufferedReader(
                                new InputStreamReader(System.in));
        System.out.print("How many darts should I toss at the board? ");
        String s = br.readLine();
        int numberOfDarts = Integer.parseInt(s.trim());
        double radius = 1.0;
        Dartboard d = new Dartboard(radius);

        for (int i=1; i <= numberOfDarts; i++) {
            Toss t = Toss.getRandom(radius);
            d.strike(t);
        }

        double fractionIn = d.getFractionIn();
        double pi = 4.0 * fractionIn;
        System.out.println("Pi is approximately "+pi);
    }
}
```

Implementing the Dartboard Class

Based on our use of the Dartboard class, we can sketch the class definition as follows:

```
class Dartboard {
    public Dartboard(double radius) {
    }
    public void strike(Toss toss) {
    }
    public double getFractionIn() {
    }
    instance variables
}
```

Furthermore, we know what behavior we desire of each method: The constructor should perform necessary initializations (it's not yet clear exactly what those will be), strike() should "process" one dart toss—in particular, it must determine whether the dart represented by `toss` struck inside or outside the circle—and `getFractionIn()` should calculate and return the fraction of darts that struck inside the circle.

From this analysis, we can begin to identify some instance variables. The value of `radius` received by the constructor is needed by `strike()` to determine whether a dart lands inside or outside the circle, so we need an instance variable

```
private double radius;
```

The `getFractionIn()` method needs to know the number of darts that struck inside or outside the circle, but these values are set by `strike()`. Furthermore, these counts should be initialized to 0 by the constructor. Thus, we need instance variables

```
private int insideCircle, outsideCircle;
```

As we start implementing the methods, we may discover that we need additional instance variables, but this is a good start.

Let's begin with the constructor. We have already determined its behavior: It needs to store the value of the `radius` parameter in the `radius` instance variable and it needs to initialize `insideCircle` and `outsideCircle` to 0:

```
public Dartboard(double radius) {
    this.radius = radius;
    insideCircle = 0;
    outsideCircle = 0;
}
```

The `strike()` method is more complicated. Given a Toss object `toss`, it must determine whether the location represented by `toss` lies within a circle with radius `radius`. Before we progress with our implementation, we must make some decisions about how locations are to be represented. To make the calculations as simple as possible, we'll imagine that our dartboard is superimposed on the (x, y) coordinate plane as shown in Figure 6.6. The point (0.0,0.0) lies at the center of

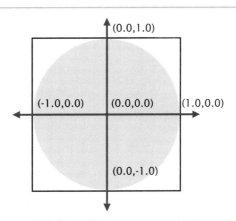

Figure 6.6
The (x, y) coordinate plane.

the circle, and the axes intersect the sides of the square at the points shown (recall that we decided to make the value of radius 1.0). A location, then, is just an (x,y) coordinate, where the values of x and y range from −1.0 to 1.0.

Before we can make any calculations, we must first learn the location represented by toss. To get the x and y values of the location from toss we'll send it two messages: getX() and getY().

```
public void strike(Toss toss) {
    double x = toss.getX();
    double y = toss.getY();
```

To determine whether a location lies within the circle, we can use the Pythagorean theorem, which says that in a right triangle with legs of lengths x and y and hypotenuse of length z,

$$x^2 + y^2 = z^2$$

Consider Figure 6.7: For any point (x,y) on the board, we can draw a right triangle with legs of length x and y. The length of the hypotenuse is the point's distance from the origin. If this length is less than the radius, then the point is in the circle; otherwise it's outside the circle. According to the Pythagorean theorem, the value of z is

$$z = \sqrt{x^2 + y^2}$$

Thus, to find out if a point is inside the circle, we just compare

$$\sqrt{x^2 + y^2}$$

to the radius.

Figure 6.7
Using the Pythagorean theorem.

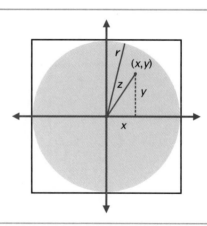

To compute the square root in Java, we use one of the many static methods provided in the Math class: Math.sqrt(). So, to compute z, we write

```
double z = Math.sqrt(x*x + y*y);
```

Then we compare z to the radius: If z is less, then the location is inside the circle, so we increment insideCircle; otherwise we increment outsideCircle:

```
if (z < radius)
    insideCircle++;
else
    outsideCircle++;
```

So the complete strike() implementation is

```
public void strike(Toss toss) {
    double x = toss.getX();
    double y = toss.getY();
    double z = Math.sqrt(x*x + y*y);
    if (z < radius)
        insideCircle++;
    else
        outsideCircle++;
}
```

Finally, we must implement getFractionIn(). This method just needs to divide the number of darts landing inside the circle (insideCircle) by the total number of darts thrown (insideCircle+outsideCircle) and return the result as a double. To ensure that floating-point arithmetic is used in the calculation, we will cast each of our results to double:

```
public double getFractionIn() {
    double total = (double) (insideCircle + outsideCircle);
    return (double) insideCircle/total;
}
```

This completes the Dartboard class:

```
class Dartboard {
    public Dartboard(double radius) {
        this.radius = radius;
        insideCircle = 0;
        outsideCircle = 0;
    }

    public void strike(Toss toss) {
        double x = toss.getX();
        double y = toss.getY();
```

```
        if (Math.sqrt(x*x + y*y) < radius)
            insideCircle++;
        else
            outsideCircle++;
    }

    public double getFractionIn() {
        double total = (double) (insideCircle+outsideCircle);
        return (double) insideCircle/total;
    }

    private double radius;
    private int insideCircle, outsideCircle;
}
```

Implementing the Toss Class

As with the Dartboard, we have already developed much of the skeleton of the Toss class:

```
class Toss {
    public double getX() {
    }
    public double getY() {
    }
    public static Toss getRandom(double radius) {
    }
    instance variables
}
```

The behaviors of getX() and getY() are straightforward: They return the *x* and *y* components, respectively, of the dart's location. The getRandom() static method must create a new instance of Toss and assign random values to its *x* and *y* coordinates. We can see that we are missing a crucial part of the class definition: a constructor. Even though no other class invokes a Toss constructor, we must define one that can be used by getRandom() to create the new instance. It is the responsibility of getRandom() to determine these random values, so our constructor must receive two parameters corresponding to the *x* and *y* coordinates of the new instance's location:

```
    public Toss (double x, double y) {
    }
```

At this point, it is clear that we will need instance variables for the *x* and *y* coordinates, because these values are set by the constructor but must be accessed by getX() and getY():

```
    private double x,y;
```

With these declared, the implementations of the constructor, getX(), and getY() are simple:

```java
public Toss(double x, double y) {
    this.x = x;
    this.y = y;
}
public double getX() {
    return x;
}
public double getY() {
    return y;
}
```

The getRandom() method is where the real work gets done: It must generate random x and y coordinates and then invoke the Toss constructor. Fortunately, Java provides a method that does most of the work of generating these random values: The static method Math.random() returns a random double value between 0.0 and 1.0. In our situation, we want random numbers between radius and −radius, so we must do a little more work. Specifically, for each coordinate we will use *two* random numbers. We will use one to determine the sign of the coordinate: If the random number is greater than 0.5 we will assign a positive sign, otherwise we will assign a negative sign. The other number will determine the size of coordinate: To transform a number between 0.0 and 1.0 into a number between 0.0 and radius, we just multiply by radius. See Figure 6.8 for a diagram of how these random numbers are used.

To calculate the x coordinate, then, we generate two random numbers between 0.0 and 1.0, size and sign. First, we multiply size by radius; then, if sign isn't above 0.5, we negate size:

```java
public static Toss getRandom(double radius) {
    double x,y;
```

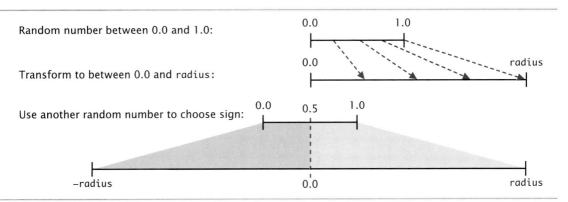

Figure 6.8   Using random numbers to generate random coordinate values.

```
double size = Math.random();
double sign = Math.random();
size = size * radius;
if (sign > 0.5)
    x = size;
else
    x = -size;
```

We perform exactly the same calculations to determine the y coordinate; before doing so, we must assign two new random numbers to size and sign:

```
size = Math.random();
sign = Math.random();
size = size * radius;
if (sign > 0.5)
    y = size;
else
    y = -size;
```

Finally, we invoke the Toss constructor with these x and y values and return a reference to the newly created object:

```
    return new Toss(x,y);
}
```

The completed Toss implementation is

```
class Toss {
    public Toss(double x, double y) {
        this.x = x;
        this.y = y;
    }
    public double getX() {
        return x;
    }
    public double getY() {
        return y;
    }
    public static Toss getRandom(double radius) {
        double x,y;
        double size = Math.random();
        double sign = Math.random();
        size = size * radius;
        if (sign > 0.5)
            x = size;
        else
            x = -size;
```

In this method, x and y refer to local variables, not instance variables

```
      size = Math.random();
      sign = Math.random();
      size = size * radius;
      if (sign > 0.5)
         y = size;
      else
         y = - size;
      return new Toss(x,y);
   }
   private double x,y;
}
```

Using the MonteCarloPi Class

Here are the results from running MonteCarloPi a few times with different numbers of darts:

NUMBER OF DARTS	APPROXIMATED VALUE OF π
100	3.28
1,000	3.196
10,000	3.1472
1,000,000	3.139568

As the number of darts increases, the quality of the approximation slowly increases.

6.4 Cascaded and Compound Conditional Statements

In Chapters 2 and 3, we briefly discussed conditional statements—statements that allow a program to choose a course of action depending on whether a condition is met—and Boolean variables and expressions—quantities that take the values true and false. In this section, we will see that both of these concepts can take more complex, and therefore more widely useful, forms.

A Car Class

To facilitate our discussion, let's consider implementing a class that models a car. This class will model only some of the aspects relevant to car ownership, specifically, the car's make, model, year, and warranty. Each of these quantities will be represented by an instance variable, and we will implement just two methods: a constructor and a chooseWarranty() method. The constructor will set the values of the make, model, and year variables, and the chooseWarranty() method will set the value of the warranty variable. Thus, the class skeleton is

```
class Car {
   public Car(String make, String model, int year);
```

```
public void chooseWarranty(parameters);
private String make;
private String model;
private int year;
private String warranty;
}
```

Implementing the constructor is straightforward:

```
public Car(String make, String model, int year) {
    this.make = make;
    this.model = model;
    this.year = year;
    warranty = "None";        No warranty given yet
}
```

Implementing `chooseWarranty()`: Multiway Tests

For our first implementation of `chooseWarranty()` we will assume that the type of warranty depends on the amount of mileage for which the owner desires coverage: 36,000 miles or less is a Standard warranty, up to 50,000 is an Extended warranty, and up to 100,000 is a Sucker warranty. The `chooseWarranty()` method will therefore receive an `int` parameter called `mileage`, and it will set the value of `warranty` to be one of "Standard", "Extended", or "Sucker". Values of `mileage` greater than 100,000 will set the value of `warranty` to "None".

The `if` statement provides a clean mechanism for selecting one of two actions based on the test of a single true/false condition. Our situation, though, is a little more involved: It resolves to more than two alternatives, so we need a *multiway test*. Here is one way to implement `chooseWarranty()` based on these rules:

```
public void chooseWarranty(int mileage) {
    if (mileage <= 36000)
        warranty = "Standard";
    else if (mileage <= 50000)
        warranty = "Extended";
    else if (mileage <= 100000)
        warranty = "Sucker";
    else
        warranty = "None";
}
```

Although this code sequence may seem obvious, let us examine it just a bit. The first `if` distinguishes the Standard case from everything else. Its true part therefore assigns "Standard" to `warranty` for `mileage <= 36000`. The false part then distinguishes two further alternatives: `36000 < mileage <= 50000` and `mileage > 50000`. We distinguish between these by a second `if` statement.

The true part of this second `if` corresponds to the case where `mileage` is greater than 36,000 (because the first condition was false) and less than or equal to 50,000. The false part corresponds to the case where `mileage` is greater than 50,000; this case is then further distinguished by the third `if`.

This style of code fragment, a sequence of conditionals taking the form

```
if (...)
    ...
else if (...)
    ...
else
    ...
```

that tests two or more conditions is often called a **cascaded if/else**. Of the various forms we will be presenting it is considered the cleanest and most understandable. Note the style of indentation; an alternative is

```
if (mileage <= 36000)
    warranty = "Standard";
else
    if (mileage <= 50000)
        warranty = "Extended";
    else
        if (mileage <= 100000)
            warranty = "Sucker";
        else
            warranty = "None";
```

This style emphasizes that the second `if` is contained within the first `else`. We usually avoid this form for the following reasons:

- Situations requiring multiple embedded conditionals such as the above occur frequently. The second style causes the code to march across the page, producing code that is unreadable and making it difficult to distinguish what code is of the same indentation level:

```
if (...)
        ...
else
    if (...)
            ...
        else
            if (...)
                    ...
                else
                    if (...)
                        ...
```

- The second conditional being embedded within the else of the first is merely a consequence of the if statement providing only two alternatives. There is really nothing subsidiary about the second conditional. All we are doing is testing the value of mileage against several ranges. Leaving the indentation at the same level and placing the if on the same line as the containing else emphasizes this.

Compound Conditions

Most warranty programs are not based solely on the mileage of the vehicle but also consider the age of the car. For example, a warranty might be valid only if the car has no more than 36,000 miles and is no more than 36 months old. Let's rewrite chooseWarranty() to accommodate these two factors. First, we will have to pass an additional parameter for the age of the car, so the new prototype will be

```
public void chooseWarranty(int mileage, int ageInMonths)
```

More importantly, we must also modify the conditional statement to use both of these values. For example, warranty should take the value "Standard" when both the mileage is no more than 36,000 *and* the ageInMonths is no more than 36. Java provides an operator, &&, which represents *and*. Using this operator, which we call the *logical and* operator, we can express the Standard condition as a single **compound condition**:

```
mileage <= 36000 && ageInMonths <= 36
```

The *logical and* operator accepts two boolean values and produces a boolean result. The && operator evaluates to true only if *both* operands are true. Thus, the Standard warranty will be chosen only if both of the conditions are true; if either or both of them is false, then the Standard warranty cannot be used and we must consider other options.

We can similarly modify the remaining two conditions: If we suppose that the Extended warranty applies only to vehicles no more than 72 months (5 years) old and the Sucker warranty applies only to vehicles no more than 84 months old, then the complete revised method is

```
public void chooseWarranty(int mileage, int ageInMonths) {
    if (mileage <= 36000 && ageInMonths <= 36)
        warranty = "Standard";
    else if (mileage <= 50000 && ageInMonths <= 72)
        warranty = "Extended";
    else if (mileage <= 100000 && ageInMonths <= 84)
        warranty = "Sucker";
    else
        warranty = "None";
}
```

Logical Operators and Conditional Statements

Logical Operators

In addition to the && operator, Java provides **logical operators** corresponding to *logical or* and *logical not*. Like the *logical and* operator, these operators are used to combine Boolean expressions. The logical or operator, written as ||, accepts two boolean values and evaluates to true if either or both value is true. The logical not, or *negation* operator, written as !, accepts a single boolean operand. The ! operator evaluates to false if its operand is true, and vice versa—that is, it "flips" the value of its operand.

Nested ifs and Dangling elses

Consider this alternative to our warranty selection code:

```
if (mileage <= 36000)
   if (ageInMonths <= 36)
      warranty = "Standard";
else if ...
```

This is an example of a **nested if**, so named because one if is nested within another. Only if the condition of the outer if is true will the inner if be tested.

This code has a subtle problem: The indentation reflects our intended meaning—the else is lined up with the if it is meant to match—but the rules for matching an else to an if will instead match the else to the most recent unmatched if, namely ageInMonths <= 36. This situation is often called the **dangling else** problem (because the else is "dangling" from the wrong if).

We can resolve this problem in a fairly simple manner. Recall that if we require more than one statement be executed within the if, they must be enclosed in braces ({}). There is nothing that prevents us from doing this even if we have only one statement. We can therefore write the above correctly as

```
if (mileage <= 36000) {
   if (ageInMonths <= 36)
      warranty = "Standard";
}
else if ...                          Note the indentation.
```

Now the braces explicitly delimit (mark off) the beginning and end of the statements belonging to the first if.

Most conditions can be designed using either cascaded or nested ifs. However, dangling elses can arise only when code contains nested ifs—they cannot arise from the cascaded if style. Furthermore, the logic of a cascaded if is easier to understand than that of a nested if. As a guideline, if your logic results in a dangling else, or even a nested if, it is likely that you can improve the readability of your code by restructuring it using cascaded ifs.

Relationship to Forms of Conditionals

As we saw earlier, the && operator is a substitute for a nested if; that is, the following are equivalent:

if (*condition1*)
    if (*condition2*)
        statement
	if (*condition1* && *condition2*)
	    statement

In general, the compound condition is easier to read than the corresponding nested if.

There is a similar relationship between the cascaded if/else and the logical or:

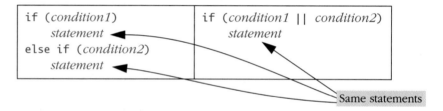

These statements are equivalent only if the indicated *statements* are the same. Unlike the && operator and nested if statements, the || operator and cascaded if/else statements are not properly viewed as substitutes for each other.

The switch Statement

The cascaded if/else often takes on the following form:

```
if (x==value1)
     statement1
else if (x==value2)
     statement2
else if (x==value3)
     statement3
else
     statement4
```

That is, it tests the same expression (in this case a single variable, x) against a series of values. Java provides a simpler construct, the **switch statement**, which eliminates a lot of the extra syntax (those else–ifs) and factors out the common expression. Here is a switch statement equivalent to the above cascaded if/else:

```
switch (x) {
case   value1:  statement1
               break;
case   value2:  statement2
               break;
case   value3:  statement3
               break;
default:        statement4
               break;
}
```

This is known as a switch statement because it allows the flow of execution to "switch" among many different cases. The various cases consist of the keyword case followed by a value, a colon, and a series of statements.

The expression is evaluated and compared with the various cases. When a match is found, the corresponding statement is executed. If no match is found, the statement associated with default is executed.

The switch expression must have a byte, char, short, or int value, and case values must be constants or literals. Associated with each case is a sequence of one or more statements—unlike the conditional, compound statements are not necessary for grouping.

The default case is optional. If it is not present and no match is found, no action is taken.

Each case should be terminated with a break. The compiler will not enforce this. If a break is omitted, execution will continue with the statements of the next cases until the next break or the end of the switch. Usually this is a disaster.

As an example, suppose we have a method that is passed an integer value from 1 to 7 that represents the day of the week. The method is to print and return a String corresponding to the name of the day; the code is as follows:

```
public String dayName(int d) {
    String dname;
    switch(d) {
    case  1:  dname  =  "Sunday";
              break;
    case  2:  dname  =  "Monday";
              break;
    case  3:  dname  =  "Tuesday";
              break;
    case  4:  dname  =  "Wednesday";
              break;
    case  5:  dname  =  "Thursday";
              break;
```

```
    case  6:  dname  =  "Friday";
              break;
    case  7:  dname  =  "Saturday";
              break;
    default:  dname  =  "Unknown  day";
              break;
    }
    System.out.println(dname);
    return  dname;
}
```

Execution of this `switch` statement causes the expression d to be compared against the various case values. The matching case assigns the corresponding day's name to the `dname` `String` variable. If the value of d is not in the range 1 through 7, the `String` "Unknown day" is assigned to `dname`.

Summary

The primitive data types `float` and `double` are used to represent floating-point values. Such values may be treated very similarly to integer-valued types, using the familiar arithmetic and relational operators, but their limited precision can result in unexpected behavior.

Complex conditional statements may be formed by cascading and/or nesting `if/else` statements. In some cases, the `switch` statement may be used as an alternative to cascaded `if/else` statements. Conditionals may also be made more complex by using compound conditions, built from simple Boolean expressions using the logical operators &&, ||, and !.

The repetition of a series of statements is one of the most powerful programming constructs. Once a task has been defined for a single object, it may be repeated for hundreds, thousands, or even millions of objects. The `for` statement provides an easy way to implement a counting loop.

Key Terms

cascaded `if/else` A sequence of `if/else` statements in which the `else` portion of one `if` statement consists of another `if` statement.

compound condition A condition (Boolean expression) containing one or more logical operators.

counter A variable that keeps count of something else.

counting loop A loop whose termination is based on executing a certain number of times.

dangling `else` A problem occurring in a nested `if`, in which the single `else` is associated with the wrong `if`.

`double` A primitive data type modeling floating-point numbers.

`float` A primitive data type modeling floating-point numbers.

floating-point number A number that models measurement with a fixed precision.

iteration The repeated execution of a section of code until some condition is satisfied.

logical operator An operator that combines Boolean expressions into larger Boolean expressions.

nested if An `if/else` or `if` statement appearing as the true portion of another `if` or `if/else` statement.

`switch` **statement** A multiway conditional. The switch allows selective execution of multiple cases based upon the value of an expression.

Questions for Review

1. What is a cascaded `if/else`? A nested `if`?
2. What is the dangling `else` problem?
3. What is a compound condition?
4. What are the logical operators?
5. Under what conditions can an `if/else` statement be replaced by a `switch` statement?
6. What are the three components of the header of a `for` statement? What are their roles?
7. Why do we need floating-point types as well as integer types?
8. When is it safe to assign a floating-point value to an integer variable? What about the other way around? When must we use casting?
9. Why are methods that manipulate primitive data types typically static methods?

Exercises

1. Write an application class (i.e., a class with a `main()` method) that uses the `Metric` class. Use `Double.parseDouble()` when you read in a measurement in feet to be converted.
2. Modify the `printFeetToMetersTable()` method of the `Metric` class so that it only prints conversions for multiples of 10 less than or equal to `maxFeet`. For example, if `maxFeet` is 37, the output table should contain values for 10, 20, and 30 feet.

3. Write a for loop that adds the values between 1 and n and stores the result in total. For example, if n is 7, then total should be 1 + 2 + 3 + 4 + 5 + 6 + 7 = 28. Assume n and total have been declared and n has been initialized.

4. Write a for loop that calculates n! (read "*n* factorial"), or $n \times (n-1) \times ... \times 2 \times 1$ and stores the result in factorial. Assume n and factorial have been declared and n has been initialized.

5. Write a for loop that prints the characters of a String, one per line. (You could use the substring(int,int) method or the charAt(int) method of the String class.)

6. Write a program that reads in an int value n and outputs a table containing the squares and cubes of integers from 1 to n. If n is less than 1, your program should produce no output.

7. Write a complete Java program that asks the user how many int values he will enter, then reads those values and prints the minimum value. Use a for loop; do not use the Minimizer class.

8. Rewrite the Minimizer class to work with doubles instead of longs.

9. Write a program that reads in an int value n and outputs a table containing the square roots of integers from 1 to n. If n is less than 1 your program should produce no output.

10. Write a program that uses Math.random() to simulate throwing two 6-sided dice.

11. When the crew of the *Millennium Falcon* aren't occupying themselves with three-dimensional chess, they might be playing three-dimensional darts. Modify the classes used to approximate π to work with a three-dimensional dartboard: Instead of a square, the dartboard is a cube, and instead of a circle, a sphere is inscribed inside the cube. Hints: The volume of a sphere with radius r is given by

$$\frac{4}{3}\pi r^3$$

In three-dimensional space, the distance from the origin to a point (x,y,z) is

$$\sqrt{x^2 + y^2 + z^2}$$

12. Modify the chooseWarranty() method so that if the make is "Ford" and the model is "Pinto" the warranty chosen is "None".

13. Implement a Date class whose constructor accepts an eight-character String in the form mm/dd/yy. The constructor checks to make sure the date is correct (i.e., the month is between 1 and 12, the month/day pair is possible—April 31, for example, is incorrect—and so on). (Hint: Use substrings and Integer.parseInt()). If the date is correct, break it up into its parts. Provide a boolean instance variable that is set to true by the constructor if the date is valid and false otherwise. You should have a method that returns

whether the object contains a valid date (by examining that instance variable). Allow the user of the class to specify whether the date is to be printed in American (mm/dd/yy) or European (dd/mm/yy) format. Finally, provide a `print()` method.

14. In Chapter 5, we implemented the `equals()` method of the `Name` class by comparing the `String` representations of two `Name` objects. Modify this method so that two `Names` are equal if the first names and last names are equal (that is, titles are irrelevant).

15. Write a program that uses `Math.random()` to generate random poker hands. A hand consists of five cards; each card is one of four suits (hearts, diamonds, clubs, or spades) and has one of 13 face values (2 through 10, jack, queen, king, ace). Use `switch` statements to help convert random numbers to card descriptions.

16. The `compareTo()` method of the `String` class accepts a `String` object as its parameter. The method returns:

   - A negative value if the receiver `String` is less than the parameter `String`
   - A positive value if the receiver `String` is greater than the parameter `String`
   - 0 if they're equal

   Write a `compareTo()` method for the `Name` class. To do this you must first decide what it means for one `Name` object to be less than another; again, the comparison should be based only on first and last names.

17. Write a method, `max()`, that accepts two integers and returns the larger of the two. Why should this method be `static`? If you were on the Java design team, where might you place such a method?

18. Write a method `max()` that accepts three integers and returns the largest. Can you write this without using nested `if`s?

19. Modify the `Minimizer` class to work with `Name` references instead of numeric values. Use the `compareTo()` method you implemented in Exercise 16.

20. Write a program that uses a `for` loop to compute the *n*th Fibonacci number. The first Fibonacci number F(1) is defined to be 1; the second Fibonacci number F(2) is also defined to be 1. Each successive Fibonacci number is defined to be the sum of the previous two Fibonacci numbers (so the next several Fibonacci numbers are 2, 3, 5, and 8).

21. Write a method `mySubStr()` that receives two `Strings` and returns a `boolean` value: `true` only if one of the `Strings` is a substring of the other. Do not use any methods of the `String` class other than `length()`.

More on Interaction

In our last GUI supplement, we introduced a rudimentary form of interaction: A single button that allowed the user to flip the color of a square. In this supplement, we will increase the level of interaction: We will write a simple graphical user interface for the `Minimizer` class from Chapter 4.

Our executing `MinimizerApplet` will look something like Figure 6.9. Users will have an area into which they can type numbers; clicking the "Minimize!" button passes the number in that area to the `Minimizer` and causes the current (updated) minimum value to be displayed next to the "Minimize!" button.

Creating and Placing the Controls

As before, our first task is to create and display the applet controls; that is, we must write the applet's `init()` method.

The applet displayed in Figure 6.9 contains three kinds of components: `Button`, which we have already seen, and two new components, `TextField` and `Label`.

As we have seen, `Button` objects model buttons in the interface. The `Button` constructor takes as an argument a `String` that will serve as a label in the button itself. So, our `init()` method will contain this `Button` constructor invocation:

```
minButton = new Button("Minimize!");
```

Note that `minButton` will *not* be declared within the `init()` method; we will see that it (and other controls) will be used by another method of our applet, so they will be declared as instance variables of the applet.

`TextField` objects model a space into which users can enter a single line of text. The `TextField` constructor takes as an argument an `int` that indicates the

Figure 6.9

The executing
`MinimizerApplet`.

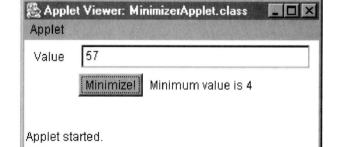

maximum number of characters that can be displayed in the field. Thus, we will need to write

```
valueField = new TextField(30);
```

in our init() method.

Finally, Label objects model a piece of text, such as "Value:" and "Minimum value is 4" in our example. The Label constructor takes as an argument a String that contains the desired text. Thus we will need constructor invocations like

```
resultLabel = new Label(" ");
```

We have provided no text at this point because when the applet begins executing, there is no sensible value to display to the user, who has not yet entered any values.

As we create each control, we pass a reference to it as a parameter to add() in order to display it. We will add() controls to the applet in the order we want them displayed (moving left-to-right, top-to-bottom). Thus, we will begin with the "Value:" Label. Because we will not need to change the text of this Label during the applet's execution (unlike the "Minimum value is" Label) we do not need to save a reference to it. We then proceed with creating and add()-ing the rest of the controls. Also, we need to create the Minimizer object that will perform the computational work of the applet; like the controls, this object will be used by more than one of the applet's methods, so it too will be declared as an instance variable. At this point, then, our MinimizerApplet looks like this:

```
import java.awt.*;
import java.applet.*;

public class MinimizerApplet extends Applet {
    public void init() {
        add(new Label("Value:"));          Don't need to save a reference
        valueField = new TextField(30);
        add(valueField);
        minButton = new Button("Minimize!");
        add(minButton);
        resultLabel = new Label(" ");
        add(resultLabel);
        m = new Minimizer();               Create Minimizer
    }
    private TextField valueField;          Applet's instance variables
    private Button minButton;
    private Label resultLabel;
    private Minimizer m;
}
```

We can compile this class, add the appropriate HTML (left as an exercise; use 300 as the width and 100 as the height), and run the applet. (Note: Depending on your local environment, `Minimizer.class` should reside in the same directory as `MinimizerApplet.class`.) The result is a very pretty but useless applet. We can type values into the text fields, but because clicking on the button does nothing, we can't perform the calculation.

Handling the Button-Clicks

To handle the button-click events, we must first identify the event source object and the listener object. In this applet, `minButton` is the event source and the `Minimizer-Applet` is the listener.

Therefore, we need to send `minButton` an `addActionListener()` message, passing a reference to the `MinimizerApplet` object as an argument. We do this in the `MinimizerApplet`'s `init()` method after creating the `minButton` object:

```
calcButton.addActionListener(this);
```

Because a `MinimizerApplet` object is the listener, we must also implement an `actionPerformed()` method in `MinimizerApplet`:

```
public  void  actionPerformed(ActionEvent  ae)  {
    code to handle the event
}
```

When the button is clicked, the applet should take the following actions:

- Read the value in `valueField`.
- Submit the value to the `Minimizer` `m` using the `check()` method.
- Query `m` for the current minimum and update the text of `resultLabel`.

The value of a `TextField` is retrieved via the `getText()` method, which returns a `String` containing the field's contents:

```
public void actionPerformed(ActionEvent ae) {
    String valString = valueField.getText();
```

Then we must convert `valString` to a `long` using the `Long.parseLong()` method and submit the result to `m`:

```
long val = Long.parseLong(valString);
m.check(val);
```

If `valString` cannot be converted to a `long`, an error will occur because the `parseLong()` will fail.

To display the current minimum value in `resultLabel`, we send a `get()` message to `m` and use the returned value to construct the new contents of `resultLabel`. The text of a `Label` is set with a `setText()` message, so we have

```
long min = m.get();
resultLabel.setText("Minimum value is " + min);
```

Finally, because the contents of resultLabel may have changed, we need to make sure the display of the applet is up to date. We do this by sending a vali-date() message to the applet, asking it to refresh the display:

```
validate();
```

Thus, the complete actionPerformed() method is

```
public void actionPerformed(ActionEvent ae) {
   String valString = valueField.getText();
   long val = Long.parseLong(valString);
   m.check(val);
   long min = m.get();
   resultLabel.setText("Minimum value is " + min);
   validate();
}
```

The final form of the applet is

```
import java.awt.*;
import java.awt.event.*          ◄──────────── Required for event-handling
import java.applet.*;
public class MinimizerApplet extends Applet
                              implements ActionListener {
   public void init() {
      add(new Label("Value:"));
      valueField = new TextField(30);
      add(valueField);
      minButton = new Button("Minimize!");
      add(minButton);
      minButton.addActionListener(this);
      resultLabel = new Label("Minimum value is ");
      add(resultLabel);
      m = new Minimizer();
   }

   public void actionPerformed(ActionEvent ae) {
      String valString = valueField.getText();
      long val = Long.parseLong(valString);
      m.check(val);
      long min = m.get();
      resultLabel.setText("Minimum value is " + min);
      validate();
   }

   private TextField valueField;
```

```
    private Button minButton;
    private Label resultLabel;
    private Minimizer m;
}
```

What About paint()?

Why didn't we implement the paint() method of MinimizerApplet? Because we didn't need to. As we saw in the Chapter 4 supplement, every applet we write, by virtue of the phrase extends Applet, contains all the methods of the Applet class, including the paint() method. All of our previous applets have provided their own implementations of paint() because they needed some customized behavior. But in this case, the default paint() behavior is adequate: The default paint() method simply sends a paint() message to each of its add()-ed components. Objects of class Button, TextField, and Label know how to paint() themselves properly, so we don't need to do any more work.

Suggested Experiments

1. Write an applet that provides a simple graphical user interface to the convertFeetToMeters() method of the Metric class. The interface should include (at least) a TextField in which a measurement in feet will be entered, a Button labeled "Convert", and a Label in which the result of the conversion will be displayed.

2. Write an applet that provides a simple graphical user interface to the Counter class. The interface should just include one Button, labeled "Increment", and one Label displaying the current value of the Counter.

3. Write an AdderApplet with two TextFields and a Button labeled "Add" (and as many Labels as you like). When the "Add" button is clicked, it computes and displays the sum of the integers entered in the TextFields.

4. Write an EvenCheckerApplet that tests a number entered in a TextField for evenness. It displays an appropriate Label depending on the result of the test.

Designing Classes

7.1 Introduction

In Chapters 4 and 5, we focused on the definition of classes and methods, instance variables, prototypes, arguments, and method invocation. This chapter concentrates on the process of developing class definitions by elaborating on the approach introduced in Chapter 4.

We start with the approach to the class definition process that we will continue to use throughout the rest of the book.

7.2 Designing Classes—An Overview

Before we start designing a class, we first require a *statement of the problem*, which describes the object or system to be modeled. Without a clear understanding of the problem, a correct solution is not possible. Next, we sketch a *sample scenario*, which illustrates how a solution might be used.

The first step in the actual class design is to *find the primary objects*. If programming is an attempt to model something, we should first determine the key elements of the model. A good starting point is to collect all the nouns in the problem statement and to choose those that are the most important.

We then *determine the desired behavior* for each of the primary objects. This step will produce our basic set of required methods for the classes that these objects will belong to. If several classes need to be designed, we proceed one class at a time.

Determining the interface is next. We determine the prototype of each method: its arguments and return-type. A good aid is to try to write sample code that uses the object and see how the method invocations naturally occur.

Once the interface has been defined, we direct our effort toward the class internals. We *define the instance variables* and finally *implement the methods*.

In this text, we will often conclude with a discussion of the solution.

7.3 The Counter Class Revisited

Before we apply this process to a new problem, let's briefly examine how it could be applied to the Counter class that we developed in Chapter 4.

Paraphrasing from Chapter 4, the problem statement is "Develop a class that models a counting device—a button on top, when clicked, causes the count to be increased by 1; another button causes the value of the counter to be reset to 0; and the face of the device displays the current value of the counter."

We introduced this class in Chapter 4 with the sample scenario of a theater usher who uses the device to count patrons entering the theater; presumably, at the end of each show the number displayed on the face of the device is recorded and the value is reset to 0 in preparation for the next show.

Although we are starting with a clear idea of the class we need to develop (Counter), we should nonetheless consider the other nouns in the problem statement, as these may suggest "auxiliary" classes that would improve the design of our solution. In this case, the nouns—*device, button, face,* and *value*—are either synonyms for the counter or describe some fundamental parts of the counter itself; *counter* is clearly the most important noun. Thus, we will begin by focusing on the design of a Counter class.

Determining the desired behavior requires analyzing the responsibilities of the class we are designing. In this case, these responsibilities are identified explicitly in the problem statement:

- increment, causing the count to increase by one
- getValue, to display the current value of the counter
- reset, to return the value of the counter to zero

We will also need a constructor, Counter, to create new Counter objects.

To determine the interface, we begin with some sample code that uses the class, such as this excerpt from our code in Chapter 4:

```
Counter purpleCounter = new Counter();
Counter yellowCounter = new Counter();
System.out.print("Person #1, do you prefer purple or yellow? ");
String response = keyboard.readLine();
if (response.equals("purple"))
    purpleCounter.increment();
else
    yellowCounter.increment();
if (purpleCounter.getValue() > yellowCounter.getValue())
    System.out.println("Purple wins.");
purpleCounter.reset();
yellowCounter.reset();
```

From this code we can derive the following interface:

```
class Counter {
    public Counter()
    {...}
    public void increment()
    {...}
    public int getValue()
    {...}
    public void reset()
    {...}
    Instance Variables
}
```

Because the counter's value must be changed by both the `increment()` and `reset()` methods, and returned by the `getValue()` method, it must be maintained in an instance variable

```
    private int count;
```

At this point we can provide the simple method implementations:

```
class Counter {
    public Counter() {
        count = 0;
    public void increment() {
        count = count + 1;
    }
    public int getValue() {
        return count;
    }
    public void reset() {
        count = 0;
    }
    private int count = 0;
}
```

7.4 An Automated Teller Machine

In this example we will design classes that model a simplified form of ATM. These machines are familiar to most people, but we still need to consider a problem statement describing exactly which features of an ATM our code is intended to model.

Statement of the Problem

An ATM allows account holders to withdraw funds from their account, deposit funds into their account, and view their current account balance. We will assume that all withdrawals, deposits, and balances are in whole dollar amounts.

A Sample Scenario

To aid in our design, we sketch a typical interaction with the ATM. First, the user is asked to enter her account number (of course, this is normally done by presenting a card with a magnetic strip, but we will limit ourselves to standard input/output). Then the user is given a menu of options (withdraw, deposit, check balance, log out). If the user selects an account transaction, she is prompted for her passcode; if it is correct, the transaction is carried out. Note that this scenario is slightly different from a typical ATM interaction: We require the passcode to be entered not when the user logs in but instead for each transaction. This results in both stricter security and a simpler class design.

Finding the Primary Objects

The nouns in the problem statement are *ATM, account holder, funds, account,* and *balance. ATM* is clearly the most important noun in the problem. Of the remaining nouns, the *account holder* is responsible only for initiating transactions and is not something that needs to be modeled explicitly; *funds* and *balance* are properties of an *account,* so we'll wait to see if they need to be modeled as separate classes. Therefore, we determine that our primary objects are ATM and account, corresponding to the classes `ATM` and `Account`:

```
class ATM {
    Class definition will go here.
    ...
}
class Account {
    Class definition will go here.
    ...
}
```

We will now design the two classes, beginning with `ATM`.

Determining the Desired Behavior—Class `ATM`

Based on the sample scenario, it appears that an ATM has two primary responsibilities: to acquire the user's account number and to present the user with a menu of possible transactions. We can decide that the `Account` class will provide methods corresponding to each type of transaction (we must make sure to incorporate this decision into our `Account` class design, of course); thus, the `ATM` class need only send the appropriate message to an `Account` object after the user makes his selection from the menu. So, our `ATM` class needs only two methods corresponding to its two responsibilities:

- `getAcctNumber`
- `getTransactionChoice`

Note that although we are focusing on the ATM class at this point, we are also making design decisions that will affect our work on the Account class later. Indeed, class design often involves refining the design of several classes as the proper delegation of responsibility becomes more evident.

Defining the Interface—Class ATM

Now that we have named the methods our class will implement, we must determine the class's interface: the signatures of each method. Neither of these methods requires any parameters or returns any value, so the interface is

```
class ATM {
    public void getAcctNumber() {...}
    public void getTransactionChoice() {...}
}
```

We haven't mentioned the constructor here because at this point it doesn't appear that the class requires a special implementation of the constructor—it's possible that the default constructor will prove adequate.

Defining the Instance Variables—Class ATM

The getTransactionChoice() method, which will carry out the transaction of the user's choice, must have access to the account information acquired by the getAcctNumber() method. Therefore, the ATM class requires an Account instance variable that will be shared by these two methods:

```
class ATM {
    public void getAcctNumber() {...}
    public void getTransactionChoice() {...}
    private Account userAcct;
}
```

Implementing the Methods—Class ATM

Because the calculations related to the transactions themselves will be carried out in the Account class, the ATM methods involve little more than interactive i/o (and therefore, each must be marked as throws Exception). First, the getAcctNumber() prompts the user for an account number, reads his response, and creates a corresponding Account object (remember, in our design, the user only enters a passcode once a transaction has been selected):

```
    public void getAcctNumber() throws Exception {
        BufferedReader kbd = new BufferedReader(
                new InputStreamReader(System.in));
        System.out.print("Enter account id: ");
```

```
        String id = kbd.readLine();
        userAcct = new Account(id);
    }
```

Will need to provide appropriate constructor

The getTransactionChoice() method first gives the user a menu of options and reads the user's response from the keyboard:

```
public void getTransactionChoice() throws Exception {
    System.out.println("Choose one of: ");
    System.out.println("W - Withdraw");
    System.out.println("D - Deposit");
    System.out.println("B - Get Current Balance");
    System.out.print("Your choice -> ");

    BufferedReader kbd = new BufferedReader(
                new InputStreamReader(System.in));
    String choice = kbd.readLine();
```

Then we determine which choice the user made and respond appropriately. If the user chooses to make a withdrawal or deposit, we must also ask for the amount of the transaction. Then we send a message to userAcct. To represent transaction amounts we will use the long primitive type.

```
    if (choice.equals("W")) {
        System.out.print("Enter amount to withdraw -> ");
        String amount = kbd.readLine();
        long longAmount = Long.parseLong(amount);
        userAcct.withdraw(longAmount);
    } else if (choice.equals("D")) {
        System.out.print("Enter amount to deposit -> ");
        String amount = kbd.readLine();
        long longAmount = Long.parseLong(amount);
        userAcct.deposit(longAmount);
    } else if (choice.equals("B")) {
        long balance = userAcct.getBalance();
        System.out.println("Balance = "+balance);
    } else
        System.out.println("--| Invalid Option |--");

    System.out.println("Thanks for using this machine!");
    System.out.println();
    }
}
```

Our design of Account must provide this interface.

With the ATM class complete, we must now consider the Account class, in which most of the real work will get done.

Determining Behavior and Defining the Interface—**Class** Account

The Account class is responsible, at the very least, for maintaining the balance of the account. Thus, this class will provide methods corresponding to the behaviors that depend on the account balance: withdraw, deposit, and get balance. We will also need to provide a constructor. Our ATM class on the previous page is an excellent source of sample code; from it we can deduce the interface that the Account class needs to provide:

```
class Account {
    public Account(String id) {...}
    public void withdraw(long amount) {...}
    public void deposit(long amount) {...}
    public long getBalance() {...}
}
```

Defining the Instance Variables—**Class** Account

We have not yet addressed one of the most important issues: How is information about each account stored and represented? In the case of a real ATM (rather than a model of one), this information is probably stored in some central location and accessed over a network connection when necessary. Such an implementation is beyond our ability at this point, so instead we will suppose that each account corresponds to a file stored in the machine itself. The name of the file will be the account number followed by an ".act" extension (e.g., account 5551212 corresponds to the file 5551212.act). The account's passcode is stored on the first line of the data file, while the second line contains the current balance.

Thus, the transaction-related methods will need access to the file corresponding to the account number provided to the constructor; this is accomplished with an instance variable:

```
private String fileName;
```

Implementing the Methods—**Class** Account

The Account constructor simply appends ".act" to id and stores the result as fileName:

```
    public Account (String id) {
        fileName = id + ".act";
    }
```

The remaining methods share a similar structure: Perform authentication (by asking the user for the correct passcode); if successful perform the transaction; and, if necessary, update the contents of the account's data file. Their implementations will look something like this:

```
    public void withdraw(long amount) throws Exception {
        if (authentication successful)
```

```
        if (amount < current balance) {
            current balance -= amount;
            update  balance in file;
        } else
            System.out.println("--| Insufficient Funds |--");
    }

    public void deposit (long amount) throws Exception {
        if (authentication successful) {
            current balance += amount;
            update balance in file;
        }
    }

    public long getBalance() throws Exception {
        if (authentication successful)
            return current balance;
    }
```

Identifying and Implementing "Helper" Methods—Class Account

Because the "if authentication successful" and "update balance in file" operations appear in multiple methods, it is sensible for us to provide these behaviors in separate methods that can be invoked from within the transaction methods. This way we not only reduce the chances of typographical mistakes, but if we decide to make a change (say, to the authentication procedure) we only need to change one method instead of three. Because these methods are "helper" methods not intended to receive messages from outside the class, we'll declare them as `private`:

```
private boolean authenticate() {...}
private void updateBalance() {...}
```

The primary behavior of `authenticate()` is to compare the user's entered passcode to the correct one. Because each transaction requires not only successful authentication but also current balance information, we will implement `authenticate()` both to check the passcode and to read in the balance. This information must be accessible to the transaction methods, so we need more instance variables:

```
private long balance;
private String correctPasscode;
```

Our implementation of `authenticate()` first prepares to read from both the account data file and the keyboard. Then it reads the correct passcode from the file and prompts the user to enter a passcode:

```
    private boolean authenticate() throws Exception {
        BufferedReader acctFile = new BufferedReader(
```

```
                        new InputStreamReader(
                        new FileInputStream(fileName)));
    BufferedReader kbd = new BufferedReader(
                        new InputStreamReader(System.in));
    correctPasscode = acctFile.readLine();
    System.out.print("Enter passcode -> ");
    String passcode = kbd.readLine();
```

Then it compares the two passcode values. If the values don't match, we set balance to 0, print out an error message, and return false, indicating that authentication failed. If the values do match, we read the value of balance from the data
file and return true:

```
    if (!(passcode.equals(correctPasscode))) {
        balance = 0;
        System.out.println("--| Password Incorrect |--");
        return false;
    } else {
        balance = Long.parseLong(acctFile.readLine());
        return true;
    }
}
```

Implementing updateBalance() is much simpler. We first open the data file, this
time using a FileOutputStream rather than a FileInputStream, then print out
the correct passcode and the value of balance (which has been updated by the
transaction):

```
private void updateBalance() throws Exception {
    PrintStream ps = new PrintStream(
                        new FileOutputStream(
                            new File(fileName)));
    ps.println(correctPasscode);
    ps.println(balance);
}
```

The Complete Implementation—Class Account

With these two helper methods, plus the instance variables used for communication between the helper methods and the transaction methods, the complete
implementation is as follows. Note that because each of the transaction methods
invoke methods that have been marked throws Exception, the invoking methods must also be marked this way:

```
public class Account {
    public Account (String id) {
        fileName = id + ".act";
    }
```

```java
public void withdraw(long amount) throws Exception {
    if (authenticate())
        if (amount < balance) {
            balance -= amount;
            updateBalance();
        } else
            System.out.println("--| Insufficient Funds |--");
}

public void deposit (long amount) throws Exception {
    if (authenticate()) {
        balance += amount;
        updateBalance();
    }
}

public long getBalance() throws Exception {
    if (authenticate())
        return balance;
}

private boolean authenticate() throws Exception {
    BufferedReader acctFile = new BufferedReader(
                        new InputStreamReader(
                        new FileInputStream(fileName)));
    BufferedReader kbd = new BufferedReader(
                        new InputStreamReader(System.in));
    correctPasscode = acctFile.readLine();
    System.out.print("Enter passcode -> ");
    String passcode = kbd.readLine();

    if (!(passcode.equals(correctPasscode))) {
        balance = 0;
        System.out.println("--| Password Incorrect |--");
        return false;
    } else {
        balance = Long.parseLong(acctFile.readLine());
        return true;
    }
}

private void updateBalance() throws Exception {
    PrintStream ps = new PrintStream(
                        new FileOutputStream(
```

```
                                        new File(fileName)));
      ps.println(correctPasscode);
      ps.println(balance);
   }

   private String fileName;
   private String correctPasscode;
   private long balance;
}
```

Using the Classes

Using these classes, we can write a simple application that models an ATM's infinite cycle of accepting new users and processing transactions. To achieve this kind of infinite loop, we will use a variation on the counting loops we studied in Chapter 6. Counting for loops include a boolean expression describing the conditions under which the loop body should be executed. For example, if the condition is i<10 then the body will be executed as long as i<10 evaluates to true. If we replace this condition by true, then we have a for loop whose condition is always true—so the loop body itself will execute until the entire program is terminated.

With this idea, we write a simple program:

```
public class ATMTestDriver {
   public static void main(String[] arg) throws Exception {
      ATM myATM = new ATM();
      for (int i=0; true; i++) {
         myATM.getAcctNumber();
         myATM.getTransactionChoice();
      }
   }
}
```

This program models a very strict ATM—it only allows users to perform one transaction per "card swipe." If we assume the file 5551212.act (in the same directory as our code's .class files) contains

```
1111
78
```

then executing our program looks something like this (user input is in bold):

```
Enter account id: 5551212
Choose one of:
W - Withdraw
D - Deposit
B - Get Current Balance
Your choice -> D
```

```
Enter amount to deposit -> 100
Enter passcode -> 1111
Thanks for using this machine!

Enter account id: 5551212
Choose one of:
W - Withdraw
D - Deposit
B - Get Current Balance
Your choice -> W
Enter amount to withdraw -> 200
Enter passcode -> 1111
--| Insufficient Funds |--
Thanks for using this machine!

Enter account id: 5551212
Choose one of:
W - Withdraw
D - Deposit
B - Get Current Balance
Your choice -> B
Enter passcode -> 1111
Current balance: 178
Thanks for using this machine!
```

Discussion

In the *determining the primary objects* step, we stated that *account* was a primary object, and that *funds* and *balance* were subordinate to that object. Let us examine the consequence of those relationships. By the time we were done, the balance was an instance variable of the Account class. In some sense we could say that an Account object possesses a balance property. We thus speak of a **has-a** property and say that Account has-a balance. The *X* has-a *Y* relationship is usually expressed in Java by having the class of *X* contain an instance variable representing *Y*.

The amount of funds deposited or withdrawn is also related to an account but not in the same "permanent" sense as balance. Although an account balance is not truly permanent, it is a value that remains the same for a relatively long period of time. Thus, the amount of funds in each transaction was made an argument rather than an instance variable.

7.5 Dispatching Repairpeople: An Example

In this example we will design some classes based on a modified version of the dispatcher/repairperson scenario discussed in Chapter 1.

Statement of the Problem

A dispatcher for a utility company is responsible for sending repairpeople to locations throughout the city. As each new repair location is reported, she must identify and send the repairperson closest to the given location.

A Sample Scenario

To aid in our design, let us imagine how we might use these classes. We will provide information about repairpersons (their names and locations), then will submit a request for a dispatch to a particular location. We will then be informed of which repairperson should be dispatched, such as

```
Send Renee Williams
```

Finding the Primary Objects

In our example, the nouns are *repairperson*, *location*, and *dispatcher*. Of these, *repairperson* and *location* seem to be the most important; our code is intended to assist the *dispatcher*, so she does not appear explicitly in our model. Therefore, we choose *repairperson* and *location* as our primary objects and introduce the classes `RepairPerson` and `Location`:

```
class RepairPerson {
    Class definition will go here.
    ...
}
class Location {
    Class definition will go here.
    ...
}
```

We now will design the two classes. Because each repairperson has location information associated with it, we will begin with the `RepairPerson` class, thereby developing a clear idea of how the `Location` class will be used before we design it.

Determining the Desired Behavior—Class `RepairPerson`

The most important responsibility of a `RepairPerson` object is to compute its distance from a given location—note that we are designing a "smart and helpful" class that doesn't simply report its location but knows how to use location information to perform useful calculations. The dispatcher also needs to be able to get a `RepairPerson`'s name and to set its location (if it is moved to a new location). We will also need a static `read()` method to allow us to create `RepairPerson` objects from input data:

- `read` (static)
- `getDistanceFrom`

- getName
- moveTo

As with the ATM class, we do not explicitly mention the constructor as part of the interface. We do expect that a constructor will be invoked by the read() method, but that does not make the constructor part of the interface.

Although we are concentrating on designing the RepairPerson class now, we are not operating in a vacuum—we are taking into account the behavior that the dispatcher requires of a repairperson. In fact, for our purposes, the *only* behavior required of the repairperson is that needed by the dispatcher. Everything else— the type of the repairperson's vehicle, the length of the repairperson's employment, and so on—can be ignored.

Defining the Interface—Class RepairPerson

The interface of the RepairPerson class consists of the signature of each Repair-Person method. It determines the way other classes communicate with a Repair-Person object.

A good starting point in defining an interface is to write some typical code that uses an object of the class being designed. Let us write a simple fragment of code that

- Creates a RepairPerson object from input (i.e., name and location data)
- Asks for its distance from Location loc
- Moves the RepairPerson to loc
- Outputs a message reporting on its actions

(Note that for the moment we won't worry about how loc is created.)

To read in a RepairPerson object we will need to create a BufferedReader object, then use the RepairPerson's static read() method:

```
BufferedReader br = new BufferedReader(
                    new InputStreamReader(System.in));
RepairPerson rp = RepairPerson.read(br);
```

Then we send rp a message asking it to calculate its distance from loc:

```
int distance = rp.getDistanceFrom(loc);
```

and move rp to loc:

```
rp.moveTo(loc);
```

Finally, we ask rp for its name (using the Name class we developed in Chapter 5) and print out a message:

```
Name n = rp.getName();
System.out.println("Moved " + n + " to new location.");
```

From this sample code we can derive the interface for the RepairPerson class. Note that we can't yet determine the signature for the constructor because, in our example, it was invoked only indirectly via the read() method:

```
class  RepairPerson {
   public static RepairPerson read(BufferedReader br)
   {...}
   public int getDistanceFrom(Location l)
   {...}
   public Name getName()
   {...}
   public void moveTo(Location l)
   {...}
   Instance variables
}
```

Defining the Instance Variables—Class RepairPerson

The information about the repairperson's name and location must be maintained within the RepairPerson object so it can provide this information when queried (by either a getDistanceFrom() or a getName() message). We therefore add instance variables to our RepairPerson class that correspond to these data:

```
class  RepairPerson {
   public static RepairPerson read(BufferedReader br)
   {...}
   public int getDistanceFrom(Location l)
   {...}
   public Name getName()
   {...}
   public void moveTo(Location l)
   {...}
   Name name;
   Location location;
}
```

Implementing the Methods—Class RepairPerson

The read() method simply invokes the respective read() methods of the Name and Location classes and uses the returned values to create a new RepairPerson object:

```
   public static RepairPerson read(BufferedReader br)
                                    throws Exception {
      Name name = Name.read(br);
      if (name == null)
         return null;
      Location location = Location.read(br);
```

```
        if (location == null)
            return null;
        return new RepairPerson(name,location);
    }
```

Now we can see that we need a constructor that takes `Name` and `Location` parameters and assigns those values to the corresponding instance variables. The `getName()` and `setLocation()` methods just work with the appropriate instance variables:

```
    RepairPerson(Name name, Location location) {
        this.name = name;
        this.location = location;
    }
    Name getName() {
        return name;
    }
    void moveTo(Location location) {
        this.location = location;
    }
```

Finally, the `getDistanceFrom()` method returns the distance between the `RepairPerson` object and the `Location` `location`. It will be the responsibility of the `Location` class actually to perform the calculation, so the `RepairPerson` will simply send a `getDistanceFrom()` message to `location`, passing its `Location` instance variable as the parameter:

```
    int getDistanceFrom(Location location) {
        return location.distanceFrom(this.location);
    }
```

The completed class definition follows:

```
class  RepairPerson {
    RepairPerson(Name name, Location location) {
        this.name = name;
        this.location = location;
    }
    Name getName() {
        return name;
    }
    void moveTo(Location location) {
        this.location = location;
    }
    public static RepairPerson read(BufferedReader br)
                                        throws Exception {
        Name name = Name.read(br);
```

```
        if (name == null)
            return null;
        Location location = Location.read(br);
        if (location == null)
            return null;
        return new RepairPerson(name,location);
    }
    int getDistanceFrom(Location location) {
        return location.distanceFrom(this.location);
    }
    Name name;
    Location location;
}
```

We now turn our attention to the Location class.

Determining the Desired Behavior—Class Location

As we have seen, the chief behavior required of a location is the ability to calculate its distance from another location. We also need to be able to read a location from input. This gives us the following set of behaviors:

- getDistanceFrom
- read (static)

Defining the Interface—Class Location

The usage of the Location class by the RepairPerson class gives us sufficient information on which to base our definition of Location's interface. In the implementation of RepairPerson's read() method we wrote

```
        Location location = Location.read(br);
```

and in the getDistanceFrom() method we wrote

```
        return location.distanceFrom(this.location);
```

where the desired return-type was int. As with RepairPerson, it appears that the Location constructor will be invoked by the read() method. We have the following interface:

```
class Location  {
    public int getDistanceFrom(Location location)
        {...}
    public static Location read(BufferedReader)
        {...}
    Instance variables
}
```

Defining the Instance Variables—Class Location

The location must maintain information that is set by the read() method and constructor and use this information in the calculation of getDistanceFrom(). We decided earlier that locations will be represented as (*x,y*) coordinates, so a Location will contain two int values, x and y:

```
class Location  {
    public int getDistanceFrom(Location location)
        {...}
    public static Location read(BufferedReader br)
        {...}
    private int x, y;
}
```

Implementing the Methods—Class Location

The read() method is responsible for creating a Location based on input values. We will assume that the (*x,y*) values for a location appear together on a line with no other data, separated by a comma, as follows:

3,7

To convert this string into a pair of int values, we will

- Use the indexOf() method to find the position of the comma
- Use the substring() method to extract the portions before and after the comma
- Use trim() to remove any extra whitespace from these substrings
- Use Integer.parseInt() to convert these substrings into int values

```
String s = br.readLine();
if (s == null)
    return null;
int comma = s.indexOf(",");
int x = Integer.parseInt(s.substring(0,comma).trim());
int y = Integer.parseInt(s.substring(comma+1).trim());
```

Once we have extracted the x and y values, we pass them to a constructor that will create the new Location value:

```
return new Location(x,y);
```

Thus, the completed read() method is

```
    public static Location read(BufferedReader br)
                                        throws Exception {
        String s = br.readLine();
        if (s == null)
            return null;
```

```
int comma = s.indexOf(",");
int x = Integer.parseInt(s.substring(0,comma).trim());
int y = Integer.parseInt(s.substring(comma+1).trim());
return new Location(x,y);
}
```

Now it is apparent that the Location constructor must take two int parameters that will be assigned to the new object's instance variables, so we can write

```
Location(int x, int y) {
    this.x = x;
    this.y = y;
}
```

The getDistanceFrom() method calculates the distance between two Locations. In Chapter 6, we used the hypotenuse of a right triangle to determine the distance between two points, but in most developed areas vehicles usually can't travel on the hypotenuse—they have to stay on the road. Because roads are often laid out on an approximate grid system, we will model the distance between two Locations as the sum of the differences between their x positions and their y positions. See Figure 7.1 for an illustration. Because the distance should always be positive, we will take the absolute value of each difference (using the Math.abs() method). Thus, the distance between (for example) the point (5,3) and (3,1) is calculated to be the same as the distance between (3,1) and (5,3).

```
int distanceFrom(Location location) {
    int xdist = Math.abs(this.x - location.x);
    int ydist = Math.abs(this.y - location.y);
    return xdist + ydist;
}
```

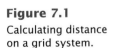

Figure 7.1
Calculating distance on a grid system.

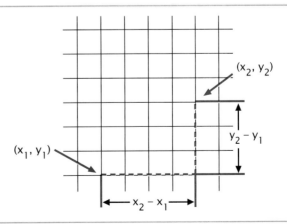

The complete `Location` class follows:

```
class Location  {
   Location(int x, int y) {
      this.x = x;
      this.y = y;
   }
   int distanceFrom(Location location) {
      int xdist = Math.abs(this.x - location.x);
      int ydist = Math.abs(this.y - location.y);
      return xdist + ydist;
   }
   public static Location read(BufferedReader br)
                                          throws Exception {
      String s = br.readLine();
      int comma = s.indexOf(",");
      int x = Integer.parseInt(s.substring(0,comma).trim());
      int y = Integer.parseInt(s.substring(comma+1).trim());
      return new Location(x,y);
   }
   private int x, y;
}
```

Using the Classes

Before we conclude, we should write a small complete program that uses all the methods defined in our new classes. This has the following benefits:

- It provides us with an initial program that tests the classes.
- By writing a complete program, we make sure the interface is consistent—all arguments make sense in the context of their methods and no arguments are superfluous or missing.

In this case, we also benefit from the opportunity to make sure the input format for our program has been adequately specified. We have decided that a `Location` will be represented as a single line containing x and y values separated by a comma; from the definition of the `Name` class we know that `Name`s are represented as two lines, the first containing the first name and the second containing the last name. In our `RepairPerson` definition we decided that a `RepairPerson` will be a `Name` followed by a `Location`.

Here is a simple program that reads in three `RepairPerson`s followed by a `Location` and outputs the name of the `RepairPerson` closest to the given `Location`:

```
public class TestRepairDispatcher {
   public static void main(String[] s) throws Exception {
```

```
    BufferedReader br = new BufferedReader(new
                        InputStreamReader(System.in));
    RepairPerson rp1, rp2, rp3;
    rp1 = RepairPerson.read(br);
    rp2 = RepairPerson.read(br);
    rp3 = RepairPerson.read(br);
    Location customer = Location.read(br);
    int d1 = rp1.getDistanceFrom(customer);
    int d2 = rp2.getDistanceFrom(customer);
    int d3 = rp3.getDistanceFrom(customer);
    System.out.print("Send ");
    if (d1<=d2 && d1<=d3) {
       rp1.getName().print(System.out);
       rp1.setLocation(customer);
    } else if (d2<=d1 && d2<=d3) {
       rp2.getName().print(System.out);
       rp2.setLocation(customer);
    } else if (d3<=d1 && d3<=d2) {
       rp3.getName().print(System.out);
       rp3.setLocation(customer);
    }
    System.out.println("");
  }
}
```

The data file read by this program looks like this:

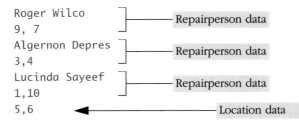

The TestRepairDispatcher class acts as an *application class*—it provides a main() method. TestRepairDispatcher uses the Location and RepairPerson classes to create a small prototype application. The only methods in the system not invoked by this class are the constructors and the getDistanceFrom() method of Location; however, those methods are used by the read() methods and RepairPerson's getDistanceFrom() method. Thus the main() method of TestRepairDispatcher invokes, directly or indirectly, the complete set of methods of the two classes.

Summary

Programming an application in Java is largely an exercise in using existing classes and defining new classes to fill in the gaps. A procedure that aids in the discovery of the relevant objects of an application and the design of any new classes is thus a valuable tool for the programmer. This chapter presents the following procedure:

- Determine the primary objects of the application by examining the nouns of the problem statement.
- Decide on the desired behavior of the classes corresponding to these objects. This provides the basic set of methods available to the user of the class.
- Define the interface. The prototypes of the methods are defined, including the nature of additional information provided as arguments.
- Instance variables are introduced to maintain the state of the class.
- The method bodies are implemented.

This process is not always followed in exactly this order; as we develop details of our class design, we may have to revisit decisions we made earlier in the process. Similarly, design decisions made while designing one class may affect the design of a related class.

Key Terms

has-a A relationship between an object and some value such that the value is part of the object's state. This is usually expressed in Java by the object possessing an instance variable corresponding to the value.

Questions for Review

1. Why is it useful to write sample code before determining a class's interface?
2. Why shouldn't we develop the "internals" of a class immediately?

Exercises

1. In our redevelopment of the Counter class, the only noun in the problem statement that became a class was *counter*. What happened to the other nouns?
2. Mimic the above process for the Minimizer class.
3. Mimic the above process for the Name class.
4. Design and implement classes to solve the following problems:
   - Many applications are *menu-driven*: they provide a list of options and ask the user to enter a choice. Design a Menu class that supports this behavior. It should provide behavior allowing the programmer to provide up to 9

options (by providing a `String` describing the option). It should also provide behavior asking the user to make a selection; the `int` value of the user's selection should be provided to the user of the class. The 0 selection should mean quit; if the user makes this choice, your code should terminate the program by invoking `System.exit(0)`.

- Write a program that models the car of tomorrow, laden with safety features. This car responds to various commands, such as "Step on the gas" (go), "Hit the brakes" (stop), "Open door," and "Close door." If it is unsafe to perform the action (for example, opening the door while the car is moving), the car doesn't perform the action and instead issues an alert. Your model should allow the user to issue a sequence of at least 10 commands (you may want to use a counting loop).

- Many toll roads allow commuters to pay their tolls via a radio transceiver, or "tag," that communicates with the tollbooth as the car containing it passes through the toll area. Each new tag is "charged" with some amount of money; each tollbooth deducts a toll from the tag (the toll charge may vary among tollbooths). If the tag has sufficient funds to pay the toll, the booth prints a "Go" message; if the tag is left with less than $10 after paying the toll, the booth prints an additional "Low Balance" message; if the tag has insufficient funds; the booth prints a "Stop: Pay Toll" message. Tags may be "recharged" with an arbitrary amount.

5. Modify the `RepairPerson` class to allow the location of a repairperson to be retrieved. Which steps of the class development procedure are changed because of this modification?

6. Modify the `RepairPerson` class to allow the dispatcher to put a repairperson on break (by sending a `goOnBreak()` message), put a repairperson back to work (by sending an `endBreak()` message), and find out whether a repairperson is on break (by sending an `isOnBreak()` message). Repairpersons on break cannot be assigned to respond to a customer. Modify `TestRepairDispatcher` to take breaks into account (note that now *no* repairpersons may be available to respond!).

7. Design and implement a class that models an employee. Creating an `Employee` object entails providing the name and hourly rate of the worker. The `Employee` object should possess a method that receives the number of hours worked as an argument and returns the earned wages.

8. Add a `read()` method to the `Employee` class.

Multiple Controls: Layout and Event Handling

Introducing Layout

In designing applets we previously paid little attention to the placement of controls—we let the applet's default behavior display the controls from left to right and from top to bottom. Sometimes the placement of graphic controls such as buttons doesn't matter, but often it does. In our next example, a simple calculator applet, the placement of the buttons that serve as the keys of the calculator is critical. (See Figure 7.2.)

The placement of the contents of an applet is guided by a LayoutManager object. When we put something into an applet using an add() message, the applet's LayoutManager determines the position of the added object. Applet is an example of a *container* class in Java—a class whose objects can graphically contain controls or other containers (as opposed to Button, for example—you can't put anything into a Button). The LayoutManager object associated with a container may be an instance of one of several different LayoutManager classes; we will discuss FlowLayout and BorderLayout here. (The relationship of these classes to each other is analogous to the relationship of the InputStream classes, Buffered-InputStream and FileInputStream.)

Programmers can control the way Applets or other container objects place their contents by creating a LayoutManager object of their choice and sending it as an argument to a setLayout() message to the container, as shown in the following code:

```
public class MyApplet extends Applet {
    public void init() {
        setLayout(new FlowLayout());  Sends a setLayout() message to itself
        ...
    }
}
```

Figure 7.2
Two calculator layouts.

```
        0.000

    C   =  /   *

    7   8  9   -

    4   5  6   +

    1   2  3
                =
      0     .

  Our goal: calculator with
  reasonably placed buttons
```

```
        0.000    C  =  /

    *   7  8  9  -  4

    5   6  +  1  2  3

            0     .
      =

   To avoid losing control over
     the placement of buttons
```

The FlowLayout manager causes the controls to be placed one after the other in the order in which they were added to the container. The controls start in the upper left corner and proceed to the right. Depending on the particular container, they may or may not "wrap around" to the space below when they reach the right end of the container. If we used a FlowLayout for our Calculator applet, its appearance would be unacceptable. (See Figure 7.3.)

Alternatively, the BorderLayout manager views the container as divided into five regions: north, south, east, west, and center. (We can, however, choose to use fewer than five positions.) It allows the programmer to assign Buttons (or other controls) to these regions. The controls assigned to the north and south are stretched out horizontally to cover the top and bottom borders of the container; the controls assigned to east and west are stretched vertically to fill the sides between the north and south controls; and the control in the center gets what's left. Obviously we can't rely solely on BorderLayout—we have 19 controls, not 5. If we put the 7, 8, 9, –, and 4 to positions north, west, center, east, and south, it would look silly (see Figure 7.4).

There are other layout manager classes available in Java, but their use is beyond the scope of this text. We are not stuck, however. Java provides a tool—the Panel class—that, when combined with the layout managers described above, allows us to accomplish our goal.

Figure 7.3
The result of using
FlowLayout for our
Calculator applet.

Figure 7.4
Two results of using
BorderLayout.

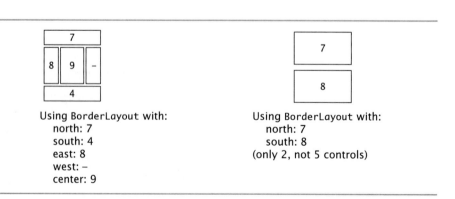

The Panel class is the simplest container class imaginable—just about the only thing we can do with a Panel object is assign it a layout manager and start adding objects. The trick to using Panels is to divide the applet region into different Panels, each containing a handful of the applet's controls. This makes it easier to lay out the controls; just a few are given to each Panel. The Panels themselves can be contained in other Panels or in the applet itself.

Our Panel strategy is shown in Figure 7.5. The first three rows of keys on the calculator are Panels containing four Buttons in a row—perfect for a FlowLayout layout manager. The 1 and 2 keys are placed in a Panel using BorderLayout and occupy west and east. This Panel is itself placed in another Panel, along with the 0 key. By using BorderLayout again with 1 and 2 in north and 0 in south, we get the effect of stretching out the 0 key.

In order for this strategy to work, we must guarantee that our Buttons have the same basic size (unless stretched by a BorderLayout). We do this by labeling each Button with a single character and using a fixed-width font (i.e., all letters are the same width, even, for example, l and W).

The Label object, which we use to display the result of a calculation, and the Panel objects that contain the Buttons are added to the applet in FlowLayout fashion.

To prevent the Panels of the applet from marching off horizontally in unfavorable ways, we can force the applet to assume a certain size by using the resize() method. The arguments to this method are the desired width and height of the calculator. We compute these by examining the components of the applet itself. For example, row1 is a variable that holds a reference to the Panel object that contains the first row of Buttons. The width of that row, plus a little bit of elbow room, is the width we desire for the applet itself. The code follows:

```
row1.getWidth();
```

Figure 7.5
Using Panels.

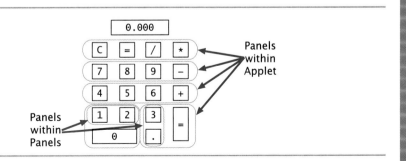

The height of a row is the same as the height of a Button. There are five rows of Buttons, plus the TextField, and there is spacing between the rows. Multiplying Button height by 8, as follows, easily accommodates the height of the applet:

```
8*d1.getHeight();
```

Once the applet is resized,

```
resize(row1.getWidth(),8*d1.getHeight());
```

all its components must be laid out again. This is accomplished by invoking the applet's validate() method.

This calculation, unfortunately, cannot be done within init()—at that point the sizes for the Panels, Buttons, and so on, have not yet been computed by the system. So we carry out this calculation and the resize() operation in the paint() method.

The code for the applet is given below. Its length is primarily a direct result of the fact that there are 19 buttons plus one Label. The code is made somewhat simpler by using the following helper methods:

- makeButton()—given a label for the button and a Color, create a Button, set its color, set its font to "Courier" and return a reference to it.
- makeButtons()—call makeButton() with different arguments 19 times in order to create all the Buttons.
- makePanel()—given a reference to some layout manager and a Color, create a Panel with the given layout manager and Color and return a reference to it.

Now init() can place the various components in their containers, as follows, in the manner sketched above:

```java
import java.awt.*;
import java.applet.Applet;
public class CalculatorApplet extends Applet {
    private Button makeButton(String label, Color color) {
        Button b = new Button(label);
        b.setBackground(color);
        b.setFont(new Font("Courier", Font.BOLD, 10));
        return b;
    }
    private Panel makePanel(LayoutManager lm, Color c) {
        Panel p = new Panel();
        p.setLayout(lm);
        p.setBackground(c);
        return p;
    }
```

```
private void makeButtons() {
    Color lightRed = new Color(255,100,100);
    Color lightBlue = new Color(100,100,255);
    Color yellow = new Color(255,255,0);

    c = makeButton("C",lightRed);
    eq = makeButton("=",lightBlue);
    div = makeButton("/",lightBlue);
    times = makeButton("*",lightBlue);
    d7 = makeButton("7",yellow);
    d8 = makeButton("8",yellow);
    d9 = makeButton("9",yellow);
    minus = makeButton("-",lightBlue);
    d4 = makeButton("4",yellow);
    d5 = makeButton("5",yellow);
    d6 = makeButton("6",yellow);
    plus = makeButton("+",lightBlue);
    d1 = makeButton("1",yellow);
    d2 = makeButton("2",yellow);
    d3 = makeButton("3",yellow);
    d0 = makeButton("0",yellow);
    dp = makeButton(".",yellow);
    eq2 = makeButton("=",lightBlue);
}

public void init() {
    background = new Color(200,255,255);
    this.setLayout(new FlowLayout(
                FlowLayout.CENTER,4,1));

    result = new Label("0.00000 ",Label.RIGHT);
    result.setBackground(new Color(255,255,255));
        add(result);
    makeButtons();

    row1 = makePanel(new FlowLayout(FlowLayout.LEFT,4,2),
                background);
    row1.add(c);
    row1.add(eq);
    row1.add(div);
    row1.add(times);

    row2 = makePanel(new FlowLayout(FlowLayout.LEFT,4,2),
                background);
    row2.add(d7);
    row2.add(d8);
    row2.add(d9);
```

```
        row2.add(minus);
        row3 = makePanel(new FlowLayout(FlowLayout.LEFT,4,2),
                         background);
        row3.add(d4);
        row3.add(d5);
        row3.add(d6);
        row3.add(plus);
        add(row1);
        add(row2);
        add(row3);
        p12 = makePanel(new BorderLayout(2,2),background);
        p12.add("West",d1);
        p12.add("East",d2);
        p120 = makePanel(new BorderLayout(2,2),background);
        p120.add("North",p12);
        p120.add("South",d0);
        p3p = makePanel(new BorderLayout(2,2),background);
        p3p.add("North",d3);
        p3p.add("South",dp);
        p3peq = makePanel(new BorderLayout(2,2),background);
        p3peq.add("West",p3p);
        p3peq.add("East",eq2);
        add(p120);
        add(p3peq);
        setBackground(background);
    }
    public void paint(Graphics g) {
        resize(row1.getWidth(),8*d1.getHeight());
        validate();
    }
    private Panel row1, row2, row3, p12, p120, p3p, p3peq;
    private Button c, eq, div, times,
                   d7, d8, d9, minus,
                   d4, d5, d6, plus,
                   d1, d2, d3,
                   d0,    dp, eq2;
    private Color background;
        private Label result;
}
```

Figure 7.6 shows the results of this code.

Figure 7.6
The final calculator result.

Handling Events from Multiple Sources

We would now like to process the button-click events. Unlike `MinimizerApplet`, this applet has many `Button`s, not just one. Again, the applet object will act as the listener, but there must be a way for it to distinguish which `Button` was clicked when `actionPerformed()` is invoked.

The `ActionEvent` object that is passed to `actionPerformed()` provides this information. The `ActionEvent` class provides a method called `getActionCommand()`, which returns an object that contains information specific to the source of the event. In the case of a clicked `Button`, `getActionCommand()` returns a `String` object that corresponds to the label of the `Button`.

We can use this to identify the individual `Button`s:

```
public void actionPerformed(ActionEvent ae) {
    String s = ae.getActionCommand();
    if (s.equals("+"))
        handle the plus operation
    ...
    else if (s.equals("1"))
        handle the one case
    ...
}
```

Setting up the cases for each of the `Button`s is easy, if tedious; figuring out to do once we know which `Button` has been clicked is an entirely different matter. We have to analyze what should happen when each of the `Button`s is clicked.

The Processing Logic

The first thing we should realize is that the behavior for each of the Buttons d0 through d9 is the same: append the digit to the display. Similarly, the plus, minus, times, and div Buttons are processed almost identically—they perform the operation; the only real difference is which operation is used. We can thus group the Buttons into several categories:

- Digit
- Operator
- Clear (C)
- Decimal (.)
- Equals (=)

We must also analyze what action should be taken for each of these categories.

When a digit is clicked, it should be incorporated into the display. If the previous Button clicked was C, =, or an operator, the clicked digit is the first digit of a new operand, and the display should be cleared and set to this digit alone. If the previous Button clicked was a digit or the decimal point, then the new digit should be added to the end of the displayed value.

If the decimal Button is clicked, a decimal point should be added to the display, but only if we have not already done so for this operand.

Clicking the clear Button should reset the calculator to its original state when the applet began.

When an operator button is pressed on a calculator, the corresponding operation cannot be performed until the *next* operand is input. However, the operator does signify the *end* of the previous operand. Furthermore, assuming there was a previous operator, *that* operator may be applied to the two previous operands. For example, suppose the user clicks the following button sequence:

```
123 + 23 *
```

When the + is first entered, the addition cannot be performed yet—we don't have the second operand, namely, 23. When the * is entered, we know that the previous operand, 23, has been completed and the addition may be performed. At this point the multiplication cannot be performed because we don't know *its* second operand.

Once an operation has been performed, its result becomes the new display and also the first operand for the next operator. In addition, as we mentioned in the context of the digit buttons, pressing an operator key signals that the next digit entered is the beginning of a new operand.

Pressing the equals button has a similar effect. The previous operator can be evaluated and the result displayed. Again, subsequent digits form a new operand.

The only difference between this button and one of the four operators is that the equals button does not perform another operation. Because the equals button is so similar to the operator buttons, we will handle it together with them.

The preceding discussion leads to the following methods:

- `handleDigit()`—processes digits
- `handleOperator()`—processes operators and equals
- `handleDecimal()`—processes decimal point
- `handleClear()`—processes clear

Rather than have `actionPerformed()` test for each individual case, we can be clever and group the cases into the above categories. We do this with the `indexOf()` method of class `String`, which tests to see whether one `String` object appears in another. We declare a constant `String`:

```
static final String digits = "0123456789";
```

Given the variable `s`, which contains a reference to the button label, the expression

```
digits.indexOf(s)
```

returns the location in `digits` of the first occurrence of `s`. If the `String` referenced by `s` does not occur in `digits`, −1 (an invalid location for a `String`) is returned. This tells us whether `s` was created from the text of a digit `Button`.

We can use a similar constant, `operators`:

```
static final String operators = "+-*/=";
```

and have the expression

```
operators.indexOf(s)
```

test whether the `Button` clicked was an operator.

We will pass the `String` `s` to `handleDigit()` and `handleOperator()` to allow them to identify the actual button pressed. These methods, therefore, each have a `String` parameter. The `handleClear()` and `handleDecimal()` methods don't need any information—in each case there is only one `Button` that would cause them to be invoked.

Here is the code for our `actionPerformed()` method:

```
public void actionPerformed(ActionEvent e) {
    String s = (String)e.getActionCommand();
    if (digits.indexOf(s) != -1)
        handleDigit(s);
    else if (s.equals("."))
        handleDecimal();
    else if (operators.indexOf(s) != -1)
```

```
        handleOperator(s);
    else if (s.equals("C"))
        handleClear();
}
```

The Instance Variables and their Initialization

Before we write the other methods, let us determine the state that must be maintained by our calculator. That will provide us with our instance variables.

We must keep track of the last operator entered because we cannot apply it until its second operand is entered.

The entry of an operator signals the end of the previous operand; we must keep track of that so that the next digit entered becomes the first digit of the next operand and not the trailing digit of the previous one.

Pressing an operator key makes sense only if at least one operand has been entered, so we must keep track of that as well. After the operator has been clicked, we must wait for the next operand to be entered—however, we must hold on to the first operand.

Pressing the decimal key should be legal only if we have not already done so for this operand.

The above leads to the introduction of a double instance variable, three boolean instance variables, and one String instance variable:

```
double opd1;                          // First operand
boolean sawDecimal, newOpd, sawAnOpd;
String lastOptr;                      // Last operator
```

These variables have the following initial values:

```
sawDecimal - false
newOpd - true
sawAnOpd - false
lastOptr - ""
```

The opd1 variable need not be initialized—it will get its value when the user enters it.

In addition, these variables should be reset to these values when the clear Button is clicked—the effect of that Button is to completely clear out the calculator's operation. We therefore introduce a method, clearCalc(), to perform this initialization:

```
private void clearCalc() {
    sawDecimal = false;
    newOpd = true;
    sawAnOpd = false;
    lastOptr = "";
```

```
        result.setText(initialString);
}
```

This method also displays the initial value in the result label, using the constant

```
static final String initialString = "0.00000";
```

The Other Methods

We must now implement the methods that process our four Button categories. Our previous analysis of the actions taken by each of the categories will help us here.

The handleClear() method is nothing more than an invocation of clearCalc():

```
private void handleClear() {
    clearCalc();
}
```

We also add an invocation of clearCalc() to the end of our init() method to initialize the calculator the first time through.

The handleDigit() method receives a String that corresponds to the text of the button pressed: "0", "1", ..., "9". If this is the beginning of a new operand (newOpd evaluates to true), we reset the display to contain the digit alone and set newOpd to false. Otherwise, we get the label text and concatenate the new digit onto the end. We must also set sawAnOpd to true to signal that an operand has been entered:

```
private void handleDigit(String s) {
    if (newOpd) {
        result.setText(s);
        newOpd = false;
    } else
        result.setText(result.getText()+s);
    sawAnOpd = true;
}
```

The method handleDecimal() checks to see whether a decimal point has already been entered. If one has not been entered, handleDecimal() operates like handle-Digit() does: If this is the beginning of a new operand, it resets the display to "0" (calculators always place a 0 in front of a leading decimal point), and newOpd is set to false. If this is not a new operand, the decimal point is concatenated to the end of the display. Once the point has been added, sawDecimal is set to true to prevent another decimal point from being added:

```
private void handleDecimal() {
    if (!sawDecimal) {
        if (newOpd) {
```

```
            result.setText("0.");
            newOpd = false;
        } else
            result.setText(result.getText()+".");
        sawDecimal = true;
    }
}
```

The `handleOperator()` method receives the text of the clicked-on operator button. However, as we discussed earlier, it is not *this* operation that is performed, but rather the previous one (if it exists). The operations must be performed on numbers. However, the operands are obtained from the display as `Strings`, through the `getText()` method. To make things nice and clean, we introduce a helper method, `getDisplay()`, which returns a `double` corresponding to the value displayed in the result `Label`:

```
private double getDisplay() {
    return Double.parseDouble(result.getText());
}
```

We can now write `handleOperator()`. If no operand has been seen yet, we ignore the operator click and return. Otherwise, we perform the appropriate operation depending upon the *last* operator, contained in `lastOptr`. In each case, the result becomes the new operand to remember for the next operation. For example, given

```
1 + 2 * 5
```

when we evaluate the +, the result, 3, becomes the first operand to the *.

If the last operator was an = or the current operator is the first to be entered (and thus `lastOptr` equals " "), the operand is simply the value already in the display.

Once the new value has been obtained, it is set as the new result value. The operator just entered becomes the last operator, and we signal that a new operand is to be entered and no decimal points have been entered:

```
private void handleOperator(String s) {
    if (!sawAnOpd)
        return;
    if (lastOptr.equals("+"))
        opd1 += getDisplay();
    else if (lastOptr.equals("-"))
        opd1 -= getDisplay();
    else if (lastOptr.equals("*"))
        opd1 *= getDisplay();
    else if (lastOptr.equals("/"))
        opd1 /= getDisplay();
```

```
        else
            opd1 = getDisplay();
        result.setText(opd1+"");
        lastOptr = s;
        sawDecimal = false;
        newOpd = true;
    }
```

Concatenation with "" converts opd1 to a `String`

The Complete Applet

Here is the completed applet, including our layout code from above. Notice that we did not pay any attention to the layout during the course of developing the event-handling logic. In this case, where the `Button`s were placed made no difference to us.

```java
import java.awt.*;
import java.awt.event.*;
import java.applet.Applet;

public class CalculatorApplet extends Applet implements
                        ActionListener {
    public void init() {
        backgroundColor = new Color(200,255,255);
        this.setLayout(new FlowLayout(FlowLayout. CENTER,4,1));
        result = new Label(initialString, Label.RIGHT);
        result.setBackground(new Color(255,255,255));
        add(result);
        makeButtons();
        row1 = makePanel(new FlowLayout(FlowLayout.LEFT,4,2),
                        backgroundColor);
        row1.add(c);
        row1.add(eq);
        row1.add(div);
        row1.add(times);
        row2 = makePanel(new FlowLayout(FlowLayout.LEFT,4,2),
                        backgroundColor);
        row2.add(d7);
        row2.add(d8);
        row2.add(d9);
        row2.add(minus);
        row3 = makePanel(new FlowLayout(FlowLayout.LEFT,4,2),
                        backgroundColor);
        row3.add(d4);
        row3.add(d5);
        row3.add(d6);
        row3.add(plus);
```

```
            add(row1);
            add(row2);
            add(row3);
            p12 = makePanel(new BorderLayout(2,2), backgroundColor);
            p12.add("West",d1);
            p12.add("East",d2);
            p120 = makePanel(new BorderLayout(2,2), backgroundColor);
            p120.add("North",p12);
            p120.add("South",d0);
            p3p = makePanel(new BorderLayout(2,2), backgroundColor);
            p3p.add("North",d3);
            p3p.add("South",dp);
            p3peq = makePanel(new BorderLayout(2,2), backgroundColor);
            p3peq.add("West",p3p);
            p3peq.add("East",eq2);
            add(p120);
            add(p3peq);
            setBackground(backgroundColor);
            c.addActionListener(this);
            eq.addActionListener(this);
            eq2.addActionListener(this);
            div.addActionListener(this);
            times.addActionListener(this);
            minus.addActionListener(this);
            plus.addActionListener(this);
            d0.addActionListener(this);
            d1.addActionListener(this);
            d2.addActionListener(this);
            d3.addActionListener(this);
            d4.addActionListener(this);
            d5.addActionListener(this);
            d6.addActionListener(this);
            d7.addActionListener(this);
            d8.addActionListener(this);
            d9.addActionListener(this);
            clearCalc();
        }
        public void paint(Graphics g) {
            resize(row1.getWidth(),8*d1.getHeight());
            validate();
        }
        public void actionPerformed(ActionEvent e) {
            String s = (String) e.getActionCommand();
```

```
        if (digits.indexOf(s) != -1)
            handleDigit(s);
        else if (s.equals("."))
            handleDecimal();
        else if (operators.indexOf(s) != -1)
            handleOperator(s);
        else if (s.equals("C"))
            handleClear();
    }
    private void handleDigit(String s) {
        if (newOpd) {
            result.setText(s);
            newOpd = false;
        } else
            result.setText(result.getText()+s);
        sawAnOpd = true;
    }
    private void handleClear() {
        clearCalc();
    }
    private void clearCalc() {
        sawDecimal = false;
        newOpd = true;
        sawAnOpd = false;
        lastOptr = "";
        result.setText(initialString);
    }
    private void handleOperator(String s) {
        if (!sawAnOpd)
            return;
        if (lastOptr.equals("+"))
            opd1 += getDisplay();
        else if (lastOptr.equals("-"))
            opd1 -= getDisplay();
        else if (lastOptr.equals("*"))
            opd1 *= getDisplay();
        else if (lastOptr.equals("/"))
            opd1 /= getDisplay();
        else
            opd1 = getDisplay();
        result.setText(opd1 + "");        Concatenation of opd1 with ""
        lastOptr = s;                     converts opd1 to String.
        sawDecimal = false;
```

```
            newOpd = true;
        }
        private void handleDecimal() {
            if (!sawDecimal) {
                if (newOpd) {
                    result.setText("0.");
                    newOpd = false;
                } else
                    result.setText(result.getText() + ".");
                sawDecimal = true;
            }
        }
        private double getDisplay() {
            return Double.parseDouble(result.getText());
        }
        private Button makeButton(String label, Color color,
                                  Font font) {
            Button b = new Button(label);
            b.setBackground(color);
            b.setFont(font);
            return b;
        }
        private Panel makePanel(LayoutManager lm, Color c) {
            Panel p = new Panel();
            p.setLayout(lm);
            p.setBackground(c);
            return p;
        }
        private void makeButtons() {
            Font   f = new Font("Courier", Font.BOLD, 10);
            Color  lightRed = new Color(255,100,100);
            Color  lightBlue = new Color(100,100,255);
            Color  yellow = new Color(255,255,0);
            c = makeButton("C",lightRed,f);
            eq = makeButton("=",lightBlue,f);
            div = makeButton("/",lightBlue,f);
            times = makeButton("*",lightBlue,f);
            d7 = makeButton("7",yellow,f);
            d8 = makeButton("8",yellow,f);
            d9 = makeButton("9",yellow,f);
            minus = makeButton("-",lightBlue,f);
            d4 = makeButton("4",yellow,f);
            d5 = makeButton("5",yellow,f);
            d6 = makeButton("6",yellow,f);
```

```
      plus = makeButton("+",lightBlue,f);
      d1 = makeButton("1",yellow,f);
      d2 = makeButton("2",yellow,f);
      d3 = makeButton("3",yellow,f);
      d0 = makeButton("0",yellow,f);
      dp = makeButton(".",yellow,f);
      eq2 = makeButton("=",lightBlue,f);
   }
   static final String initialString = "0.00000";
   static final String digits = "0123456789";
   static final String operators = "+-*/=";
   private String lastOptr;
   private String Filler = "        ";
   private boolean sawDecimal, newOpd, sawAnOpd;
   private double opd1;
   private Panel row1, row2, row3, p12, p120, p3p, p3peq;
   private int    appletWidth, appletHeight;
   private Button c, eq, div, times,
                  d7, d8, d9, minus,
                  d4, d5, d6, plus,
                  d1, d2, d3,
                  d0,     dp, eq2;
   private Color  backgroundColor;
   private Label  result;
}
```

Summary

We developed this calculator applet in two phases: First we designed the display layout, then we developed the code for the actual processing. It is interesting to note that the "layout-only" applet was a full applet: It compiled cleanly and could even be executed, it just couldn't respond to button clicks, perform the operations, or do anything remotely useful. The second phase of development focused solely on those very tasks. What we see is a clear and clean separation of the part of the applet that is responsible for the display and input from the portion that does the actual processing required by the application. This separation will be a recurring theme in several of the applets we develop in the rest of this text.

Suggested Experiments

1. Design and implement a GUI front end for the Counter class. It should include at least two buttons, corresponding to the *increment* and *reset* operations, as well as a Label in which the current value of the Counter is displayed.
2. Add a remainder function to the calculator applet.
3. Modify the calculator applet to allow a unary minus to be entered.

4. Implement a cash register applet. A cash register has buttons for the 10 digits plus a button for double zeroes ("00"). It has four "operational" buttons: "taxable," "non-tax," "total," and "tendered." Its behavior is as follows: Because every value is in dollars and cents, there is no need for a decimal-point button; instead, the last two digits of every value entered are interpreted as cents and displayed to the right of the decimal point. Thus, entering "15" causes the display to show 0.15, and entering "21000" causes the display to show 210.00. After a price is entered, either the "taxable" or "non-tax" button is pressed. The display then shows the total of all prices entered so far. After all prices have been entered, the "total" button is pressed, which computes and displays the total cost for the transaction: the total cost of all non-tax items, plus the total cost of all taxable items, plus sales tax on the taxable items. Then the amount of cash tendered is entered, followed by the "tendered" button. The cash register then displays the amount of change to be provided.

Verifying Object Behavior

8.1 Introduction

All applied sciences possess the concept of a *testing phase:* determining whether a hypothesis, product, or design is correct and behaves in the expected manner. Pharmaceutical companies test new drugs first on laboratory animals and then possibly on a select segment of the population, prior to a general marketing of the product. Aircraft manufacturers test new designs of planes endlessly, first using computers, then in physical mock-ups, and finally in full prototypes.

Testing is a crucial part of the software cycle. It is too often overlooked by students who have unique time and effort constraints. Yet it is precisely those students who, as the programmers of the future, will bear the responsibility for creating code that is safe to operate. Code with errors can have disastrous consequences. A computerized stock-trading program that malfunctions could cause the loss of millions of dollars if trade is interrupted for even the shortest period of time. The computer that monitors the heart rate of an intensive care patient and triggers an alarm in the event of heart failure cannot afford to malfunction.

It is the goal of this chapter to impress on you the importance of testing. From the outset, therefore, let us state: *Testing is not an afterthought or something that you do* after *you've finished developing the program.* Rather, it is an integral part of the program development process, for which time and effort must be allocated. Any thought to the contrary will guarantee the failure of your programming effort.

Beginners sometimes think that once their code has compiled with no errors, they are almost finished. Nothing could be further from the truth. If we developed a class using the steps outlined in the previous chapters for developing code, it would be a fairly straightforward matter to remove any compilation errors. The class is not ready to be released, however. It must first be tested to ensure that it behaves in the expected manner. In an industrial setting, a set of tests known as a **test suite** is usually created, and we speak of *running the code against the test suite.*

Testing is an attempt to minimize the errors in our programs. However, as a famous computer scientist, Edsgar Djikstra, once said, "Testing merely confirms the presence of errors, never their absence." That is, if during testing an error is discovered, we determine its cause and fix it. However, if no errors arise during the testing phase, there is no guarantee that the code has no errors, merely that our tests have not exposed any.

Errors come in all varieties. Sometimes they are trivial to fix, sometimes they take days to discover and then correct, and sometimes they force us to go back to the drawing board and redo some of our design. Having to do that can be enormously costly—that's one reason for having a careful approach to class design.

Testing is more than simply running a few arbitrarily chosen cases. It involves careful thought and a good knowledge of both the application and the software solution. With improperly designed testing, the most obvious errors can and will remain in our programs. Consider the following class, which contains an (admittedly stupid) erroneous method:

```java
class DoubleTrouble {
    public DoubleTrouble(int value) {
        this.value = value;
    }
    // doubleIt returns the value instance variable multiplied by 2.
    public int doubleIt() {
        this.value += 2;        Ooops! Adding 2, not doubling.
        return this.value;
    }
    private int value;
}
```

together with a fragment of code that is supposed to test it:

```java
DoubleTrouble t = new DoubleTrouble(2);
System.out.println(t.doubleIt());   Prints 4, looks OK.
```

Executing this test fragment produces the correct result, even though the method is completely wrong. The moral of this story is that it is easy for a small set of test cases to falsely validate the code.

8.2 Categories of Errors

Although errors arise in a number of ways, they all fall into one of three basic categories. Errors that occur during the translation of the source (e.g., during compilation) are, appropriately enough, known as *compilation errors*. Errors that cause a program to abruptly terminate during execution without completing its task are called *run-time* errors. In a Java program this is usually accompanied by an announcement of an "Exception" followed by a torrent of error messages. Finally there are errors that don't cause any explicit error but rather cause the program to produce an incorrect result. This kind of an error is known as a *logic error*. Run-time and logic errors are commonly referred to as *bugs*.

Compilation-Time Errors—Syntax and Semantics

As the name implies, compilation errors occur at compile or program translation time. Such errors range from the trivial omission of a semicolon to the use of an uninitialized variable.

Let us examine several examples of compilation errors, beginning with the missing semicolon:

```
x = 5    No semicolon
```

Roughly speaking, this mistake corresponds to leaving out a period or comma in a sentence. We thus further categorize this as a *syntax error,* the word *syntax* meaning sentence structure or grammar. In other words, leaving out a semicolon is a grammatical error as far as the Java compiler is concerned—the statement has not been formed correctly. We may understand the intent of the statement (just as we understand the grammatically incorrect sentence, "The boy have a toy"), but the compiler still generates the error message.

Other examples of syntax errors include

- Omitting a comma between arguments in an argument list: `f(a b)`
- Badly parenthesized expressions: `(3 + 5 or 3 + 5)`
- Other badly formed expressions: `3 + % 5`

Syntax errors are usually easy to fix—they are often caused by typing mistakes. On occasion, however, the compiler does get tripped up by a syntax error and has a difficult time getting back on track. This in turn can cause it to generate (or *cascade*) numerous additional, spurious error messages (i.e., messages that are caused by the compiler's "confusion" rather than by any real errors in the subsequent source). If during compilation you see an error message that is followed by a slew of additional messages (beginning with the same or next statement as the first error), none of which seem to make sense, try fixing the first error—many of the others will often disappear as well.

Another kind of error, using an uninitialized variable, does not arise as a result of a badly formed statement:

```
int i;
i++;    i was never assigned an initial value.
```

Although the structure of each of the statements is correct, there is a mistake in the meaning, or *semantics*, of the code. The above fragment makes no sense: The value of `i` cannot be meaningfully incremented if it has no meaningful value in the first place.

Other examples of semantic errors are

- Forgetting to declare a variable—it makes no sense to assign to or from a variable that has not been declared to exist.

- Assigning a String constant to an int variable—the assignment makes no sense.

The majority of semantic errors (including the last error above) fall into a category known as *type errors*. These are errors resulting from an attempt to use a variable in a manner that is incompatible with its type. For example, String values may not be assigned to int variables. Other examples of type errors include

- Using an object in an arithmetic expression—it makes no sense to apply an arithmetic operator to an instance of a class.
- Invoking a method of an object whose class does not possess such a method—it makes no sense to ask the object to do something for which it was not defined.
- Sending a message to a primitive data type—message sending is incompatible with such types.
- Assigning a double to an int—the resulting possible loss of precision is too dangerous for the compiler to allow without any complaint.

Unlike syntax errors, the intended meaning behind a semantic error is not always clear. For example, given the error

```
int i = "Hello";
```

what was the intent of the programmer? Because of this, semantic errors are usually somewhat more difficult to correct than syntax errors. They reflect some mistake in our understanding of the meaning of a particular construct or variable or of the relationships between variables. That the compiler detects such errors and prevents us from running our code until they have been eliminated is extremely important. A semantically incorrect construct by definition is one that makes no sense, and executing such a construct would surely result in incorrect results.

Run-time Errors

The second general category of errors arises during the execution of the Java code. These are errors that could not be detected during translation time. An example of such an error is

```
int w, x;
x = Integer.parseInt(...);
w = 10 / x;
```

Suppose the value 0 is read into x. The third statement then results in a division by zero, which is illegal (mathematically as well as in Java) and results in the program terminating abruptly with an error message from the Java interpreter such as

```
java.lang.ArithmeticException:  divide  by  zero
    at Test.main(TrivialApplication.java:10)
```

(different Java interpreters on different platforms may generate somewhat different messages).

Run-time errors are usually the most difficult to correct. Unlike compile-time errors, with run-time errors it is not always clear what the true source of the error is. As an extremely simple example, suppose the preceding code were instead

```
int w, x, y, z;
x = Integer.parseInt(…);
y = Integer.parseInt(…);
z = Integer.parseInt(…);
…
```

Code that manipulates x, y, *and* z *using* if *statements*

```
…
w = 10 / ((x – y) * z);
```

A division by zero error here can arise either from x being equal to y or from z being zero. Before we can fix the error we first have to determine how it arose. Even once we know the nature of the error, it is not always clear how we should remedy the situation. For example, in the division by zero example, what are we supposed to do when a zero value for z occurs?

The process of fixing such errors or **bugs** is called **debugging**, and often is the most time-consuming aspect of the software development process. But even before we can fix such errors, we must be made aware of their existence. This can only be done properly through a thorough testing of the code.

Logic Errors

Even worse than run-time errors are those errors that do not reveal themselves in any obvious fashion. They often arise as a result of the requirements of the software being incorrectly implemented. In our context, this would mean not following the statement of the problem correctly. The example at the beginning of our chapter was just such a situation. If the statement of the problem calls for a method that doubles the instance variable and instead we produce a method that adds 2 to the variable, the only way we will detect such a mistake is through the execution of test cases and an examination of the results. No run-time error will occur to notify us that something is wrong.

These last two categories, run-time and logic errors, are the subject of the rest of this chapter. Unlike compile-time errors, which are revealed and eliminated in the safety and comfort of our development environment, run-time and logic errors can occur at any time and seem mostly to reveal themselves once the code has been released to the general user population. Although we can never be sure that no errors exist, we must still test our code to the utmost to minimize the existence of such errors.

Java Interlude

Java's Assertion Facility

Java (specifically, versions 1.4 and later) includes an *assertion facility* that programmers can use to make some logic errors easier to detect. You should consult your instructor or lab administrator to find out how to enable assertions (if possible) for the version of Java you are using.

Rather than using only comments to describe how our code is intended to work, we can incorporate `assert` statements to alert us if our code does not meet our expectations. An `assert` statement is composed of a `boolean` expression and, optionally, an expression that has some printable value. For example, we might use this `assert` statement:

assert x < MAXVAL : x + " < " + MAXVAL; ◄──────── Optional

When this statement is executed, the expression preceding the colon is evaluated. If it is `true`, nothing happens and control passes to the next statement. If the expression is `false`, the program will stop executing. If the optional expression is provided, its `String` representation is output before the program terminates.

Note that assertions are intended to be used almost exclusively for debugging: They are not a way to deal with illegal input values or issue error messages. Instead, they provide a way for us as programmers to describe our assumptions about the program logic. If our assumptions are wrong (as they often are!), a failed assertion gives us a very precise indication of the nature of our faulty assumption.

This mechanism does not replace the techniques of testing we discuss in the rest of the chapter, but can make it easy for us to catch many errors quickly—freeing us to focus on tracking down the especially subtle problems in our code.

8.3 Test Drivers

An application like `LonelyLapRunner` in Chapter 4 can and should be tested by repeatedly giving it various combinations of input and comparing the actual results with the expected results. What about utility classes, such as `Name` or `Minimizer`? These classes exist primarily for use by other classes. We can't execute these classes until they are actually incorporated into a larger program. Giving in to the temptation to avoid testing such a class until absolutely necessary is unwise for several reasons:

- Testing is part of the development phase of software. After software is released, there is less opportunity to do thorough testing because the programmers are under great pressure to fix bugs discovered by customers.
- When you use a utility class, you need a high degree of confidence in its correctness. If you discover an error in the behavior of your code, finding the error is substantially more difficult if you have to worry about both the correctness of the utility classes *and* that of the newly created code.
- Creating the test cases works best when the class is fresh in your mind. Testing in a production environment, that is, where the code will actually be used (in contrast to assignments in a programming class in school), is usually done in stages:

first by the creator of the code, then by some other member of the group, and finally by some dedicated test group within the company. Although the others will test only the external behavior of the class and how it *integrates* or fits with the rest of the software being designed, you as the designer can test other aspects of the class as well—for example, the values of instance variables.

Therefore, all code, even utility classes, should be thoroughly tested before actual use. So, how do we test a class whose usefulness is limited to being incorporated into larger programs? By creating a **test driver** for the class, that is, a method whose sole purpose is to test the class. For convenience, this method can be incorporated into the class that it is testing:

```java
class Dartboard {
    ...
    public static void testDriver() {
        Dartboard d = new Dartboard(1.0);
        System.out.println("Radius: 1.0");
        Toss t = new Toss(0.0,0.0);
        System.out.println("Toss 1: <0.0, 0.0>");
        d.strike(t);
        t = new Toss (0.5,0.5);
        System.out.println("Toss 2: <0.5, 0,5>");
        d.strike(t);
        t = new Toss(1.0,1.0);
        System.out.println("Toss 3: <1.0, 1.0>");
        d.strike(t);
        System.out.print("Fraction in circle: ");
        System.out.println(d.getFractionIn());
    }
}
```

This way, a class can carry around its own test driver.

The test driver method is `static` because it is not invoked with a receiver. Rather we invoke the method as follows:

```java
Dartboard.testDriver();
```

Thus, a program that tests the `Dartboard` class is just

```java
class TestDartboard {
    public static void main(String[] a) {
        Dartboard.testDriver();
    }
}
```

The driver itself merely invokes the methods of the class and prints out the results (along with the input values); the user of the test driver must check that the results are correct.

Some Advantages of Test Drivers

Testing is not particularly glamorous or enjoyable. We want to produce good software; testing makes it work. Like anything unglamorous and unenjoyable (taking out the trash, for example), the trick is to make it as convenient as possible. Writing a test driver helps us in the following ways:

- A test driver at least partially automates the testing of a class.
- A test driver eliminates the need to remember which tests were originally run on the class. This makes it easier to retest the class after fixing a bug just in case a "fix" messed something else up. This process is known as *regression testing.*
- A class with a test driver benefits other programmers who use the class because they can run the driver to confirm the class's correctness—and then look elsewhere for their bugs.

8.4 Automatic Testing

Even with a test driver, we still have the problem of determining whether the class successfully passed the test. In the preceding example, we had the input data as well as the results printed, thus allowing us to perform the necessary calculations and determine whether the fraction was correctly computed. This approach has the following drawbacks:

- If the calculation is a relatively simple one, as is the case for our dartboard example, it is easy to calculate the proper answer and compare it against the one displayed by the test driver. However, if the calculation is even moderately complex (such as calculating the interest on a student loan over 10 years), recalculating the value each time the code is to be retested is not desirable.
- A good test driver typically performs many tests on the class. As discussed earlier, each method representing some external behavior must be tested. Any special cases must be also be tested. The verification of even simple calculations becomes difficult when there are many.

One solution is to calculate the correct answers once, embed them in the test driver, and print out those values as well as those computed by the class:

```
class Dartboard {
    ...
    public static void testDriver() {
        Dartboard d = new Dartboard(1.0);
        System.out.println("Radius: 1.0");
        Toss t = new Toss(0.0,0.0);
        System.out.println("Toss 1: <0.0, 0.0>");
        d.strike(t);
```

```
        t = new Toss (0.5,0.5);
        System.out.println("Toss 2: <0.5, 0,5>");
        d.strike(t);
        t = new Toss(1.0,1.0);
        System.out.println("Toss 3: <1.0, 1.0>");
        d.strike(t);
        double correctAnswer = 2.0/3.0;
        System.out.print("Fraction in circle (computed): ");
        System.out.println(d.getFractionIn());
        System.out.print("Fraction in circle (correct): ");
        System.out.println(correctAnswer);
    }
}
```

This way both the correct and computed values are printed, eliminating the need to constantly recalculate the results each time we run the test. However, this doesn't solve our second problem, the difficulty of comparing all the computed and calculated results for a large number of tests. To solve this problem, we can have the computer check the computed values with the correct ones for us and notify us only when there is a problem:

```
public static void testDriver() {
    Dartboard d = new Dartboard(1.0);
    System.out.println("Radius: 1.0");
    Toss t = new Toss(0.0,0.0);
    System.out.println("Toss 1: <0.0, 0.0>");
    d.strike(t);
    t = new Toss (0.5,0.5);
    System.out.println("Toss 2: <0.5, 0,5>");
    d.strike(t);
    t = new Toss(1.0,1.0);
    System.out.println("Toss 3: <1.0, 1.0>");
    d.strike(t);
    double correctAnswer = 2.0/3.0;
    double calcFraction = d.getFractionIn();
    System.out.print("Fraction in circle (computed): ");
    System.out.println(calcFraction);
    if (calcFraction != correctAnswer) {
        System.out.print("*** Error – computed fraction does not ");
        System.out.print("match correct answer of ");
        System.out.println(correctAnswer);
        System.out.println("Test failed!");
    } else
        System.out.println("Test completed successfully!");
}
```

Check computed answer against my calculation.

This method now does all the work except for the original calculation of the correct answer. It performs the test *and* checks the answer for us.

The testing approach in which a test driver checks the results for correctness is often known as **automatic testing**. That is not to say that the test driver determines the test automatically—that can only be done by someone who knows the class. In fact, the ability to create a proper test suite is quite a talent and is a bit of an art in itself. Rather, when we speak of an automatic test, we mean that the test driver checks the correctness of the results, and the human tester is informed only when something is amiss.

Test Drivers Made Easier

It is quite cumbersome to repeatedly write a sequence of the form

```
if (theCorrectAnswer != theComputedAnswer) {
        a series of System.out.print() statements
            displaying the error.
}
```

For the reader of the test driver, this is a distraction in the logical flow.

To facilitate the writing of an automatic test driver, we would like a method that performs the above test and subsequent action. In addition, it would be useful to know the chain of method invocations (and line numbers) that led to the error. We can obtain this using the static `dumpStack()` method of the predefined class `Thread`:

```
class TestHelper {
   public static void verify(boolean testCondition, String message) {
      if (!testCondition) {
         System.out.print("*** Error - test failure: ");
         System.out.println(message);
         Thread.dumpStack();
      }
   }
}
```

Because `verify()` depends solely on its arguments, it has no need for a receiver object and should therefore be declared `static`. Furthermore, this method will be used by many test drivers of various classes, so we place it in its own class, `TestHelper`. For example, executing the following simple program

```
public class Test {
   public static void main(String args[]) {
      int x = 5, y = 0;
      TestHelper.verify(x==y,"Just a test");
   }
}
```
Here's an invocation of `verify()` that causes a test failure.

yields

```
*** Error - test failure: Just a test
java.lang.Exception: Stack trace
    at java.lang.Thread.dumpStack(Thread.java:534)
    at TestHelper.verify(TrivialApplication.java:20)
    at Test.main(TrivialApplication.java:9)
```

Reading from the bottom up, we see that at line 9 in main() we invoked verify(). It was that invocation that detected the failure of the test condition and invoked dumpStack().

Returning to our test driver, the fragment

Check computed answer against my calculation.

```
if (calcFraction != correctAnswer) {
    System.out.print("*** Error - computed fraction does not ");
    System.out.print("match correct answer of ");
    System.out.println(correctAnswer);
    System.out.println("Test failed!");
}
```

could then be replaced by the less verbose (and more readable)

```
TestHelper.verify(calcFraction == correctAnswer,"calcPay test");
```

The easier it is to write a test, the more likely it is for the programmer to do so; a method such as verify() can be a very handy tool in the creation of a test driver.

8.5 What to Test and How to Test It

By now you should be convinced that testing is both useful and crucial to the development of successful software. Furthermore, we can attempt to alleviate some of the problems inherent in testing—laziness, boredom, manual checking of results, and so on—through the use of test drivers and, whenever possible, the automation of the tests themselves. What we haven't yet discussed are the following questions:

- What constitutes a good and thorough test?
- What values should be used for the various tests?

Let us now address these issues. Be cautioned, however, that we are merely touching the surface of testing techniques. And once again, don't forget Djikstra's statement regarding testing. In general, we can never be absolutely certain there are no errors in our code.

What Constitutes a Good and Thorough Test?

As we've said, you can never test too much. However, because we are usually unable to perform an exhaustive test, how do we determine the point at which we've sufficiently tested our code? We will present several standard testing guidelines to help you.

All Behavior Must Be Tested

Recall the Dartboard class of Chapter 6. It contains the following methods:

- Dartboard (constructor)
- strike()
- getFractionIn()

Our initial temptation might be to test only the getFractionIn() method; after all, that method is what the class is all about. Ignoring the other methods, however, is just asking for trouble. An incorrect constructor, for example, one that incorrectly initializes the insideCircle and outsideCircle values, would prove disastrous. Similarly, if the strike() method were incorrect, the values used by the calculation in getFractionIn() might be based on incorrect values.

If a method is invoked by a user of the class, it *must* be directly tested in the test suite. If the method is not used by the outside, but rather exists as a helper method called by other methods of the class, that method should also be tested whenever possible.

Try to Find a Logical Test Order

Many tests are independent of each other. For example, it does not really matter in which order we test strike() with inside and outside positions. On the other hand, it makes more sense to test the constructor prior to testing strike(); after all, if the former doesn't work, the latter will definitely produce an incorrect result. Often the methods of a class can be ordered on the basis of how *primitive* they are, that is, how much their implementation depends on other methods in the class. The more primitive the method, the less it uses other methods of the class. Because all (non-static) methods of a class ultimately depend on the constructor properly initializing the object, its proper operation is vital to the correct operation of the class.

The more primitive the method, the earlier it should be tested in the test suite. If we are testing a method that uses other methods of the class, any debugging is made easier if we have already tested those methods.

In addition, we would like to be able to print out the value of our object for the purpose of debugging. We would like to have confidence in any methods that print the object, and those should therefore also be tested early in the suite.

Make Sure Each Statement Has Been Executed At Least Once

Every-statement testing is a useful approach, and when there are conditionals, it is quite an important approach. This technique requires that every statement in the code has been executed at least once during the test. The idea is that an

untested statement is an incorrect statement. Look at the following code from the
strike() method of the Dartboard class:

```
if (Math.sqrt(x*x + y*y) < radius)
    insideCircle++;
else
    outsideCircle++;
```

If no test of strike() involves a position outside the circle (i.e., one that causes
the condition of the if statement to evaluate to false), there is an untested statement in the program:

outsideCircle++;

Untested statements can be disastrous. Some application of this class will eventually
have a situation in which a dart strikes outside the circle. If you have never encountered that case during testing, the user is essentially executing untested code.

Sufficient tests must be used to ensure that at least each alternative of a conditional (one for an if, two for an if/else) has been executed at least once during
some test. Choosing such data can often be challenging, but overlooking it during development guarantees doing it later. After all, the conditional is there for a
reason—do not lull yourself into a false sense of security by deciding that case
will *never* happen.

There is an alternative to the every-statement testing technique, known as **all-
paths testing**. In this approach, not only is every statement tested, but *every
sequence of statements in the program is tested as well.* To see the difference
between the two techniques, consider the following code:

```
int i1,i2,i3, smallest;
...
if (i1 < i2)
    smallest = i1;          // (1)
else
    smallest = i2;          // (2)
if (i3 < smallest)
    smallest = i3;          // (3)
```

The every-statement approach requires that each statement be executed at least
once. In particular, we are interested in making sure the true and false parts of
the if statements—the statements labeled (1), (2), and (3)—are each executed at
least once during our tests. We can guarantee this with merely two tests. For
example, the test data

```
i1: 407
i2: 635
i3: 202
```

causes the execution of (1) and (3); the test data

```
i1: 547
i2: 212
i3: 989
```

forces the execution of (2).

The all-paths approach, however, goes even further. It requires the testing of the following sequences:

- (1) followed by (3)
- (2) followed by (3)
- (1) alone (the condition of the second if evaluates to false)
- (2) alone

This is a minimum of four sets of test data to cover all cases.

While all-paths testing is certainly a more comprehensive testing approach than every-statement testing, this technique quickly becomes overwhelming in size.

What Values Should Be Used for the Various Tests?

The ideal answer to this one is the values that uncover all the bugs. Unrealistic as it may be, however, this answer provides us with a good criteria for selecting test cases.

Look for and Test Special Cases

In addition to testing each alternative of a condition, it is a good idea to test the value, if one exists, that lies on the boundary of the conditional. For example, to test the strike() method (assuming radius has been initialized to 1.0), we might have a test for the point (0.0,0.0) corresponding to the true alternative of the conditional, and a test for (1.0,1.0) for the false. In addition, we should test a point such as $(\sqrt{2.0}, \sqrt{2.0})$, because this point is on the border between the two categories. We call such cases *boundary conditions* because they are at the boundary between the alternatives of a conditional. Incorrect treatment of the values of boundary conditions is often the origin of logic errors. For example, a careless implementor of strike() might have written

```
if (Math.sqrt(x*x + y*y) <= radius)   // Note the equality.
```

A toss landing exactly on the circle would now (incorrectly) fall into the inside category. Simply testing the case for (0.0,0.0) and (1.0,1.0) would not have exposed the error. (In this case, although there is a logic error, the results would probably still be correct because tosses landing *exactly* on the circle will be too rare to affect the calculation.)

Values sometimes require special consideration even if there are no overt conditionals present. One of the most common examples is the division operation. Division by zero is undefined mathematically, and thus dividing by zero is always an error. In the context of division, we might then think of int values as falling into two categories: zero and everything else. A method that uses the division operator must ensure that it is never applied when the divisor is zero. So, if we are testing this method, we should construct a data set that causes the divisor to be zero and another that causes it to be nonzero. If the division is not prevented in the zero case, the method has an error.

The value `null` is another special case that arises in the context of reference variables. Attempting to send a message using a reference variable whose value is `null` results in a run-time error in Java. Whenever possible, the `null` value should be used as a test case to determine its effect on the code. If nothing else, you might wish to ask yourself, "Can this reference variable ever assume the `null` value, and if so, what happens?"

Do Not Be Concerned with the Efficiency of the Test

Unlike other applications in which execution time can and usually does play a role, the sole purpose and goal of testing software is to verify behavior. We would rather have a slow but comprehensive test than one that, although lightning fast, performs only a cursory check.

8.6 Debugging Techniques

No matter how well we design our code, errors will arise. As testing proceeds and the code matures and is used more and more, the frequency of discovering errors should decrease. However, those errors that *do* arise after reasonable testing are often very difficult to pin down. The process of discovering an error is known as debugging.

Although specialized tools known as debuggers exist to aid in the tracking down of errors, they are not always available. A universal method of finding bugs, regardless of the computer system or language being used, is to print out values at appropriate points in the program's execution. Finding those *appropriate* points is a skill that improves with practice.

As an example, suppose when implementing the `Account` class of Chapter 7, we left out the line that decreases `balance`.

```
class Account {
   public Account (String id) {
      fileName = id+".act";
   }

   public void withdraw(long amount) throws Exception {
      if (authenticate())
         if (amount < balance) {
            // balance -= amount;          Suppose we omitted this
                                           line? Oops!
```

```
            updateBalance();
        } else
            System.out.println("--| Insufficient Funds |--");
    }
    ...
```

Discovering the Bug

In order to comply with every-statement testing, we must ensure that the condition `amount < balance` evaluates to `true` for some test and `false` for some test. The following test driver fragment should do that; we'll assume that as part of our testing process we have created some mock data files, including one for account 9999 with initial balance 100:

```
class Account {
    public static void testDriver() {
        Account acct = new Account("9999");
        acct.withdraw(100);
        acct.withdraw(75);
        ...
    }
    ...
}
```

This *should* cause `amount < balance` to be `true` in the first invocation of `withdraw()` but `false` in the second. Instead, when we run the test driver, we notice the expected warning message `"Insufficient Funds"` is not issued. This is a bug.

Hunting for the Error

If we examine the code of `withdraw()`, we see that if no message was printed out, somehow the condition `amount < balance` is not `true`. If the condition is not `true`, somehow `amount` is at least `balance`. How could this be? We specifically designed our test so that from an initial balance of 100 we attempted to withdraw first 100 and then an additional 75. Somehow the value of `amount` or the value of `balance` (or both) is in error.

To see which variable is the culprit, we can print their values just before the condition is tested:

```
class Account {
    public Account (String id) {
        fileName = id+".act";
    }

    public void withdraw(long amount) throws Exception {
        if (authenticate()) {
            System.out.println("Amount: "+amount);
            System.out.println("Balance: "+balance);
```

```
        if (amount < balance) {
            // balance -= amount;          ◄── Suppose we omitted this
            updateBalance();                    line? Oops!
        } else
            System.out.println("--| Insufficient Funds |--");
    }
}
...
```

When we repeat the test, we will see that `balance` is unchanged. Fixing the error requires an analysis of the problem similar to the one we presented in Chapter 7, when we developed a correct implementation of `withdraw()`.

Summary

Code testing is an integral and essential part of the software development process. Code that has not been tested must be assumed to be flawed. Even tested code cannot truly be said to be error-free—at most we can minimize the number of errors and their frequency of occurrence. As we become more and more dependent on software in our lives, the potential for disaster resulting from poorly tested code becomes more pronounced.

Any application or class definition should have an associated collection of tests known as a test suite. While a test suite cannot guarantee that no errors exist, it does provide some measure of confidence in the software, especially if it contains a comprehensive set of tests.

The test suite itself automatically verifies the success or failure of each test. It relieves the programmer of having to do each verification and makes it possible to run thousands of test cases against the software, a daunting task for the most dedicated programmer. It also allows for convenient regression testing—testing performed after the elimination of a bug to ensure no old bugs have reappeared as a result of the fix. A method that allows the tester to easily specify conditions that *must* hold true, and that provides useful diagnostics when such conditions fail, aids in the testing process.

There are several items to keep in mind when testing:

- Test all behavior.
- Find a logical order for the tests, typically testing simpler methods before more complex ones.
- Ensure each statement has been executed at least once.
- Look for special cases.
- Do not worry about the test's efficiency.

Once a bug has been discovered, it must be tracked down. Printing relevant values is an invaluable aid to hunting down the source of an error.

Key Terms

all-paths testing An approach to testing in which every possible sequence of statements is tested at least once.

automatic testing An approach to testing in which the test suite verifies the correctness of the test results.

bug A run-time error in a program.

debugging The process of finding and fixing bugs.

every-statement testing An approach to testing in which every statement is tested at least once.

test driver A method (or collection of methods) whose purpose is to test the behavior of one or more utility classes.

test suite A set of tests.

Questions for Review

1. What is the purpose of testing?
2. What is the purpose of a test driver?
3. Where might a test suite of a class be placed?

Exercises

1. List some more syntax and semantic errors.
2. Would you rather have an error discovered at compile time or run time? Explain your answer.
3. Add a test driver to each of the classes you have written.
4. We suggested that the test driver for a class be placed into the class itself so that it is carried along with the class definition. Can you think of another reason to have the test driver be a part of the class? (Hint: Think of `public` and `private`.)
5. Implement the `TestHelper` class and use it to automate as much as possible the test drivers of Exercise 3.
6. Write a test driver for the `Name` class of Chapter 5.
7. Write a test driver for the `RepairPerson` and `Location` classes of Chapter 7.

Separating Display and Control

In the last GUI supplement, we observed that our development of `Calculator-Applet` proceeded in two nearly independent phases: We designed the layout and display, then we implemented the calculator logic. In this supplement we separate those two steps even further by placing the calculator logic in a separate class. This separation allows us to make changes to the display without worrying about the underlying logic. To demonstrate this we will write another version of `CalculatorApplet` that has a more complex display.

Extracting the Calculator Logic

Our first task is to design and implement the class that contains only the calculator logic. Such classes are often called *models* because they model essential behavior. Because it is completely independent from the display, our calculator model doesn't need to address complicated issues such as how numbers are entered (especially the decimal points). Instead, the model will implement only numerical operations.

As we noted in Chapter 7, the result of each calculation becomes both the new displayed value *and* the first operand of the next operation. Because this value must be remembered for the next operation, the calculator needs to retain this value as part of its state. Because this value will be used as the first operand for each operation, the methods implementing these operations require only a single parameter corresponding to the second operand. In addition to these methods, our model needs a method to clear the calculator, a method to retrieve the stored value (so it can be displayed, for example), and a method to set the stored value (to be used at the beginning of the calculator's operation or after the calculator has been cleared).

The class can be implemented as follows:

```
class Calculator {
   public Calculator() {
      value = 0.0;
   }
   public void clear() {
      value = 0.0;
   }
   public double getValue() {
      return value;
   }
   public void setValue(double v) {
      value = v;
```

```
    }
    public void add(double d) {
        value += d;
    }
    public void subtract(double d) {
        value -= d;
    }
    public void multiply(double d) {
        value *= d;
    }
    public void divide(double d) {
        value /= d;
    }
    private double value;
}
```

Using the Calculator Model

Rewriting our original `CalculatorApplet` to take advantage of the new `Calculator` class requires only a few changes. First, we need to declare a `Calculator` instance variable:

private Calculator calc;

and initialize it at the end of `init()`:

public void init() {

    ...

    d9.addActionListener(this);
    calc = new Calculator();
    clearDisplay();
}

Because the `Calculator` keeps track of the current value as part of its state, we can remove the declaration of `opd1`: Its role in `handleOperator()` will be taken over by `calc`. We also change the name of `clearCalc()` to reflect more accurately the role of the applet (as the calculator's display).

Notice that the `Calculator` object is created before the `clearDisplay()` message is sent; this is because the `clearDisplay()` method sends a `clear()` message to the `Calculator` object:

```
private void clearDisplay() {
    sawDecimal = false;
    newOpd = true;
    sawAnOpd = false;
    lastOptr = "";
```

```
        calc.clear();
        result.setText(initialString);
    }
```

The final change is in the implementation of `handleOperator()`, where `calc` replaces `opd1`:

```
private void handleOperator(String s) {
    if (!sawAnOpd)
        return;

    if (lastOptr.equals("+"))
        calc.add(getDisplay());
    else if (lastOptr.equals("-"))
        calc.subtract(getDisplay());
    else if (lastOptr.equals("*"))
        calc.multiply(getDisplay());
    else if (lastOptr.equals("/"))
        calc.divide(getDisplay());
    else
        calc.setValue(getDisplay());

    result.setText(calc.getValue()+"");

    lastOptr = s;
    sawDecimal = false;
    newOpd = true;
}
```

Changing the Display: Adding a (Virtual) Paper Tape

With the essential logic of the calculator separated into its own class, it's straightforward to implement changes to the display without affecting the underlying model (that is, without altering the calculator logic). For example, we can augment the calculator with a simulated paper tape (see Figure 8.1). The paper tape is used to keep a record of each operation performed by the calculator.

Before we begin changing the applet code, we should determine the desired behavior of the tape: What should be printed on it, and when? We make the following design decisions:

- When the C button is pressed, as well as when the applet starts executing, the string 0.000000 C will be displayed on the tape.
- When a button corresponding to one of the four arithmetic operations is pressed, the string containing the current display (on the calculator's "screen") followed by the operator will be displayed on the tape.

Figure 8.1
Calculator applet
with virtual paper
tape.

- When one of the = buttons is pressed, two lines will be displayed on the tape:
first, the string containing the current display (i.e., the last operand in the calculation) followed by =, and second, the string containing the result of the calculation followed by T (for "total").

From Figure 8.1, it should be clear that this approach conveys information about
the calculations in a reasonable way.

Implementing the Tape

The most obvious change to be made to the display is the addition of the element that displays the contents of the tape. This control is a List, which allows
us to display an arbitrarily long sequence of strings. To incorporate the List into
the applet display, we need to make a number of small changes. First, we need
to declare a List instance variable:

```
private List tape;
```

Then we need to modify the init() method to include the List in the applet's
display:

```
public void init() {
    backgroundColor = new Color(200,255,255);
    this.setLayout(new FlowLayout(FlowLayout.CENTER,4,1));
```

```
tape = new List();
tape.setBackground(backgroundColor);
add(tape);
result = new Label(initialString, Label.RIGHT);
    ...
```

We also need to modify the size calculation in the paint() method so that the applet sizes itself to accommodate the List:

```
public void paint(Graphics g) {
    resize(row1.getWidth(),
            8 * (d1.getHeight()) + tape.getHeight());
    validate();
}
```

Finally, we need to add code to implement the tape display behavior we discussed above. To add a new line to a List, we use the method

```
void add (String s);
```

A string added this way is inserted at the bottom of the List display. However, the new string may not be visible in the display: A List can display only a few lines of its contents at any moment; unless it happens to be displaying the last few lines at the moment when a new line is added, the addition will not be visible. To solve this problem, we will make use of two more List methods:

```
int getItemCount(void);
void makeVisible(int);
```

As part of its state, a List object maintains a count of the number of lines it contains; further, it assigns each line a number, or *index*. The first line in the display has index 0; in general the nth line in the display has index $n-1$. The getItemCount() method returns the number of lines in the List, and the makeVisible() method takes an index value as a parameter and ensures that the line with that index is visible in the List's display.

Thus, to display the last line of the List (i.e., the most recently added line), we first send a getItemCount() message to the List, then we subtract 1 from the result to get the index of the last line and pass this value as a parameter of a makeVisible() message. Because we want to treat every line we add to the List in this manner, we can write a simple method to accomplish the complete add-and-display process (see Figure 8.2):

```
private void printToTape(String s) {
    tape.add(s);
    tape.makeVisible(tape.getItemCount()-1);
}
```

0	allegro		0	allegro
1	lento		1	lento
2	presto		2	presto
3	rubato		3	rubato
4	andante		4	andante
5	ritardando		5	ritardando
6	largo		6	largo

List displaying lines 2 through 5. `getItemCount()` returns 7.   same `List` after `makeVisible(6)`

Figure 8.2
Adjusting the
`List` display.

Now we can use this method to implement the three tape behaviors—clear, arithmetic operations, and equals. We called for the clear behavior to be invoked under precisely the conditions that the `clearCalc()` method is invoked, so we can just add a `printToTape()` message to the definition of `clearCalc()`:

```
private void clearCalc() {
    ...
    calc.clear();
    result.setText(initialString);
    printToTape(initialString + " C");
}
```

(Note the `List` object itself is responsible for deciding when to display the scrollbar, and for responding appropriately when the user moves the scrollbar's "handle.")

The arithmetic operation and equals behaviors can both be implemented in the `handleOperation()` method. In both cases, we want to add a line to the tape containing the current display followed by the operator. Thus, we need to add a `printToTape()` message at the start of the `handleOperation()` definition:

```
private void handleOperator(String s) {
    if (!sawAnOpd)
        return;
    printToTape(getDisplay() + " " + s);
    ...
```

In the case of the equals behavior, we also need to add a line to the tape containing the result of the calculation. Thus must be done after the calculation is performed; we can just extract the updated value from `result` and print it to the tape:

```
    ...
    result.setText(calc.getValue()+"");
    if (s.equals("="))
        printToTape(getDisplay() + " T");
    lastOptr = s;
    sawDecimal = false;
    newOpd = true;
}
```

The complete applet for the calculator with virtual tape is

```java
import java.awt.*;
import java.awt.event.*;
import java.applet.Applet;
public class CalculatorAppletWithTape extends Applet
                            implements ActionListener {
    public void init() {
        backgroundColor = new Color(200,255,255);
        this.setLayout(new FlowLayout(FlowLayout.CENTER,4,1));
        tape = new List();
        tape.setBackground(backgroundColor);
        add(tape);
        result = new Label(initialString, Label.RIGHT);
        result.setBackground(new Color(255,255,255));
        add(result);
        makeButtons();
        row1 = makePanel(new FlowLayout(FlowLayout.LEFT,4,2),
                    backgroundColor);
        row1.add(c);
        row1.add(eq);
        row1.add(div);
        row1.add(times);
        row2 = makePanel(new FlowLayout(FlowLayout.LEFT,4,2),
                    backgroundColor);
        row2.add(d7);
        row2.add(d8);
        row2.add(d9);
        row2.add(minus);
        row3 = makePanel(new FlowLayout(FlowLayout.LEFT,4,2),
                    backgroundColor);
        row3.add(d4);
        row3.add(d5);
        row3.add(d6);
        row3.add(plus);
        add(row1);
        add(row2);
        add(row3);
        p12 = makePanel(new BorderLayout(2,2),backgroundColor);
        p12.add("West",d1);
        p12.add("East",d2);
        p120 = makePanel(new BorderLayout(2,2),backgroundColor);
        p120.add("North",p12);
        p120.add("South",d0);
        p3p = makePanel(new BorderLayout(2,2),backgroundColor);
        p3p.add("North",d3);
```

```java
            p3p.add("South",dp);
            p3peq = makePanel(new BorderLayout(2,2),backgroundColor);
            p3peq.add("West",p3p);
            p3peq.add("East",eq2);
            add(p120);
            add(p3peq);
            setBackground(backgroundColor);
            c.addActionListener(this);
            eq.addActionListener(this);
            eq2.addActionListener(this);
            div.addActionListener(this);
            times.addActionListener(this);
            minus.addActionListener(this);
            plus.addActionListener(this);
            dp.addActionListener(this);
            d0.addActionListener(this);
            d1.addActionListener(this);
            d2.addActionListener(this);
            d3.addActionListener(this);
            d4.addActionListener(this);
            d5.addActionListener(this);
            d6.addActionListener(this);
            d7.addActionListener(this);
            d8.addActionListener(this);
            d9.addActionListener(this);
            calc = new Calculator();
            clearDisplay();
        }

        public void paint(Graphics g) {
            resize(row1.getWidth(),
                    8 * (d1.getHeight()) + tape.getHeight());
            validate();
        }

        public void actionPerformed(ActionEvent e) {
            String s = (String)e.getActionCommand();
            if (digits.indexOf(s) != -1)
                handleDigit(s);
            else if (s.equals("."))
                handleDecimal();
            else if (operators.indexOf(s) != -1)
                handleOperator(s);
```

```
        else if (s.equals("C"))
            handleClear();
}

private void handleDigit(String s) {
    if (newOpd) {
        result.setText(s);
        newOpd = false;
    } else
        result.setText(result.getText()+s);
    sawAnOpd = true;
}

private void handleClear() {
    clearDisplay();
}

private void clearDisplay() {
    sawDecimal = false;
    newOpd = true;
    sawAnOpd = false;
    lastOptr = "";
    calc.clear();
    result.setText(initialString);
    printToTape(initialString+" C");
}

private void handleOperator(String s) {
    if (!sawAnOpd)
        return;

    printToTape(getDisplay()+" "+s);

    if (lastOptr.equals("+"))
        calc.add(getDisplay());
    else if (lastOptr.equals("-"))
        calc.subtract(getDisplay());
    else if (lastOptr.equals("*"))
        calc.multiply(getDisplay());
    else if (lastOptr.equals("/"))
        calc.divide(getDisplay());
    else // this is first operator, or last op was =
        calc.setValue(getDisplay());
```

```java
            result.setText(calc.getValue()+"");

            if (s.equals("="))
                printToTape(getDisplay()+" T");

            lastOptr = s;
            sawDecimal = false;
            newOpd = true;
    }
    private void handleDecimal() {
        if (!sawDecimal) {
            if (newOpd) {
                result.setText("0.");
                newOpd = false;
            } else
                result.setText(result.getText() + ".");
            sawDecimal = true;
        }
    }

    private double getDisplay() {
        return Double.parseDouble(result.getText());
    }

    private void printToTape(String s) {
        tape.add(s);
        tape.makeVisible(tape.getItemCount()-1);
    }

    private Button makeButton(String label, Color color,
                              Font font) {
        Button b = new Button(label);
        b.setBackground(color);
        b.setFont(font);
        return b;
    }
    private Panel makePanel(LayoutManager lm, Color c) {
        Panel p = new Panel();
        p.setLayout(lm);
        p.setBackground(c);
        return p;
    }
```

```java
    private void makeButtons() {
        Font    f = new Font("Courier", Font.BOLD, 10);
        Color  lightRed = new Color(255,100,100);
        Color  lightBlue = new Color(100,100,255);
        Color  yellow = new Color(255,255,0);
        c = makeButton("C",lightRed,f);
        eq = makeButton("=",lightBlue,f);
        div = makeButton("/",lightBlue,f);
        times = makeButton("*",lightBlue,f);
        d7 = makeButton("7",yellow,f);
        d8 = makeButton("8",yellow,f);
        d9 = makeButton("9",yellow,f);
        minus = makeButton("-",lightBlue,f);
        d4 = makeButton("4",yellow,f);
        d5 = makeButton("5",yellow,f);
        d6 = makeButton("6",yellow,f);
        plus = makeButton("+",lightBlue,f);
        d1 = makeButton("1",yellow,f);
        d2 = makeButton("2",yellow,f);
        d3 = makeButton("3",yellow,f);
        d0 = makeButton("0",yellow,f);
        dp = makeButton(".",yellow,f);
        eq2 = makeButton("=",lightBlue,f);
    }
    static final String initialString = "0.000000";
    static final String digits = "0123456789";
    static final String operators = "+-*/=";
    private String lastOptr;
    private String Filler = "        ";
    private boolean sawDecimal, newOpd, sawAnOpd;
    private Calculator calc;
    private Panel row1, row2, row3, p12, p120, p3p, p3peq;
    private int    appletWidth, appletHeight;
    private Button c, eq, div, times,
                   d7, d8, d9, minus,
                   d4, d5, d6, plus,
                   d1, d2, d3,
                   d0,     dp, eq2;
    private Color  backgroundColor;
    private Label  result;
    private List   tape;
}
```

Note that what we have accomplished in this supplement—the separation of control logic from display logic—we accomplished implicitly in the Chapter 6 supplement, in which we implemented a GUI front end for the `Minimizer` class. In that case, the model was our starting point, and our task was only to implement an appropriate display.

Suggested Experiments

1. Rewrite the `ButtonFlipperApplet` of Chapter 5 to use separated control logic and display logic. The control logic should be in a class called `FlipRectangle` that provides methods `flipColor()` and `getColor()`.

2. Rewrite the cash register applet you wrote in Chapter 7 to use separated control and display logic.

3. Create an applet that displays a list of names in a `List`.

4. Investigate selection from a `List`. Selecting (double-clicking) an item from a `List` generates an `ActionEvent`. Modify the applet of the previous exercise to display the name selected by the user.

Working with Multiple Objects

9.1 Introduction

In this chapter, we will focus on iteration, the ability to perform an action repeatedly. We saw one form of iteration—the counting loop—in Chapter 6; in this chapter we will look at a broader range of applications and programming techniques. As we saw earlier, much of the power of programming comes from the ability to automate repetition: It's not hard to imagine tossing 10 or 20 darts at an actual dartboard in order to estimate the value of π, but 100 darts starts to sound tiring, and 10,000 is clearly impractical. Computers, though, don't get tired or bored.

We start by considering repetitive processing in the context of multiple instances of a class. This processing includes

- Processing multiple objects created by input
- Maintaining multiple instances
- Processing the multiple objects in some manner (for example, calculating the payroll of all the employees of a company)

9.2 Processing Multiple Objects

We begin with the simple but common case of multiple objects that

- Can be processed independently of each other
- Once processed, are no longer needed

For example, suppose the utility company in our repairperson example wanted to collect some data on the distribution of repairpeople across its service area at some given moment. We can write code to process the data file containing current information about the repairpeople, measuring the distance of each one from a given location (such as the town center) and printing the results. Each RepairPerson will be processed independently, and once the result of the distance calculation is printed out, the RepairPerson object may be discarded. We have the code that processes a single RepairPerson object:

```
Repairperson  rp  =  RepairPerson.readIn(br);
int distance = rp.getDistanceFrom(loc);
System.out.println(rp.getName()+": "+distance);
```

br and loc
already declared

We now want to be able to repeat this piece of code for each object to be processed. If we have five objects, we will repeat the process five times, for 1,000 objects, 1,000 times, and so on:

```
Repairperson  rp  =  RepairPerson.readIn(br);
int distance = rp.getDistanceFrom(loc);
System.out.println(rp.getName()+": "+distance);
```

Repeat as necessary

Because we have a sequence of code to repeat, we know that we need to write a **loop**. In this situation, we don't know ahead of time how many repetitions will be necessary, so we cannot use a counting loop; instead, we must turn to a more general looping structure. If we examine the above, we see that a loop consists of two parts:

- The *body* of the loop, that is, the sequence of code we wish to be able to repeat. In the above example, the body consists of the three boxed statements.
- The code for the looping mechanism itself. Although we wish to repeat the body of the loop, we do want the loop to *terminate* eventually, at which point execution moves to the code after the loop. In the above sample, "Repeat as necessary" and the arrow constitute an informal *loop construct*.

A loop construct must, therefore, specify what constitutes the body of the loop and under what circumstances the loop terminates.

The while Statement

The most versatile loop construct is the **while statement**. Its general form is

while   (*condition*)
        body

Condition and *body* are the same constructs as those that are present in the if statement:

- *Condition* is a Boolean-valued expression. It is also called the *loop test*.
- *Body* is a single statement or a compound statement.

The phrase while (*condition*) is called the *loop header*. As in the case of the conditional, the *body* should be indented for clarity.

The execution of the while statement proceeds as follows:

1. The condition is tested.

2. If the condition evaluates to `false`, the loop is *terminated*; execution continues with the statement immediately following the loop (i.e., the statement after the body of the loop).

3. On the other hand, if the condition evaluates to `true`, the body of the loop is executed (we often say "the loop is entered") and these steps are repeated.

This repetition proceeds until the condition evaluates to `false` in the second step.

Back to the `RepairPerson` Loop

Let us now use a `while` statement to code the loop introduced at the beginning of the section. First, recall our discussion in Chapter 5 about returning `null` as the result of a `read()` method for which no data are present in the file. When `read()` returns `null`, there is no more repairperson data and our loop should terminate:

```
(1)   RepairPerson rp = RepairPerson.read(br);   ◄──────── Read first object.
(2)   while (rp != null) {   ◄──────────────────────────── Was an object read?
(3)       int distance = rp.getDistanceFrom(loc);   ◄────── Process object.
(4)       System.out.println(rp.getName()+": "+distance);  ◄─ Process object.
(5)       RepairPerson rp = RepairPerson.read(br);   ◄───── Read next object.
(6)   }
```

The loop proper consists of lines (2) through (6). Line (1) invokes the `read()` method of `RepairPerson` in order to read the first object. The condition of the `while` tests whether a `RepairPerson` object has been successfully read. If so, the loop is entered and the `RepairPerson` object is processed. Prior to returning to line (2), another `RepairPerson` object is read, and the process repeats.

The first `RepairPerson` object is read *before* the loop body—in line (1). This is to guarantee that the condition `rp != null` is meaningful, that is, that `rp` has been given a value (either a reference to a `Name` object or `null`) that can be tested.

Your first intuition might have been to write

```
// This code is INCORRECT!!!
RepairPerson rp;
while (rp != null) {   ◄──────────────────────────────── Was an object read?
    rp = RepairPerson.read(br);   ◄─────────────────────── Read next object.
    int distance = rp.getDistanceFrom(loc);   ◄─────────── Process object.
    System.out.println(rp.getName()+": "+distance);   ◄─── Process object.
}
```

This, however, results in an undefined value for `rp` the first time it is used in the condition of the `while`. Fortunately, the Java compiler would issue an error message to that effect, preventing the error from becoming a serious bug.

An equally incorrect loop is

Also INCORRECT!!!

```
RepairPerson rp  =  RepairPerson.read(br);◄──────────Read first object.
while  (rp  !=  null)  {◄──────────────────────────Was an object read?
    int distance = rp.getDistanceFrom(loc);◄───────Process object.
    System.out.println(rp.getName()+": "+distance);◄──Process object.
}
```

In this instance, only the first `RepairPerson` object is read—the loop body does not contain an invocation of the `read()` method and no additional objects are read. Assuming there are data corresponding to at least one name in the data file, this loop will never terminate. Such a situation is known as an *infinite loop.* (What happens if the data file contains *no* data?)

In this example, we must read the first object *prior* to the loop body (this is often called a "priming read") and then read subsequent objects at the very end of the body *immediately before* retesting the `while` condition.

9.3 Loop Patterns

Reading in a series of data items and processing them, as we did with `Repair-Person` data in the previous section, is a fairly common task. This sort of loop can be easily adapted to handle other types of objects as well as other types of processing. For example, the following reads names from a file and prints them out with the title "Dr.":

```
Name n;
n  =  Name.read(...);◄───────────────────────────Read first.
while  (n  !=  null)  {◄─────────────────────────Test for termination.
    n.setTitle("Dr.";◄─────────────────────────Processing...
    n.print(System.out);
    n = Name.read(...);◄───────────────────────Read next.
}
```

This reads `Strings` and prints them out:

```
String  s;
s  =  br.readLine();◄────────────────────────────Read first.
while  (s  !=  null)  {◄─────────────────────────Test for termination.
    System.out.print(s);◄──────────────────────Processing
    s  =  br.readLine();◄──────────────────────Read next.
}
```

Consider a loop that reads a series of integers and prints their squares. Recall that our method for reading in integers consists of reading in a line as a `String` object and then using the `parseInt()` method to produce the `int` value:

```
int  i;
i  =  Integer.parseInt(br.readLine());
```

However, if we want to test for end-of-file, we must check for a `null` value returned from the `readLine()` method. Furthermore, this must be done *prior* to invoking `parseInt()`—attempting to invoke that method with a `null` argument produces a run-time error. We must break up the two steps of the integer input:

```
int  i;
String  temp;
temp  =  br.readLine();◄─────────────────────── Read first.
while  (temp  !=  null)  {◄─────────────────── Test for termination.
    i  =  Integer.parseInt(temp);◄─────────── Processing—first convert to int.
    System.out.print(i * i);◄──────────────── Now print square.
    temp  =  br.readLine();◄───────────────── Read next.
}
```

We first read the line into the `String` object, `temp`. This value is used as the controlling condition of the loop. The processing portion in the body of the loop consists of converting the `String` into an integer and then printing out the square. We then read the next `String`.

If we knew that the integers to be processed were all non-negative, we could use a negative value to indicate the end of the data. In this situation, there is no need to break up the `readLine()` and the subsequent `parseInt()`. In fact, to do so would be wrong. The `parseInt()` must immediately precede the test because the test is performed on the result of `parseInt()` rather than on the result of `read-Line()`:

```
int  i;
i  =  Integer.parseInt(br.readLine());◄──────────── Read first.
while  (i  >=  0)  {◄──────────────────────────── Test for termination.
    System.out.print(i * i);◄──────────────────── Print square.
    i  =  Integer.parseInt(br.readLine());◄────── Read next.
}
```

Although the exact type of data, the condition for loop termination, and the actual processing differ among these examples, they all have much in common. In all cases, the purpose of the loop is to read and process successive data items. The basic structure of the loop is the same: read first item, test for termination, process, read next item, repeat test, and so on. We can depict this sequence of actions with a generalized sketch of such a loop:

```
// Loop Pattern: read/process
read first item
while  (a  valid  item  has  been  read)  {◄──────────── Test for termination.
    process  the  item
    read  the  next  item
}
```

We call such a sketch a **loop pattern** because it provides us with a starting point for the construction of a loop whose purpose is to read and process multiple data items. To use this pattern, we supply the following:

- The means of reading the item
- The condition that will determine that no valid item has been read
- The code that specifies the processing

By plugging these into the pattern, we create a working loop.

We will give names to our various patterns so that we can speak about them. We call our first pattern *read/process* because that is precisely what it does: reads data and processes the objects created from that data. In this chapter we will present several loop patterns that perform other common tasks.

9.4 The Impact of Loops on Testing

We call a code fragment that contains no conditionals or loops *straight-line* because execution moves in a straight line—no statements are skipped or repeated. When we introduced conditionals, we began writing programs that were no longer strictly linear in nature: Different states of the program can cause alternate sequences of execution. However, we could test all possible paths of execution by running the program several times and supplying the appropriate data that would cause a particular path to be taken. For example, given the condition

```
if (x < 10)
```

we could test the program twice—once making sure x is less than 10, and once with x equal to or greater than 10.

With the introduction of loops, however, this exhaustive testing approach no longer works. The looping construct allows us to repeat a block of code an arbitrary number of times (our RepairPerson example, for instance, would loop for as many times as there are entries in the input file). We can thus no longer test every possible scenario (the all-paths approach)—the very nature of an arbitrary loop precludes us from performing such an exhaustive test.

The other side of the coin is that we can use loops to automate our testing processes even further. Recall the concept of automatic testing introduced in Chapter 8. Using that technique, we set up test cases that could verify themselves. Assuming such verification could be performed, we could create a loop that might run hundreds or even thousands of test cases without us having to endure the tedium of checking each and every one.

Regardless of the number of test cases we might run against our software, the existence of loops within the code makes it unlikely that we will be able to test *every* case. To increase our confidence in our code, we must therefore be very careful in the construction of loops. In this chapter, we restrict ourselves to a small number of very specific loop designs. In the next chapter, we will present a more general approach to loop design, one that will provide guidance in the development of correct loops.

However, no matter how good our loop design is, we still must methodically test our loops. The all-paths approach is impossible, but as a minimum, we should test the following cases:

- The loop condition is false the first time, and the loop body is never executed.
- The loop body is executed exactly once.
- The loop body is executed more than once.

9.5 A Telephone Book

In this section, we develop an example of the read/process loop pattern in the context of our class design approach.

Statement of the Problem

A telecommunications startup wants to provide a computerized telephone book service that supports both "standard" lookup (by name) and reverse lookup (by telephone number). They have purchased a data file with entries consisting of names and telephone numbers.

A Sample Scenario

Here's how a user might interact with the telephone book service:

```
Entry to lookup:  Edward Kaspel
Phone number:  5556789
Entry to lookup:  5554321
Owner:  Katell Keineg
```

Determining the Primary Objects

The relevant nouns of the problem are *telephone book, file, entry, name,* and *telephone number. Name* and *telephone number* are subsidiary to *entry. Entry* and *file* are the data on the disk, representing the telephone book; they will be read in and assigned to objects. Our primary class will thus be TelephoneBook.

Determining the Desired Behavior

We want to be able to create a TelephoneBook as well as look up an entry. Our methods are

- TelephoneBook (constructor)
- lookup

Defining the Interface

Here is some typical usage code:

```
TelephoneBook kingsCounty = new TelephoneBook("kings.dat");
kingsCounty.lookup("Marty Markowitz");
kingsCounty.lookup("5556263");
```

A TelephoneBook is associated with a particular input file whose name is given to the constructor. The lookup() method accepts a String that is either a name or a telephone number and prints the results to System.out. Here is the interface:

```
class TelephoneBook {
    public TelephoneBook(String fileName) {...}
    public void lookup(String data) {...}
}
```

Defining the Instance Variables

Each time lookup() is invoked, it will create a new BufferedReader that is associated with the disk file named in the constructor's parameter. This name, therefore, must be maintained as part of the state of the TelephoneBook object:

```
class TelephoneBook {
    public TelephoneBook(String fileName) {...}
    public void lookup(String data) {...}
    private String fileName;                    Instance variable
}
```

Implementing the Methods

The constructor is just an assignment of its argument to the fileName instance variable:

```
public TelephoneBook (String fileName)  {
    this.fileName = fileName;
}
```

The lookup() method must create a BufferedReader from fileName. It then reads entries from the BufferedReader, looking for an entry containing a value matching data. Specifically, if data is a phone number, we must look for an entry with a matching phone number and (if one is found) output its owner; if data is a name, we must output the corresponding phone number. For the sake of simplicity, we will decide that if the first character of data is a digit, then data represents a phone number; otherwise it is a name. Using a couple of String methods, we can determine which case applies:

```
String digits = "0123456789";
String firstChar = data.substring(0,1);     Extract first character.
int position = digits.indexOf(firstChar);   Check—is it a digit?
```

```
if (position < 0)
    process as name
else
    process as number
```

To perform the processing, we require a class that models entries; let us call this class `Entry`. Given such a class, we might then apply our read/process loop pattern. Below is a sketch of the loop that reads in the entries, searching for the desired data:

```
public void  lookup(String data) throws Exception {
    BufferedReader  br  =
                new BufferedReader(
                  new InputStreamReader(
                    new FileInputStream(fileName)));
    String digits = "0123456789";
    String firstChar = data.substring(0,1);
    int position = digits.indexof(firstChar);
```

Using read/process loop pattern

```
    Entry e  =  Entry.read(br);            ← First object
    while  (e != null)  {                  ← Was an object read?
        if (position < 0)                  ← If looking up name
            Check entry's name and print out if matches
        else
            Check entry's number and print if matches
        e  =  Entry.read(br);              ← Read next object.
    }
}
```

Before we begin to develop our `Entry` class, however, let us more carefully examine what behavior we want this class to have. To do this, we complete the above sketch of the `lookup()` loop:

```
    Entry e  =  Entry.read(br);
    while  (e != null)  {
        if (position < 0) {
            if (data.equals(e.getName()))     ← Compare data with
                System.out.println("Phone number: " + e.getNumber());   entry's name
        }
        else {
            if (data.equals(e.getNumber())    ← Compare data with
                System.out.print("Owner: " + e.getName());   entry's number
        }
        e = Entry.read(br);
    }
```

That is, in order to compare the entry's name, we will need a method that returns the entry's name. If the name matches the one we are looking for, we then need to print out the corresponding number; thus, we also need a method that returns the entry's number. To perform the reverse lookup, we will use these methods in the opposite way. Finally, we require a method that creates an `Entry` object from input.

Notice that the preceding code completes the implementation of the `lookup()` method and thus the definition of the `TelephoneBook` class. In order to complete our application, we must now define the `Entry` class.

Determining the Desired Behavior—The `Entry` Class

As discussed above, we require the following methods:

- read
- getName
- getNumber

Defining the Interface—The `Entry` Class

We don't need to imagine "typical usage code"—we have very specific usage code in the `lookup()` method above that was the actual motivation for our class:

```
...
Entry e  =  Entry.read(br);
while  (e != null)  {
   if (data.equals(e.getName())) {
      System.out.print("Phone number: ");
      System.out.println(e.getNumber());
   }
   e  =  Entry.read(br);
}
...
```

This shows the argument and return-types of the `read()`, `getName()`, and `get-Number()` methods. So our interface must include

```
class  Entry  {
   public static Entry read(BufferedReader br)  {...}
   public String getName() {...}
   public String getNumber() {...}
}
```

Defining the Instance Variables—The `Entry` Class

The `Entry` class is relatively simple. We require only a name and a number. Note that in this case there is no constructor to motivate our instance variables; instead the requirements of the TelephoneBook's lookup() method determine the information that needs to be maintained in Entry:

```
class  Entry  {
    Methods specified above
    private String  name,  number;
}
```

Implementing the Methods—The Entry Class

In order to implement the read() method, we must decide the format of the data file. For simplicity, we will say that an entry occupies two lines: The first line contains a name and the second line contains the corresponding number.

```
public static Entry read(BufferedReader br) throws Exception {
    String name = br.readLine();
    if (name == null)
        return null;
    String number = br.readLine();
    return new Entry(name, number);
}
```

We leave the implementation of the Entry constructor and the methods getName() and getNumber() as an exercise.

Using the Methods—The Entry Class

The lookup() method of TelephoneBook provided us with a full usage of the Entry class. We might also want to create a test driver for Entry. We leave this as an exercise as well.

Discussion

Our solution introduced two classes: TelephoneBook and Entry. The Entry class was not introduced until a need for it arose when the methods for the TelephoneBook class were implemented. Our repairperson example in Chapter 7 also required the development of two classes: RepairPerson and Location; however, in that example, we made the determination from the outset while determining the primary object.

If we review the problem statement for the telephone book, we see that the need to model an entry is present (the noun *entry* does appear), so we might indeed have been able to deduce the need for a second class when we determined the primary objects. However, because entries are subsidiary to the telephone book, we elected to address the issues of the telephone book first.

Finally, a slight change in TelephoneBook's behavior could cause us to discover the need for a Entry class at a different step in the development process (see the exercises).

The Nature of the Class Development Procedure

Our class design procedure is not simply following a sequence of steps; it may involve some repetition and refinement of earlier decisions. During the course of designing a class, we might require some object (as an instance variable, for example) that exhibits a specific behavior. We would then have to either find an existing class that supplies that behavior or, failing that, create a new class. The telephone book application that we just developed was such a case. While implementing the methods for class TelephoneBook, we introduced a local variable, e, when we wrote the lookup() method. This variable was used to model an entry. We didn't really expect to find an appropriate predefined Java class; the desired behavior was fairly specific to this particular application, whereas the Java classes are more general purpose. We therefore had to create a new class, Entry.

As our applications get more and more sophisticated, this iterative process will often extend to many more steps. A typical commercial system may have hundreds of classes, many of which are created specifically for that system.

9.6 Maintaining Multiple Values

Our manipulation of multiple objects has so far consisted of working with an individual object to completion and only then moving on to the next object. There are times, however, when we must maintain a reference to an object even after we move on to the remaining objects.

Another Look at TelephoneBook

Although the TelephoneBook class does provide the necessary behavior of looking up names and numbers, lookup() is quite slow (i.e., it takes several seconds before the entries are displayed on the screen). The reason for this is that each time lookup() is invoked, the data file is reopened (by creating the FileInputStream) and its entire contents are processed.

Input/output (i/o), the reading or writing of data to or from a file, is a very expensive—that is, slow—task compared to the manipulation of objects stored in memory. This is because memory is an electronic device, and i/o usually involves some form of mechanical device subject to the physical laws of inertia and friction. A faster implementation of the TelephoneBook class reads the data file in once (say, during creation of the TelephoneBook object) and then performs the lookup completely in memory. Because the input file consists of pairs of lines, with each pair containing the data necessary to create an Entry object, reading in the file involves creating multiple Entry objects. The number of Entry objects is, however, unknown—it depends on the number of entries in the file. Thus, we cannot simply declare two or five or any other specific number of Entry instance variables for our TelephoneBook. Rather, we must maintain a **collection** of objects.

A collection is a group of objects that can be declared as a single entity. The collection itself is an object that may be created and for which a reference variable may be declared. The individual objects in a collection are known as the **elements** of the collection.

Collections of Dependent Objects

In our earlier repairperson example, the specific repairperson information being processed during a particular pass through the loop was no longer necessary once that repairperson information had been processed. Once the distance had been calculated and printed, the repairperson data could be discarded. The next time through the loop, the variable rp was reassigned to reference a new RepairPerson object. In this case, the various RepairPerson objects are independent of each other.

There are times, however, when the objects created during each pass are dependent on each other and cannot be discarded immediately. Here are some examples:

- When reading in a list of names and printing them in reverse order of appearance, we must retain all the names until the last one has been read (because it must be the first printed out).
- More realistically, suppose we must read a list of names and then print them out alphabetically. We are faced with the same problem because until the last name has been read, we cannot be sure which name should be printed first.
- Suppose we have a roster file for a college course. Each student registered in the course has the following pair of lines in the file:

  name

  average

  We want to determine which students are performing above and which are below the average of the class. To do this, we must first calculate the average of the class, a process entailing reading in all the students' grades, summing their averages (i.e., accumulating a total), and dividing by the number of students (obtained by maintaining a counter). Only after we have done this can we examine *each* student's average to see whether it's above or below that of the class. (This example is discussed later in this chapter.)
- A *concordance* is a list of all the words in a document together with their frequency of occurrence. To create a concordance for a document contained in a file, the list of words encountered must be maintained until the entire document has been read.

These examples seem somewhat more compelling in their need for a collection than the revision of TelephoneBook, for which a collection is a matter of efficiency.

In these cases it seems that a collection is unavoidable. We now present our first example of a collection in Java.

9.7 `Vector`—A Simple Collection Class

Working with collections of objects is somewhat different from working with the type of code we've been writing until now. However, using our standard approach, we can try to come up with a list of the behaviors we would like the collection to exhibit. To do this let us examine in a bit more detail what a collection does for us:

- Create a new collection (i.e., the constructor)
- Add an object to the collection
- Process the objects in a collection

The important point here is that once we have added an object to a collection, we can come back later and process it and all the others in the collection. We can do this as often as is needed.

Java supplies several collection classes as part of the `java.util` package. The simplest of these—the one we are interested in—is the **Vector** class. We can easily create a `Vector` object, add elements to it, and go through the collection processing those elements.

The `Vector` constructor takes no arguments. Thus to declare a `Vector` reference variable and create a new `Vector`, we can write (see also Figure 9.1):

```
Vector  v  =  new  Vector();
```

Let us now read some `String` objects and add them to `v`. This is just another application of the read/process loop pattern. In this case, the processing involved is adding the `Strings` to the `Vector`. To add an element to a `Vector` we use the method `add()`, passing the object to be added as an argument (see also Figure 9.2):

```
String  s;
s  =  br.readLine();  ◄────────────────── Read first string
while  (s  !=  null)  {
```

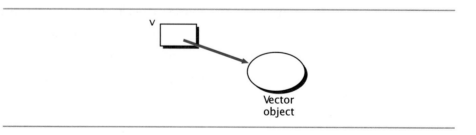

Figure 9.1
A `Vector`, just created.

v

Vector
object

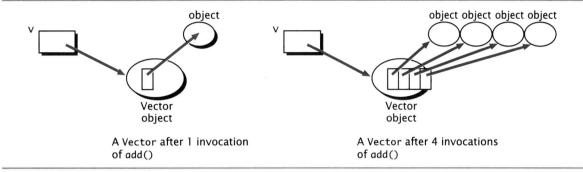

A Vector after 1 invocation of add()

A Vector after 4 invocations of add()

Figure 9.2 A Vector, after add().

```
        v.add(s);  ◄───────────────────────── Processing—adds s to v
        s = br.readLine();  ◄──────────────── Read next string.
}
```

Again, this is just another example of our read/process loop pattern. The reading in each String object is straightforward; the processing portion of the loop is the addition of the object to the collection.

The Vector collection models elements that are arranged in a sequence, so we can think of the *first* element, the *second* element, and so on. The add() method adds a new element at the end of the sequence.

9.8 Traversing Vectors Using for Loops

The process of going through a collection of objects is known as a **traversal** of the collection, and we thus speak of *traversing the collection* and *visiting* (processing) each element. A traversal is a repetitive process (visit *each* of the elements), and thus we should not be surprised that a loop is involved. If we knew how many elements the collection contained, we could accomplish this traversal with a counting loop:

```
for (i = 0; i < size of collection; i++)
     process element number i
```
Remember that Java numbers things from 0 (like the characters in a String)

In order to visit each of the elements of a Vector we need to be able to

- Learn how many elements the Vector contains
- Get the element at a particular position

The Vector class provides methods corresponding to these behaviors:

- int size()
- *ReturnType* elementAt(int index)

The size() method returns the number of elements in the Vector, and the elementAt() method returns the element at a given position, or **index**, where the elements are numbered from 0. Note that because elements are numbered from 0, the highest *index* value of a Vector element is always one less than its size(). (See Figure 9.3.)

The return-type of elementAt() is a bit problematic: It needs to be able to return a reference to an object of *any* class. This is a marvelous flexibility! It means that today we can make a Vector of Name objects and retrieve references to them using elementAt(), and tomorrow we can do the same for String objects. But how can elementAt() return String references, Name references, and *anything-else* references? So far, all our experience with methods shows that if they return a reference, it is always the same kind of reference.

Collection classes such as Vector must work with any object class. Java provides a predefined class, called Object, that models *any* object. Name, Employee, and String references are also Object references. When the elementAt() method returns a reference, it is returning a reference to an Object object. Hence its prototype is

```
Object elementAt(int index);
```

We deliberately use the phrase "an Object object" to emphasize that Object is a class (as is String), and just as there are String objects, so are there Object objects. In fact, every object—String, Name, Employee, and so on—is also an Object object. Because elementAt() is declared as returning a reference to an Object, it can return references to String objects when we use a Vector to store Strings, and it can return references to Name objects when we use a Vector to store Names—all because a reference to a Name object is also a reference to an Object object.

Similarly, when we pass a String reference to the add() method of Vector, as far as add() is concerned, we are just passing a reference to an instance of the Object class.

Figure 9.3
The size() and elementAt() methods of Vector.

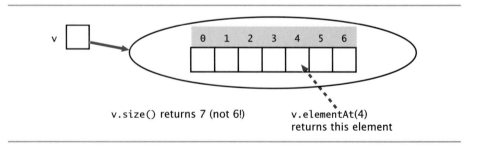

v.size() returns 7 (not 6!) v.elementAt(4) returns this element

We have to pay a small price for this flexibility. This is illustrated in the following snippet of code, which creates a Name object, adds it to a Vector object (making it an element of the collection), and then gets a reference to that element (the original Name object):

```
Name n = new Name("Gerald","Weiss");
Vector v = new Vector();          Add a Name reference to the Vector—but to the
v.add(n);◄──────────────────────── Vector we are just adding another Object reference.
Name n2 = (Name) v.elementAt(0);◄──────────── What is the purpose of (Name)?
```

Because elementAt() is declared as returning a reference to an Object and we are assigning it to n2, a Name reference variable, we must inform Java that the kind of Object reference we are expecting to get from elementAt() is a Name reference. As long as we are sure we put only Name references into the Vector (using add()), we know we are correct. So the extra work is simply

- Making sure that, for any given Vector object, we add only references to one kind of object
- Inserting the phrase (*ClassName*) in front of any invocation of elementAt(), where *ClassName* is the name of the class of object stored in the Vector

The action of informing the system of the true nature of an object reference is known as casting. For example, in the statement

```
Name n2 = (Name) v.elementAt(0);
```

we speak of *casting the first element of v to a* Name. When we cast we are making a promise about the type of a value when the program eventually runs. If it turns out that our promise is broken, and the run-time type is different, then an exception will be thrown and our program will fail. We have used this technique before to convert one type of numeric value to another (e.g., long to int, or int to double); casting can be applied to references as well as to primitive values.

We can now write the code to traverse a collection. As a first example, let's print the Strings in the Vector we created above. The following is a sketch of a traversal loop:

```
for (i = 0; i < size of collection; i++)
    process element number i
```

It now translates to

```
for (i = 0; i < v.size(); i++  {
    String s = (String) v.elementAt(i);
    System.out.println(s);
}
```

Another Loop Pattern—Traversing a Vector

Traversing a collection is the third of our loop patterns. Its general form is

```
// Loop pattern - traverse
for (i=0; i < v.size(); i++  {
    ElementType e = (ElementType) v.elementAt(i);
    process the element
}
```

Extract element.

9.9 Revisiting the TelephoneBook Class

The point of this example is to use a Vector. It is also an example of software refinement—providing a more efficient implementation.

A Better Implementation

As our first application of Vector, let's return to the example that led us to collections: the TelephoneBook class. Recall that rather than having the lookup() method read through (i.e., traverse) the file each time, we instead wish to read the file once and maintain it in memory as a collection. If we examine our original development of TelephoneBook, we see that this change becomes relevant only when we must define the instance variables. Prior to that step, we were defining the behavior and interface to the outside world. These are not and must not be affected by our proposed change. It is the instance variables that must change, as we shall now see.

Defining the Instance Variables

We originally introduced a String instance variable that contained the name of the disk file. This was necessary because each time lookup() was invoked, we had to create the BufferedReader (for subsequent reading) from that name. This is no longer necessary: We will be reading the input file once, using a static read() method; after that we no longer need to know the name of the file. We do, however, need an instance variable to maintain the collection of data read from the file. We use a Vector and name the variable entries:

```
class TelephoneBook  {
    public TelephoneBook()  {...}
    public static TelephoneBook read(String filename) {...}
    public void lookup(String data)  {...}
    private Vector entries;
}
```

Implementing the Methods

The read() method will be responsible for reading the input file into entries:

```
public static TelephoneBook read (String  fileName) throws Exception {
    TelephoneBook tb  =  new  TelephoneBook();
    BufferedReader br =
            new BufferedReader(
                new InputStreamReader(
                    new FileInputStream(fileName)));
    Entry e =  Entry.read(br);
    while  (e != null)  {                   ◄──────────── Read/process loop pattern.
        tb.entries.add(e);
        e = Entry.read(br);
    }
    return tb;
}
```

Once the collection has been created and read, lookup() needs only to traverse the collection in its data search using the traverse loop pattern:

```
public void  lookup(String  data)  {
    String digits = "0123456789";
    String firstChar = data.substring(0,1);
    int position = digits.indexof(firstChar);
    for (int i=0; i< entries.size(); i++) { ◄──────── Traverse loop pattern.
        Entry e = (Entry) entries.elementAt(i);
        if (position < 0) {
            if (data.equals(e.getName()))
                System.out.println(e.getNumber());
        } else {
            if (data.equals(e.getNumber()))
                System.out.println(e.getName());
        }
    }
}
```

Discussion

Along with the efficiency gained by this reimplementation, the most important lesson of this example is that the user of the class sees absolutely no change in the class. The behavior is the same, and the interfaces (i.e., the arguments to the methods) are the same. No code changes are needed wherever the Telephone-Book class is used when we go to this more efficient implementation.

Java Interlude

Primitive Types and Collections: Revisiting the Wrapper Classes

Suppose we want to maintain a collection of some primitive data type, say int. Although a Vector is an obvious choice, we have to deal with one serious obstacle: A Vector accepts an object (Object) as its element type, while an int is a primitive data type, not an object.

To solve this problem, Java introduces a set of classes known as wrapper classes. There is one per primitive data type: Integer corresponds to int, Boolean to boolean, and so on. These classes play two important roles. First, as discussed in Chapter 5, they provide a logical place to keep static methods related to the corresponding primitive data type. Thus, the method parseInt() is logically located in the Integer class.

The second function of the wrapper class is to provide the ability to maintain collections of primitive data types such as int and boolean. For example, to maintain a Vector of integer values, we create instances of the Integer class to "wrap" the various int values we wish to have in the collection. These instances are proper objects and can thus be added to a Vector. The basic mechanism is the same for all the wrapper classes. Here's how to do it for integers:

```
Vector  vi  =  new  Vector();
int  w;
w  =  1;
vi.add(new Integer(w));              Wrap the int value
w  =  2;                             within an Integer object.
vi.add(new Integer(w));
w  =  3;
vi.add(new  Integer(w));
for (int i=0; i < vi.size(); i++)  {
    Integer intObj = (Integer) vi.elementAt(i);   Unwrap the Integer object,
    System.out.println(intObj.intValue());        retrieving the int value.
}
```

The constructor of the Integer class accepts an int argument that corresponds to the integer value to be wrapped in the new object. The new object can then be added to the Vector. We can now traverse the Vector, retrieving the Integer objects and extracting the wrapped value using the intValue() method of the Integer class.

Analogous methods in the Boolean, Double, Float, and Long wrapper classes provide a similar capability for wrapping boolean, double, float, and long values.

9.10 An Example—Determining a Student's Relative Performance

In this section we have more examples of the read/process and traversal loop patterns.

As another example of using Vector, we implement one of the applications that motivated the use of collections.

Statement of the Problem

Suppose we have a roster file for a college course. Each student registered in the course has the following pair of lines in the file:

name
average

We want to determine which students are performing above and below the average of the class.

Determining the Primary Object

The nouns are *roster file*, *student*, *name*, and *average*. *Name* and *average* are subsidiary to *student*, which is in turn subsidiary to the *roster file* (the roster consists of a sequence of student data). We will therefore introduce a class, Student-Roster, which will be associated with the input file.

As we gain experience in designing and writing classes, we begin to see and exploit similarities when creating new classes. Looking back at TelephoneBook, we see a similarity to our current application. In both cases, subsidiary objects (entries there, students here) are read from a file, after which operations are performed upon them. Associated with the file is an object (TelephoneBook and Student-Roster, respectively) that will provide the necessary behavior.

Determination of the Behavior

We want to be able to evaluate the students in the roster. In addition we have a constructor, as follows:

- StudentRoster (constructor)
- evaluate (goes through the roster and evaluates the student)

Notice we haven't yet discussed when the class average will be calculated, when the student information will be read, or whether there will be a collection—none of that is relevant to the user of the class and does not belong in a discussion of the behavior. Rather, it will be introduced when we define instance variables and implement methods.

Defining the Interface

As usual, we write some typical code to help us determine the interface. We are taking our lead from the TelephoneBook class—creating the roster entails associating it with the appropriate input file. After the object is created, we may invoke its evaluate method:

```
StudentRoster  roster  =  new  StudentRoster("CS1.f02");
roster.evaluate();
```

Our interface is as follows:

```
class  StudentRoster  {
    public StudentRoster(String  rosterFileName)  {...}
    public void  evaluate()  {...}
}
```

Defining the Instance Variables

In order to evaluate each student, we must first compute the class average. This average can be calculated in the constructor as soon as the student data are available. So that the average can be used later in the evaluate() method, it is stored in an instance variable.

The information associated with each student is required twice: first to compute the class average in the constructor and then later for the assessment. This student information must also be maintained as part of the StudentRoster's state. Because this information consists of many objects, one per student, a collection is in order:

```
class  StudentRoster  {
    Methods

    ...
    private Vector  studentColl;
    private int  classAverage;
}
```

Implementing the Methods

Using TelephoneBook as a guide, we create the studentColl collection and load it up in the constructor. In the course of writing the loop that reads in the input, the need arises for a class, Student, that models a student:

```
public StudentRoster(String rosterFileName) throws Exception {
    studentColl  =  new Vector();
    BufferedReader  br =
            new BufferedReader(
                new  InputStreamReader(
                    new FileInputStream(rosterFileName)));
    Student  student  =  Student.read(br);
```

```
    while  (student  !=  null)  {                          Read/process loop pattern.
        studentColl.add(student);
        Any other processing
        student  =  Student.read(br);
    }
}
```

Once again, we have encountered an application of the read/process pattern. This constructor, however, has more to do. It must calculate the class average. To do this, we maintain a total of the individual averages read as well as a count of the number of students. Thus, we initialize an int variable, count, to zero, reflecting that at the outset no students have been processed. Each time we successfully read a student, we increment this variable. Similarly, we initialize an int variable, total, to zero, reflecting that at the outset the sum of the averages of the students read is zero—because no students have yet been read. Each time we successfully read a student, we add the student's average to this variable. Once the input has been completely read, we can compute the class average by dividing total by count. Here is the full constructor:

```
StudentRoster(String rosterFileName) throws Exception {      A second look
    studentColl  =  new Vector();
    BufferedReader  br =
            new BufferedReader(
                new  InputReaderStream(
                    new FileInputStream(rosterFileName)));
    int  total  =  0;  // accumulated total of averages
    int  count  =  0;  // count of students
    Student  student  =  Student.read(br);
    while  (student  !=  null)  {                          Read/process loop pattern.
        total  +=  student.getAverage();
        count++;
        studentColl.add(student);
        student  =  Student.read(br);
    }
    classAverage  =  total  /  count;
}
```

Besides fleshing out the implementation of StudentRoster, this additional code in the constructor provides us with more behavior for the Student class that we must write (the method getAverage()).

We can now write evaluate(), using the traverse loop pattern. Processing each student consists of comparing the student's average against the class average and displaying the appropriate results:

```
public void  evaluate()  {
    for (int i=0; i<studentColl.size(); i++) {            Traverse loop pattern
```

```
        Student student  =  (Student) studentColl.elementAt(i);
        System.out.print(student.getName());
        System.out.print("  is  performing  ");
        if  (student.getAverage()  >=  classAverage)
            System.out.println("above average.");
        else
            System.out.println("below average.");
        }
    }
```

Again, evaluate() has also introduced further required behavior for the Student class (method getName()).

Using the Class

We introduce another class, Evaluator, whose sole purpose is to contain a main method that will use our StudentRoster class. We could have just as easily placed the main method in the StudentRoster class itself:

```
class Evaluator  {
    public static void main(String[] args) throws Exception {
        StudentRoster roster = new StudentRoster("CS1.f02");
        roster.evaluate();
        roster = new StudentRoster("CS2.f02");
        roster.evaluate();
    }
}
```

We leave the design of the Student class as an exercise.

Discussion

Our applications are growing in complexity. As we progress, we should be collecting techniques and design ideas from the classes we create and using these ideas in future class designs. TelephoneBook and StudentRoster were somewhat similar. Having implemented one, we were able to glean ideas from it for the other. In some sense, when we look at classes we have already implemented to get ideas for new classes, we are working with patterns—class patterns, rather than the loop patterns we have been discussing.

When we first introduced collections, we presented the StudentRoster application as one that seemed to *require* a collection because of the dependent nature of the student objects. However, this is not strictly the case. In our implementation of the methods, we discussed the possibility of evaluate() traversing the studentColl collection twice: once to calculate the average and once to evaluate the individual students. Another possibility might have been to eliminate the collection entirely and have evaluate() read the roster file twice: once to calculate the average and once to evaluate the students. Although this would be highly inefficient, it is no more so than our original `TelephoneBook` implementation, which constantly read through the data file every time `lookup()` was invoked. Furthermore, it emphasizes an interesting point: *Files are in essence nothing more than collections stored on disk.* The primary reason we use collections (when working with files) is for efficiency; it is just too expensive to keep reading in the same file over and over again.

9.11 Another Vector Application

If we flip a coin many times (say, 100), how many of those flips yield a head? On average, we would expect to see 50 heads and 50 tails. If we actually perform this experiment, though, often we won't get exactly 50 heads—sometimes we'll get 48, or 53, and very occasionally we might get just a few heads, or even none at all. That is, if we perform this experiment hundreds of times and draw a graph of the number of heads we get in each experiment, we'd expect to see a curve that looks something like Figure 9.4.

We can use Monte Carlo methods (as we did to approximate the value of π in Chapter 6) to approximate this curve as closely as we would like. This time, instead of keeping track of one value (the number of darts landing inside the circle) we'll keep track of several: We need to count how many times we get 0 heads, how many times we get 1, how many times we get 2, and so on. This is

Figure 9.4
Expected results of flipping a coin 100 times.

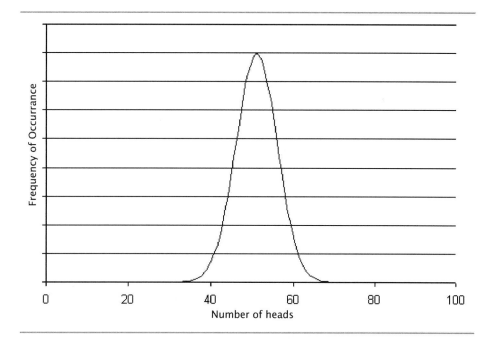

another application of a Vector: Instead of using it to store a sequence of values, we will use the indices of the Vector elements very intentionally. That is, when we finish with our series of experiments, the *i*th element of the Vector will tell us how many times our experiment yielded *i* heads. When the experiments are completed, we can output the results in some useful way.

We'll begin by asking the user to choose how many experiments to perform and how many flips to execute in each experiment:

```java
import java.io.*;
import java.util.*;

class CoinFlips {
    public static void main(String[] a) throws Exception {
        BufferedReader  kbd = new BufferedReader(
                            new InputStreamReader(System.in));
        System.out.print("How many experiments? ");
        String expString = kbd.readLine();
        int numExp = Integer.parseInt(expString);
        System.out.print("How many coins per experiment? ");
        String flipString = kbd.readLine();
        int numFlips = Integer.parseInt(flipString);
        System.out.println(numExp + " experiments and "
                                + numFlips + " flips.");
```

Before we begin performing experiments, we must declare a Vector to hold the results, and we also need a simple counting loop to ensure that all values of the Vector are initially zero:

```java
Vector headsCount = new Vector(numFlips);       // Overloaded constructor
for (int i=0; i < numFlips; i++)
    headsCount.add(new Integer(0));
```

Then we can perform the experiments, again using a counting loop. We will use a helper method, doExperiment() (to be defined shortly), to do the work; it will take as an argument the number of flips to perform, and it will return the number of heads that occurred during the experiment:

```java
for (int i=0; i < numExp; i++) {
    int numHeads = doExperiment(numFlips);
    Integer currCount = (Integer)headsCount.elementAt(numHeads);
    headsCount.setElementAt(
        new Integer(currCount.intValue()+1), numHeads);
}
```

Finally, we pass numHeads to another helper method, doOutput(), which will display the results.

```
        doOutput(headsCount);
    }
}
```

The doExperiment() Method

This method will also use a counting loop to generate a sequence of random values. Because we are only interested in two values (heads or tails) we will simply test the random value to see whether it is greater than or less than 0.5. We'll decide (arbitrarily) that values less than 0.5 are heads, and the rest are tails. Thus, we can implement doExperiment() as

```
static int doExperiment(int flips) {
    int heads = 0;
    for (int i=0; i < flips; i++)
        if (Integer.random() < 0.5)
            heads++;
        // otherwise do nothing...

    return heads;
}
```

The doOutput() Method

We have several options for implementing the doOutput() method. The simplest is just to print out the elements of headsCount in order:

```
static void doOutput(Vector v) {
    for (int i=0; i<v.size(); i++)
        System.out.println((Integer) v.elementAt(i));
}
```

But this implementation doesn't make it very easy to see the shape of the curve. Instead, we could replace the numerical values with a sequence of symbols, such as

```
static void doOutput(Vector v) {
    for (int i=0; i < v.size(); i++) {
        Integer heads = (Integer) v.elementAt(i);
        for (int j=0; j < heads.intValue(); j++)
            System.out.print('*');
        System.out.println();
    }
}
```

Of course, if there are a sizable number of experiments (say, more than 100), then it is likely that some of these lines of stars will be too long to fit on the screen. To prevent this, we can let each star represent several heads, depending on the number of experiments (in which case we will need to pass the number of experiments as a parameter). A very safe implementation might be

```
static void doOutput(Vector v, int numExp) {
    int scaleFactor =  numExp/80+ 1;
    for (int i=0; i < v.size(); i++) {
        Integer heads = (Integer) v.elementAt(i);
        for (int j=0; j < heads.intValue()/scaleFactor; j++)
            System.out.print('*');
        System.out.println();
    }
}
```

Running this program gives output like this:

```
How many experiments to be performed? 1000
How many coins in each experiment? 20
1000 experiments and 20 flips.
```

```
*
***
****
********
************
**************
************
********
*****
**
*
```

These curves are obviously on the "wrong" axis: we prefer to see curves that move from left to right (as in Figure 9.4) rather than from top to bottom. This is a more complicated problem, which we leave as an exercise.

Our final version of the coin-flipping program, then, is shown here:

```
import java.io.*;
import java.util.*;

class CoinFlips {
    public static void main(String[] a) throws Exception {
        BufferedReader  kbd = new BufferedReader(
```

```
            new InputStreamReader(System.in));
        System.out.print("How many experiments to be performed?");
        String expString = kbd.readLine();
        int numExp = Integer.parseInt(expString);
        System.out.print("How many coins in each experiment?");
        String flipString = kbd.readLine();
        int numFlips = Integer.parseInt(flipString);
        System.out.println(numExp + " experiments and " +
                                        numFlips + " flips.");
        Vector headsCount = new Vector(numFlips);
        for (int i=0; i < numFlips; i++)
            headsCount.add(new Integer(0));

        for (int i=0; i < numExp; i++) {
            int numHeads = doExperiment(numFlips);
            Integer currCount = (Integer)headsCount.elementAt(numHeads);
            headsCount.setElementAt(
                new Integer(currCount.intValue()+1),numHeads);
        }
        doOutput(headsCount,numExp);
    }

    static int doExperiment(int flips) {
        int heads = 0;
        for (int i=0; i < flips; i++) {
            if (Math.random() < 0.5)
                heads++;
        }
        return heads;
    }

    static void doOutput(Vector v, int numExp) {
        int scaleFactor =  numExp/80+ 1;
        for (int i=0; i < v.size(); i++) {
            Integer heads = (Integer) v.elementAt(i);
            for (int j=0; j < heads.intValue()/scaleFactor; j++)
                System.out.print('*');
            System.out.println();
        }
    }
}
```

*Object **Methods***

Because *all* objects are considered as instances of class `Object`, any methods defined for that class must be universally applicable. In particular, we wish to examine two of these `Object` class methods: `equals()` and `toString()`.

The purpose of the `toString()` method is to create a `String` representation of the object for which this method is invoked. Invoking `toString()` on an `Integer` object that contains the integer value 275 thus produces the `String` "275". Invoking `toString()` on a `String` object merely produces the same object.

Because the `toString()` method provided by the `Object` class knows nothing about the actual class of the object, it produces a `String` with minimal information—essentially the name of the object's actual class. For example, suppose we have the following (useless) class:

```java
class  Test  {
    public Test()  {          This class has no behavior or state.
    }
}
```

The result of executing `toString()` on a `Test` object

```java
Test  t;
String  s  =  t.toString();
```

causes the `Object` class `toString()` method to be invoked, producing a `String` of the form

```
Test@15368
```

(The 15368 could be any number; it is tied to the particular object and is meaningless to us.)

If we want `toString()` to produce a `String` that is customized to our `Test` class, we have to implement such a method in the class itself. To do this *we have to match exactly the signature of the `toString()` method as implemented in class `Object`*. This signature can be seen in the prototype

```java
public String  toString();       The prototype of the toString()
                                 method as specified in class Object.
```

By adding this method to our class, we are indicating that an invocation of `toString()` on a `Test` object should invoke the version in `Test`, not the one in the `Object` class. This is known as *overriding*, and we will see a lot more of this in later chapters.

```java
class  Test  {
    public Test()  {}
    public  String  toString()  {
```

```
        return  "I  am  a  Test  object";
    }
}
```

Invoking `toString()` upon a `Test` object now produces the `String` "I am a Test object". This is not much better, but then the class is a trivial one. Let us write a `toString()` method for our `RepairPerson` class. We (somewhat arbitrarily) decide that `toString()` for `RepairPerson` objects should return the name followed by the location, separated by spaces:

```
class  RepairPerson  {
    ...
    public String  toString()  {
        String  result  =  name;
        result += "  " + location;
        return  result;
    }
    ...
}
```

Now any user of the class who wants to get a custom `String` representation of a `RepairPerson` (say, for debugging purposes) can do so by invoking `toString()`.

In fact, the `toString()` method is invoked automatically whenever the compiler detects the need for a `String`. Note that in the statement

```
        String  result  =  name;
```

we are taking advantage of the fact that we already defined a `toString()` method for `Name` in Chapter 5; this method is invoked by the compiler when it sees that we're trying to assign a `Name` reference to a `String`. Similarly, when we write

```
        result += "  " + location;
```

the compiler will try to invoke the `toString()` method of `Location`. We leave the implementation of this method as an exercise.

The `equals()` Method

The second `Object` class method of interest is `equals()`. The intent of this method is to allow the comparison of two objects for equality. As we saw with `Telephone-Book`, this function is particularly useful when searching for a particular element of a collection. The signature of this method can be seen in the prototype

```
public boolean  equals(Object  o) ◄───
```
The prototype of the `equals` method as specified in class `Object`

Because this method is defined in class `Object`, all we can say is that we are comparing two objects—the receiver and the argument—and thus the `Object` type for the parameter. Lacking any detailed information regarding the actual class of the two objects, the `Object` class `equals()` method merely checks to see whether the receiver and argument reference the same exact object. Suppose we have the following two objects of our `Location` class:

```
Location  loc1  =  new  Location(4, 7);
Location  loc2  =  loc1;
```

The invocation

```
loc1.equals(loc2)
```

results in `true` because `loc1` and `loc2` reference the exact same object. However, given the two `Location` objects

```
Location  loc1  =  new  Location(4, 7);
Location  loc2  =  new  Location(4, 7);
```

the invocation

```
loc1.equals(loc2)
```

results in `false` because `loc1` and `loc2` refer to different objects. The fact that they contain the same information and would thus be equal in terms of the "meaning" of a `Location` does not matter.

As with `toString()`, if we want to have a customized version of `equals()`, one that works with our understanding of what it means for two `Location` objects to be equal, we must supply our own version in the `Location` class itself. The only problem, again, is that the signature must exactly match the one in the `Object` class that accepts an `Object` argument. We resolve this by taking the argument and casting it to a `Location` object. The receiver *is* a `Location` object (the method is defined in the `Location` class; thus the receiver must be a `Location`). We can then access the instance variables to perform our `Location`-specific equality test:

```
class  Location  {
    ...
    public boolean  equals(Object  o)  {
        Location  loc = (Location) o;
        return  (this.x == loc.x  && this.y == loc.y);
    }
    ...
}
```

Note that we made a small but significant change from our discussion of the `equals()` method in Chapter 5. Before, the signature of our `equals()` method for the `Name` class was

```
public boolean equals (Name n)
```

While that method worked perfectly well in the context of Chapter 5, from now on all `equals()` methods should accept an `Object` parameter to guarantee proper compilation.

9.12 Introducing Arrays

An **array** is a language feature that uses indexing to support collections of data. An array shares some characteristics with a `Vector`:

- It consists of one or more positions.
- Each position is indexed by an integer.
- The first position's index is 0.
- It must be created with the `new` operation.
- It is an object.
- It is referenced using a reference variable.

There are also many differences between the two:

- There is no array class. Arrays are not defined in a class library; they are built into the language itself.
- There are no "array methods" to work with arrays or their elements; instead, special symbols are provided by the language that allow us to access array elements.
- An array has a *field*, called `length`, that indicates the number of elements of the array—in contrast to a `Vector`, which uses a *method*, `size()`, to provide this information.
- Array elements can hold primitive data such as `int` values as well as references to objects.
- The type of the elements of an array must be specified in the array's declaration. Everything stored in its elements must be of that type.
- Arrays can't grow—once an array has been created, it has a fixed number of elements.

Declaring and Creating Arrays

To declare an array reference variable, we write the type of data each element will hold, followed by an empty pair of square brackets and then the name of the reference variable:

```
int[]     lotteryNumbers;  // This can refer to an array whose elements are all ints.
String[] winners;          // This can refer to an array whose elements are
                           //     all references to String objects.
Name[]    personnel;       // This can refer to an array whose elements are
                           //     all references to Name objects.
```

Of course, you have been seeing such declarations since Chapter 1: The parameter to main in a stand-alone application is String[] a. These declarations don't create arrays, just variables that can refer to them.

To *create* an array we use the new operator, followed by the element type and a pair of square brackets enclosing an integer that specifies the number of elements the array will have. For example, the following code creates an array of six elements, each of which may be assigned an integer value:

```
new  int[6]
```

As in the creation of any object, if we don't save the reference to the new object, we won't be able to do anything, so we normally would write something like the following:

```
lotteryNumbers = new  int[6];
```

Now lotteryNumbers refers to this six-element array. (See Figure 9.5.)

The expression

arrayReferenceVariable.length

yields the size of the array that the array reference variable refers to. There are no parentheses after length: It is not a method, just a value.

So, the value of

```
lotteryNumbers.length
```

is 6, given the assignment above. As in the case of Vectors and the result of the size() method, the value yielded by length is not a valid position—it is 1 more than the index of the last position in the array.

Array Elements

To set the element in position k of array z to a particular value we write

```
z[k]  =  value;
```

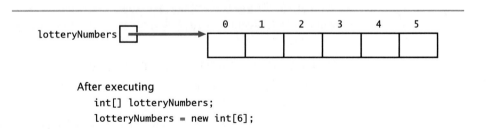

After executing
```
int[] lotteryNumbers;
lotteryNumbers = new int[6];
```

The value assigned must match the type the array was declared to have. To use the value of the element in position k of array z we simply write

```
z[k]
```

as in

```
int  x  =  3*z[k];
int  y  =  z[k];
```

This square bracket element selection is analogous to the `elementAt()` method of Vectors.

Array elements—`lotteryNumbers[3]`, `winners[2]`, and `z[k]`, for example—are very much like variables. They can be assigned values, and when they are used in an expression, these values are retrieved. In fact, sometimes arrays are called indexed variables.

9.13 Vectors and Arrays

In this section we compare arrays and Vectors and look at how code using Vectors can be converted to code using arrays.

Arrays or Vectors?

Arrays offer three advantages over Vectors:

- You can store primitive data values (such as `int`) in arrays.
- Their elements can be accessed without sending a message, so code using an array will be somewhat faster than code using a Vector.
- Arrays, because they are typed, offer a kind of checking at compile time that Vectors don't. If you have a Vector that is intended to store references to Name objects, Java does not prevent you from mistakenly storing a String or Entry reference because Vector elements can be assigned any reference to an object. But Java will give you a compile-time error if you try storing one of those references into an array that is declared to hold Name references. You might not like getting the error message, but at least it allows you to catch your mistake early. This also eliminates the need for casting, which can make array code a little cleaner.

On the other hand, arrays have the following disadvantages when compared to Vectors:

- Arrays are fixed in size and will not grow.
- Arrays do not offer the rich set of operations that the methods of the Vector class offer—for example, `insertElementAt()`.

Table 9.1 summarizes the differences between arrays and Vectors.

TABLE 9.1 DIFFERENCES BETWEEN ARRAYS AND VectorS

	ARRAY a	Vector v
Element type	Established by declaration of a	Reference to object
Element referenced by	a[index]	v.elementAt(index)
Element assigned by	a[index] = value	v.setElementAt(value)
Number of elements	a.length	v.size()
Can store primitive data types?	Yes	No
Can grow dynamically?	No	Yes
Defined by	The Java language	The Java class library

From Vectors to Arrays

Much code written using Vectors can be converted to code using arrays. The first step is to create an array that is large enough to store all the elements that will be needed. The second step is to eliminate all method invocations other than size(), elementAt(), and setElementAt(). Doing this requires replacing add() with setElementAt(). The third step is to replace size() with the length array notation, and the elementAt() and setElementAt() methods with the square-bracket index notation.

Code involving some of the more powerful Vector methods, such as insert-ElementAt(), requires more work to convert. In general, if the type and number of elements in the collection are known and fixed, an array is often the best choice.

9.14 Coin Flipping with Arrays

In this section, we'll convert our coin-flipping example from a Vector-based application to an array-based application.

Declaring and Initializing the Array

The initial prompting of the user, of course, remains the same, but declaring and initializing heads as an array now looks like this:

```
import java.io.*;
import java.util.*;

class CoinFlips {
    public static void main(String[] a) throws Exception {
        BufferedReader  kbd = new BufferedReader(
                    new InputStreamReader(System.in));
        System.out.print("How many experiments to be performed?");
```

```
    String expString = kbd.readLine();
    int numExp = Integer.parseInt(expString);
    System.out.print("How many coins in each experiment?");
    String flipString = kbd.readLine();
    int numFlips = Integer.parseInt(flipString);
    System.out.println(numExp + " experiments and " +
                                    numFlips + " flips.");

    int[] headsCount = new int[numFlips];

    for (int i=0; i < numFlips; i++)
        headsCount[i] = 0;
```

Recording the results of the experiments is now straightforward: Rather than extracting an `Integer` value from the collection, converting it to an `int`, adding 1, and replacing the incremented value in the collection, we can now increment the appropriate element of the array directly:

```
    for (int i=0; i < numExp; i++) {
        int numHeads = doExperiment(numFlips);
        headsCount[numHeads]++;
    }
    doOutput(headsCount,numExp);
}
```

Finally, the `doExperiment()` method is unchanged, but the `doOutput()` method receives an array parameter rather than a `Vector`:

```
static int doExperiment(int flips) {
    int heads = 0;
    for (int i=0; i < flips; i++) {
        if (Math.random() < 0.5)
            heads++;
    }
    return heads;
}

static void doOutput(int[] a, int numExp) {
    int scaleFactor =  numExp/80+ 1;
    for (int i=0; i < a.length; i++) {
        int heads = a[i];
        for (int j=0; j < heads/scaleFactor; j++)
            System.out.print('*');
        System.out.println();
    }
}
}
```

Summary

The repetition of a series of statements is one of the most powerful programming constructs. Once a task has been defined for a single object, it may be repeated for hundreds, thousands, or even millions of objects. A loop is a language construct that supports such repetition. It consists of a body—the statements to be repeated—and a termination condition.

One application of a loop is to read in a series of objects belonging to the same class or primitive data type and process them individually. Once an object has been processed, it is no longer needed. We say such objects are independent of each other. Though the exact processing or method of input may vary depending on the nature of the object, the basic structure of the loop in all such cases is the same, and to emphasize this similarity, we introduce the concept of a loop pattern. Such patterns give the programmer a starting point for designing simple loops. The basic structure is provided by the pattern; the programmer must provide the read and processing logic to complete the loop.

Often we must maintain multiple objects, as for example, when we wish to read in a list of numbers and print it in reverse. In this case, we cannot discard each object as it is read in. Because there is an arbitrary number of such objects to be processed, declaring individual variables for each object is impossible. A collection is an object that models a number of related objects. The simplest collection class in Java is the Vector. Objects may be added to the Vector object using the add() method.

The objects of a Vector may be processed by traversing through them using the elementAt() method. This method takes an index value as a parameter and returns a reference to the object in that position. The size() method may be used to determine when there are no more objects left to process.

In order to allow primitive data types to be added to a Vector that requires its elements be objects, Java provides wrapper classes Integer, Long, Double, Byte, Short, Float, and Boolean for each of the primitive types.

Key Terms

array A programming language feature that provides an indexed collection of data values.

collection A class or language construct that manages one or more objects.

elements The individual objects contained within a collection.

index An integer that denotes a position in an ordered collection.

loop A language construct that repeatedly executes a section of code.

loop pattern The code structure of a loop that is frequently used.

traversal The process of listing or going through all members of a collection.

Vector A particular collection class in the java.util package.

while statement A particular loop construct in the Java language.

Questions for Review

1. How does a while statement work?
2. Why are programs that contain loops difficult to test thoroughly?
3. When is a collection necessary?
4. What is the read/process loop pattern?

Exercises

1. Write a program that reads in a series of int values using the technique presented in Section 5.3 for performing integer input. Do you see any difference in structure between this program and the one presented that read repairperson data?

2. Can we put the read() in the repairperson-processing loop at the beginning of the loop, as follows?

```
RepairPerson rp  =  RepairPerson.read(br);
while  (rp  != null)  {
    rp = RepairPerson.read(br);
    int distance = rp.getDistanceFrom(loc);
    System.out.println(rp.getName()+": "+distance);
}
```

3. Explain how each of the three loop test categories apply to the read/process loop pattern. That is, what sort of data must be in the file for each of the cases to occur?

4. Apply the test method outlined in Section 9.4 to our repairperson loop.

5. How do the three minimal loop test categories approximate *all-paths* testing?

6. Complete the implementation of the Entry class by implementing the constructor and getName() and getNumber() methods.

7. Write a test driver for the Entry class.

8. Rework the behavior of the TelephoneBook class so that lookup() returns the entry it found, rather than simply printing out the name or number. Does this change the point at which the need for an Entry class is discovered?

9. Write code to read a series of Name objects into a Vector and then traverse the Vector, printing out the values.

10. Write code to read a series of Location objects into a Vector, then traverse the Vector, printing them out.

11. Can we add an int value to a Vector? What about double?

12. Complete the design and implementation of the Student class that is required by StudentRoster.

13. Can you think of any reason not to place a main() method in StudentRoster that simply demonstrates the use of the class? (Hint: Go back and look at Section 8.3 on test drivers.)

14. Write a program that reads in customer information from a file. The information for each customer includes a name, address, and amount purchased over the last three months. Calculate the average purchasing amount for each customer. If particular customers have purchased more than the average, send those customers letters thanking them for their patronage. Otherwise, send the customers letters notifying them that they will receive 5% off their next purchases (in an attempt to get them to buy more).

15. Implement the toString() method of the Location class.

16. Why can't you rewrite the TelephoneBook class to use arrays?

17. If the TelephoneBook data file contained one extra line of information at the beginning, *could* you rewrite the class to use arrays? What would this line contain? Rewrite the TelephoneBook class to use this modified data format and arrays.

18. Modify the TypingTutor class of Chapter 4 so that every incorrect string typed by the user is saved. Add a method to the class that outputs all the incorrect strings typed so far. Rewrite the Test class (which uses TypingTutor) to read practice strings from a file and test the user five times on each practice string.

19. Write a program that reads integers from a data file and uses Minimizer to identify the smallest value read.

Positioning Text

In this supplement we will focus on some of the challenges of writing applets that manipulate and display text. We'll design an applet that implements a few of the functions of a word processor; in the next supplement we'll add some more features.

Specifically, we'll write an applet that displays a few lines of text and allows the user to choose their position: left-justified, right-justified, or centered; at the top, middle, or bottom of the display. When running, this applet should look something like Figure 9.6.

Mixing Graphics with GUI Components

Applets and panels are examples of *container* components—other components may be placed within them, using a layout manager and the *add()* method.

User interface components, such as buttons, text fields, and panels, are maintained as objects distinct from the container component on which they are

Figure 9.6
Executing the Text-JustifierApplet.

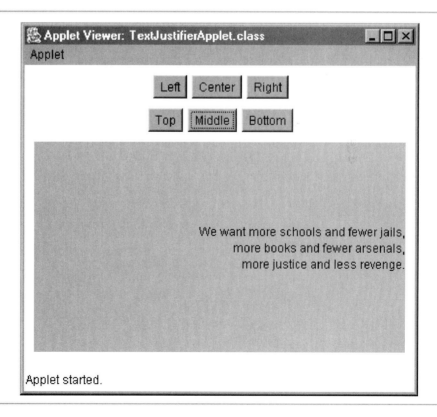

placed. Their primary responsibility is to provide a mechanism for the user to interact with the program, and therefore each component has its own specific behavior provided by the corresponding class: Button for buttons, Panel for panels, and so on. These components may be placed within a container, but they maintain their own identity.

In contrast, text and the graphic shapes such as lines, rectangles, and ovals have no existence independent of the component they are drawn on. For example, they cannot be given their own background color—they use the color of the component they are drawn on. We can change that color using the setBackground() method of the Graphics class but then the background color of the whole component would change as well, not just that of the text string or shape.

In summary, components are created and placed on their containers using a layout manager. Graphical shapes (including text), on the other hand, are drawn directly on the display surface—the layout manager knows nothing of them. When a component is created, it has its own display surface, and when it is placed into position by the layout manager, it hides the portion of the display surface directly beneath it. If there is text in that area, the text will be hidden by the component. The following table compares components and graphical shapes:

	COMPONENTS	GRAPHICAL SHAPES
Associated with objects	Yes	No
Have properties	Yes	No
Generate events	Yes	No
Positioned by	Layout manager	Programmer

If we add GUI components to an applet and then draw text (or other graphics) on it, the layout manager, which knows nothing of the text, will position the components without regard to the underlying text. For example, suppose we write an applet with three buttons that also displays the three lines of text shown in Figure 9.7 :

```java
import java.awt.*;
import java.applet.*;

public class TextAndButtonsApplet extends Applet {
    public void init() {
        add(new Button("Previous"));
        add(new Button("Next"));
        add(new Button("Cancel"));
    }
```

Figure 9.7
A clash of components and text.

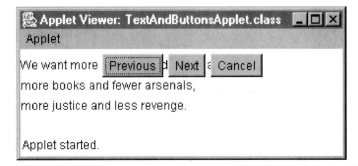

```
public void paint(Graphics g) {
    g.drawString("We want more schools and fewer jails,",0,20);
    g.drawString("more books and fewer arsenals,",0,40);
    g.drawString("more justice and less revenge.",0,60);
    }
}
```

Running the resulting applet produces a display in which the text and buttons clash.

The Canvas Component

To prevent the clash shown in Figure 9.7, we must isolate the shapes and text from the GUI components. We accomplish this with a Canvas component, whose behavior models a drawing canvas—we can draw our text and shapes on it. Because a Canvas is a component, it may be added to the panel and will be known to the layout manager. Layout managers never allow components to overlap each other. Thus, when the buttons are added, the layout manager will prevent them from overlapping the Canvas, preserving our display.

Each time we created a new applet, we defined a new applet class. In a similar fashion, each time we wish to draw a new type of canvas, we define a new canvas class. In our case, we will have a class, TextCanvas, whose responsibility is the display of our text.

Laying out TextJustifierApplet

Before we begin implementing our applet's behavior, we first create the layout. Our approach will be to create a panel containing the buttons; this panel itself will use a BorderLayout object to position two smaller panels, each of which will contain one row of buttons. We will also create a new TextCanvas object (the behavior of which we'll describe below) and add it to the display. Thus, our applet will have the following init() method and instance variables:

```
public class TextJustifierApplet extends Applet  {
    public void init() {
        setBackground(new Color(255,255,255));

        Panel horiz = new Panel();
        leftButton = new Button("Left");
        centerButton = new Button("Center");
        rightButton = new Button("Right");
        horiz.add(leftButton);
        horiz.add(centerButton);          Buttons for horizontal
        horiz.add(rightButton);           positioning.

        Panel vert = new Panel();
        topButton = new Button("Top");
        middleButton = new Button("Middle");
        bottomButton = new Button("Bottom");
        vert.add(topButton);
        vert.add(middleButton);           Buttons for vertical
        vert.add(bottomButton)            positioning.

        Panel position = new Panel();
        position.setLayout(new BorderLayout());
        position.add("North",horiz);
        position.add("South",vert);       Layout button panel.
        tc = new TextCanvas();
        add(position);                    May need to modify constructor signature.
        add(tc);

        register buttons with some listener
    }

    private Button leftButton,centerButton,rightButton;
    private Button topButton,middleButton,bottomButton;
    private TextCanvas tc;
}
```

We will postpone registering the buttons with an event listener until we begin a more detailed analysis of the applet's behavior.

Setting Sizes in the start() Method

Notice that the layout manager for the applet itself is the default FlowLayout. Thus, when we add() the position Panel and the TextCanvas tc we have no guarantee that they'll be laid out vertically. One way to force a vertical layout is to adjust the size of tc to be almost as wide as the applet itself, so there will be no room to the right of the buttons to position tc. We can also set the height of tc to be sure there will be room for both the buttons and the canvas. Because the buttons are not given a size during the init() method, we must wait to set the sizes. We could set the size of tc in the paint() method, but that would cause the size calculations to be made *each* time paint() is called rather than just once. Instead, we will put the size calculation in the body of the applet's start() method. This method is automatically invoked after init() and is also invoked each time the page containing the applet is reloaded by the browser:

```
public void start() {                        A little narrower than the applet.
    tc.setSize(getWidth()-20,
               getHeight()-(4*leftButton.getHeight()));
}                                            Leave four button-heights at the top.
```

Of course, we could have used a BorderLayout manager instead, but we chose to illustrate manipulating component sizes rather than organizing more Panels in a BorderLayout.

Handling Events

What happens when a button is clicked? The display of the text within the Text-Canvas might change, but nothing else should. Therefore, the proper listener for the button events is the canvas rather than the applet itself. It's both more logical and more efficient to register the canvas as the buttons' ActionListener. Thus, the last few lines of the applet's init() method are

```
leftButton.addActionListener(tc);
centerButton.addActionListener(tc);
rightButton.addActionListener(tc);
topButton.addActionListener(tc);
middleButton.addActionListener(tc);
bottomButton.addActionListener(tc);
```

A TextCanvas Skeleton

The TextCanvas is a component that is used for drawing, so we clearly must provide a paint() method. Because it is the listener for the applet's buttons, we must provide an actionPerformed() method (and mark the class as implements ActionListener). So far, then, we have

```
class TextCanvas extends Canvas implements ActionListener {
    public void actionPerformed(ActionEvent e) {...}
    public void paint(Graphics g) {...}

    other methods?

    instance variables
}
```

Implementing `actionPerformed()`

Because most of TextCanvas's behavior will occur in response to button clicks, we'll start our method implementation with `actionPerformed()`. As in our `Calculator-Applet` implementation, we'll design our `actionPerformed()` to determine the source of the event, then delegate the response to an appropriate method. There are essentially two kinds of events: one that asks for the horizontal position to be changed, and one that asks for the vertical position to be changed. Therefore, we will provide two additional methods, `setHorizJust()` and `setVertJust()`, for handling each type of event; these methods will each receive a single parameter representing the desired new position. To make the communication among methods (`actionPerformed()` to `setHorizJust()` to `paint()`, which will display the text with appropriate justification) easier, we will define some constant (i.e., `static final`) values in the TextCanvas class. Constants defined in a class are often declared as `public` to allow users of the class access to their values, but because these constants are only going to be used *within* the class, we will declare them `private`:

```
private static final int LEFT = 0;
private static final int CENTER = 1;
private static final int RIGHT = 2;
private static final int TOP = 0;
private static final int MIDDLE = 1;
private static final int BOTTOM = 2;
```

Identifying the Source of the Event

In our calculator applets, we used the `getActionCommand()` method to return the *label* of the Button that generated the event we were handling. In those applets, the button labels carried important information, especially the labels of the digit buttons. This technique has disadvantages, however: If the interface designer changes the labels on the buttons, the event-handling code must also change. Java therefore provides an alternative technique for identifying the source of an event: The `ActionEvent.getSource()` method returns a *reference* to the event-generating object. This allows us to identify the source of the event without regard to its label.

Because we need to compare this reference to references to the applet's buttons, the applet must provide these references to the TextCanvas object; a natural time to do this is when the applet creates the TextCanvas object. Thus, we will provide TextCanvas with a constructor that receives six Button references as parameters; we will also declare six instance variables to store these references:

```
public TextCanvas(Button l, Button c, Button r,
                  Button t, Button m, Button b) {
    leftButton = l;
    centerButton = c;
```

```
        rightButton = r;
        topButton = t;
        middleButton = m;
        bottomButton = b;
    }

    private Button leftButton,centerButton,rightButton;
    private Button topButton,middleButton,bottomButton;
```

Here is our implementation of actionPeformed():

```
    public void actionPerformed(ActionEvent e) {
        Object source = e.getSource();

        if (source == leftButton)
            setHorizJust(TextCanvas.LEFT);          Horizontal
        else if (source == centerButton)            adjustment
            setHorizJust(TextCanvas.CENTER);
        else if (source == rightButton)
            setHorizJust(TextCanvas.RIGHT);

        else if (source == topButton)
            setVertJust(TextCanvas.TOP);            Vertical
        else if (source == middleButton)            adjustment
            setVertJust(TextCanvas.MIDDLE);
        else if (source == bottomButton)
            setVertJust(TextCanvas.BOTTOM);
    }
```

What should setHorizJust() and setVertJust() do? The effect of clicking the button will not be apparent to the user until the canvas repaints itself, so the main job of these methods is to ensure that TextCanvas's paint() method will be invoked. In addition, these methods must make sure that paint() knows where the text is supposed to be positioned. Thus, we will declare two instance variables, horiz and vert, which indicate where the text should appear. setHorizJust() and setVertJust() assign values to horiz and vert (respectively), then send a repaint() message. Here is our TextCanvas implementation so far:

```
public class TextJustifierApplet extends Applet  {
    public void init() {
        setBackground(new Color(255,255,255));

        Panel horiz = new Panel();
        leftButton = new Button("Left");
```

```
        centerButton = new Button("Center");
        rightButton = new Button("Right");
        horiz.add(leftButton);
        horiz.add(centerButton);
        horiz.add(rightButton);

        Panel vert = new Panel();
        topButton = new Button("Top");
        middleButton = new Button("Middle");
        bottomButton = new Button("Bottom");
        vert.add(topButton);
        vert.add(middleButton);
        vert.add(bottomButton);

        Panel position = new Panel();
        position.setLayout(new BorderLayout());
        position.add("North",horiz);
        position.add("South",vert);
        tc = new  TextCanvas(leftButton,centerButton,rightButton,
                            topButton,middleButton,bottomButton);
        add(position);
        add(tc);

        leftButton.addActionListener(tc);
        centerButton.addActionListener(tc);
        rightButton.addActionListener(tc);
        topButton.addActionListener(tc);
        middleButton.addActionListener(tc);
        bottomButton.addActionListener(tc);
    }

    public void start() {
        tc.setSize(getWidth()-20,
                 getHeight()-(4*leftButton.getHeight()));
    }

    private Button leftButton,centerButton,rightButton;
    private Button topButton,middleButton,bottomButton;
    private TextCanvas tc;
}

class TextCanvas extends Canvas implements ActionListener {
    public TextCanvas(Button l, Button c, Button r,
```

```
                        Button t, Button m, Button b) {
      leftButton = l;
      centerButton = c;
      rightButton = r;
      topButton = t;
      middleButton = m;
      bottomButton = b;
   }

   public void actionPerformed(ActionEvent e) {
      Object source = e.getSource();

      if (source == leftButton)
         setHorizJust(TextCanvas.LEFT);
      else if (source == centerButton)
         setHorizJust(TextCanvas.CENTER);
      else if (source == rightButton)
         setHorizJust(TextCanvas.RIGHT);

      else if (source == topButton)
         setVertJust(TextCanvas.TOP);
      else if (source == middleButton)
         setVertJust(TextCanvas.MIDDLE);
      else if (source == bottomButton)
         setVertJust(TextCanvas.BOTTOM);
   }

   public void paint(Graphics g) {...}

   private void setHorizJust(int j) {
      horiz = j;
      repaint();
   }

   private void setVertJust(int j) {
      vert = j;
      repaint();
   }

   private int horiz = TextCanvas.LEFT;
   private int vert = TextCanvas.TOP;

   public static final int LEFT = 0;
```

Display text in top left corner when applet starts.

```
public static final int CENTER = 1;
public static final int RIGHT = 2;
public static final int TOP = 0;
public static final int MIDDLE = 1;
public static final int BOTTOM = 2;

private Button leftButton,centerButton,rightButton;
private Button topButton,middleButton,bottomButton;
}
```

Implementing paint(): Getting Text Measurements

At this point, all that remains in our development of TextCanvas is the paint() method. Its primary responsibility is the correct positioning of text, so we must begin by determining the size of the strings to display. As we saw in the Chapter 2 supplement, we can get text dimensions by sending a getFontMetrics() message to g, then using the returned FontMetrics object to measure text. For our purposes in this supplement, we will need not only the getHeight() and stringWidth() methods of the FontMetric class but also the getAscent() method, which returns the height of the portion of the text that extends up from the baseline. (See Figure 9.8.)

The paint() method begins, then, by getting measurements both of the text and of the canvas itself:

```
public void paint(Graphics g) {
    String line1 = "We want more schools and fewer jails,";
    String line2 = "more books and fewer arsenals,";
    String line3 = "more justice and fewer revenge.";

    int myWidth = getWidth();
    int myHeight = getHeight();          TextCanvas dimensions

    FontMetrics fm = g.getFontMetrics();
```

Figure 9.8
Some text measurement methods.

```
int lineHeight = fm.getHeight();
int ascent = fm.getAscent();            Text-related dimensions
int l1Width = fm.stringWidth(line1);
int l2Width = fm.stringWidth(line2);
int l3Width = fm.stringWidth(line3);
```

Then we can begin positioning the text. First, we'll calculate the horizontal position of the strings. Specifically, we must calculate the *x*-coordinate of the left end of each string. This value depends both on the horizontal position desired by the user and on the width of each string itself, so we must calculate a separate position for each string (see Figure 9.9 for a diagram of these calculations for line3):

```
if (horiz == LEFT) {
    l1Margin = 0;
    l2Margin = 0;
    l3Margin = 0;
} else if (horiz == CENTER) {
    l1Margin = (myWidth - l1Width) / 2;
    l2Margin = (myWidth - l2Width) / 2;
    l3Margin = (myWidth - l3Width) / 2;
} else {
    l1Margin = myWidth - l1Width;
    l2Margin = myWidth - l2Width;
    l3Margin = myWidth - l3Width;
}
```

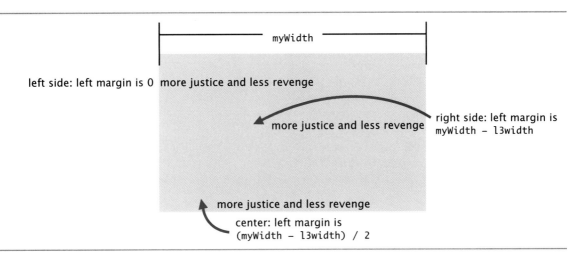

Figure 9.9 Calculating horizontal position of line3.

Next, we must calculate the vertical position: we will determine the *y*-coordinate for the baseline of the top line, then determine the positions of the remaining lines by moving down from there. If the text is to be positioned at the top, then the vertical margin is 0. Otherwise we perform a calculation similar to those for determining the horizontal position: We determine the height of the text (which is simply 3*lineHeight) and subtract it from the height of the canvas. These calculations give us the position of the top of the text; to determine the coordinate of the baseline (as needed by drawString(), we add the distance from the top of a line to the baseline, which is the ascent:

```
int textHeight = 3 * lineHeight                     Determine coordinate
if (vert == TOP)                                    of top of text
    vertMargin = 0;
else if (vert == MIDDLE)
    vertMargin = (myHeight - textHeight) / 2;
else
    vertMargin = myHeight - textHeight;

int vertPos = vertMargin + ascent;                  Determine coordinate
                                                    of baseline
```

Now all that remains is the actual display. We will display the canvas itself with a gray background so that we can confirm that the text is located correctly with respect to the edges of the canvas. Then we draw the strings:

```
    setBackground(new Color(190,190,190));
    g.drawString(line1,l1Margin,vertPos);
    g.drawString(line2,l2Margin,vertPos+lineHeight);
    g.drawString(line3,l3Margin,vertPos+2*lineHeight);
}
```

Below is the complete applet. Note that we can define TextCanvas in the same file as TextJustifierApplet:

```
import java.applet.*;
import java.awt.*;
import java.awt.event.*;

public class TextJustifierApplet extends Applet  {
    public void init() {
        setBackground(new Color(255,255,255));

        Panel horiz = new Panel();
        leftButton = new Button("Left");
        centerButton = new Button("Center");
        rightButton = new Button("Right");
        horiz.add(leftButton);
```

```
            horiz.add(centerButton);
            horiz.add(rightButton);

            Panel vert = new Panel();
            topButton = new Button("Top");
            middleButton = new Button("Middle");
            bottomButton = new Button("Bottom");
            vert.add(topButton);
            vert.add(middleButton);
            vert.add(bottomButton);

            Panel position = new Panel();
            position.setLayout(new BorderLayout());
            position.add("North",horiz);
            position.add("South",vert);
            tc = new TextCanvas(leftButton,centerButton,rightButton,
                            topButton,middleButton,bottomButton);
            add(position);
            add(tc);

            leftButton.addActionListener(tc);
            centerButton.addActionListener(tc);
            rightButton.addActionListener(tc);
            topButton.addActionListener(tc);
            middleButton.addActionListener(tc);
            bottomButton.addActionListener(tc);
        }

        public void start() {
            tc.setSize(getWidth()-20,
                    getHeight()-(4*leftButton.getHeight()));
        }

        private Button leftButton,centerButton,rightButton;
        private Button topButton,middleButton,bottomButton;
        private TextCanvas tc;
}

class TextCanvas extends Canvas implements ActionListener {
        public TextCanvas(Button l, Button c, Button r,
                            Button t, Button m, Button b) {
            leftButton = l;
            centerButton = c;
            rightButton = r;
```

```
            topButton = t;
            middleButton = m;
            bottomButton = b;
        }

        public void actionPerformed(ActionEvent e) {
            Object source = e.getSource();

            if (source == leftButton)
                setHorizJust(TextCanvas.LEFT);
            else if (source == centerButton)
                setHorizJust(TextCanvas.CENTER);
            else if (source == rightButton)
                setHorizJust(TextCanvas.RIGHT);

            else if (source == topButton)
                setVertJust(TextCanvas.TOP);
            else if (source == middleButton)
                setVertJust(TextCanvas.MIDDLE);
            else if (source == bottomButton)
                setVertJust(TextCanvas.BOTTOM);
        }

        public void paint(Graphics g) {

            String line1 = "We want more schools and fewer jails,";
            String line2 = "more books and fewer arsenals,";
            String line3 = "more justice and less revenge.";

            int myWidth = getWidth();
            int myHeight = getHeight();
            FontMetrics fm = g.getFontMetrics();
            int lineHeight = fm.getHeight();
            int ascent = fm.getAscent();
            int l1Width = fm.stringWidth(line1);
            int l2Width = fm.stringWidth(line2);
            int l3Width = fm.stringWidth(line3);

            int vertMargin;
            int l1Margin,l2Margin,l3Margin;

            if (horiz == LEFT)
                l1Margin = l2Margin = l3Margin = 0;
```

```
        else if (horiz == CENTER) {
           l1Margin = (myWidth - l1Width) / 2;
           l2Margin = (myWidth - l2Width) / 2;
           l3Margin = (myWidth - l3Width) / 2;
        }
        else {
           l1Margin = myWidth - l1Width;
           l2Margin = myWidth - l2Width;
           l3Margin = myWidth - l3Width;
        }

        int textHeight = 3*lineHeight;
        if (vert == TOP)
           vertMargin = 0;
        else if (vert == MIDDLE)
           vertMargin = (myHeight - textHeight) / 2;
        else
           vertMargin = myHeight - textHeight;

        int vertPos = vertMargin+ascent;

        setBackground(new Color(190,190,190));
        g.drawString(line1,l1Margin,vertPos);
        g.drawString(line2,l2Margin,vertPos+lineHeight);
        g.drawString(line3,l3Margin,vertPos+2*lineHeight);
    }

    private void setHorizJust(int j) {
        horiz = j;
        repaint();
    }

    private void setVertJust(int j) {
        vert = j;
        repaint();
    }

    private int horiz = TextCanvas.LEFT;
    private int vert = TextCanvas.TOP;
    public static final int LEFT = 0;
    public static final int CENTER = 1;
    public static final int RIGHT = 2;
    public static final int TOP = 0;
```

```
public static final int MIDDLE = 1;
public static final int BOTTOM = 2;

private Button leftButton,centerButton,rightButton;
private Button topButton,middleButton,bottomButton;
}
```

Suggested Experiments

1. Extend this applet so that instead of displaying three lines, it displays an arbitrary number of lines that are stored in a `Vector`. Also add a `TextField` and an "Add" button that will allow users to add lines to the display

2. Write an applet that implements a simple form of *full* justification—that is, text that extends all the way from the left to the right side of the canvas. Your applet should have a single text field and four buttons (labeled "First Word," "Second Word," "Third Word," and "Fourth Word" for example), as well as a canvas on which text is displayed. Entering a word in the text field and clicking a button should change the corresponding word in the displayed line. To maintain proper aesthetics, the amount of space between each word should be equal; this space will change as the lengths of the words change. Which class should be the listener?

3. This is significantly more challenging. Write another full-justification applet. This one should just have a single text field, a button labeled "Add Word," and a canvas. The "Add Word" button should cause the word in the text field to be added to the sequence of words that are displayed. Each time a word is added, one of two things will happen: It will be added to a line of the display, causing the words in that line to be respaced, or there won't be room to add the word to the line, and it will be displayed as the *first* word on the next line. Should you use a collection?

Designing Iteration

10.1 Introduction

The for statement (from Chapter 6) and the while statement (from Chapter 9) allow us to implement methods that use iteration. In our previous discussions, we have looked at three loop patterns:

- Counting: performing a task a fixed number of times
- Read/process: constructing and processing objects read from input
- Traverse: iterating through a collection, that is, applying a piece of code to every object in the collection

Although these patterns are very common, other situations arise that require different patterns or significant variations of the above. However, it is neither possible nor desirable to memorize all possible loop, or iteration, patterns. Therefore, we now introduce an approach that can be fruitfully employed to construct while statements when one doesn't know of or can't recall the appropriate loop pattern. This approach for writing loops not only works well for the simple loops that appear in this chapter but for the more complex ones that appear later in this text.

10.2 Designing Loops

Suppose we were defining a class with several methods that needed to calculate the value of one nonnegative integer raised to the power of another:

$$x^y$$

such as 5^7 or 23^4. (We exclude 0^0 because that is mathematically undefined.) We can implement a helper method specifically to perform this task:

```
private int power(int x, int y) { // y>=0 returns x**y.

    ...

}
```

(The notation x**y is widely used to represent x^y when superscripts are not available.) This method could be invoked by other methods to compute various exponentiations as illustrated by the following code:

375

```
int     a,b,w,z;
...
z = power(5,7);
w = power(a,b+2);
```

One way to begin to implement the power() method is to view exponentiation as repeated multiplication and to use **iteration** to repeat, in a controlled way, code that carries out multiplication.

Our approach to developing this iteration involves several stages. Each stage will be described in general terms and then applied to the problem at hand, exponentiation.

Informal Procedure

We begin by asking ourselves how we, as humans, could solve the problem. At this point we don't worry about specific coding issues such as variables, loops, and assignments. *We are working with our intuition, not with code.*

How do we compute x^y by hand? We recognize that exponentiation is repeated multiplication, that is,

$$x^y == 1{*}x{*}x{*}x{*}{\cdots}{*}x \quad \text{1 multiplied by } x, y \text{ times}$$

The use of 1 in the definition of exponentiation allows us to cover the case when $y{==}0$: 1 is multiplied by x *no* times and so $x^0{==}1$. An informal procedure immediately presents itself: Start with 1 and multiply it by x, then multiply the result by x, and continue multiplying subsequent results by x until y multiplications have been performed. The *last* result is the value to return. The remaining steps of our approach will transform this intuition into working code.

Choosing and Defining Variables

We identify the information items that our informal procedure requires us to keep track of. These items become our variables. We choose names for them, write declarations for them, and most important, we write down precise definitions of their meanings as comments.

In this case, we need to keep track of the *result of the most recent multiplication* (note that we do not need remember all the intermediate multiplication results, just the most recent one). We also need to keep track of *the number of multiplications that we have done so far*. So, we need two variables that we call result and count:

```
int count,   // count==the number of multiplications done.
    result; // result==1*x*x*...*x (count times), that is, result==x**count.
```

Notice that our comments use equality notation (==). This style of comment for numerical variables, which means this variable is equal to . . ., tends to encourage the kind of precision we seek in our definitions. Furthermore, as you will see, we will make good use of this form of comment to guide our code development.

At this point our comments are not statements of fact but statements of *intent.* So far, both `count` and `result` remain uninitialized, so it is not yet true that `result==x`^{count}. We have to write code that makes this intention a reality.

Skeleton of the Code

We write a skeleton of the code of the method, including the method header, the declarations, and a skeleton of a `while` statement.

Here we write the following code:

```
private int power(int x, int y) {
    int count, // count==the number of multiplications done.
        result; // result==1*x*x*...*x (count times), that is,
                // result==x**count.
    ...
    while (condition)
        body
    ...
}
```

The `while` Condition

Next comes the crucial question: What do we want to be the case *after* the `while` statement terminates? To answer this question, we must express what it means for our task to be completed in terms of the values of our variables and any input/output that we are doing.

In the case of `power()`, our informal procedure calls on us to carry out y multiplications. According to our variable definitions (see the declarations), our intention is for `count` to equal the number of multiplications done at any given point. So, it seems that we are finished when `count` equals y.

Let's verify that we are really finished when `count==y`. According to the definition for `result` in the comment, `result==x`^{count}. If and when `count` equals y, `result==x`^{y}. This value is exactly what we want to return. So, after the `while` statement, we want `count` to equal y. To remind ourselves of this as we write our code, we add a comment to that effect immediately after the `while` statement:

```
private int power(int x, int y) {
    int count, // count==the number of multiplications done.
        result; // result==1*x*x*...*x (count times), that is,
                // result==x**count.
    ...
    while (condition)
        body
    // At this point, after the loop terminates, count==y.
    ...
}
```

The condition that controls the `while` statement's execution is called the `while` condition, or **loop condition**. The `while` statement terminates when its loop condition is false. So we can guarantee that a condition X will be true *after* the `while` statement by making the `while` loop condition the negation of condition X.

In our case, we want `count==y` to be true after the `while` statement. So our `while` condition becomes its negation: `count!=y`. This guarantees that when the `while` statement terminates, `count==y` and hence `result==x`^{y}. We can therefore return `result` immediately after the `while` statement. Our code now is as follows:

```
private int power(int x, int y) {
    int count, // count==the number of multiplications done.
        result; // result==1*x*x*...*x (count times), that is,
                //    result==x**count.

        ...
    while (count!=y)
        body
    // count==y, result==x**y
    return result;
}
```

Initialization

When execution reaches the `while` statement, the variables that appear in its condition must have values—otherwise the condition will not be meaningful. Parameters receive values from arguments, but local variables must be initialized prior to the `while` statement.

In this case, we must assign `count` a value before the `while` statement. Your intuition might tell you that this value should be 1, or it might tell you 0. Actually, it is possible to do it either way, depending on what code we write later. But the best way of proceeding and the best way of making sure that the code we write now is consistent with the code we write later is to *consult our variable definitions.*

According to these, `count==` the number of multiplications done. Before the `while` statement, no multiplications have been performed. So the initial value of `count` should be 0. Our `power()` method so far is

```
private int power(int x, int y) {
    int count, // count==the number of multiplications done.
        result; // result==1*x*x*...*x (count times), that is,
                //    result==x**count.
    count = 0;
    while (count!=y)
        body
    // count==y, result==x**y
    return result;
}
```

Guaranteeing Termination

Now we turn to the body of the loop. A good way of getting started is to guarantee **loop termination**, that is, to make sure that the loop will *terminate* (we almost never want a loop to be *infinite*—never ending). A loop terminates when its condition is tested and is found to be false. So the loop body must contain some code that makes *progress toward termination,* that is, some code that guarantees that the loop condition will eventually become false.

In our case, the `while` statement will not terminate until `count` equals y. We need to write code in the loop that will eventually make `count` equal to y. Our informal procedure and our intuition tells us that we should increment `count` by 1 in the loop body. We can readily see that if we do that, `count` will eventually equal y (provided y is non-negative, which is a requirement of the method). Our loop then is

```
while (count!=y) {
    rest of body
    count++;
}
// count==y, result==x**y
```

Completing the Loop Body

We complete the body of the `while` statement. We are guided both by our informal procedure and by the definitions of our variables. In particular, we take into account the effect that the code in the previous step (guaranteeing termination) might have on the equalities that appear in the definitions of the variables.

One of our variable definitions tells us that `count` should be the number of multiplications we have carried out. Thus, every time that we increment `count`, we should have done another multiplication by x in the loop body—this is certainly consistent with our informal procedure too.

Furthermore, the definition of `result` tells us that $result==x^{count}$. If we increment `count`, the equality is broken: The right side is too large by a factor of x. To restore this equality we multiply `result` by x so that `result` can "catch up." The following code completes our loop body:

```
result *= x;
count++;
```

Recheck Initialization

Variables must have values before they are used. Any variables that are used in the loop body must be given appropriate values prior to entering the loop. Our last step is to recheck our variables to make sure all of them have been initialized before being used. Guided by our variable definitions and our informal procedure, we write assignment statements needed to initialize variables referred to in the `while` statement body.

The variables used in the loop body here are result, x, and count. The latter has already been initialized, and x receives its value from the argument to the power method, so we have only to initialize result. What should its value be, before entering the loop?

To answer this question, we *turn again to the definition* of result: $result == x^{count}$. Prior to the loop, count is 0, so, according to this definition, prior to the loop $result == x^0$, or 1. So we initialize result to 1 before the loop, and our code is finished:

```
private int power(int x, int y) {
    int count,   // count==the number of multiplications done.
        result;  // result==1*x*x*···*x (count times), that is,
                 //   result==x**count.
    count = 0;
    result = 1;
    while (count!=y) {
        result *= x;
        count++;
    }
    // count==y, result==x**y
    return result;
}
```

Discussion

The advantage of this approach is that it allows a programmer to start with an intuitive and informal solution and work toward a complete solution in Java. Furthermore, the approach accommodates some gaps in our intuition. For example, suppose our intuition had been less clear on the matter of incrementing count. How can we guarantee termination? We could consider different alternatives. For example, most naively we could propose simply to assign count=y. That guarantees that count==y eventually, but it disregards the requirement that count must equal the number of multiplications—how could we possibly do y multiplications at once? Other alternatives could also be ruled out: For example, if we increment count by 2 in the body, count+=2, we have to worry about y being odd and never reaching count==y. We therefore recognize incrementing by 1 as the only viable approach.

| Java Interlude | ***Two Loop Statements*** |

for **is Equivalent to** while

In fact, this example can also be implemented as a counting loop using a for statement:

```
private int power(int x, int y) {
    int count,result;
```

```
   result = 1;
   for (count = 0; count != y; count++)
      result *= x;
   }
   return result;
}
```

In general, counting loops are often implemented as `for` statements and other loop patterns are implemented as `while` statements, but any loop pattern can be implemented using either statement.

The `for` statement

for (*initialization assignment*; *loop condition*; *increment*)
    body

can be understood in terms of a `while` statement:

initialization assignment;
while (*loop condition*) {
    body
    increment;
}

Similarly, the `while` statement

while (*loop condition*)
    body   -

can be expressed as a `for` statement:

for (; *loop condition* ;) | Semicolons required even though ini-
    body | tialization and increment are "empty."

In the next several examples, we will discuss the loop design process primarily in terms of the `while` statement

The Flexibility of the `for` Statement

As we saw above, the `for` statement header does not have to contain all three elements (although two semicolons are *always* required). The `for` statement is actually very flexible. For example, the *initialization* does not have to be a single assignment to a counter. Several assignments may be supplied by separating them with commas:

```
for (i=0, sum=0; i<100; i++)    // Compute the sum from 0 through 99.
   sum += i;
```

Similarly, the *increment* does not have to be a single increment—it too can be a comma-separated sequence of statements:

```
for (i=0, powOf2=1; i<10; i++, powOf2*=2)   // Print table of powers of 2.
    System.out.println("2 to the "+ i + " is " + powOf2);
```

10.3 Another Simple Example

Our approach involves the following eight steps:

1. Informal procedure
2. Choosing and defining variables
3. The `while` sketch
4. The `while` condition
5. Initialization
6. Guaranteeing termination
7. Completing the loop body
8. Recheck initialization

Of these eight, the first four should be undertaken in the order shown, but the remaining four can be done in any order that is convenient. Also, if we get stuck, we can always revisit an earlier step. The willingness to rethink is an important quality for programmers. In fact, even if we do not get stuck at any point, we should, when we are finished, go back to step 1 and try to improve the informal procedure in light of our experience developing the loop.

In this section and the exercises at the end of the chapter, we look at a group of easy problems in order to further illustrate this approach and to make some broader points about computer science.

Multiplication

Suppose there were no multiplication operator. In that case, in order to implement classes that require multiplication, we would write a helper method, `multiply()`, whose arguments are two integers and whose return value is the integer product of its arguments:

```
private int multiply(int x, int y) { // y>=0, returns x*y.
    ...
}
```

To complete this method definition, we take the same approach that we used for exponentiation.

Informal Procedure

We start with the observation that multiplication is repeated addition, that is,

$$x*y == 0+x+x+\cdots x \qquad x \text{ added to } 0, \ y \text{ times}$$

(The use of 0 in the definition of multiplication allows us to cover the case when *y*==0: *x* is added to *0 no* times, and so *x**0 == 0.) So an informal procedure immediately presents itself: Start with zero and add *x* to it, then add *x* to the result, then add *x* to *that* result, and so on, until *y* additions have been performed. The *last* result is the value to return.

Choosing and Defining Variables

We need to keep track of the result of the most recent addition and the number of additions done so far. Therefore, we need two variables, which we call `result` and `count`:

```
int count,   // count==the number of additions done.
    result; // result==0+x+x+...+x (count times), that is, result==x*count.
```

In this exercise, we are assuming that there is no * operator available. However, in a comment we can use any notation we choose; hence * is used in the definition of `result`.

Skeleton of the Code

We write

```
private int multiply(int x, int y) {
    int count, // count==the number of additions done.
        result; // result==0+x+x+...+x (count times), that is,
                //    result==x*count.

    ...
    while (condition)
        body
    ...
}
```

The `while` Condition

Our informal procedure calls on us to carry out y additions. According to our variable definitions, it is our intention that `count` equal the number of additions done so far at any given point. Therefore, it seems that we are finished when `count` equals y.

Indeed, according to the definition for `result` in the comment, `result==x*count`. If and when `count` equals y, `result==x*y`. This value is exactly what we want to return. So we want

```
count==y
```

to be true immediately after the `while` statement. We note this with a comment immediately after the `while` statement:

```
private int multiply(int x, int y) {
    int count, // count==the number of additions done.
```

```
        result;  // result==0+x+x+···+x (count times), that is,
                 //    result==x*count.
    ...
    while (condition)
        body
    // count==y
    ...
}
```

Our `while` condition then is `count!=y`. This will guarantee that when the `while` statement terminates, `count==y` and hence `result==x*y`. We can therefore return `result` immediately after the `while` statement. Our code now is

```
private int multiply(int x, int y) {
    int count,  // count==the number of additions done.
        result;  // result==0+x+x+...+x (count times), that is,
                 //    result==x*count.
    ...
    while (count!=y)
        body
    // count==y, result==x*y
    return result;
}
```

Initialization

According to our variable definitions, `count==` the number of additions done. Before the `while` statement, no additions have been performed. So the initial value of `count` should be 0:

```
private int multiply(int x, int y) {
    int count,  // count==the number of additions done.
        result;  // result==0+x+x+...+x (count times), that is,
                 //    result==x*count.
    count = 0;
    ...
    while (count!=y)
        body
    // count==y, result==x*y
    return result;
}
```

Guaranteeing Termination

The `while` statement we have written will not terminate until `count` equals `y`. Following our informal procedure and our intuition, we increment `count` by 1 in the loop body. Doing this makes `count` eventually equal to `y`, provided `y` is non-negative. If y is negative, the loop will not terminate. (Addressing this problem is left as an exercise.) Our loop then is

```
while (count!=y) {
    rest of body
    count++;
}
```

Completing the Loop Body

One of our variable definitions tells us that count should be the number of additions we have carried out. Thus, each time we increment count, we should do another addition of x in the loop body. Furthermore, the definition of result tells us that result==x* count. If we increment count, the equality is broken: The right side is too large by x. To restore this equality we add x to result so that result can "catch up." The following code completes our loop body:

```
result += x;
count++;
```

Recheck Initialization

The variables used in the loop body here are result, x, and count. The latter has already been initialized, and x receives its value from the argument to the multiply method, so we have only to initialize result. Its definition is result==x*count. Prior to the loop, count is 0; therefore, according to this definition, prior to the loop result==0. So we initialize result to 0 before the loop, and our code is finished:

```
private int multiply(int x, int y) {
    int count,   // count==the number of additions done.
        result;  // result==0+x+x+...+x (count times), that is,
                 //    result==x*count.
    count = 0;
    result = 0;
    while (count!=y) {
        result += x;
        count++;
    }
    // count==y, result==x*y
    return result;
}
```

Discussion

In the exercises at the end of the chapter, you are asked to apply the above approach to implement methods that add, subtract, and divide. The fact that we can do this demonstrates the power of iteration. All the operations of arithmetic can be implemented merely with increments and decrements of 1, provided iteration is available. The discovery by logicians in the 1930s that all computation ultimately requires only iteration and a tiny handful of elementary operations is one of the cornerstones of modern computer science.

10.4 Revisiting Loop Patterns

In Chapter 9, we presented two loop patterns. In this section, we apply our systematic approach to derive them.

The Traverse Pattern: Looking Up an Entry

We encountered this pattern in the `TelephoneBook` class in Chapter 9. There we wrote a method, `lookup()`, that receives a `String` parameter, `data`, and has access to an instance variable, `entryColl`, which is a `Vector` of `Entry` objects. Each of these `Entry` objects provides a `getName()` and a `getNumber()` method. To access these objects we use the `elementAt()` method provided by the `Vector`. We will focus here on the loop for looking up all the entries with a particular name; we'll develop the loop as a `while` statement rather than as a `for` statement.

Informal Procedure

We could accomplish this task manually if the `Vector` object were a stack of numbered index cards, labeled with name and number. Starting with the first index card, we could take one index card after the other, checking to see whether the name matched the one we were interested in. Where there was a match, we would write down the number on the index card.

Choosing and Defining Variables

We need a variable to refer to our current position in the `Vector`, and we also need a variable to refer to the most recent `Entry` object that we have taken from the `Vector`:

```
int i;      // Refers to current position in the Vector
Entry e;    // Refers to the most recent Entry object taken from the Vector
```

Skeleton of the Code

Our loop so far is as follows:

```
int i;      // Refers to current position in the Vector
Entry e;    // Refers to the most recent Entry object taken from the Vector
while (condition)
     body
}
```

The while Condition

Informally, our task is complete when there are no more index cards; in the program, the corresponding condition is when our current position is past the end of the Vector—that is, when i >= entryColl.size(). The negation of this condition—and the condition for the while statement here—is that our position in the Vector is still valid:

```
while (i < entryColl.size())
    body
//  i >= entryColl.size().
```

Initialization

Because i is used in the while condition, it must first be initialized:

```
i = 0;
```

Guaranteeing Termination

Termination can come only when i reaches entryColl.size(). In order to progress to this point, we must increment i each time the loop body is executed:

```
while (i < entryColl.size()) {
    ...
    i++;
    ...
}
//  i >= entryColl.size().
```

Completing the Loop Body

According to its definition, e is the most recent Entry object taken from the Vector. Hence the value of e must be assigned as

```
e = (Entry) entryColl.elementAt(i);
```

At this point, our code is

```
while (i < entryColl.size()) {
    e = (Entry) entryColl.elementAt(i);
    ...
    i++;
    ...
}
//  i >= entryColl.size().
```

At this point, we are stuck. Certainly our intuition may suggest what we do next, but let us pause and consider what our approach tells us in the absence of intuition.

In the previous examples, whenever we added code to the loop body to guarantee termination, we disturbed one or more of the definitions of our variables. For example, when we incremented `count` by 1 in the multiplication example, it was no longer the case that `result==x*count` and we were forced to add x to `result` to restore this equality.

In other words, in the previous examples, the definitions themselves were enough to drive the development of the `while` statement.

Here, however, they are not enough. The preceding code does not result in the violation of any of the meanings of the variables, but we can be certain that it does not yet accomplish our objective. The code as it stands just looks through each entry in the telephone book but does not do any meaningful processing.

Our final condition (our position, i, is at the end of the `Vector`) is useful only if we know that all the data have been processed at that point, not just ignored. In fact, our informal procedure explicitly tells us to process each entry as we encounter it. Implicit in that directive is the understanding that when we test to see whether we can terminate the loop (test whether i < `entryColl.size()`), we are confident that all the `Entry` objects prior to the one e refers to have been processed.

This assumption is extremely important and should be stated as a comment prior to the loop. We also add to the loop body the code that outputs the telephone number if the name matches. The complete loop is as follows:

```
// All Entrys before the ith one have been processed.
while (i < entryColl.size()) {
   e = (Entry) entryColl.elementAt(i);
   if (data.equals(e.getName()))
      System.out.println(e.getNumber());
   i++;
}
```

The Read/Process Pattern: Repairperson Distance

This pattern was introduced in the repairperson example of Chapter 9. The problem was as follows. Given the following input

- Information that defines repairperson 1 (name)
- Location of repairperson 1
- Information that defines repairperson 2 (name)
- Location of repairperson 2

and so on, we print each repairperson's distance from a given location. Assume the availability of the `RepairPerson` and `Location` classes (from Chapter 7).

Informal Procedure

This task can be accomplished by repeatedly reading the data for a repairperson, computing the resulting distance, and printing it out until there are no more data left.

Choosing and Defining Variables

We need two variables. One is a reference to the most recent RepairPerson object returned by RepairPerson.read(), which we will use to read employee-defining data, and the other is an int, the distance that corresponds to the most recently read RepairPerson object. We may call these variables rp and distance:

```
RepairPerson rp;  // rp refers to the most recently read RepairPerson object
                  //    or is null.
int distance;     // distance is the distance from the given location of the most
                  //    recently read RepairPerson.
```

Skeleton of the Code

We write

```
RepairPerson rp;  // rp refers to the most recently read RepairPerson object
                  //    or is null.
int distance;     // distance is the distance from the given location of the most
                  //    recently read RepairPerson.
...
while (condition)
    body
...
```

The while Condition

Our informal procedure calls on us to continue reading information, processing it, and printing out results until there are no more data left to read. Accordingly, we want to write the following with confidence after our while statement:

```
// No more data to read.
```

How can we express in Java code the condition "no more data to read"? The possibility that there are no more data was considered in the design of the RepairPerson class in Chapter 7. When an attempt to read data and construct a RepairPerson object fails because there are no more data, the RepairPerson.read() method returns null. Thus, rp will equal null when there are no more data and will not equal null when data are available to construct a RepairPerson object. So, the above comment can be rewritten (in more Java-like terms) as

```
// rp==null
```

Accordingly, the while condition is the negation of this, and we now have

```
RepairPerson rp;  // rp refers to the most recently read RepairPerson object
                  //    or is null.
int distance;     // distance is the distance from the given location of the most
                  //    recently read RepairPerson.
...
```

```
while (rp!=null)
    body
// No more data to read, i.e., rp==null.
```

Initialization

Because rp is used in the loop condition, it must be initialized prior to the loop. In order for it to refer to the most recently read RepairPerson object at that point, we initialize it from RepairPerson.read():

```
RepairPerson rp;  // rp refers to the most recently read RepairPerson object
                  //    or is null.
int distance;     // distance is the distance from the given location of the most
                  //    recently read RepairPerson.
rp = RepairPerson.read(br);
while (rp!=null)
    body
// No more data to read, i.e., rp==null.
```

Guaranteeing Termination

The loop terminates only when there are no more data to read. To guarantee that this eventually happens, we must continue reading data. With this in mind and following our intuition and our informal procedure, we attempt to read data and create a new RepairPerson object in the loop body:

```
RepairPerson rp;  // rp refers to the most recently read RepairPerson object
                  //    or is null.
int distance;     // distance is the distance from the given location of the most
                  //    recently read RepairPerson.
rp = RepairPerson.read(br);
while (rp!=null) {
    rest of body
    rp = RepairPerson.read(br);
}
// No more data to read, i.e., rp==null.
```

Completing the Loop Body

Again we are stuck. There is nothing in the definition of the variables that demands further code, yet we know that we are not finished. All that the above code will do is read the data and create RepairPerson objects.

As we've done before, we consult our informal procedure and see that we are instructed to process each RepairPerson as it is read. The instruction assumes that this has been done for all the entries considered to date. We express this assumption in a comment before the loop.

With this comment in mind (along with our own intuition), we are compelled to process the RepairPerson object to which rp refers *before* carrying out the RepairPerson.read() in the loop body. After the RepairPerson.read(), however, there is nothing to do but retest the loop condition and continue. The loop's structure is as follows:

```
// All RepairPerson objects created prior to the one rp refers to have been processed.
while (rp!=null) {
    process the object to which rp refers
    rp = RepairPerson.read(br);
}
```

Our understanding of what it means to process repairperson information requires that we compute the repairperson's distance from a given location (loc) and print the result. The following statements accomplish this:

```
distance = rp.getDistanceFrom(loc);
System.out.println(rp.getName() + ": " + distance);
```

Recheck Initialization

In this case, there are no variables used in the loop body that are not initialized. (The distance variable is initialized in the loop body itself.) Our final code is

```
RepairPerson rp;   // rp refers to the most recently read RepairPerson object
                   //    or is null.
int distance;      // distance is the distance from the given location of the most
                   //    recently read RepairPerson.
// All RepairPerson objects created prior to the one rp refers to have been processed.
rp = RepairPerson.read(br);
while (rp!=null) {
    distance = rp.getDistanceFrom(loc);
    System.out.println(rp.getName() + ": " + distance);
    rp = RepairPerson.read(br);
}
```

This code is virtually identical to the code given in Chapter 9.

10.5 Variations on the Repairperson Loop

In this section we consider a few of the many possible variations on the repairperson loop.

Counting Repairpersons Within 30 Blocks

Here's another variation of the repairperson problem. Let's write a loop to count the number of repairpersons that are within 30 blocks of loc. (This would include those who are exactly 30 blocks away.) For brevity, we present only the additional considerations resulting from this requirement, not the full development.

Informal Procedure

In addition to everything else, we must remember the number of repairpersons that we have encountered so far who are within 30 blocks.

Choosing and Defining Variables

We require another variable to hold our count:

```
int count30;     // count30== the number of repairpersons processed so far whose
                 //     distance is within 30 blocks.
```

Skeleton of the Code

The skeleton is not changed in this variation, except for the addition of the above declarations. The `while` condition, initialization of the `while` condition variables, and code to guarantee termination do not change in this variation.

Completing the Loop Body

According to its definition, `count30` is the number of repairpersons processed whose distance is within 30 blocks. So, in the loop, after a repairperson whose distance is within 30 blocks is processed, `count30` must be incremented:

```
if (distance <= 30)
    count30++;
```

Recheck Initialization

Because `count30` appears in the loop body but is not initialized there, it must be initialized before the loop. Prior to the `while` statement, no repairpersons have been processed; therefore the number of repairpersons whose distance is within 30 blocks is 0. We therefore initialize `count30` to 0:

```
int count30 = 0;    // count30== the number of repairpersons processed so far
                    //     whose distance is within 30 blocks.
RepairPerson rp;    // rp refers to the most recently read RepairPerson object
                    //     or is null.
int distance;       // distance is the distance from the given location of the most
                    //     recently read RepairPerson.
// All RepairPerson objects created prior to the one rp refers to have been processed.
rp = RepairPerson.read(br);
while (rp!=null) {
    distance = rp.getDistanceFrom(loc);
    if (distance <= 30)
        count30++;
```

```
    rp = RepairPerson.read(br);
}
System.out.print("Number whose distance is within 30: ");
System.out.println(count30);
```

Finding the Nearest Repairperson

Now suppose we want to identify the one repairperson who is nearest to loc. As we did in the previous example, we present only the additional considerations resulting from this requirement, not the full development.

Informal Procedure

Now, along with everything else, we must remember the repairperson who is nearest. We must also remember that repairperson's distance so that, as we encounter other repairpersons, we can compare their distance with the distance of the nearest one so far.

Choosing and Defining Variables

We therefore require two more variables. One variable either refers to a repairperson (who is nearest among those repairpersons considered) or is null (in the case where no repairpersons have yet been considered) and an int to hold that repairperson's distance (assuming there is such a repairperson):

```
RepairPerson    rpMin;  // rpMin== the nearest repairperson (so far)
                        //     or null if none have been considered so far.
int minDist;            // minDist== the distance of repairperson rpMin
```

Skeleton of the Code

The skeleton is not changed in this variation, except for the addition of the above declarations. The while condition, initialization of the while condition variables, and code to guarantee termination do not change in this variation.

Completing the Loop Body

According to its definition, rpMin refers to the repairperson who is nearest (of the repairpersons seen so far). So, after reading another repairperson and calculating his distance, we need to check to see if the new repairperson's distance exceeds the largest seen so far. However, if rpMin is null, we haven't yet considered any repairpersons and the one we just read is the largest so far (in distance). So, if rpMin is null or if the new value for distance is less than minDist, we take appropriate action and recognize the newly read repairperson as the nearest one:

```
if (rpMin==null || distance<minDist) {
    minDist = distance;
    rpMin = rp;
}
```

Recheck Initialization

Because rpMin and minDist both appear in the loop body but are not initialized there, they must be initialized before the loop. Prior to the while statement, no employees have been processed, so rpMin should be initialized to null:

```
rpMin = null;
```

At this point there is no meaningful value to assign to minDist. However, because minDist is used in a condition in the loop, Java requires that it be initialized to some value (Java doesn't and can't know that the only time that minDist would be uninitialized is when rpMin is null and the condition is thereby true). We therefore choose a dramatically meaningless value to assign to minDist and note this anomaly with a comment:

```
minDist  =  -999;     // No meaningful value for minDist at this point.
```

The completed code follows:

```
RepairPerson rp;      // rp refers to the most recently read RepairPerson object
                      //    or is null.
int distance;         // distance is the distance from the given location of the most
                      //    recently read RepairPerson.
RepairPerson rpMin;   // rpMin== the nearest repairperson (so far)
                      //    or  null if none have been considered so far.
int minDist;          // minDist== the distance of repairperson rpMin
rpMin  =  null;
minDist  =  -999;     // No meaningful value for minDist at this point.

// All RepairPerson objects created prior to the one rp refers to have been processed.
rp = RepairPerson.read(br);
while (rp!=null) {
   count++;
   distance = rp.getDistanceFrom(loc);
   if (rpMin==null || distance<minDist) {
      minDist = distance;
      rpMin = rp;
   }
   rp = RepairPerson.read(br);
}
System.out.print("Nearest repairperson: ");
System.our.println(rpMin.getName());
```

10.6 Totaling a Bank's Accounts

Consider the Account class from Chapter 7. Suppose a banking application maintained a Vector of Account objects, to represent all the checking accounts in the bank. We'll assume that `checkingAccounts` is the reference variable to such a `Vector`. Let's write the code that would compute the total dollar amount in all the accounts.

Informal Procedure

Our plan is to traverse `checkingAccounts` and consider each of its elements. We are thus using the traverse pattern encountered in Chapter 9 and rederived in this chapter. In addition, for each element (an `Account` object) we will note its balance and add this value to a growing sum of that we will maintain.

Choosing and Defining Variables

Besides the usual variables for traversing `checkingAccounts`, we will require an `int` variable to hold the growing sum as the loop executes:

```
int balanceSum; // balanceSum== the sum of all the balances seen so far.
```

Skeleton of the Code

We take as our code skeleton the traverse pattern loop as developed earlier, suitably modified for `checkingAccounts` and `Account`, along with the above declaration:

```
int balanceSum; // balanceSum== the sum of all the balances seen so far.
int i;          // Refers to current position in checkingAccounts
Account a;      // Refers to the most recent Account object taken from
                //    checkingAccounts

i=0;
while (i<checkingAccounts.size())
    a = (Account) checkingAccounts.elementAt(i);
    rest of body
    i++;
}
```

Completing the Loop Body

According to its definition, `balanceSum` must equal the total sum of the balances calculated so far. Therefore, as soon as we get an `Account` object, we should get its balance and add it to `balanceSum`.

```
int balance = a.getBalance();
balanceSum += balance;
```

Recheck Initialization

`balanceSum` appears in the loop body but is not initialized there. Its initial value is easily inferred from its definition. Prior to the `while` statement, no balances have been summed—so the variable is initialized to 0. The resulting code follows:

```
int balanceSum=0; // balanceSum== the sum of all the balances seen so far.
int i;             // Refers to current position in checkingAccounts
```

```
Account a;        // Refers to the most recent Account
                  //          object taken from checkingAccounts
i=0;
while (i<checkingAccounts.size())
    a = (Account) checkingAccounts.elementAt(i);
    int balance = a.getBalance();
    balanceSum += balance;
    i++;
}
```

After the loop has completed we can print the the sum of the balances:

```
System.out.print("Sum of all the balances is: ");
System.out.println(balanceSum);
```

10.7 More Loop Patterns: Counters, Accumulators, and Extremes

The loops we have developed in the previous sections exhibit patterns that we frequently see in programming.

Loop Pattern: The Counter

We often need to count objects. The objects we count might be the elements of a collection for which a particular condition holds. Alternatively, the objects might be values read from an input source. To do this we need a loop that will iterate through the entire group of objects (whether obtaining them from input or from a collection such as a Vector) and a variable, called a **counter**. The counter equals the number of occurrences encountered at any given point. The counter is an int variable and must be initialized to 0. It is incremented, sometimes conditionally, in the loop body:

```
int countSomething = 0; // countSomething== the number of
                        //     somethings encountered so far.
  ...
while (...) {
    ...
    if (something we're interested in)
        countSomething++;
    ...
}
```

We have used counters to count the number of repairpersons in the system and the number of repairpersons less than 30 blocks away from a given location.

Loop Pattern: The Accumulator

We often wish to apply a binary operation—such as multiplication, addition, or even concatenation—to a group of values or objects, that is, to add, multiply, or concatenate them together. To do this we need a loop that iterates through the entire group of objects or generates the entire group of values and a variable, called an **accumulator**. The accumulator equals the result of applying the binary operation to all the objects or values so far encountered. The accumulator's type is usually determined by the type of the other operand. If a product of doubles is being computed, the accumulator is a double; if a bunch of Strings are being concatenated, the accumulator is a String reference variable. Its initial value depends on the operation. If the accumulator is a *sum,* 0 is an appropriate initial value, because 0 is the only number that does not contribute to the result. If the accumulator is a *product,* the appropriate initial value is 1, for similar reasons. If the accumulator is a String that results from concatenation, an empty String is the appropriate initial value.

In the loop body, the accumulator is assigned a new value, resulting from applying the given operation to it and the next value or object in the group that is being iterated:

```
SomeType accumulator;     // accumulator== the application of operation to
                          //     set of objects or values encountered so far.
  ...
while (...) {
      ...
    accumulator = apply operation to both accumulator and next object
                     or value
      ...
}
```

We have used accumulators to compute the total balance for a collection of Account objects as well as to maintain a product of one value that is repeatedly multiplied (to compute the exponential) and to maintain a sum of one value that is repeatedly added (to compute the product).

Accumulators need not be applied to all the values or objects encountered in the iteration. Like counters, they can be applied conditionally. For example, suppose we wanted to concatenate all the lines of input from a BufferedReader, br, that start with the character ":":

```
String s = "";
String line;
line = br.readLine();
while (line!=null) {
    if (line.substring(0,1).equals(":"))
        s = s.concat(line);
    line = br.readLine();
}
```

Loop Pattern: Extremes Among Objects

Some loops seek an object that is an **extreme**. An extreme object is one that in comparison with other objects in the group under consideration is the most extreme in some sense. Examples are

- A String that has more vowels than all the other Strings
- An employee who worked more hours than every other employee

To find an extreme object, we need a loop to iterate over a group of objects and a variable (such as rpMin) to remember the most extreme object encountered so far. In addition, we need a way of determining whether the current object under consideration is more extreme than the one that was most extreme so far. Sometimes, as in the case of our repairperson problem (where the RepairPerson object had no knowledge of the repairperson's distance from another location), this requires maintaining an additional variable (such as minDist). At other times—when the object provides more information—that is not necessary. The general pattern is

```
SomeType    extreme; // extreme== a reference to the object that is most
                     //     extreme among the set of objects encountered so far
                     //     or that is null if no objects have been considered.
extreme = null;
```

If other variables are required to represent the extreme character of the object, initialize them as required by Java (their value is not significant because at this point extreme is null).

```
while (...) {
    ...
    if (extreme==null || current object is more extreme  than extreme)
        extreme = current object
    ...
}
```

As a further example of this pattern, suppose we wanted to print the longest String in a Vector of references to String objects v:

```
String  s;
String  longest = null; // The longest String encountered so far or null if no
                        //     String has been encountered.
for (int i=0; i<v.size(); i++) {
    s = (String) v.elementAt(i);
    if (longest==null || s.length()>longest.length())
        longest = s;
}
System.out.println("Longest String is ".concat(longest));
```

Loop Pattern: Extremes Among Primitive Data Values

The construction of a loop that seeks an extreme primitive data type value among a set of such values is quite similar to the search for an extreme object, except for one problem. When searching for an extreme object, we used a special value, null, that indicated that we had not yet examined any objects in our search for the extreme. Often no such value exists for primitive data types. In this case we need a boolean variable, called foundExtreme, perhaps, that is true once some extreme has been found (on examining the first value) and until then is false. The general pattern is

```
boolean    foundExtreme;     // true if an extreme has been found so far;
                             //    false otherwise.
SomeType    extreme;         // extreme== the most extreme value
                             //    encountered so far if foundExtreme is
                             //    true; otherwise its value is meaningless.
extreme = some arbitrary and meaningless value;
foundExtreme  =  false;
while (...) {
    ...
    if (!foundExtreme  ||  current value is more extreme than extreme) {
        extreme = current value
        foundExtreme  =  true;
    }
    ...
}
```

As an example of this pattern, suppose we wanted to print the largest integer read from a BufferedReader br:

```
boolean    foundExtreme;
int        largest;
int        x;
foundExtreme  =  false;
largest  =  0;
String  line;
line  =  br.readLine();
while (line!=null) {
    x  =  Integer.parseInt(line);
    if (!foundExtreme  ||  x>largest) {
        largest = x;
        foundExtreme  =  true;
    }
    line = br.readLine();
}
System.out.println("Largest integer is " + largest);
```

10.8 Iterating Through Arrays

As another illustration of our procedure for developing loops, let's use an array to write the following tiny program: Read in a list of 100 integers, one to a line, and print the list in reverse, again, one integer to a line.

We begin with a counting loop to read in the integers:

```
import   java.lang.*;
import   java.io.*;
class   ReverseIntegers   {
    public   static   void   main(String[]   a)  throws Exception {
        BufferedReader kb   =   new   BufferedReader(
                        new InputStreamReader(System.in));
        int[]   z = new int[100];
        for (int i=0 ; i<100; i++)
            z[i]   =   Integer.parseInt(kb.readLine());
```

Informal Procedure

To print the elements of an array in reverse order, we first print the element in the last position (given by z.length-1), then the one in the second to last position, and so on, until we print out the first element of the array at position 0. At that point, having printed all of the elements out, we stop.

Choosing and Defining Variables

We need to keep track of the position we are up to. Position is given by an index, so we will need an integer variable. We must be very precise here. Should this integer denote the next position to print or should it denote the position printed most recently? Either meaning is fine so long as we are consistent. We will choose the first one:

int k; // k== the index of the next position in the array to print.

According to our informal procedure, if k is the *next* position to print, all the positions after k, starting with z.length-1, then z.length-2, and on down to k+1, must already have been printed. This observation is worth adding as a comment to the declaration because it gives further information about the meaning of k. We might also remark that, according to our informal procedure, if k is the next position to print, then all the positions that remain to be printed are k, k-1, and on down to 0:

int k; // k== the index of the next position in the array to print.
       // Positions z.length-1, z.length-2, ..., k+1 have already been printed.
       // Positions k, k-1, ..., 0 remain to be printed.

The first comment describes the next step of the task that is to be performed, the second describes the work that has already been performed, and the third describes the work that remains.

The while Condition

We are finished when all the array elements have been printed, that is, when positions

```
z.length-1, z.length-2, ..., 0
```

have been printed. Our understanding of k is that positions

```
z.length-1, z.length-2, ..., k+1
```

have been printed. These expressions are identical when k is −1. So, when k is −1, k+1 is 0 and we are done. To guarantee that k equals −1 when the loop terminates, our loop condition is k!=−1:

```
int k; // k== the index of the next position in the array to print.
       // Positions z.length-1, z.length-2, ..., k+1 have already been printed.
       // Positions k, k-1, ..., 0 remain to be printed.
...
while (k != -1)
       body
       // k== -1 and therefore z.length-1, z.length-2, ..., 0 have already been
       //     printed.
```

Initialization

The definition of k indicates that it is the index of the next position to print. Our informal procedure tells us that at the outset this must be z.length-1:

```
k = z.length-1;
```

Guaranteeing Termination

Decrementing k by 1 in the loop body guarantees that eventually k will fall to −1:

```
int k;     // k== the index of the next position in the array to print.
           // Positions z.length-1, z.length-2, ..., k+1 have already been printed.
           // positions k, k-1, ..., 0 remain to be printed.
k = z.length-1;
while (k != -1) {
    body
    --k;
}
// k== -1 and therefore z.length-1, z.length-2, ..., 0 have already been printed.
```

Completing the Loop Body

Decrementing k means that what was position k is now position k+1; in order for this to be justified, that position must have been printed out before the decrement:

```
System.out.println(z[k]);
```

Copying the code from the beginning of this section, our completed code is as follows:

```
class ReverseLines {
    public static void main(String[] a) throws Exception {
        BufferedReader in = new BufferedReader(
                        new InputStreamReader(System.in));
        int[]  z = new int[100];
        for (i=0 ; i<100; i++)
            z[i]  =  Integer.parseInt(kb.readLine());
        int k;      // k== the index of the next position in the array to print.
                    // Positions z.length–1, z.length–2, …, k+1 have already been
                    //     printed.
                    // Positions k, k–1, …, 0 remain to be printed
        k = z.length–1;
        while (k != –1) {
            System.out.println(z[k]);
            --k;
        }
        // k== –1 and therefore z.length–1, z.length–2, …, 0 have already
        //        been printed.
    }
}
```

Java Interlude   *Short Circuits, break, and continue*

Short-Circuiting

Java evaluates compound conditions in a strict left-to-right order. In addition, it evaluates only as much of the condition as necessary to arrive at the boolean result. Consider the following condition:

```
atBat!=0  &&  hits/atBat>0.300
```

Java evaluates atBat!=0 first. If it is false, there is no need to go further because the && must be false if the first operand is false. If atBat!=0 is true, Java will go further and evaluate hits/atBat>0.300. Notice that the first condition guarantees that a division by 0, which is a fatal error, will not be performed.

Conditions involving the || operator are evaluated similarly. Consider the following condition:

```
person.age()>=17   ||   person.accompaniedByAdult()
```

Java evaluates person.age()>=17 first. If it is true, there is no need in going further because the || must be true if the first operand is true. If person.age()>=17 is false, Java will go further and evaluate person.accompaniedByAdult().

This way of evaluating compound conditions is called **short-circuiting**. We took advantage of short-circuiting when we searched for an extreme object:

```
if (longest==null || s.length()>longest.length())
```

This condition is safe to execute only because the first clause, longest==null, is tested first. If the clause is true, that is, if longest is null, the second clause is not tested at all. If this were not the case and both clauses were always tested, when longest was null, the second clause, which uses longest as a reference, would be in error for sending a message to a null reference.

The break and continue Statements

The **break statement** consists of a single keyword, break:

```
break;
```

When Java encounters this statement in a loop body, the loop is immediately terminated. The following loop terminates either when the loop condition is tested and k equals 5 or when end-of-file is reached, causing s to be assigned null:

```
int     k=0;
while  (k!=5) {
    String s = infile.readLine();
    if (s==null)
        break;
    process s
    k++;
}
// k==5 or s==null
```

Although there may be some occasions when using the break statement is justified, we caution beginning and intermediate programmers not to employ it. Its use leads to two problems. First, when there is more than one exit from the loop, the code becomes more complex and harder to analyze. The reader of the above loop has to mentally construct an *or* termination condition implicitly. If the loop had been written as

```
int     k=0;
String s = infile.readLine();
while (!(k==5 || s==null)) {
    process s
    k++;
```

```
        s = infile.readLine();
    }
```

the reader could see the termination condition explicitly: (k==5 || s==null).

Secondly, programmers who rely on using the break statement often gloss over the step of determining the while condition. We have seen, however, that this step, although not hard, is an essential part of the design process.

Java also provides a **continue statement**, consisting of the single keyword, continue:

```
continue;
```

When Java encounters this statement in a loop, the remaining part of the loop body is skipped for this cycle. If the loop is a for statement, the increment is carried out, and then the condition is retested. In a while statement, there is no increment in the loop header, and so the condition is retested immediately after the continue:

```
for  (i=0;  i<100;  i++)  {
    if  (i%2==1)
        continue;
    if  (!veryComplicatedCondition(i))
        continue;
    process i
}
```

In the loop above, i is processed only if it is even and if the veryComplicated-Condition is true for i. The loop could have been written equivalently as follows:

```
for  (i=0;  i<100;  i++)  {
    if  (i%2==0  &&  veryComplicatedCondition(i))  {
        process i
    }
}
```

The advantage of continue is that it can reduce levels of nesting and indentation within a loop body. Its danger is that the conditions for executing the rest of the loop body are not explicit—they must be inferred by the programmer reading the different conditions that result in continue statements.

The continue statement can be downright dangerous, particularly when used in a while statement. Consider the following loop:

```
String  s =  keybd.readLine();
while (s!=null)  {
    if  (!someCondition1(s))
        continue;
    if  (!someCondition2(s))
```

```
        continue;
    process s
    s = keybd.readLine();
}
```

The intent here is that s should be processed only when someCondition1 and someCondition2 are true. However, when we use the continue statement, the entire loop body is skipped, including the read of the next String! Thus, s is never changed, and the loop is an infinite loop.

We therefore strongly advise beginners and intermediate programmers not to use the continue statement. Instead, work with explicit conditionals in the loop body.

The break and continue statements can be the inadvertent source of serious bugs. For example, a considerable portion of the long distance network of a major long distance provider went down in 1990 as a result of software error stemming from improper use of the break statement.

10.9 A Loop Design Strategy: Refining an Imperfect Solution

Many computing problems may be solved by starting with an imperfect provisional solution and then improving (or refining) it. We call this *successive refinement*. This approach requires the following three capabilities:

- The ability to *construct* an initial provisional, albeit imperfect, solution
- The ability to take a provisional solution and *improve* it, thus yielding a new provisional solution that is, in some way, closer to an actual solution of the given problem
- The ability to *determine* whether a given provisional solution is actually a solution of the problem, that is, an ability to know when the job is done

We use the term *provisional solution* broadly. A provisional solution could be a very crude approximation or an extremely incomplete result—usually it is not close at all to the true solution. For example, if our goal was to compute the square root of a number x, a provisional solution might be the number x itself—certainly close to the solution if x is close to 0 or 1 but very crude if x is large.

To make our discussion of successive refinement concrete, we consider the problem of calculating the non-negative square root of a real number x. The three capabilities mentioned above may be developed in any order. For the square root, we start with the third one first.

How do we determine whether a double value stored, say, in y is the square root of a double value stored, say, in x? We might be tempted to write the condition

```
y*y == x
```

as our measure of success, but given the peculiarities of floating-point arithmetic, it is more practical to ask not whether y*y equals x but rather whether y*y is very close to x. Remember, when floating-point arithmetic is used, approximations are usually inevitable and, provided they are good enough, always acceptable. By writing

```
Math.abs(y*y-x) <= p
```

we can determine whether y*y is within a distance of p from x. If p is quite small (for example, 1.0e-10), we know that y is a close, perhaps a sufficiently close, approximation of the square root of x. The value of p determines the precision of our assessment.

A helper method that checks whether one value, y, is within a given precision of the square root of x, is

```
private boolean closeEnough(double x, double y, double precision) {
    return Math.abs(y*y-x) <= precision;
}
```

So we now have a method that tells us *when our job is done,* that is, whether our (square root) problem has been solved. Now we turn to improvement: Given a provisional solution that is not "good enough," how can we improve it? We base the method of improvement on an algorithm attributed to the great seventeenth-century scientist Isaac Newton.

The essence of the algorithm lies in the observation that if y is an approximation of the square root of x that is greater than the true square root of x, then x/y will be smaller than the true square root. Likewise, if y is too small, x/y will be greater than the true square root. Furthermore, the average of the approximation y and x/y

$$(y + x/y) / 2$$

is a closer approximation of the square root of x than either y or x/y. This is illustrated in Figure 10.1. For example, suppose we seek the square root of 100 and we approximate it as 20. With y as 20 and x as 100, we calculate

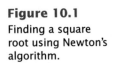

Figure 10.1

Finding a square root using Newton's algorithm.

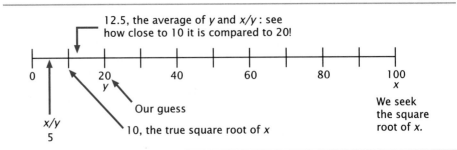

$$(20 + 100/20) / 2$$

which is 12.5—much closer to the true square root of 100 than 20. What we have, then, is a means for taking one approximation and producing a better one.

A helper method that uses this to improve a provisional solution to the square root of x is

```
private double improveSolution(double y, double x) {
    return (y+x/y) / 2.0;
}
```

We thus have our second capability: We can *improve our provisional solution* to the square root of x. Finally, we need to start somewhere, to come up with an *initial provisional solution* to the square root of x. It need not be a good one, because we know we can improve it. Any positive value here will do and so we may start with x itself.

In general, given these capabilities, it is often possible to solve the problem with iteration. Let's work through the general case with our loop-constructing approach and then apply it to our square root problem.

Informal Procedure

We start with our provisional solution and improve it. As long as our provisional solution is not good enough, we keep improving it. When it *is* good enough, the job is done and we stop.

Choosing and Defining Variables

We are talking in generalities now, so we can't describe specific variables—each particular problem will have its own set of variables to represent a provisional solution (in the square root problem, a single variable, y, is all that is required). For purposes of discussion, let's have one variable, s, here that represents the provisional solution to our problem:

SomeType s;   // Provisional solution to the problem at hand

Skeleton of the Code

Given our expectation of using iteration, we have

SomeType s;   // Provisional solution to the problem at hand
while (*condition*)
    body

The while Condition

Our informal procedure tells us that our job is complete when the solution is good enough:

```
while (condition)
     body
// closeEnough(s)
```

So the negation of this is our loop condition:

```
while (!closeEnough(s))
     body
// closeEnough(s)
```

Initialization

Because s is used in the while condition, it must first be initialized. Our first required capability, the ability to start with a provisional solution, allows us to do this:

```
s = provisional solution
while (!closeEnough(s))
     body
// closeEnough(s)
```

Guaranteeing Termination

According to our informal procedure, we repeatedly improve the provisional solution in hopes of reaching a solution that is good enough:

```
s = provisional solution
while (!closeEnough(s))
     s = improveSolution(s);
// closeEnough(s)
```

It is correct, however, to ask whether continually improving a solution is enough to guarantee termination. In some cases, it will not be. To take a silly but illustrative example, suppose that our goal was for s to reach the value 2, starting from 1.0. If we added successively 0.1, 0.01, 0.001, 0.0001, and so on, with each addition s gets closer to 2, but it never reaches that value. The question of whether the improvement necessarily leads to termination must always be examined carefully.

Finding the Square Root

Following this discussion, we write our square root method:

```
// squareRoot returns square root of x within the given precision.
private double squareRoot(double x, double precision) {
```

```
    double y;
    y = x;
    while (!closeEnough(x, y, precision))
        y = (y+x/y) / 2.0;
    return y;
}
```

Given the nature of the `while` statement, there is no question that if `squareRoot()` returns, it will return a value that equals the square root of *x* within the given precision. It is thanks to Isaac Newton that we know that our method of improvement leads to a sequence of approximations that converges to the square root of *x* and hence that the `while` loop will indeed terminate.

A Broader View

Actually all the loops we have encountered in this and the preceding chapter may be viewed in this light. Each of these loops in a sense takes a provisional solution to a problem and incrementally improves it. Consider, for example, the code that multiplies by repeated addition:

```
private int multiply(int x, int y) {
    int count,   // count== the number of additions done.
        result;  // result==0+x+x+...+x (count times), that is,
                 //      result==x*count.
    count = 0;
    result = 0;
    while (count!=y) {
        result += x;
        count++;
    }
    // count==y, result==x*y
    return result;
}
```

Our task is to make `result` equal x*y. In terms of the successive refinement,

- The provisional solution is 0.
- The way we improve our provisional solution is to add x.
- We test whether count!=y to determine whether our provisional solution is the actual solution to the problem.

The first two of these are straightforward, but how does testing count!=y show whether our provisional solution is the correct solution or not? The answer lies in the meaning of count and result—information that is provided in the comments associated with their definition and that is implicit in the code that was developed: result==x*count. Given that information, of course count!=y is a measure of whether the job has been done. The central role played by this fact of our design, `result==x*count`, underscores the importance of thinking carefully about the meaning of our variables and expressing those meanings, with an equality if possible, in a comment.

10.10 Example: The LOGO Turtle

LOGO is a programming language developed in the 1970s as part of an effort to introduce basic programming concepts at the elementary school level. The LOGO language revolves around the concept of a "turtle" moving about on a surface. The turtle has a pen on its underside, which can be raised or lowered to allow it to draw a line as it moves. The surface that the lines are drawn on is called the turtle's *world*. LOGO statements are commands to the turtle: turn left, move forward some distance, raise the pen, and so on. In addition, several basic programming constructs such as conditionals and looping are provided to allow more complex shapes (such as squares) to be conveniently drawn. The result is an environment that is both motivating and encouraging to a young would-be programmer, providing instant positive feedback in the form of the interesting shapes that can be drawn.

Our next example develops a very simple turtle object modeled after this language.

Statement of the Problem

Create an object that models the turtle of the LOGO language. The commands that the turtle should respond to are turn left or right, move forward some distance, and raise or lower the pen.

Scenario

We will provide the various commands as methods. An application could then create a turtle object and control it through invocations of the methods:

```
Turtle t = new Turtle(40);      The world should be 40 x 40 units.
t.penUp();
t.move(5);
t.left();
t.move(5);
t.penDown();
for (int i = 0; i < 4; i++) {
    t.move(10);
    t.left();
}
```

We do not propose conditional or loop capabilities because we can use Java features such as the loop in this code fragment.

The turtle output might be a display of the world on System.out that uses some character to represent the pen line. See Figure 10.2.

Finding the Primary Object

This is a straightforward task. We are trying to model the LOGO turtle. We will introduce a Turtle class. We use the simple output to System.out described above.

Determining the Behavior

The behavior required by our problem statement is as follows:

- Turtle (constructor)
- left (turn left)
- right (turn right)
- move (move forward)
- penUp (lift pen—subsequent moves do not draw lines)
- penDown (lower pen—subsequent moves do draw lines)

Output Behavior

The simplest output is to print the turtle's world on System.out. Unfortunately, we don't have full control over movement on that device. We can't move up a line or to the left because output to System.out models that of a typewriter—strictly left-to-right, up-to-down. We often refer to such devices as TTY devices. (TTY stands for teletype, meaning a computer-linked typewriter.)

Therefore, because the Turtle cannot display each move as it occurs, our class will provide a method that displays the turtle's world in its entirety. We thus have an additional behavior:

- display the turtle's world

Determining the Interface

The above behavior translates neatly into methods. Only the move() method requires additional information—the distance the turtle is supposed to move. In

Figure 10.2

A textual display of the turtle's world. The pen mark generated by the turtle at a position is represented by an *.

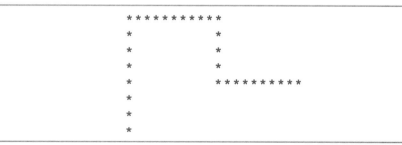

addition, to make things interesting, we will allow the user to specify the size of the turtle's world as an argument to the constructor (we'll assume the world is square):

```
class Turtle {
    Turtle(int size) {...}          // Creates turtle in a world of the size
                                    //     given by size
    void move(int distance) {...}   // Move distance squares in the
                                    //     current direction.
    void penUp() {...}              // Raises drawing pen
    void penDown() {...}            // Lowers drawing pen
    void left() {...}               // Turn left.
    void right() {...}              // Turn right.
    void display() {...}            // Display turtle's world
}
```

Representing the World

The `display()` method will need information that represents the turtle's world. This information will be needed by each invocation of `display()` and may be modified by `move()`. We therefore need an instance variable that represents the turtle's world.

A square itself is quite simple—it is either blank or it has been drawn on. We can represent a square using a `boolean`, with the understanding that `true` means drawn on and `false` means blank.

We know how to represent more than one thing—we need a collection. Because the things we are representing are primitive data types (`booleans`) we will use an array, not a `Vector`.

If our world was one-dimensional, that is, if our world consisted of a single row of squares (see Figure 10.3), we could represent it simply as an array of `booleans`:

```
private boolean[]      world;     // Good for a one-dimensional world
```

However, the world consists of many rows. Again, we know how to represent many things. If each row is an array of `booleans`, the world is an array of arrays of `booleans`:

```
private boolean[][]  world;     // Good for a two-dimensional world
```

Figure 10.3
A one-dimensional world. Such a world could be represented by an array of `boolean`: `boolean[] world;`.

A one-dimensional world: just a row of squares

Multidimensional Arrays

The preceding declaration can be read as follows: *The identifier world is declared as an array of arrays of type boolean.* Instead of each element of world being a primitive type or a reference to an individual object of some class, each element is itself an array that has boolean as *its* element type. The identifier world represents a reference variable to an array, whose elements are referred to as world[0], world[1], and so on. In the arrays we have encountered so far, these elements contained either primitive data values, such as int, or references to objects of some class. In our world array, the elements are themselves references to arrays of boolean. Thus world[0] is a reference to an array, world[1] is a reference to an array, and so on. The elements of the world[0] array, as in any other array, begin with subscript 0, and are referred to as world[0][0], world[0][1], and so on. (See Figure 10.4.) Although the abundance of brackets may be somewhat confusing, the concept is a straightforward consequence of our notion of an array.

An array of arrays is often called a *two-dimensional array*, or *matrix*. One could also have three-dimensional arrays, four-dimensional, and so on. There is nothing mysterious about them—the dimension is nothing more than the number of subscripts used to access an individual element.

Working with such an array is not much different from working with a one-dimensional array: The subscripts for each dimension begin at 0. To access an individual element of the array, a subscript must be supplied for each dimension:

```
int i = 2, j = 1;
System.out.print(a[i][j]);   // Prints a[2][1]
```

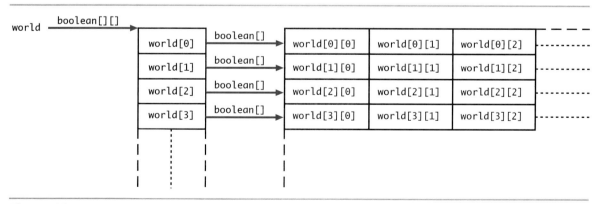

Figure 10.4 An array of arrays of booleans.

Creating a multidimensional array is analogous to a standard (one-dimensional) array, with the addition of having to specify the size of both dimensions. To create a world array whose first dimension (the rows in the figure) is of size 10, and whose second dimension (the columns) is of size 20, we write

```
boolean[][] world = new boolean[10][20];
```

(We could also allocate the individual world[i] arrays, but we will not explore that approach.)

Iterating through a multidimensional array is an extension of the technique used for the single dimensional case—for each dimension, a loop is used to iterate through that dimension. These loops are nested to provide a full iteration of the array. For example, the following code iterates through the array world allocated above:

```
for (int i = 0; i < world.size; i++) ◄──────────── Iterates through world
    for (int j; j < world[i].size; j++) ◄────────── Iterates through world[i]
        world[i][j] = 0; ◄──────────── Don't forget world[i] is also an array
```

Defining the Other Instance Variables

We have to keep track of whether the pen is raised or lowered and we have to remember the turtle's current position, represented by a pair of subscript values for the world array:

```
boolean penLowered;
int x, y; // x is horizontal position (first subscript), y is vertical (second subscript).
```

We also need to keep track of the direction the turtle is facing. We choose to speak of the turtle facing north, east, south, or west (as shown in Figure 10.5).

Figure 10.5

The turtle's position and direction. The turtle occupies one of the world positions. It may face one of the four compass directions; that direction becomes its direction of movement.

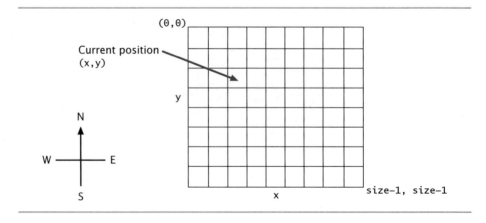

We could represent the current direction as a string: "North", "East", "South", "West". The problem with this approach is that it requires remembering the exact strings, for example, "North" versus "north." Furthermore, this representation precludes using a switch based upon the direction, an approach we will show to be useful.

Instead, we represent the direction using an integer, for example, 0 for north, 1 for east, and so on. To avoid having to remember which value represents which direction, we use integer constants:

```
private int direction;
private static final int NORTH=0, EAST=1, SOUTH=2, WEST=3;
```

This approach allows us to perform a switch based on the direction. In addition, mistakes in the spelling of the directions, for example North rather than NORTH, will generate an "Undeclared identifier" compiler error.

Implementing the Methods

The constructor creates the world, and it initializes a starting position, direction, and pen position. We choose to place the turtle initially in the center of the world facing north with the pen down.

```
public Turtle(int size) {
    world = new boolean[size][size];
    int i, j;
    for (i = 0; i < size; i++)
        for (j = 0; j < size; j++)
            world[i][j] = false;          ◄——————  Iterate through the world array,
    direction = NORTH;                              setting each square to false.
    x = size / 2;
    y = size / 2;
}
```

The world, x, and y instance variables depend on the value of the size argument supplied to the constructor and thus must be initialized there. The penLowered variable, however, is always initialized to true, and this initialization may therefore be performed at the point of declaration as follows:

```
class Turtle {

    ...
    // Instance variables
    private boolean penLowered = true;

    ...
}
```

The penUp() and penDown() methods modify the pen position to the appropriate value:

```java
public void penUp() {      // Raises drawing pen
    penLowered = false;
}
public void penDown() {   // Lowers drawing pen
    penLowered = true;
}
```

Turning to the left or right causes a change to the current direction. We take the straightforward, though somewhat lengthy approach of listing all the possible cases and explicitly setting the new direction based upon the current direction:

```java
public void left() { // Turns left
    switch (direction) {
        case NORTH:
            direction = WEST; break;
        case WEST:
            direction = SOUTH; break;
        case SOUTH:
            direction = EAST; break;
        case EAST:
            direction = NORTH; break;
    }
}
public void right() { // Turns right
    switch (direction) {
        case NORTH:
            direction = EAST; break;
        case EAST:
            direction = SOUTH; break;
        case SOUTH:
            direction = WEST; break;
        case WEST:
            direction = NORTH; break;
    }
}
```

The `display()` method iterates through the array row by row, printing the contents of the elements as shown in Figure 10.6:

```java
public void display() { // Displays turtle's world on System.out
    int i, j;
    for (i = 0; i < world.length; i++) {
        for (j = 0; j < world.length; j++)
            if (world[i][j])
                System.out.print("*");
```

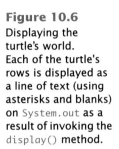

Figure 10.6
Displaying the turtle's world. Each of the turtle's rows is displayed as a line of text (using asterisks and blanks) on System.out as a result of invoking the display() method.

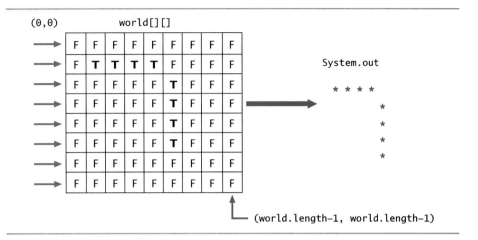

```
        else
            System.out.print(" ");
        System.out.println();
    }
}
```

The move() method performs the following three tasks:

- Calculates the starting and end positions of the line to be drawn.
- Draws the line, if the pen is down.
- Updates the state of the Turtle object.

To draw, we will rely on a helper method, draw(), that is passed the starting and end positions of the line to be drawn:

```
private void draw(int startX, int startY, int destX, int destY)
```

To calculate these positions we save the indices of the starting position in two int variables, startX and startY. We calculate the indices of the end position and place their values directly into this.x and this.y, thereby updating the state:

```
public void move(int distance) {
    int startX = this.x,
        startY = this.y;
    Calculate new values of this.x and this.y.
    if (penDown)
        draw(startX,startY,this.x,this.y);
}
```

The details of the calculation of the end points depend on the direction of movement. Because we only allow the turtle to face one of the four primary compass directions, only one coordinate varies as we move forward. The rules for moving in the various directions are as follows (see Figure 10.7):

- North—y coordinate decreases as we move forward; edge is encountered when y == 0.
- East—x coordinate increases as we move forward; edge is encountered when x == world.length–1.
- South—y coordinate increases as we move forward; edge is encountered when y == world.length–1.
- West—x coordinate decreases as we move forward; edge is encountered when x == 0.

We will handle each direction as a separate case:

```
switch(this.direction) {
    case NORTH:
            Handle northward move.
            break;
    case EAST:
            Handle eastward move.
            break;
    case SOUTH:
            Handle southward move.
            break;
    case WEST:
            Handle westward move.
            break;
}
```

Figure 10.7

Coordinate changes corresponding to movement in the various directions. Either the x or the y coordinate changes with movement in a particular direction; the other coordinate remains fixed.

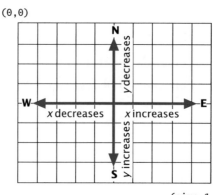

(0,0)

(size–1, size–1)

We will develop the eastward movement; the other directions are similar. When the turtle moves eastward, the x coordinate increases, while the y coordinate remains constant; see Figure 10.8.

The diagram shows that if we disregard the edge of the world, our destination square's x coordinate could be calculated this way:

```
this.x = this.x + distance;
```

However, we must take the edge of the world into consideration and stop at the edge if we reach it. Our rules tell us that the edge of the world, when we are heading east, is encountered when x is equal to world.length–1. Therefore, when calculating the x coordinate of the destination square, we can go no further than the end of the world, and we therefore revise the assignment of this.x to

```
this.x = Math.min(x + distance, world.length–1);
```

Here the (static) method Math.min() returns the smaller of its two values.

The other directions are analogous, the only changes being the subscript (y for north/south, x for east/west), the manner in which the subscript is changed (increment for south/east, decrement for north/west), and the test for the edge of the world. The resulting method is

```
// Move distance squares in the current direction.
public void move(int distance) {
```

Figure 10.8
The squares visited during an eastward movement (edge ignored). If we ignore the edge of the world, moving dis-tance squares in the eastward direction takes us to square this.x + distance. The result of per-forming a move(4) is shown.

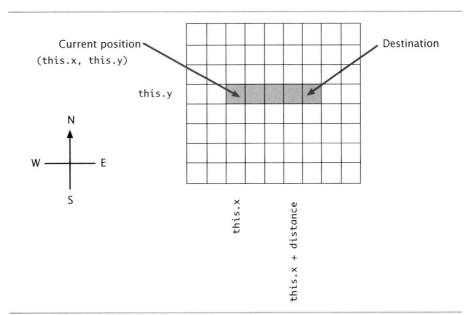

```
        int startX=this.x,
            startY=this.y;
        switch (direction) {
            case NORTH:
                this.y = Math.max(this.y - distance, 0);
                break;
            case SOUTH:
                this.y = Math.min(this.y + distance, world.length-1);
                break;
            case WEST:
                this.x = Math.max(this.x - distance, 0);
                break;
            case EAST:
                this.x = Math.min(this.x + distance, world.length-1);
                break;
        }
        if (penLowered)
            draw(startX, startY, this.x, this.y);
}
```

All that is left is the implementation of our draw() method. Based on the current direction we use a simple for loop to drop a mark in each intervening position:

```
private void draw(int startX, int startY, int destX, int destY) {
    switch (direction) {
        case NORTH:
            for (int i = startY; i >= destY; i--)
                world[destX][i] = true;
            break;
        case SOUTH:
            for (int i = startY; i <= destY; i++)
                world[destX][i] = true;
            break;
        case WEST:
            for (int i = startX; i >= destX; i--)
                world[i][destY] = true;
            break;
        case EAST:
            for (int i = startX; i <= destX; i++)
                world[i][destY] = true;
            break;
    }
}
```

The Complete Implementation

Putting the pieces together, the complete implementation of the Turtle class is as follows:

```java
import java.io.*;
class Turtle {
    // Creates turtle in a world size-by-size squares
    public Turtle(int size) {
        world = new boolean[size][size];
        int i, j;
        for (i = 0; i < size; i++)
            for (j = 0; j < size; j++)
                world[i][j] = false;
        direction = NORTH;
        x = size / 2;
        y = size / 2;
    }
    // Move distance squares in the current direction.
    public void move(int distance) {
        int startX = this.x,
            startY = this.y;
        switch (direction) {
            case NORTH:
                this.y = Math.max(this.y - distance, 0);
                break;
            case SOUTH:
                this.y = Math.min(this.y + distance, world.length-1);
                break;
            case WEST:
                this.x = Math.max(this.x - distance, 0);
                break;
            case EAST:
                this.x = Math.min(this.x + distance, world.length-1);
                break;
        }
        if (penLowered)
            draw(startX, startY, this.x, this.y);
    }
    private void draw(int startX, int startY, int destX, int destY) {
        switch (direction) {
            case NORTH:
```

```
                for (int i = startY; i >= destY; i--)
                    world[destX][i] = true;
                break;
            case SOUTH:
                for (int i = startY; i <= destY; i++)
                    world[destX][i] = true;
                break;
            case WEST:
                for (int i = startX; i >= destX; i--)
                    world[i][destY] = true;
                break;
            case EAST:
                for (int i = startX; i <= destX; i++)
                    world[i][destY] = true;
                break;
        }
    }

    // Raises drawing pen
    public void penUp() {
        penLowered = false;
    }

    // Lowers drawing pen
    public void penDown() {
        penLowered = true;
    }

    // Turns left
    public void left() {
        switch (direction) {
            case NORTH:
                direction = WEST; break;
            case WEST:
                direction = SOUTH; break;
            case SOUTH:
                direction = EAST; break;
            case EAST:
                direction = NORTH; break;
        }
    }

    // Turns right
    public void right() {
        switch (direction) {
            case NORTH:
```

```
                direction = EAST; break;
            case EAST:
                direction = SOUTH; break;
            case SOUTH:
                direction = WEST; break;
            case WEST:
                direction = NORTH; break;
        }
    }
    public void display() { // Displays turtle's world on System.out
        int i, j;
        for (i = 0; i < world.length; i++) {
            for (j = 0; j < world.length; j++)
                if (world[i][j])
                    System.out.print("*");
                else
                    System.out.print(" ");
            System.out.println();
        }
    }
    // Instance variables
    private boolean[][] world;
    private int x, y;
    private int direction;
    private boolean penLowered = true;

    // Static variables
    private static final int NORTH=0, EAST=1, SOUTH=2, WEST=3;
    public static void main(String[] args) {
        Turtle t = new Turtle(40);
        t.penUp();
        t.move(5);
        t.left();
        t.move(5);
        t.penDown();
        for (int i = 0; i < 4; i++) {
            t.move(10);
            t.left();
        }
        t.display();
    }
}
```

Summary

Although familiarity with common patterns of loops in programs is helpful, a methodical approach to loop construction is an essential tool for the programmer. We advocate that a programmer start by considering an informal solution to a problem requiring a loop and then follow these steps:

- Identify the needed variables and write down precise definitions of their meaning.
- Make an overall sketch of the `while` statement and its context (the method it appears in).
- Determine the loop condition by taking the negation of the condition that should be true when the loop terminates.
- Write code before the loop to make sure any variables used in the loop condition are properly initialized.
- Write code in the loop body that guarantees termination—that is, that guarantees that the loop condition eventually will be false.
- Complete the loop body by adding code that maintains the consistent meaning of the variables.
- Write additional initialization code as needed.

In each step, particularly the last four, insight from the informal solution can and should be used.

Key Terms

accumulator A variable that holds a partial sum, product, or analog for another binary operation besides + or *.

break statement A statement that forces immediate termination of a loop.

continue statement A statement that forces Java to skip the remainder of the loop body in the current iteration.

counter A variable that keeps count of something.

counting loop A loop whose termination is based on executing a certain number of times.

extreme A value in a set that is no greater or no less than all the other elements.

iteration The repeated execution of a section of code until some condition is satisfied.

loop condition The condition that controls the loop statement's execution.

loop termination The property of eventually completing execution of a loop.

short-circuiting Ending the evaluation of a condition without evaluating all its clauses as soon as the value of the condition is determined.

Questions for Review

1. What can we be sure is the case when a `while` statement terminates?
2. Is the definition of n violated at any point in the code below? Is this a problem? Explain.

```
int n=0;      // Number of stars printed out
while (n!=5)  {
    System.out.print("*");
/   n++;
}
```

Exercises

1. Rework the `power()` example by modifying the definition of `count` so that it must be initialized to 1.
2. The condition for termination was `count!=y`. Compare this with the condition `count<y`. Is the result the same? Does this change our reasoning about the value of `result` after the loop terminates?
3. Correct the `multiply()` method so that it handles negative values in its second argument. (*Hint:* One approach might be to make part of the loop body conditional on the sign of the second argument.)
4. Implement an `add()` method that adds two arbitrary integers using only increment and decrement.
5. Implement a `subtract()` method that subtracts arbitrary integers using only increment and decrement.
6. Implement a `quotient()` method that returns the quotient of two integers; the method may not use the divide (/) or modulus (%) operators.
7. Implement a `remainder()` method that returns the remainder of dividing two integers.
8. Implement an integer log-base-2 method. The log (base 2) of an integer is the number of times the integer can be divided by 2 before the integer result becomes 1. For example, the integer log-base-2 of 6 is 2 because 6 can be divided by 2, yielding 3, which can be divided by 2, yielding 1 (integer division).

9. Extend the method of the previous exercise to any positive base.

10. Write the code needed to read in a list of RepairPerson objects, and compute and print out their average distance from a Location, loc.

11. Write a static method that receives the name of a file and an integer N as arguments. The method returns a Vector of the first N Strings read from the file. If the file has fewer than N Strings, the Vector contains all the Strings it does have.

12. Write a static method that receives an integer N as argument and returns the sum of the first N cubes: $1^3 + 2^3 + 3^3 + \cdots + N^3$.

13. Write a static method that receives a filename as an argument. Assume that the file consists solely of integers. The method returns the product of the smallest and largest integers in the file.

14. Write a program that reads exactly one hundred integers into an array and then prints out the odd-numbered integers, followed by the even-numbered integers. Thus, if the first 10 integers read in were 8, 18, 23, –8, 44, 2, 101, 17, 19, 72 then the first five integers printed out would be: 8, 23, 44, 101, 19.)

15. Reimplement your solutions using the *other* kind of loop statement. Are some solutions easier to read or understand using one kind of loop statement?

16. The criterion for y being a satisfactory approximation for the square root of x is

    `Math.abs(y*y–x) <= precision`

    for some value of precision. Suppose precision is 0.000001. Can you think of a number for which this is a very poor criterion? Suppose the criterion was

    `Math.abs(y*y–x) <= 1.0`

    Can you think of a number for which this is a very poor criterion? Can you think of a number for which this criterion is quite reasonable?

17. Come up with a better criterion for a satisfactory approximation.

18. Change the Turtle class so that the turtle's world does not have to be square but can be any rectangle.

19. Add an overloaded Turtle constructor that accepts no arguments and creates a world of some default size.

20. Add an overloaded move() method that accepts no arguments. Instead the turtle is to be moved forward by the same distance as the most recent move() message. Does this new condition require a change to the internal state of the class? Why is this method useful?

21. Rewrite the left() and right() methods so that they do not use a conditional. (*Hint*: Take advantage of the int representation of the direction instance variable.)

22. Our implementation treated the world as flat and we "clipped" the turtle's movement at the edge. Implement a "round" world, one without edges. That is, when the turtle reaches an edge, it simply continues to the opposite side. (See the diagram on the following page.)

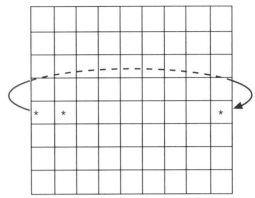

move(3) direction is west

23. Define a class called `Smiley` whose objects, when constructed, create a `Turtle` object and use it to create a smiling face. The turtle display should then be followed by the message *Have a nice day!!* Thus

```
Smiley sm = new Smiley();
```

produces the following output:

```
* * * * * * * * * * * * * * * *
*                             *
*    * *             * *      *
*                             *
*                *            *
*    *                  *     *
*     *               *       *
*        *   *   *            *
*                             *
* * * * * * * * * * * * * * * *
        Have a nice day!!
```

24. Consider the fragment of code below. Unfortunately, we spilled some coffee on it and it can't all be seen. Can you tell what will be printed out even though some code is covered by coffee? (Assume that the loop does terminate.)

```
int      i, j;
i = 19;
j = 3;
while (i!=7)
    i += j;
```

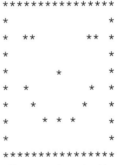
coffee stain !

```
}
System.out.println(i);
```

More Text Manipulation

In this supplement, we will extend our "text justifier" applet from the previous chapter, adding the following features:

- Adjustable line spacing
- Adjustable text size
- Adjustable left and right margins

The new version of our applet will look like Figure 10.9.

Behavior

The additional behaviors of this applet are not the full-strength versions found in commercial word processing programs—users can't choose arbitrary text size or line spacing—but with these additional features we will be able to explore a broad range of issues in positioning text.

Specifically, the line spacing and text size buttons allow the user to choose among only three options; the applet implementation details determine precisely what "double spacing" or "large text" mean. The user *is* able to set the margin sizes (using pixel measurements, not inches) by entering a margin value in the "Width" text field then clicking the appropriate button ("Set Left" or "Set Right").

Layout

The new layout is similar to the original, with more elaborate Panel organization to achieve an appropriate grouping of the buttons. We will postpone the code

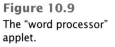

Figure 10.9
The "word processor" applet.

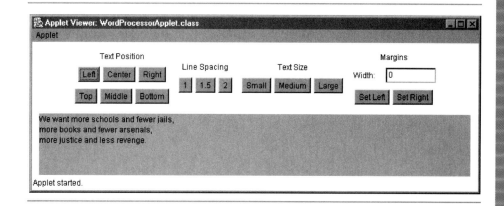

listing until we have developed the entire applet, but here are the instance variables we need:

```
// buttons for horizontal position
private Button leftButton,centerButton,rightButton;

// buttons for vertical position
private Button topButton,middleButton,bottomButton;

// buttons for line spacing
private Button singleButton,oneAndHalfButton,doubleButton;

// buttons for text size
private Button smallButton,mediumButton,largeButton;

// buttons for margins
private Button setLeftButton,setRightButton;
private TextField marginSize;
private TextCanvas tc;
```

We also need to alter our sizing calculations in the `start()` method. Here is one set of values that works:

```
public void start() {
    setSize(14*middleButton.getWidth(),20*middleButton.getHeight());
    tc.setSize(getWidth()-20,15*middleButton.getHeight());
}
```

Handling Events

Again, the `TextCanvas` is the most sensible responder to events, because it is the only object that needs to take action in response to these events. This version of the applet introduces a complication, however: Responding to a "changing margin" event requires access to the contents of the `marginSize` field. To provide this access, we'll add a parameter to the `TextCanvas` constructor: a reference to the `TextField` containing the margin size. The revised constructor (which now also receives references to the additional buttons) looks like this:

```
public TextCanvas(Button l,Button c,Button r,
                  Button t,Button m,Button b,
                  Button one,Button oneAndHalf,Button two,
                  Button sm,Button med,Button lg,
                  Button setl,Button setr,TextField ms) {
    leftButton = l;
    centerButton = c;
```

```
        rightButton = r;
        topButton = t;
        middleButton = m;
        bottomButton = b;
        singleButton = one;
        oneAndHalfButton = oneAndHalf;
        doubleButton = two;
        smallButton = sm;
        mediumButton = med;
        largeButton = lg;
        setLeftButton = setl;
        setRightButton = setr;

        marginSize = ms;
}
```

and `TextCanvas` will include the additional instance variables

```
private Button singleButton,oneAndHalfButton,doubleButton;
private Button smallButton,mediumButton,largeButton;
private Button setLeftButton,setRightButton;
private TextField marginSize;
```

Our implementation of `actionPerformed()` will simply be an extended version of the method we wrote in the previous supplement: We just have a few more kinds of events to handle. Specifically, we need to handle additional events corresponding to line spacing, text size, and margin size. As before, we will assume that Text-Canvas provides methods to handle the details of each kind of event; our `action-Performed()` method will be responsible for sending an appropriate message (with appropriate arguments) to the `TextCanvas`. We'll assume that these `TextCanvas` methods (which we will implement shortly) have the following signatures:

```
        public void setSpacing(double s) {
        public void setTextSize(int s) {
        public void setLeftMargin(int m) {
        public void setRightMargin(int m) {
```

Here is the new `actionPerformed()` method:

```
        public void actionPerformed(ActionEvent e) {
          Object source = e.getSource();

          if (source == leftButton)
             setHorizJust(TextCanvas.LEFT);
          else if (source == centerButton)
             setHorizJust(TextCanvas.CENTER);
```

```
    else if (source == rightButton)
        setHorizJust(TextCanvas.RIGHT);

    else if (source == topButton)
        setVertJust(TextCanvas.TOP);
    else if (source == middleButton)
        setVertJust(TextCanvas.MIDDLE);
    else if (source == bottomButton)
        setVertJust(TextCanvas.BOTTOM);
```

> Identical to first version up to this point.

```
    else if (source == singleButton)
        setSpacing(1.0);
    else if (source == oneAndHalfButton)
        setSpacing(1.5);
    else if (source == doubleButton)
        setSpacing(2.0);
```

> Translate clicked button into a double value indicating desired spacing.

```
    else if (source == smallButton)
        setTextSize(TextCanvas.SMALL);
    else if (source == mediumButton)
        setTextSize(TextCanvas.MEDIUM);
    else if (source == largeButton)
        setTextSize(TextCanvas.LARGE);
```

> Another set of constants defined in `TextCanvas`.

```
    else if (source == setLeftButton)
        setLeftMargin(Integer.parseInt(marginSize.getText()));
    else if (source == setRightButton)
        setRightMargin(Integer.parseInt(marginSize.getText()));
}
```

> Extract text from `Text-Field` and convert to `int` equivalent.

Changing Text Characteristics

Before we turn to the `TextCanvas` implementation, let's briefly review what we know about working with fonts in the context of applet development. As we saw in the Chapter 2 supplement, changing the characteristics of the text drawn by a `Graphics` object is a two-step process: creating a new `Font` object corresponding to the desired text characteristics, then passing this `Font` object to the `Graphics` with the `setFont()` method.

Creating a new `Font` is a matter of providing three parameters: the font *family* (e.g., Times, Dialog, Helvetica), the *face* (plain, italic, bold, etc.), and the *size* (measured in *points*). For our purposes, we are interested only in the size, so we will use the default values for the other two parameters: the `Dialog` family, and the `Font.PLAIN` face. The size will ultimately be determined by the `setText-Size()` method, so we will need an instance variable

```
private int textSize;
```

to communicate between the setTextSize() method, which determines the size of the text, and the paint() method, which draws the text on the screen.

Partial Implementation of TextCanvas

At this point, we can write all of the TextCanvas class except the modified paint() method. In particular, we have added four set...() methods (which are very similar in form and purpose to the existing ones) and corresponding instance variables, as well a few more static final instance variables:

```
public void setHorizJust(int j) {
    horiz = j;
    repaint();
}

public void setVertJust(int j) {
    vert = j;
    repaint();
}

public void setSpacing(double s) {
    lineSpacing = s;
    repaint();
}

public void setTextSize(int s) {
    textSize = s;
    repaint();
}

public void setLeftMargin(int m) {
    leftMargin = m;
    repaint();
}

public void setRightMargin(int m) {
    rightMargin = m;
    repaint();
}
```

New set...() methods

```
private int horiz = TextCanvas.LEFT;
private int vert = TextCanvas.TOP;
private double lineSpacing = 1.0;
private int textSize = TextCanvas.MEDIUM;
```

New instance variables

```
private int leftMargin=0, rightMargin=0;
public static final int LEFT = 0;
public static final int CENTER = 1;
public static final int RIGHT = 2;
public static final int TOP = 0;
public static final int MIDDLE = 1;
public static final int BOTTOM = 2;
public static final int SMALL = 10;
public static final int MEDIUM = 12;
public static final int LARGE = 20;
```

New constants

Implementing paint(): Some New Text Measurements

Our modified paint() begins in much the same way as the previous version, recording some basic measurements of the text. In this new version, we must first create a new Font object corresponding to the font we wish to display (i.e., based on the textSize instance variable) before we can take our measurements:

```
public void paint(Graphics g) {

    String line1 = "We want more schools and fewer jails,";
    String line2 = "more books and fewer arsenals,";
    String line3 = "more justice and less revenge.";

    int myWidth = getWidth();
    int myHeight = getHeight();

    Font f = new Font("Dialog", Font.PLAIN, textSize);
    g.setFont(f);
    FontMetrics fm = g.getFontMetrics();
    int lineHeight = fm.getHeight();
    int ascent = fm.getAscent();
    int l1Width = fm.stringWidth(line1);
    int l2Width = fm.stringWidth(line2);
    int l3Width = fm.stringWidth(line3);
```

Create new Font based on size.

Now we have two new computations to perform. First, because the user may change the line spacing, we must compute the amount of space to insert between each line. Notice that if the desired line spacing is 1, then the amount of additional space is 0; if the desired line spacing is 1.5, we must insert 0.5 lines of space. That is, the amount of inter-line space is lineHeight multiplied by lineSpacing − 1:

```
int interLineSpace = (int) (lineHeight*(lineSpacing-1.0));
```

We must cast the result to `int` to indicate to the compiler that we are willing to accept the possible loss of precision in storing the `double` result of our calculation in an `int` variable.

Second, our horizontal position calculations are a bit more complicated due to the presence of margins—centering, for example, must take place with respect to the margins, not the edges of the canvas. To assist in these calculations, we compute an intermediate value: the width of the text area (`writeAreaWidth`), defined as the width of the canvas minus the margin widths:

```
int writeAreaWidth = myWidth-leftMargin-rightMargin;
```

Now we proceed by calculating the horizontal and vertical position of the text. The horizontal position is straightforward: If the text is to appear on the left, then we move the text over `leftMargin` units. Otherwise, we use `writeAreaWidth` and the width of the string to find out how much blank space should appear to the left of the string in the write area, and add the width of the left margin (see Figure 10.10):

```
int l1Margin,l2Margin,l3Margin;

if (horiz == LEFT)
    l1Margin = l2Margin = l3Margin = leftMargin;
else if (horiz == CENTER) {
    l1Margin = (writeAreaWidth-l1Width)/2+leftMargin;
    l2Margin = (writeAreaWidth-l2Width)/2+leftMargin;
    l3Margin = (writeAreaWidth-l3Width)/2+leftMargin;
```

Figure 10.10
Horizontal text position.

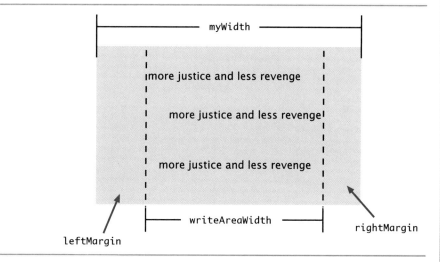

```
    }
    else {
        l1Margin = writeAreaWidth - l1Width + leftMargin;
        l2Margin = writeAreaWidth - l2Width + leftMargin;
        l3Margin = writeAreaWidth - l3Width + leftMargin;
    }
```

To determine the vertical position, we first determine the height of the text, which is

```
    int textHeight = 3*lineHeight + 2*interLineSpace;
```

Then, just as before, we determine the distance to the top of the displayed text:

```
    int vertMargin;
    if (vert == TOP)
        vertMargin = 0;
    else if (vert == MIDDLE)
        vertMargin = (myHeight - textHeight) / 2;
    else
        vertMargin = myHeight - textHeight;
    int vertPos = vertMargin + ascent;
```

To display the text, we first make the background gray, then draw the strings. The only difference from the original version is that the vertical distance between strings is not just `lineHeight` but `(lineHeight+interLineSpace)`:

```
    setBackground(new Color(190,190,190));
    g.drawString(line1,l1Margin,vertPos);
    g.drawString(line2,l2Margin,vertPos+lineHeight+interLineSpace);
    g.drawString(line3,l3Margin,
                    vertPos+2*(lineHeight+interLineSpace));
    }
```

Here is the complete applet:

```
import java.applet.*;
import java.awt.*;
import java.awt.event.*;

public class WordProcessorApplet extends Applet {
    public void init() {
        setBackground(new Color(255,255,255));

        Panel horiz = new Panel();
        leftButton = new Button("Left");
        centerButton = new Button("Center");
        rightButton = new Button("Right");
```

```
horiz.add(leftButton);
horiz.add(centerButton)    // buttons for horiz. pos.
horiz.add(rightButton);

Panel vert = new Panel();
topButton = new Button("Top");
middleButton = new Button("Middle");
bottomButton = new Button("Bottom");
vert.add(topButton);
vert.add(middleButton);
vert.add(bottomButton);   // buttons for vert. pos.

Panel position = new Panel();
position.setLayout(new BorderLayout());
position.add("North",horiz);
position.add("South",vert);
Panel labelPosition = new Panel();
labelPosition.setLayout(new BorderLayout());
labelPosition.add("North",
           new Label("Text Position",Label.CENTER));
labelPosition.add("South",position);

singleButton = new Button("1");
oneAndHalfButton = new Button("1.5");
doubleButton = new Button("2");

Panel lineSpacing = new Panel();
lineSpacing.add(singleButton);
lineSpacing.add(oneAndHalfButton);
lineSpacing.add(doubleButton);
Panel labelSpacing = new Panel();
labelSpacing.setLayout(new BorderLayout());
labelSpacing.add("North",
           new Label("Line Spacing",Label.CENTER));
labelSpacing.add("South",lineSpacing);

Panel textSize = new Panel();
smallButton = new Button("Small");
mediumButton = new Button("Medium");
largeButton = new Button("Large");
textSize.add(smallButton);
textSize.add(mediumButton);
textSize.add(largeButton);
Panel labelTextSize = new Panel();
```

```
labelTextSize.setLayout(new BorderLayout());
labelTextSize.add("North",
            new Label("Text Size",Label.CENTER));
labelTextSize.add("South",textSize);

Panel marginValue = new Panel();
marginValue.add(new Label("Width:"));
marginSize = new TextField("0",8);
marginValue.add(marginSize);
Panel marginSet = new Panel();
setLeftButton = new Button("Set Left");
setRightButton = new Button("Set Right");
marginSet.add(setLeftButton);
marginSet.add(setRightButton);

Panel margins = new Panel();
margins.setLayout(new BorderLayout());
margins.add("North",marginValue);
margins.add("South",marginSet);
Panel labelMargins = new Panel();
labelMargins.setLayout(new BorderLayout());
labelMargins.add("North",
            new Label("Margins",Label.CENTER));
labelMargins.add("South",margins);

Panel controls = new Panel();
controls.add(labelPosition);
controls.add(labelSpacing);
controls.add(labelTextSize);
controls.add(labelMargins);
tc = new TextCanvas(leftButton,centerButton,rightButton,
                topButton,middleButton,bottomButton,
                singleButton,oneAndHalfButton,doubleButton,
                smallButton,mediumButton,largeButton,
                setLeftButton,setRightButton,marginSize);
add(controls);
add(tc);

leftButton.addActionListener(tc);
centerButton.addActionListener(tc);
rightButton.addActionListener(tc);
topButton.addActionListener(tc);
middleButton.addActionListener(tc);
```

```java
        bottomButton.addActionListener(tc);
        singleButton.addActionListener(tc);
        oneAndHalfButton.addActionListener(tc);
        doubleButton.addActionListener(tc);
        smallButton.addActionListener(tc);
        mediumButton.addActionListener(tc);
        largeButton.addActionListener(tc);
        setLeftButton.addActionListener(tc);
        setRightButton.addActionListener(tc);

    }

    public void start() {    // make layout work
        setSize(14*middleButton.getWidth(),
                20*middleButton.getHeight());
                tc.setSize(getWidth()-20,
                15*middleButton.getHeight());
    }

    private Button leftButton,centerButton,rightButton;
    private Button topButton,middleButton,bottomButton;
    private Button singleButton,oneAndHalfButton,doubleButton;
    private Button smallButton,mediumButton,largeButton;
    private Button setLeftButton,setRightButton;
    private TextField marginSize;
    private TextCanvas tc;
}

class TextCanvas extends Canvas implements ActionListener {
    public TextCanvas(Button l,Button c,Button r,
                      Button t,Button m,Button b,
                      Button one,Button oneAndHalf,Button two,
                      Button sm, Button med, Button lg,
                      Button setl, Button setr,TextField ms) {
        leftButton = l;
        centerButton = c;
        rightButton = r;
        topButton = t;
        middleButton = m;
        bottomButton = b;
        singleButton = one;
        oneAndHalfButton = oneAndHalf;
        doubleButton = two;
```

```
        smallButton = sm;
        mediumButton = med;
        largeButton = lg;
        setLeftButton = setl;
        setRightButton = setr;

        marginSize = ms;
    }
    public void paint(Graphics g) {

        String line1 = "We want more schools and fewer jails,";
        String line2 = "more books and fewer arsenals,";
        String line3 = "more justice and less revenge.";

        int myWidth = getWidth();
        int myHeight = getHeight();
        Font f = new Font("Dialog", Font.PLAIN, textSize);
        g.setFont(f);
        FontMetrics fm = g.getFontMetrics();
        int lineHeight = fm.getHeight();
        int ascent= fm.getAscent();
        int l1Width = fm.stringWidth(line1);
        int l2Width = fm.stringWidth(line2);
        int l3Width = fm.stringWidth(line3);

        int interLineSpace = (int) (lineHeight*(lineSpacing-1.0));
        int writeAreaWidth = myWidth - leftMargin - rightMargin;

        int vertMargin;
        int l1Margin,l2Margin,l3Margin;

        if (horiz == LEFT)
            l1Margin = l2Margin = l3Margin = leftMargin;
        else if (horiz == CENTER) {
            l1Margin = (writeAreaWidth - l1Width) / 2 + leftMargin;
            l2Margin = (writeAreaWidth - l2Width) / 2 + leftMargin;
            l3Margin = (writeAreaWidth - l3Width) / 2 + leftMargin;
        }
        else {
            l1Margin = writeAreaWidth - l1Width + leftMargin;
            l2Margin = writeAreaWidth - l2Width + leftMargin;
            l3Margin = writeAreaWidth - l3Width + leftMargin;
        }
```

```
        int textHeight = 3*lineHeight + 2*interLineSpace;
        if (vert == TOP)
            vertMargin = 0;
        else if (vert == MIDDLE)
            vertMargin = (myHeight - textHeight) / 2;
        else
            vertMargin = myHeight - textHeight;

        int vertPos = vertMargin + ascent;

        setBackground(new Color(190,190,190));
        g.drawString(line1,l1Margin,vertPos);
        g.drawString(line2,l2Margin,vertPos+lineHeight+interLineSpace);
        g.drawString(line3,l3Margin,
                     vertPos+2*(lineHeight+interLineSpace));
    }

  public void actionPerformed(ActionEvent e) {
        Object source = e.getSource();

        if (source == leftButton)
            setHorizJust(TextCanvas.LEFT);
        else if (source == centerButton)
            setHorizJust(TextCanvas.CENTER);
        else if (source == rightButton)
            setHorizJust(TextCanvas.RIGHT);

        else if (source == topButton)
            setVertJust(TextCanvas.TOP);
        else if (source == middleButton)
            setVertJust(TextCanvas.MIDDLE);
        else if (source == bottomButton)
            setVertJust(TextCanvas.BOTTOM);

        else if (source == singleButton)
            setSpacing(1.0);
        else if (source == oneAndHalfButton)
            setSpacing(1.5);
        else if (source == doubleButton)
            setSpacing(2.0);

        else if (source == smallButton)
            setTextSize(TextCanvas.SMALL);
```

```
      else if (source == mediumButton)
         setTextSize(TextCanvas.MEDIUM);
      else if (source == largeButton)
         setTextSize(TextCanvas.LARGE);

      else if (source == setLeftButton)
         setLeftMargin(Integer.parseInt(marginSize.getText()));
      else if (source == setRightButton)
         setRightMargin(Integer.parseInt(marginSize.getText()));

   }
   public void setHorizJust(int j) {
      horiz = j;
      repaint();
   }

   public void setVertJust(int j) {
      vert = j;
      repaint();
   }

   public void setSpacing(double s) {
      lineSpacing = s;
      repaint();
   }

   public void setTextSize(int s) {
      textSize = s;
      repaint();
   }

   public void setLeftMargin(int m) {
      leftMargin = m;
      repaint();
   }

   public void setRightMargin(int m) {
      rightMargin = m;
      repaint();
   }
```

```
    private int horiz = TextCanvas.LEFT;
    private int vert = TextCanvas.TOP;
    private int leftMargin=0, rightMargin=0;
    private double lineSpacing = 1.0;
    private int textSize = TextCanvas.MEDIUM;

    public static final int LEFT = 0;
    public static final int CENTER = 1;
    public static final int RIGHT = 2;
    public static final int TOP = 0;
    public static final int MIDDLE = 1;
    public static final int BOTTOM = 2;
    public static final int SMALL = 10;
    public static final int MEDIUM = 12;
    public static final int LARGE = 20;

    private Button leftButton,centerButton,rightButton;
    private Button topButton,middleButton,bottomButton;
    private Button singleButton,oneAndHalfButton,doubleButton;
    private Button smallButton,mediumButton,largeButton;
    private Button setLeftButton,setRightButton;

    private TextField marginSize;
}
```

Maintaining Collections of Objects

11.1 Overview

In this chapter, we focus on two of the most common (by far) applications of collections and iteration: searching and sorting.

11.2 Searching

People spend much of their lives searching for keys, for a parking spot, for a biology lab section that is not closed and that doesn't meet on Friday afternoons, and so on. Programs spend even more time searching for a bank record corresponding to a customer number, for an inventory record corresponding to a part number, for the web page that a client browser has requested, and so on. Often the objects that programs search for are stored in collections such as `Vectors` and arrays.

To illustrate how a search might be carried out, let's write a method, `search()`, that receives a `String` parameter and searches for it in an array, z, that contains references to `Strings`. The method returns the index of the `String` if it finds the `String` in the array and returns −1 otherwise. We choose −1 to represent "not found" because a negative integer cannot possibly be a legitimate index in Java—any other negative integer would work as well. The prototype for `search` is as follows:

```
private int search(String z[], String s) {
                              // Returns the index of a match to s in z
                              //    or –1 if there is no match.
      ...
}
```

We now turn to our standard approach to loop design to construct this code.

Informal Procedure

We must check every element in the array until we find a match or until there are no more elements to check. One way to do this methodically is to check the

445

element in position 0, then the element in position 1, then 2, and so on. By proceeding from 0 and going up, checking every position as we go, we will eventually get to each element: We'll either find our match or get to the end of the array without skipping any elements.

Choosing and Defining Variables

We need to keep track of our current position and so we need an integer variable to hold this index. Should this integer denote the next position to check or the position checked most recently? Either meaning is fine, so long as we are consistent. We will choose the first one:

```
int k;      // k== the index of the next position in the array to check.
```

According to our informal procedure, if k is the next position to check, we have already checked all the positions before k, that is, 0, ..., k−1, and we haven't found a match in those positions. We add this observation as an additional comment. (See Figure 11.1.)

```
int k;      // k== the index of the next position in the array to check.
            // No match has been found in positions 0 through k−1.
```

Skeleton of the Code

We write

```
// Returns the index of a match to s in z or −1 if there is no match
private int search(String z[], String s) {
    int k;      // k== the index of the next position in the array to check.
                // No match has been found in positions 0 through k−1.

        ...
    while (condition)
        body
        ...
}
```

Figure 11.1

The meaning of the index in searching an array. The array is logically divided into two regions by k: (1) 0 through k−1, where no match has been found (shaded) and (2) k through z.length−1, where a match may yet by found (unshaded).

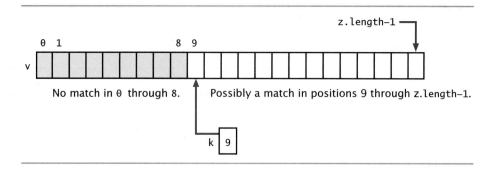

The while Condition

We are finished when the object in the next position to check matches the parameter *or* when there are no more positions to check. The object in the next position is given by

```
z[k]
```

To see if this object and the parameter object, s, are equal we may write

```
s.equals(z[k])
```

If this condition is true, we have found a match to the parameter and are finished—we can return true.

On the other hand, if

```
k==z.length
```

we are confident that no match exists. That's because the definition of k tells us that there is no match in positions 0 through k–1; with k==z.length, no match has been found in positions 0 through z.length–1—there is no match anywhere in the array. Thus, we are finished when

```
// k==z.length OR s.equals(z[k])
```

(See Figure 11.2.)

Figure 11.2
When the search is complete. (Top) The search is complete when we see that the object has no match in the array *or* (bottom) the object's match in the array has been found in position k.

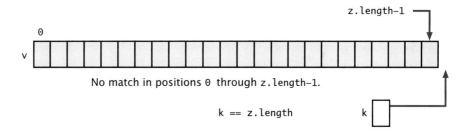

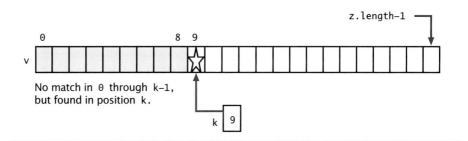

To guarantee that this is true when the loop terminates, the loop condition is

```
!(k==z.length || s.equals(z[k]))
```

Our code now is

```
// Returns the index of a match to s in z or –1 if there is no match
private int search(String z[], String s) {
    int k;       // k== the index of the next position in the array to check.
                 // No match has been found in positions 0 through k–1.

        ...
    while (!(k==z.length || s.equals(z[k])))
        body
    // k==z.length OR s.equals(z[k])
}
```

Note that we test k==z.length first because z[k] is illegal if k==z.length. By testing k's value first we make sure—thanks to short-circuiting—that s.equals(z[k]) will not be evaluated when k==z.length.

Before continuing our development, let's make sure that we can easily complete the method once it is known that

```
k==z.length OR s.equals(z[k])
```

In fact, we can. One or the other of the above conditions is true—they can't be true simultaneously because if k is equal to z.length, it is the index of the position after the last valid position of the array and there is no element at that position—in that case we should return –1. If k is not equal to z.length, we know that the second clause in the OR is true and k must be the index of the match we found—in that case we should return k:

```
if (k==z.length)
    return –1;
else
    return k;
```

Initialization

The definition of k indicates that it is the index of the next position to check. Our informal procedure tells us that this must be 0:

```
k = 0;
```

Guaranteeing Termination

By incrementing k by 1 in the loop body, we know that eventually k will equal z.length or that we will find a match to s in position k.

```
// Returns the index of a match to s in z or –1 if there is no match
private int search(String z[], String s) {
```

```
int k;      // k== the index of the next position in the array to check.
            // No match has been found in positions 0 through k-1.
k = 0;
while (!(k==z.length || s.equals(z[k])))
   k++;
// k==v.size OR s.equals(z[k])

if (k==z.length)
   return -1;
else
   return k;
}
```

Completing the Loop Body

Usually, this step is taken because the code that guarantees termination (k++ here) causes a momentary violation of the definition of one of our variables. Here, however, this violation does not occur because the loop condition itself has already ascertained that position k does not match the parameter and so incrementing k is safe—it will not violate the claim that no match has been found in positions 0 through k–1. Remarkably, perhaps, the loop is already complete. Because we added no new code, there is no need for additional initializations, and the method above is complete.

Discussion

The loop in our new search() method starts in position 0 and accesses elements of the array from lower to higher index. The search() method gives us the index of the element, unlike the contains() method, which merely indicated whether the element was present or not. The search algorithm used here is called the **sequential search** because the elements are searched in the sequence in which they are stored in the array.

Notice that we redeveloped as a while loop a pattern we originally presented as a for loop. You should be able to confirm that the two loop forms are *almost* equivalent. Our effort at careful loop design did pay off, though: The version above is more efficient that our original version. Here, once we find the element we are looking for, our loop stops; before, our for loop continued until we had looked at all elements in the array.

11.3 Binary Search

The sequential search algorithm is simple, but it can be slow. If we have to search an array containing several thousand elements, we may notice a bit of a delay before the result is returned—especially if the element we're searching for isn't in the array, in which case the search looks at every element before it gives up.

If a computer takes a detectable amount of time to perform this search, then how is it possible for humans to search, say, a phonebook containing 100,000 entries? If it takes a computer a second or two to do this, then why doesn't it take us several months to perform one search?

It *would* take us several months—if we used a sequential search algorithm. But most people don't search a telephone book by examining the first entry, then the second entry, and so on. Instead, we take advantage of the fact that the phonebook is sorted. (Specifically, a phonebook is sorted by name—if we wanted to look for a particular number, we'd have no choice but to use some form of sequential search.) When collections are sorted, a search can be extremely efficient.

Suppose the `Strings` in our array had been added in alphabetical order:

```
...
z[56] = "manlius";
z[57] = "marlboro";
z[58] = "melville";
z[59] = "midwood";
...
```

How can we rewrite our search method to take advantage of this? Think of how people search for a listing in a phonebook. We may use intuition to guide the search. For example, if the name is *Whitman*, we start near the end of the book. What is most important is that as we search, we divide the phonebook into three parts:

- The portion of the book that the search has been narrowed down to
- The portion of the book before that
- The portion of the book after that

For example, in a search for *Whitman*, at one point we might have a finger on a page that starts with *Van Dyke* and another finger on a page that starts with *Wolsey*. *Whitman* could not appear in the pages before *Van Dyke* or in the pages after *Wolsey*, but it might appear in between.

The search proceeds by taking a look at a page roughly in the middle of the "might be" zone. In the search for *Whitman*, we might find *Webster* between *Van Dyke* and *Wolsey*. Because *Whitman* comes after *Webster*, we narrow down the "might be" zone to between *Webster* and to *Wolsey*. (See Figure 11.3.) The search continues until the "might be" zone has been narrowed to a single page.

Guided by this strategy, let's construct a loop to carry out a search for a `String s` in an array.

Informal Procedure

Just as the phone book search in Figure 11.3 depended on two pages that defined the part of the book where the name might be found, so will our search through the array depend on two positions between which the `String` we are

Figure 11.3
Searching a phone-book for a name. (Left) Locate an initial zone. Then (right), pick a page in the middle of where *Whitman* might be and use that page to narrow down the search.

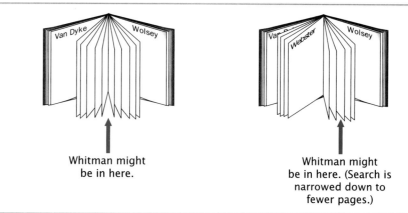

Whitman might be in here.

Whitman might be in here. (Search is narrowed down to fewer pages.)

searching for might be found. For the sake of discussion, let's call these positions `left` and `right`. (See Figure 11.4.)

At each step we will look in the middle between `left` and `right`. If the `String` in the middle position comes before `s`, the middle position becomes the new left position. If the `String` in the middle position comes after `s`, the middle position becomes the new right position. (See Figure 11.5.) We repeat this procedure until we have narrowed the search down to a single position, at which point we stop and check that position for a match to `s`.

Choosing and Defining Variables

We need integer variables to keep track of `left` and `right`. As always, precision in their meaning is essential. Does the middle region, where a match to `s` might be, include `left`? Does it include `right`? We may be guided by sketches we made in the diagrams that outlined our informal procedure, but we are not bound by them. Any decision on the precise meaning for `left` and `right` is fine, so long as we stick to that decision as we develop our code. We will choose the following definition:

```
int     left, right;    // If the String is anywhere, it's in positions left
                        //      through right-1.
                        // The String is not in a position before left.
                        // The String is not in a position after right-1.
```

Figure 11.4
Searching a sorted array for a `String`. If it is anywhere, *Whitman* is in the shaded region, between `left` and `right`.

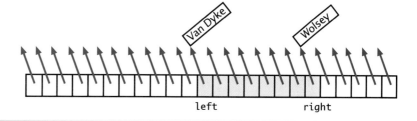

left   right

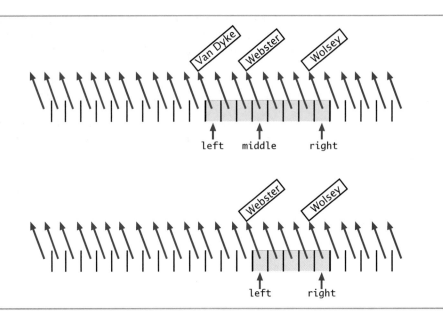

Figure 11.5

Narrowing down the search. (Top) Because *Whitman* comes after *Webster,* the middle becomes the new left. (Bottom) The part of the array that we still must search through is narrowed down.

This choice differs from the above diagrams in that it excludes position right from the middle (shaded) region, which now only goes as far as right-1. We revise our diagram to match our choice. (See Figure 11.6.)

We could just as easily have defined the middle to include right. Our choice—and this is not much more than a matter of whim—was made because the length field of an array represents the index of the position after the last position in the array. By analogy, right here is the index of the position after the last position in the middle region.

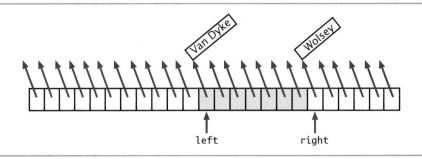

Figure 11.6

Searching a sorted array for a String (revised). If it is anywhere, *Whitman* is in the shaded region, from left up to but not including right.

Our informal procedure tells us that we keep shrinking the middle region until we have narrowed it down to a single element. So `left` must never equal or exceed `right`, and we add the following comment:

```
// left<right
```

The `while` Condition

We stop when we have narrowed the search down to a single element. We will be down to a single element when `left` and `right-1` are the same element; that is, when

```
left==right-1
```

Our loop so far is

```
while (left!=right-1) {
    ...
}
// left==right-1
```

When the loop terminates, the only position that might match `s` is `left`. So the method can, at that point, test the element at this position:

```
if (s.equals(z[k]))
    return  left;
else
    return  -1;
```

Note that when there is only one element in the array, the loop condition is `false` from the outset and the loop body will not be executed, as shown in Figure 11.7.

Initialization

At the outset, the match to `s` could be anywhere in the array, from position 0 to position `z.length-1`. Consistency with the definitions of our variables, `left` and `right`, calls for

```
left = 0;
right = z.length;
```

Figure 11.7
Searching an array of size 1. When the array has a size of 1, the termination condition, `left==right-1`, is immediately `true`.

left   right

These assignments make it true that the match to s could be anywhere from left (0) to right–1 (z.length–1).

There is one special case we must check. If the array is empty, that is, if its size is 0, the above assignments violate our requirement that left<right always. In this case, however, we know that there is no match to s. We therefore precede these assignments with the following code:

```
if  (z.length==0)  {
    return -1;
}
```

Guaranteeing Termination

We must make sure that, as we are guided by our informal procedure, the distance between left and right shrinks (that is, we narrow down the search region) but that left and right never meet or cross (left<right). We must also guarantee that the element for which we search is never before left or after right–1. That is,

- right–left must be smaller each time around the loop.
- left<right always.
- The value we seek is between left and right–1, or it is nowhere to be found.

Our informal procedure asks us to find the element midway between left and right. We can think of that as the position that is the "average" of left and right (see Figure 11.8):

```
m  =  (left+right)/2;
```

We need to compare s, the String we search for, with the String at position m:

```
z[m].compareTo(s)
```

Comparing z[m] to s will provide us with valuable information about where the element we're searching for might be. We make use of this information to modify left or right or possibly both to narrow down the search range.

Figure 11.8
Finding the middle
of the search area.
m is the index of the
location.

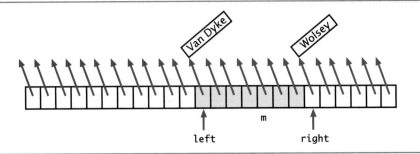

If s comes after z[m], left moves to the middle (see Figure 11.9):

```
if  (z[m].compareTo(s)<0)
    left  =  m;
```

If s comes before z[m], right moves to the middle:

```
else  if  (z[m].compareTo(s)>0)
    right  =  m;
```

and if s and z[m] are equal, we've found a match and we can set the left and right so that the range has been reduced to a single element:

```
else  {
    left  =  m;
    right  =  m+1;
}
```

The code that we write, influenced by our informal procedure, is as follows:

```
while  (left!=right-1)  {
    m  =  (left+right)/2;
    if  (z[m].compareTo(s)<0)
        left  =  m;                    // Move left to the middle.
    else  if  (z[m].compareTo(s)>0)
        right  =  m;                   // Move right to the middle.
    else  {
        left  =  m;
        right  =  m+1;
    }
}
```

We must make sure that this code guarantees that right-left decreases each time around the loop but that left<right always. To do this, we have to look closely at the value of m in relation to the values of left and right.

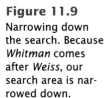

Figure 11.9
Narrowing down the search. Because *Whitman* comes after *Weiss*, our search area is narrowed down.

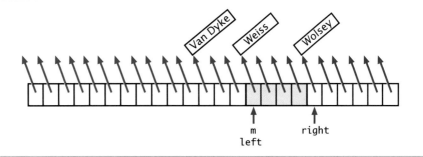

For the moment, assume that left<right is true when the loop condition is evaluated. Then when we start executing the loop, we know that left<right–1, because

- We are, for the moment, assuming that left<right was true when we evaluated the loop condition, and it still will be true in that case.
- The loop condition, left!=right–1 must be true in order to execute the loop body.

If left<right–1, we have left<right–1<right: There is at least one value between left and right. In that case, m, which is assigned (left+right)/2 will take on one of these intermediate values. (See Figure 11.10.) So m will be greater than left and less than right:

left < m < right

The only way that the loop body ever changes left or right is by assigning one of them m. However, because left<m<right, left cannot be assigned a value as big as right and right can't be assigned a value as small as left. At the end of the loop body, left is still less than right.

Of course, the conclusion that left<right at the end of the loop body's execution depends on the assumption that left<right going in. Fortunately, our code initializes left and right so that at the outset left<right. And we see that once left<right is true, this relationship won't vary as the loop is executed. Because the loop preserves this relationship and because we start out with that relationship we can be confident that left<right throughout the execution of the loop.

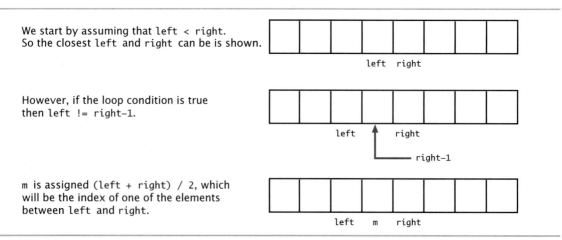

Figure 11.10 The relationships between left, right, and m.

Because left<m<right, we also see that each time the loop body is executed, the search range, left through right–1, is narrowed down. That's because we either assign m to left, making left greater, or we assign m to right, making right smaller.

Completing the Loop Body

We have not violated any of the definitions of the variables, and so there is nothing more to add to the loop. The loop is complete and the method is

```
// Returns true if and only if s equals one of the Strings in z.
private int bsearch(String z[],String s) {
    int    left, right;
                    // If the String is anywhere, it is in positions left through right–1.
                    // The String is not in a position before left.
                    // The String is not in a position after right–1.
    if (z.length == 0)
    return–1;
    left = 0;
    right = z.length;
    while  (left!=right–1)  {
        int  m  =  (right+left)/2;
        if  (z[m].compareTo(s)<0)
            left  =  m;          // Move left to the middle.
        else  if  (z[m].compareTo(s)>0)
            right  =  m;         // Move right to the middle.
        else  {
            left  =  m;
            right  =  m+1;
        }
    }
    if (s.equals(z[left]))
      return left;
    else
      return –1;
}
```

Binary Search: What's in a Name?

Suppose the array we are searching has 4,000 elements. Initially, left is 0 and right is 4,000, and the range of elements to consider is 4,000. However, the first time around the loop, m has the value 2,000 and either left or right assumes this value, leaving a range of just 2,000 elements to consider. Suppose that after the first pass left is 2,000 and right still is 4,000. In the second pass, m will be 3,000 and the range of elements to consider is reduced to 1,000. In each pass through the loop body, the range to consider is cut in two. The algorithm's name, **binary search**, comes from this cutting-in-two characteristic.

Efficiency

Starting with a value N, how many times can you divide by 2 before reaching 1? Consider 4,000:

$$4000 \rightarrow 2000 \rightarrow 1000 \rightarrow 500 \rightarrow 250 \rightarrow 125 \rightarrow 62 \rightarrow 31 \rightarrow 15 \rightarrow 7 \rightarrow 3 \rightarrow 1$$

Just 11. Imagine! To find out whether a particular String is stored among 4,000 others requires just 11 executions of the loop body. In contrast, the search() method of Chapter 10 requires 4,000 executions of its loop body to discover that a particular String is not in the array, and on the average it requires 2,000 executions to find a String that is there. Thus, 2,000 versus 11 is a staggering ratio: about 180. A binary search executes its loop body 180 fewer times than the sequential search in this case. Of course, the loop body in the binary search is longer than the one in search() and may take more time. But even if the loop body of the binary search is four times as slow (which it isn't) as that of search(), it will run 180/4 = 45 times faster than search().

How does a speed factor of 45 translate into hardware prices? At the time of writing this text, 2.5GHz Pentium 4 machines are just appearing on the market. Their cost is in the neighborhood of $2,000. They are roughly 45 times faster than 50MHz 486 machines that cost next to nothing. So a "worthless" machine running a binary search is approximately the equivalent of a $2,000 machine running search() for data in this quantity.

The point of this comparison is to illustrate the profound impact that software has on a system. A good algorithm can be far more important to the efficiency of a system than the latest, most expensive hardware.

In mathematics, there is a function called log-base-2 that is written

$$\log_2$$

It equals the number of times its argument can be divided by 2 before reaching 1. So if the array's size is N, the binary search requires **$\log_2 N$** passes through the loop. In contrast, the sequential search of Chapter 10 requires $N/2$ passes through the loop on the average to find a String that is there and N passes to discover that a String is not present in the array.

The table below compares $\log_2 N$ and $N/2$ for different values of N:

N	$\log_2 N$	$N/2$	$(N/2)/\log_2 N$
100	7	50	7
500	9	250	27
1,000	10	500	50
5,000	13	2,500	192
10,000	14	5,000	357

The last column shows how many times greater $N/2$ is than $\log_2 N$. As is evident, the significance of using binary search becomes greater as the size of the array increases. In going from 5,000 to 10,000 elements, although the cost of a sequential search doubles, the cost of a binary search increases by a small fraction, 1/13.

11.4 Finding the Index of an Extreme

Chapter 10 presented several loop patterns for finding extremes. In those examples, our goal was to obtain an extreme value. Suppose, however, we have an array, z, of Strings and we want a method that returns the *index* of the "smallest" String—smallest in the sense of the alphabetical order, for example, "elephant" is smaller than "mouse":

```
int getSmallest(String z[]) {
    if (v==null || z.length==0)
        return -1;
    ... rest of the method goes here ...
}
```

We adopt the same convention that we used in search() previously: We return –1 if no extreme can be found—either because the array doesn't exist or because it has no elements.

Informal Procedure

To complete the method, we examine elements in successive positions, remembering the index of the smallest one encountered so far. We start at position 1, with the element in position 0 considered the smallest—so far. We stop when all positions have been examined.

Choosing and Defining Variables

We need two integer variables—one to store the index of the next element to examine and the other to hold the index of the smallest element that we know of.

```
int     k;      // Index of next element to examine; all elements at positions
                //    less than k have been examined already.
int     small;  // Index of smallest element that we know of
```

The while Condition

We stop when we have examined all the elements, that is, when k==z.length):

```
while (k!=z.length) {
    ...
}
// k==z.length
```

At this point, small is the index of the smallest element in the array and can be returned:

```
return  small;
```

Initializing Variables

Before the loop, we write

```
k  =  1;
small  =  0;
```

Although we never actually examined the element at position 0, when k is 1 and only one position (0) is in question, that position contains the smallest (and for that matter the largest) element. Hence, we set small to 0.

Guaranteeing Termination

In the loop body, we write

```
k++;
```

Completing the Loop Body

To preserve the meaning of small, before incrementing k we must compare the String at position k with the smallest one encountered so far:

```
String current  =  (String)  z[k];
String  smallest  =  (String)  z[small];
if  (current.compareTo(smallest)<0)
    small  =  k;
```

Putting all the pieces together, we have

```
// Returns the index of the smallest element in z or -1 if none exist
int  getSmallest(String z[])  {
    if  (z==null  ||  z.length==0)
        return -1;
    int    k;        // Index of next element to examine; all elements at
                     //      positions less than k have been examined already.
    int    small;    // Index of smallest element examined so far
    k  =  1;
    small  =  0;
    while  (k!=z.length)  {
        String current  =  (String)  z[k];
        String  smallest  =  (String)  z[small];
        if  (current.compareTo(smallest)<0)
            small  =  k;
```

```
        k++;
    }
    // k==z.length
    return small;
}
```

11.5 Sorting

The binary search is a powerful, efficient search algorithm, but it requires that the array be sorted. What if the data that are read and placed in the array are not sorted? In that case, we need to sort the array ourselves. That means that we have to rearrange the references in the array.

A sorted array has the following properties that we will make use of:

- First, given any two integers, j and k, where j<k and where both identify positions of elements within the array, the element at position j will be less than or equal to the element at position k.
- Phrased more formally, if we have integers j and k where $0 <= j < k < z.length$, z[j] is less than or equal to z[k].
- Any element that appears before position k is less than or equal to any element that appears after position k.

There are dozens of sorting algorithms—we will use one of the simplest, the **selection sort**. The basic idea of this sort is given in the informal procedure discussed below.

Informal Procedure

Given an array z of *n* elements, we take the following steps:

- *Put the correct element in position 0.* Find the position of the smallest of the *n* elements in positions 0 through *n* – 1 and exchange the element in that position with the element in position 0. (At that point, position 0 is taken care of because it has the smallest of the elements.)
- *Put the correct element in position 1.* Find the position of the smallest of the *n* – 1 remaining elements in positions 1 through *n* – 1 and exchange the element in that position with the element in position 1. (At that point, positions 0 and 1 are taken care of and contain, in sorted order, the two smallest elements.)
- *Put the correct element in position 2.* Find the position of the smallest of the *n* – 2 remaining elements in positions 2 through *n* – 1 and exchange the element in that position with the element in position 2. (At that point, positions 0, 1, and 2 are taken care of and contain, in sorted order, the three smallest elements.)

- *Continue doing this until position $n - 2$ has been given the correct element.* At that point position $n - 1$ must contain the largest element because all the smaller ones were placed in positions $0, \ldots, n - 2$.

Figure 11.11 shows the changes an array of names undergoes as a result of this procedure.

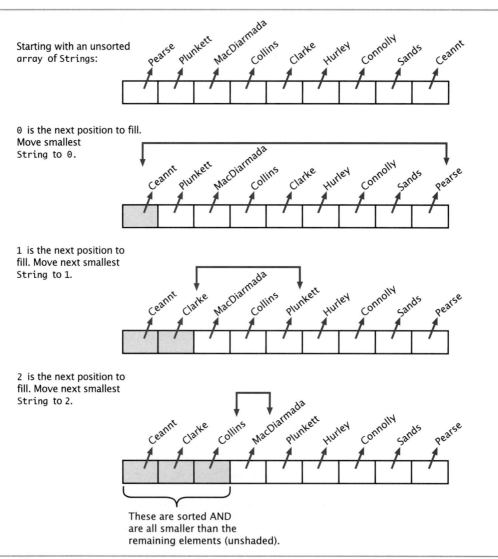

Starting with an unsorted array of Strings:

Pearse Plunkett MacDiarmada Collins Clarke Hurley Connolly Sands Ceannt

0 is the next position to fill. Move smallest String to 0.

Ceannt Plunkett MacDiarmada Collins Clarke Hurley Connolly Sands Pearse

1 is the next position to fill. Move next smallest String to 1.

Ceannt Clarke MacDiarmada Collins Plunkett Hurley Connolly Sands Pearse

2 is the next position to fill. Move next smallest String to 2.

Ceannt Clarke Collins MacDiarmada Plunkett Hurley Connolly Sands Pearse

These are sorted AND are all smaller than the remaining elements (unshaded).

Figure 11.11 The state of an array after three steps in the selection sort. The shaded elements are those that have been sorted. Each step extends this group by one element.

Choosing and Defining Variables

We need to keep track of the position we are up to, and so we will need an integer variable, which we will call k. The position that k refers to divides the array into two regions:

```
int k;    // k== the index of the next position in the array to take care of.
          // All elements to the left of k are less than or equal to the
          //    elements at k or to the right of k.
          // All elements to the left of k are in ascending order.
```

For convenience, we also have a variable, n, which we will set to the size of the array:

```
int n=z.length;        // n== number of elements in the array.
```

Skeleton of the Code

We write

```
private void sort(String z[])   { // On return, the elements of z are
                                  //      sorted in ascending order.
    int k;            // k== the index of the next position in the array to
                      //    take care of.
                      // All elements to the left of k are less than or equal
                      //    to the elements at k or to the right of k.
                      // All elements to the left of k are in ascending order.
    int n=z.length; // n== number of elements in the array.
    ...
    while (condition)
        body
    ...
}
```

(See Figure 11.12.)

Figure 11.12
The significance of the index in the simple selection sort. All the elements of the index lower than k (shaded boxes) are sorted and are less than or equal to the elements at position k or beyond (unshaded).

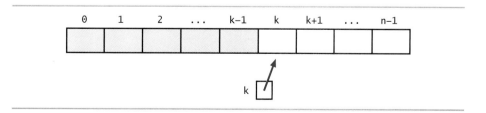

The while Condition

We are finished when the object in the next position to take care of is the last one, $n - 1$.

```
while  (k!=n-1)
     body
// k==n-1 and therefore elements 0, ..., n-2 are sorted; but because these
// elements are also less than the element in position n-1 (the last element), the
// entire array is sorted.
```

Initialization

The definition of k indicates that it is the index of the next position to take care of. Our informal procedure tells us that in the beginning this must be 0:

```
k = 0;
```

Guaranteeing Termination

By incrementing k by 1 in the loop body, we know that eventually k will equal $n - 1$.

```
k=0;
while  (k!=n-1) {
     process
     k++;
}
// k==n-1 and therefore elements 0, ..., n-2 are sorted; but because these
// elements are also less than the element in position n-1 (the last element), the
// entire array is sorted.
```

Completing the Loop Body

Before we increment k, however, we must make sure that position k is given the smallest of the elements in positions k, ..., n–1. Finding the smallest elements in a subportion of an array is a task by itself. We will use a helper method, get-Smallest(), that is a slight modification of the getSmallest() method we wrote earlier.

This method will return the index of the smallest element of z from position k forward:

```
int    j  =  getSmallest(z,k);
```

This is in contrast to the earlier version that returns the index of the smallest element from position 0 forward.

Once we have that index, we can use an exchange() method to swap elements j and k:

```
private void  exchange(String z[],  int  k,  int  j)  {
    String temp = z[k];
    z[k] = z[j]
    z[j] = temp;
}
```

The sort() method then becomes

```
private void sort(String z[]) {  // On return, the elements of z are
                                 //     sorted in ascending order.
    int k;              // k== the index of the next position in the array
                        //     to take care of.
                        // All elements to the left of k are less than or
                        //     equal to the elements at k or to the right of k.
                        // All elements to the left of k are in ascending
                        //     order.
    int n=z.length;  // n== number of elements in the array.
    k = 0;
    while  (k!=n-1)  {
        int j  =  getSmallest(z,k);
        exchange(z,k,j);
        k++;
    }
    // k==n-1 and therefore elements 0, ..., n-2 are sorted; but because
    //     these elements are also less than the element in position n-1 (the
    //     last element), the entire array is sorted.
}
```

The Modified getSmallest() Method

The original method searched for the smallest method from position 0 forward. So k now plays the role of 0 and k+1, the role of 1; that is, at the outset, the smallest element we know of is at position k and the next position to examine is k+1:

```
// Returns the index of the smallest element in z or –1 if none exist
private int  getSmallest(String z[],  int  k)  {
    if  (z==null  ||  z.length==k)
        return  -1;
    int    i;        // Index of next element to examine; all elements at positions
                     //     less than k have been examined already.
    int    small;  // Index of smallest element examined so far
    i  =  k+1;
    small  =  k;
    while  (i!=z.length)  {
        String current  =  (String)  z[i];
        String  smallest  =  (String)  z[small];
```

```
        if  (current.compareTo(smallest)<0)
            small  =  i;
        i++;
    }
    //  i==z.length
    return small;
}
```

Efficiency

A quick look at the sort() method tells us that $n - 1$ steps are carried out. However, these steps include the invocation of the getSmallest() method. This method searches positions k through $n - 1$ for the smallest element. To do that, every one of the k through $n - 1$ positions must be checked, for $n - k$ positions in all. When k is small, this is a big number, close to n; when k is large, that is, close to $n - 1$, this is a small number.

Over the course of the sort, k ranges from 0 to $n - 2$. So the number of elements checked in search of the smallest is shown in the following table:

WHEN k IS	NUMBER CHECKED IS
0	n
1	$n - 1$
2	$n - 2$
...	...
$n - 4$	4
$n - 3$	3
$n - 2$	2

How big is $2+3+4+...+(n - 2)+(n - 1)+(n)$? The answer is $\frac{(n)(n+1)}{2} - 1$. If n is large, this value is approximately $n^2/2$. This analysis shows that the number of steps needed to carry out this sort is proportional to n^2, where n is the number of elements in the collection. This is a terrible state of affairs. Suppose the collection doubles in size. In place of n we have $2n$; and $(2n)^2$ equals $4n^2$; four times the cost of sorting the original collection.

Although we would anticipate that doubling the size of our collection could easily double the time it takes to sort it, quadrupling the time for sorting seems quite unfair and prohibitive. Fortunately, there are more efficient (but more complicated) sorting algorithms that are much faster than the one presented here.

11.6 Searching Files

Searches are not only carried out on arrays or collections such as Vectors. Searching one or more files is quite common. We'll take a quick look at file searching in this section by considering a simple problem.

Write a program, FileSearch, that takes two or more command-line arguments. The first argument is some search String. The second argument is the name of a file containing plain text. The program searches the file to see whether the search String appears anywhere in the file. If there are additional arguments, they are also assumed to be the names of files to be searched. The program prints the names of the files in which the search String is found.

Suppose for example, we have two files, file1 and file2, whose contents are as follows:

file1:

```
Where was the first computer built? In
the U.S. or the U.K.?
```

file2:

```
1 half gallon milk
dozen bagels, assorted but no "salt"
cream cheese (1/3 less fat)
coffee beans (regular, not flavored)
```

Given these two files, if we were to invoke the FileSearch program,

```
java FileSearch regul file1 file2
```

the output would be

```
file2
```

because the search String here ("regul") appears in file2 but not in file1.

We start by sketching our application class—that is the class that will provide the main method—focusing on defining the roles played by the command-line arguments:

```java
import java.io.*;

public class FileSearch {
    public static void main(String[] args) throws Exception {
        String pattern = args[0];        // The pattern to search for
        Now search for the String pattern in each of the
        files named by args[1] ... args[args.length–1]
    }
}
```

We now need to traverse the elements of the args array. This is similar to traversing the elements of a Vector (see Chapter 9); the difference lies only in how we access the elements (indices) and how we determine the number of elements (length instead of size()):

```
// search files args[1], args[2], ... args[args.length–1]
for (int i=1; i<args.length; i++) {
    Search for pattern in the file whose name is args[i]
    if the pattern is found, print the name of the file
}
```

In this code we initialized the index variable, i, to be 1 instead of 0 so that we would not treat args[0] as one of the filenames.

To implement the body of the loop, we need to search a file for a pattern and determine whether the search was successful. We propose therefore to define a class that provides this behavior. Calling this class FileSearcher and using the most natural words for its method names, we can write the loop body as follows:

```
FileSearcher fs = new FileSearcher(args[i]);
fs.search(pattern);
if (fs.found())
    System.out.println(args[i]);
```

We create a FileSearcher object, telling the constructor the name of the file to search (the FileSearcher object will certainly need to know the name of the file). We then send it a search() message with pattern as an argument. Then we ask the object whether the pattern was found(). We will have to implement the FileSearcher class, but we have at least completed the FileSearch application class:

```java
import java.io.*;

public class FileSearch {
    public static void main(String[] args) throws Exception {
        String pattern = args[0];        // The pattern to search for
        // search files args[1], args[2], ... args[args.length–1]
        for (int i=1; i<args.length; i++) {
            FileSearcher fs = new FileSearcher(args[i]);
            fs.search(pattern);
            if (fs.found())
                System.out.println(args[i]);
        }
    }
}
```

Implementing the FileSearcher Class

The use of the FileSearcher class in the FileSearch class's main() method defines the interface of the class. We see that we must provide a constructor that gets as an argument the name of the file to be searched, a search() method that gets as an argument the pattern to be searched for and returns nothing, and a predicate method found() that returns true or false, depending on whether the pattern was found:

```
import java.io.*;

public class FileSearcher {
    public FileSearcher(String filename) {
    }
    public void search(String pattern) throws Exception {
    }
    public boolean found() {
    }
}
```

Identifying the instance variables here is a matter of recognizing what information needs to be preserved from one method to another. The constructor gets the file-name as an argument, but it is the search() method that is going to need that information when it creates a BufferedReader to actually read the file. So we will have an instance variable, filename, that will maintain that information. Similarly, the search() method does the searching and will therefore discover whether the pattern has been found or not, but it is the found() method that needs to access that information so it can return true or false accordingly. So we will have an instance variable, foundIt, that maintains that information. With this in mind we can declare the instance variables, and complete the constructor and the found() method:

```
import java.io.*;

public class FileSearcher {
    public FileSearcher(String filename) {
        this.filename = filename;
    }
    public void search(String pattern) throws Exception {
        use filename to create a BufferedReader
        read from that BufferedReader, looking for pattern
        set foundIt to be true or false, accordingly
    }
    public boolean found() { return foundIt; }
    private String  filename;
    private boolean foundIt;
}
```

Now, all that remains is implementing the body of the search() method: looking for a pattern in a file that we are reading from a BufferedReader. Our strategy for looking for a String in the file is to read the file, line by line, and in each line use the indexOf() method of String to see whether our pattern is in the file. We will know when we've reached the end of the file when the BufferedReader returns null.

This is a problem and the plan is identical to the sequential search we developed in the beginning of the chapter. The differences lie only in how the elements being searched are accessed (through readLine() messages, not array indices) and how the end of the search is recognized (by getting null back from the BufferedReader instead of comparing an index with the length of the array). Thus, we can write

```java
String line = br.readLine();
while (line!=null && line.indexOf(pattern)==-1)
    line = br.readLine();
foundIt = line!=null;
```

In the last line, we exploit the fact that if line really is null, then we've read through the entire file without indexOf() returning any value other than –1. This would mean that pattern was never found in any of the lines of the file. So the truth value of line!=null is the value we need to assign to foundIt(). If line!=null (is true) then the loop terminated before reaching the end of the file and so foundIt() is assigned true.

We can complete the the definition of the search() method by creating the BufferedReader from the filename instance variable. The complete class definition for FileSearcher then is:

```java
import java.io.*;

public class FileSearcher {
    public FileSearcher(String filename) {
        this.filename = filename;
    }
    public void search(String pattern) throws Exception {
        BufferedReader br = new BufferedReader(
                new InputStreamReader(
                new FileInputStream(filename)));
        String line = br.readLine();
        while (line!=null && line.indexOf(pattern)==-1)
            line = br.readLine();
        foundIt = line!=null;
        br.close();
    }
    public String getFileName() { return filename; }
    public boolean found() { return foundIt; }
    private String  filename;
    private boolean foundIt;
}
```

11.7 Threads: Computing in Parallel

Much of the time when we program, we consciously ignore the underlying nature of the computer and focus, appropriately, on building a logical, elegant, and efficient solution. Sometimes, however, additional efficiency can by obtained by awareness of machine architecture. In particular, many modern computers are capable of executing more than one sequence of instructions simultaneously. These computers can do this because they contain multiple processing units (or processors), each of which can execute a program independently and in parallel to the other processors. This presents the software developer with an interesting opportunity: orchestrate the processors to make the application run faster. Let's take a look at a couple of human analogies and then explore Java's tools for parallel processing.

Consider the chefs working in the kitchen for a large restaurant. Each of them has a recipe and is following it while the others do the same. The chefs don't wait for each other to finish a task—they are all working simultaneously. If the restaurant is quite large, there may be times when more than one chef is following the same recipe for different customers.

Now consider a football team. When play starts, each member is following a set of instructions, given by the coach or the captain. We see that when there is more than one task to carry out at a time, it is commonplace to have several people working, each following the instructions to handle a single task.

The same is true in programming. Let's start with a definition: a **thread** is the process of carrying out a set of instructions one at a time. Using this term in the above examples, we might see that each chef or football player is a separate thread carrying out his or her own set of instructions. These examples involve multiple threads, more than one chef or player. In contrast, the programs that we have written and worked with in the non-GUI parts of this book have all consisted of a single thread. This has worked out because they only had to perform a single task at a time.

However, programs are often required to carry out more than one task at the same time. For example, a multimedia application might need to perform the following tasks simultaneously:

- Play background music
- Display a sequence of images
- Scroll text that explains the images

This application might employ three threads, one for each of these tasks.

As another example of an application that benefits from more than one thread, consider a web browser such as Netscape Navigator. Suppose you are using Navigator and you click on a link to load in a new page. While Navigator is finding the source of the new page and establishing a connection, you can still scroll through the old page, type a new URL in the locator bar, or click the stop button to abort the new page. Navigator here is carrying out at least two tasks at once:

- Network input/output—accessing the new page
- Responding to controls (the stop button, the scroll bar, and so on)

The application we have been working on in the previous section involved searching files for the presence of a String. In that case, we could imagine two or more threads dividing the work—each thread taking the responsibility for searching some, but not all, of the files.

Introducing the Thread **Class**

Java provides a class, called Thread, that models threads and allows us to build applications and applets in which more than one thread is at work. Using this class, we can create Thread objects that are associated with a particular piece of code that we want to execute as a thread, simultaneously with other threads. In the multimedia example, we might have one Thread object that executes the code to play music, a second Thread object that executes the code to display a sequence of images, and a third Thread object that executes the code that scrolls text. Each Thread object will execute its code at the same time as the other Thread objects and therefore carry out its task simultaneously.

Simultaneity and Concurrency

Simultaneity—literally carrying out instructions from different codes at exactly the same time—is not possible on the majority of desktops at this time. This does not mean, however, that we cannot use threads in our programs. The Java Interpreter, which implements the Java Virtual Machine, repeatedly cycles through the various threads in a given program, doing a bit of work on each thread before going to the next. In doing so, it simulates simultaneity. Thus, we can use Java Threads to design our application as if they were multiple, simultaneously executing codes, and the Java Interpreter does all the work of making these codes execute not simultaneously but concurrently—running in an interwoven fashion, overlapped in time. If implemented correctly, the concurrent execution of these codes can be made to appear as if it were simultaneous execution.

Interweaving code is done quite differently from one desktop machine to the next. As a result, applications using Threads on these machines may vary considerably in their time-dependent behavior.

Threads considerably expand the opportunities available to the programmer. Without Threads, our code carries out a single task at a time. It is like a band that consists of a single musician, say a bass player, just playing a bass line. With Threads, our program can carry out multiple tasks simultaneously (or at least concurrently). It's as if the one-player band can now acquire a drummer, rhythm and lead guitarists, a saxophonist, and several vocalists.

The Thread class provides a method, start(), that starts the execution of the Thread. Until this method is invoked, the Thread may exist as an object, but the code it is associated with—the code that we want to execute simultaneously—has not yet started executing.

Here is a simple example of a non-GUI application that creates two Threads and starts them executing:

```
class DoNothingThreadExample {
    public static void main(String[] a) {
        Thread t1 = new Thread();
        Thread t2 = new Thread();
        t1.start();
        t2.start();
    }
}
```

If we run this program, nothing happens—the program terminates almost immediately. That's because the code that a Thread object executes by default is empty, so it completes immediately and does nothing. To make a Thread object that does something useful, we need to define our own customized Thread class:

```
class SimpleCounter extends Thread {
    rest of the definition
}
```

The clause "extends Thread" will be explained in the next chapter. We then provide the class with a method called run() with the following prototype:

```
public void run()
```

It is the run() method that contains the code that the Thread object executes simultaneously. The run() method defines the customized actions our Thread is to carry out.

A Simple Thread Example

In this example, the code our Thread executes just prints out integers, starting from 0, incremented by a quantity given in the constructor:

```
class CountingThread extends Thread {
    public CountingThread(int x) {
        this.x = x;
```

```
        }
    public void run() {
        int     i=0;
        while (i<15) {
            System.out.println(i);
                i+=x;
        }
    }
    private int x;
}
```

The code below creates two `CountingThread` objects, with different increments (2 and 3), and starts each object executing:

```
class CountingThreadExample {
    public static void main(String a[]) {
        CountingThread  t1 = new CountingThread(2);
        CountingThread t2 = new CountingThread(3);
        t1.start();
        t2.start();
    }
}
```

The output of this program on a typical desktop computer depends on the way the Java Interpreter interweaves the two executing Threads. The Java rules give it quite a bit of leeway in this regard. In fact, a likely output is

```
0
2
4
6
8
10
12
14
0
3
6
9
12
```

There is no interweaving at all. The rules of the Java interpreter require that if an executing Thread object becomes temporarily unable to proceed (for example, it is waiting for input or is temporarily suspended), any Thread that is able to execute will then do so.

We can force our Thread objects to become temporarily unable to proceed by making them *sleep*—that is, suspend their own execution for a time that we specify. The Java code that does this is

```
try {
    sleep(35);        Suspend my execution for 35 milliseconds.
} catch(Exception e) {}
```

The extra syntax here (try...catch) is unfortunate but necessary. Its meaning, which we can ignore for now, will be made clear in Chapter 13.

Using this feature to suspend execution for 1 millisecond after each increment of i, we rewrite the run() method of CountingThread as follows:

```
public void run() {
    int     i=0;
    while (i<15) {
        System.out.println(i);
        i+=x;
        try {
            sleep(1);
        } catch(Exception e) {}
    }
}
```

Executing the program now, the output is

```
0
0
2
3
4
6
6
9
8
12
10
12
14
```

and the interweaving is apparent.

11.8 Threads: A Parallel File Search

Returning to our problem of file searching, we may decide to create a different thread for each file we are asked to search. This way, if there are enough processors on our machine, each file can be searched in parallel. Our first requirement is to define a Thread class that will take the responsibility for doing one, and exactly one, search. We will therefore need to define two methods:

- A constructor, which will save the essential information of the search in some instance variable
- A run() method, which will be executed (in parallel) once we send the Thread object a start message.

```java
import java.io.*;

public class SearcherThread extends Thread {
    public SearcherThread(FileSearcher fs, String pattern) {
        this.fs = fs;
        this.pattern = pattern;
    }
    public void run() {
        try {
            fs.search(pattern);
            if (fs.found())
                System.out.println(fs.getFileName());
        } catch (Exception e) {}
    }
    private FileSearcher    fs;
    private String          pattern;
}
```

We need a constructor here to save the references to the FileSearcher object and the String pattern because we are not allowed to pass arguments to the run() method—in fact, we never directly invoke the run() method; it is only executed when we send a start() message to the Thread. The constructor saves its two arguments in instance variables so that the run() method will be able to access the FileSearch and the pattern.

The run() method itself just carries out the work that the main() method in FileSearch used to do: sends a search message (with the pattern) to the FileSearcher object (fs) and then queries the object to see if the pattern was found, in which case it prints out the file's name.

Because the FileSearch object carries out input/output, we would normally have to add a "throws Exception" clause to the definition of run(). However, in creating our customized Thread classes, we are not allowed to change the signature of run() in any way—it must be "public void run()" with no throws clause. For that reason, we surround the body of the method with a "try … catch" clause. This is explained in Chapter 13 in more detail, but here it essentially means that we will ignore any exceptions (problems) that arise in input/output.

Now we can revise our FileSearch program to create a thread object for each file to be searched:

```java
import java.io.*;

public class FileSearch {
    public static void main(String[] args) throws Exception {
        String pattern = args[0];
        for (int i=1; i<args.length; i++) {
            FileSearcher fs = new FileSearcher(args[i]);
            SearcherThread searcher =
                    new SearcherThread(fs, pattern);
            searcher.start();
        }
    }
}
```

To confirm that there really is a difference in execution speed between the two verions of FileSearch, we created two 80 megabyte files and ran the threaded and the non-threaded version of FileSearch on a two-processor Sun computer. A search through two files that took 42 seconds on in the non-threaded version took only 23 seconds in the threaded version—a fairly dramatic speedup, though nothing compared to the speedup resulting from using a binary search in place of a sequential one!

Summary

The most important applications of indexed collections are searching and sorting. By putting into the programmer's hands the ability to rearrange the order in which elements are checked in the course of a search, indexing allows a programmer to move through and rearrange the elements of an array in a way that makes searching efficient.

Searching need not be confined to searching arrays and Vectors. We have seen that it is possible to search external files. In general, wherever there is data, searching is possible and not unusual.

Finally, Java provides a Thread class that allows programmers to define threads of execution that can execute concurrently or, if there is more than one processor, in parallel. This can potentially lead to programs that execute faster.

Key Terms

binary search An algorithm for efficiently searching a sorted collection by repeatedly dividing the region where the item might be found in half and reducing consideration to one half or the other.

$\log_2 N$ The number of times one can start with N and successively divide by 2 before reaching 1. The $\log_2$ is the inverse of exponentiation with 2 as the base: If 2^x is N, $\log_2 N$ is x.

search An algorithm for finding a particular item that is stored in a collection of related values or objects.

selection sort An algorithm for sorting where one successively selects progressively ascending elements of a collection.

sequential search An algorithm for searching an indexed collection, checking the elements in the same sequence that they are stored in the collection.

thread The process of carrying out a set of instructions one at a time.

Questions for Review

1. How dos a binary search work? What special requirement does it make of the array or Vector being searched?
2. Why is a binary search so much more efficient than a sequential search?
3. Why the name "binary" search?
4. How does the selection sort work? Why the name "selection" sort?
5. What is a thread?
6. How does the Java Thread class support threads?
7. Under what conditions can Threads make a program run faster?
8. Besides speeding up programs in some circumstances, what other use do Threads have?

Exercises

1. Rewrite the search() method so that it starts its search at the end of the array and searches backward toward position 0. In doing this, start from scratch, following the approach to loop construction that we have been following. Do not try to use the search() method from the text as a starting point and then just modify it here and there. That path is error prone.
2. Write a predicate method, vContains(), that receives two arguments: a String and an array of Strings. The method returns true if the first argument matches one of the elements of the array; otherwise it returns false.

3. Write a method, vSearch(), that receives two arguments: Each is an array of Strings. The method returns the index of a String in the first array that matches an element of the second array. Use the vContains() method you wrote in the previous exercise.

4. The binary search loop in the binary search method can be sped up slightly if we assign m+1 to left and m–1 to right. Would these assignments violate the requirement that left<right? Use the inequality

   left < left+1 <= m <= right–1 < right

   to guide your answer and rewrite the method with the improvements that don't violate the requirement that left<right.

5. In our development of the binary search we made the following definitions of left and right:

   int   left, right;
                    // If the String is anywhere, it is in positions left through right–1.
                    // The String is not in a position before left.
                    // The String is not in a position after right–1.

   Redevelop the binary search from scratch, using the following definitions of left and right:

   int   left, right;
                    // If the String is anywhere, it is in positions left through right.
                    // The String is not in a position before left.
                    // The String is not in a position after right.

   (right–1 has been replaced by right.)

6. What must be changed in getSmallest() to transform it to getLargest()—a method that returns the largest element in an array?

7. Write a method getSecondSmallest() that returns the index of the second smallest element or, if none exists, –1.

8. Write the definition for the following method

   private int   getSmallest(Vector v,   int k)

   that receives a Vector of Strings and returns the index of the smallest (alphabetically) String among those stored in v[k] through the end of the array.

9. Show that $1+2+3+\ldots+(n-2)+(n-1)+(n)$ equals $(n)(n+1)/2$. Use this trick: Assume that n is even and pair 1 with n, 2 with $n-1$, 3 with $n-2$, and so forth. What is the sum of each of these pairs? How many pairs are there? What is the total? Now address the case where n is odd. Leave out n and pair 1 with $n-1$, 2 with $n-2$, 3 with $n-3$, and so forth. What is the sum of each pair? How many pairs are there? Taking into account n, what is the total?

10. Write a method called fixOnePair() as follows. The method receives an array of Strings as a parameter. It searches the array for an adjacent pair of Strings that are out of order. If it finds none, it returns false. When it does find a pair, it exchanges the elements so that they are in (ascending) order and returns true.

11. Write a method called sort() as follows. The method receives an array of Strings as a parameter and returns nothing. It sorts the array by repeatedly calling fixOnePair() (from the previous exercise) until it returns false.

12. Compare the sort developed in the previous two exercises with the selection sort developed earlier in the chapter. Under what circumstances would one be more efficient than the other? Explain.

13. Write a program that gets two Strings as arguments, followed by a list of file-names. In each of the files indicated, the program replaces every occurence of the first String with the second String. Write a non-threaded and a threaded version of this program.

Threads

Consider the applet shown in Figure 11.13, which consists of a Canvas and a single button. Initially, the button's label is "start." When the user clicks the button the label changes to "stop," the applet's paint() method is invoked, and an alternating sequence of red and green rectangles is drawn on the Canvas.

The button changes to "stop" and an alternating sequence of red and green rectangles is drawn.

When the user clicks the button again, the label should change to "start" and the paint() method should cease to draw:

```
import java.awt.*;
import java.awt.event.*;
import java.applet.*;
public class RedGreen extends Applet implements ActionListener{
    public void init() {
        setLayout(new BorderLayout(2,2));
        b = new Button("start");
        b.addActionListener(this);
        c = new Canvas();
        add("West",b);
        add("East",c);
        c.setSize(100,50);
    }
    public void paint(Graphics g) {
        Graphics gc = c.getGraphics();
        while (keepGoing) {
            gc.setColor(new Color(200,50,50));
            gc.fillRect(5,5,90,40);
```

Figure 11.13

The RedGreen applet after the start button has been clicked. The button changes to "stop" and an alternating sequence of red and green rectangles is drawn.

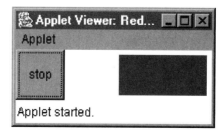

481

```
            gc.setColor(new Color(50,200,50));
            gc.fillRect(5,5,90,40);
        }
    }
    public void actionPerformed(ActionEvent ae) {
        String s = ae.getActionCommand();
        if (s.equals("start"))
            handleStart();
        else if (s.equals("stop"))
            handleStop();
    }
    private void handleStart() {
        keepGoing = true;
        b.setLabel("stop");
    }
    private void handleStop() {
        keepGoing = false;
        b.setLabel("start");
    }
    private Button   b;
    private Canvas   c;
    private boolean keepGoing=false;
}
```

If we run this applet and click the start button, the paint() method is invoked and a sequence of red and green rectangles is rapidly drawn. However, clicking the stop button elicits no response. The applet does not work properly.

The problem here is that the applet is written as a single thread—only one sequence of instructions is being executed at a time. Once paint() is entered and its while loop starts executing, there is no chance for actionPerformed() to execute and therefore no way that keepGoing can be made false again—the loop executes forever.

In this example there really are two tasks that must be carried out concurrently:

- Drawing the rectangles on the Canvas
- Responding to the user's actions

Building the applet to use two threads instead of one is a good way to address this.

The RedGreen Applet with Threads

Let's use our thread technology to fix the RedGreen applet that we considered earlier. As we pointed out, there are two tasks:

- Drawing the rectangles on the `Canvas`
- Responding to the user's actions

If we make a separate thread for drawing that runs concurrently with the applet itself, the applet will be free to respond properly to button clicks. To do this, we define another class, a `RedGreenThread` class, extended from `Thread`. Its `run()` method will contain code that is similar to that of the earlier applet's `paint()` method. However, we will make the loop condition always `true` so that the thread never terminates as long as the applet is running. We also add a 50-millisecond `sleep` to the loop to improve the appearance of the alternating colors. Our first draft of this class is as follows:

```
class RedGreenThread extends Thread {
    RedGreenThread(Canvas c) {
        this.c = c;
    }
    public void run() {
        Graphics gc = c.getGraphics();
        while (true) {
            gc.setColor(new Color(200,50,50));
            gc.fillRect(5,5,90,40);
            try {
                sleep(50);
            } catch(Exception e) {}
            gc.setColor(new Color(50,200,50));
            gc.fillRect(5,5,90,40);
            try {
                sleep(50);
            } catch(Exception e) {}
        }
    }
    private Canvas c;
}
```

The applet will create the `Canvas` and add it to its display. It will have to pass a reference to it to the `RedGreenThread` constructor so that the `run()` method can display rectangles on it.

We need to provide a way for the applet to suspend and resume execution of this thread. The `Thread` class provides `resume()` and `suspend()` methods. However, for security reasons, applets are not allowed to directly suspend, resume, or stop other threads (you wouldn't want to download some stranger's applet onto your machine and have it start suspending other threads on your browser, would you?). We can, however, provide our own version of these methods. They can set a `boolean` instance variable, `amRunning`, to `true` or `false`, and we can use this variable to control whether any painting actually gets done:

```
class RedGreenThread extends Thread {
    RedGreenThread(Canvas c) {
        this.c = c;
    }
    public void run() {
        Graphics gc = c.getGraphics();
        amRunning = true;
        while (true)
            if (amRunning) {
                gc.setColor(new Color(200,50,50));
                gc.fillRect(5,5,90,40);
                try {
                    sleep(50);
                } catch(Exception e) {}
                gc.setColor(new Color(50,200,50));
                gc.fillRect(5,5,90,40);
                try {
                    sleep(50);
                } catch(Exception e) {}
            }
    }
    public void mySuspend() {
        amRunning=false;
    }
    public void myResume() {
        amRunning=true;
    }
    private Canvas c;
    private boolean amRunning=false;
}
```

The `RedGreen` applet can then be rewritten using this class. The `paint()` method is no longer needed because the red and green squares are constantly being redrawn by the `run()` method in our thread. When the start button is clicked, the button's label is changed to stop, and the thread is created and started. When the stop button is clicked, the label is changed to resume, and the thread is suspended. When the resume button is clicked, the thread is resumed and the button label changed back to stop. (See Figure 11.14.) The actions for resume and stop now are taken in terms of the `RedGreenThread`:

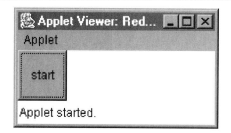

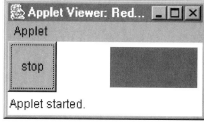

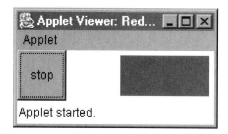

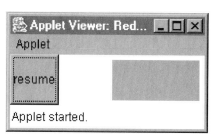

Figure 11.14
Threaded version of RedGreen. Using a separate thread for painting allows the applet user to start, stop, and resume the alternation of red and green images.

```java
import java.awt.event.*;
import java.applet.*;

public class RedGreen extends Applet implements ActionListener {
    public void init() {
        setLayout(new BorderLayout(2,2));
        b = new Button("start");
        b.addActionListener(this);
        c = new Canvas();
        add("West",b);
        add("East",c);
        c.setSize(100,50);
    }
    public void actionPerformed(ActionEvent ae) {
        String s = ae.getActionCommand();
        if (s.equals("start"))
            handleStart();
        else if (s.equals("resume"))
            handleResume();
        else if (s.equals("stop"))
            handleStop();
    }
    private void handleStart() {
        b.setLabel("stop");
```

```
            rgt = new RedGreenThread(c);
            rgt.start();
        }
        private void handleResume() {
            b.setLabel("stop");
            rgt.myResume();
        }
        private void handleStop() {
            b.setLabel("resume");
            rgt.mySuspend();
        }
        private Button           b;
        private Canvas           c;
        private RedGreenThread   rgt=null;
}
```

Note that in the course of using this applet, many `RedGreenThread` threads may be created, one for each time the start button is clicked.

Multiple Clocks: A More Elaborate Example

We close this supplement with one more example of a thread-based applet. The applet shown in Figure 11.15 displays two digital clocks, each with its own start/stop button. One clock displays eastern standard time (EST), the other Greenwich mean time (GMT).

The architecture of this applet is essentially identical to the threaded RedGreen applet above. There are two classes, `ClockApplet` and `ClockAppletThread`. For each clock, the `ClockApplet`'s `init()` method creates a button for control and a `Label` for display. The `init()` method goes through the usual gyrations to place these components properly. In addition, it sets the applet up as a listener for action events associated with the buttons. The `actionPerformed()` method of the

Figure 11.15
A multiple clock applet. This applet displays time in two time zones: EST and GMT. Each clock has its own start and stop buttons. Once started, the time is updated constantly and displayed in hours/minutes/seconds and hundredths of seconds.

Before clicking Start:

After clicking Start for EST and Start and Stop for GMT:

ClockApplet determines the event that occurred and invokes the handleStart() or handleStop() helper method accordingly, passing an int argument to indicate which clock the event was associated with. These methods relabel the relevant button so that start becomes stop, stop becomes resume, and resume becomes stop. In addition, the handleStart() method creates and starts a ClockThread object, associating it with the appropriate Label and giving it a String indicating the time zone (GMT or EST). The handleStop() method simply invokes the mySuspend() method of the appropriate ClockThread object. The handleResume() method invokes the myResume() method. All this is analogous to the RedGreen applet that we studied above.

The ClockAppletThread's constructor stores its parameter values, a reference to the Label for the clock and a String representing the time zone, in its instance variables. The run(), mySuspend(), and myResume() methods and the boolean instance variable amRunning all play the same roles that they did in the RedGreenThread above.

The actual work done by the run() method is repeated invocations of the helper method oneTick(), which models a single tick of the clock. This method makes use of the GregorianCalendar and TimeZone classes that Java provides. The remainder of oneTick() builds the needed display String for the time using the integers extracted from the GregorianCalendar object. To handle the case of single-digit hours, minutes, and seconds it uses the leadingDigit() helper method.

The Complete Applet

Here is the complete code for the ClockApplet:

```java
import java.util.*;
import java.awt.*;
import java.awt.event.*;
import java.applet.*;
public class ClockApplet extends Applet implements ActionListener {
    public void init() {
        Color backgroundColor = new Color(200,255,255);
        setLayout(new FlowLayout(FlowLayout.CENTER,4,1));
        clock1 = new Label("EST: 00:00:00.00", Label.CENTER);
        clock2 = new Label("GMT: 00:00:00.00", Label.CENTER);
        clock1Button = new Button(start1ButtonCommand);
        clock1Button.addActionListener(this);
        clock2Button = new Button(start2ButtonCommand);
        clock2Button.addActionListener(this);
        clock1Panel = new Panel();
        clock1Panel.setLayout(new BorderLayout(2,2));
        clock2Panel = new Panel();
        clock2Panel.setLayout(new BorderLayout(2,2));
        clock1Panel.add("West",clock1Button);
```

```java
        clock1Panel.add("East",clock1);
        clock2Panel.add("West",clock2Button);
        clock2Panel.add("East",clock2);
        mainPanel = new Panel();
        mainPanel.setLayout(new BorderLayout(2,2));
        mainPanel.add("North",clock1Panel);
        mainPanel.add("South",clock2Panel);
        add(mainPanel);
        setBackground(backgroundColor);
    }
    public void actionPerformed(ActionEvent ae) {
        String whichButton = ae.getActionCommand();
        if (whichButton.equals(start1ButtonCommand))
            handleStart(1);
        else if (whichButton.equals(resume1ButtonCommand))
            handleResume(1);
        else if (whichButton.equals(stop1ButtonCommand))
            handleStop(1);
        else if (whichButton.equals(start2ButtonCommand))
            handleStart(2);
        else if (whichButton.equals(resume2ButtonCommand))
            handleResume(2);
        else if (whichButton.equals(stop2ButtonCommand))
            handleStop(2);
    }
    private void handleStart(int n) {
        if (n==1) {
            clock1Button.setLabel(stop1ButtonCommand);
            clockTicker1 = new ClockThread(clock1,"EST");
            clockTicker1.start();
        } else if (n==2) {
            clock2Button.setLabel(stop2ButtonCommand);
            clockTicker2 = new  ClockThread(clock2,"GMT");
            clockTicker2.start();
        }
    }
    private void handleResume(int n) {
        if (n==1) {
            clock1Button.setLabel(stop1ButtonCommand);
            clockTicker1.myResume();
        } else if (n==2) {
            clock2Button.setLabel(stop2ButtonCommand);
            clockTicker2.myResume();
```

```java
        }
    }
    private void handleStop(int n) {
        if (n==1) {
            clock1Button.setLabel(resume1ButtonCommand);
            clockTicker1.mySuspend();
        } else if (n==2) {
            clock2Button.setLabel(resume2ButtonCommand);
            clockTicker2.mySuspend();
        }
    }
    private Panel   clock1Panel,clock2Panel,mainPanel;
    private Button clock1Button,clock2Button;
    private String start1ButtonCommand= "Start EST",
                   resume1ButtonCommand= "Resume EST",
                   stop1ButtonCommand= "Stop EST",
                   start2ButtonCommand= "Start GMT",
                   resume2ButtonCommand= "Resume GMT",
                   stop2ButtonCommand= "Stop GMT";
    private Label   clock1, clock2;
    private ClockThread clockTicker1,clockTicker2;
}
class ClockThread extends Thread {
    ClockThread(Label theLabel, String timeZone) {
        this.clock = theLabel;
        this.timeZone = timeZone;
    }
    public void run() {
        amRunning = true;
        while (true)
            if (amRunning) {
                oneTick();
                try {
                    this.sleep(20);
                } catch (Exception e) { }
            }
    }
    public void mySuspend() {
        amRunning = false;
    }
    public void myResume() {
        amRunning = true;
```

```
        }
      private void oneTick() {
         GregorianCalendar gc = new GregorianCalendar(
                             TimeZone.getTimeZone(timeZone));
         int      h = gc.get(Calendar.HOUR);
         int      m = gc.get(Calendar.MINUTE);
         int      s = gc.get(Calendar.SECOND);
         int     ms= gc.get(Calendar.MILLISECOND);
         String  hms = leadingDigit(h," ") + ":" +
                       leadingDigit(m,"0") + ":" +
                       leadingDigit(s,"0") + "." +
                       leadingDigit(ms/10,"0");
         clock.setText(hms);
      }
   private String leadingDigit(int n, String leader) {
      if (n<10)
         return leader+n;
      return ""+n;
   }
   private Label    clock;
   private boolean amRunning;
   private String timeZone;
}
```

Extending Class Behavior

12.1 Introduction

U p to this point, we have developed every class starting from scratch: We explicitly defined every method and instance variable of the class, even if there might have been a class with similar methods or variables. This approach did not allow us to build on previous effort. We want the ability to define a new class by starting from an existing class and adding behavior and state to it. This new class would be an *extension* of the original.

Building a Better BufferedReader

The BufferedReader class provides a base set of behavior for reading Strings. Whenever we read a value, either from the keyboard or a disk file, we must first create a BufferedReader object. In Chapter 3 we showed how to do this, and we explained why several intermediate objects such as FileInputStream and InputStreamReader must be created in the process.

After we have a BufferedReader, we can invoke the readLine() method to read a line of text. To read an integer, however, we must first read the line, using readLine(), and then convert the returned String to an int value, using Integer.parseInt().

In both of these situations—creating the BufferedReader object and reading integers—all we are really interested in is the final product: a BufferedReader object and an int value. The intermediate steps are just a necessary annoyance.

We thus wish to transform those intermediate steps required to create the Buffered-Reader object or read an integer into behavior that can be invoked by a user; that is, we wish to turn them into methods. One possible solution is to add these methods to the existing class. For various reasons, this solution may not be appropriate:

- The class may have been rigorously tested. Adding even a single line of code (not to speak of entire methods) changes the behavior of the class and will require a full retesting of the class. Programmers often make the error of assuming that the change they are making "could not possibly affect the rest of the class." Confidence in the modified class can only result from testing that is as rigorous as the testing that was originally performed.

- Others may be using this class and not want the additional behavior, either because of performance costs or increased complexity.

- It may not be possible or advisable to modify the class. For example, modifying a Java predefined class is definitely not a recommended action. Any mistakes can affect all of your programs in strange and mysterious ways. Furthermore, the sources of the class definitions are not always available. You may be supplied with the *.class* file (the output of the Java compiler), rather than the *.java* file (the actual source text). Our example is such a case: We cannot modify the BufferedReader class.

In general, modifying an existing class, especially one we did not create, requires a full understanding of the class's implementation, and such an understanding may not be possible or practical.

Object-oriented languages such as Java provide a very powerful mechanism for the extension of class behavior. In fact, this mechanism, known as *inheritance*, is one of the crucial elements required for a language to be called object-oriented.

12.2 Extending Classes—Inheritance I

Class behavior may be extended through a process known as **inheritance**. In the following class definition

```
class BetterBR extends BufferedReader {
}
```

the keyword extends is followed by the class name BufferedReader. This defines BetterBR as a class that automatically inherits all the methods and instance variables of the BufferedReader class; that is, objects of class BetterBR possess all methods and instance variables of class BufferedReader.

This means that without even declaring a method, we have defined a new class, BetterBR, that contains a full set of behavior—the behavior inherited from BufferedReader.

We say that BufferedReader is the **superclass** of BetterBR, and BetterBR is a **subclass** of BufferedReader.

After the BetterBR class has been defined, we can use it like any other class. We can create objects of the class and invoke methods upon them. In the case of a subclass, objects of the class have available to them all the methods defined in the superclass:

```
BetterBR bbr = new BetterBR(...);      We'll talk about the constructor later.
String s = bbr.readLine();             A method inherited from BufferedReader.
```

A subclass is everything the superclass is. In our example, the BetterBR subclass contains all the behavior of the BufferedReader superclass.

If a subclass were to provide only the methods inherited from its superclass, there would be no point to the inheritance. For example, the `BetterBR` class would provide us with no behavior beyond that of the original `BufferedReader` class. However, by defining additional instance variables and methods in the subclass, we introduce new behavior, unique to the subclass:

```
class BetterBR extends BufferedReader {
    int readInt() {...}              Method unique to BetterBR.
    instance variables unique to BetterBR
}
```

Now, given the `BetterBR` reference variable `bbr` declared above, we can invoke the new methods with code such as the following:

```
int i = bbr.readInt();              Using a BetterBR method.
```

Now let's develop a `BetterBR` class that contains the additional behavior we spoke of above.

12.3 A Better BufferedReader

The following example provides an introduction to the process of inheritance.

Statement of the Problem

Create a more convenient `BufferedReader` class that possesses the following behavior:

- All the behavior of class `BufferedReader`, in particular the `readLine()` method
- The ability to create a reader object associated with a file specifying the filename only. If no filename is specified, we create a reader associated with `System.in`.
- A method that provides direct reading of `int` values

Scenario

The following is a sample scenario of using this class. Here we illustrate the intended usage of the `readLine()` method inherited from `BufferedReader`, the constructor that receives a filename argument, and the new `readInt()` method.

```
BetterBR   bbr = new BetterBR("data13");    Just the filename. The
String name = bbr.readLine();               constructor takes care of
int sales1 = bbr.readInt();                 everything else.
int sales2 = bbr.readInt();                 Inherited
System.out.println("Total sales for " + name +   New method
              " = " + sales1 + sales2);
```

Finding the Primary Object

Our problem statement provides us with the primary object, namely a smart
`BufferedReader` class. We'll name the class `BetterBR` and have it inherit from
`BufferedReader`:

```
class BetterBR extends BufferedReader {
    ...
}
```

Determining the Behavior

Our desired behavior is also obtained from the problem statement as follows:

- `BetterBR` (constructor)
- `readInt()`—Read an integer, returning it as an `int`.
- All the behavior of the `BufferedReader` class (We get that automatically
  through the inheritance process.)

Defining the Interface

We wish to be able to create a `BetterBR` object by specifying simply a filename.
Alternatively, if we specify nothing, we want the input source to be `System.in`.
We therefore overload our constructor:

```
BetterBR(String fileName) {...}
BetterBR() {...}
```

Our `readInt()` method requires no arguments and should return as its result an
`int` corresponding to the integer value read in:

```
int readInt() {...}
```

This code completes the interface of the methods introduced by the `BetterBR`
class. Again, in addition to these methods, we inherit all the functionality of the
`BufferedReader` class.

Defining the Instance Variables

Defining class `BetterBR` by extending class `BufferedReader` means that all of
`BufferedReader`'s instance variables and methods are inherited and thus become part
of any `BetterBR` object. Remember—a `BetterBR` object is a `BufferedReader` object.
We can think of no new state information for our extended behavior. However, we
may have to introduce instance variables as we implement our new methods.

Implementing the Methods

None of the behavior being implemented is unfamiliar to us. We have been creating `BufferedReader` objects from filenames or `System.in` since Chapter 3, and

reading in `int` values since Chapter 5. What is new here is the packaging of this behavior into a subclass's methods.

The Constructors

The job of a constructor is to provide a valid initial state for the newly created object. Because a `BetterBR` object is a `BufferedReader` object, we must make sure that this `BufferedReader` object is properly initialized. Normally, the invocation of the `BufferedReader` constructor is performed automatically when a user of the class creates a `BufferedReader` object:

```
BufferedReader br;                               The constructor for BufferedReader
br = new BufferedReader(new InputStreamReader(System.in)); ◄─ is invoked.
```

In our situation the user is not directly creating a `BufferedReader` object. Instead, it is being created automatically as part of the creation of a `BetterBR` object:

```
BetterBR bbr = new BetterBR();   ◄─────────   BufferedReader object created
                                              as part of this object.
```

The `BetterBR` constructor is invoked because we are creating a `BetterBR` object; however, there is no invocation of the `BufferedReader` constructor. It therefore becomes the responsibility of the `BetterBR` constructor to invoke the `BufferedReader` constructor as follows:

```
public BetterBR() throws IOException {           Another sort of
    super(new InputStreamReader(System.in));     invocation of
}                                                BufferedReader's
                                                 constructor
```

The first action taken by the `BetterBR` constructor is to invoke the constructor of its superclass, `BufferedReader`, providing any necessary arguments, in this case the `InputStreamReader` object created from `System.in`. Rather than invoking the constructor in the usual way, that is, through `BufferedReader(new InputStream-Reader(System.in))`, a different invocation is used. When a superclass's constructor is invoked from a subclass's constructor, the keyword `super` is substituted for the name of the superclass. This usage emphasizes the inheritance relationship between the subclass and its superclass.

Following the invocation of the superclass's constructor, the subclass constructor performs any initialization specific to the subclass. As we have no state information new to our subclass, no further initialization is necessary.

The second `BetterBR` constructor accepts a filename that is used to construct the object. The sequence of steps is as follows:

- Create a `File` object from the name.
- Create a `FileInputStream` from the `File` object.
- Create an `InputStreamReader` object from the `FileInputStream` object.
- Create a `BufferedReader` object from the `InputStreamReader` object.

Our constructor therefore is

```
BetterBR(String fileName) throws IOException {
    super(new InputStreamReader(
            new FileInputStream(new File(fileName))));
}
```

Again, no further initialization is required beyond the invocation of the `Buffered-Reader` superclass's constructor.

The readInt() Method

We read in a line with the `readLine()` method and then use `Integer.parseInt()` to convert the line into an `int`. Here is the code:

```
int readInt() throws IOException {
    String line;
    line = readLine();
    return Integer.parseInt(line);
}
```

Turning this behavior into a method, however, introduces the problem of how to handle the end-of-file condition. Until now, we could test whether the value returned by the `readLine()` method was equal to `null`. If it was, there were no more data to read, and no `int` was produced. How does the `readInt()` method indicate this situation to the caller? That is, what value could it return to indicate that no number was read? We cannot return `null` as we do for methods that read in objects—null is not a valid `int` value! Values like –1 or even –999999 are not really special: They could legitimately appear as numeric data.

One solution to this problem will be presented in Chapter 13. For the moment, we leave the responsibility of detecting the end of numeric input to the caller of `readInt()`. The `main()` method of the full class implementation in the next section illustrates how this responsibility can be assumed by the caller.

The Full Class Implementation

Here is the complete code for the `BetterBR` class. The sample code in the `main()` method creates a `BetterBR` object associated with the file `data12`, whose contents follow the class definition. The `main()` method then reads integers until a negative value is read, after which it simply reads lines until the end of the file is encountered. Here, `main()`—the caller of `readInt()`—assumes that a negative number will signal the end of the numeric input.

```
import java.io.*;

class BetterBR extends BufferedReader {
    public BetterBR() throws IOException {
        super(new InputStreamReader(System.in));
    }
    public BetterBR(String fileName) throws IOException {
```

```
                super(new InputStreamReader(
                    new FileInputStream(new File(fileName)))));
        }
    public int readInt() throws IOException {
        String line;
        line = readLine();
        return Integer.parseInt(line);
    }
    public static void main(String[] arg) throws IOException {
        int i;
        String s;
        BetterBR bbr = new BetterBR("junk");
        i = bbr.readint();
        while (i >= 0) {
            System.out.println("i = " + i);
            i = bbr.readInt();
        }
        s = bbr.readLine();
        while (s != null) {
            System.out.println("s = " + s);
            s = bbr.readLine();
        }
    }
}
```

while (i >= 0) — Positive numbers only—a negative value signals the end of the input.

System.out.println("s = " + s); — Read in strings until the end of the file.

Contents of the data12 File

Here are the contents of the data12 file:

```
3
5
237
-1
A line
Line #2
This is the last line
```

12.4 Adding State to the Subclass—Accessing the Superclass's State

The BetterBR class extended its BufferedReader superclass through the addition of methods only. These methods performed their tasks by invoking the superclass's own methods and using local variables. The new class required no state of its own nor any knowledge of the superclass's state.

The extension of behavior, however, usually requires that the subclass introduce some additional instance variables of its own in order to maintain the state associated with the new behavior. For example, in the next section, we will develop an extended Name class, based on the class introduced in Chapter 5. The extended state will add a middle name to the information maintained by the original Name class, and this new information will be maintained in the subclass:

```
class ExtendedName extends Name {
    ...
    private String middleName;          Introduced by ExtendedName
}
```

Furthermore, in order for a subclass to implement its additional behavior, it often needs to access the state of the superclass. While the methods provided by the superclass provide "packaged" behavior suitable for a user, the methods may not (and usually do not) supply direct access to the underlying instance variables—access often required by the subclass. Again, looking ahead, our extended Name class will require access to the title and first and last name of the superclass if it wishes to create a String composed of title, first, middle, and last name.

As matters stand, however, the subclass is unable to access the instance variables of its superclass because they were declared private. To solve this problem, Java possesses an additional access keyword, protected, which is similar to private except that access is provided to subclasses as well as to the class itself. Thus, given the following pair of class definitions:

```
class Name {
    ...
    protected String last;
}
class ExtendedName extends Name {
    ...
}
```

The methods of the ExtendedName class have access to the last instance variable of class Name, because it has been declared protected.

12.5 Revisiting the Name Class—Adding Additional State

We now develop a class that introduces additional state information as well as new methods. This example shows a subclass that adds state (instance variables) of its own.

Statement of the Problem

Extend the Name class developed in Chapter 5 so that it supports a middle name. In addition to the behavior provided by the Name class, the new class should provide methods to return the middle initial and a formal name consisting of title, first, middle, and last names.

Finding the Primary Object

As with our previous example, our problem statement provides us with our primary object—an extended name class that we call ExtendedName.

Determining the Behavior

Our desired behavior is also obtained from the problem statement as follows:

- ExtendedName (constructor)
- middleInitial—Returns middle initial
- formalName—Returns title followed by first, middle, and last name
- All the behavior of the Name class (We get that automatically through the inheritance process.)

Defining the Interface

Our original Name constructor required two arguments: the first and last names. These must be supplied to our ExtendedName constructor so that the Name constructor (invoked as super(...) in ExtendedName constructor) can be passed these values. In addition, we must supply the middle name to our ExtendedName constructor:

```
ExtendedName(String firstName, String middleName,
             String lastName) {...}
```

It is also possible that someone has no middle name, so we overload the constructor to allow the user to specify a first and last name only:

```
ExtendedName(String firstName, String lastName) {...}
```

The getFormalName() method, like the other get...() methods inherited from the Name class, requires no arguments and returns a String object. Our completed interface is

```
class ExtendedName extends Name {
    public ExtendedName(String firstName, String
                        middleName, String lastName) {...}
    public ExtendedName(String firstName, String lastName) {...}
    public String getFormalName() {...}
        Instance variables
    ...
}
```

This completes the interface of the methods introduced by the ExtendedName class. Again, in addition to these methods, we automatically acquire, through inheritance, all the functionality of the Name class.

Defining the Instance Variables

We need to maintain the middle name in our class, so we introduce an instance variable, middleName. This instance variable is present *only* at the subclass level—objects of type Name do not possess such a value. However, ExtendedName objects do inherit the lastName, firstName, and title instance variables from their superclass. In order to allow the methods of ExtendedName to access these variables, we must change their access to protected. Here are the two classes:

```
class Name {
      Methods
    ...
    protected String firstName, lastName, title;
}
class ExtendedName extends Name {
      Methods
    ...
    private String middleName;
}
```

Implementing the Methods

In addition to invoking the Name constructor, the constructor for ExtendedName must also initialize its own middleName instance variable. Initialization is done after the superclass constructor invocation:

```
public ExtendedName(String firstName, String middleName,
                    String lastName) {
    super(firstName, lastName);
    this.middleName = middleName;
}
```

The second constructor, which accepts just a first and last name, initializes the middle name to the empty string:

```
public ExtendedName(String firstName, String lastName) {
    super(firstName, lastName);
    this.middleName = "";
}
```

The getMiddleInitial() method checks whether there is a middle name and returns the first initial; otherwise, the empty string is returned.

```
public String getMiddleInitial() {
    if (!middleName.equals(""))
        return middleName.substring(0, 1);
```

```
    else
        return "";
}
```

The getFormalName() method simply returns the concatenation of the title, first, middle, and last names. Declaring the Name class's instance variables protected allows getFormalName() to access those variables.

```
public String getFormalName() {
    return title + " " + firstName + " " + middleName + " " + lastName;
}
```

The Complete Class

Here is the completed ExtendedName class together with the Name class, which has been modified so that its instance variables are now declared protected. Note that we have declared the middleName instance variable of the Extended-Name class to be private.

The sample code in the main() method of the ExtendedName class creates a pair of ExtendedName objects, one with a middle name, the other without. It then invokes both ExtendedName methods, getMiddleInitial() and getFormalName(), as well as the getLastFirst() method defined in the Name class.

```
class ExtendedName extends Name {
    public ExtendedName(String firstName, String middleName,
                        String lastName) {
        super(firstName, lastName);
        this.middleName = middleName;
    }
    public ExtendedName(String firstName, String lastName) {
        super(firstName, lastName);
        this.middleName = "";
    }
    public String getMiddleInitial() {
        if (!middleName.equals(""))
            return middleName.substring(0, 1);
        else
            return "";
    }
    public String getFormalName() {
        return title + " " + firstName + " " + middleName +
                       " " + lastName;
    }
```

```java
    public static void main(String [] args) {
        ExtendedName en = new ExtendedName("Anna", "Louise","Strong");
        System.out.println(en.getMiddleInitial());
        System.out.println(en.getFormalName());
        System.out.println(en.getLastFirst());
        en = new ExtendedName("Gerald", "Weiss");
        System.out.println(en.getMiddleInitial());
        System.out.println(en.getFormalName());
        System.out.println(en.getLastFirst());
    }
    private String middleName;
}
class Name{
    public Name(String first, String last){
        firstName = first;
        lastName = last;
        title = "";
    }
    public String getInitials(){
        String s;
        s = firstName.substring(0,1);
        s = s.concat(".");
        s = s.concat(lastName.substring(0,1));
        s = s.concat(".");
        return s;
    }
    public String getLastFirst(){
        return lastName.concat(",").concat(firstName);
    }
    public String getFirstLast(){
        return title.concat("").
                    concat(firstName).
                        concat("").concat(lastName);
    }
    public void setTitle(String newTitle){
        title = newTitle;
    }
    protected String firstName;
    protected String lastName;
    protected String title;
}
```

> The middle name of an `ExtendedName`

> Refers to the first name of this `Name`
> Refers to the last name of this `Name`
> Refers to the title part of this `Name`

Inheritance

Basic Mechanics and Terminology

If we use our ExtendedName class as an illustration, the class definition:

```
class ExtendedName extends Name {
    ...
}
```

causes the class ExtendedName to inherit all of the Name class's instance variables and methods.

We say that ExtendedName extends Name. Thus, ExtendedName is a subclass of Name, and Name is a superclass of ExtendedName. In addition to the inherited items, ExtendedName may define its own instance variables and methods.

Creating an ExtendedName object such as

```
ExtendedName en = new ExtendedName("David", "Moss", "Arrow");
```

causes a *single* object to be created. This object consists of the Name superclass object augmented with the instance variables and methods of the ExtendedName subclass (see Figure 12.1). All Name-defined methods may be directly invoked on the object, in addition to those methods defined specifically for an ExtendedName:

```
en.getLastFirst();          Invokes a Name-defined method
en.getMiddleInitial();      Invokes an ExtendedName-defined method
```

Within the ExtendedName's methods, the methods and instance variables defined by the Name superclass may be referred to using either this as the receiver or no receiver

Figure 12.1
The anatomy of a subclass object. An ExtendedName subclass object can be thought of as consisting of the Name superclass object augmented with the instance variables and methods introduced in the ExtendedName class. The methods defined in the Name superclass can only refer to those instance variables in the superclass, because they know nothing of the subclass's state.

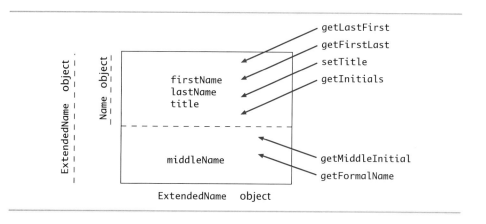

at all, exactly as would be done for Name objects. Thus, our getFormalName() method can refer to the title instance variable either as title or this.title.

Constructors

Until now, we explicitly created each object by invoking the new operator, passing the appropriate arguments to the object's constructor:

```
Employee e = new Employee("Zvi Weiss", 23);
Location l = new Location (10 , 7);
```

In the presence of inheritance, matters become slightly more complicated. Suppose we create an ExtendedName object:

```
Extended en = new ExtendedName("Scott", "David", "Dexter");
```

Although a *single* object is created, in some sense that object is composed of a pair of *nested* parts: a Name object within an ExtendedName object, the latter consisting only of methods and instance variables defined within the ExtendedName class. Although both portions require proper initialization, it is only the ExtendedName constructor that is explicitly invoked during the creation. It thus becomes the responsibility of the ExtendedName constructor to ensure that the constructor of the embedded Name object is invoked. It does this without an invocation of the new operator because the Name object is already created as part of the new ExtendedName invocation. Therefore, Java introduces a new syntax to allow a subclass to invoke the constructor of its superclass with the proper arguments. The invocation emphasizes the sub/superclass relationship of the two classes:

super(*arguments to the superclass's constructor*);

We usually get the arguments to super from the arguments to the subclass's *own* constructor, as we did with the firstName and lastName arguments to the ExtendedName constructor.

The invocation of the superclass's constructor must be the first action of the subclass's constructor:

```
public ExtendedName(String firstName, String middleName,
                    String lastName) {
    super(firstName, lastName);            This must be invoked first.
    this.middleName = middleName;
}
```

To invoke a superclass constructor that accepts no arguments we just write the following:

```
super();
```
Invoking the superclass's constructor without arguments.

Alternatively, we can omit such an invocation without arguments entirely, in which case it is performed automatically for us.

Inheritance and the *is-a* Relationship

We created the ExtendedName class by extending the Name class in order to provide additional behavior. The ExtendedName class, however, still retains all the methods and instance variables of the Name class (in addition to its own) and we say that any object of class ExtendedName ***is-a*** Name object. The term *is-a* is widely used to denote the subclass/superclass relationship. An ExtendedName object may therefore be freely used as a Name object. For example, the following code creates an ExtendedName and assigns it to a Name reference variable. This **assignment** is legal because Name reference variables may contain references to Name objects, and an ExtendedName object is a Name object:

```
Name n = new ExtendedName("Yocheved", "Chaya", "Weiss");
```

This illustrates a very important and powerful aspect of inheritance: *the ability to use an object of a subclass anywhere a superclass object is allowed.*

As another example, an array declared to contain an element type of Name objects may contain ExtendedName objects as well:

```
Name[] na = new Name[10];
na[0] = new Name("George", "Washington");          No surprises here.
na[1] = new ExtendedName("George", "Washington", "Carver");
                                          ExtendedNames are Names too!
```

Code that was written even before the class ExtendedName was defined can still properly operate on objects of that class. However, in the context of a Name reference variable, ExtendedName objects can only behave as the more restricted Name objects. For example:

```
Name n = new ExtendedName("Wolfgang", "Amadaeus", "Mozart");
n.getInitials();         OK, Name objects can return initials.
n.getFormalName();       Wrong!! We are acting as a Name now.
                         No such method in Name.
```

Fortunately, this mistake will be caught by the compiler.

The protected Keyword

In addition to public, which permits all classes to access a method or instance variable, and private, which restricts access to members of the class only, Java provides the keyword protected to permit access by subclasses but not other classes. This keyword allows a subclass to provide extended behavior that requires access to the instance variables of its superclass.

There are two basic problems with the use of protected. First, the designer of a class is assumed to have foreknowledge of two possible eventualities:

- There may eventually be a subclass defined extending this class.
- The subclass will require access to the state (instance variable) of this class.

Although this information may be available under certain circumstances, we cannot be sure that this information is available in general. There is a school of thought that recommends that *all* instance variables be declared `protected` to allow for eventual subclass definition.

The second problem associated with the use of `protected` is one of responsibility and integrity of state. If we view a class as being the sole entity responsible for its behavior, then it is not clear that even subclasses should have access to its internal state. Once a subclass is able to access the instance variables of its superclass, the superclass can no longer guarantee that its state is always correct. No matter how much the superclass's own methods are tested, the variables can be corrupted by the methods of the subclass. That is why the "all protected" school is a small minority. In fact, there is another school of thought that frowns on *any* use of `protected`.

Inheritance versus Composition

Defining an `ExtendedName` class as inheriting from a `Name` object is completely different from defining a class that contains a reference to a `Name` object as an instance variable:

```
class Name2 {
    public Name2(String firstName, String middleName,String lastName)
    {...}
    public String getMiddleInitial() {...}
    public getFormalName() {...}
    private Name n;
    private String middleName;
}
```

This code shows the type of construction we have been using all along. It declares a reference variable of one class as an instance variable of a second class. This is the *has-a* relationship we spoke of in Chapter 7. In the above class definition, the class `Name2` *has-a* `Name` object as part of its state.

Building classes in this way is called **composition** because the class is *composed* of instance variables that are objects of other classes. Again, the `Name2` class is composed of a `Name` object, as well as a `String` object.

In this case, the `Name2` does not inherit the methods and instance variables of the `Name` object. When it is created, only a *reference* to a `Name` object is created (see Figure 12.2). An actual `Name` object must be created as a separate step, usually within the constructor:

```
Name2(String firstName, String middleName, String lastName) {
    n = new Name(firstName, lastName);
    this.middleName = middleName;
}
```

Same as `this.n` ➔ `n = new Name(firstName, lastName);`

Figure 12.2

Using composition to define a new class. With composition, an object of the existing class is used as an instance variable of the new class.

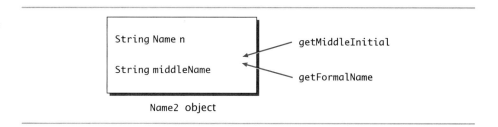

In addition, the only methods directly available to the object are those defined in the new Name2 class. The original Name class methods are not inherited and cannot be invoked upon an Name2 object:

```
Name2 n2 = new Name2("Louisa", "May", "Alcott");
n2.getMiddleInitial();          Okay, getMiddleInitial defined for Name2.
n2.getLastFirst();              Error—no such method for Name2.
```

Finally, when composition is used, the protected keyword does not buy us anything. That access is only granted to subclasses, not classes that incorporate the object as an instance variable.

Inheritance or Composition?

Inheritance and composition each have their applications; one is not necessarily superior to the other. The thing to remember is that inheritance models an *is-a* relationship whereas composition models a *has-a* relationship. Given an existing class, X, and the need for a related new class, Y, the following guidelines can help you to decide whether to use composition or inheritance.

- If *all* the methods of the original class X should be methods of the new class Y, then use inheritance.
- If *some* of the methods of the original class X make no sense as methods of the new class Y, use composition.
- If it feels right to say that "a Y is an X" (as in "a part-timer is an employee"), then use inheritance.
- If it feels right to say that "a Y has an X" (as in "an employee has a name"), then use composition.

Furthermore, when you are deciding on inheritance versus composition, in Java a class may have only one superclass; that is, it may inherit from one class only. On the other hand, a class may contain instance variables of many classes. Thus, composition is not restricted to an object of a single class. It often turns out that a particular class uses both techniques: inheriting from one class and using composition for several others.

A Common Mistake

Programmers new to inheritance often forget that the instance variables of the extended class (Name in our case) are *automatically inherited*. A common mistake is to repeat the declarations of these variables in the inheriting class:

```
class ExtendedName extends Name {
    Methods
        ...
    String title, lastName, firstName;
    String middleName;
}
```

INCORRECT! These are already inherited from Name!

This is the only instance variable that should be explicitly defined by ExtendedName.

What's even worse, the Java compiler will not complain about this situation. The result is that we have introduced a new set of instance variables, unique to Extended-Name objects, which have names identical to those of Name.

Class Hierarchies

There is no reason why subclasses cannot themselves be extended. We might decide at some later date to extend the behavior of our ExtendedName to provide even more behavior (see Exercise 7 on page 528 and Figure 12.3):

```
class SuffixedName extends ExtendedName {
    ...
}
```

It's also possible to have two *different* classes inherit from the same class (see Figure 12.4):

```
class SuffixedName extends Name {
    ...
}
```

Figure 12.3

A subclass with its own subclass. The subclass ExtendedName can itself be extended. It then becomes a superclass to the new subclass SuffixedName.

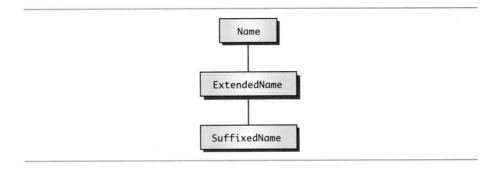

Figure 12.4
A superclass with two subclasses. A class can be extended by more than one class.

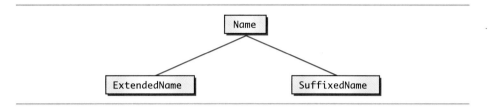

The resulting class relationship is called a **class hierarchy** and is illustrated graphically using a structure known as a **class hierarchy tree**. Figures 12.3 and 12.4 are both examples of a hierarchy tree. This tree can extend to multiple levels.

The Object Class

We can now finally provide a full explanation of the Object class with which we became acquainted back in Chapter 9.

Every class in Java, with one exception, must be a subclass of some other class. The resulting class hierarchy is what we call the **Java class hierarchy**. The one exception is the class that resides at the top, or **root** position of the hierarchy. In Java, the Object class occupies this distinguished position in the class hierarchy (see Figure 12.5). This means that all classes in Java have Object as a superclass (though usually with several classes intervening).

Before we reached this chapter our class definitions did not contain the extends clause. Whenever this clause is omitted, the class is assumed to inherit directly from the Object class:

```
class MyClass {          Same as class MyClass extends Object
    ...
}
```

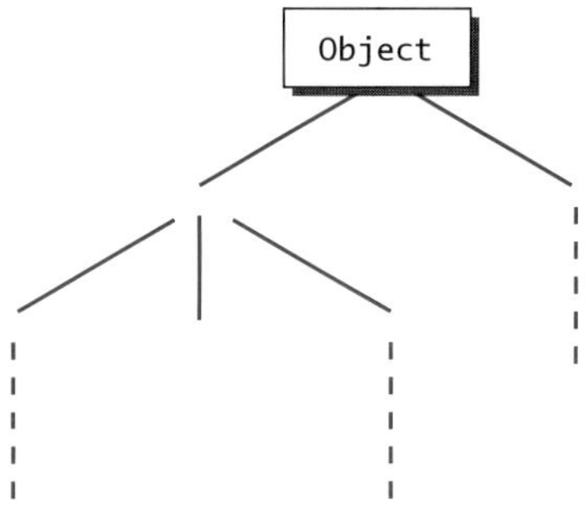

Figure 12.5
The root of the Java class hierarchy.
Class Object is the root of the Java hierarchy tree. All classes inherit, directly or indirectly, from this Object class.

12.6 Overriding Methods

The behavior of the ExtendedName class was a strict extension of the Name class. ExtendedName added new behavior only; there was no modification of the original Name behavior.

With a little thought, however, we can uncover a discrepancy in the behavior of ExtendedName, in particular in the behavior of the getInitials() method inherited from the Name class. This method returns a String corresponding to the first and last initials of the Name object. With the introduction of the ExtendedName class, however, the getInitials() method should properly return all three initials—first, middle, and last. What we must do is modify the behavior of the getInitials() method for ExtendedName objects. However, we don't wish to modify the behavior of the getInitials() method for Name objects—in fact, we can't because they have no middle name in their state.

What we must do in this situation is *replace* the original getInitials() method with one defined in ExtendedName that incorporates a middle initial. In order for this replacement to work, the getInitials() method that we will define in ExtendedName must match the signature of the original getInitials() of Name. We write it as follows:

```
class ExtendedName extends Name {
    ...
    public String getInitials() {
        return firstName.substring(0,1) + "." +
            getMiddleInitial() + "." + lastName.substring(0,1);
    }
    ...
}
```

This technique of redefining a method in a class further down the hierarchy is known as **overriding**. Overriding refers to the act of reimplementing a method in a subclass with the same signature of a method in the superclass. In effect, we are circumventing the superclass's original method. In our situation, invoking the getInitials() method on an ExtendedName object causes the new method, defined in ExtendedName, to be invoked.

Java Interlude   *Polymorphism*

The Mechanics of Overriding

Let us consider a simplified but useful way to understand how overriding works. During execution, when a message is passed to an object, the message is compared against the object's class's own message signatures (name plus argument list). If a match is found, the corresponding method is invoked. If not, the message is compared against the prototypes of the superclass's messages. The process repeats until a match is encountered. A match is guaranteed because the Java compiler will issue a compile-time error if a message is invoked upon an object that does not have the message name defined within either itself or some superclass.

Let us apply this to the context of Name and ExtendedName objects. Suppose we have the following declarations:

```
Name n = new Name("Shlomo","Weiss");
ExtendedName en = new ExtendedName("William","Tecumseh","Sherman");
```

Let us invoke a getInitials() method on each of these objects and examine the effect.

First we invoke the method on the Name object:

```
String initials = n.getInitials();   Invokes the getInitials() method in Name
```

The Java interpreter looks up the getInitials() method, with no arguments, in class Name (which is the object upon which the method was invoked) and finds that such a method exists. That method is therefore invoked.

Now let us invoke this method on the ExtendedName object:

```
initials = en.getInitials();   Invokes the getInitials() method in ExtendedName
```

The interpreter again finds a matching method immediately, this time in the ExtendedName class and that is the one that is then invoked.

Compare this second call to the following invocation:

```
String s = en.getLastFirst();       Invokes the getLastFirst() method in Name
```

This time the Java interpreter looks up the getLastFirst() method in class ExtendedName and does not find any such method. The interpreter then moves up to ExtendedName's superclass, Name, where it finds a matching getLastFirst() method and invokes it.

Polymorphism

It gets even better than that! Let's look at the following declaration:

```
Name n = new ExtendedName("Thomas","Alva","Edison");
```
An ExtendedName object referenced by a Name variable

Again, this code is perfectly legal because *a subclass object may be used wherever an object of its superclass is allowed.* Because an ExtendedName *is-a* Name, it may be assigned to a Name reference variable. Now here's where the fun begins. Invoking the getInitials() method on n

```
n.getInitials();
```
Invokes the getInitials() method in ExtendedName!

causes the interpreter to begin searching for a matching method *in the object upon which the method was invoked*—the receiver. Now n may be a Name reference variable, but the object it references is an ExtendedName (see Figure 12.6). This means that the class in which the method matching begins is ExtendedName, and the method invoked is the getInitials() method defined in that class.

This leads to the following important rule:

> When invoking overridden methods, the type of the actual object is what counts, not the type of the reference variable. Method matching thus begins in the object's class, not the class of the reference variable.

This means that invoking the *same* method on the *same* reference variable will invoke *different* methods depending on the object being referred to:

```
Name n = new Name("James","Michener");
String s = n.getInitials();              Invokes getInitials defined in Name.
n = new ExtendedName("James","Clerk","Maxwell");
s = n.getInitials();              Invokes getInitials defined in ExtendedName.
```

All of the above hinges on our ability to override methods. As we have said, the search for the matching method is performed by the Java interpreter and is thus performed at run time. The ability to override methods coupled with the run-time determination of which method to invoke means that different objects (even when using the same reference variable) can respond to the same message in different ways. This capability is known as **polymorphism** (literally "many forms") because the same message can evoke different behavior depending upon the receiver. Polymorphism is a feature of object-oriented languages in which the exact method to be invoked is determined at run time by the class of the receiving object.

Another example of polymorphism is the familiar toString() method. This method is defined in the Object class with the intention that it be subsequently overridden by subclasses. The purpose of toString() is to construct a String representation of an object, usually for the purpose of printing:

```
while (i<v.size())
    System.out.println((v.elementAt(i)).toString());
```
Invokes the
toString()
method of the
element's class.

Figure 12.6

A Name reference variable referencing an ExtendedName object.

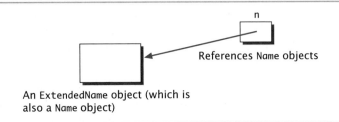

n

References Name objects

An ExtendedName object (which is also a Name object)

The method toString() returns a String representation of an object. This method was introduced in Chapter 9 as being available to all objects, as it was defined in class Object. Furthermore, any class could rewrite that method to provide its own behavior for that method, providing the exact same signature as the one defined in class Object.

During execution, sending the message toString() to an object causes the Java interpreter to check whether the object's class possesses such a method, and if so, it invokes that method. If the method is not found in that class, the immediate superclass is checked. This process repeats itself until a class is found with a toString() method. If no class defined its own toString() method, eventually the Object class will be encountered and its toString() method (which returns as its value a not-very-descriptive string) will be invoked.

Overriding versus Overloading

Overriding differs from overloading in that overriding requires signatures to be identical whereas overloading requires signatures to be different. From a usage point of view, the two have completely different applications. Overloading allows the programmer to use the same name for two distinct methods. The invoker of the method implicitly specifies which method is being invoked by the argument list passed in the message, which is then compared against the prototypes of the various candidate methods until a match is found. The determination of which is the correct method is performed at compile time (by the Java compiler).

In contrast, overriding provides the programmer with the ability to redefine the behavior of a particular method in a subclass. When overriding methods are employed, the method invoked is determined at run time in the manner described above.

12.7 Factoring Out Common Behavior—Inheritance II

The inheritance encountered by the beginning Java programmer is usually of the form presented in the previous sections. An existing class provides a base of behavior and the programmer extends it to provide additional behavior. In our examples, we extended the existing Name class to create an ExtendedName class and the Java predefined BufferedReader class to create a BetterBR class.

This ability to build on previous effort provides unprecedented power to the relative beginner. For example, Java provides a powerful graphical interface class called Applet. This class can be extended by a novice who provides only the specifics of the application at hand—the sophisticated window management is automatically inherited.

There is another common use for inheritance, one that arises during the design of applications involving numerous related classes. Because the beginner does not usually encounter such applications (entry-level positions usually do not involve large-scale design), this form of inheritance is seen less often. It is, however, a critical part of understanding class hierarchies in an object-oriented system, and we therefore provide an introduction to it.

As our example, let us assume we are designing an inventory system for a camera store that is to track the various items in the warehouse. Different categories of items require different information be maintained. For example, we might have the following categories and information:

- Lenses will possess a focal length and may or may not zoom.
- Film must remain cool and thus has a recommended storage temperature, as well as a film speed and number of exposures.
- Cameras may or may not come with a lens, and have a maximum shutter speed and body color.

In addition, all inventory items must contain the following information:

- A description of the item
- An inventory identification number
- The quantity on hand
- The price of the item

Each information element associated with an inventory item can be maintained as an instance variable. Our example has three distinct categories of items: lens, film, and camera, and we will define three corresponding classes, Lens, Film, and Camera.

It makes little sense to lump them all into the same class because that class would have to maintain the union of *all* the instance variables for all three types of items.

Here is a brief sketch of the proposed classes. We will not be developing a full application using these classes, so we ignore the constructor details as well as the methods that are specific to the different classes.

```
class Lens {
    public Lens(...) {...}          Constructor
    public String getDescription() {return description;}
    public int getQuantityOnHand() {return quantityOnHand;}
    public int getPrice() {return price;}

    ...
    methods specific to Lens
    ...

    private String description;
    private int inventoryNumber;
    private int quantityOnHand;
    private int price;
    private boolean isZoom;
    private double focalLength;
}
```

```
class Film {
    public Film(...) {...}          Constructor
    public String getDescription() {return description;}
    public int getQuantityOnHand() {return quantityOnHand;}
    public int getPrice() {return price;}
    ...
    methods specific to Film
    ...
    private String description;
    private int inventoryNumber;
    private int quantityOnHand;
    private int price;
    private int recommendedTemp;
    private int numberOfExposures;
}
class Camera {
    public Camera(...) {...}          Constructor
    public String getDescription() {return description;}
    public int getQuantityOnHand() {return quantityOnHand;}
    public int getPrice() {return price;}
    ...
    methods specific to Camera
    ...
    private String description;
    private int inventoryNumber;
    private int quantityOnHand;
    private int price;
    private boolean hasLens;
    private int maxShutterSpeed;
    private String bodyColor;
}
```

While the three classes do model the three separate types of inventory items, there is a significant amount of repetition regarding their common elements: description, inventoryNumber, quantityOnHand, and price. This repetition is reflected in both instance variables and methods operating on those variables. If an additional piece of information is to be maintained for all inventory items, we must add another instance variable, together with any associated methods to *all three classes*. In short, all three classes are required to model behavior common to all inventory items, and it seems a waste of effort to have each of them accomplish this individually.

Each of the three classes is actually modeling two related, but distinct concepts: a general inventory item and the specific sort of item (lens, film, and camera). This is where inheritance can help. We create a superclass, InventoryItem, which models the behavior of a generic inventory item:

```
class InventoryItem {
    InventoryItem(...) {...}          Constructor
    String getDescription() {return description;}
    int getQuantityOnHand() {return quantityOnHand;}
    int getPrice() {return price;}

    ...
    String description;
    int inventoryNumber;
    int quantityOnHand;
    int price;
}
```

This class knows nothing of specific items; it is responsible solely for behavior common to all inventory items. Any modifications to the behavior of all inventory items need be maintained by this class only.

We can now define three subclasses that extend the InventoryItem class:

```
class Lens extends InventoryItem {
    Lens(...) {...}                   Constructor
    ...
    methods specific to Lens
    ...
    boolean isZoom;
    double focalLength;
}
class Film extends InventoryItem {
    Film(...) {...}                   Constructor
    ...
    methods specific to Film
    ...
    int recommendedTemp;
    int numberOfExposures;
}
class Camera extends InventoryItem {
    Camera(...) {...}                 Constructor
    ...
    methods specific to Camera
    ...
    boolean hasLens;
    int maxShutterSpeed;
    String bodyColor;
}
```

These three classes model the specifics of the individual types of items. The general behavior of inventory items is inherited from the InventoryItem class.

What we have done here is to recognize that our original classes were abstracting two sets of behavior, one of which was common to all of them. We then factored that common behavior out to a common superclass.

We haven't introduced anything new here—all we have done is shown a different use of inheritance. Our original motivation for using inheritance was to take advantage of existing class behavior when creating new classes. What we have done here is to use inheritance to factor out common behavior when we are designing logically related classes. In both cases, we are trying to share as much code as possible.

As with any subclass/superclass, the *is-a* relationship holds between the Lens, Film, and Camera subclasses and the InventoryItem superclass. A reference variable of type InventoryItem may reference an object of any of the three classes:

```
InventoryItem ii;
ii = new Lens(…);       Okay—Lens objects are InventoryItem objects.
ii = new Film(…);       Okay—Film objects are InventoryItem objects.
ii = new Camera(…);     Okay—Camera objects are InventoryItem objects.
```

As we have already seen, the *is-a* relationship allows for some fairly powerful programming capabilities. Consider the following array declaration and initialization:

```
InventoryItem[] invarr = new InventoryItem[3];
invarr[0] = new Lens(…);
invarr[1] = new Film(…);
invarr[2] = new Camera(…);
```

We can now iterate through the array and print out the element's description and quantity on hand:

```
for (int i = 0; i < invarr.length; i++)
    System.out.println(invarr[i].getDescription() + ": " +
        invarr[i].getQuantityOnHand() + " available");
```

12.8 Abstract Methods and Classes

Let's take a closer look at this array code:

```
InventoryItem[] invarr = new InventoryItem[3];
invarr[0] = new Lens(…);
invarr[1] = new Film(…);
invarr[2] = new Camera(…);
for (int i = 0; i < invarr.length; i++)
    System.out.println(invarr[i].getDescription() + ": " +
        invarr[i].getQuantityOnHand() + " available");
```

This code prints out only the information that is available in the InventoryItem superclass. This is because in the context of the InventoryItem array, invarr, the various items are viewed as InventoryItems and not as objects of the individual subclasses.

Suppose we wanted to be able to go through the array and print out detailed information for the individual objects: the temperature, the number of exposures of Film objects, the focal length and zoom capability of a Lens object, and so on. To accomplish this task, we need to do the following:

- Define a method called print() in each of the subclasses Lens, Film, and Camera.
- In order to invoke these print() methods polymorphically using an Inventory-Item reference variable, we must define a print() method in the Inventory-Item class.
- The print() methods of the subclasses therefore override the Inventory-Item's print() method.

We thus require print() methods in both the subclasses and the superclass:

```
class InventoryItem {

    ...
    void print() {...}
    ...

}

class Lens extends InventoryItem {

    ...
    void print() {...}          Overrides print() of InventoryItem
    ...                          and prints Lens-specific data.

}

class Film extends InventoryItem {

    ...
    void print() {...}          Overrides print() of InventoryItem
    ...                          and prints Film-specific data.

}

class Camera extends InventoryItem {

    ...
    void print() {...}          Overrides print() of InventoryItem
    ...                          and prints Camera-specific data.

}
```

Note, however, that the print() method in the superclass exists only so that it can be overridden. It cannot by itself provide any behavior specific to the individual classes. So, we actually don't want to implement the print() method in the InventoryItem class. It is the responsibility of each subclass to provide an over-ridden method customized to itself. What we really want is to specify the existence of such a print() method, but require that it be overridden by a subclass.

Java provides this capability through the use of the abstract keyword in the method header. Declaring a method to be abstract announces that the class recognizes the existence of the method, *but its implementation is left to the subclass*. No method body is supplied; instead, the method header is followed by a semicolon. An **abstract method** is thus a method that is declared with the keyword `abstract`. It has no method body and must be overridden by a subclass:

```
abstract void print();
```

Because no implementation exists for the `print()` method in class `Inventory-Item`, it makes no sense to be able to create an object of that class—its behavior is incompletely specified. A class that contains one or more abstract methods is an **abstract class**, and the Java compiler requires that we indicate it in the definition of the class with the keyword `abstract`.

With `print()` an abstract method, our `InventoryItem` class becomes

```
abstract class InventoryItem {
    ...
    abstract void print();      No method body for an abstract method.
    ...
}
```

Because we can't create objects that are instances of an abstract class, the following code is in error:

```
InventoryItem inv = new InventoryItem(...);   Incorrect—will generate
                                              a compiler error!
```

We may, however, declare reference variables whose type is of an abstract class:

```
InventoryItem inv;          OK, not creating InventoryItem object
```

However, because no `InventoryItem` objects can exist, such a variable can only reference objects belonging to subclasses. This is another consequence of the *is-a* relationship.

```
inv = new Lens(...);          OK—a Lens is an InventoryItem too
```

Suppose we are given our abstract `print()` method and let us assume it has been implemented in the `Lens`, `Film`, and `Camera` subclasses. We can then write the printing iteration code for our array:

```
for (int i = 0; i < invarr.length; i++)
    invarr[i].print();
```

The above code exploits both the *is-a* relationship and polymorphism. The *is-a* relationship allows us to store the subclass objects in a superclass array. Polymorphism ensures that the actual `print()` method invoked is determined at run time by the type of the receiver object, the object referred to by `invarr[i]`. When i equals 0, the object referenced by `invarr[i]` is a `Lens`, and thus the `print()` method defined in the `Lens` class is invoked. When i equals 1, the `Film` class `print()` method is invoked. And, finally, when i equals 2, the `Camera` class `print()` method is invoked.

12.9 Specifying Common Behavior—Interfaces

Abstract methods allow us to state in a superclass that a particular method must exist and may be invoked on a reference variable belonging to the superclass. The actual implementation of the method remains the responsibility of the subclasses. In essence, we are requiring that all subclasses implement behavior that is only being specified (not implemented) in the superclass.

There is a constraining element to working with abstract methods: the superclass/ subclass relationship. When the superclass declares an abstract method, the requirement that the method be implemented applies only to its subclasses—no other class in the hierarchy is required to implement that method.

There are times, however, when we wish to impose the requirement that certain behavior be adhered to for objects that have no direct relationship to each other in the hierarchy. One common example is the Enumeration (see Appendix D). Enumerations model iteration behavior through some collection, such as a Vector. The various Enumerations we define have no relationship to each other; rather they are more closely tied to the collection objects they enumerate over. What Enumerations *should* have in common is the ability to get the next element, nextElement(), and test for termination, hasMoreElements(). We can't provide a *single* implementation for these because the implementation really depends on the type of collection we intend to enumerate over. Nonetheless, we would like to require that any candidate Enumeration object provide these methods. In other words, we are specifying a set of abstract methods that must be implemented by any class wishing to call itself an Enumeration. We could write this as

```
abstract class Enumeration {
    abstract Object nextElement();
    abstract boolean hasMoreElements();
}
```

A class implementing these methods would not be inheriting anything because there are no instance variables or implemented methods. The relationship would thus be quite different than the usual subclass/superclass one. There is no extension of existing behavior. This relationship is one of *conforming to a specified set of behaviors,* namely the abstract methods in the class.

Remember, however, that Java allows a class to have only one superclass. If we defined a class to be an extension of the above Enumeration class, we would be wasting the one superclass from which we would like to inherit all sorts of useful behavior. We would be wasting our choice on a class that provides no behavior yet forces us to implement two methods.

Rather than extend an abstract class that contains only abstract methods, Java allows us to define a nonclass type that consists only of abstract methods. Such a type is called an **interface**. An interface corresponding to the above abstract class is as follows:

```
interface Enumeration {
    Object nextElement();
    boolean hasMoreElements();
}
```

A class can be declared to implement the set of methods specified in an interface by adding the keyword `implements` followed by the name of the interface:

```
class VectorEnumeration implements Enumeration {
    ...
}
```

The above declaration states that the `VectorEnumeration` class guarantees that it will implement every method declared in the `Enumeration` interface. That is, we are guaranteed that there will be a pair of methods, `nextElement()` and `hasMoreElements()`, inside the class as follows:

```
class VectorEnumeration implements Enumeration {
    VectorEnumeration(...) {...}        Whatever the constructor does
    Object nextElement() {
        Here we would implement getting the next element for the Vector
    }
    boolean hasMoreElements() {
        Here we would implement the test for termination
    }
}
```

The commitment of a class to implement the methods of an interface does not prevent the class from inheriting from a superclass. One could write

```
class VectorEnumeration extends OtherClass implements Enumeration {
    ...
}
```

Interfaces do not reside in the class hierarchy—they are not classes. They inherit nothing and possess nothing to inherit. Classes do not extend interfaces because there is no implemented behavior to extend. Rather we say they **implement** the interface.

We can declare the type of a reference variable to be an interface. We have already seen this whenever we declared an `Enumeration` reference variable:

```
Enumeration e;
```

This declaration is similar to the declaration of a reference variable whose type is that of an abstract class. Even though there are no objects of the interface itself, the reference variable may be used to refer to an object of any class implementing the interface.

Furthermore, while the relationship between an interface and the class that implements it is not one of subclass/superclass, it is still an *is-a* relationship. Any object of a class that implements an interface is considered an object of the interface as well and therefore may be assigned to a reference variable of the interface type:

```
VectorEnumeration ve = new VectorEnumeration(…);
Enumeration e = ve;
```

Java's usage of the interface and implements keywords in this context corresponds nicely with the way we have used those terms until now. An interface is merely the specification of some behavior. That specification must then be implemented in order for a user to evoke the behavior.

We conclude this chapter with one last example that defines an interface.

12.10 A Generic Sorting Method

Recall the selection sort of Chapter 11:

```
void sort(String z[]) {   // On return, the elements of v are
                          //     sorted in ascending order.
    int k;                // k== the index of the next position in the array
                          //     to take care of.
                          // All elements to the left of k are less than or
                          //     equal to the elements at k or to the right of k.
                          // All elements to the left of k are in ascending
                          //     order.
    int n=z.length;       // n== number of elements in the array.
    k = 0;
    while  (k!=n−1)  {
       int j = getSmallest(z,k);
       exchange(z,k,j);
       k++;
    }
            // k==n−1 and therefore elements 0, …, n−2 are sorted; but because
            //     these elements are also less than the element in position n−1 (the
            //     last element), the entire array is sorted.
}
// Returns the index of the smallest element in v or −1 if none exist
int  getSmallest(String z[],  int  k)  {
    if  (z==null  ||  z.length==k)
        return  −1;
    int i;      // Index of next element to examine; all elements at positions
                //     less than i have been examined already.
    int small;  // Index of smallest element examined so far
    i  =  k+1;
    small  =  k;
    while  (i!=z.length)  {
```

```
        String current  =  (String) z[i];
        String smallest =  (String) z[small];
        if (current.compareTo(smallest) < 0)
            small = i;
        i++;
    }
    // i==z.length
    return small;
}
```

This sort was constrained to work on a Vector of Strings only. This restriction stems from the code in the getSmallest() method

```
if (current.compareTo(smallest) < 0)
    smallest = current;
```

which compares the current String element against the smallest String encountered to that point. The sort() method itself is oblivious to the element type of the Vector.

We could not use this pair of methods to sort ints because the elements of a Vector must be objects, whereas int is a primitive data type. We could, however, use the Integer wrapper class. Its primary purpose is to allow integer-valued collections. We would then have to modify the getSmallest() method. The variables current and smallest need to be redeclared as Integers. We must also cast the extracted elements to Integer. Finally, the comparison operation must be changed. We use the intValue() method of the Integer class, which returns the integer value of the object as int. Here is the resulting method:

```
// Returns the index of the smallest element in v or −1 if none exists
int getSmallest(Vector v, int k) {
    if (v==null || v.size()==k)
        return −1;
    int i;      // Index of next element to examine; all elements at positions
                //   less than i have been examined already.
    int small;  // Index of smallest element examined so far
    i = k+1;
    small = 0;
    while (i!=v.size()) {
        Integer current = (Integer) v.elementAt(i);
        Integer smallest = (Integer) v.elementAt(small);
        if (current.intValue() < smallest.intValue() 0)
            small = i;
        i++;
    }
    // i==v.size()
    return small;
}
```

Now suppose we wish to sort a Vector whose elements are of some other class, say, our old friend Name of Chapter 5. The variables and casts must change and we must have a method that compares two Name objects, allowing us to determine which was the smaller of the two.

The problem with this scheme is that every time we wish to sort a Vector with a different element type, we must either modify getSmallest() or make a copy of it. (Overloading doesn't help here because the signature will always be the same, and we'd have to come up with a different name for each copy.)

The answer to our problem is to introduce an interface; let's call it Sortable. The purpose of an interface is to provide a specification of required behavior. The behavior we require of an object that is sortable is that it possesses a method that allows it to be compared against another sortable object. Calling that method lessThan(), we get

```
interface Sortable {
    boolean lessThan(Sortable s);  // Returns true if receiver < s
}
```

All we are doing is requiring that a sortable object provide a lessThan() method; the implementation of that method is the responsibility of the implementing class. Thus a lessThan() for Strings would use compareTo(), for Integers, a comparison using intValue(), and so on. Our getSmallest() then becomes the following:

```
// Returns the index of the smallest element in v or −1 if none exists
int getSmallest(Vector v, int k) {
    if (v==null || v.size()==k)
        return -1;
    int    i;        // Index of next element to examine; all elements at
                     //     positions less than i have been examined already.
    int    small;    // Index of smallest element examined so far
    i = k+1;
    small = 0;
    while (i!=v.size()) {
        Sortable current = (Sortable) v.elementAt(i);
        Sortable smallest = (Sortable) v.elementAt(small);
        if (current.lessThan(smallest))
            small = i;
        i++;
    }
    // i==v.size()
    return small;
}
```

This method will correctly sort any Vector whose elements are Sortable, that is, objects of a class implementing that interface.

Before we finish, let us define a class `MyInteger` that implements the `Sortable` interface for integer values. The constructor stores its argument in the `int` instance variable. The `lessThan()` method casts its argument to a `MyInteger`. (Implementing the methods of an interface is like overriding. The signature of `lessThan()` in the implementing class must match the signature of the interface's `lessThan()`, that is, the parameter must be declared a `Sortable`.) The `less-Than()` method then compares the `MyInteger` value to the receiver.

```
class MyInteger implements Sortable {
    public MyInteger(int val) {this.val = val;}
    boolean lessThan(Sortable s) {
        MyInteger mi = (MyInteger)s;
        return this.val < mi.val;
    }
    private int val;
}
```

Summary

Inheritance provides a mechanism to extend the behavior of an existing class. A new class may be defined that inherits all the methods and instance variables of the existing class. In addition, the new subclass may provide additional behavior through the introduction of its own methods and instance variables. Using inheritance, classes with immensely rich behavior can be quickly and easily defined by extending existing classes that provide the bulk of that behavior—the programmer need only add the behavior specific to the application at hand.

In addition to extending behavior, a subclass must often modify the existing behavior of its superclass. This often occurs because additional state information introduced at the subclass level requires a change in the subclass's behavior. A subclass may override a method of its superclass by redefining that method, making sure that the method's signature matches that of the original method in the superclass. When the method is invoked on objects of the subclass, it is the new, overriding method that is invoked.

Inheritance is a reflection of an *is-a* relationship between the subclass and the superclass. This means that any object of the subclass is also an object of the superclass. An object of the subclass may thus be used anywhere the superclass's objects can be used. In particular, references to objects of the subclass may be assigned to superclass reference variables. Invoking an overridden method on a subclass object referenced through a superclass variable causes the subclass's overriding method to be invoked. This mechanism is known as polymorphism and allows different objects to behave in their own different and appropriate ways, even when referenced through the same object.

Inheritance also allows the class designer to move behavior common to several related classes into a superclass. This helps avoid code redundancy and often provides for a more realistic modeling of behavior.

If a method is to be invoked through a superclass variable, the method must be known to the superclass. Often, however, the behavior is dependent upon the particular subclass and thus the implementation of the method can only be completed at the subclass level. Abstract methods allow the designer to specify that a method with a particular signature must be defined by any extending subclass. A class containing one or more abstract methods is known as an abstract class. No instance of an abstract class may be created because the class's behavior is incomplete.

If all the methods of a class are abstract, there is nothing to inherit. Rather than wasting a class's one superclass on such a class, we instead define an interface consisting solely of the method specifications. Classes implement interfaces, that is, they provide the bodies of the specified methods. Unlike inheritance, which allows a class to have only one superclass, a class may implement many interfaces.

Table 12.1 provides a roadmap to the various examples in this chapter. Each of the sample classes is presented along with the section in which the class is developed and the features illustrated by the example.

TABLE 12.1 A GUIDE TO CHAPTER 12 EXAMPLES AND FEATURES

CLASS	SECTION	FEATURE ILLUSTRATED
BetterBR	A Better BufferedReader	Inheritance—behavior extension
ExtendedName	Revisiting the Name Class	Inheritance—additional state
InventoryItem	Factoring Out Common Behavior Inheritance II	Inheritance—common behavior
Enumeration	Specifying Common Behavior—Interfaces	Interface
Sortable	A Generic Sorting Method	Interface

Key Terms

abstract class A class that contains at least one abstract method.

abstract method A method declared but not implemented by a superclass. It is the responsibility of a subclass to implement the method.

class hierarchy The structure resulting from the subclass/superclass relationships of a set of classes.

class hierarchy tree A graphical depiction of a class hierarchy. Each class is displayed below its superclass and above its subclasses.

composition A technique in which a class is defined using instance variables that are references to objects of other classes.

implement The guarantee that a class makes that it will provide the methods specified in an interface.

inheritance A technique in object-oriented languages in which one class assumes all the methods and instance variables of another class as its own. The inheriting class may also provide its own additional behavior.

interface An abstract class containing only abstract methods.

is-a The relationship between subclass and superclass. An object of a subclass *is-a* object of the superclass and may be used wherever an object of the superclass may be used.

Java class hierarchy The class hierarchy composed of Java's classes.

overriding The act of reimplementing a method in a subclass with the *exact* same signature of a method in the superclass.

polymorphism A feature of object-oriented languages in which the exact method to be invoked is determined at run time by the class of the receiving object.

root The class at the top of a class hierarchy. The root has no superclass.

subclass A class that inherits from some other class.

superclass A class that is inherited from.

Questions for Review

1. How is inheritance specified in Java?
2. What is a class hierarchy?
3. What is the root of the Java class hierarchy?
4. Does every class in Java have a superclass? a subclass?
5. How is an interface specified in Java? How does a class implement an interface in Java?
6. What is the difference between overriding and overloading? Which is done at compile time? at run time?
7. Can you create a object whose type is an abstract class? an interface?
8. Can you declare a reference variable whose type is an abstract class? an interface?
9. How does an interface differ from an abstract class?

Exercises

1. Modify the readInt() method so that an integer may be placed anywhere on the line. (Hint: Look at the trim method of class String.)

2. Modify the readInt() method so that blank lines are ignored.

3. In the main() method in Section 12.3, what would happen if the file date12 did not have a negative value at the end of the numeric section? That is, what if the −1 in the file were omitted?

4. Add a readDouble() method to the BetterBR class that reads in and returns a double value using the technique presented in Chapter 6.

5. Extend the Stopwatch class of Chapter 4 to provide "split time" behavior, i.e., the ability to display elapsed time without resetting the watch.

6. Extend the Name class to create a new class, SuffixedName, that provides for a suffix, for example, M.D., Esq., Ph.D., and so on. Introduce a method that prints out a name with the suffix.

7. Have the SuffixedName class of Exercise 6 extend the ExtendedName class rather than the Name class. Do any issues arise?

8. There are some subtle output mistakes in the ExtendedName class. Apply the testing techniques of Chapter 8 to uncover and fix them.

9. Extend the Location class of Chapter 7 to create a ThreeDLocation class. This class contains 3 coordinate values—a z coordinate in addition to the x and y coordinates of the Location clss. Override the distanceFrom() method to use all 3 coordinates.

10. Think about it: If we override a method of a superclass, are we *really* able to say that the *is-a* relationship holds?

11. Define a class that implements lessThan() for String objects.

12. Define a class that implements lessThan() for Name objects. What is a reasonable meaning for one Name to be less than another?

13. Extend the Turtle class developed in Chapter 10 to provide a method move(x,y) that raises the pen and moves to the given coordinates. What changes must be made to the Turtle superclass to permit this movement?

14. Extend the Turtle class to allow a character to be specified for the penmark instead of "*".

15. Consider classes Book, Periodical, and Multimedia. What behavior might they have in common as class/interface LibraryHoldings? Does it make more sense to specify this common behavior in an abstract class or in an interface? Implement the common-behvaior portions of these classes and their common interface or abstract class.

Exploring the Abstract Window Toolkit of the Java Class Hierarchy

In this GUI supplement, we're going to do something a little bit different. Rather than presenting yet another applet that introduces a new graphic technique or component, we're going to explore the Abstract Window Toolkit (AWT) portion of the Java class hierarchy, focusing on the inheritance and interface issues.

The AWT Hierarchy—A Brief Overview

Recall that when we introduced the `BufferedReader` class in Chapter 3, we pointed out that the various intermediate classes used in the creation of a `BufferedReader` model different ways of looking at an input source. In the same way, the different layers in the Java class hierarchy model the different roles that objects play. For example, consider the following portion of the hierarchy corresponding to a text area component:

```
class  Object
    class  Component
        class  TextComponent
            class  TextArea
```

A text area is a graphic component that allows the user to enter and edit multiple lines of text.

The above hierarchy indicates the following:

- A text area is first of all an object and thus inherits behavior from the `Object` class, which models *all* objects in the system. For example, we can store references to a text area in a `Vector`, as we can do with any object.
- A text area is a graphic component and therefore it also inherits behavior from the `Component` class, which models graphic components in the AWT. For example, a text area may be moved—a behavior associated with all components.
- A text area is a text component and therefore it also inherits behavior from the `TextComponent` class, which models a graphic component that allows text editing. For example, the text area may change the text cursor—a behavior common to all text components.
- Finally, a text area is an area containing text and whose specific behavior is provided by the `TextArea` class that models behavior specific to the text area itself. For example, a text area may be created with a scrollbar—behavior that is specific to a multiline text component.

This layering of classes and behavior is an application of using inheritance to factor common behavior out to a superclass. Each class in a hierarchy models behavior common to all classes below it. By placing that behavior into a single class—the superclass—we are placing the responsibility for that behavior in exactly one place. Inheritance then allows each subclass requiring the behavior to possess it.

The Interfaces

Interfaces are not part of the class hierarchy. However, they can form hierarchies of their own. One interface can extend another interface using the same sort of syntax for class extension (inheritance). For example, the following code declares the `ActionListener` interface to be an extension of the `EventListener` interface:

```
interface ActionListener extends EventListener {
    Method specifications unique to ActionListener
}
```

This code states that the `ActionListener` is a specification of all the methods that are specified by the `EventListener` interface. It is also a specification of any new methods introduced in `ActionListener`. Any class that implements `Action-Listener` must therefore implement all the methods of the `EventListener` interface as well. Interface extension allows us to add a new set of method requirements to an existing one.

Methods That Query or Modify Behavior

The classes in the AWT maintain different properties associated with the interface: component size, color, font, and so on. Many of these properties are made accessible to the user of the class through *get/set* methods, that is, methods that allow the user to query (*get*) or modify (*set*) the value of a property. These methods usually travel in get/set pairs.

A Very Brief Look at Packages

The Java predefined class hierarchy consists of several hundred classes and interfaces—and that's not counting any classes you may write. To maintain some order among this huge collection, Java provides a mechanism that logically groups related classes—the package. The packages provided by Java along with some of their related classes include

- `java.applet`—Applet-related classes: `Applet`
- `java.awt`—AWT-related classes: `Button`, `Checkbox`, `Color`
- `java.awt.event`—Event-related classes: `ActionEvent`, `MouseEvent`
- `java.io`—Input/output-related classes: `BufferedReader`, `File`
- `java.lang`—Java language-related classes: `String`, `Integer`, `Object`
- `java.math`—Math-related classes: `BigInteger`
- `java.net`—Network-related classes: `URL`, `URLConnection`
- `java.text`—Text-related classes: `DateFormat`, `DecimalFormat`
- `java.util`—Utility and collection classes: `Date`, `Vector`

There are several other packages predefined by Java, but their description is beyond the scope of this book.

We will not go into any detail here regarding the creation or use of packages beyond noting that when we used import, we were effectively informing the compiler of the identities of the packages whose classes we were using.

The full name of a class is actually the class name with the package name as a prefix. Thus, the text area hierarchy could have been written:

```
class  java.lang.Object
    class  java.awt.Component
        class  java.awt.TextComponent
            class  java.awt.TextArea
```

Note that it is possible to define a class in one package that inherits from a class in a different package.

The Graphical Components

Here is the portion of the hierarchy modeling the various graphical components. The classes in bold are the ones we discuss.

```
class  java.lang.Object
    class  java.awt.Component
        class  java.awt.Button
        class  java.awt.Canvas
        class  java.awt.Checkbox
        class java.awt.Choice
        class  java.awt.Container
            class  java.awt.Panel
                class  java.applet.Applet
            class  java.awt.ScrollPane
            class  java.awt.Window
                class  java.awt.Dialog
                    class java.awt.FileDialog
                class  java.awt.Frame
            class  java.awt.Label
            class  java.awt.List
            class  java.awt.Scrollbar
            class  java.awt.TextComponent
                class  java.awt.TextArea
                class  java.awt.TextField
```

Class Component is the superclass for all graphic component classes, the classes that model windows, buttons, list boxes, and so on. The Component class models behavior common to all graphic components. Methods defined in this class deal with properties such as visibility, size, colors, and font. A paint() method is provided. It

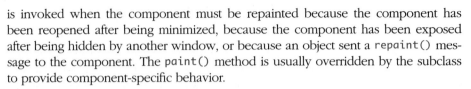

is invoked when the component must be repainted because the component has been reopened after being minimized, because the component has been exposed after being hidden by another window, or because an object sent a `repaint()` message to the component. The `paint()` method is usually overridden by the subclass to provide component-specific behavior.

The `Component` class also provides methods for registering a listener of various component-related events: hiding, showing, moving, or resizing a component. Other events specific to particular component subclass are registered by using methods defined in that component's class.

By virtue of being in the superclass of every component, the above methods are inherited by every component class, providing a rich base set of behavior.

Component Subclasses

Each of the subclasses of `Component` models a specific graphical component and therefore provides behavior specific to that component. We now very briefly describe some of the more commonly used component classes and their behavior.

The `Button` class models a clickable command button. The class provides methods to modify or query the button's label, as well as a method that allows an object to register as a listener of button clicks.

The `Canvas` class models a surface on which graphic shapes, such as circles, lines, and text. A primary purpose of the component is to isolate the drawn items from other graphical components. This class primarily serves as a superclass to programmer-defined classes that override the `paint()` method to draw application-specific information on the canvas.

The `Checkbox` class models a check box that can be selected or deselected. Several `Checkbox` objects can be used together with the `CheckBoxGroup` class to provide a set of mutually exclusive boxes: clicking one deselects the previous clicked box. Methods are provided to select and deselect the box, access the box's text label, register event listeners, and obtain information about the related `CheckboxGroup` object.

Class `Container` is the superclass for all classes that model components that may contain other components: for example, windows and panels. The methods provided therefore focus on the relationship between a container and its embedded components: specification of layout managers, addition and removal of components, and registration of container-related events. In addition, the `paint()` method is overridden so that it contains code to invoke the `paint()` method of the container's components.

The `Panel` class provides the most basic of container functionality. It essentially does nothing more than inherit its methods from its superclass. Its main purpose is to provide a convenient mechanism to break up a larger container into groups of components, each in its own panel, that can be laid out independently of the rest of the container.

The `Applet` class models an applet—a program that executes while embedded within a browser. It inherits from `Panel` all the basic container behavior so that components may be added to the applet, providing a graphical interface. Methods defined at the `Applet` level include those that deal with the program perspective of this class: initialization code to be performed when the applet is initially loaded and when it begins execution.

Class `Window` provides the basic functionality of a window residing on the desktop. Its methods deal with displaying the window, moving the window to the front or back of its desktop position—that is, whether the window is below or above all other windows residing at the same location—and registration of window-related events.

The `Dialog` class models the behavior of a window whose purpose is to accept user input. Often this input is required before the program can proceed, in which case we want no other user activity to be allowed in any other window of the program until the user has completed the dialog window. In such a situation, we say the dialog is *modal*. If the user can perform action in another window, it is *nonmodal*. The methods of the `Dialog` class include testing and setting modality as well as manipulating the text in the title bar of the window.

In Java, a *frame* is a window with a title bar; various control elements to minimize, maximize, and close the window; and possibly a menu bar across the top. The `Frame` class models the behavior of a frame. The methods deal with manipulating the title and menu bar as well as event registration.

In an applet, an `Applet` object is the top-level container. Stand-alone applications, that is, programs with a `main()` method, can also use a graphical user interface. The top-level container in that case is a programmer-defined subclass of the `Frame` class. The constructor of this subclass typically contains the code that would appear in an applet's `init()` method.

The `Label` class models a component consisting of text that is displayed but that cannot be edited by the user. Methods include obtaining or setting this text.

The `List` class provides the functionality of a box displaying a list of items from which one or more selections may be made. Scrollbars are automatically added to the list as it grows beyond the number of items that can be displayed in the box. Methods include manipulating and selecting the list items, specifying whether multiple items may be selected, and list-specific event registration.

The `TextComponent` class is the superclass for editable text components. Its methods provide manipulation of the text, positioning of the text cursor, controlling whether the text may be modified, selecting portions of the text, and text-specific event registration. The `TextArea` component class extends `TextComponent` to model a multiline text field and thus supplies methods dealing with scrollbars. The TextField class restricts the text component to a single line.

The Event Classes

Here is the event portion of the hierarchy. The occurrence of an event within the AWT environment causes the system to create an object in this hierarchy whose state contains information specific to the event. Thus, moving the mouse causes the AWT environment to create a MouseEvent object with information regarding the mouse move, such as the position of the mouse.

```
class  java.util.EventObject
    class  java.awt.AWTEvent
        class  java.awt.event.ActionEvent
        class  java.awt.event.AdjustmentEvent
        class  java.awt.event.ComponentEvent
            class  java.awt.event.ContainerEvent
            class  java.awt.event.FocusEvent
            class  java.awt.event.InputEvent
                class  java.awt.event.KeyEvent
                class  java.awt.event.MouseEvent
            class  java.awt.event.PaintEvent
            class  java.awt.event.WindowEvent
        class  java.awt.event.ItemEvent
        class  java.awt.event.TextEvent
```

The Event class is the superclass of the event portion of the hierarchy and as such models the behavior common to *all* events. Its primary method, get-Source(), returns the object, known as the *event source,* that generated the event.

The AWTEvent class is the superclass for all AWT-related events; these are the only ones we are examining. The method of interest is getID(), which returns an integer identifying the sort of event that occurred. These integer values usually are declared as constants in the specific event subclass.

The ActionEvent class models an action event specified by the user, such as a button click. Its methods provide access to what is known as the *command name* associated with the event. In the case of a button click, the command name is the text of the button. Any special keys, such as the ALT or CTRL keys, known as modifiers, held down during the click may also be obtained through the getModifiers() method.

The AdjustmentEvent class maintains information about events generated by components that can be adjusted, most notably scrollbars. The methods include querying the type of adjustment and the current value. For example, a scrollbar can generate a small or large motion, depending on where the bar is clicked.

The ComponentEvent class deals with component-related events. The events associated with this class include hiding, moving, or resizing the component.

Events associated with the ContainerEvent class include the addition or removal of a component in the container.

The FocusEvent class maintains the information associated with a component gaining the *focus*. That is, the component becomes the active element of the interface. The two basic events are gaining and losing the focus.

The InputEvent class is the superclass of events involving user input. Methods include the ability to test whether special modifier keys were held down at the time of the event.

The KeyEvent class extends the behavior of its InputEvent superclass by adding behavior specific to keyboard input. The methods include querying for the key that was pressed to generate this event. Constants are defined in this class corresponding to the various function keys, allowing the user to refer to these keys.

The MouseEvent class is the other subclass of InputEvent; it maintains the state of a mouse-generated event. Event types include clicking, dragging, moving, pressing, and releasing the mouse. Associated with the event and accessible through methods are the coordinates of the mouse position, and the number of clicks causing the event (for example, single- versus double-click).

The WindowEvent class maintains window-related events: closing, minimizing, and restoring a window.

The ItemEvent handles events generated by making a selection, for example, from a list box. The events of interest are selecting and deselecting.

The TextEvent class models an event generated through the manipulation of text. The single event type defined in this class is the text-changed event. The associated text can be obtained through the methods of the component generating the event.

The Listener Interfaces

In order to handle an event generated by a component object, an object must register itself as a *listener* of the component object. It accomplishes this by invoking the listener registration method of the component object. The method name is of the form set*EventType*Listener or add*EventType*Listener. In addition, the class of the listener object must support a standard set of methods to handle the events when they occur. The listener class is usually already a subclass of some superclass that provides it with the bulk of its nonevent-related behavior. Therefore, the listener method-set is specified as an interface that the listener object must implement.

We've said that interfaces can form their own hierarchies representing increasing sets of required methods. Here is the interface hierarchy corresponding to listeners. The root of the hierarchy is the `EventListener` interface. The indentation reflects the hierarchy of the interfaces.

```
interface  java.util.EventListener
    interface  java.awt.event.ActionListener
    interface  java.awt.event.AdjustmentListener
    interface  java.awt.event.ComponentListener
    interface  java.awt.event.ContainerListener
    interface  java.awt.event.FocusListener
    interface  java.awt.event.KeyListener
    interface  java.awt.event.MouseListener
    interface  java.awt.event.MouseMotionListener
    interface  java.awt.event.TextListener
    interface  java.awt.event.WindowListener
```

Each listener interface specifies one or more event-handling methods that must be provided by an implementing class. These event-handling methods accept as an argument an object of an event class corresponding to the listener type, such as an `ActionEvent` for the `ActionListener` methods. These methods are invoked when the corresponding event occurs. Thus, the `actionPerformed()` method of the `ActionListener` interface is invoked when an action event—a button click, for example—occurs. This invocation is performed by the AWT environment, which is also responsible for creating and initializing the associated event object.

The `ActionListener` interface requires an implementing class to provide a single method, `actionPerformed()`, that accepts an `ActionEvent` object as its single argument. The class implementing this method can use the argument to obtain information regarding the event in order to process it.

The `AdjustmentListener` interface requires that one method, `adjustmentValueChanged()`, be implemented. Its accepts an `AdjustmentEvent` object as its argument.

The `ComponentListener` interface has four required methods corresponding to hiding, displaying, resizing, and moving a component. Each of these methods accepts a `ComponentEvent` argument.

The `ContainerListener` requires two event-handling methods corresponding to adding an interface and removing an embedded component. The methods accept a `ContainerEvent` argument.

The `FocusListener` interface specifies two methods: gaining and losing the focus. They accept a `FocusEvent` argument.

An `ItemEvent` is associated with a component from which a selection may be made. The `ItemListener` interface requires that a single method be implemented.

This method is invoked when some change has been made regarding the selection, for example, if the user has changed the highlighted selection in the list box. The method accepts an `ItemEvent` as its argument.

The `KeyListener` interface requires three methods to be implemented corresponding to pressing, releasing, or the combined press-and-release of a key, called *typing a key* (a combination of the other two). The methods accept a `KeyEvent` as their argument.

The `MouseListener` interface contains method specifications corresponding to all mouse-related events except mouse movement. The methods correspond to pressing, releasing, and clicking (similar to the typing of the `KeyListener` in that it involves a press/release event pair occurrence), as well as the mouse entering or exiting the boundaries of a component. The methods accept a `MouseEvent` as argument.

The `MouseMotionListener` interface handles mouse movement. Moving the mouse is handled through a separate mechanism because of the large number of mouse movement events generated and the consequent effect on performance. There are two events associated with mouse movement—simple movement and dragging a component. Each is specified in a separate method that accepts a `MouseEvent` as its argument.

The `TextListener` interface specifies a single method corresponding to the event occurring when a text-related event occurs. The method accepts a `TextEvent` as its argument.

The `WindowListener` interface specifies a number of methods corresponding to window-related events: minimizing, restoring, closing, opening, and so on. Each accepts a `WindowEvent` as its argument.

The Adapter Classes

Although many of the listener interfaces specify only a single method, several of them require that multiple methods be provided by an implementing class. It is often the case that an application is only interested in handling one or two of these event types, and thus only wishes to provide the methods corresponding to these. However, neglecting to implement the remaining methods will cause a compile-time error because the interface is incompletely specified. To reduce the burden on a class implementing an interface with multiple methods, Java provides a set of classes, known as the *adapter* classes, which provide empty method bodies for each of the methods specified in a listener interface. For example, the `ComponentAdapter` class, which implements the `ComponentListener` interface, appears this way:

```
class ComponentAdapter implements ComponentListener {
    public void componentResized(ComponentEvent e) {}
```

```
    public  void  componentMoved(ComponentEvent  e)  {}
    public  void  componentShown(ComponentEvent  e)  {}
    public  void  componentHidden(ComponentEvent  e)  {}
}
```

A class that is intended to be a `ComponentListener` without implementing all of the required methods can then inherit from the `ComponentAdapter` class and override only those methods it is interested in. For example, the following class wishes only to handle the resize event:

```
class  MyComponentListenerClass  extends  ComponentAdapter  {
    public  void  componentResized(ComponentEvent  e)  {
        code to handle the resize event
    }
}
```

The remaining (empty) event-handling methods are inherited from the `Component-Adapter` superclass.

One word of caution about using adapter classes—they are inherited, which means the subclass cannot inherit behavior from any other class. Because the behavior inherited from the adapter class consists of empty method bodies, their usefulness is limited.

Exceptions

13.1 Expect the Unexpected

I magine the following code, which might appear in an inventory program:

```
int numberInStock = Integer.parseInt(br.readLine());
```

We expect that all is well with the input source represented by the `Buffered-Reader` object referenced by `br` and that eventually it will produce a line containing a number. We generally don't expect the following to occur:

- The `BufferedReader` object represents a file on a floppy disk that has been erroneously ejected from the computer by the user.
- The `BufferedReader` object represents a network connection that has suddenly failed because a leaky pipe suddenly ruined one of the campus routers.
- The `BufferedReader` object represents a file on a hard disk that has just failed.

We don't expect circumstances such as these unless we are professional programmers, that is. Professional programmers must learn to *expect the unexpected.*

The unexpected does not consist only of physical interferences such as those mentioned above. When we write

```
int numberInStock = Integer.parseInt(br.readLine());
```

we are expecting that a number will appear in the input at this point. Consider, however, the following possibilities:

- What if the data entry operator types a "w" instead of a "2" by mistake?
- What if the operator had been distracted while typing and had accidentally held the "3" key down too long, adding twenty-two 3s to the end of the number?

The context in which software executes is not as predictable as we would like. Good software is designed to take this into account. In this chapter we examine the mechanism that Java provides to handle unexpected circumstances.

13.2 Encountering the Unexpected

Responding to the unexpected is as much a part of the required behavior of our "smart and helpful" objects as dealing with the expected. Behavior, as we know, is implemented in methods. But what can methods do when they encounter the unexpected?

Let's consider a method from the `Integer` class that we've been using since Chapter 5, `parseInt()`. Its argument is a `String`—hopefully one that is a well-formed decimal representation of an integer. But what if it's not? What should `parseInt()` do, for example, if its argument is "eggplant"?

One thing `parseInt()` cannot do is correct the error—it has no way of knowing what the argument should have been. Nor could `parseInt()` query the user for the correct argument with code such as the following:

```
System.err.print("Hi, parseInt here. I have a
                  bad non-numeric argument");
System.err.print(... argument goes here ...);
System.err.print("Please type in the proper value: ");
... = ...readLine();          Read new String from keyboard.
```

First, there may not be any available user. The invocation of `parseInt()` may be in a program that is processing files or carrying out network operations. Second, it is impossible for `parseInt()` to let a user know the context in which this problem has occurred because `parseInt()` doesn't know whether it is converting a pay-rate value, an hours-worked value, a number-of-dependents value, or something else. There may be hundreds of places in the program where integers are read in. That being the case, how could the user possibly know the correct value to type in?

In sum, *it is not the responsibility of `parseInt()` to correct or even identify the ultimate source of the error.* The argument came from its invoker, so the responsibility therefore rests on the invoker of `parseInt()`. Thus, `parseInt()` must inform its invoker that a problem has occurred. How can that be done?

Normally, information from a method is communicated to its invoker by a return value. Perhaps an unexpected situation could be communicated via a return value that the invoker could test. But the unexpected does not occur "normally." The designer of `parseInt()` could not specify that if the method encounters an error it will return a `String` "bad number format" because `parseInt()`'s prototype demands that it always return an `int`. Nor could the designer arrange for some special `int` value like –999 to be returned in the event of an error. What if the `String` argument was –999—how could the resulting integer be distinguished from an error?

Throwing Exceptions

To allow methods to respond to the unexpected, Java provides an alternate means of terminating the execution of a method. This is accomplished with the throw statement

throw *reference*

where the reference is to an object of a subclass of the class Exception—a class that represents unexpected situations. (We discuss Exception classes in the Java Interlude later in this chapter). The throw statement usually takes on the following form:

throw new *Exception-class*(*String-Argument*);

where *Exception-class* is a subclass of Exception. When a method executes the throw statement, we say that it *throws an exception.*

Picture the chain of method invocations that leads to the invocation of a particular method, known as the **invocation chain**. The first method that executes is main(). It invokes a method that in turn invokes a method, and so on until the method that encounters the unexpected situation is invoked (see Figure 13.1).

Figure 13.1
A chain of method invocations leading to an unexpected circumstance. The main method invoked methodA, which invoked another method, which eventually invoked methodX, which invoked methodY. Now methodY encounters an unexpected situation—what happens?

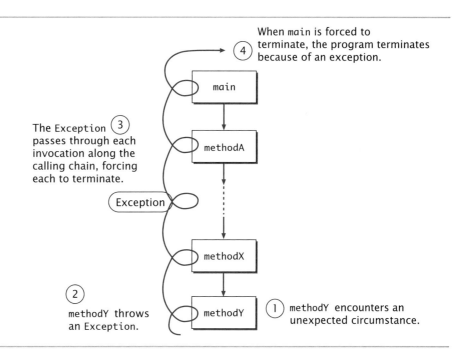

Throwing an Exception causes the executing method to terminate immediately. However, the throw statement does not return a value, nor does the sender resume execution from the point where the invocation occurred. Instead, the thrown Exception passes through each invocation along the chain, forcing each invoked method to terminate. To each method along the way, it appears as if the method it had invoked had thrown the Exception. In fact, we say that each method along the way throws the Exception. Eventually this cascades all the way back to the main() method that started the program's execution, at which point the program terminates.

Thus the statement

throw *reference-to-Exception-object*

causes the program to terminate. You might think of it as an escape hatch. Java systems typically respond to such an outcome by displaying on standard output (or in a window) the Exception being thrown, followed by the names of the methods that terminated their execution by throwing an Exception. The following is an example of this display:

```
SomeException
        at TryThrow.method2(TryThrow.java:18)
        at TryThrow.method1(TryThrow.java:15)
        at TryThrow.main(TryThrow.java:12)
```

You might recognize this as the same output generated by the Thread.dumpStack method introduced in Chapter 8.

The above output is typical and serves as text representation of the invocation chain that led to method2(). It shows that in line 12 of TryThrow.java, the main() method invoked method1(), and in line 15 of TryThrow.java, method1() invoked method2(). In line 18 of TryThrow.java, method2() threw a SomeException object. This terminated method2(), method1(), and main().

EXAMPLE parseInt(). The parseInt() method contains a statement similar to

throw new NumberFormatException(*String-Argument*);

This creates a new NumberFormatException object and throws the reference to this object. NumberFormatException is a subclass of Exception.

The throws Clause

The verb *throw* is not altogether unfamiliar to you—you have undoubtedly noticed that Java often requires that we include a throws clause in the header of a method declaration. For example,

public static void main(String[] a) (throws Exception){

We can now (finally!) explain this requirement: Any method that might throw an Exception must acknowledge it in its declaration with a **throws clause**. A throws clause consists of the keyword throws and a list of subclasses of Exception that could be thrown by the method. This requirement applies not only to methods that contain a throws statement but to methods that may throw an Exception because they invoke other method's throws Exceptions.

ava Interlude

The Exception *Class*

The reference that appears in a throws statement must refer to an object of the Exception class. Because of the rules of inheritance, any object that is an instance of a subclass of the Exception class is also an Exception object.

Why have different Exception classes? These classes allow us to make distinctions between the different kinds of unexpected situations that arise. For example, the requirement for throws clauses forces programmers to be more aware of the possibility of unexpected situations. If every throws clause simply had Exception, the programmer would not receive or convey specific information as to what type of exception could arise. Writing

```
... throws  IOException
```

uses the IOException class, which models problems that pertain to an i/o operation. However, writing

```
throws  FileNotFoundException,  RemoteException
```

uses subclasses of IOException that model even more specific unexpected circumstances.

Labeling Exceptions

One Exception constructor takes as an argument a String that is printed out when the invocation chain is displayed. This allows the thrower of the Exception to label the Exception in order to convey additional information:

```
throw new FileNotFoundException("log file is always "necessary");
```

Checked Exception Versus RuntimeException

The Java class library defines a RuntimeException class that is an extension of Exception. Going further down the hierarchy, Exception subclasses like Null-PointerException, IOException, NumberFormatException, and so on are defined as extensions to RuntimeException. Unlike other Exceptions, the compiler does not require that any of these be mentioned in a throws clause. The reason is that these exceptions generally represent coding errors. Because such errors could occur anywhere, *every* method would have to mention RuntimeException in its declaration. Thus no distinctive information would be provided, and so the throws requirement is waived.

Exceptions that must be mentioned in a throws clause are called **checked Exceptions** because the compiler checks that the throws clauses match any throws statements or throws clauses of other methods invoked.

13.3 Handling the Unexpected

By default, the throws statement launches a chain of method terminations, beginning with the method executing the throws statement, ending with the main() method of the program, and terminating the program itself. This is usually too harsh a way of handling an unexpected situation. Often it is possible for the program to respond to the unexpected and recover. How can a method respond to an Exception thrown by another method that it invokes?

Java provides a way for methods to *catch* any Exception that is thrown their way by methods that they invoke. Catching an Exception means breaking the cascade of Exception-throwing that leads to the termination of the program. Instead, the method catching the Exception regains control and can then—hopefully—handle the situation in a less extreme way than abrupt program termination.

To catch an Exception, the statements containing invocations of Exception-throwing methods must be surrounded by braces and preceded with the keyword try:

```
try {
    someObject.someMethod();
}
```

Following this is the keyword catch and a parenthesized declaration of a reference variable that will refer to the thrown Exception object:

```
try {
    someObject.someMethod();
} catch (Exception e)
```

After that comes a group of statements surrounded by braces. If an exception is thrown, these statements will be executed when the Exception object reaches this method:

```
try {
    someObject.someMethod();
} catch (Exception e) {
    Statements that are executed if and only if an exception
    is thrown by the code within the try
}
```

The code that appears in the braces that follow the keyword try is called the *try part*; we also say that this code is surrounded by a *try catch*. The code that appears after the catch is called the *catch part*.

EXAMPLE Improved Error Messages. Let us take a simple example. Suppose we have a Movie class that has a static method readMovie(). This method is passed a BufferedReader and returns a Movie object. It is expected to read the name of the movie and the number of minutes of playing time from the BufferedReader, pass these values (String reference and int) to the Movie constructor, and return the resulting Movie reference. If end-of-file is reached, a null reference is returned.

Ignoring the unexpected, we have

```
static Movie readMovie(BufferedReader br) throws IOException {
    String name;
    int playingTime;
    Movie  newMovie;

    name = br.readLine();
    if (name==null)
        return null;
    playingTime = Integer.parseInt(br.readLine());
    newMovie = new Movie(name,playingTime);
    return newMovie;
}
```

Recognizing the possibility of data error in the integer input, we note that it is possible for parseInt() to throw a NumberFormatException. We don't want the program to terminate without some explanation for the user.

We therefore enclose the statement that invokes parseInt() within a try and catch any NumberFormatException that it throws:

```
static Movie readMovie(BufferedReader br) throws IOException {
    String name;
    int    playingTime;
    Movie  newMovie;

    name = br.readLine();
    if (name==null)
        return null;
    try {
        playingTime = Integer.parseInt(br.readLine());
    } catch (NumberFormatException e) {
        System.err.println("Bad playingTime format for "+ name);
        throw e;
    }
```

```
    newMovie = new Movie(name,playingTime);
    return newMovie;
}
```

After writing out a meaningful error message to the user, we rethrow the `Exception` and let it continue to take its course. We do this because we have not fully handled the error.

EXAMPLE Recovering from an Error.   Now let's consider a more involved example. It might not be reasonable to allow a single error in the data to terminate an entire run. Rather, we would like to display a warning message, skip the erroneous data, go on and read the next movie entry, and process it. We write:

```
static Movie readMovie(BufferedReader br) throws IOException {
    String name;
    int playingTime;
    Movie  newMovie;

    name = br.readLine();
    if (name==null)
        return null;
    try {
        playingTime = Integer.parseInt(br.readLine());
    } catch (NumberFormatException e) {    // Skip this movie; do  next one.
```

```
        System.err.print("Bad playing time data for "+name);
        System.err.println(" -- movie skipped");
        name = br.readLine();
        if (name==null)
            return null;
        playingTime = Integer.parseInt(br.readLine());
        newMovie = new Movie(name,playingTime);
        return newMovie;
```

This code is executed if `parseInt()` throws a `NumberFormat-Exception`.

```
    }
```

```
    newMovie = new Movie(name,playingTime);
    return newMovie;
```

This code is executed if `parseInt()` does not throw a `NumberFormatException`.

```
}
```

Can you see the problem here? The code that skips the movie with bad input and goes onto the next movie also calls `parseInt()` and faces the same possibility of bad input. If there were two instances of bad data in a row, the program would terminate.

Let's take a step back from this code. What we really want to do is keep trying to get some good movie data. This may conceivably (though hopefully not!) take many reads. A loop is needed, therefore, one that ends either when there are no more data (`name` is `null`) or when good data (`String` and `int`) have been successfully read. To keep track of the second condition, we will use a boolean variable, got-GoodData.

At this point we have

```
boolean gotGoodData;      // True if and only if both name and playingTime
                          //     have valid data.
...
while (name!=null && !gotGoodData)) {
     ...
}
```

After the loop, we can check name and either return null or a new Movie based on the good data we have:

```
if (name==null)
    return null;
else
    return new Movie(name,playingTime);
```

We must initialize name before the loop. Because we don't yet have a good value for playingTime, gotGoodData is initialized to false. Our method at this point is as follows:

```
static Movie readMovie(BufferedReader br) throws IOException {
    String name;
    int playingTime;
    boolean gotGoodData; // True if and only if both name and playingTime
                         //     have valid data.
    Movie  newMovie;
    name = br.readLine();
    gotGoodData = false;
    while (!(name==null || gotGoodData)) {
         ...
    }
    if (name==null)
         return null;
    else
         return new Movie(name,playingTime);
}
```

The loop's termination is guaranteed by trying to complete the reading of the movie input data:

```
try {
    playingTime = Integer.parseInt(br.readLine());
} catch (NumberFormatException e) { // Skip this movie; do next one.
```

... exception handling code goes here ...
```
}
```

If `parseInt()` throws an `Exception`, we warn the user, set `gotGoodData` to `false` and read in the name of the next movie in the input. The body of the catch part then is as follows:

```
System.err.print("Bad playing time data for " + name);
System.err.println("--movie skipped");
gotGoodData = false;
name = br.readLine();
```

The definition of `gotGoodData` requires that it be `true` when the movie data are good, that is, when no `Exception` has been thrown. We therefore, rather optimistically, set `gotGoodData` to be `true` before trying to read `playingTime`. If the attempt to read `playingTime` fails, then catching the `Exception` will set `gotGoodData` back to `false`.

The completed method is as follows:

```
static Movie readMovie(BufferedReader br) throws IOException {
    String name;
    int playingTime;
    boolean gotGoodData; // True if and only if both name and playingTime
                         //     have valid data.
    Movie  newMovie;

    name = br.readLine();
    gotGoodData = false;
    while (!(name==null || gotGoodData)) {
        gotGoodData = true; // Optimistic! but if an Exception
                            //     is thrown, it will be set to false.

        try {
            playingTime = Integer.parseInt(br.readLine());
        } catch (NumberFormatException e) { // Skip this movie; do next one.
            System.err.print("Bad playing time data for "+ name);
            System.err.println(" -- movie skipped");
            gotGoodData = false;
            name = br.readLine();
        }
    }
    if (name==null)
        return null;
    else
        return new Movie(name,playingTime);
}
```

13.4 Responsibility for the Unexpected

In object-oriented programming, each object takes "responsibility" for its behavior. Handling unexpected circumstances is often part of the behavior we desire from our "smart and helpful" objects. For example, imagine the following group of objects:

- The NetHeadlineScanner object models a network headline service. A NetHeadlineScanner object continuously displays headlines containing certain keywords. These headlines are obtained from a NetHeadlines object.
- The NetHeadlines object obtains continual headline news from any one of several alternative sources. Such an object is implemented using a NetReader.
- The NetReader object reads continuously updated information from a source on the network. The NetReader in turn may be implemented using a BufferedReader.
- The BufferedReader object is constructed from an InputStream delivered by a connected Socket object. Socket is a Java predefined class that models low-level network connections.

Thus, the NetHeadlineScanner object invokes a readLine() method of the NetHeadline class, which in turn invokes a readLine() method of the NetReader class, which in turn invokes BufferedReader's readLine() method.

The "unexpected" in this case is the current news source going down, that is, suddenly becoming unavailable, while it is being accessed. Which classes should take responsibility for this occurrence? What should their behavior be?

One way to approach this question is to note where the Exception is generated and then consider the objects along the invocation chain, including which object is in a position—in terms of the scope of its responsibility—to do something about the exception. Let's try that here.

BufferedReader.readLine() throws the Exception, so we can hardly expect it to catch the Exception. But why does it throw the Exception? Why couldn't it handle the network data source going down? It could not simply because a BufferedReader is itself an idealized data source and has no knowledge of whether it is providing data from a network, a file, or a keyboard. It can only know that there has been an abnormal interruption of data (as distinct from an end-of-file). It can only throw up its hands—and throw an Exception.

What about NetReader? The description above tells us that the NetReader object knows that it is reading from the network location of its source. But getting data from that particular source is the entire behavior of a given NetReader object. If data from that source are now not available, the NetReader object too can only throw up its hands—and rethrow the Exception generated by BufferedReader.

What about NetHeadlines? According to the description, a NetHeadlines object knows about several alternative news sources on the network. Therefore, the

NetHeadlines object could conceivably respond to the situation by catching the Exception, selecting a different network address, creating a different NetReader object based on that address, and continuing as before—the NetHeadlineScanner need never know that this happened.

Let's still consider NetHeadlineScanner. Perhaps it would do as well or better than NetHeadlines in handling this Exception. That, however, turns out not to be the case. The NetHeadlineScanner takes a source of headlines for granted. Its responsibility is the selection of headlines based on keywords.

Thus, we see that the place that ought to deal with the Exception is the readLine() method of NetHeadlines (see Figure 13.2).

13.5 Exceptions Are Not Always Errors

In this chapter we have adopted Java's rather optimistic view that errors are exceptions. However, the Exception mechanism is flexible and powerful, and its use goes beyond handling errors.

As an example, let's write a simple program that gets an URL as its single command-line argument and prints the evaluation "good" or "bad," depending on whether the URL is the address of a web page that exists and is accessible to us.

To do this, we make use of the integer *response codes* that web servers send when web clients (like browsers) make connections to them. Response codes of 300 or greater signify some kind of error in the URL. For example, 404 means the resource does not exist. The HttpURLConnection class in the java.net package models HTTP connections to web resources that are specified by URLs. We can create such an object by sending an openConnection() message to an URL object. Once we have an HttpURLConnection object, we can send it a getResponseCode() message to get the response code resulting from an attempt to connect to the URL. Testing the resulting integer allows us to determine whether the URL is good or bad:

Figure 13.2

Where should an Exception be caught? The Exception pictured here is thrown in BufferedReader's readLine() method, but it can only be handled in the read-Line() method of NetHeadlines. So it is caught in that method.

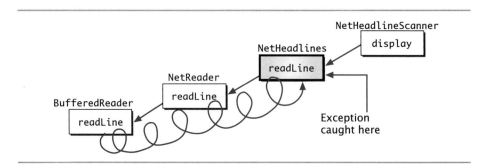

```
import java.net.*;
import java.io.*;
class CheckURL {
   public static void main(String[] a) throws Exception {
      URL u = new URL(a[0]);
      HttpURLConnection uC = (HttpURLConnection) u.openConnection();
      int responseCode = uC.getResponseCode();
      System.out.println(responseCode);
      if (responseCode>=300)
         System.out.println("bad");
      else
         System.out.println("good");
   }
}
```

Unfortunately, our program will print out "bad" or "good" only if it actually can make a connection to an HTTP server. If the machine address part of the URL doesn't exist or if that machine is not an HTTP server, the program will throw an Exception instead of printing "bad." This is not an error however, merely a result of a bad URL. So we solve this problem by enclosing all the statements in the method in a try clause and printing the appropriate message if an Exception occurs:

```
import java.net.*;
import java.io.*;
class CheckURL {
   public static void main(String[] a) {
      try {
         URL u = new URL(a[0]);
         HttpURLConnection uC = (HttpURLConnection) u.openConnection();
         int responseCode = uC.getResponseCode();
         System.out.println(responseCode);
         if (responseCode>=300)
            System.out.println("bad");
         else
            System.out.println("good");
      } catch (Exception e) {
            System.out.println("bad");
      }
   }
}
```

This use of Exception catching illustrates an important point. Although most of the discussion of Exceptions in this chapter was in the context of errors, not all Exceptions are errors. Here, for example, the purpose of the program is to find bad URLs lurking in a set of web pages. Finding them is hardly an error. Yet we use the Exception mechanism quite conveniently here to identify them.

For that matter, the Exceptions here are not particularly unexpected either.

Summary

How an object handles unexpected circumstances is as much a part of its behavior as how it responds to messages in normal situations. Java provides a class, Exception, that models unexpected situations. Along with this class, Java provides the throw statement, a mechanism for abruptly changing the flow of control. When a method encounters a situation that it cannot handle in the normal way, it may create and throw an Exception object. The throw statement transfers control to the first enclosing try-catch statement for that particular Exception. If none is found in the current method, the method terminates, throwing the same Exception and the search for a try-catch continues in the invoking method. This process will continue all the way up the chain of invocation until a matching try-catch is found. If none is found, the main() method itself throws the Exception and the program terminates.

Key Terms

checked Exception An Exception that, if thrown by a method, must appear in the method's throws clause; so called because the Java compiler checks for its presence in the clause.

Exception An object that represents an unexpected circumstance or an out-of-the-ordinary situation.

invocation chain The sequence of method invocations starting with main() that leads to and includes the invocation of the currently executing method.

Runtime Exception An Exception that reflects a programming error that typically can occur "anywhere" and ought to occur "nowhere" in the code and therefore is not required to be in the throws clause.

throws clause A clause in a method declaration that identifies all the checked exceptions the method might throw.

Questions for Review

1. What happens when an Exception is thrown?
2. Why isn't the normal return mechanism sufficient for handling out-of-the-ordinary situations?

3. How can a method handle Exceptions thrown by methods it invokes?
4. What is a checked Exception? Give an example of an Exception that is not a checked Exception.
5. How can a method attach additional information to an Exception that it throws?
6. Why do we need different Exception classes that are extensions of Exception?

Exercises

1. Return to the ATM example of Chapter 6. What unexpected circumstances could occur in the methods of its classes?
2. Return to the WHWWW example program at the end of Chapter 3. What unexpected circumstances could arise in executing that program?
3. Write a method that receives a nonnegative integer as an argument and returns true if the integer is a perfect square and returns false otherwise. The method, isPerfectSquare(), should throw an Exception if the argument is negative. Test this method using both acceptable and unacceptable values as arguments.
4. Write a method that receives an array of nonnegative integers as an argument and returns true if every integer in the array is a perfect square and returns false otherwise. The method, areAllPerfectSquares(), repeatedly invokes isPerfectSquare() (see Exercise 3). Test this method using both acceptable and unacceptable values in the elements of the array argument.
5. Modify the method you wrote in Exercise 3 so that the Exception thrown is labeled with an explanatory String.
6. Define a new class, NegativeIntegerException, that is an extension of the Exception class. Modify the isPerfectSquare() method so that it throws a NegativeIntegerException instead of simply throwing an Exception.
7. Rewrite the RepairPerson.read() method from Chapter 7 so that it can recover from input errors.
8. Reconsider the Location class from Chapter 7. Define a LocationException class and rewrite the methods of the Location class to throw a Location-Exception when their arguments violate the assumptions (requirements) of the methods. For example, the Location.read() method assumed that its input was of the form <int>,<int>. Verify this in the method body now and, if the argument doesn't have this form, throw a LocationException. Make this analysis and carry out this rewrite for each of the Location methods.

The Model-View-Controller (MVC) Paradigm

In this supplement we'll discuss the Model-View-Controller paradigm, a technique for designing GUI programs (such as applets) that is surprisingly powerful. We'll begin by developing a simple CounterApplet, using the Counter class from Chapter 4 and applying the principle of separating display and control we introduced in the Chapter 8 supplement.

A Simple CounterApplet

Figure 13.3 shows the execution of our CounterApplet: buttons corresponding to the increment() and reset() methods, and a TextField in which the current Counter value is displayed. Here is the code for this applet (including the Counter class itself):

```java
import java.applet.*;
import java.awt.*;
import java.awt.event.*;

public class CounterApplet extends Applet implements ActionListener {
    public void init() {
        incButton = new Button("+");
        resetButton = new Button("reset");
        valField = new TextField();
        valField.setText(Integer.toString(ctr.getValue()));
```

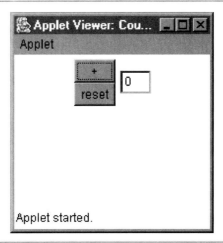

Figure 13.3
The executing
CounterApplet.

```
        Panel p = new Panel();
        p.setLayout(new BorderLayout());
        p.add(incButton, "North");
        p.add(resetButton, "South");
        add(p);
        add(valField);

        ctr = new Counter();

        incButton.addActionListener(this);
        resetButton.addActionListener(this);
    }

    public void actionPerformed(ActionEvent ae) {
        String s = ae.getActionCommand();
        if (s.equals("+"))
            ctr.increment();
        else if (s.equals("reset"))
            ctr.reset();
        valField.setText(Integer.toString(ctr.getValue()));
    }

    Button incButton, resetButton;   // Instance variables
    TextField valField;
    Counter ctr;
}

class Counter {
    public void reset() {
        count = 0;
    }
    public void increment() {
        count = count + 1;
    }
    public int getValue() {
        return count;
    }
    private int count = 0;
}
```

Some Limitations

As we discussed in Chapter 8, separating the "control" part of the applet's behavior from the "display" part allows us to design applets that are both conceptually simpler and easier to modify. But even this separation has some limitations; in particular, the `actionPerformed()` method must not only respond to button clicks (which is the primary responsibility of the method) but also update the display. Thus, if at some point we decide to change the display (say, to a scrollbar or some kind of gauge) we will have to remember to modify the `actionPerformed()` implementation. To overcome this kind of limitation, we will turn to a design technique that allows us to separate completely the input, the model, and the display.

Model-View-Controller

Model-View-Controller applications are designed based on three conceptually distinct components:

- *Model.* As before, the model contains the application data and logic, independent of any user interface. For example, a Microsoft Word document is a model that represents a sequence of formatted text; our `Counter` class is also a model.
- *View.* The view provides the user with a display of the model. Word provides several different displays (outline view, page view) and permits multiple simultaneous views by allowing the user to split the document window. We expect the view always to be up to date, so the view must be notified each time the model changes.
- *Controller.* The controller is the source of input and therefore the usual source of changes to the model.

In many cases, it is easier to combine the view and the controller into one class; this is sometimes known as the *Document-View* paradigm.

Implementing this paradigm requires some modifications to the model class—in addition to its primary responsibility, the model must also be able to notify the view whenever the model changes. Conceptually, we can think of the view as an "observer" that is observing the model. This is very similar to Java's event-handling mechanism: For each object that might generate an interesting event, we must provide a "listener"; furthermore, we must tell each event-generating object (by sending an `addActionListener()` message) which object is listening to it. By analogy, our model must know which object is "observing" it, so that it can notify this object whenever the model is changed. This table summarizes the similarities between event handling and view notification:

EVENT HANDLING	VIEW NOTIFICATION
Who is the listener?	Who is the view/observer?
Must notify listener of event.	Must notify view/observer of update.
Listener registers with event source.	View/observer registers with model.
Listener implements `Listener` interface.	View implements `Observer` interface.

So, just as event listeners must implement some kind of `Listener` interface (such as the `ActionListener` interface, which consists only of the `actionPerformed()` method), our view must implement some kind of `Observer` interface. This interface, unlike the `Listener` interfaces, is not predefined by Java—it's just another common programming pattern that is part of the Model-View-Controller paradigm.

Solution Skeleton

Let's summarize what we know about our solution so far. The `Counter` class is the model. In addition to the `reset()`, `increment()`, and `getValue()` methods that are part of the model's responsibility, `Counter` will provide a method that will allow an observer to register; we'll call this method `registerAsObserver()`. In addition, we will implement a private helper method, `notifyObserver()`, that we'll use to notify any registered observer of updates to the model.

The `CounterApplet` class will serve as both the controller and the view. Its functionality as controller will be unchanged—when a button is clicked, it will send the appropriate message to the `Counter`. The `TextField` will not be updated directly; this is now the responsibility of the view.

The `CounterApplet` serves as the view by implementing an appropriate interface (which we must define). We will call this interface `CounterObserver`; it will consist of the single method `counterHasChanged()` (in analogy with the `action-Performed()` method of the `ActionListener` interface). Thus, the complete definition of `CounterObserver` is

```
interface CounterObserver {
    public void counterHasChanged(Counter ctr);
}
```

Just as `actionPerformed()` takes as a parameter an `ActionEvent` reference, the `counterHasChanged()` method takes a `Counter` reference. Figure 13.4 gives a schematic of the relationship among the model, view, and controller in our solution.

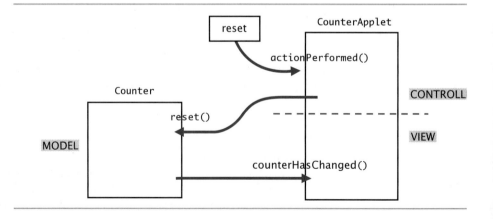

Figure 13.4
Counter MVC design.

The Counter Class

Here is what we know about the signatures of the methods of the revised Counter class:

```
class Counter {
    public void reset() {...}              These methods must notify
    public void increment() {...}          observer that model has changed.
    public int getValue() {...}
    public void registerAsObserver(CounterObserver co) {...}
    private void notifyObserver() {...}
}
```

Because the notifyObserver() method must have access to the Counter-Observer reference passed to registerAsObserver(), we will also need an instance variable

```
private CounterObserver observer;
```

The implementations of reset() and increment() are *almost* unchanged—after they adjust the value of count, they must then invoke the notifyObserver() helper method to ensure that the registered observer takes appropriate action:

```
public void reset() {
    count = 0;
    notifyObserver();
}
public void increment() {
    count = count + 1;
    notifyObserver();
}
```

Note that in fact we are notifying the observer that the Counter's state *might* have changed—it's possible that the Counter would receive, for example, two reset() messages in a row, in which case the second reset() message would not cause the Counter's state to change.

The implementation of getValue() is unchanged; because it does not alter the Counter's state, it doesn't need to communicate with the observer:

```
public int getValue() {
    return count;
}
```

The registerAsObserver() method has two responsibilities: It must record the parameter reference in the instance variable observer, and it must invoke notify-Observer() in order to ensure that the view's initial display is correct:

```
    public void registerAsObserver(CounterObserver co) {
        observer = co;
        notifyObserver();
    }
```

Finally, the `notifyObserver()` method itself just invokes `observer`'s `counterHasChanged()` method:

```
    private void notifyObserver() {
        observer.counterHasChanged(this);
    }
```

The CounterApplet class

In revising the `CounterApplet` class, we must make three significant changes:

- It must `implement` the `CounterObserver` interface.
- It must register with the `Counter` during initialization.
- The display is updated in the `counterHasChanged()` method rather than in the `actionPerformed()` method.

The revised applet is as follows, with new code in bold:

```
import java.applet.*;
import java.awt.*;
import java.awt.event.*;

public class CounterApplet extends Applet
                implements ActionListener, CounterObserver {
    public void init() {
        incButton = new Button("+");
        resetButton = new Button("reset");
        valField = new TextField();

        Panel p = new Panel();
        p.setLayout(new BorderLayout());
        p.add(incButton, "North");
        p.add(resetButton, "South");
        add(p);
        add(valField);

        ctr = new Counter();
        ctr.registerAsObserver(this);

        incButton.addActionListener(this);
        resetButton.addActionListener(this);
    }
```

```
public void actionPerformed(ActionEvent ae) {
    String s = ae.getActionCommand();
    if (s.equals("+"))
        ctr.increment();
    else if (s.equals("reset"))
        ctr.reset();
}

public void counterHasChanged(Counter ctr) {
    valField.setText(Integer.toString(ctr.getValue()));
}

Button incButton, resetButton;   // Instance variables
TextField valField;
Counter ctr;
}
```

Extensions

This completes our introduction to MVC programming. By imposing a little bit more separation on the behaviors of our original CounterApplet application, we developed a cleaner design, one in which the model (the Counter) knew nothing about either the view or the controller. By making a small change to the observer-related parts of the Counter class, we can create a framework that is even more flexible and sophisticated. Specifically, instead of allowing only one CounterObserver to register, we will store a Vector of CounterObservers in the Counter class. Thus, we can have several simultaneous views of the Counter, all of which respond immediately when the Counter itself is updated.

To implement this change, we need to do the following:

- Change the instance variable

  private CounterObserver observer

  to

  private Vector observers = new Vector();
- Revise registerAsObserver() and notifyObserver() method to use Vector (and rename notifyObserver() to notifyObservers())

Here are the two revised methods:

```
public void registerAsObserver(CounterObserver co) {
    observers.add(co);
    co.counterHasChanged(this);
}
```

```
public void notifyObservers() {
  CounterObserver co;
  for (int i=0; i < observers.size(); i++) {
    co = (CounterObserver) observers.elementAt(i);
    co.counterHasChanged(this);
  }
}
```

With this change, we can now implement an applet that has multiple controllers and views for each counter. Specifically, we'll create an applet with two counters; each counter will have two synchronized "control panels," plus a "logger" that prints a message each time the counter changes. See Figure 13.5.

The CounterLogger

The CounterLogger's behavior is simple: When we create a CounterLogger object, we give it a Counter reference and a name for this Counter; each time the Counter changes, it prints a message to System.out with the new value of the Counter:

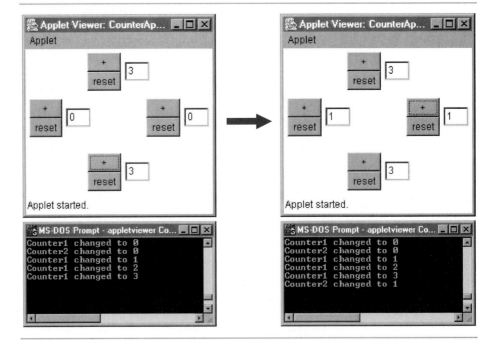

Figure 13.5
CounterApplet with multiple controllers and views.

```
class CounterLogger implements CounterObserver {
   public CounterLogger(Counter ctr, String counterName) {
      this.counterName = counterName;
      ctr.registerAsObserver(this);
   }

   public void counterHasChanged(Counter ctr) {
      System.out.print(counterName+" changed to ");
      System.out.println(ctr.getValue());
   }
   private String counterName;
}
```

Note that the `CounterLogger` doesn't need to save the `Counter` reference in an instance variable—when the `Counter` notifies its observers of an update, it passes a reference to itself to each of the observers.

The CounterPanel

Just as we were able to create our own "custom" `Canvas` in Chapters 9 and 10 by subclassing the `Canvas` class, we can create a custom `Panel` by subclassing the `Panel` class. (Remember, a `Canvas` only allows us to place graphics; if we want to place components such as buttons and text boxes, we must use `Panel`). Each of the four panels in Figure 13.5 closely resembles the previous version of `CounterApplet`; the implementation of `CounterPanel` will closely resemble the implementation of `CounterApplet`. The only significant difference is that the initialization code will be placed in the `CounterPanel` constructor rather than in an `init()` method:

```
class CounterPanel extends Panel
            implements ActionListener,CounterObserver {
   public CounterPanel(Counter ctr) {
      incButton = new Button("+");
      resetButton = new Button("reset");
      valField = new TextField();

      Panel p = new Panel();
      p.setLayout(new BorderLayout());
      p.add(incButton, "North");
      p.add(resetButton, "South");
      add(p);
      add(valField);
```

> Observed `Counter` passed as argument, not created by `CounterPanel`.

```
            incButton.addActionListener(this);
            resetButton.addActionListener(this);

            this.ctr = ctr;
            ctr.registerAsObserver(this);
        }

        public void actionPerformed(ActionEvent ae) {
            String s = ae.getActionCommand();
            if (s.equals("+"))
                ctr.increment();
            else if (s.equals("reset"))
                ctr.reset();
            valField.setText(Integer.toString(ctr.getValue()));
        }

        public void counterHasChanged(Counter ctr) {
            valField.setText(Integer.toString(ctr.getValue()));
        }

        Button incButton, resetButton;   // Instance variables
        TextField valField;
        Counter ctr;
    }
```

The CounterPanel is not responsible for creating the Counter object itself; instead its constructor receives a reference to a Counter. This will allow us to create multiple panels for each Counter.

Modifying the Applet

Because all the controller/view functionality has been moved into the Counter-Logger and CounterPanel, the applet itself is much simplified. Its only responsibilities are creating the Counters and their observers and laying out the display:

```
public class CounterApplet extends Applet {
    public void init() {
        Counter ctr1 = new Counter();
        CounterLogger cl1 = new CounterLogger(ctr1,"Counter1");
        CounterPanel nPanel = new CounterPanel(ctr1);
        CounterPanel sPanel = new CounterPanel(ctr1);
```

```
        Counter ctr2 = new Counter();
        CounterLogger cl2 = new CounterLogger(ctr2,"Counter2");
        CounterPanel ePanel = new CounterPanel(ctr2);
        CounterPanel wPanel = new CounterPanel(ctr2);

        setLayout(new BorderLayout());
        add(nPanel,"North");
        add(sPanel,"South");
        add(ePanel,"East");
        add(wPanel,"West");
    }
}
```

Suggested Experiments

1. Implement a CounterAlarmCanvas (implementing the CounterObserver inter-face) that takes a Counter and a threshold value. If the Counter's value is below the threshold, the Canvas displays a green circle; if the Counter's value is at or above the threshold, the Canvas displays a red circle. Incorporate this class into an applet.

2. Reimplement the MinimizerApplet from the Chapter 6 supplement using an MVC design.

3. Reimplement the calculator applet using an MVC design. In the MVC solution, what changes need to be made in order to switch from the original "simple" display to the "virtual paper tape" display?

4. Implement the Logo turtle as an applet. Have a Canvas upon which the turtle moves, and buttons for the various commands. You will also need a Vector to remember all the moves the turtle has made. When the Canvas's paint() method is called, you must redo all those moves.

Recursion

14.1 Introduction

Imagine that you are at a big family or friends' reunion. Dinner is over and the sink is filled with a stack of dishes that seems a mile high. You walk by the kitchen at an inopportune moment and someone possessing a certain amount of authority tells you to *do the dishes*.

So what do you do? You might take the *lazy* approach:

- Wash one dish.
- Find the nearest person and, with all the authority you can muster, tell him or her to *do the dishes*.

You duck out of there as quickly as possible, but perhaps the person you passed the job to follows the same lazy approach you did:

- Wash one dish.
- Find the nearest person and, with all the authority you can muster, tell him or her to *do the dishes*.

Of course the newest "victim" can follow this same procedure—as can all succeeding dishwashers. This procedure might work out rather nicely—no one ends up having to do the whole sinkload—provided that each person called on can recognize an empty sink when it finally appears, in which case the lucky soul neither washes a dish nor gets someone else to do the rest of the job. Taking this into account, we amend the lazy approach as follows.

To do the dishes:

- If the sink is empty, then there is nothing to do.
- If it is not empty, then
    - Wash one dish.
    - Find the nearest person and, with all the authority you can muster, tell him or her to *do the dishes*.

The lazy approach contains a reference to itself (to do the dishes, we tell someone else to do the dishes). To guarantee that this approach does not become an endless passing of the buck, *each person does some of the work, and so the job given to the next person is somewhat smaller.*

Because the job gets smaller each time, eventually it is completed and the chain of getting another person to do the rest of the work can be broken.

A procedure that does part of a task and then gets the rest done by referring to itself is called a **recursive procedure** and the execution of such a procedure is called **recursion**. The procedure to do the dishes is recursive because one of its steps includes "do the dishes"—a reference to itself.

14.2 Example: Exponentiation

Recursion is not only an easy way to get out of doing a lot of dishes but also an easy and powerful way of tackling many difficult computing problems. Rather than starting our exploration of recursion using these difficult problems, we'll start with easier ones—problems for which iteration is well-suited and recursion not needed. We do this because it is easier to learn a new tool using easy problems than using hard ones. We'll look at some more challenging problems later in this chapter. Therefore, let's start with a simple example: the problem of writing a helper method to compute the value of one nonnegative integer raised to the power of another. As in our implementation in Chapter 11, this method receives two int parameters, x and y, and returns an integer value, x raised to the power of y:

$$x^y$$

An outline of the method is:

```
private int power(int x, int y) {      // y>=0 returns x**y

    ...

}
```

(When we don't have superscripts available, the notation x**y is widely used to represent x^y.)

The definition of exponentiation is

$$x^y = 1*x*x*\cdots*x \ (y \text{ times})$$

In English, we say that x raised to the power of y equals 1 multiplied by x, y times.

To use recursion to write this method, we start by imagining that we have to do the process ourselves by hand (without a calculator). It seems like quite a bit of work, especially if y is large. Let's take the lazy approach and get someone else to do most of the work. We have to compute x^y, but if we could get an assistant to compute x^{y-1}, all we would have to do is multiply the assistant's result by y.

Of course, our assistant might get an assistant to compute x^{y-2} and so on by following the same procedure. And what is this procedure exactly? If we take into account that each assistant should check for the easy case of x^0, where the result is 1, the procedure could be stated as follows.

To compute the power of x to the y

- If y is 0 then there are no multiplications to do, and the result is 1.
- If y is greater than 0, then
    - Tell an assistant *to compute the power of* x *to the* y–1.
    - The result is x times the assistant's result.

So, using the procedure to compute 4^3, we hire an assistant (A) to compute 4^2, who hires an assistant (B) to compute 4^1, who hires an assistant (C) to compute 4^0. The last assistant recognizes that y is 0, and so the result is 1. B's result is 4*1 (==4), and A's result is 4*4 (==16), and so our result is 4*16 or 64, which is indeed 4^3. See Figure 14.1.

This procedure is recursive because it includes a reference to itself and it is valid for the following reasons:

- The procedure gives the assistant a smaller problem to compute.
- The procedure provides a way to check whether there is no more work to be done.

To express this procedure in a Java method is straightforward:

```
if (y==0)
    return 1;
else {
    assistantResult = power(x,y-1);
    return x*assistantResult;
}
```

If y is 0 then there are no multiplications to do and the result is 1.

Else (if y is greater than 0), tell an assistant to compute x to the y–1 power. The result is x times the assistant's result.

Adding the required declaration, the `power()` method is:

```
private int power(int x, int y) {    // y>=0, returns x**y
    int    assistantResult;
```

Figure 14.1

Recursion in exponentiation. To compute 4^3, we must compute 4^2. To compute 4^2 we must compute 4^1. To compute 4^1 we must compute 4^0.

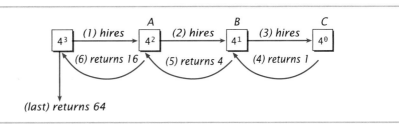

```
    if  (y==0)
        return 1;
    else {
        assistantResult = power(x,y-1);
        return x*assistantResult;
    }
}
```

The Recursive Call

The power() method invokes itself:

```
private int power(int x, int y) {    // y>=0 returns x**y
    ...
        assistantResult = power(x,y-1);
    ...
}
```

An invocation of a method from within that method is a **recursive call**. A recursive call is legal in Java and it corresponds to the passing of the job on to an assistant. The arguments that are passed to a method determine the task it must perform. The arguments in a recursive call must define a task that is smaller or easier than the task given to the caller. Note that the caller must calculate x^y, but the recursive call involves an easier task, x^{y-1}.

Termination

The power method has a conditional return that does not involve a recursive call:

```
private int power(int x, int y) {    // y>=0 returns x**y
    if  (y==0)
        return 1;
    ...
    }
}
```

This code corresponds to checking whether there is a need to hire another assistant. This **termination step** is essential in any viable recursive procedure. It checks the task to see whether it can be carried out without resorting to recursion. If so, it terminates the recursion; that is, it prevents further recursive calls from being made. The termination code must appear before the recursive call—otherwise the recursive call would be repeatedly invoked and the termination code would never be reached.

14.3 How to Design a Recursive Method

In order to design a recursive solution to a problem, we must find a way to do the following:

- Use a solution to a smaller or easier version of the problem to arrive at the solution to the problem itself.
  - This step leads to the recursive call.
  - Usually laziness can be an inspiration at this step.
- Know when the problem is small enough to solve directly.
  - This step leads to the termination code.
  - Laziness can help here too. Ask, What is the easiest version of the problem to solve?

In the exponentiation example in the previous section we applied this approach.

- We multiplied x^{y-1}, an easier exponentiation problem than x^y, by x to get our result.
- We were able to solve x^0 directly.

Let's apply this approach to some more examples.

Reading Data to Construct a Collection of RepairPerson Objects

Let's write a helper method that receives a BufferedReader object and a Vector as arguments. Its task is to read all the RepairPersons from the BufferedReader and add them to the Vector.

```
private void getRepairPersons(BufferedReader br, Vector  v)
```

Step 1: Getting Lazy

With a long stream of data to read, we take inspiration from the dishwasher. We read just one RepairPerson object from br and add it to v,

```
RepairPerson rp  =  RepairPerson.read(br);
v.add(rp);
```

We then let someone else (our recursive call) process the rest of the input, which is now slightly smaller because we have read and processed one RepairPerson. So our recursive call will be

```
getRepairPersons(br,v);
```

The arguments don't seem to make the problem smaller, but br refers to a BufferedReader that has one less RepairPerson in it.

Step 2: Knowing When to Quit

When is the task so small that we can solve it directly? That's easy! We can quit when there is no more input and the `RepairPerson.read()` method returns `null`; there is nothing to add to v, so there is no need to have someone else process the rest of the input. Our termination code is as follows:

```
if (rp==null)
    return;
```

The termination code must come after the attempt to read but before we add to v or make the recursive call. The following is the completed method.

```
private void getRepairPersons(BufferedReader br, Vector v)
    RepairPerson rp = RepairPerson.read(br);
    if (rp==null)
        return;
    v.add(rp);
    getRepairPersons(br,v);
}
```

Searching a Collection for the Nearest RepairPerson

Let's write a helper method that receives a `Location` and an `Enumeration` object for a group of employees and returns a reference to the `RepairPerson` object that is closest to the given `Location` or returns `null` if the `Enumeration` is empty:

```
private RepairPerson getNearest(Enumeration e, Location loc)
```

Step 1: Getting Lazy

We don't want to look at all the `RepairPerson` objects and make comparisons. We could, however, take just one `RepairPerson` object from the `Enumeration` and let someone else find the nearest of those left:

```
RepairPerson rp, nearestOfThoseLeft;
rp = (RepairPerson) e.nextElement();
nearestOfThoseLeft = getNearest(e, loc);
```

The argument doesn't seem to define a smaller task, but the `Enumeration` e has become smaller because we removed rp from it—e may in fact now be empty.

We now find out who is nearer: rp or nearestOfThoseLeft. If nearestOfThoseLeft is `null`, there is no contest. Otherwise, we have to compare its distance with that of rp.

```
if (nearestOfThoseLeft==null ||
    nearestOfThoseLeft.getDistanceFrom(loc) > rp.getDistanceFrom(loc))
    return rp;
else
    return nearestOfThoseLeft;
```

Step 2: Knowing When to Quit

The easiest form of this task is when the Enumeration has no more elements, in which case the only thing to do is return null. Our termination code is:

```
if (!e.hasMoreElements())
    return null;
```

This check for termination must be placed before we attempt to remove an element from e, so the completed method is as follows:

```
private RepairPerson getNearest(Enumeration e, Location l) {
    if (!e.hasMoreElements())
        return null;

    RepairPerson rp, nearestOfThoseLeft;
    rp = (RepairPerson) e.nextElement();
    nearestOfThoseLeft = getNearest(e, loc);
    if (nearestOfThoseLeft==null
            || nearestOfThoseLeft.getDistanceFrom(loc)
                            > rp.getDistnaceFrom (loc))
        return rp;
    else
        return nearestOfThoseLeft;
}
```

Two Recursion Patterns

We have encountered four recursion examples, counting our dishwasher. Two patterns emerge, shown in Figure 14.2.

Pattern 1 is simple. We solve the problem by handling a small part of it and making a recursive call to solve the rest. This is the way getRepairPersons() and the dishwasher worked. In pattern 2, a smaller version of the problem is passed in the recursive call and the resulting solution is used to solve the problem at hand. This is the way power() and getNearest() worked.

```
method (problem)          {              method (problem)          {
    if (problem is very easy)                if (problem is very easy)
        solve it and return                      return solution to easy problem
    solve part of the problem,               solution to smaller problem=method (smaller problem);
            leaving a smaller problem        solve problem, using solution to smaller problem
    method (smaller problem);                return solution
}                                        }
        Pattern 1                                    Pattern 2
```

Figure 14.2 Two patterns of simple recursion.

14.4 Recursive Methods: Under the Hood

We have yet to meet the student who is not curious to know how recursion works, that is, how it is possible for a method to invoke itself. We explain that in this section with a stern warning:

Understanding how recursion actually works is of little help in using it to solve problems. To use recursion *to solve problems, use the lazy approach* given in the previous section.

Remember what happens when a method is invoked:

- A message is sent to a receiving object; the sender of the message suspends execution.
- The receiver gets the message and arranges for the correct method to execute.
- The receiver *creates* the local variables of the method (parameters and other local variables).
- The parameters get the values from the arguments.
- The method executes.
- The method completes and destroys the local variables of the method; any return value replaces the expression that sent the message.
- The sender of the message resumes execution.

In order for this to work, every time a method is invoked, the system allocates a new piece of memory for the method to store the following:

- The local variables that it creates
- The parameters it uses
- The location in the code of the sender of the message

Such pieces of memory are called activation records. An **activation record** is a block of memory holding the parameters and local variables of a method, along with the return address of the invoker of the method.

Let's look again at the power() method.

```
private int power(int x, int y) {     // y>=0 returns x**y
    if  (y==0)
        return 1;
    else {
        int    assistantResult;
        assistantResult = power(x,y-1);              Method power, line 5
        return  x*assistantResult;
    }
}
```

and let's assume that it is invoked by method f() as follows:

```
void  f(...) {
    ...
    int  q  =  power(3,2);          Method f, line N
    ...
}
```

Thus, the power() method is first invoked as power(3,2). Consider the structure of memory once power() starts executing. There is an activation record for f(), the sender of the message, and there is an activation record for power() as well. See Figure 14.3.

When the recursive call, power(x,y–1), is made in line 5, a message is sent to same object that is executing power(3,2), telling it to execute power(3,1). So the object takes the following steps:

- It suspends its execution of power(3,2).
- It sends the power(3,1) message to itself.
- It receives the power(3,1) message.
- It creates a new activation record with x==3, y==1, and sender: method power, line 5.
- It starts executing the power() method from the beginning.

The resulting structure of memory is shown in Figure 14.4.

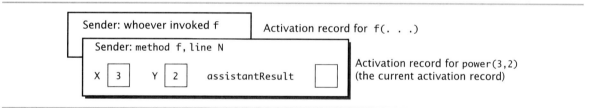

Figure 14.3   A stack of activation records after invoking power(3,2). After invoking power(3,2), the activation record for power(3,2) is on top of the stack.

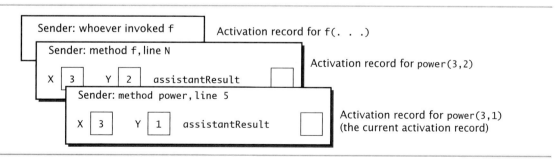

Figure 14.4   A stack of activation records after invoking power(3,1). Now the activation record for power(3,1) is on top of the stack.

Now there are two activation records for power()—one for the invocation by f(), the other for the recursive invocation by power() itself. The contents of the two activation records are different and reflect this distinction.

There are two x, two y, and two assistantResult variables now that belong to the different activation records. Only the most recent activation record, the **current activation record**, is used. So when power() refers to x, there is never any ambiguity; the reference is always to the x in the current activation record.

As execution continues, power(), discovering that y, which now equals 1, is not equal to 0, makes another recursive invocation: power(3,0). So the object takes the following steps:

- It suspends its execution of power(3,1).
- It sends the power(3,0) message to itself.
- It receives the power(3,0) message.
- It creates a new activation record with x==3, y==0, and sender: method power, line 5.
- It starts executing the power() method from the beginning.

The resulting structure of memory is shown in Figure 14.5.

The power() method starts executing now for the third time—it has yet to return. However, this time, the y in the current activation record is 0, so the test y==0 succeeds. The method then executes

return   1;

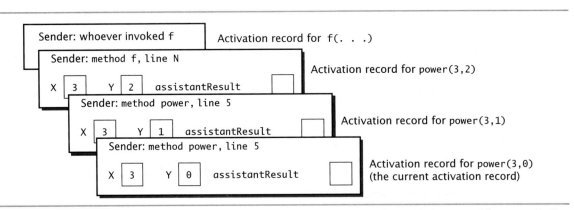

Figure 14.5   A stack of activation records after invoking power(3,0). Now the activation record for power(3,0) is on top of the stack.

The return statement does each of the following:

- It evaluates the return value (in this case 1).
- It destroys the current activation record.
- It replaces the expression that invoked the method with the return value.
- It resumes execution of the sender.

The resulting structure of memory is shown in Figure 14.6.

Then power(3,1) resumes executing on line 5:

```
assistantResult  =  1;
```

The value returned by power(3,0), 1, replaces power(3,0) in the execution. See Figure 14.7.

power() now executes

```
return  x*assistantResult;
```

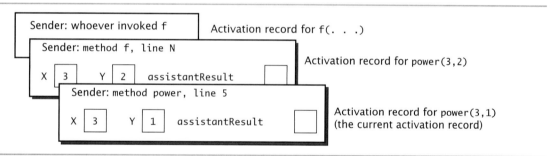

Figure 14.6 A stack of activation records after return from power(3,0). The activation record for power(3,0) has been discarded, leaving the activation record for power(3,1) at the top of the stack once more.

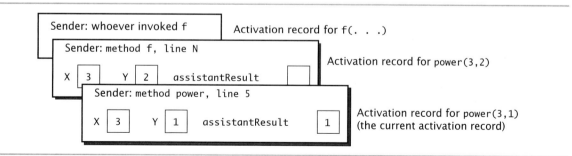

Figure 14.7 A stack of activation records: assistantResults gets the return value. The return value of power(3,0) is stored in a local variable of the activation record of power(3,1), at the top of the stack.

which does the following steps:

- It evaluates the return value (in this case, 3).
- It destroys the current activation record.
- It replaces the expression that invoked the method with the return value.
- It and resumes execution of the sender.

These steps lead to the state shown in Figure 14.8.

Finally, the original invocation of power(), power(3,2), resumes and executes

`return  x*assistantResult;`

At this point, assistantResult is 3 and so 9 (the correct evaluation of 3^2) is returned to f(), which resumes its execution. Its activation record is once again the current activation record. See Figure 14.9.

As you can see, the implementation of recursion, that is, what's "under the hood," is quite involved. Keep the following important guideline in mind as you work:

> Thinking about the implementation when you are designing a recursive method will distract you from the real task; instead, focus on finding a procedure that contributes a little to the solution and has an "assistant" do the rest by carrying out the same procedure.

In other words, we've shown you how recursion actually is implemented. Now let's forget it and go back to the business of designing recursive solutions to problems.

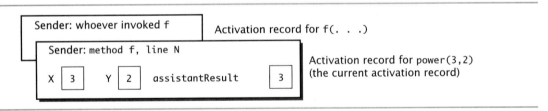

Figure 14.8 A stack of activation records after return from power(3,1). The activation record for power(3,1) has been discarded, leaving the activation record for power(3,2) at the top of the stack once more. The return value of power(3,1) is stored in a local variable of the activation record of power(3,2).

Sender: whoever invoked f

Activation record for f(. . .)
(the current activation record)

Figure 14.9 A stack of activation records after return from power(3,2). When the first invocation completes, there are no activation records of the recursive procedure still on the stack.

14.5 Recursion with Vectors, Arrays, and Strings

Recursion is often fruitfully applied to collections, particularly ones with indices such as Vectors, arrays, and Strings. Typically, the original task involves the entire collection. The smaller versions of the task passed to an "assistant" usually involve a subsection of the collection. One can specify a subsection of a collection with the following three arguments (see Figure 14.10):

- A reference to the collection itself
- The index of the first position in the subsection
- The first position after the subsection or the number of elements in the subsection

The third argument can be omitted if it is assumed that the subcollection goes to the end of the original collection itself. Thus, recursive methods for a collection will have the first two or all three arguments as well as any additional ones needed for the particular task.

EXAMPLE Reading Integers from a BufferedReader into an Array. The helper method will require a reference to a BufferedReader as well as the other arguments, and we will have it return the number of elements it has read:

```
// Read integers (one per line) from br and store in a[first], ..., a[beyond-1];
// Read until end-of-file or until no more elements are available.
```

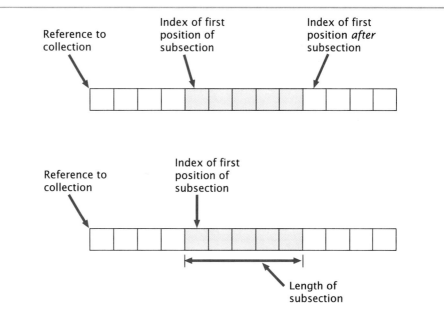

Figure 14.10
Two ways of specifying a subsection of a collection. Subsections of a collection can be specified by starting point and ending point (top) or starting point and length (bottom) of the subcollection.

```
//  Return the number of integers read and stored.
private int  readIntArray(int[]  a,  int  first,
                          int  beyond, BufferedReader  br)  {

}
```

Step 1: Getting Lazy

The laziest thing we can do is to read a single integer and store it in the first element of the subcollection. Then we can give our assistant a slightly smaller subcollection to work on:

```
String  s  =  br.readLine();
a[first]  =  Integer.parseInt(s);
return  1+readIntArray(a,first+1,beyond,br);
```

The assistant tells us how many integers it read. So we add 1 to that number, because we also read in one integer, and we return the sum to our invoker. We give the assistant exactly the same arguments given to us, except that first becomes first+1, reflecting the fact that we have stored a value in a[first].

Step 2: Knowing When to Quit

There are two situations that require us to quit: when the array is full, that is, first is up to beyond (first==beyond) and when there are no more data (s==null).

The test for the array being full must be done *before* we invoke readLine(). If we did it afterward, our method would be reading data and then not doing anything with them (and hence losing data) in the event that the array is full.

On the other hand, the test for end-of-data must be done after readLine() has been invoked. The only way we can tell if the data have ended is to see whether readLine()'s return value is null. In both cases we return without reading integers and so we return 0. The method then is as follows:

```
//  Read integers (one per line) from br and store in a[first], ..., a[beyond-1];
//  Read until end-of-file or until no more elements are available.
//  Return the number of integers read and stored.
private int  readIntArray(int[]  a,  int  first, int  beyond,
                          BufferedReader  br) throws Exception {
  if  (first==beyond)
     return  0;
  String  s  =  br.readLine();
  if  (s==null)
     return  0;
  a[first]  =  Integer.parseInt(s);
  return 1+readIntArray(a,first+1,beyond,br);
}
```

and would be invoked as

```
int[]   x  =  new int[50];
int     count;
count  =  readIntArray(x,0,x.length,br);
```

We can now note that beyond never changes—it is always the length of the array. We may therefore leave it out as a parameter and replace it with a.length in the readIntArray() method body:

```
//  Read integers (one per line) from br and store in a[first], ..., a[a.length-1];
//  Read until end-of-file or until no more elements are available.
//  Return the number of integers read and stored.
private int  readIntArray(int[]  a,  int  first,
                          BufferedReader br) throws Exception {
  if  (first==a.length)
     return  0;
  String  s  =  br.readLine();
  if  (s==null)
     return  0;
  a[first]  =  Integer.parseInt(s);
  return  1+readIntArray(a,first+1,a.length,br);
}
```

EXAMPLE Binary Search, Again. The method requires the item we are looking for and three arguments that specify the part of the array we are searching:

```
//  Returns true if s is among z[first], ..., z[beyond-1]
private int  bsearch(String z[], String s, int  first,  int  beyond)  {
}
```

As in Chapter 11, we pick the middle element and, by comparing it with s, determine in which half of z[first], ..., z[beyond-1] s might be found.

Step 1: Getting Lazy

Taking the lazy approach, however, we do hardly more work than that. After we identify the half to search, we get our assistant to do the rest, returning whatever the assistant returns to us.

First find the index of the middle element:

```
int  m  =  (first+beyond)/2;
```

If the middle element is less than what we are searching for, the assistant should search after position m (from m+1 on):

```
if  (z[m].compareTo(s)<0)
     return  bsearch(s,z,m+1,beyond);
```

If the middle is more than what we are searching for, then position m could be considered "beyond" where the item may be found and the assistant should search from position first up to m:

```
if  (z[m].compareTo(s)>0)
    return  bsearch(s,z,first,m);
```

Step 2: Knowing When to Quit

When is the task so small that we can solve it directly? As usual, that's pretty easy! When there are no elements at all to look for, that is, when first==beyond or first>beyond we know the item won't be found, so we can return –1. On the other hand, if the element we are looking for matches the one in the middle, we can return m—it's been found.

The check to see whether first>=beyond should be done first because it is meaningless to compute the middle if there is nothing there. We don't need to directly check the middle element for a match. If the compareTo() invocations do not yield <0 or >0, then we know we have a match and can just return true.

```
// Returns true if s is among z[first], ..., z[beyond–1]
private int  bsearch(String z[], String s, int  first,  int  beyond)  {
        if  (first>=beyond)
            return;
        int  m  =  (first+beyond)/2;
        if  (z[m].compareTo(s)<0)
            return  bsearch(s,z,m+1,beyond);
        if  (z[m].compareTo(s)>0)
            return  bsearch(s,z,first,m);
        return  m;
}
```

14.6 Permutations

In the game of Scrabble, each player has a rack of seven letter tiles. In each move the player uses the letters to make a word on a board. There is a premium for using all seven letters. A program playing Scrabble might search for seven-letter words by checking every permutation of its letters, that is, every possible ordering of the seven letters, and look each one up in a dictionary. A method to help it do this is

```
public static Vector getWords(Vector dictionary, String letters)
```

The method is passed a Vector of words that we call dictionary and a String of seven letters that we call letters. It returns a Vector of Strings. Each of these Strings corresponds to a word in the dictionary Vector and is a permutation (see Exercise 19 in Chapter 2) of the seven letters in the letters String.

Given a set of letters, say, A B C D E F G, how could we construct a permutation? At the outset, our permutation is empty, and we have no letters in it. Our situation is

permutation: letters left: A B C D E F G

We could start by choosing a letter, say D, to add to the permutation:

permutation: D   letters left: A B C E F G

Then we could choose another letter, say B:

permutation: DB   letters left: A C E F G

And then another, say F:

permutation: DBF   letters left: A C E G

And so it would go until the permutation contained seven letters and there were no letters left:

permutation: DBFAEGC   letters left:

The problem is to methodically generate all permutations.

Step 1: Getting Lazy

Suppose we viewed our job as the following:

- We are given a string, p, and a group of letters.
- Find all the strings that consist of the String p concatenated with a permutation of the letters in the group.

If our string were the empty string, then this job would simply amount to finding all the permutations of the letters in the group. Now we can find a role for some assistants.

Keeping track of permutations is hard, but choosing letters is easy. Let's follow this procedure:

- Pick one of the letters and give the following to an assistant:
  - A string consisting of p concatenated with the letter we picked
  - A new set of letters consisting of our letters minus the one we appended to p
- The assistant carries out this same procedure, of course.
- Then we do the same for all the other letters.

Step 2: Knowing When to Quit

When there are no more letters left, the String p is a complete permutation of the original letters. At that point we need to see whether it is actually a word, and if it is, we need to add it to our Vector. Either way, we return.

From this informal outline, we see that our recursive method, which we will call permutations(), needs four parameters:

- The Vector to which a word should be added
- The dictionary that we use to check if a permutation is a word or not
- The String p that has been constructed so far
- The set of letters still available for choosing

Because the String class offers so many convenient methods for manipulating a sequence of characters, we will use String objects for the last two. Our method then is

```
private static void permutations(Vector v, Vector dict,
                                 String perm, String letters)
```

and getWords() can be implemented with it:

```
static Vector getWords(Vector dictionary, String letters)  {
    Vector  v  =  new  Vector();
    permutations(v,dictionary,"",letters);
}
```

Now we must turn steps 1 and 2 above into code to implement permutations(). Step 2 is easy:

```
private static void permutations(Vector v, Vector dict,
                                 String perm, String letters) {
    if  (letters.length()==0)   {
        if  (dict.contains(perm))
            v.add(perm);
        return;
    }
```

Note our usage of the Vector method contains(). This is not a method we have used previously; we found ourselves in a situation in which such a method would be useful. In such a situation, the first thing to do is consult the documentation to see if the method we desire exists; in this case we were in luck.

Step 1 is more difficult. We have to set up an assistant for each one of the characters in the letters:

```
int     i;
i  =  0;
while   (i<letters.length())   {
    String newPermutation  =  The permutation we have with
                                    the ith letter added
        String  newLetters  =  The letters we have with
                                    the ith letter deleted
```

```
        permutations(v,dict,newPermutation,newLetters);
        i++;
    }
}
```

Adding the ith letter to perm is just a matter of appending the substring of the ith character in the letters:

```
perm + letters.substring(i,i+1)
```

and creating a String with all the characters in letters but the ith one is a matter of joining the substring of characters before i with the substring of characters after i:

```
letters.substring(0,i) + letters.substring(i+1)
```

The finished method is

```
private static void permutations(Vector v, Vector dict,
                                String perm, String letters) {
    if  (letters.length()==0)  {
        if  (dict.contains(perm))
            v.add(perm);
        return;
    }
    int    i;
    i  =  0;
    while  (i<letters.length())  {
        String  newPermutation  =  perm + letters.substring(i,i+1);
        String  newLetters = letters.substring(0,i) +
                                letters.substring(i+1);
        permutations(v,dict,newPermutation,newLetters);
        i++;
    }
}
```

14.7 Towers of Hanoi

The Puzzle

The Towers of Hanoi is a puzzle that consists of three poles, or "towers," and seven disks, no two of which are the same size. Each disk has a hole in the center so that a pole can go through it. The puzzle starts with all the disks placed on tower 1; we must move them all to tower 3 with the following constraints:

- No disk can ever be on top of a smaller disk.
- Only one disk can be moved at a time.

- A disk must always be placed on a tower, never off to the side.
- Only the disk at the top of a tower can be moved, never a lower one.

Disks can be moved to tower 2, and may be moved back and forth off of towers 1 and 3 as needed. See Figure 14.11.

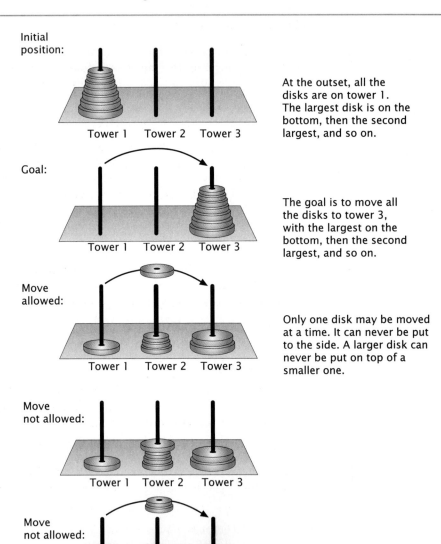

Figure 14.11
The Towers of Hanoi puzzle. The Towers of Hanoi puzzle requires the player to move all the disks from one pole to another, subject to several constraints.

Initial position:

At the outset, all the disks are on tower 1. The largest disk is on the bottom, then the second largest, and so on.

Goal:

The goal is to move all the disks to tower 3, with the largest on the bottom, then the second largest, and so on.

Move allowed:

Only one disk may be moved at a time. It can never be put to the side. A larger disk can never be put on top of a smaller one.

Move not allowed:

Move not allowed:

A solution to the puzzle consists of a sequence of directions that accomplishes the goal given the constraints. Here is an example of a solution.

- Move a disk from tower 1 to tower 3.
- Move a disk from tower 1 to tower 2.
- Move a disk from tower 3 to tower 2.
- Move a disk from tower 1 to tower 3.
- Continue . . .

Note that because only the top disk can be moved, we never have to specify which disk is moved from a tower, we just need to specify the source and target towers.

Our goal is to define a class whose objects can produce a solution to this puzzle.

This puzzle is relevant to the study of recursion because, like the permutation problem earlier, it is a good example of how recursion makes an otherwise extremely difficult puzzle become relatively easy. Before taking the recursive approach, however, take some time to think about this puzzle yourself.

- Try solving it yourself. Use concrete objects, coins, tokens, dishes—whatever is available. Start with using only three objects, then try solving the puzzle with four, and work up to seven.
- Try writing code using one or more loops that would solve this puzzle. Be warned: It is extremely difficult, but worth trying anyway.
- Try thinking of a recursive procedure that solves this puzzle. (The procedure need not be in Java code; an informal one is fine).

Taking the Easy Way Out

A good strategy in recursive design is to let one's assistant do as much of the work as possible. Our problem is to move seven disks from one pole to the other. Let's imagine an assistant who could move six disks. For starters, we come up with the following procedure (see Figure 14.12):

To move seven disks from tower 1 to tower 3, using tower 2 as a holding tower:

- Step 1: Move six disks from tower 1 to tower 2 (the assistant).
- Step 2: Move the remaining disk from tower 1 to tower 3 (our contribution).
- Step 3: Move six disks from tower 2 to tower 3 (the assistant).

The following aspects of this procedure are worth noting:

- The task we give the assistant, though still challenging, is smaller than the task we have to do.
- We invoke the assistant before we do any work ourselves.
- We invoke the assistant twice.

Initial
position:

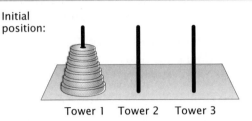

Tower 1 Tower 2 Tower 3

Figure 14.12
Toward a recursive solution of the Towers of Hanoi puzzle. To work toward a recursive solution, we imagine how to make use of an assistant who can move six disks.

After
step 1:

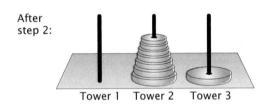

Tower 1 Tower 2 Tower 3

The assistant somehow moves six disks from tower 1 to tower 2, one at a time following the rules of the puzzle.

After
step 2:

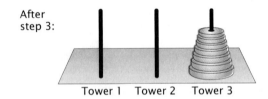

Tower 1 Tower 2 Tower 3

We can then move the seventh disk from tower 1 to tower 3.

After
step 3:

Tower 1 Tower 2 Tower 3

The assistant somehow moves six disks from tower 2 to tower 3, one at a time following the rules of the puzzle.

- Tower 2 is used as a temporary holding tower for the six smaller disks until the largest one is moved to tower 3.
- This approach requires that initially, on towers 2 and 3, there are no disks smaller than any of the six disks being moved. If there were, the assistant would not necessarily be able to move the six disks.

For this to be an acceptable recursive procedure, the task we give the assistant must be of the same form as the task we give ourselves. In the above procedure, we move disks from 1 to 3, and the assistant moves disks from 1 to 2 and from 2 to 3. We are responsible for seven, our assistant is responsible for six. By changing the task statement, we put it into a form that is applicable to both ourselves and our assistant.

The new statement of the task is: Move *n* disks from the source tower to the target tower, using the other tower as a holding tower. The steps are as follows:

- Step 1: Move *n*–1 disks from *source* to *holding*.
- Step 2: Move 1 disk from *source* to *target*.
- Step 3: Move *n*–1 disks from *holding* to *target*.

We also have to know when to quit. That's easy: When *n* is 0, there are no disks to move and we don't have to do anything. Our procedure now becomes as follows:

- Move *n* disks from *source* to *target*.
- If *n* is 0 do nothing. Otherwise:
- Determine which tower is the *holding* tower: It's the one that is not *source* or *target* (a preliminary to steps 1–3).
- Step 1: Move *n*–1 disks from *source* to *holding*.
- Step 2: Move 1 disk from *source* to *target*.
- Step 3: Move *n*–1 disks from *holding* to *target*.

The solution to the Towers of Hanoi puzzle comes from using this procedure with *n* set to 7, *source* set to 1, and *target* set to 3.

At different points in the computation, the three towers switch their respective roles as *source*, *target*, and *holding*. For example, in the recursive invocation in step 1, *source* is still 1, but *target* is 2 and *holding* is 3. In step 3, *source* is now 2, *target* is 3, and *holding* is 1. See Figure 14.13.

We will now design a class that solves the Towers of Hanoi. The point of this example is to introduce another example of solving a hard problem with recursion and illustrate the concept of separating display from calculation.

Statement of the Problem

Create an object that models the Towers of Hanoi and produces a solution by starting from the initial configuration and then generating a sequence of moves, consistent with the game's rules. Display each move and the resulting picture of the towers.

Scenario

We want the Towers object to generate the moves. We also want to see these moves on a display. Because we are working with System.out, the display is primitive. Just printing the source and target of the move of a single disk and then representing the towers and their disks in some simple fashion is sufficient. As an extra feature, when we create the Towers object, we want to specify the number of disks it starts with. Thus we should be able to make requests such as the following:

- Set up a Towers object with *n* disks and a display.
- Solve the puzzle, using the above information.

To move seven disks from tower 1 to tower 3:

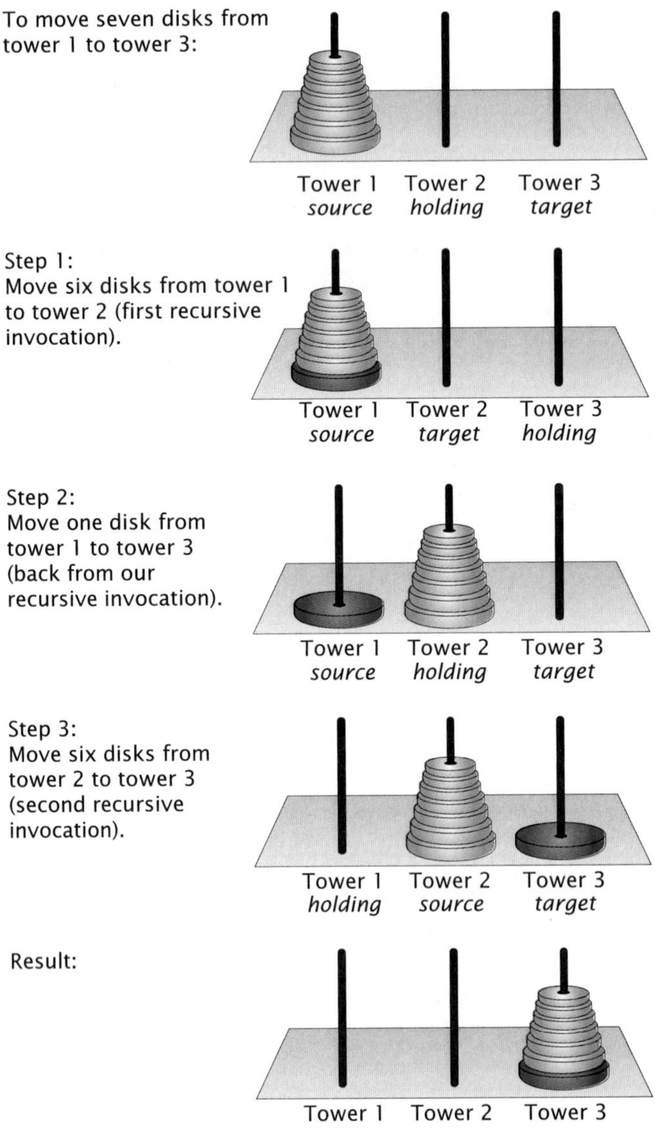

Tower 1   Tower 2   Tower 3
source   *holding*   *target*

Step 1:
Move six disks from tower 1 to tower 2 (first recursive invocation).

Tower 1   Tower 2   Tower 3
source   *target*   *holding*

Figure 14.13

The changing roles of the towers. At different points in the computation, the three towers switch their respective roles as *source*, *target*, and *holding*.

Step 2:
Move one disk from tower 1 to tower 3 (back from our recursive invocation).

Tower 1   Tower 2   Tower 3
source   *holding*   *target*

Step 3:
Move six disks from tower 2 to tower 3 (second recursive invocation).

Tower 1   Tower 2   Tower 3
holding   *source*   *target*

Result:

Tower 1   Tower 2   Tower 3

In addition, a `TowerDisplay` object will need to access some information about the current state of the solution; specifically it may need

- Source and target towers of the current move
- Current contents of each tower

Finding the Primary Object

We will introduce a `Towers` class. Another noun, however, that also appeared in the statement of the problem and the scenario is "display." We will develop a separate class, `TowerDisplay`, for handling that.

Determining the Behavior

Our problem statement provides us with the necessary behavior:

- Tower (constructor)—Set up the puzzle.
- Solve It—Figure out the moves and display them, along with the changes to the towers as they are made.
- Get From, Get To—Return the towers involved in the current move.
- Get Tower—Return some representation of the contents of a tower.

Determining the Interface

The above behavior translates neatly into methods. The only methods that receive arguments are the constructor (a reference to the `TowerDisplay` object that `Towers` will use to display its moves, and the number of disks) and get-`Tower()` (the number of tower to return). Our interface is as follows:

```
class Towers  {
    public Towers(TowerDisplay td, int nDisks) {...}
    public void solveIt()  {...}
    public int getFrom() {...}
    public int getTo() {...}
    public ToBeDetermined getTower(int index) {...}
}
```

We will decide on the return-type of the `getTower()` method once we consider the instance variables of the class.

Defining the Instance Variables

The `solveIt()` method will need the values of the constructor's parameters: the reference to the display object and the number of disks. So these must be stored in instance variables:

```
private int nDisks;
private TowerDisplay td;
```

What about instance variables to keep track of the disks that are on each tower? Interestingly, solving the puzzle doesn't require that we maintain this information. The informal recursive procedure we developed above never needed to know where any particular disk was located. The problem statement, however, requires some kind of display of the towers' contents at each point; this information will be updated by the `solveIt()` method but used by the `get...()` methods, so we need some instance variables.

The key issue to address here is how to represent the towers and their disks. If we choose to display the disks as single-digit numbers (and thereby restrict this class's usefulness to representing at most nine disks) we can make use of String objects and their methods in a rather neat way. If we are doing the standard version of the puzzle, a tower holding all seven disks is represented and displayed by the String "1234567". A tower with no disks is just the empty String "". Moving a disk from one tower to another is a matter of removing the last character of the String of one and concatenating it to the other. See Figure 14.14.

With this in mind, we choose to represent the towers with three Strings. The getTower() method will return a single String, and its argument will be either 1, 2, or 3, indicating which tower to return. If we use an array of four elements to

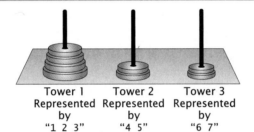

Each disk can be represented by a single digit. "1" represents the largest disk, "7" the smallest. A String of digits can represent the disks on a particular tower.

Figure 14.14

Representing the disks on towers with String objects. The towers can be represented by Strings and movement can be represented by changes to the Strings.

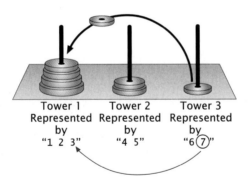

To represent the movement of a disk, we remove a digit from the String representing the tower of origin and place it at the end of the String representing the destination.

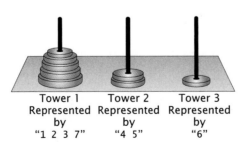

store our Strings, we can use integers to index the array and access the String representing the tower indicated by the parameter. So our instance variable is

```
private String[] towers;
```

Tower 1 is represented by towers[1], tower 2 by towers[2], tower 3 by towers[3] (towers[0] is unused).

We will also use two int variables to represent the source and target of each move:

```
private int from;
private int to;
```

Thus, our class skeleton so far is as follows:

```
class Towers  {
    public Towers(TowerDisplay td, int nDisks) {...}
    public void solveIt() {...}
    public int getFrom() {...}
    public int getTo() {...}
    public String getTower(int index) {...}

    private int nDisks;
    private TowerDisplay td;
    private int from;
    private int to;
    private String[] towers;
}
```

Implementing the Methods

The constructor must save the values of the parameters in the instance variables. In addition, at some point before the solution is generated, the contents of the towers array must be initialized; because our solution can't display more than nine disks, we must also check the value of nDisks. The constructor therefore is as follows:

```
public Towers(TowerDisplay td, int nDisks) {
    this.td = td;
    this.nDisks = nDisks;
    if (nDisks>9)
        nDisks = 9;
    towers = new String[4];
    towers[1] = "123456789".substring(0,nDisks);
    towers[2] = "";
    towers[3] = "";
}
```

Put the right number of disks on the first tower.

The informal recursive procedure we developed on the previous page can be coded as a recursive method. However, this method requires the same parameters as our procedure: number of disks, source tower, target tower.

```
void solveIt(int  nDisks,  int  source,  int  target)  {...}
```

The Towers interface calls for a different prototype for solveIt():

```
void solveIt()  {...}
```

Apparently we need two versions of solveIt(): one to serve as part of the interface, the other to get the job actually done by implementing our recursive procedure:

```
public void solveIt() {...}          // Invoked by the outside to display a
                                     //      solution
private void solveIt(int nDisks, // Recursively generate a solution.
        int source, int target) {...}
```

Fortunately, Java allows overloading.

To make sure that the job gets done when the public solveIt() method is invoked, we implement it as a single invocation of the private solveIt() method:

```
public void solveIt() {
    solveIt(nDisks, 1, 3);
}
```

We start with nDisks on tower 1 and ask for them to be moved to tower 3. The implementation of the recursive solveIt() method follows from the informal recursive procedure. We check to see whether there is no work to do:

```
if (nDisks<=0)
    return;
```

We figure out whether tower we should use as the holding tower. That will require a few messy if statements, so we encapsulate that in a private helper method. This way we won't obscure the recursive structure of the solveIt() method:

```
int holding = getHoldingTower(source,target);
```

We solve the problem of moving *n*–1 disks from *source* to *holding* (generating all the moves to do that):

```
solveIt(nDisks-1,source,holding);
```

We then move a disk from *source* to *target*. First we need to update the model; this involves a few string operations, so we'll encapsulate this step, too, in its own helper method, updateModel(). Then we can inform the TowerDisplay object of the move:

```
td.displayMove(this);
```

Finally, we solve the problem of moving *n*–1 disks from *holding* to *target*:

```
solveIt(nDisks-1,holdingTower,target);
```

The completed method is as follows:

```
private void solveIt(int nDisks, int source, int target) {
    if (nDisks<=0)
        return;
    int holding = getHoldingTower(source,target);
    solveIt(nDisks-1,source,holding);
    updateModel(source,target);
    td.displayMove(source,target);
    solveIt(nDisks-1,holding,target);
}
```

To complete the class, we implement the two helper methods. The getHolding-Tower() method involves a straightforward though messy pair of if statements; the updateModel() method updates the values of from and to, and moves one digit from the end of the source-tower String to the end of the target-tower String (see Figure 14.15). The complete Towers class is as follows:

```
class Towers {
    public Towers(TowerDisplay td, int nDisks) {
        this.td = td;
        this.nDisks = nDisks;
        if (nDisks>9)
            nDisks = 9;
        towers = new String[4];
        towers[1] = "123456789".substring(0,nDisks);
        towers[2] = "";
        towers[3] = "";
    }

    public void solveIt() {
        solveIt(nDisks, 1, 3);
    }

    private void solveIt(int nDisks, int source,int target) {
        if (nDisks<=0)
            return;
        int holding = getHoldingTower(source,target);
        solveIt(nDisks-1,source,holding);
        updateModel(source,target);
        td.displayMove(this);
        solveIt(nDisks-1,holding,target);
```

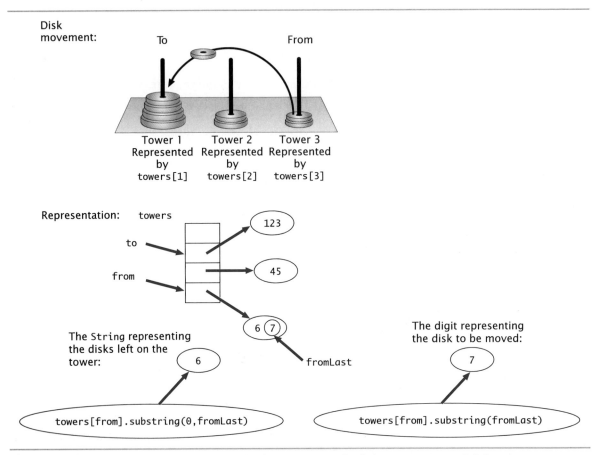

Figure 14.15 Manipulating Strings to model the movement of a disk. In removing a disk from a tower, we need an expression that represents the disk to be moved and another expression that represents the disks left on the tower.

```
    }

    public int getFrom() {
        return from;
    }
    public int getTo() {
        return to;
    }
    public String getTower(int index) {
        return towers[index];
    }
```

```
    private int getHoldingTower(int source, int target) {
       if ((source == 2 && target == 3) ||
           (source == 3 && target == 2))
          return 1;
       if ((source == 1 && target == 3) ||
           (source == 3 && target == 1))
          return 2;
       return 3;
    }

    private void updateModel(int source, int target) {
       from = source;
       to = target;
       int fromLast = towers[from].length()-1;
       towers[to] = towers[to].concat(
                          towers[from].substring(fromLast));
       towers[from] = towers[from].substring(0,fromLast);
    }

    private int nDisks;
    private String[] towers;
    private int from,to;
    private TowerDisplay td;
}
```

Implementing the TowerDisplay Class

The interface and behavior of the TowerDisplay class has been determined by the above discussion. It is just this:

```
class TowerDisplay {
    public void displayMove(Towers t) {…}
}
```

The displayMove() method queries t for information about the current state, then writes a simple description of the move to standard output. The code for displayMove() is as follows:

```
    public void displayMove(Towers t) {
       System.out.println("MOVE from " + t.getFrom() +
                                    " to " + t.getTo());
       System.out.println("   tower 1:" + t.getTower(1));
       System.out.println("   tower 2:" + t.getTower(2));
       System.out.println("   tower 3:" + t.getTower(3));
    }
```

The full solution to the problem is as follows, with the addition of a main()
method to the Towers class so that it can be directly executed:

```java
import  java.io.*;
import  java.util.*;

class Towers {
    public static void main(String[] a) {
        if (a.length!=1)
            System.err.println(
                    "Usage: java Towers <number of disks> ");
        else {
            int nDisks = Integer.parseInt(a[0]);
            Towers th = new Towers(new TowerDisplay(), nDisks);
            th.solveIt();
        }
    }

    public Towers(TowerDisplay td, int nDisks) {
        this.td = td;
        this.nDisks = nDisks;
        if (nDisks>9)
            nDisks = 9;
        towers = new String[4];
        towers[1] = "123456789".substring(0,nDisks);
        towers[2] = "";
        towers[3] = "";
    }

    public void solveIt() {
        solveIt(nDisks, 1,  3);
    }

    private void solveIt(int nDisks, int source,int target) {
        if (nDisks<=0)
            return;
        int holding = getHoldingTower(source,target);
        solveIt(nDisks-1,source,holding);
        updateModel(source,target);
        td.displayMove(this);
        solveIt(nDisks-1,holding,target);
    }

    public int getFrom() {
```

```
          return from;
      }
   public int getTo() {
      return to;
   }
   public String getTower(int index) {
      return towers[index];
   }

   private int getHoldingTower(int source, int target) {
      if ((source == 2 && target == 3) ||
          (source == 3 && target == 2))
         return 1;
      if ((source == 1 && target == 3) ||
          (source == 3 && target == 1))
         return 2;
      return 3;
   }

   private void updateModel(int source, int target) {
      from = source;
      to = target;
      int fromLast = towers[from].length()-1;
      towers[to] = towers[to].concat(
                        towers[from].substring(fromLast));
      towers[from] = towers[from].substring(0,fromLast);
   }

   private int nDisks;
   private String[] towers;
   private int from,to;
   private TowerDisplay td;
}

class TowerDisplay {
   public void displayMove(Towers t) {
      System.out.println("MOVE from " + t.getFrom() +
                                   " to " + t.getTo());
      System.out.println("   tower 1:" + t.getTower(1));
      System.out.println("   tower 2:" + t.getTower(2));
      System.out.println("   tower 3:" + t.getTower(3));
   }
}
```

14.8 Recursion and Iteration

Recursion and iteration both result in the controlled repeated execution of a body of code—the method body in the case of recursion, and the loop body in the case of iteration. In both techniques, a terminating condition that ends the repeated execution is essential to the design.

Any iteration can be implemented with recursion. Consider the following general form for iteration:

```
while  (condition)                    Using variables v1, v2, ..., vN and p1, p2, ..., pN
      body
```

where

- v1, v2, ..., vN are the variables that appear in the condition and the body whose values will be needed after the loop terminates.
- p1, p2, ..., pN are the variables that appear in the condition and the body whose values will *not* be needed after the loop terminates.

The equivalent recursive solution is to declare v1, v2, ..., vN as instance variables and write the following method:

```
private void  recursiveWhile (declaration of parameters p1,
                                                      p2, ..., pN) {
      if  (!condition)
          return;
      body
      recursiveWhile(p1, p2, ..., pN);
}
```

The original loop is replaced by the following invocation:

```
recursiveWhile(p1, p2, ..., pN);
```

Each recursive invocation corresponds to another evaluation of the loop condition and execution of the loop body. Note that each loop body execution in the recursive equivalent requires its own activation record in memory.

As an example, let's consider the following method that returns the sum of the first *n* elements of an array of integers, x, that is declared as an instance variable:

```
class SomeClass {
    ...
    public int getSum(int n) {
        int i = 0;
        int sum = 0;
        while (i!=n) {
            sum += x[i];
```

```
            i++;
        }
        // sum == x[0] + x[1] + ... + x[n-1]
        return sum;
    }
    ...
    private int[] x;
}
```

The variables n and i are used in the loop but their values are not needed after the loop, so i and n become parameters to the recursive method. The variable sum is needed after the loop, so it becomes an instance variable. We replace the loop with an invocation of a recursive method, recComputeSum(), which we add to the class as a helper method. The implementation of recComputeSum() follows the pattern presented above:

```
class SomeClass {
    ...
    public int getSum(int n) {
        int i = 0;
        sum = 0;
        recComputeSum(i,n);                    recursiveWhile (p1, p2)
        // sum == x[0] + x[1] + ... + x[n-1]
    }
    private void recComputeSum(int i, int n) {  recursiveWhile (p1, p2)
        if (!(i!=n))                               if (!condition)
            return;                                    return
        sum += x[i];                                   body
        i++;                                           body
        recComputeSum(i,n);                        recursiveWhile (p1, p2);
    }
    ...
    private int    sum;                         v1, made an instance variable
    private int[]  x;
}
```

Performance

Recursion can, in principle, compute anything that iteration can compute and is comparable in speed to iteration. However, as the diagrams in Figures 14.3 through 14.8 show, recursion can demand a lot of memory. In general, the amount of memory required by a loop is independent of the number of times the loop body executes, but the "further down" we go in the recursion process, the more memory is needed to save all the previous activation records.

Memory demand is a peculiar kind of cost. As long as you have enough memory, using it has little impact on performance. However, once memory is exhausted, the cost of needing more is catastrophic—the program fails!

A recursive method that replaces a simple iteration of 50,000 loop cycles is a silly waste of space because the simple iteration is fine and 50,000 activation records have to be created and stored while the recursion proceeds. On the other hand, the recursive solution to the Towers of Hanoi never requires more than eight activation records at a time. Each recursive invocation decreases nDisks by 1 and returns if nDisks is 0. Of course, many more than eight activation records are created, but there are never more than eight at a time. This recursive method therefore uses very little memory.

Transforming recursion in general into iteration is much harder, as you will see if you try it for our Towers of Hanoi problem! It is possible, however, to do it using techniques for manipulating collections that you will learn later in your career.

Most computer scientists and programmers would regard the use of recursion in the simple kinds of problems that we examined in the beginning of the chapter as overkill. On the other hand, recursion can often be the easiest way to solve a problem, and it is usually much easier to verify the correctness of a recursive solution than an iterative one. Certainly, for problems such as generating permutations and the Towers of Hanoi recursion is the method of choice.

Summary

Recursion is a convenient yet powerful technique for designing methods. Both its convenience and power derive from the fact that the designer of a recursive method need only write code that does part of the task or makes the task smaller in some way. The remainder of the work is done by reapplying the same method to the smaller task—we have whimsically called this part of the process "giving the work to an assistant" in this chapter.

Key Terms

activation record A block of memory holding the parameters and local variables of a method, along with the return address of the invoker of the method.

current activation record The most recently allocated activation record, which corresponds to the currently executing method.

recursion The process of using a recursive procedure; the carrying out of a recursive call.

recursive call An invocation of a method from within that method.

recursive procedure A procedure that carries out a part of a task and refers to itself to carry out the rest of the task.

termination step An essential step in any viable recursive procedure, in which the task is checked to see if it can be carried out without resorting to recursion.

Questions for Review

1. What is a recursive method?
2. In what sense is recursion a "lazy" approach?
3. What is the termination step? Why must it always be present?
4. What are the two key steps to take in designing a recursive solution?
5. Why does recursion require more memory than iteration? When is the increased memory requirement a problem? When is it not a problem?
6. What is an activation record?

Exercises

1. Suppose you have a stack of 500 advertisement flyers that must be stuffed into 500 envelopes for mailing. Take the lazy approach and describe a recursive procedure for carrying this out. Assume you have at least 499 friendly coworkers willing to lend a small helping hand.
2. Suppose you have two stacks of index cards, each with a name written on it. The stacks are not sorted. Your task is to write up a sorted list of the names that appear in both stacks. Take the lazy approach and describe a recursive procedure for carrying out this task.
3. Write a recursive method that receives two nonnegative integer arguments and returns their product. The method does not use the * operator. Instead, it relies on the fact that $x*y = x + x + \cdots + x$ (where there are y terms in the sum). Here are some hints:
   - Think of the sum as equivalent to $0 + x + x + \cdots + x$.
   - If you could hire an assistant to help you, what would you have the assistant do so that you would have to do only one addition?
   - For what value of y would it be silly to hire an assistant?
4. Write a recursive method that receives a nonnegative integer argument, n, and prints n hyphens, all on the same line.
5. Consider the methods you wrote in the previous exercises. (If you have not written them, do so now!) Which of the patterns of Figure 14.2 characterizes each of them?

6. Write a recursive method that receives two nonnegative integer arguments, x and y, and returns their sum, $x + y$. The method is not allowed to use the + or – operators, but it may use ++ and --. *Hint:* Note that $x + y$ is equal to $x + 1 + 1 + \cdots + 1$ (where there are y 1s in the sum).

7. Write a recursive method that receives an array of ints and initializes each element to 0.

8. Write a recursive method that receives two Strings and determines whether the first is a substring of the second.

9. Write a program that opens a file called dictionary that contains a list of words in English, one per line. The program creates a Vector object containing the words in this file. The program then reads in a seven-letter "word" and uses the getWords() and permutations() methods to print out all the permutations of these seven letters that appear in the dictionary file.

10. Our permutations() method does not guarantee that each "word" added to the Vector is unique. Under what circumstances would there be duplicate words? Modify the permutations() method so that no word in the Vector appears more than once.

11. How many permutations are there of a set of two elements? Three? Four? Seven? Write and run a program that uses the permutations() method for a set of seven elements. Time the program (a rough estimate should do).

12. Implement a more general TowerDisplay class that is not limited to a maximum of nine disks. Do not, of course, change the interface of the class!

13. Try writing a different Towers class for the following variation of Towers of Hanoi. The disks on tower 1 are alternating red and black. In addition to the other rules of the game, no two disks of the same color can ever be placed one on top of the other.

14. If there is just one disk in the Towers of Hanoi, how many invocations of solveIt() will there be? What if there are two disks? How about three disks? How about seven disks? n disks?

15. Write a recursive method that is equivalent to the following loop:
```
int i=0,  sum=0;
while (i!=1000) {
    sum+=a[i];
    i++;
}
```

16. Consider the permutations() method. What is the greatest number of activation records of permutations() if it is invoked for a set of five elements?

17. Write a recursive method that receives an array of integers and returns their sum.

18. Write a recursive method that returns the smallest value in a subsection of an array.

19. Write a method that prints out all possible 3 × 3 "magic squares." An $n \times n$ magic square is an $n \times n$ grid with the numbers 1 through n^2 placed in each square of the grid and where all the rows, columns, and diagonals add up to the same number. Below is one example.

```
8   1   6
3   5   7
4   9   2
```

You can view any 3 × 3 magic square as a permutation of the integers 1 to 9. For example, the above square is 8 1 6 3 5 7 4 9 2. So, one strategy might be to generate all permutations of the integers 1 to 9 and test each one to see whether it satisfies the requirements for a magic square. It would be a good idea to have a separate method do that part.

Towers of Hanoi Applet

In this supplement we develop a graphical implementation of the Towers of Hanoi program, using an MVC design.

The Towers of Hanoi Applet Design

Our Towers of Hanoi applet presents a Canvas on which textual descriptions of the moves are printed and the configuration of the disks on the towers displayed. After displaying each move, there is a delay (see below) followed by a redrawing of the differently colored disks, to update the tower configuration. It also provides two buttons and two textfields for controlling the applet (see Figure 14.16):

- Start/restart button—Initially labeled "start," this button starts the solution of a puzzle. Once started, the button's label is changed to "restart."
- Pause/resume button—Initially labeled "pause," this button suspends activity and changes its label to "resume." When the resume button is pressed, activity resumes and the button changes its label back to "pause."
- Number of disks textfield—Initially set at 7, this field determines the number of disks in the puzzle. The user can edit this number and by pressing the RETURN key to inform the applet that there is a new value. The new value will be used the next time the start/restart button is pressed.
- Delay (millisecs) textfield—Initially set at 1,000, this field determines the number of milliseconds delay between steps in the display of the solution to the puzzle.

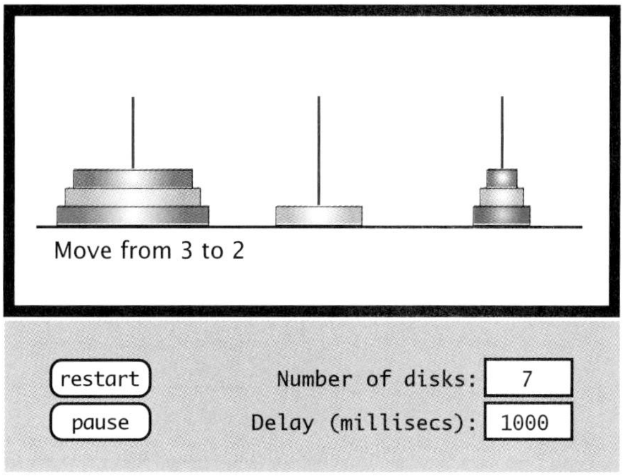

Figure 14.16

A moment in the execution of the Towers of Hanoi applet.

607

The Architecture of the Towers of Hanoi Applet

There are three classes in this model:

- An extended Thread class that serves as the *model*
- An extended Canvas class that serves as the *view*
- An extended Applet class that serves as the *controller*

Our extended Thread class, TowerThread, contains the same methods and code as the Towers class, along with the usual methods for thread control: myResume(), mySuspend(), and myStop(), as well as a registerAsObserver() method.

Our extended Canvas class, TowerDisplay, plays the same role that the non-GUI TowerDisplay did earlier in this chapter. Instead of writing moves to System.out and displaying towers as strings of digits written to System.out, it paints these onto a Graphics object. Because it provides a view of a TowerThread model object, TowerDisplay also implements the TowerObserver interface.

Our extended Applet class, TowerApplet, creates the TowerDisplay object, the buttons, and the textfields. It places these controls and handles button and textfield action events. It responds to these events by creating, starting, suspending, resuming, and altogether stopping TowerThread objects, and by notifying the TowerDisplay object of the new delay time value when the delay time has been changed.

The TowerApplet Class

The init() method, though messy as ever, should be familiar by now. It creates the TowerDisplay, the Buttons, the Textfields, and the Labels that label them. Various Panels that use BorderLayout are created to place the controls in a reasonable way (see Figure 14.17).

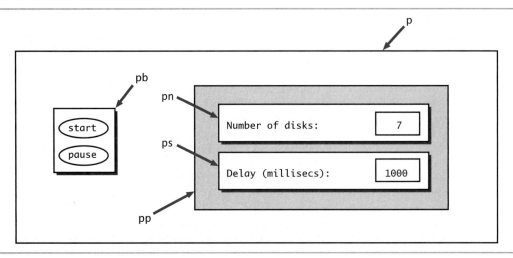

Figure 14.17 Use of Panels in the TowerApplet layout. The layout of the controls is organized using multiple nested Panels: pb, pn, ps, pp, and p.

Likewise, the general idea of the implementation of `actionPerformed()` and the various handler methods should be familiar to you. Although there are only two `Button`s, there are four handler methods associated with them. That's because we alter the labels of the `Button`s, depending on the state of the applet's execution (for example, after we click the "pause" button, its label is changed to "resume" and vice versa). Because each label indicates a different behavior, each label corresponds to a different handler method. The `handlePause()` method here corresponds to the `ClockApplet`'s `handleStop()` method. The `handleStop()` method here allows to us to completely shut down the thread, something we did not do in the `ClockApplet`. It accomplishes this by sending a `myStop()` message to the existing `TowerThread`, then creating and starting a new `TowerThread`.

The two `TextField`s are handled differently. A change in the number of disks affects only the initial setup of a Towers of Hanoi puzzle, so the applet does not respond to those changes immediately. It just uses the value in that `TextField` when creating a `TowerThread`. On the other hand, any keyboard action causes the applet to read the number in the delay textfield and immediately send a `setDelay()` message to the `TowerDisplay` object. That guarantees an immediate response to the user setting the delay. Figure 14.18 illustrates the role of the applet's methods in responding to button clicks.

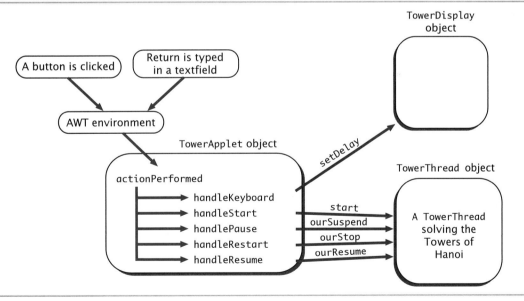

Figure 14.18 How the `TowerApplet` responds to buttons and textfields. The `actionPerformed()` method is invoked by the AWT environment in response to action events. This method handles the different action events that occur by invoking various helper methods that control the `TowerThread` or modify the display. The `handleStart()` method also creates the `TowerThread` object before sending it a `start()` message. After sending a `myStop()` message to stop the current `TowerThread`, the `handleRestart()` method invokes `handleStart()` to start up a new `TowerThread` object.

In the Chapter 13 supplement, the view was able to register with the model as soon as the view was created; that is, we passed a reference to the model as an argument to the view's constructor. Here, that is impossible: the view is created in the applet's init() method, but the model is created in the handleStart() method:

```
private void handleStart() {
    int nDisks = Integer.parseInt(numDisks.getText().trim());
    handleKeyboard();
    towersTicker = new TowerThread(nDisks);
    td.replaceModel(towersTicker);  ◄────── Rough equivalent to passing
    towersTicker.start();                    model to view constructor
    startButton.setLabel("restart");
    pauseButton.setLabel("pause");
}
```

Even worse, each invocation of handleStart() causes the creation of a *different* model, even though the display remains fixed. Therefore, we need view registration to take place each time a new model is created; we will need to provide a replaceModel() method in the TowerDisplay class. Because the TowerDisplay object created in init() is used in the handleStart() method, its reference must be saved as an instance variable.

The code for TowerApplet follows:

```
import java.util.*;
import java.awt.*;
import java.awt.event.*;
import java.applet.*;

public class TowerApplet extends Applet implements ActionListener {
    public void init() {
        setBackground(new Color(200,255,255));
        this.setLayout(new BorderLayout(20,2));
        td = new TowerDisplay();
        add("Center",td);

        startButton = new Button("start");
        pauseButton = new Button("pause");
        Panel pb = new Panel();
        pb.setLayout(new BorderLayout(2,2));
        pb.add("North",startButton);
        pb.add("South",pauseButton);
        startButton.addActionListener(this);
        pauseButton.addActionListener(this);
```

```
    numDisks = new TextField(" 7");
    numDisks.setFont(new Font("Courier",Font.BOLD,10));

    Label numDisksLabel = new Label(
                        "Number of disks:",Label.RIGHT);
    Label stepDelayLabel = new Label(
                      "Delay (millisecs):",Label.RIGHT);
    numDisksLabel.setFont(new Font("Courier",Font.BOLD,10));
    stepDelayLabel.setFont(new Font("Courier",Font.BOLD,10));

    Panel pn = new Panel();
    pn.setLayout(new BorderLayout(2,2));
    pn.add("East",numDisks);
    pn.add("West",numDisksLabel);

    stepDelay = new TextField("1000");
    stepDelay.addActionListener(this);
    stepDelay.setFont(new Font("Courier",Font.BOLD,10));
    Panel ps = new Panel();
    ps.setLayout(new BorderLayout(2,2));
    ps.add("East",stepDelay);
    ps.add("West",stepDelayLabel);
    Panel pp = new Panel();
    pp.setLayout(new BorderLayout(2,2));
    pp.add("North",pn);
    pp.add("South",ps);
    Panel p = new Panel();
    p.setLayout(new  FlowLayout(FlowLayout.CENTER,50,20));
    p.add(pb);
    p.add(pp);
    p.setBackground(new Color(255,200,200));
    add("South",p);
  }

  public void actionPerformed(ActionEvent ae) {
    String whichButton = ae.getActionCommand();
    if (whichButton.equals("start"))
      handleStart();
    else if (whichButton.equals("restart"))
      handleRestart();
    else if (whichButton.equals("pause"))
      handlePause();
    else if (whichButton.equals("resume"))
      handleResume();
```

```
        else
          handleKeyboard();
      }
      private void handleStart() {
        int nDisks = Integer.parseInt(numDisks.getText().trim());
        handleKeyboard();
        towersTicker = new TowerThread(nDisks);
        td.replaceModel(towersTicker);
        towersTicker.start();
        startButton.setLabel("restart");
        pauseButton.setLabel("pause");
      }
      private void handleRestart() {
        towersTicker.myStop();
        handleStart();
      }
      private void handlePause() {
        towersTicker.mySuspend();
        pauseButton.setLabel("resume");
      }
      private void handleResume() {
        towersTicker.myResume();
        pauseButton.setLabel("pause");
      }
      private void handleKeyboard() {
        int sDelay = Integer.parseInt(stepDelay.getText().trim());
        td.setDelay(sDelay);
      }
      private   Button startButton, pauseButton;
      private   TextField numDisks, stepDelay;
      private   TowerDisplay td;
      private   TowerThread towersTicker = null;
    }
```

The line `td.replaceModel(towersTicker);` is annotated: Rough equivalent to passing model to view constructor

The TowerDisplay Class

This class is a close analog of the TowerDisplay class from the non-GUI Towers of Hanoi. It provides the same services to the TowerThread that the non-GUI class provided the Tower class: a graphical realization of the sequence of moves. Because it must implement the TowerObserver interface

```
interface TowerObserver {
    public void towerHasChanged(TowerThread tower);
}
```

it must provide a `towerHasChanged()` method. As we saw earlier, it must also provide a `replaceModel()` method. Because `TowerDisplay` extends `Canvas`, we also provide a customized `paint()` method.

The `TowerDisplay` constructor creates an array of nine different `Color` objects so that the disks can be painted later with different colors.

The `setup()` method computes a large set of locations on the `Canvas` to facilitate displaying the moves and the towers later.

The `displayMove()` method does the actual display of the move and the towers. It draws a `String` that indicates the move to be made. It pauses for the user-specified delay time and then invokes `paint()` to draw the towers. The reason `paint()` doesn't handle the display of the move, but just the display of the towers, is that it is also invoked by the AWT environment, which has no idea about the current move. There may, in fact, not be a current move. Figure 14.19 illustrates the role the `TowerDisplay` methods have in displaying the moves and towers.

The `TowerDisplay` class here uses the same array of four `Strings` technique that the non-GUI `TowerDisplay` class used to maintain its internal picture of the state of the three towers.

The `replaceModel()` Method

The `replaceModel()` method calculates the sizes and positions of the various graphical elements in the display, for use in the `paint()` and `displayMove()` methods. These variables containing these quantities and their relation to the graphical display are shown in Figures 14.20 and 14.21. Because some of these quantities depend on the number of disks in the problem, we must query the

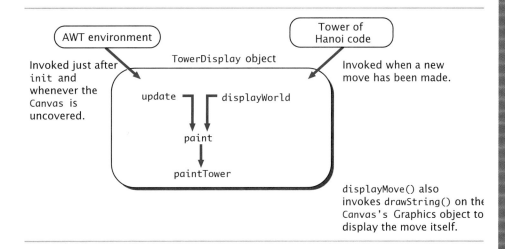

Figure 14.19
How the move and towers get displayed.

Figure 14.20
The principal size and position variables of Tower-Display (I). Achieving an appealing display requires careful planning in advance. Here we show the basic sizes of the graphical objects in the display.

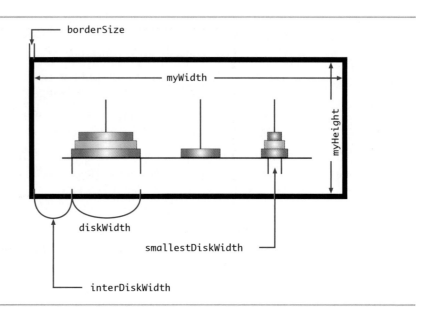

Figure 14.21
The principal size and position variables of Tower-Display (II). Here we show the positions of the baseline's end points and the horizontal positions of the three towers: towerLeft[1], towerLeft[2], and towerLeft[3].

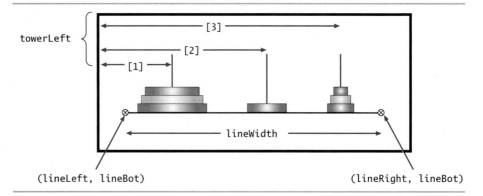

model for the number of disks; this will require an additional accessor method getNDisks() in the TowerThread class.

At the end of the method, paint() is invoked to display the towers before the solution is generated. After paint() returns, delay() is invoked so that the display will persist for a bit before being changed.

The basic drawing layout strategy is to divide the width of the Canvas and subdivide it into three regions for displaying towers, with each region separated from the other or the border by the same amount of space. The lengths of the four intertower regions add up to the size of one of the tower regions. This scheme is shown in Figure 14.22.

Figure 14.22
Partitioning the width of the Canvas. The maximum disk width—the width of each tower—is calculated from the width of the applet. The spaces separating the towers from each other and from the borders are the same and add up to one disk width.

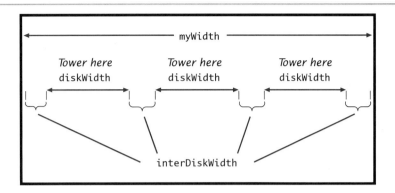

The width and height of the area available for display is calculated by subtracting twice the borderSize from the actual width of the Canvas and storing the result in myWidth:

```
myWidth  = this.getWidth() - borderSize;
myHeight = this.getHeight() - 2*borderSize;
```

This width is divided by 4 to reflect the division of the Canvas into three tower regions and a set of intertower regions whose combined width is the same as a tower region:

```
diskWidth = myWidth / 4;
```

This quantity is divided by the number of disks to yield the width of the smallest disk:

```
smallestDiskWidth = diskWidth / nDisks;
```

The width of the largest disk is also the width of the tower region. Our strategy calls for each of the four intertower distances to be one fourth this size:

```
interDiskWidth = diskWidth/4;
```

Regardless of the number of disks our problem has, we choose the height of each disk to be 10:

```
diskHeight = 10;
```

We want the towers to extend one disk height past the top disk, even when all the disks are stacked on the same tower. So the height of the tower is

```
towerHeight = (nDisks+1) * diskHeight;
```

The left and right positions of the baseline for the towers are then calculated. The line is inset one interDiskWidth past the border:

```
lineLeft = borderSize + interDiskWidth;
```

Vertically it is positioned so that the poles of the towers (whose height is tower-Height) are centered:

```
lineBot  = myHeight - (myHeight-towerHeight)/2;
```

(*Remember.* Position 0 is at the top of the Canvas, and myHeight marks the bottom.) This scheme is shown in Figure 14.23.

The width of the line is just enough to hold three towers and two intertower distances. The right position of the line is just the left position plus the width:

```
lineWidth = 3*diskWidth + 2*interDiskWidth;
lineRight = lineLeft+lineWidth;
```

Finally, we allocate an array to store the horizontal coordinates of each tower, taking into account their widths and the intertower distances between them:

```
towerLeft = new int[4];
towerLeft[1] = lineLeft + diskWidth/2;
towerLeft[2] = towerLeft[1] + diskWidth + interDiskWidth + diskWidth/2;
towerLeft[3] = towerLeft[2] + diskWidth + interDiskWidth + diskWidth/2;
```

After these calculations, we can then register with the TowerThread, save the reference t in an instance variable so that paint() will have access to it, then invoke paint() to paint the initial configuration of the disks on the towers:

```
t.registerAsObserver(this);
tower = t;
paint(this.getGraphics());
delay(1000);
```

Figure 14.23

Partitioning the height of the Canvas. Here we show the calculation of the tower baseline and the vertical positions of the bases of the towers. It is calculated so that the towers are centered vertically in the display.

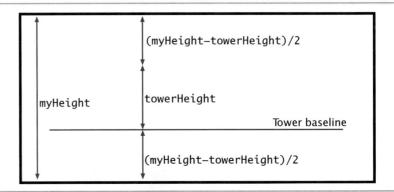

The `towerHasChanged()` and `paint()` Methods

The `towerHasChanged()` method is invoked from the `TowerThread`. Its first task is to determine the color of the disk that was just moved in the model; this color will be used to display the textual description of the move. To do this, it queries the model for the most recent source and target towers, and also gets the `String` representation of the target tower. The most recently moved disk is at the top (i.e., the end) of the target tower:

```
int from = t.getFrom();
int to = t.getTo();
String toTower = t.getTower(to);
int toLast = toTower.length()-1;
```

With the tower and the index on that tower of the disk whose color we want, we can invoke a helper method `getDiskColor()` (which we will also use later) to return the appropriate `Color` object:

```
Color   c = getDiskColor(to,toLast);
```

To prepare for drawing, we then access the `Graphics` object associated with the `TowerDisplay`:

```
Graphics g = this.getGraphics();
```

In order to clear any residual display of a previous move, `paintLowerBackground()` is invoked:

```
paintLowerBackground(g);
```

`paintLowerBackground()` just fills a white rectangle over the area below the tower baseline, the area where the moves are printed out. The color is then set along with a nice clear font, and the move description is drawn, with a starting position directly below the left end of the tower baseline and halfway between the baseline and the bottom of the display:

```
g.setColor(c);
g.setFont(new Font("Helvetica",Font.BOLD,18));
g.drawString("Move from " + from + " to " + to, lineLeft,
             myHeight - (myHeight-towerHeight)/4);
```

Once the description is drawn, we delay, letting the user anticipate the change in the towers displayed by `paint()`. The delay, `sdelay`, is set by the `setDelay()` method that is invoked by the `handleKeyboard()` method of the `TowerApplet`. Before painting, we save `t` in an instance variable for use by `paint()`; after painting, there is another, shorter delay before returning to the `solveIt()` method of the `TowerThread`:

```
delay(sdelay);
tower = t;
paint(g);
delay(sdelay/3);
```

The paint() method itself invokes paintBackground() to clear the background of the towers with a white rectangle, redraws the borders by invoking paint-Borders(), draws the tower baseline using the drawLine() method, and then invokes paintTower() for each of the towers. The paintTower() method iterates over each digit in the String representing a tower and uses that digit to determine the color (via getDiskColor()) and size of a disk to draw. The coordinates of each disk are determined using the variables whose values were given in the replaceModel() method.

The Complete TowerDisplay Class

The code for the TowerDisplay class is as follows:

```
class TowerDisplay extends Canvas implements TowerObserver {
    public TowerDisplay() {
        c = new Color[10];
        c[0] = new Color(255,0,0);
        c[1] = new Color(0,255,0);
        c[2] = new Color(0,0,255);
        c[3] = new Color(255,255,0);
        c[4] = new Color(255,0,255);
        c[5] = new Color(0,255,255);
        c[6] = new Color(44,150,44);
        c[7] = new Color(44,44,150);
        c[8] = new Color(150,150,44);
        c[9] = new Color(150,44,150);
    }
    public void replaceModel(TowerThread t) {
        nDisks = t.getNDisks();
        myWidth = this.getWidth() - 2*borderSize;
        myHeight = this.getHeight() - 2*borderSize;

        diskWidth = myWidth / 4;
        smallestDiskWidth = diskWidth / nDisks;
        interDiskWidth = diskWidth / 4;

        diskHeight = 10;
        towerHeight = (nDisks+1) * diskHeight;
        lineLeft = borderSize + interDiskWidth;
        lineBot  = myHeight - (myHeight-towerHeight)/2;
```

```
      lineWidth = 3*diskWidth + 2*interDiskWidth;
      lineRight = lineLeft+lineWidth;
      towerLeft = new int[4];
      towerLeft[1] = lineLeft + diskWidth/2;
      towerLeft[2] = towerLeft[1] + diskWidth + interDiskWidth
      towerLeft[3] = towerLeft[2] + diskWidth + interDiskWidth
      t.registerAsObserver(this);
      tower = t;
      paint(this.getGraphics());
      delay(1000);
   }
   public void setDelay(int d) {
      sdelay = d;
   }

   public void towerHasChanged(TowerThread t) {
      int from = t.getFrom();
      int to = t.getTo();
      String toTower = t.getTower(to);
      int toLast = toTower.length()-1;
      Color   c = getDiskColor(to,toLast);
      Graphics g = this.getGraphics();
      paintLowerBackground(g);
      g.setColor(c);
      g.setFont(new Font("Helvetica",Font.BOLD,18));
      g.drawString("Move from " + from + " to " + to, lineLeft,
                   myHeight - (myHeight-towerHeight)/4);
      delay(sdelay);
      tower = t;
      paint(g);
      delay(sdelay/3);
   }

   public void paint(Graphics g) {
      paintBackground(g);
      paintBorder(g);
      g.setColor(new Color(0,0,0));
      if (tower==null)
         return;
      g.drawLine(lineLeft,lineBot,lineRight,lineBot);
      paintTower(g,1);
      paintTower(g,2);
      paintTower(g,3);
   }
```

```java
private void paintTower(Graphics g, int whichTower) {
    int j;
    String s = tower.getTower(whichTower);
    g.setColor(new Color(0,0,0));
    g.drawLine(towerLeft[whichTower],lineBot,
               towerLeft[whichTower],lineBot-towerHeight);
    for (int i=0;i<s.length();i++) {
        j = nDisks-Integer.parseInt(s.substring(i, i+1));
        g.setColor(getDiskColor(whichTower,i));
        int jWidth = (1+j)*smallestDiskWidth;
        int jLeft = towerLeft[whichTower]-jWidth/2;
        int jBot = lineBot - diskHeight - i*diskHeight;
        g.fill3DRect(jLeft,jBot,jWidth,diskHeight,true);
    }
}
private void paintLowerBackground(Graphics g) {
    g.setColor(new Color(255,255,255));
    g.fillRect(lineLeft-2, lineBot+4,
               lineWidth+4,(myHeight-towerHeight)/4);
}
private void paintBackground(Graphics g) {
    g.setColor(new Color(255,255,255));
    g.fillRect(5,5,this.getWidth()-10,this.getHeight()-10);
}
private void paintBorder(Graphics g) {
    g.setColor(new Color(0,0,0));
    g.fillRect(0,0,this.getWidth(),borderSize);
    g.fillRect(0,this.getHeight()-borderSize,
               this.getWidth(),borderSize);
    g.fillRect(0,0,borderSize,this.getHeight());
    g.fillRect(this.getWidth()-borderSize,0,
               borderSize,this.getHeight());
}
private Color getDiskColor(int whichTower, int n) {
    String s = tower.getTower(whichTower);
    int j = nDisks-Integer.parseInt(s.substring(n,n+1));
    return c[j%10];
}

private void delay(int n) {
    try {
        Thread.sleep(n);
    } catch(Exception e) {}
}
```

```
    private TowerThread   tower;

    private final   int    borderSize = 5;
    private int          sdelay=100;
    private int          nDisks;
    private Color[]      c;
    private int          myHeight;
    private int          myWidth;
    private int          diskWidth;
    private int          smallestDiskWidth;
    private int          interDiskWidth;
    private int          diskHeight;
    private int          towerHeight;
    private int          lineBot;
    private int          lineLeft;
    private int          lineRight;
    private int          lineWidth;
    private int[ ]       towerLeft;
}
```

The TowerThread Class

This class is based on the Towers class from the non-GUI version, with the addition of both those methods needed to make this class function in the MVC framework and those methods needed to make the class a Thread. The getHoldingTower() methods are identical in both classes, as are the instance variables nDisks, towers, from, and to.

The constructor is identical, except that the TowerDisplay is not mentioned in the new version. The new methods registerAsObserver() and (helper method) notifyObserver() are responsible for communication with the display(s).

The usual thread-control methods, mySuspend(), myResume(), and myStop() and the instance variables they manipulate, amRunning and amStopped, are provided.

The run() method—required by a Thread class—replaces and plays the role of the public solveIt() method in the non-GUI version of Towers. It sets the boolean thread-control variables to their proper initial values and invokes the private recursive solveIt() method.

The solveIt() method here is identical to its non-GUI counterpart, except that before invoking the display of a move, the following code is executed:

```
if (amStopped)
    return;
while (!amRunning)
    delay(80);
```

This code allows an appropriate and rapid response to changes in the thread-control variables amStopped and amRunning. As long as amRunning is false, we repeatedly invoke the delay() method, which happens to be identical to the delay() method in the TowerDisplay class.

The complete code for the TowerThread class is as follows:

```
class TowerThread extends Thread {
    public TowerThread(int nDisks) {
        this.nDisks = nDisks;
        if (nDisks>9)
            nDisks = 9;
        towers = new String[4];
        towers[1] = "123456789".substring(0,nDisks);
        towers[2] = "";
        towers[3] = "";
    }

    public void registerAsObserver(TowerObserver observer) {
        observers.addElement(observer);
    }

    public void run() {
        amRunning = true;
        amStopped = false;
        solveIt(nDisks, 1, 3);
    }

    public void mySuspend() { amRunning = false;}
    public void myResume()  { amRunning = true;}
    public void myStop()    { amStopped = true;}

    private void delay(int n) {
        try {
            Thread.sleep(n);
        } catch(Exception e) {}
    }

    private void solveIt(int nDisks,int source,int target) {
        if (nDisks<=0)
            return;
        int holdingTower = getHoldingTower(source,target);
        solveIt(nDisks-1,source,holdingTower);
        if (amStopped)
```

```
            return;
        while (!amRunning)
            delay(80);
        updateModel(source,target);
        notifyObservers();
        solveIt(nDisks-1,holdingTower,target);
    }

    public int getFrom() {
        return from;
    }
    public int getTo() {
        return to;
    }
    public int getNDisks() {
        return nDisks;
    }
    public String getTower(int index) {
        return towers[index];
    }

    private int getHoldingTower(int source, int target) {
        if ((source == 2 && target == 3) ||
            (source == 3 && target == 2))
            return 1;
        if ((source == 1 && target == 3) ||
            (source == 3 && target == 1))
            return 2;
        return 3;
    }

    private void updateModel(int source, int target) {
        from = source;
        to = target;
        int fromLast = towers[from].length()-1;
        towers[to] = towers[to].concat(
                        towers[from].substring(fromLast));
        towers[from] = towers[from].substring(0,fromLast);
    }

    private void notifyObservers() {
        TowerObserver to;
        for (int i=0; i < observers.size(); i++) {
```

```
            to = (TowerObserver) observers.elementAt(i);
            to.towerHasChanged(this);
        }
    }

    private boolean amRunning, amStopped;
    private int nDisks;
    private String[] towers;
    private int from,to;
    private Vector observers = new Vector();
}
```

The Threads and Threads

Where there is execution, there is a thread. All code executes as part of some thread. The Thread class provides a static method, currentThread(), that returns a reference to a Thread object that is currently executing (the one that invokes currentThread()). We can use the getName() method of the Thread class to get the unique name of the currently executing thread. The following program uses this to illustrate the fact that there is always a thread executing:

```
class  Sample  {
    public  static  void  main(String[]  a)  {
        System.out.println(Thread.currentThread().getName());
    }
}
```

The output of this program is the word *main,* the name of the thread executing this program. From this little experiment we make the following observations:

- A thread does not only execute the code that is defined in a Thread class—here, for example, the main thread is executing the main() method in the Sample class.
- When our programs run, there may be threads that we did not create and that are not defined by any Thread class of ours.

When our TowerApplet executes, there are at first two threads present:

- The main applet thread—it loads the applet, invokes init(), and then invokes start().
- The AWT-environment thread—this thread runs AWT code that detects events associated with the user (button clicks, typing in textfields, and so on) and determines when our applet or parts of it need to be redrawn (for example, when another window that covered our applet is moved and exposes part or all of the applet). This thread invokes actionPerformed(), paint(), and other AWT methods as needed.

These two threads are present when any applet executes, including the first one we wrote in Chapter 3. These threads, like the main thread that was revealed by the Sample class on the previous page, are not created by our code or defined by a Thread class that we wrote. They are "given" to us by the execution environment.

When the TowerApplet executes, there may be additional threads executing, as our code creates new threads to solve the Towers of Hanoi.

Creating a thread involves two steps:

- Creating a Thread object
- Sending a start() message to the Thread object

There is a difference between a Thread (an object) and a thread (an independent execution of code). When we create a Thread object, using the new operator, we have not yet created a new thread—just a new object. It is not until we send the Thread object a start() message that a new *thread* is actually created.

The code executed by the threads we create is defined by but not limited to the run() method of the Thread class we define. This run() method invokes other methods within its own class and in other classes as well. The tower-HasChanged() method in our TowerDisplay class is executed by the TowerThread threads that we create in response to the start and reset buttons.

Figure 14.24 shows some methods of the three classes we defined in making the TowerApplet and the threads that execute them. Note that there are some methods that are executed by more than one thread, such as paint().

Repaint, Paint, Update, and Drawing Things Directly

The AWT environment thread takes responsibility for drawing all components (such as Buttons and Canvases) that are added to a Container. This includes Applet objects because they are components and they too are added to a Container—the browser window. The AWT thread does this by invoking the paint() method of each such component. Every component is responsible for providing a paint() method that draws itself on the Graphics object that the AWT thread passes to the method.

For components whose appearance does not rapidly change—like Buttons and Labels—it is sufficient to simply provide a paint() method. When such methods do need to redraw themselves, they usually just invoke the repaint() method. This method tells the AWT environment that the component needs to be updated. As a result, the AWT method will eventually invoke the component's update() method, which in turn invokes the component's paint() method.

We could have taken this approach in TowerDisplay, by replacing our tower-HasChanged() method,

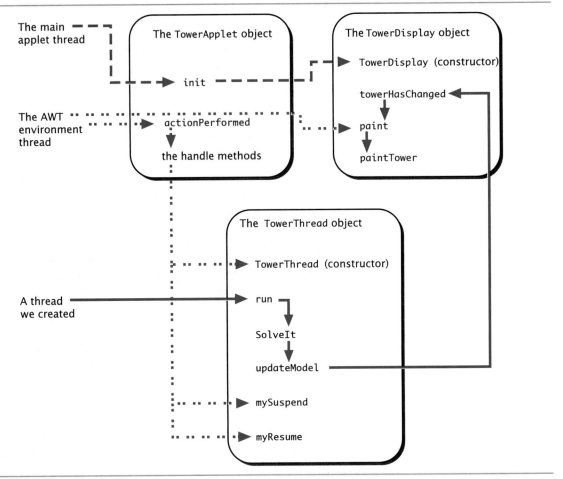

Figure 14.24 The threads of the TowerApplet and the methods they execute. Not all the methods of every class are shown here.

```java
public void towerHasChanged(TowerThread t) {
    ...
    Graphics g = this.getGraphics();
    paintLowerBackground(g);
    ...
    paint(g);
    delay(sdelay/3);
}
```

with a simple version that invoked `repaint()`.

Had we done this, the redrawing of the world would not have been carried out by the current `TowerThread` (remember, `TowerThread` executes `towerHasChanged()`). Instead, the AWT environment thread would eventually invoke `TowerDisplay`'s `update()` method.

We didn't write the `update()` and `repaint()` methods because when we create a class by extending another class, as we did in `TowerDisplay` (and `TowerThread` and `TowerApplet`), we inherit the methods of the other class. In this case, `update()` and `repaint()` are examples of those methods.

Using `repaint()` here is inappropriate, however. That's because the Towers of Hanoi display is rapidly changing. The AWT environment is not always in a hurry to do updates. By the time it invoked `update()` and `paint()`, the model could have changed, and we would miss some of the moves. Worse, while `paint()` is drawing the display, the model could have changed, resulting in a picture that is partly one state, partly the next—ugly and inconsistent. Finally, while we wait for the AWT to get around to invoking `update()`, the `TowerThread` could have made multiple invocations to `towerHasChanged()` and therefore to `repaint()`. Many invocations of `update()` would then be scheduled. As a result, when we paused or stopped the solution, we would observe many redrawings of the same world.

This is all a consequence of the fact that our `Canvas` might be rapidly recomputed. If we knew it was going to change only once every few hundred milliseconds (i.e., if we forced a lower limit on the delay period), we could use `repaint()` in `towerHasChanged()` and leave all the painting to `paint()`.

Suggested Experiments

1. Write an applet that challenges the user's reflexes. Display a circle that is constantly changing color. When the circle is red, the user is supposed to click a button. If the user succeeds, he or she gets a point. Display the score in a textfield. To do this nicely, you may wish to use the `Random` class in the `java.util` package.

2. Based on your knowledge of how multiple threads execute, why might the previous exercise not work quite as well as you would like?

Client–Server Computing

15.1 Clients and Servers

One of the reasons for the continually increasing interest in Java is its delivery mechanism. Java applets do not reach their users on diskettes or CD-ROMs in shrink-wrapped software. Nor are they downloaded once from some network source to be used over and over again. Instead, they are embedded within a web page and downloaded anew with each loading of the web page. Java applets are not only on the Internet but are creatures of the Internet as well.

In this final chapter, we will explore further some of the technology underpinning the Internet and therefore this aspect of Java.

15.2 Internet Communication

Communication on the Internet is the transfer of data from one machine to another. This encompasses downloading of web pages and applets, as well as email, remote logins, chat rooms, and all other Internet applications. Communication is accomplished by breaking up the data to be transferred into small pieces called **packets** and transferring these packets. The sending machine is almost never directly connected to the receiving machine, so these packets actually are transferred from one machine to another on the Internet until they arrive at their destination. The machines involved in the process must have specialized routing software that enables them to transfer the data packets. These machines are called **routers** and are usually dedicated to this purpose. Every machine on the Internet must be on a local area network with at least one router—and every router must be connected to at least one other router so that there can be a path of routers between any two machines. See Figure 15.1.

Unfortunately, the transfer of packets is unreliable—packets can get lost on the way. Not only are the communication connections unreliable, but the routers and the receiving machine themselves have limited memory. If packets arrive faster than they can be processed, there may not be enough memory to hold them and some packets will be lost.

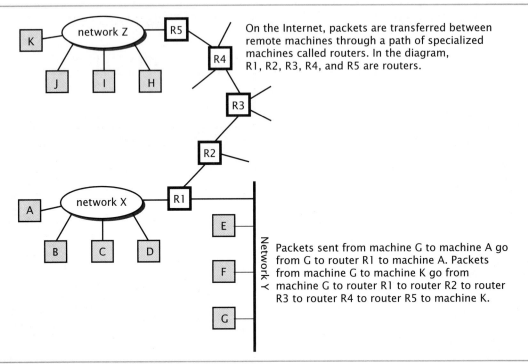

On the Internet, packets are transferred between remote machines through a path of specialized machines called routers. In the diagram, R1, R2, R3, R4, and R5 are routers.

Packets sent from machine G to machine A go from G to router R1 to machine A. Packets from machine G to machine K go from machine G to router R1 to router R2 to router R3 to router R4 to router R5 to machine K.

Figure 15.1 Routing packets on the Internet.

This underlying reality of Internet communication—individual packets unreliably moved through many intermediate machines—is a very poor facility for most Internet applications. From the application's point of view, a better facility would be a reliable, direct connection between two programs on different machines, allowing a stream of data in both directions. All machines on the Internet run software that uses the actual Internet communication facility, called **Internet Protocol** or IP, to provide this better facility, called **Transmission Control Protocol** or TCP, for applications (see Figure 15.2). Together these facilities are referred to as TCP/IP.

Sockets

A TCP connection between two programs in many ways is like a phone connection. Data can move reliably and continuously in both directions simultaneously. Furthermore, before communication can take place a connection has to be made—one party must call the other. Finally, both parties need something besides the connection. In phone connections, both parties need a telephone—a device that allows someone to hear and speak on a phone line. In TCP connections, Java programs need objects of the Socket class—objects that model telephones in that they allow programs to communicate across a connection.

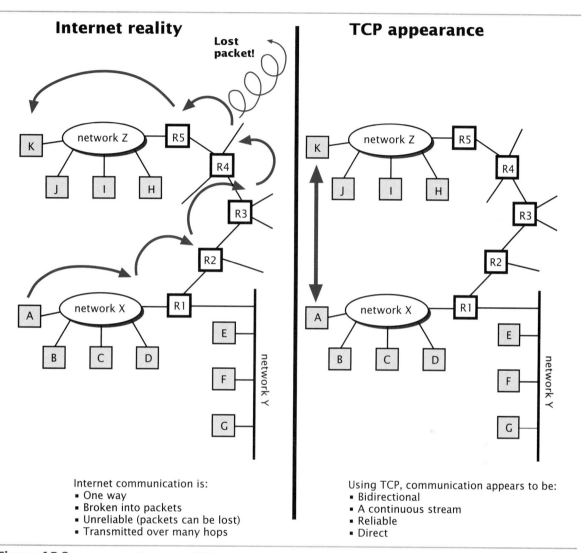

Figure 15.2 Internet reality versus TCP appearance.

The Socket class (found in the java.net package) models a disposable telephone. A Socket object is created for making a single TCP connection. In fact, the arguments to the constructor are the name of the machine being contacted and the port number to which the answering program will be responding. (You can think of the port number as analogous to an extension in a large phone system. For example, the following code creates a Socket that makes a TCP connection to the web server at www.yahoo.com:

```
new  Socket("www.yahoo.com",80);
```

80 is the standard port number for web servers.

The Socket class provides getInputStream() and getOutputStream() methods from whose return values BufferedReader objects and PrintStream objects can be constructed. These objects use the TCP connection as their input source or output target.

A TCPConnection Class

We can use Java's predefined Socket class to develop a class, TCPConnection, that models a TCP connection. Later we can use TCPConnection objects to build simple Internet application classes.

The behavior of a TCPConnection is straightforward:

- Create a connection to a particular machine and port.
- Read a line in the form of a String from the connection.
- Write a line in String form to the connection.

The interface of the class then is as follows:

```
class TCPConnection {
    public TCPConnection(String hostname, int portnumber) {}
    public String readLine() {}
    public void println(String s) {}
}
```

The repeated calls to readLine() and println() require that references to a BufferedReader object and a PrintStream object be maintained as instance variables:

```
private BufferedReader    br;
private PrintStream       ps;
```

The BufferedReader and PrintStream objects must be associated with the actual TCP connection, so that, for example, a read from the BufferedReader involves reading data from the TCP connection itself.

Given these instance variables, the implementation of readLine() and println() is as follows:

```
public String readLine() throws Exception {
    return br.readLine();
}
public void println(String s) {
    ps.println(s);
}
```

It is the responsibility of the constructor to initialize the instance variables. To do this, it creates a socket using the address and port number given, and then sends it getInputStream() and getOutputStream() messages to get InputStream and OutputStream objects from which a BufferedReader and PrintStream are constructed. The complete class definition is as follows:

```java
import java.net.*;
import java.io.*;
class TCPConnection {
    public TCPConnection(String hostname, int portnumber)
                                            throws Exception {
        Socket s = new Socket(hostname,portnumber);
        br = new BufferedReader(
                new InputStreamReader(
                    s.getInputStream()));
        ps = new PrintStream(s.getOutputStream());
    }
    public String readLine() throws Exception {
        String s;
        try {
            s = br.readLine();
        } catch (IOException ioe) {
            System.err.println("TCP input failure: network error");
            throw new Exception("Input Failure: Network I/O Error");
        }
        return s;
    }
    public void println(String s) {
        ps.println(s);
    }
    private BufferedReader  br;
    private PrintStream     ps;
}
```

We can write the following simple, though limited, test program for this class. It creates a TCPConnection object to model a connection to a well-known web server, sends a two-line HTTP request on the connection, and then reads from the connection:

```java
import java.net.*;
import java.io.*;
class TestTCPConnection {
    public  static  void  main(String[]  a)  throws  Exception  {
        TCPConnection  tc = new TCPConnection("www.yahoo.com",80);
```

```
            tc.println("GET "+"/"+" HTTP/1.0\n");
            String  s  =  tc.readLine();
            while  (s!=null)  {
                System.out.println(s);
                s = tc.readLine();
            }
        }
    }
```

> Note the \n—we're sending two lines, the second of which is blank.

15.3 Client-Server Computing

Sockets and TCP connections allow programs to communicate across the Internet, but they don't determine any particular style of communication or relationship between the programs. There is a widely used design approach for Internet applications—called the **client-server model**—that does just that, however. In the client-server model, an application consists of one program running as server—a program that provides a service—and another program running as a client—a program that requests a service.

To accomplish its mission, a client takes the following steps:

- It creates a Socket object with the machine address and appropriate port number of the server. (There are standards that determine what port number to use for what service. For example, the standard port number for the web is 80.)
- It sends a message to the server on the TCP connection that is associated with the Socket.
- It waits for the server to respond by indicating a need for more information, indicating that the requested action has been performed, or providing the data requested.

Depending on the application, the conversation between client and server may be more elaborate, with variations of the last two steps being repeated several times.

The client-server model works very nicely for the Internet because the most common Internet applications involve users either seeking data from some source (for example, web browsing or receiving email) or seeking to transfer data to some place (sending email for example). Thus, a web browser is a client. It accomplishes its task by repeatedly (for each new URL) creating Socket objects that make TCP connections to successive web servers, sending these servers requests for data, and receiving the responses and displaying them.

Client-Server Protocols

Each client-server application has its own rules (or protocol) governing the conversation between client and server. So the web clients and servers use one protocol called **HyperText Transport Protocol** or HTTP. Email clients and servers use a different protocol, called **Simple Mail Transfer Protocol** or SMTP. The protocols are fairly elaborate and a detailed discussion is beyond the scope of this text. However, let's listen in on a few client-server conversations and infer a few of the rules in these protocols so that we can experiment with some client and server programs of our own.

EXAMPLE A Web Client-Server Exchange. When a web client just wants an HTML file to display, all it has to do is make a TCP connection to the appropriate web server and send two lines of text:

- The first line starts with the word GET, then has the name of the file sought, and finally indicates the name of the protocol (just so the server really knows it is speaking the same language).
- The second line is blank. The blank line indicates the end of the request to the server.

In fact, our test program for the TCPConnection class sent these two lines.

Here is a hypothetical exchange between a web client and server:

```
client:GET  /~arnow/answers/answer15.html HTTP/1.0
client:  ◄——————————— Blank line signifies end of client request.
server:HTTP/1.0  200  Document  follows
server:Date:  Mon,  13  Jan  2003  23:26:47  GMT
server:Server:  NCSA/1.5.2
server:Last-modified:  Fri,  18  Dec  2002  01:18:38  GMT
server:Content-type:  text/html
server:Content-length:  110
server:  ◄——————————— Blank line signifies that the HTML content follows.
server:<HTML>
server:<HEAD>
server:<TITLE>Answer  to  Question  15</TITLE>
server:</HEAD>

server:

server:<BODY>

server:Answer to question 15: YES

server:</BODY>

server:</HTML>
```

Information about the server and the data sent in the transmission

The contents of the file requested.

At that point the server breaks off the connection.

EXAMPLE Email Client-Server Exchange. Email protocol, SMTP, is downright chatty compared to the web's HTTP. In SMTP, the server starts with a brief introduction of itself—its Internet address—and the protocol it is using. Here, as in all its messages, the SMTP server's message starts with a number code. The email client responds with EHLO (an anagram of a misspelled "HELLO") and its machine address. The mail server answers with a lengthy list of information about its configuration.

At this point the niceties (often called "handshaking") end and the client gets down to business. It sends a MAIL From: line and a RCPT To: line. These lines indicate who the sender and recipient are. To each, the server merely responds that the information is ok.

The email client then sends a DATA line followed by the contents of the email. A period by itself in a line indicates the end of the mail contents. Finally, the client sends a QUIT line and the server terminates the connection.

```
server:220 mailhost.mycollege.edu ESMTP
client:EHLO m3.mycollege.edu
server:250-mailhost.mycollege.edu Hello
        arnow@m3.mycollege.edu
        [146.245.37.30], pleased to meet you
server:250-EXPN
server:250-VERB
server:250-8BITMIME
server:250-SIZE
server:250-DSN
server:250-ONEX
server:250-ETRN
server:250-XUSR
server:250 HELP
client:MAIL From: <arnow@m3.mycollege.edu>
server:250 <arnow@m3.mycollege.edu>... Sender ok
client:RCPT To: <weiss>
server:250 <weiss>... Recipient ok
client:DATA
server:354 Enter mail, end with "." on a line by itself
client:I hope the students liked this book.
client:.
server:250 SAA05661 Message accepted for delivery
client:QUIT
server:221 mailhost.mycollege.edu closing connection
client:Connection closed by foreign host.
```

Introductions in conversation between client and server

Specifying sender

Specifying recipient

Content of email

Signifies end of email

Request termination

15.4 Some Simple Client Classes

In this section, we develop classes that model a web client and an email client. The WebClient object will model a web client's access of a single HTML file. A web client application could then repeatedly create WebClient objects as the user surfs from one HTML file to the next. The MailClient object will model an email client's sending of a single email. An email client application could then repeatedly create MailClient objects as the user sends different emails to various recipients.

The WebClient **Class**

The behavior that we desire from a WebClient is as follows:

- Create a WebClient based on a hostname, a portnumber, a resource (file) name; it should also be possible to leave out either the portnumber or the file-name or both and have these replaced by appropriate default values (80 and /, respectively).
- Read lines of HTML from the page accessed by the WebClient.

The interface for the class is as follows:

```
class WebClient {
    public WebClient(String hostname, int portnumber,
                     String resource) {}
    public WebClient(String hostname, String resource) {}
    public WebClient(String hostname, int portnumber) {}
    public WebClient(String hostname) {}
    public String readLine()  {}
}
```

Web clients, like most Internet client applications, use a TCP connection to get data from their server. Repeated invocations of readLine() will therefore require that WebClient maintain a TCPConnection object as an instance variable as follows:

```
private  TCPConnection  tc;
```

The readLine() method is no more than the following wrapper to a readLine() invocation using tc:

```
public String readLine()  {
   return tc.readLine();
}
```

The constructor's task is to create the TCPConnection and to make sure subsequent invocations of readLine() will return the successive lines of the HTML file. The constructor thus carries out the following steps:

- Create the TCPConnection.
- Send the HTTP request for resource desired.
- Read up through and including the blank line that signifies that the HTML content follows.

The constructor with the full set of arguments can therefore be implemented as follows:

```
public WebClient(String hostname, int portnumber, String resource)
                                    throws Exception {
    tc  =  new  TCPConnection(hostname,  portnumber);     Create connection.
    tc.println("GET  " + resource + "  HTTP/1.0\n");      Send request.
    String  s  =  tc.readLine();
    while  (s!=null  &&  !s.equals(""))                   Read up through
        s  =  tc.readLine();                             blank line.
}
```

The remaining constructors can be implemented by invoking the above constructor, substituting default values when necessary:

```
public WebClient(String hostname, String resource) throws Exception {
    this(hostname,80,resource);
}
public WebClient(String hostname, int portnumber) throws Exception {
    this(hostname,portnumber,"/");
}
public WebClient(String hostname) throws Exception {
    this(hostname,80,"/");
}
```

The complete class, with a simple test driver, is as follows:

```
class WebClient {
    public WebClient(String hostname, int portnumber, String resource)
                                        throws Exception {
        tc  =  new  TCPConnection(hostname,  portnumber);
        tc.println("GET  " + resource + "  HTTP/1.0\n");
        String  s  =  tc.readLine();
        while  (s!=null  &&  !s.equals(""))
            s  =  tc.readLine();
    }
    public WebClient(String hostname,  String resource)
                                        throws Exception {
        this(hostname,80,resource);
    }
    public WebClient(String hostname,  int portnumber)
                                        throws Exception {
        this(hostname,portnumber,"/");
    }
    public WebClient(String hostname) throws Exception {
        this(hostname,80,"/");
    }
    public String readLine() {
```

```
        return  tc.readLine();
    }
    private  TCPConnection tc;
    public static void main(String[] a) throws Exception {      Test driver
        if (a.length!=2)
            System.err.println("usage: java WebClient " +
                                    "host resource");
        else {
            WebClient wc = new WebClient(a[0],80,a[1]);
            String s = wc.readLine();
            while (s!=null) {
                System.out.println(s);
                s = wc.readLine();
            }
        }
    }
}
```

The MailClient Class

The behavior that we desire from a MailClient is as follows:

- Create a MailClient based on the address of a recipient and a sender.
- Write a line of the email content to the MailClient with the expectation that it will send these to the recipient.
- Indicate the end of the message by sending a period and a QUIT.
- Find the status of our interaction with the server (success or failure).

The interface for the class, therefore, is as follows:

```
class MailClient {
    public MailClient(String toAddress, String fromAddress) {}
    public void println(String s) {}
    public void close() throws Exception {}
    public boolean success() throws Exception {}
}
```

Like the web client, the mail client uses a TCP connection to send data and receive data from the server. Our implementation of MailClient will be illustrative, but crude. For example, it has the following requirements:

- The full email address of both sender and recipient must be specified.
- The hostname part of the recipient's address must be the address of the actual mail server used by the recipient's system. (Usually all that is required is the name of the network rather than that of the specific server.)

It has a similar structure to that of the WebClient. A TCPConnection object is maintained as an instance variable, allowing for an easy implementation of println() and close() as follows:

```
class  MailClient  {
    ...
    public void println(String  s) {
        tc.println(s);
    }
    public void close() {
        println("\n.\nQUIT");
    }
    private TCPConnection tc;
}
```

The success() method makes use of two facts:

- Every message from the mail server starts with a three-digit number.
- Error messages from the mail server always start with a number in the 500s.

So the success() method just reads server responses from the TCP connection until it reaches end-of-file or it finds a 5 at the beginning of the line:

```
public boolean success() throws Exception {
    String  s  =  tc.readLine();
    while  (s!=null  &&  !s.substring(0,1).equals("5"))
        s  =  tc.readLine();
    return  s==null;            null means no 5 was found;
}                               therefore, it was successful.
```

The MailClient constructor carries out the following steps:

- Create the TCPConnection.
- Send the SMTP information announcing identity, sender, and recipient.
- Send the DATA line indicating that the content of the email message is coming next.

Much of the work in the constructor involves extracting the sender's machine, the recipient's machine, and the recipient from the to and from addresses. The position of the "@" (as in *someone@somewhere.org*) is used to distinguish the user from the machine. We write the constructor as follows:

```
public MailClient(String to, String from) throws Exception {
    int    atInTo  =  to.indexOf("@");        Location of @ in to address
    int    atInFrom  =  from.indexOf("@");    Location of @ in from address
    String  serverHost  = to.substring(atInTo+1);
    String  senderHost  = from.substring(atInFrom+1);
```

```
    String  recipient  =  to.substring(0,atInTo);
    tc = new TCPConnection(serverHost, 25);    Create connection.
    println("EHLO " + senderHost);             Identify our machine.
    println("MAIL From: <" + from + ">");      Announce mail with
    println("RCPT To: <" + recipient + ">");   sender's address.
    println("DATA");                           Specify recipient on mail server.
}                                              Content of email follows.
```

The complete `MailClient` class, including a simple test driver, is as follows:

```
class MailClient {
    public MailClient(String to, String from) throws Exception {
        int    atInTo   = to.indexOf("@");     Location of @ in to address
        int    atInFrom = from.indexOf("@");   Location of @ in from address
        String serverHost = to.substring(atInTo+1);
        String senderHost = from.substring(atInFrom+1);
        String recipient = to.substring(0,atInTo);
        tc = new TCPConnection(serverHost, 25); Create connection.
        println("EHLO " + senderHost);          Identify our machine.
        println("MAIL From: <" + from + ">");   Announce mail with
        println("RCPT To: <"+to+">");           sender's address.
        println("DATA");                        Specify recipient on mail server.
    }                                           Content of email follows.
    public boolean success() throws Exception {
      String s  =  tc.readLine();
      while  (s!=null  &&  !s.substring(0,1).equals("5"))
         s = tc.readLine();
      return  s==null;                          null means no 5 was found;
    }                                           therefore, it was successful.
    public void println(String s) {
        tc.println(s);
    }
    public void close() {
        println("\n.\nQUIT");
    }
    private TCPConnection tc;
    public static void main(String[] a) throws Exception {
        MailClient mc = new MailClient(a[0],a[1]);
        mc.println("Subject: test message!");
        mc.println("Just let me know if you received this. Thanks!");
            mc.close();
            if (mc.success())
                System.out.println("mail success");
```

```
            else
               System.out.println("mail failure");
      }
}
```

Handling Client Exceptions

In the classes we developed above, we have continued to take the approach we have followed throughout most of the book; that is, wherever a method might encounter an exception, we added the `throws Exception` clause to the method header. Now that we know more about exceptions in Java, we can take a more refined approach. We will consider the `TCPConnection` class, and leave the client classes as exercises.

One problem with our `TCPConnection` class is that its constructor gives up too easily. For example, the `Socket` constructor may throw an exception for several reasons. On the one hand, the `hostname` may be invalid. In that case, there is no possible recovery. On the other hand, the host machine being contacted may not be responding. That might be just because of transient network problems. Rather than throwing an exception, we might wish for more patient behavior—several retry attempts before giving up, for example.

To achieve this, we will define our own private method, `makeSocket()`, for creating a `Socket`, and we will use this method in our `TCPConnection` constructor as follows:

```
public TCPConnection(String hostname, int portnumber)
                                      throws Exception {
    Socket   s=makeSocket(hostname,portnumber);
    br = new BufferedReader(
              new InputStreamReader(
                   s.getInputStream()));
    ps = new PrintStream(s.getOutputStream());
}
```

The essence of the `makeSocket()` method is the creation of a `Socket`:

```
Socket   s = null;
...
s   = new Socket(hostname, portnumber);
...
return   s;
```

However, the `Socket` constructor may throw an exception. We don't want to terminate in that case; instead, we want to examine the exception. If the exception reflects an improper `hostname`, we will issue a diagnostic to the user and give up, that is, rethrow the exception. If failure occurred for another reason, we will try again:

```
while (...) {
    try {
        s  = new Socket(hostname, portnumber);
    } catch (UnknownHostException uhe) {
        System.err.println("Cannot make TCP connection." +
                        "Reason: Unknown Host: " + hostname);
        throw new TCPException("Connection Failure: " + Unknown Host");
    } catch (IOException ioe) {
        System.err.println("Connection failed " +
                        "due to Network I/O Error: retrying ...");
    }
}
```

We don't want to keep trying forever, though. We will keep track of the number of attempts with a local variable, attempts, and we will declare an instance variable to define the maximum number of attempts to connect as follows:

```
private final int maxAttempts = 5;
```

Then, when the loop terminates we should either have our Socket, that is, s should no longer be null, or attempts should equal maxAttempts. Our loop then is

```
int     attempts = 0;
while (s==null && attempts<maxAttempts) {
    try {
        s = new Socket(hostname, portnumber);
    } catch (UnknownHostException uhe) {
        System.err.println("Cannot make TCP connection." +
                        "Reason: Unknown Host: "+ hostname);
        throw new TCPException("Connection Failure: Unknown Host");
    } catch (IOException ioe) {
        System.err.println("Connection failed " +
                        "due to Network I/O Error: retrying ...");
    }
    attempts++;
}
```

When the loop terminates we check the value of s and either rethrow an IOException or return s. The revised implementation of TCPConnection is as follows:

```
import java.net.*;
import java.io.*;
class TCPConnection {
    public TCPConnection(String hostname, int portnumber)
                                        throws Exception {
        Socket  s = makeSocket(hostname,portnumber);
```

```java
            br = new BufferedReader(
                    new InputStreamReader(
                        s.getInputStream()));
            ps = new PrintStream(s.getOutputStream());
        }
        public String readLine() throws Exception {
            String  s;
            try {
                s = br.readLine();
            } catch (IOException ioe) {
                System.err.println("TCP input failure: network error");
                throw new Exception("Input Failure: Network I/O Error");
            }
            return s;
        }
        public void println(String s) {
            ps.println(s);
        }
        private Socket makeSocket(String hostname, int portnumber)
                                            throws Exception {
            Socket s=null;
            int    attempts = 0;
            while (s==null && attempts<maxAttempts) {
                try {
                    s = new Socket(hostname, portnumber);
                } catch (UnknownHostException uhe) {
                    System.err.println("Cannot make TCP connection" +
                                    "Reason: Unknown Host: " + hostname);
                    throw new TCPException("Connection " +
                                        "Failure: Unknown Host");
                } catch (IOException ioe) {
                    System.err.println("Connection failed " +
                        "due to Network I/O Error: retrying ...");
                }
                attempts++;
            }
            if  (s==null)
                throw new IOException("Connection Failure: " +
                                    "Net I/O Errors");
            else
                return  s;
```

```
        }
        private final int      maxAttempts=5;
        private BufferedReader  br;
        private PrintStream     ps;
}
```

Summary

The fundamental mode of information transmission on the Internet is the unreliable delivery of packets specified by the Internet Protocol (IP). For scenarios that require guarantees of delivery, the Transmission Control Protocol (TCP) provides a reliable communications link; this type of connection is modeled in Java by the Socket class.

Sockets can be used to implement many forms of communication across the Internet; one of the most common applications is client-server computing, in which two programs (a client and a server) use the Internet to request and transmit data. Both the web and email are client-server applications; each uses its own special-purpose communication protocol (the HyperText Transport Protocol and the Simple Mail Transfer Protocol, respectively) to govern client-server interactions.

Key Terms

client-server model A program design approach in which one program, the sender, provides a service to another program, the client, which is requesting that service.

HyperText Transport Protocol The protocol used by web servers and their clients.

Internet Protocol A method of communication used by the Internet, in which information is moved unreliably through intermediate machines.

packet A small piece of data resulting from breaking up information for communication across a network.

router A machine on a network that transfers (routes) packets.

Simple Mail Transfer Protocol The protocol used by email servers and their clients.

Transmission Control Protocol A reliable, conceptually direct communication between two machines that is coded on top of the Internet Protocol.

Questions for Review

1. What is the function of a router? Why aren't routers considered in the Transmission Control Protocol?

2. What is a protocol?

3. Based on what you have learned in this chapter, how do you suppose the URL class (discussed briefly at the end of Chapter 3) works?

Exercises

1. Revise the WebClient and MailClient classes so that they catch all exceptions and write appropriate diagnostic messages.

2. Write a web client that prints an outline of the requested resource by printing only the text that appears between header tags <H1>...</H1> through <H6>...</H6>.

Swing

Introduction

Up to now, our GUI supplements have used the AWT—the Abstract Window Toolkit—Java's basic graphic user interface. It is important to remember that the AWT is not part of the Java language proper, but rather a package of classes that is provided as part of the "predefined" Java environment. It is thus possible to substitute a new graphical user interface package for the AWT by developing a different set of classes for handling a GUI. In fact, the Java Development Kit versions 1.2 and above, collectively known as Java 2, provide exactly that: a replacement for the AWT. This replacement, known as *Swing*, offers many enhancements over the AWT: a much broader choice of controls, a more polished appearance, and in general a greater degree of programmer control over the appearance and operation of the interface. Each of the basic AWT controls such as `Button` or `TextField` has a Swing counterpart, making it fairly easy to move from an AWT-based GUI to one that is Swing-based. In addition, there are a number of controls that are new to Swing and that provide the programmer with a very rich and powerful set of tools for GUI development.

In this supplement, we examine some of the new features introduced in Swing:

- The *look-and-feel* facility
- Swing's improved component hierarchy
- One or two of the new controls and features

Swing, however, is not just a better GUI package. It's also a rich case study of the power of object-oriented design. From this perspective, the most interesting thing about Swing is that there's no new Java, just a new set of classes. As Java matured, its designers decided to produce a more powerful GUI, but to do so they didn't make changes to the language or even the AWT—instead they wrote a new set of classes—the Swing package. As we will see, the new package uses behavior of AWT such as layout managers and events. Far from throwing out or even ignoring the AWT, Swing's designers incorporated whatever useful behavior they could from the AWT. In several places they extended existing AWT classes or implemented AWT interfaces, thus reducing the amount of code that had to be written and tested. If the AWT is a superb example of designing a class hierarchy that takes advantage of inheritance and polymorphism, Swing is the perfect example of exploiting and extending behavior and proof that object-orientation is an invaluable design and programming approach. We will continue to emphasize this point throughout the supplement.

We first present the basic mechanics of writing a Swing-based applet and then we'll explore some of the enhancements.

A Simple Swing-Based Applet

Coding simple Swing-based applets is not that much different than coding applets using AWT—Swing was designed that way to ease the transition.

Let us start with a very simple applet that displays a button and changes the button's text when clicked. We will code it in both AWT and Swing and compare the results. We'll look at the code (what we have to be concerned about) and at what the user sees (which is the ultimate point of having a different interface). Here is the AWT-based version:

```java
import java.awt.*;          // AWT classes ...
import java.awt.event.*;    //... and events
import java.applet.*;       // Applet-related classes

public class PushApplet extends Applet implements ActionListener {
    public void init() {
        theButton = new Button("Push Me!");
        add(theButton);
        theButton.addActionListener(this);
    }
    public void actionPerformed(ActionEvent e) {
        theButton.setLabel("Ouch!");
    }
    Button theButton;
}
```

Here is the applet in action before clicking (Figure 15.3) and after clicking (Figure 15.4).

Figure 15.3
Before clicking.

Figure 15.4
After clicking.

Now let's take a look at the Swing-based version. For this and many applets, much of the coding is the same as for the AWT-based version. Event handling, layout management, and the logic specific to the applet are the same. There are differences, but many of them are straightforward, requiring little in the way of actual design of logic changes. Here are the principal differences:

- The basic Swing classes and, in particular, the components (buttons, text boxes, and so forth) are imported from the package `javax.swing`. The name `javax` indicates that the package is a Java *extension*, that is, a package of classes that has been added to the predefined Java class environment, which is known as the *core*. This exact distinction is not important to us—what is important is to remember that the Swing's package name begins with `javax`, not `java`.

- For each of the AWT components, buttons, textfields, lists, and so on, there is a corresponding Swing component. The name of the Swing component is the same as its AWT counterpart, prefixed with a J. Thus we have `JButton`, `JText-Field`, and so on. There is also a Swing-based applet class, `JApplet`, that should be used whenever Swing components are employed.

- In AWT, components may be placed directly upon the `Applet`'s surface, using the `add()` method. In Swing, the `JApplet` does not act as a container for its components. Rather, the `JApplet` contains a single `Container` object, known as the *content pane*, and it is the content pane upon which all of the `JApplet`'s components are placed, again using the `add()` method. A reference to the content pane can be obtained from the `JApplet` via the `getContentPane()` method.

- The default layout manager for the `JApplet`'s content pane is `BorderLayout`, whereas `Applet`'s default layout manager is `FlowLayout`. Therefore, if we wish to lay out components on the content pane in the same way as they are laid out on the applet, we must set the content pane's layout manager to `FlowLayout`.

  `JApplet` extends the `Applet` class and therefore inherits all standard applet behavior. The `JApplet` class need only add new behavior specific to Swing, in particular to the presence of the new Swing components.

- The superclass of Swing components is the `JComponent` class, which itself derives from the standard AWT `Container` class and thus from the AWT `Component` class as well. This means that all Swing components inherit all AWT component behaviors, including the ability to set foreground and background colors, generate events, and so on.

Taking into account the above differences, we have the following Swing code for our applet. We've highlighted the Swing-related changes.

```
import java.awt.*;        // Still use some AWT classes
import java.awt.event.*;  // (Container) and events
                          // (ActionEvent)
import javax.swing.*;     // For Swing components and
                          // JApplet

public class PushJApplet extends JApplet implements
                                    ActionListener {
```

```
public void init() {
   Container contentPane = getContentPane();
   contentPane.setLayout(new FlowLayout());
   theButton = new JButton("Push Me!");
   contentPane.add(theButton);
   theButton.addActionListener(this);
}
public void actionPerformed(ActionEvent e) {
   theButton.setText("Ouch!");
}
JButton theButton;
}
```

As you can see, the code modifications are relatively simple. This makes it easy for a programmer to make the initial transition from AWT to Swing simply by making the above changes. More advanced Swing-specific features can then be introduced as desired.

Here is the output of the Swing-based applet before clicking (Figure 15.5) and after clicking (Figure 15.6).

Figure 15.5
Before clicking.

Figure 15.6
After clicking.

The applet looks quite similar to the AWT one, the primary differences being the background color and the appearance of the button. Such differences give the user interface its *look and feel*. This change in appearance is one of the prominent features of Swing, and is discussed in the next section.

Look and Feel (L&F)

If you've ever worked on more than one type of machine, for example on a PC and a Macintosh, you may have noticed that the graphical components look somewhat different. A button is recognizable as a button, but its exact appearance will usually differ from one system to the next. For example, Figure 15.7 shows what a button looks like in Microsoft Windows and Figure 15.8 shows a

Figure 15.7
A Windows-style
button.

Figure 15.8
A Motif-style
button.

button in Motif, a Unix-based interface. Although they both look like buttons, there is a distinctive difference between the two. In fact, with a bit of experience on both systems, it is easy to look at a display and say which system is running—Windows or Motif, or some other. Each interface is said to have its own distinctive *look and feel*, or L&F for short. We also refer to the look and feel as the *user interface*.

Java is designed to be cross-platform, and so it has a bit of an identity problem when it comes to GUI: Which look and feel should it use? The AWT took the approach of using the look and feel of the machine it is running on, what the Java documentation speaks of as the *native*, or *system*, look and feel. Thus an applet running on a Windows platform looked like Windows, one running on a Mac looked like a Mac, and so on. The native look and feel is accomplished by using the graphic components of the native system: a `Button` is displayed using a Windows button when running on Windows. While this solves the identity problem, it doesn't provide a uniform look to the applet as we move from one platform to another.

Swing provides *pluggable look and feel*, that is, the ability for the programmer to choose a particular look and feel. There are several look and feels distributed with the JDK:

- The Java look and feel (JLF). This is the default and is meant to be cross-platform, giving the interface a uniform appearance regardless of platform. This look and feel is also called the *cross-platform look and feel*. The actual name of this look and feel is *Metal* because the surface and components have a metallic appearance.
- The Windows look and feel
- The Motif look and feel

When we introduced canvases, we explained that what distinguishes a component from simple graphic shapes such as lines, ovals, or text is the association of a component with a class and its ability to generate events. The actual appearance of the component on the display, however, is itself nothing more than a series of graphic shapes. The display of a button, for example, is nothing more than a rectangle (the border of the button), some text (the label), and some shading in a contrasting color (giving the button its 3D appearance). It is *not* a real button. Changing the set of graphic shapes associated with a component can thus change its appearance.

A particular look and feel is implemented by first designing the appearance of the various components. A graphic artist rather than a programmer would typically be responsible for this task. The components are designed around some uniform theme, just like the characters of a single font. Once the "look" of the components has been designed, the programmer implements that design by coding the logic to paint the component shapes.

The above technique is not restricted to the JDK-supplied L&Fs. We can produce our own look and feel by coding the painting of our components. Although this is not terribly difficult, it does get somewhat involved and is beyond the scope of our present discussion.

Instead, let us develop a Swing-based applet that will demonstrate some typical components using the L&Fs provided by Java. The applet provides a four-button interface, allowing the user to choose among the various L&Fs. Initially, the applet is displayed using the default L&F, as shown in Figure 15.9.

Three classes are of importance when working with L&F:

- The abstract superclass `LookAndFeel` models the notion of L&F. Subclasses of this class implement particular L&Fs: Windows, JLF, and so on.
- The `UIManagerClass` is responsible for maintaining the current look and feel of the applet. The behavior of this class includes
  - Retrieving the current L&F (`getLookAndFeel()`)
  - Changing the L&F (`setLookAndFeel()`)
  - Retrieving a reference to a `LookAndFeel` instance corresponding to the native L&F (`getSystemLookAndFeel()`)
- The `SwingUtilities` class contains useful Swing-related utility methods that don't quite belong anywhere else. In particular, `SwingUtilities` contains the `updateComponentTreeUI()` method that causes a component to update its current look and feel.

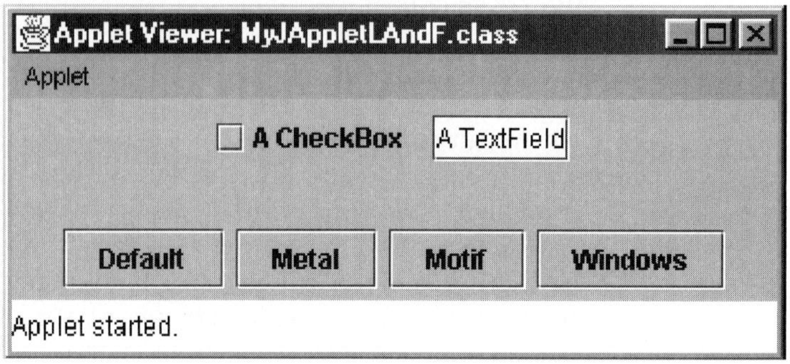

Figure 15.9
The default (Metal) cross-platform look and feel.

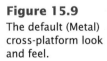

Changing an applet's L&F involves finding a subclass of LookAndFeel that provides the desired L&F (or creating a new one), invoking setLookAndFeel(), and finally, invoking updateComponentTreeUI().

```java
import javax.swing.*;
import java.awt.*;
import java.awt.event.*;
// Different 'look-and-feel' packages
import com.sun.java.swing.plaf.windows.*;
import com.sun.java.swing.plaf.motif.*;
import javax.swing.plaf.metal.*;
public class MyJAppletLAndF extends JApplet implements
                                        ActionListener {
    public void init() {
        Container contentPane = getContentPane();
        defaultLookAndFeel =
                        UIManager.getLookAndFeel();
        defaultButton = new JButton("Default");
        metalButton = new JButton("Metal");
        motifButton = new JButton("Motif");
        windowsButton = new JButton("Windows");

        // Create panel of sample components, some
        // with borders
        JPanel components = new JPanel();
        JCheckBox checkBox = new JCheckBox("A CheckBox");
        components.add(checkBox);
        JTextField textField = new JTextField("A TextField");
        components.add(textField);

        // Create panel of buttons
        JPanel buttons = new JPanel();
        buttons.add(defaultButton);
        buttons.add(metalButton);
        buttons.add(motifButton);
        buttons.add(windowsButton);

        // Add the panels to the content pane
        contentPane.add("North", components);
        contentPane.add("South", buttons);

        // Register with the buttons as a Listener
        defaultButton.addActionListener(this);
        metalButton.addActionListener(this);
        motifButton.addActionListener(this);
        windowsButton.addActionListener(this);
    }
```

```
    public void actionPerformed(ActionEvent ev) {
        try {
            if (ev.getSource() == motifButton)
                UIManager.setLookAndFeel(new MotifLookAndFeel());
            else if (ev.getSource() == windowsButton)
                UIManager.setLookAndFeel(new WindowsLookAndFeel());
            else if (ev.getSource() == defaultButton)
                UIManager.setLookAndFeel(defaultLookAndFeel);
            else
                UIManager.setLookAndFeel(new MetalLookAndFeel());
            SwingUtilities.updateComponentTreeUI(this);
            validate();
        } catch (UnsupportedLookAndFeelException e) {
            System.out.println("UnsupportedLookAndFeelException");
        }
    }

    LookAndFeel defaultLookAndFeel;
    JButton defaultButton, metalButton, motifButton,
            windowsButton;
}
```

The basic logic of the applet is straightforward. When a button is clicked, the corresponding L&F is set and the components updated by invoking Swing-Utilities.updateComponentTreeUI(this). This causes the applet and all the components within it to change their L&F. During applet initialization, we obtain the current (default) L&F and save it in an instance variable for use if the user clicks the Default button.

Here is the applet using the Motif L&F (Figure 15.10) and the Windows L&F (Figure 15.11).

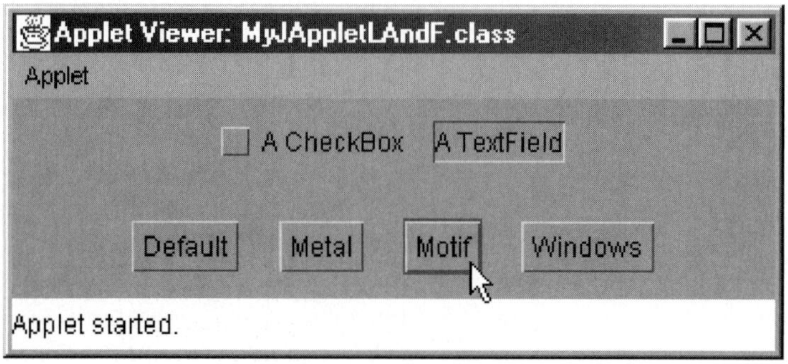

Figure 15.10
The Motif look and feel.

Figure 15.11
The Windows look and feel.

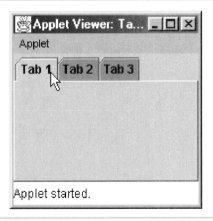

Swing's Enhanced Controls

While pluggable L&F provides great flexibility in the appearance of the interface, Swing's most popular feature is probably its introduction of numerous additional controls as well as its enhancements to the AWT controls. We now present a small applet that demonstrates some of these features. Though relatively simple to code, the applet contains a sophisticated control—the tabbed pane.

Despite larger displays and increased screen resolutions, screen real estate is always at a premium. It always seems that no matter how big our screen is, we always manage to fill it, and even want more. If the components of our interface require a window larger than our screen, we could always add scrollbars; however, it's awkward to be constantly scrolling through the window trying to find a particular component. One solution adopted by many graphic interfaces such as Motif and Windows is to use a *tabbed pane* (see Figure 15.12). Windows may be added as separate tabs to the pane; clicking a tab exposes the associated window.

Figure 15.12
A tabbed pane.

Our applet contains a tabbed pane of two tabs: one with a pair of buttons, the other a single line textfield and a multiline text area. Each button contains a small picture, or *icon*, in addition to the button's text. The multiline text area has a border containing a title, while the single-line textfield has a slightly thicker, colored border. Finally, pausing the cursor over the textfield causes a small help box, known as a *tool tip*, to appear. We won't bother responding to the buttons, we're just interested in displaying the various controls. Figures 15.13 and 15.14 show some displays of the applet.

One of the new control classes introduced with Swing is the TabbedPane. Components—usually panels—may be added with the addTab() method. The complexity of the tab switching and the exposing of the correct window is all handled by the code in the TabbedPane class. The applet programmer does not have to do anything.

Although the behavior of the tabbed pane is complex, it is completely implemented by the TabbedPane class. A few wisely chosen public methods are all the programmer using the control requires in order to work with it. This is the big advantage of interface versus implementation—the user works with the former and is protected from the latter by use of private and protected access control.

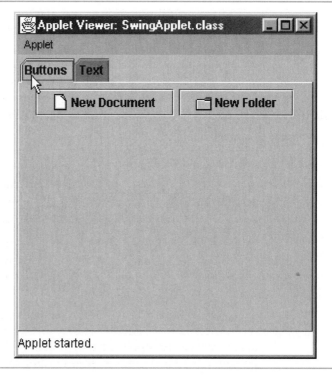

Figure 15.13
The Buttons tab exposed.

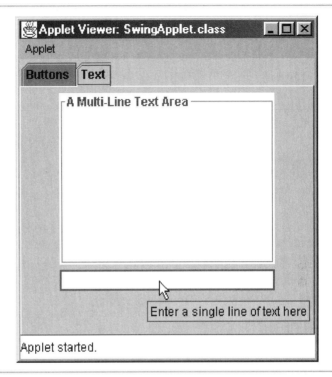

Figure 15.14
The Text tab exposed
and a visible tool tip.

In the AWT, only `Window`, `Frame`, `Panel`, `Applet`, and a few other classes were derived from `Container`. Controls such as `Button` or `TextField` derived directly from `Component` and thus were not subclasses of `Container`, and could not have other components added to them. While the inability to add a component to a button may at first not seem very restrictive, it does prevent us from adding a picture to the button's surface.

Swing's hierarchy removes this and other related restrictions. `JComponent`, the superclass of all Swing components, extends the AWT `Container` class, and therefore all Swing components can act as a GUI container.

The `JButton` method `setIcon()` is used to place the icon on the button's surface. Although the programmer could do this directly with the `add()` method, `setIcon()` makes sure the icon does not interfere with the button's text. Our applet uses two icons present in the JDK, primarily to ensure that it runs correctly on any installation.

The structure of a system's class hierarchy can have far-reaching, and sometimes unexpected, consequences. The AWT's restriction on which components are containers can impact upon a totally unrelated feature. The larger a software problem, the more important the need to carefully design its class structure.

We're also adding some borders to our controls—Swing allows us to specify a border for any component. Adding a border to, say, a button in AWT is possible, but somewhat cumbersome. Swing, on the other hand, abstracts the job of maintaining a border into an AbstractBorder superclass. There are several subclasses of AbstractBorder: LineBorder and TitledBorder are two. LineBorder models a simple line border with a color and border width, while TitledBorder allows for a border with a text heading. A programmer can create instances of these border classes and associate them with components, using the setBorder() method. Similarly, using the setToolTipText() method, a programmer can associate with any Swing component a piece of text to act as a tool tip.

All Swing components derive from the JComponent class. The setBorder() and setToolTipText() methods are defined at the JComponent level and therefore are inherited by all Swing components. Having all border classes derive from a single superclass, AbstractBorder, allows all Swing components to treat all border objects in the same way and with the same methods.

As before, the applet is surprisingly simple, given its relative sophistication. Its basic logic is also quite similar to an AWT applet's, the primary difference being the use of Swing rather than AWT components. Components are declared, created, and added to various GUI containers. The applet code follows.

```java
import java.awt.*;
import java.awt.event.*;
import javax.swing.*;
import javax.swing.border.*;
// Accesses two predefined icons
import javax.swing.plaf.metal.MetalIconFactory.*;
public class SwingApplet extends JApplet {
    public void init() {
        JTabbedPane tp = new JTabbedPane();
        getContentPane().add("Center", tp);
        JPanel buttons = new JPanel(); // Create the button panel
        tp.addTab("Buttons", buttons); // Add it as a new tab
        // Add buttons to the button tab
        JButton b1 = new JButton("New Document");
        b1.setIcon(new FileIcon16());// Add icon
        buttons.add(b1);
        JButton b2 = new JButton("New Folder");
        b2.setIcon(new FolderIcon16());// Add icon
        buttons.add(b2);
        // Add text components to the text tab
        JPanel texts = new JPanel();
```

```
        tp.addTab("Text", texts);
        JTextArea textArea = new JTextArea(10, 20);
        textArea.setBorder(new TitledBorder("A Multiline Text Area"));
        texts.add(textArea);
        JTextField textField = new JTextField(20);
        // Add a red border of thickness 2
        textField.setBorder(new LineBorder(Color.red, 2));

        // Add a tool tip to the text field
        textField.setToolTipText(
        "Enter a single line of text here");
        texts.add(textField);
    }
}
```

With all the increased sophistication of the Swing GUI, all that is really new here is the behavior of the Swing classes. While the new controls are much more powerful than those of the AWT, working with them is not much different. Components are still laid out, colored, and sized, and event handlers written. The beauty of object-oriented programming lies with the objects' assuming responsibility for their own actions and allowing their user to concentrate on the important part—composing, combining, and extending them into applications.

Suggested Experiments

1. Reimplement some earlier applets (such as `MinimizerApplet`, `Calculator-Applet`, and `WordProcessorApplet`) to use Swing rather than the AWT.

Appendix A

Glossary of Terms

abstract class A class that contains at least one abstract method.

abstract method A method declared but not implemented by a superclass. It is the responsibility of a subclass to implement the method.

access The ability to use a method or variable.

access control The ability to allow or prevent access to a method or variable.

accessor method A method whose behavior is either to assign a value to or return the value of one of the class's instance variables.

accumulator A variable that holds a partial sum, product, or analog for another binary operation besides + or *.

activation record A block of memory holding the parameters and local variables of a method, along with the return address of the invoker of the method.

all-paths testing An approach to testing in which every possible sequence of statements is tested at least once.

argument Information provided in a message in addition to the method-name.

array A programming language feature that provides an indexed collection of data values.

assignment The association of a value with a variable; the new value replaces any previous value associated with the variable.

assignment statement A statement that results in an assignment; the statement consists of the name of the variable being assigned, the assignment operator =, and an expression that gives the value that is assigned to the variable.

automatic testing An approach to testing in which the test suite verifies the correctness of the test results.

behavior Any action that the object may take; any change it may undergo or characteristic it may reveal as a result of a method being invoked..

binary search An algorithm for efficiently searching a sorted collection by repeatedly dividing the region where the item might be found in half and reducing consideration to one half or the other.

boolean A primitive data type modeling true and false values.

boolean expression An expression evaluating to a `boolean` value.

break statement A statement that forces immediate termination of a loop.

bug A run-time error in a program.

cascaded `if/else` A sequence of `if/else` statements in which the `else` portion of one `if` statement consists of another `if` statement.

cascading A technique in which the result of one method invocation is used as the receiver of a second method invocation.

casting A notation indicating to the compiler the true nature of a value.

character A distinct elementary symbol, often corresponding to a single keyboard keystroke; letters, digits, punctuation marks, spaces, and tabs are all examples of characters.

checked `Exception` An `Exception` that, if thrown by a method, must appear in the method's `throws` clause; so called because the Java compiler checks for its presence in the clause.

class A category of objects that share the same behavior.

class hierarchy The structure resulting from the subclass/superclass relationships of a set of classes.

class hierarchy tree A graphical depiction of a class hierarchy. Each class is displayed below its superclass and above its subclasses.

class method A method that is not associated with any particular object of a class but rather with the class itself. As a result, it can be invoked without reference to an object. Such a method is also called a static method.

class variable A variable that is not associated with any particular object of a class but rather with the class itself. As a result, it can be manipulated without reference to an object. Such a variable is also called a static variable.

client-server model A program design approach in which one program, the sender, provides a service to another program, the client, which is requesting that service.

code A section of text written in some programming language such as Java.

collection A class or language construct that manages one or more objects.

common behavior The behavior shared by objects in the same class. It is this behavior that defines the class.

compiler A program that translates code written in a high-level programming language into machine language.

composition A technique in which the result of one method invocation is used as an argument in a second method invocation.

composition A technique in which a class is defined using instance variables that are references to objects of other classes.

compound condition A condition (Boolean expression) containing one or more logical operators.

compound statement One or more statements surrounded by braces that are thereby treated as a single statement.

computer network A collection of computers, connected by wires, that can exchange data with each other.

conditional execution The ability to selectively execute code depending on some true or false condition.

constant An entity whose value may not be changed after initialization.

constructor A method that is invoked when an object is created. The name of the constructor method is the same as the corresponding class name.

`continue` statement A statement that forces Java to skip the remainder of the loop body in the current iteration.

counter A variable that keeps count of something.

counting loop A loop whose termination is based on executing a certain number of times.

current activation record The most recently allocated activation record, which corresponds to the currently executing method.

dangling `else` A problem occurring in a nested `if`, in which the single `else` is associated with the wrong `if`.

debugging The process of finding and fixing bugs.

declaration A Java statement that introduces a variable into a Java program. A declaration of a reference variable specifies the name (identifier) of the variable and the class of object to which it may refer.

default constructor The constructor automatically provided for a class if the programmer does not specify one; it takes no arguments.

delimiter A marker indicating a beginning or ending; in Java, braces mark the beginning and ending of method bodies and class definitions.

double A primitive data type modeling floating-point numbers.

elements The individual objects contained within a collection.

end-user A person who is using a program, usually not the author of the code.

Exception An object that represents an unexpected circumstance or an out-of-the-ordinary situation.

every-statement testing An approach to testing in which every statement is tested at least once.

execute To carry out instructions of program code.

extreme A value in a set that is no greater or no less than all the other elements.

file A named collection of data on the disk.

float A primitive data type modeling floating-point numbers.

floating-point number A number that models measurement with a fixed precision.

has-a A relationship between an object and some value such that the value is part of the object's state. This is usually expressed in Java by the object possessing an instance variable corresponding to the value.

HyperText Transport Protocol The protocol used by web servers and their clients.

identifier A sequence of characters which may be used as a name in a Java program. An identifier typically consists of an alphabetic characters (A–Z, a–z) followed by zero or more alphanumeric characters (A–Z, a–z, 0–9).

imperative programming Programming by commanding the computer to perform a fundamental computational task.

implement Provide the code that realizes a design.

implement The guarantee that a class makes that it will provide the methods specified in an interface.

import directive A statement that permits classes in a package to be named using its simple name rather than its full name.

index An integer that denotes a position in an ordered collection.

inheritance A technique in object-oriented languages in which one class assumes all the methods and instance variables of another class as its own. The inheriting class may also provide its own additional behavior.

initializer An optional portion of a variable declaration specifying the variable's initial value.

input Information from outside the program that is provided to the program.

instance A particular object of a class.

instance method A method that is associated with a particular object of a class and therefore must be invoked via a reference to an object.

instance variable A variable that is declared within a class but outside of any method; its purpose is to store information needed by methods to be preserved in between invocations. Each object has its own set of instance variables that have their own unique values—it is these values that distinguish one object from another. The entire set of the instance variables of an object define its state.

interactive An arrangement of bidirectional and alternating data flow between user and program.

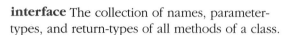

interface The collection of names, parameter-types, and return-types of all methods of a class.

interface An abstract class containing only abstract methods.

Internet A rapidly growing, very widely used global network of networks.

Internet address A `String`, such as `www.aw.com`, that identifies a machine on the Internet.

Internet Protocol A method of communication used by the Internet, in which information is moved unreliably through intermediate machines.

interpreter A program that directly carries out the statements of a high-level programming language.

invocation chain The sequence of method invocations starting with `main()` that leads to and includes the invocation of the currently executing method.

is-a The relationship between subclass and superclass. An object of a subclass *is-a* object of the superclass and may be used wherever an object of the superclass may be used.

iteration The repeated execution of a section of code until some condition is satisfied.

Java The name of one of the most recent and popular programming languages; also the one used in this text.

Java class hierarchy The class hierarchy composed of Java's classes.

keyword A word with a special, predefined meaning in Java language.

local variable A variable that is declared within a method; it exists only during the invocation of the method and is used as a temporary convenient holder of information.

$\log_2 N$ The number of times one can start with N and successively divide by 2 before reaching 1. The $\log_2$ is the inverse of exponentiation with 2 as the base: If 2^x is N, $\log_2 N$ is x.

logical operator An operator that combines Boolean expressions into larger Boolean expressions.

loop A language construct that repeatedly executes a section of code.

loop condition The condition that controls the loop statement's execution.

loop pattern The code structure of a loop that is frequently used.

loop termination The property of eventually completing execution of a loop.

message The mechanism by which a method is invoked. A message consists of a method name followed by a (possibly empty) argument list.

method A self-contained section of code belonging to a class that achieves a specific behavior for that class. A method consists of a return type, method-name, and parameter list, all of which form the method's signature, and the section of code that is called the body of the method.

method-name The identifier associated with a method.

model A representation of something. Models are usually simpler than the object they are representing; they contain only those aspects relevant to the user of the model.

nested if An `if/else` or `if` statement appearing as the true portion of another `if` or `if/else` statement.

network resource A resource, usually a file, that is available to users on machines other than the one on which the file is stored.

object An entity in Java that models something; a member of a class.

operation An action in Java that results in a value.

operator A symbol or keyword representing an operation (e.g., the identifier `new` represents the operation that creates an object).

overloading The practice of having a class provide different—though highly related—methods of the same name; the methods are distinguished by the types of arguments they receive, that is, their signatures.

overriding The act of reimplementing a method in a subclass with the *exact* same signature of a method in the superclass.

package A named group of related classes.

packet A small piece of data resulting from breaking up information for communication across a network.

parameter A variable that is declared in the parentheses of a method signature and whose purpose is to store the value of the corresponding argument; naturally, the type of the argument and the parameter must match in some sense.

polymorphism A feature of object-oriented languages in which the exact method to be invoked is determined at run time by the class of the receiving object.

precedence rules Rules describing the order in which to perform a sequence of operations.

predicate method A method whose return value is `boolean`.

primitive data type A data type provided as part of the language definition rather than through a class definition. No class or methods are associated with the data type.

private A keyword modifier in a method definition or instance variable declaration that *prevents* access to a method or variable from any code outside the class.

program A Java text that can be compiled and executed.

programming language A specialized language for writing programs.

prompt A `String` that is written to the screen to tell an end-user what kind of input should be entered next.

prototype Part of a method definition that consists of return-type, method-name, and argument list in parentheses.

public A keyword modifier in a method definition or instance variable declaration that *allows* access to a method or variable from any code outside the class.

receiver An object to which a message is sent.

recursion The process of using a recursive procedure; the carrying out of a recursive call.

recursive call An invocation of a method from within that method.

recursive procedure A procedure that carries out a part of a task and refers to itself to carry out the rest of the task.

reference A value or expression that refers to an object, thereby allowing us to send messages to the object.

reference variable An identifier that may be assigned a reference to an object of a particular class.

responsibility The set of behaviors that a class provides.

return A verb keyword that allows a method to terminate its own execution and allows the sender of the message to resume execution; additionally, the `return` statement allows the method to send some information back to the receiver.

return-type The first part of the prototype; it specifies what kind of information will be returned by the method.

return value The value given back to the sender by the receiver of a message.

root The class at the top of a class hierarchy. The root has no superclass.

router A machine on a network that transfers (routes) packets.

runtime Exception An Exception that reflects a programming error that typically can occur "anywhere" and ought to occur "nowhere" in the code and therefore is not required to be in the throws clause.

search An algorithm for finding a particular item that is stored in a collection of related values or objects.

selection sort An algorithm for sorting where one successively selects progressively ascending elements of a collection.

sequential search An algorithm for searching an indexed collection, checking the elements in the same sequence that they are stored in the collection.

short-circuiting Ending the evaluation of a condition without evaluating all its clauses as soon as the value of the condition is determined.

signature A method's name along with a description of its arguments.

Simple Mail Transfer Protocol The protocol used by email servers and their clients.

state The collection of values of the instance variables of an object at any given time.

statement A sentence of the Java programming language. A statement represents an action to be carried out.

static method A class method.

static variable A class variable.

string A group of characters written between double quotes.

String constant A sequence of characters embedded in double quotes, e.g., "Hello". The constant is a reference to the String object consisting of the characters between the quotes, in our case, the characters Hello.

subclass A class that inherits from some other class.

superclass A class that is inherited from.

switch statement A multiway conditional. The switch allows selective execution of multiple cases based upon the value of an expression.

termination step An essential step in any viable recursive procedure, in which the task is checked to see if it can be carried out without resort to recursion.

test driver A method (or collection of methods) whose purpose is to test the behavior of one or more utility classes.

test suite A set of tests.

Thread The process of carrying out a set of instructions one at a time.

throws clause A clause in a method declaration that identifies all the checked exceptions the method might throw.

Transmission Control Protocol A reliable, conceptually direct communication between two machines that is coded on top of the Internet Protocol.

traversal The process of listing or going through all members of a collection.

URL A unique identification of a network resource, including the Internet address of the machine on which the resource is stored, the filename of the resource, and the protocol (such as HyperText Transfer Protocol, or HTTP) that should be used to access the resource.

variable An identifier that can be given a value.

Vector A particular collection class in the java.util package.

void Return-type of methods that do not return a value.

while statement A particular loop construct in the Java language.

Appendix B

Three Java Environments

Introduction

This appendix illustrates how to create, compile, and execute Java programs. We will use the first program presented in Chapter 1 as an example:

```
class  Program0  {
    public  static  void  main(String  arg[])  {
        System.out.println("Welcome  To  Java!");
    }
}
```

We present the development of this program for three operating systems: MacOS X, UNIX/Linux, and Windows. We use the Java Development Kit (JDK) from Sun Microsystems for its simplicity and because it can be downloaded without cost from the Java web site at java.sun.com. There are several integrated development environments (IDEs) available for these platforms (including some, themselves written in Java, which will run on all these platforms). An IDE provides editing, compiling, and execution in a single program. If you are using one of these environments, please consult your instructor about its use.

Macintosh

The newest version of the Macintosh operating system, MacOS X, is based on the UNIX operating system. Furthermore, Java is always provided with the MacOS X distribution, so there is no need to download anything.

Using Java in MacOS X, then, is almost identical to using Java in a traditional UNIX-like operating system. We will access Java through the UNIX *shell*, called the Terminal application. You can find the Terminal application by opening the Applications folder (in Finder, select the Go menu, followed by Applications, or press SHIFT-APPLE-A), then opening the Utilities folder. Double-click the Terminal icon and a new window will appear; this is the UNIX shell.

From this point, follow the instructions below.

UNIX/Linux

Step 1: Edit and save the program as a .java source file.   Create this file using any one of the of UNIX editors. For example, if you use vi, then type the following from the UNIX shell command line:

```
vi  Program1.java
```

In general, Java source files must have the same name as the class followed by the suffix *.java*.

Step 2: Compile the .java source file.   From the UNIX shell command line, run the Java compiler by typing

```
javac  Program1.java
```

Any errors are displayed by the compiler accompanied by their line numbers. For example, forgetting the semicolon in the fifth line of the program produces this output

```
>  javac  Program1.java
Program1.java:5:  ';'  expected.
    System.out.println("Welcome  To  Java!")
                                              ^

1 error
>
```

Fix any errors by going back into the editor, and then recompile. When the program is error-free, the compiler issues no error output:

```
>  javac  Program1.java
>
```

Step 3: Execute the .class file.   From the UNIX shell command line, execute the program by typing the following:

```
java  Program1
```

Do *not* include the *.class* suffix. The output of the program is displayed on the screen as follows:

```
>  java  Program1
Welcome  To  Java!
>
```

Windows

Step 1: Edit and save the program as a .java source file. Type in the program using the Windows notepad editor. From the Start Menu/Run dialog box, type the following:

```
notepad  path\Program1.java
```

The path is the directory in which you wish the source file to be created. For example, if you have a directory \Java\Programs on the C drive, you would type:

```
notepad  C:\Java\Programs\Program1.java
```

In general, Java source files must have the same name as the class, followed by the suffix *.java.*

Step 2: Open a command prompt window and move to the proper directory. From the Start Menu/Programs popup menu, open a command prompt window. At the command prompt, change directories to the one containing the source file you have created. For example, using the directory example of step 1, type the following:

```
C:\>  cd  C:\Java\Programs
```

Step 3: Compile the .java source file. Remaining in the command prompt window, run the Java compiler by typing:

```
javac  Program1.java
```

Any errors are displayed by the compiler accompanied by their line numbers. For example, forgetting the semicolon in the fifth line of the program produces the output:

```
C:Java\Programs\>  javac Program1.java
Program1.java:5:  ';'  expected.
   System.out.println("Welcome  To  Java!")
                                           ^
1 error
C:\Java\Programs>
```

Fix any errors by going back into the editor, and then recompile. When the program is error-free, the compiler issues no error output:

```
C:\Java\Programs>  javac  Program1.java
C:\Java\Programs>
```

Step 3: Execute the .class file.   From the command prompt shell command line, execute the program by typing:

java   Program1

Do *not* include the *.class* suffix. The output of the program is displayed on the screen:

```
C:\Java\Programs>  java   Program1
Welcome   To   Java!
C:\Java\Programs>
```

Appendix C

AWIO

Introduction

This appendix provides an alternative input/output technique to that introduced in Chapter 3. In this appendix we introduce the AWIO package, a package of predefined Java classes written specially for this book. These classes allow the student to write programs that perform the same input and output that is discussed in Chapter 3 without having to learn the important lessons in object-oriented programming concepts and techniques developed in that chapter.

Using AWIO for Output

We create a new file or overwrite an existing one in the same way in Java. Both require a pathway (or *stream*) for output from the program to provide the newly created or existing file with content.

The AWPrinter Class

The AWIO package provides a predefined class, similar to `PrintStream`, for modeling a stream of output. This class is called `AWPrinter`. There are two constructors for `AWPrinter`—another example of overloading. One constructor has no arguments:

```
new AWPrinter()
```

This creates an `AWPrinter` object that has the same behavior as `System.out`: You can send it `println()` and `print()` messages and they will cause output to display on standard output (usually the monitor). For example

```
AWPrinter awout = new AWPrinter();
awout.println("Just like PrintStream!");
```

creates an `AWPrinter` object associated with standard output and displays the string `"Just like PrintStream!"`.

The other constructor accepts a reference to a `String` object as its argument, as follows:

```
new AWPrinter(String)
```

This creates an AWPrinter object that also has the same PrintStream-like behavior as System.out except that the object is associated with a file on disk. You can still send it println() and print() messages, but now these will cause output to be stored in the file named by the String. An example of this follows:

```
AWPrinter awout = new AWPrinter("Simplicity");
```

This code opens the disk file Simplicity so that it can receive output; it creates the file if it doesn't already exist. The reference to the new AWPrinter object is returned and stored in awout. As soon as the AWPrinter is constructed, the file is created if it did not exist before or its contents are removed if the file already exists. Now a statement such as

```
awout.println("You should still read Chapter 3 sometime!");
```

will store the string "You should still read Chapter 3 sometime!" in the disk file Simplicity.

EXAMPLE Maintaining a Backup of Screen Output.   Suppose we want our program to maintain a disk file copy (named "backup") of the screen output that it generates. Let's assume this is an improvement of Program1. We write the program as before but add the code needed to create a new file, backup, with an associated AWPrinter. Then, whatever we write to System.out, we also write to this AWPrinter object, as follows:

```
import AWIO.*;
class Program1Backup {
   public static void main(String arg[]) throws Exception {
       AWPrinter backup;
       backup = new AWPrinter("backup");
       System.out.println("This is my first Java program");
       backup.println("This is my first Java program");
       System.out.println("... but it won't be my last.");
       backup.println("... but it won't be my last.");
   }
}
```

What Can Go Wrong?

As our programs interact further with their computing environment—creating new files, for example—there are more opportunities for them to fail through no fault of their own. For example, the program above is perfectly correct, but if someone runs it in a directory where he or she doesn't have permission to create files, the program will fail. Java requires that the programmer acknowledge potential failures of this kind by adding the phrase throws Exception to the boilerplate, as we have done above. If the phrase is omitted, the compiler will issue an error. The phrase means that it is conceivable that an unrecoverable error might occur because of a problem in the computing environment and, as a result, the program might terminate abruptly. We learn more about this issue and exceptions in general in Chapter 14. See the exercises at the end of Chapter 3.

Using AWIO for Keyboard Input

We have not yet considered how to use *input*—information coming from a keyboard or stored in a file—to create objects. We have been forced to place all information into the programs themselves. If we could get information, such as Strings, from input, our programs could be more general. For example, instead of writing a program that changes a file's name from ford to lincoln by specifying the names, we could write a program that reads in two Strings from the keyboard (what the user types) and treats them as the old and new names of a file that is renamed. We'll learn how to read input in this and the next two sections.

In the preceding section, we introduced a class, AWPrinter, that we used to write Strings either to standard output or to a file. Here we introduce a class, AWReader, that we can use to read Strings either from the keyboard (standard input) or a file.

An AWReader object models a stream of input coming from a file or the keyboard. As is the case for AWPrinter, AWReader has two constructors—yet another example of overloading.

One constructor has no arguments:

```
new AWReader()
```

This creates an AWReader object that is associated with the keyboard, or, more generally, standard input. Let's store the resulting reference in a variable as follows:

```
AWReader keyb = new AWReader();
```

Once we have an AWReader object, we can use its ability to read in a line from some source of input and create a String object, whose characters are those that appeared in the input line. The method that models this behavior is called readLine(). Because it creates an object, it returns a reference to that object, just as the String methods toUpperCase() and substring() return references to the new String objects that they create. Therefore, the following is a reference to the String:

```
keyb.readLine()
```

The String is returned by AWReader when it reads in the next line of input from the keyboard in response to the readLine() message.

To use the `String` object that `keyboard` creates, we declare a `String` reference variable, as follows:

```
String      inputLine;      // Models a line of input
```

We use it to save the `String` reference that the `AWReader` returns, as follows:

```
inputLine = keyb.readLine();
```

Let's use these new tools to write a program that reads in a singular noun from the keyboard and displays its plural on the screen. We don't yet have the tools to come close to doing this correctly, so we will assume that merely adding the letter *s* to a word correctly results in the plural form (thereby ignoring words like *fox* and *baby*).

We write a comment defining the meaning of the program followed by the usual first two lines of boilerplate notation and then the above four pieces of code, as follows:

```
import java.io.*;
import AWIO.*;
/*
* Program4:  Displays the plural form of the word typed on
*               the keyboard. Uses the naive and wrong(!)
*               approach of just adding s.
*/
class Program4 {
   public static void main(String arg[]) throws Exception {
      AWReader       keyboard;   // Models a keyboard that
                                 // reads in lines as Strings
      String         inputLine;  // Models a line of input.
      keyboard = new AWReader();
      inputLine = keyboard.readLine();
      //
      // Rest of the program goes here ...
      //
   }
}
```

All that remains is to arrange to display the `String` as intended. We will send a `print()` (not a `println()`) message to `System.out` with the word read from input as an argument. We send `print()` instead of `println()` because we want the *s* to appear on the same line as the word, not on the succeeding line. Then we will send a `println()` message with `"s"` as an argument in order to display the *s* and complete the line, as follows:

```
System.out.print(inputLine);
System.out.println("s");
```

Here is the complete program:

```
import java.io.*;
/*
 * Program4: Displays the plural form of the word typed on
 *              the keyboard. Uses the naive and wrong(!)
 *              approach of just adding s.
 */
class Program4 {
    public static void main(String arg[]) throws Exception {
        AWReader      keyboard;   // Models a keyboard that
                                  // reads in lines as Strings.
        String        inputLine; // Models a line of
                                  // input.
        keyboard = new AWReader(isr);
        inputLine = keyboard.readLine();
        System.out.print(inputLine);
        System.out.println("s");
    }
}
```

Interactive Input/Output

Keyboards are only one source of input for programs. Other sources include data files on disk and even other programs that are running on the computer. We will explore all of these other sources as we proceed in this book.

One characteristic distinguishing keyboard input is that it directly involves a human being, often termed an *end-user* (of the program). In practice, end-users are almost never the authors of the programs that they use. Millions of people use WordPerfect; only a handful of them had a role in writing that program.

Because end-users (or users for short) are not the authors of the programs they use, they cannot be expected to automatically know what to type on the keyboard and when to type it. A program that expects input from a keyboard must, in order to be useful, provide that information to the users as it runs. It must display messages such as "Please enter your PIN now" and "Sorry, that choice is not correct – please make your selection again." These *prompts* tell the user what to type on the keyboard. The flow of data between users and programs is referred to as *interactive* input and output.

Consider `Program4` from the previous section. The program includes the following line:

```
inputLine = keyboard.readLine();
```

It expects the user to type in a word that is to be made plural. But how will the user know that this is expected? The `readLine()` method waits silently for the user to type in a line—it cannot offer any guidance. The solution is to display a prompt, such as, "Type in a word to be made plural, please" just before the `readLine()` message is sent to `keyboard`. We know how to display such a `String` to the user: We must send a `print()` message to `System.out` prior to reading in the line, as follows:

```
System.out.println("Type in a word to be made plural, please ");
inputLine = keyboard.readLine();
```

A general form for interactive input and output is as follows:

```
System.out.println(prompt goes here);
string reference variable = keyboard.readLine();
possibly compute something (using, for example, concatenation)
System.out.println(output string goes here);
```

Using AWIO for Disk File Input

Obtaining input from a disk file is as easy as writing output to one. All you need to do is create an `AWReader` object with the name of the file as an argument to the constructor, as follows:

```
AWReader awin = new File("Americas.Most.Wanted");
```

The object that `awin` references is an `AWReader`, just like the one `keyboard` referenced earlier. We can send `readLine()` messages to this object to read successive lines from the file, which we will print out, as follows:

```
String line;
line = awin.readLine();
System.out.println(line);
line = awin.readLine();
System.out.println(line);
```

EXAMPLE Making a Copy of a File.   Let's write a program that reads, interactively from the keyboard, the name of a file that contains two lines. The program creates a copy of the file whose name is the original name with `.copy` added to it. We write it using sections of code based on the various examples we have seen so far in this chapter. Here is the program:

```
import java.io.*;
import AWIO.*;
class CopyFile {
    public static void main(String arg[]) throws Exception {
        AWReader keyboard;
        String fileNameOrig;
        AWReader rdrOrig;
        String fileNameCopy;
        String s;
        AWPrinter awout;
        keyboard = new AWReader();
        System.out.print("name of file to copy: ");
        fileNameOrig = keyboard.readLine();
        fileNameCopy = fileNameOrig.concat(".copy");
        rdrOrig = new AWReader();
        awout = new AWPrinter(fileNameCopy);
        s = rdrOrig.readLine();
        awout.println(s);
        s = rdrOrig.readLine();
        awout.println(s);
    }
}
```

Using AWIO in the Rest of the Book

This appendix has described the use of the AWIO package, a collection of classes that reduce the amount of code that must be typed for a program to do file output, keyboard input, and file input. This appendix serves, therefore, as a limited alternative to the techniques of Chapter 3.

In those places where input/output appears in examples in Chapters 4 through 15, the techniques of Chapter 3 are used, not the AWIO package. However, it is fairly straightforward to use the AWPrinter and AWReader classes as alternatives in those situations.

For example, throughout the text, BufferedReader objects are used to perform input. Wherever you see BufferedReader in the text, replace it with AWReader (both provide the same readLine() method). Similarly, wherever you see PrintStream, replace it with AWPrinter.

Furthermore, replace the creations of BufferedReader objects such as

```
BufferedReader br = new BufferedReader(
                    new InputStreamReader(
                      new FileInputStream(
                        new File("SomeFileName"))));
```

with

```
AWReader br = new AWReader("SomeFileName");
```

By not changing the name of the instance variable, br, you can use code such as

br.readLine()

without modification.

Similarly, replace the creations of BufferedReader objects such as

```
BufferedReader br = new BufferedReader(
                        new InputStreamReader(System.in));
```

with

```
AWReader br = new AWReader();
```

and creations of PrintStream objects such as

```
PrintStream ps = new PrintStream(
                        new FileOutputStream(
                            new File("SomeFileName")));
```

with

```
AWPrinter ps = new AWPrinter("SomeFileName");
```

Again, by not changing the names of the instance variables, you minimize the need for other changes.

Appendix D

Traversing Collections Using **Enumeration**s

Traversing a Vector—Enumerations

In Chapter 9, we discuss the *traversal* of a collection (in particular, the `Vector` collection), and note that a `for` loop is a natural structure for traversing the `Vector`:

```
for (i = 0; i < size of collection; i++)
    process element number i
```

We can take another view of the traversal algorithm, however, one that doesn't rely explicitly on knowledge of the size of the collection:

```
while (we still have more elements to visit)
    visit the next element
```

In order to visit each of the elements of a collection such as `Vector` we need to be able to

- Get the *next element*, that is, visit an element that has not yet been visited
- Test whether the collection *has more elements* to be visited

We might expect `Vector` to provide these methods. However, `Vector` is not the only collection class that Java defines, and the above behavior (that is, visiting all the elements) is common to all collections.

Java therefore provides an interface, `Enumeration`, which models this traversal behavior. Each collection class provides a method that creates and returns a reference to an object of class `Enumeration`. It is the `Enumeration` object that provides the methods to get the next element and test for more elements.

In particular, the `Vector` class contains a method, `elements()`, that returns a reference to an `Enumeration` object:

```
Enumeration elements() {...}◀──────── Returns an Enumeration for the Vector
```

679

In turn, `Enumeration` provides the following methods:

```
boolean  hasMoreElements()    // Returns true if there are more
                             // elements to visit; returns false otherwise.
Object nextElement()          // Returns reference to next element.
```

Note that the return-type of `nextElement()` is `Object`, for the same reasons that the return-type of `Vector`'s `elementAt()` method is `Object`: This method must be able to return a reference to any kind of object, so it returns a reference to `Object` that the programmer may then cast to the appropriate type.

We can now write the code to *enumerate* (traverse) through a collection. As an example, let's write an alternative loop for printing the elements of a `Vector` of `String`s, as we do in Chapter 9. The following is a sketch of a traversal loop:

```
while (there are more elements)  {
    x = get the next element
    process x
}
```

It now translates to

```
Enumeration  enum  =  v.elements();
while (enum.hasMoreElements()) {
    String s = (String) enum.nextElement();
    System.out.print(s);
}
```

Another Loop Pattern—Enumerating through a Collection

Enumerating through a collection is another loop pattern. Its general form is

```
// Loop pattern - enumerate
Enumeration enum = get an Enumeration reference from the collection
while  (enum.hasMoreElements())  {
    String  s  =  (String)enum.nextElement();     ←——— Extracts
    process the element                                 elements
}
```

Index

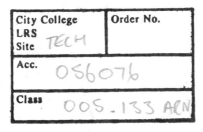